# The NIV®
# Standard
# Lesson Commentary
# 1996-97

## International Sunday School Lessons

published by

**Standard Publishing**

Eugene H. Wigginton, *Publisher*

Richard C. McKinley, *Director of Curriculum Development*

Jonathan Underwood, *Editor*  Hela M. Campbell, *Office Editor*

*Third Annual Volume*

STANDARD
PUBLISHING
Cincinnati, Ohio

Lessons based on International Sunday School Lessons © 1990 by the Lesson Committee.

Cover design by Listenberger Design Associates, Indianapolis.

© 1996
The STANDARD PUBLISHING Company
division of STANDEX INTERNATIONAL Corporation
8121 Hamilton Avenue, Cincinnati, Ohio 45231
Printed in U.S.A.

# In This Volume

## Special Features

## Autumn Quarter, 1996
### Theme: God's People Face Judgment

**Writers**

Lesson Development............................*Orrin Root*      Discovery Learning ........................*Mark A. Taylor*
Verbal Illustrations ..................*Charles R. Boatman*      What Do You Think? ...................*Kenton K. Smith*

## Winter Quarter, 1996-97
### Theme: New Testament Personalities

**Writers**

Lesson Development........*Dale Cornett (1, 6), Lloyd*      Discovery Learning.............*Alan Weber (1-6), Mark*
*Pelfrey (2), Johnny Pressley (3-5), David Morley (7-9)*      *Plunkett (8, 9, 11), Phil Haas (10, 13),*
*Jerran Jackson (10, 11), Dennis Gaertner (12, 13)*      *Jonathan Underwood (7, 12)*
Verbal Illustrations.....................*Richard W. Baynes*      What Do You Think? ......................*Richard A. Lint*

## Spring Quarter, 1997
### Theme: Hope for the Future

**Writers**

Lesson Development ...................*Edwin V. Hayden*      Discovery Learning...............*Dennis E. Glenn (1-5),*
Verbal Illustrations....................*James G. VanBuren*      *Timothy Heck (6-9), Thomas G. May (10-13)*
What Do You Think? ....................*Kenton K. Smith*

## Summer Quarter, 1997
### Themes: Guidance for Ministry
### A Call to Faithfulness

**Writers**

Lesson Development.......................*John W. Wade*      Discovery Learning........................*Ronald G. Davis*
Verbal Illustrations .....................*C. Barry McCarty*      What Do You Think? ...................*David A. Baynes*

# A Christ for All Time

"Who am I?" "Where am I going?" These are crucial questions. Because there is such uncertainty today as to how to address these concerns about the *past* and the *future*, the *present* has become saturated with futility and hopelessness for many.

This year's lessons offer a life-enriching perspective on the past, present, and future. The autumn quarter, drawn from the Old Testament, focuses on messages of judgment on Israel and Judah. Theirs is a history we should desire *not* to repeat.

The good news is that even though one's past has been marked by similar defeat and failure, in Christ there is forgiveness of that past and a refreshing hope for the future! Such hope is powerfully exemplified in the lives of many of the "New Testament Personalities" highlighted in our winter quarter. The theme of hope continues in the spring quarter, featuring studies from 1 and 2 Thessalonians and Revelation.

The summer quarter presents "Guidance for Ministry" from the Pastoral Epistles and "A Call to Faithfulness" from Hebrews. Not only does Jesus cleanse us from our past and give hope for the future; he also calls us to a day-by-day experience of fruitful service in his name. May these perspectives on the past, present, and future give you and your students much encouragement throughout the year!

## International Sunday School Lesson Cycle
## September, 1992—August, 1998

| YEAR | AUTUMN QUARTER (Sept., Oct., Nov.) | WINTER QUARTER (Dec., Jan., Feb.) | SPRING QUARTER (Mar., Apr., May) | SUMMER QUARTER (June, July, Aug.) |
|---|---|---|---|---|
| 1992-1993 | Old Testament Personalities (Old Testament Survey) | Good News for All (New Testament Survey) | Believing in Christ (John) | Following God's Purpose (Ephesians, Philippians, Colossians, Philemon) |
| 1993-1994 | The Story of Beginnings (Genesis) | The Story of Jesus (Luke) | Good News for God's People (Romans) Set Free by God's Grace (Galatians) | God Redeems a People (Exodus, Leviticus, Numbers, Deuteronomy) |
| 1994-1995 | From the Conquest to the Kingdom (Joshua, Judges, 1 and 2 Samuel, 1 Kings) | Jesus the Fulfillment (Matthew) | Christians Living in Community (1 and 2 Corinthians) | A Nation Turns From God (1 and 2 Kings, Amos, Hosea, Micah, Isaiah) |
| 1995-1996 | The Story of Christian Beginnings (Acts) | God's Promise of Deliverance (Isaiah) God's Love for All People (Jonah, Ruth) | Teachings of Jesus (Matthew, Mark, Luke) | A Practical Religion (James) God Is With Us (Psalms) |
| 1996-1997 | God's People Face Judgment (2 Kings, Jeremiah, Lamentations, Ezekiel, Habakkuk) | New Testament Personalities | Hope for the Future (1 and 2 Thessalonians, Revelation) | Guidance for Ministry (1 and 2 Timothy, Titus) A Call to Faithfulness (Hebrews) |
| 1997-1998 | God Leads a People Home (Major Prophets, Minor Prophets, Nehemiah) | God's People in a Troubled World (1 and 2 Peter, 1, 2, 3 John, Jude) | The Gospel of Action (Mark) | Wisdom for Living (Job, Proverbs, Ecclesiastes) |

# Introducing *The NIV Standard Lesson Commentary*

Look at all the features that will make *The NIV Standard Lesson Commentary* a great help as you prepare your Sunday school lessons.

## LESSON DEVELOPMENT

The first page of each lesson gives the title, Scripture, current unit, and lesson aims for the session. The date in the thumb tab is repeated at the top of each page.

The lesson aims cover all the bases. Ordinarily there are three aims: a **content** aim, what the student should *know* about the content of the lesson text; a **concept** aim, what the student should *understand* about the content; and the **conduct** aim, what the student is expected to *do* with the information presented. These aims are restated on the discovery learning page of each lesson.

The first item in the lesson development is **"Why Teach This Lesson?"** Tying the lesson theme to contemporary life, this puts application at the forefront. Then comes the **introduction,** which provides background and other useful information to give you a handle on the context for the lesson.

What follows is a **verse-by-verse Scripture exposition.** The text is printed in the *New International Version,* usually one verse at a time. Commentary is interspersed so you can relate each comment to the specific Scripture passage it illuminates.

The **conclusion** leans heavily toward **application,** giving specific examples of how the principles of the lesson Scripture can be put to practice in real life.

## MARGINAL NOTES

Occasionally the text suggests some interesting point for discussion. These issues are raised in the margin under the heading of **"What Do You Think?"** No answers are given because these are questions without pat answers. These will encourage your students to wrestle with the big issues without being trite.

**"Visuals"** are pictured in the margins, also. These are reproductions of the classroom visuals available from Standard Publishing each quarter to help your students visualize the points being made. **Daily Bible readings,** points to remember, and even prayer ideas are included in the margin near the end of each lesson.

## DISCOVERY LEARNING

The page of **Discovery Learning** included in each lesson will get the students involved with an opening activity, a Bible study activity, and an application activity.

The last page of each lesson is a **reproducible page.** These may help to involve the students in discovery learning or provide detailed information not available elsewhere. Sometimes they are an integral part of the discovery learning plan. At other times, they provide optional activities that may be introduced at various points in the lesson. Marginal "Option" notes frequently call your attention to an activity on this page. Or you can start with the whole page and build your lesson plan around it, using the other resources in this book.

## PLANNING SHEET

Use the lesson planning sheet on page 10 to plan each of your lessons. The page is reproducible, so you can use it to fill in the blanks and plan out your complete lesson each week. List the options and features you have chosen for each lesson, and use it to guide you quickly and easily from one activity to the next.

# Index of Printed Texts, 1996-97

The printed texts for 1996-97 are arranged here in the order in which they appear in the Bible. Opposite each reference is the page number on which the passage begins in this volume.

# Cumulative Index

A cumulative index for the Scripture passages used in *The NIV Standard Lesson Commentary* for September 1994—August 1997 is presented here for your convenience.

# Lesson Planning Page

*List the aims here, either directly from the lesson or revised to suit your individual needs.*

## LESSON AIMS

*Begin with an opening activity like the illustration from the beginning of the lesson, "Into the Lesson" from the Discovery Learning page, a discussion question, or some other appropriate opener.*

## GETTING STARTED

*List in order the activities you will use. These include discussion questions, activities from the discovery learning page and the reproducible page—as well as key points from the commentary section.*

## LESSON DEVELOPMENT

I.

II.

III.

*How will you bring the lesson to a climax, stressing the key point and desired action steps?*

## CONCLUSION & APPLICATION

*Dismiss the class with an activity that reinforces the Bible lesson.*

## CLOSING ACTIVITY

# Autumn Quarter, 1996

## Theme: God's People Face Judgment

### Special Features

### Lessons

#### Unit 1. Responses to Wrong

#### Unit 2. Judah's Internal Decay

#### Unit 3. The Fall of Jerusalem

## ABOUT THESE LESSONS

This series of studies focuses on the history of the southern kingdom (Judah) from the time that the north (Israel) fell in 722 B.C. to the fall of Jerusalem in 586 B.C. The reigns of Kings Hezekiah and Josiah are highlighted, along with the prophetic ministries of Jeremiah, Habakkuk, and Ezekiel, who tried in vain to turn their countrymen from the path of certain doom.

Sep 1

Sep 8

Sep 15

Sep 22

Sep 29

Oct 6

Oct 13

Oct 20

Oct 27

Nov 3

Nov 10

Nov 17

Nov 24

# Lessons for Our Learning

*by Orrin Root*

Christians may disagree on many topics, but most agree that the Bible deserves more time and attention than we give it. We know it is supremely important for time and eternity, but other things demand our attention—things we have to do and things we want to do. So our Bible study often becomes crowded into a corner with other matters that we promise to get to "someday."

Having only a little time to study God's Word, we prefer to use most of that time with the New Testament. There we find the teaching of Jesus and the apostles, our best guide in Christian living. Yet we know that the Old Testament was also written for our learning (Romans 15:4), so we should want to include it in our study as well. Our Sunday school lessons are planned in accordance with the need to study and learn God's Word in its entirety.

## A LONG VIEW

The Sunday school lessons that we study are arranged in cycles, each cycle continuing for six years. Each year is divided into three-month quarters, with each quarter focusing on a particular topic. This September we are beginning the fifth year of the current cycle.

Fifteen quarters of this cycle are devoted to the New Testament, and only nine quarters to the Old. This means that more than sixty percent of our time is devoted to the New Testament and less than forty percent to the Old, though the Old offers more than three times as much material as the New does. In proportion to the number of pages in each Testament, we are giving more than five times as much attention to the New Testament.

If the nine quarters of study in the Old Testament were all grouped together, we would have more than two years of Old Testament study only. That is not too long to study the Old Testament, but it is too long to neglect the New. The lessons are arranged to give at least half of each year to the New Testament. In half of the six years of the current cycle, three quarters of the year are devoted to the New Testament and only one quarter to the Old.

## OLD TESTAMENT LESSONS

The quarter beginning with this September is one of those devoted to the Old Testament. Before we start, let's look quickly at the other Old Testament studies within the cycle.

**Autumn 1992.** A quick survey of Old Testament history, each lesson centering on an important person.

**Autumn 1993.** The book of Genesis, beginning with creation and ending with the migration of Jacob and his family to Egypt.

**Summer 1994.** The escape from Egypt and the journey to the promised land.

**Autumn 1994.** The battles that won the promised land, and Israel's life in that land until it became a kingdom and Solomon brought it to the peak of its power.

**Summer 1995.** The division of Israel and the growth of sin, in spite of urgent warnings by the prophets, until the northern kingdom was destroyed.

**Winter 1996.** Lessons from Isaiah, Jonah, and Ruth.

**Autumn 1996.** This is the quarter we are now beginning. It traces the history of the southern kingdom (Judah) after the northern kingdom (Israel) was destroyed, and it ends with Judah's captivity in Babylon. The current cycle contains only two more quarters with lessons from the Old Testament.

**Autumn 1997.** Lessons from Nehemiah and the prophets concerning Israel's return from Babylon.

**Summer 1998.** Lessons from Old Testament wisdom literature: Job, Proverbs, Ecclesiastes.

## WHAT NOW?

Now here is a brief preview of the thirteen lessons we shall be studying in September, October, and November.

SEPTEMBER

## UNIT 1. RESPONSES TO WRONG

**Lesson 1.** At the age of twenty-five, Hezekiah became king of Judah. The nation had drifted deep into idolatry and sin, and was facing constant pressure from Assyria. Hezekiah's response to Judah's sin was to get rid of it. Vigorously he restored the worship of Jehovah and led his people in living by Jehovah's Law. The Lord warned that evil would still bring Judah to ruin, but not in Hezekiah's lifetime.

**Lesson 2.** Two bad kings followed Hezekiah, and idolatry and corruption became the norm once again. During Josiah's reign, however, the forgotten book of the Law was found in the temple, and Josiah enforced it with enthusiasm. Again disaster was delayed.

**Lesson 3.** While Josiah was king, Jeremiah was called to support his reforms with messages from the Lord. His mission was to proclaim God's messages fearlessly, though many in Judah would oppose him.

**Lesson 4.** Jeremiah sounded God's call: "Reform your ways and your actions!" If Judah would not do so, the fabulous temple where they pretended to worship would be destroyed. Jeremiah continued to give God's messages after Josiah died, and even after Judah was taken captive to Babylon.

**Lesson 5.** The prophet Habakkuk spoke during a time when Judah was mired in sin, perhaps after good king Josiah had died. He asked how long the Lord would let this wickedness go on. The answer was grim. Babylonians were going to destroy the nation. This troubled Habakkuk even more; how could God let those wicked Babylonians do that? But God was firmly in control: Babylon would be destroyed in its turn. Sooner or later, doing wrong always comes back to haunt the wrongdoer.

OCTOBER

## UNIT II. JUDAH'S INTERNAL DECAY

**Lesson 6.** This lesson shows how deeply sin was embedded within the people of Judah. Jeremiah was invited to search Jerusalem for a good man, but none could be found. Therefore disaster was certain.

**Lesson 7.** This message belongs to the time when ten thousand people of Judah had already been taken captive to Babylon. A false prophet in Jerusalem was preaching that Babylon would soon be crushed and the captives would be free. The true message from God was that the captivity would continue for some time.

**Lesson 8.** Ezekiel was one of those ten thousand captives in Babylon. God called him to proclaim the truth to his fellow captives, but warned him that they would not welcome his message.

**Lesson 9.** The captives in Babylon wanted to believe that they were there because of their ancestors' sins, not their own. God corrected that belief. The exiles were there because they had continued to commit the sins of their fathers. Each person is responsible for what he himself does.

| ## UNIT III. THE FALL OF JERUSALEM

**Lesson 10.** In Babylon the prophet Ezekiel made a little clay model of Jerusalem being besieged. This was a visualized prophecy of how the Babylonians would one day besiege Jerusalem and capture it. The survivors would then join the captives already in Babylon.

**Lesson 11.** After a siege of about a year and a half, the city of Jerusalem was captured and destroyed. Most of the survivors were driven away to Babylon to join those already in exile there.

**Lesson 12.** Here we have a sample (from the book of Lamentations) of Jeremiah's sorrow over the disaster that had come to his people. He acknowledged that their fate was due to their sin, but still he prayed that they would be forgiven and restored.

**Lesson 13.** The nation of Israel was no more; a remnant of its people were helpless captives in a foreign land. Subjection to Babylon would last for seventy years. That would be approximately fifty years after the final stage of Judah's captivity. Yet God gave Ezekiel a clear prophecy of restoration. The nation would live again. God still had a purpose for his people.

### LESSONS TO BE LEARNED

Mindful of the fact that the Old Testament records were written for our learning, we shall be looking for what they teach us. What do these lessons say to our nation, to our church, and to ourselves?

No other nation was chosen of God as Israel was, but other nations have risen and fallen as it did. Nebuchadnezzar's Babylonian empire took Judah into captivity, yet Nebuchadnezzar's own dream foretold three empires that would follow his (Daniel 2:26-45). History records that they rose and fell, each in its turn: the empire of the Medes and Persians, the Greek empire of Alexander the Great, and the magnificent empire of Rome. Like Israel, each of these was weakened by corruption within before it was destroyed by attack from without. Is there a lesson here for our nation?

Nebuchadnezzar's dream also foretold a kingdom that will never be destroyed (Daniel 2:44). This is God's kingdom, the kingdom of Heaven. It is eternal, but that does not mean it is immune to corruption. Jesus called his disciples the salt of the earth, but he warned, "If the salt loses its saltiness, how can it be made salty again? It is no longer good for anything, except to be thrown out and trampled by men" (Matthew 5:13). Syria and North Africa once were solidly Christian. But the salt that was present there lost its saltiness. Officials of the church allied themselves with the secular government and shared its corruption until these lands were trampled by Moslem hordes. Is there a lesson here for the church of today?

Both church and nation are made up of individual people; thus, the corruption of individuals becomes the corruption of church and nation. In a few weeks we will read God's rebuke to people who wanted to blame others for their troubles. Loud and clear came the message: "The soul who sins is the one who will die" (Ezekiel 18:4). Through centuries that stern sentence has not been revoked, yet there is a way of escape. In God's kingdom and by his grace there is forgiveness. Sinners can live if their sins are taken away through Jesus, but not if they prefer to continue in their sins. To us the message is as loud and clear as it was to Judah.

The lessons ahead of us are for our learning. Are we ready and willing to listen?

# HOLDING FAST TO THE LORD

**LESSON 1**

## WHY TEACH THIS LESSON?

"When you reach the end of your rope, tie a knot and hang on!" The advice started out as a joke, but it really is good advice. Perseverance is a rare commodity today, but it is essential. The key is having something worth waiting for—and Christians surely do!

Times may be tough, but hold on. Government and media pressures may press, but hold on. Family and friends may oppose, but hold on. Hezekiah, one of Judah's greatest kings, was the son of one of the worst. But he held fast to the Lord. Society had dismissed worship of the true God as old fashioned, but Hezekiah held fast. His example can help you and your students hold fast as well.

## INTRODUCTION

### A. TWO KINDS OF HISTORY

One of the great testimonies for the truth of the Bible is its history. Ancient historians, usually employed by kings who wanted to be fondly remembered, often distorted the facts to paint their monarch in as favorable light as possible. Often they exaggerated the ruler's triumphs and ignored his failures. To do so made the king look good and the historian wealthy. A more honest approach could even be hazardous to the historian's health!

The inspired men who wrote Bible history were of a different kind. Their books "tell it like it is." The primal sin of Adam and Eve is recorded with no attempt to excuse it. So is the sin of David, though he was a man after God's own heart. And when we come to good king Hezekiah, we see his blunders along with his goodness.

### B. LESSON BACKGROUND

Two years ago we began a series of studies that showed how Israel became a kingdom, and how David and Solomon brought that kingdom to the peak of its power and glory. The following summer we saw how that power and glory faded. The great nation was split into two little ones—Israel in the north and Judah in the south.

Idolatry quickly invaded the northern kingdom. Encouraged by the government, it grew worse and worse. Greed and immorality increased as well.

In Judah, the government swung wildly from bad to good and back again. When the government was bad, the people quickly followed it into evil ways. When it was good, the people were more apt to follow God's ways.

Now we take up the story more than two centuries after the kingdom was divided. Hezekiah was one of Judah's good kings—one of the best. Yet Hezekiah erred, and the historian does not hide it.

DEVOTIONAL READING
DEUTERONOMY 10:12-22

LESSON SCRIPTURE
2 KINGS 18—20

PRINTED TEXT
2 KINGS 18:1-8; 20:16-21

**OPTION**

*Expand on this concept with the reproducible avctivity, "The Good and the Bad," on page 22.*

**LESSON AIMS**

*As students participate in today's class session, they should do the following:*

*1. List specific ways found in 2 Kings 18 that show how Hezekiah held fast to the Lord.*

*2. Explain what it means to hold fast to the Lord.*

*3. Decide how they themselves can hold fast to the Lord in at least one specific way.*

**KEY VERSE**

*He held fast to the LORD and did not cease to follow him; he kept the commands the LORD had given Moses.* 2 Kings 18:6

**Lesson 1 Notes**

## I. GOOD KING (2 KINGS 18:1-6)

Ahaz was one of Judah's worst kings. He turned away from the Lord, becoming an enthusiastic idol worshiper. He even sacrificed one of his sons (2 Kings 16:1-4).

When Ahaz died, the new king had the task of turning the government and the whole nation back to the Lord and to honesty, decency, and morality. It was no small task.

### A. STATISTICAL SUMMARY (vv. 1, 2)

**1. In the third year of Hoshea son of Elah king of Israel, Hezekiah son of Ahaz king of Judah began to reign.**

*The third year of Hoshea.* This was most likely 728-727 B.C., since in Hoshea's ninth year (722 B.C.) Israel fell to Assyria (2 Kings 17:6). This, however, creates certain problems with the dating of Hezekiah's reign. In this difficult area of chronology, competent scholars disagree. Probably the problems are caused by coregencies (fathers and sons serving together) that are not specified or defined, but the particulars are beyond the scope of what we can discuss here.

**2. He was twenty-five years old when he became king, and he reigned in Jerusalem twenty-nine years. His mother's name was Abijah daughter of Zechariah.**

Most heads of state are in at least middle age. A president of the United States, for example, by law must be at least thirty-five years old—and most presidents have been much older. But in Judah a youngster of twenty-five stepped to the throne and resolved to make a change that would reverse the whole course of his country.

The new king's mother is named, probably because his father had more than one wife. *Abijah* is named in 2 Chronicles 29:1 also, but nothing more is known of either this lady or her father *Zechariah.*

### B. RIGHT ACTION (vv. 3, 4)

**3. He did what was right in the eyes of the LORD, just as his father David had done.**

Thus the general character of Hezekiah's reign is briefly described. *David* had ruled close to three centuries earlier. He was not the actual *father* of Hezekiah, but Hezekiah was a direct descendant of that great king. David was the head of the dynasty. From the time Israel and Judah separated into two nations, Israel had been served by several dynasties. Only Judah could claim an unbroken succession of kings descended from David.

More important than biological heritage, however, was the spiritual kinship between Hezekiah and David. Both of them served *the Lord* and *did what was right.*

**4. He removed the high places, smashed the sacred stones and cut down the Asherah poles. He broke into pieces the bronze snake Moses had made, for up to that time the Israelites had been burning incense to it. (It was called Nehushtan.)**

*The high places* were places of worship on hilltops or artificial mounds. Some of them may have been used for the worship of the Lord; but in the time of Hezekiah's evil father, the high places were devoted mainly to heathen worship. *The sacred stones* were idols representing imaginary gods. The typical *Asherah pole* was a wooden pole erected at one of the high places to represent an imaginary goddess named Asherah.

We read about *the bronze snake Moses had made.* in Numbers 21:4-9. It had provided healing for anyone bitten by the poisonous snakes the Lord had sent to punish the Israelites for their grumbling. Now, in a time of general idolatry, people had begun to look on this bronze snake as an idol. They *had been burning incense to it.* This was an act of worship, the smoke of the incense representing the prayers of the people. Hezekiah broke this snake and contemptuously called it "a piece of bronze." It was no more a god than any other lump of bronze was!

**What Do You Think?**

Given the example of his wicked father Ahaz, isn't it remarkable that Hezekiah became a such good king? How might this circumstance have come about? Discuss the influence each of the following might have had in producing this result.

The role of Hezekiah's mother Abijah. (What, then, would you advise godly wives of ungodly men in regard to bringing up faithful children? How about single moms?)

Advisors who urged Hezekiah toward a course of righteousness. (Where are we to find godly advisors for young people seeking the way of the Lord?)

Hezekiah's own observation of the disastrous effects of his father's policies. (See 2 Chronicles 29:1-11.)

The visual for lesson 1 in the visuals packet shows a high place with an altar, perhaps similar to the high places destroyed by Hezekiah. The inset picture of a copper snake found in southern Palestine may also give us some idea of the bronze snake that Hezekiah destroyed.

### TWISTED SYMBOLS

One December recently, a school board acting in its collective wisdom decided to ban all references to Santa Claus from the classrooms that fell under its authority. The basis for their action was a misunderstanding of the principle of the separation of church and state. How ironic that one of the major symbols of the secularization of Christmas in America had come to be seen by some as a religious symbol!

Symbols only suggest meaning. Thus they can come to symbolize something other than what they were originally intended to mean. Judah's twisting of Moses' bronze snake into a pagan idol is an example. This snake had originally symbolized God's power to save the Israelites when they were bitten by poisonous snakes in the wilderness. Jesus would much later refer to this same snake and give it new meaning as a prophetic symbol of his own death by crucifixion (John 3:14, 15).

The nations of Judah and Israel turned from God to serve idols and became, in themselves, twisted symbols. The people who were to be a sign to the nations of God's providence denied him and forced him to bring ruin and desolation upon them.

All who wear the name of Christ are symbols of God's redeeming power. Let us wear the name carefully and not twist it into a symbol of hypocrisy or faithlessness.

—C. R. B.

### C. RIGHT TRUST (vv. 5, 6)

**5. Hezekiah trusted in the LORD, the God of Israel. There was no one like him among all the kings of Judah, either before him or after him.**

Judah had other good kings. Hezekiah's great-grandfather Uzziah was notable among them, and so was his great-grandson Josiah.

Some Bible students see a contradiction here with 2 Kings 23:25. There it is said that "neither before nor after Josiah was there a king like him who turned to the Lord as he did." How could Hezekiah be better than anyone before or after him if Josiah was better than any king before or after him?

Two explanations have been offered to resolve the conflict. First, the Hebrew language is given to hyperbole—deliberate exaggeration for emphasis. It may be that neither description is to be taken as a literal comparison but simply as an emphatic statement of approval. We use a similar figure of speech when we say a baseball player "hit the ball a mile!" We do not mean that the ball traveled 5,280 feet—just that it went an impressively long distance.

A second explanation notes that Hezekiah *trusted in the Lord* and "held fast to the Lord" (verse 6) like no other while Josiah "turned to the Lord" like no other. Thus, there is no real contradiction. Hezekiah was best in one specific way and Josiah was best in another.

Either explanation satisfactorily refutes the idea of a contradiction.

**6. He held fast to the LORD and did not cease to follow him; he kept the commands the LORD had given Moses.**

More than seven hundred years had passed since the Lord gave his Law to Moses; but that Law was still the law of the land, and King Hezekiah obeyed it.

### II. REWARD OF GOODNESS (2 KINGS 18:7, 8)

#### A. NATIONAL FREEDOM (v. 7)

**7. And the LORD was with him; he was successful in whatever he undertook. He rebelled against the king of Assyria and did not serve him.**

*The Lord was with him.* With the Lord, a young man of twenty-five became a capable and successful king. *He was successful in whatever he undertook.* We have seen his great campaign against spiritual enemies (v. 4); verse 8 records another campaign against national enemies (the Philistines).

### HOW TO SAY IT

*Abijah.* Uh-BYE-juh.
*Ahaz.* AY-haz.
*Asherah.* Uh-SHE-ruh.
*Assyria.* Uh-SEER-ee-uh.
*Elah.* EE-lah.
*eunuchs.* YOU-nicks.
*Hezekiah.* Hez-eh-KYE-uh.
*Hoshea.* Ho-SHE-uh.
*Isaiah.* Eye-ZAY-uh.
*Josiah.* Jo-SYE-uh.
*Leah.* LEE-uh.
*Manasseh.* Muh-NASS-uh.
*Nehushtan.* Nee-HUSH-tun.
*Nineveh.* NIN-uh-vuh.
*Philistines.* Fih-LISS-teens or FIL-us-teens.
*Uzziah.* Uh-ZYE-uh.
*Zechariah.* Zek-uh-RYE-uh.
*Zedekiah.* Zed-uh-KYE-uh.

### VISUALS FOR THESE LESSONS

The Adult Visuals/Learning Resources *packet contains classroom-size visuals designed for use with the lessons in the Autumn Quarter. The packet is available from your supplier. Order no. ST 192.*

## WHAT DO YOU THINK?

*"Like father, like son."
Hezekiah proves this is not always the case. Tragically, his own son proves it as well. Still, there is no doubt that children are strongly influenced by the examples their parents offer them. If parents want Jesus Christ to occupy a place of high importance in their children's lives, those parents need to demonstrate their own genuine commitment to Christ. If parents envision a life of purity and honesty for their children, those parents dare not compromise in their own quest for holiness.*

*What specific actions do you think parents should take to ensure faithfulness in the next generation? Do you think the church needs to do more to help parents? If so, what?*

Verse 7 records that *he rebelled against the king of Assyria.* Assyria was a growing empire with its capital at Nineveh. With formidable armies, it was pushing to add more nations to its territory. Ahaz, Hezekiah's father, had made a costly treaty with Assyria. Attacked by the combined forces of Israel and Syria, Ahaz did not trust in the Lord but appealed to Assyria for help. Assyria's help cost Ahaz a huge sum of silver and gold, much of it coming from the temple (2 Kings 16:5-9). Apparently Ahaz had continued to pay tribute to Assyria. Hezekiah, however, refused to pay. That brought the fury of Assyria's army against him. Hezekiah trusted the Lord, who drove the Assyrians back to Nineveh (2 Kings 18:13—19:36).

### B. NATIONAL VICTORY (v. 8)

**8. From watchtower to fortified city, he defeated the Philistines, as far as Gaza and its territory.**

The Philistines lived along the coast of the Mediterranean Sea. They were constant enemies of Judah. Probably they had occupied some of Judah's territory while king Ahaz had been busy with the attack by Israel and Syria. Hezekiah not only drove them out, but also followed them into their own territory and defeated them thoroughly. His campaign reached *as far as Gaza,* far to the southwest.

*The watchtower* symbolizes the most remote rural area. There a tower built in a vineyard provided shelter for workers, and from its top a watchman could see thieves if they entered a secluded part of the vineyard. (See Matthew 21:33.) *The fortified city* was a city with a strong stone wall to protect it from attack. So *from watchtower to fortified city* means "throughout the whole land," from the most isolated rural part to the biggest city. Hezekiah's victory over the Philistines was complete.

### CLEANING UP A MESS

Dolores Zarley's son was not a disorderly adolescent with a messy room. He was a forty-year-old whose sloppiness spilled over into the front yard. There, his collection of junk cars and trucks was an eyesore that grated on his mother's nerves. When her patience wore out, she launched a campaign to get rid of the visual abominations. Her first step was to throw a match into the back seat of the graffiti-covered junker that bothered her the most. Her efforts resulted in a family fight, five stitches on her husband's chin, and her arrest on arson charges!

King Hezekiah, on the other hand, was a *young* man who was embarrassed because his *elders* had allowed Judah to become a religious "junkyard." The people of God had cluttered up their land and their lives with idols of many kinds. The spiritual life of this covenant people was a humiliation to those who loved God. So Hezekiah began cleaning up Judah's "front yard."

Hezekiah got better results than Mrs. Zarley: his cleanup succeeded and he gained an honored reputation for doing "what was right in the eyes of the Lord." Our calling as Christians is similar to Hezekiah's: to be a positive influence on God's people and the society in which we worship and work. But let us do it as Hezekiah did—in such a way as to be honored (because our love for God brings needed change), not hated (because of a contentious attitude).     —C. R. B.

## III. BAD NEWS AND GOOD (2 KINGS 20:16-21)

The first part of 2 Kings 20 tells us that Hezekiah was sick and near death. In response to his fervent prayer, the Lord gave him fifteen more years on earth (verse 6). As a sign that this message came from God, the shadow on the stairway moved backward (verses 8-11).

Later, ambassadors from the king of Babylon came to congratulate Hezekiah upon his recovery from his sickness (2 Kings 20:12). They also wanted to know more about "the miraculous sign that had occurred in the land" (2 Chronicles

32:31). Was that sign the backward motion of the shadow (2 Kings 20:11)? Was it the miraculous defeat of the Assyrian army (2 Kings 19:35, 36)? Was it simply Hezekiah's marvelous growth in wealth and power (2 Chronicles 32:27-30)? Any of these was enough to excite the interest of the king of Babylon.

Hezekiah then displayed a regrettable measure of pride. He showed the men from Babylon all he had—his treasures of silver and gold and other precious items, including "his armory" with his battle equipment. "There was nothing in his palace or in all his kingdom  that Hezekiah did not show them" (2 Kings 20:13).

When the emissaries had gone back to Babylon, Isaiah the prophet came to Hezekiah with sharp questions: Who were those men? Where did they come from? What did you show them? Hezekiah's answer was plain and honest: I showed them everything I have. Thus the stage was set for the final scene of our text.

## A. BAD NEWS (vv. 16-18)

**16. Then Isaiah said to Hezekiah, "Hear the word of the LORD.**

Isaiah himself had no criticism or comment. He was simply a messenger, bringing *the word of the Lord.*

**17. "The time will surely come when everything in your palace, and all that your fathers have stored up until this day, will be carried off to Babylon. Nothing will be left, says the LORD.**

All the wealth that Hezekiah had so proudly shown the Babylonians, all the royal treasures stored up through generations, would finally *be carried off to Babylon.* Babylon would one day take Assyria's place, conquer Judah, and despoil it.

**18. And some of your descendants, your own flesh and blood, that will be born to you, will be taken away, and they will become eunuchs in the palace of the king of Babylon."**

Not only Hezekiah's treasures, but also his sons would be included in the spoil taken to Babylon. The princes of Judah would become menial slaves in the palace of a foreign king. It was more than a century after Hezekiah died when the last of Judah's treasures were taken to Babylon (2 Kings 25:13-17). The king of Judah at that time was Zedekiah. He belonged to the fourth generation after Hezekiah. Some ten years before that King Jehoiachin, also a descendant of Hezekiah, was captured by the Babylonians and the temple treasures were plundered (2 Kings 24:10-17).

The Hebrew word for *eunuchs* is rendered "officers" in 1 Samuel 8:15. In connection with the Babylonians' future treatment of Hezekiah's descendants, the term may imply the actual physical procedure that would make a man a eunuch. King Jehoiachin did receive a position of honor in the Babylonian palace (2 Kings 25:27-30). Whether he was literally made a eunuch or the term applies to him as an "officer" cannot be stated with certainty, but he does fulfill the prophecy. Others of Hezekiah's descendants, as well as Daniel and his friends, probably received similar treatment (Daniel 1:1-7).

## B. GOOD NEWS (v. 19)

**19. "The word of the LORD you have spoken is good," Hezekiah replied. For he thought, "Will there not be peace and security in my lifetime?"**

Bad as the news was, Hezekiah called it *good.* Of course, even a word of condemnation from the Lord is good in that it is just and right. But Hezekiah found something else that was good. The disaster would be postponed until a later generation. *Peace and security* would remain as long as Hezekiah lived.

While Hezekiah's reply appears selfish, it seems that Hezekiah overcame his unseemly pride and humbled himself (2 Chronicles 32:26). "Peace and security" were then granted, and he was able to reign until the end of the years allotted him.

---

### WHAT DO YOU THINK?

Hezekiah's reaction to Isaiah's prophecy regarding coming disaster was curious: "'The word of the Lord . . . is good,' Hezekiah replied. For he thought, 'Will there not be peace and security in my lifetime?'" (2 Kings 20:19). For us the idea that our children or grandchildren may have to face disaster is an appalling one. We desire peace in our time, but we desire it also in their time.

What do you think is the proper role for the church in working for "peace and security" for future generations? How much should the church be involved in political issues? Economic issues? Educational issues? Why? What about individual Christians—is their role any different from the role of the church itself? Why or why not?

### WHAT DO YOU THINK?

Even good king Hezekiah fell victim to the temptations of pride. The result was disastrous, even if "peace and security" remained in his day. Do you think Christians today are generally concerned with the danger of pride? Why or why not?

What situations are most likely to tempt you to become excessively proud? How can—or should— you deal with those temptations? How does Hezekiah's example instruct you in this matter?

## THOUGHT TO REMEMBER

Yesterday is gone, but we can use today to make a better tomorrow.

## DAILY BIBLE READINGS

**Monday, Aug. 26**—Rabshakeh Mocks the Living God (2 Kings 18:26-36)

**Tuesday, Aug. 27**—Rabshakeh Rebuked by God (2 Kings 19:1-7)

**Wednesday, Aug. 28**—Hezekiah Prays for God's Deliverance (2 Kings 19:14-19)

**Thursday, Aug. 29**—God Promises to Save Jerusalem (2 Kings 19:29-34)

**Friday, Aug. 30**—God Heals Hezekiah (2 Kings 20:1-6)

**Saturday, Aug. 31**—The Sign of Hezekiah's Healing (2 Kings 20:7-11)

**Sunday, Sept. 1**—Hezekiah's Great Riches (2 Chronicles 32: 27-41)

## C. THERE'S MORE (vv. 20, 21)

**20. As for the other events of Hezekiah's reign, all his achievements and how he made the pool and the tunnel by which he brought water into the city, are they not written in the book of the annals of the kings of Judah?**

It appears that *the book of the annals of the kings of Judah* was a much more extensive record than any of the biblical books that record events of the same time period. Perhaps it was a diary kept by the royal scribes. This longer record may have perished in the flames when Jerusalem was burned about a century later. We must be content with the shorter records we have in Kings and Chronicles, plus chapters 36-39 of Isaiah.

Additional details concerning Hezekiah's reconstruction of Jerusalem's water source are found in 2 Chronicles 32:1-5, 30.

**21. Hezekiah rested with his fathers. And Manasseh his son succeeded him as king.**

*Rested with his fathers* is a gentle way of saying that he died. With but few blunders, Hezekiah had ruled nobly for twenty-nine years (2 Kings 18:2). Sad to say, his son Manasseh proved to be as bad as Hezekiah was good. This bad son of a good father led Judah far down the road to ruin (Jeremiah 15:1-4).

## CONCLUSION

### A. BEWARE OF PRIDE!

A cute little first grader was telling me about her school. "I'm the best reader in my class," she confided. "But that's all right, because I don't know it."

In a second she realized that something was amiss with that statement. Maybe my chuckle tipped her off. "I guess I do know it," she amended, "but I act as if I didn't."

How neatly her alert mind caught one of the lessons we learn from king Hezekiah! Doing well is dangerous. It can make us proud. If you're the best, probably you're smart enough to know you're the best. It's hard to act as if you don't know it, and to act that way without being seen as a hypocrite or a pretender.

Then what? Do you stop being the best? Of course not. You keep on being the best, but you're careful not to brag about it. You're the same sweet, friendly, and helpful person you were before you became the best. Then people like you even if you are the best, and you like them even if they're not. More than that, people admire you and try to be as good as you are—and that may be the best of the good things you do.

### B. LOOK AHEAD

"Like father, like son." That's what "they say," but it's not always true. Hezekiah was the best of kings, while his father Ahaz was a bad king and his son Manasseh was even worse. What happened to "like father, like son"?

Every parent needs to be looking ahead and thoughtfully planning to make the next generation better than this one. The Lord tells how. His words are basic. You cherish them in your heart, and you plant them in the hearts of your children. You talk of them when you're sitting at home, even if you have to turn off the TV sometimes. When you're not at home, you show how they're applied. You think of them when you go to bed and when you get up (Deuteronomy 6:6, 7). And of course you do all this without nagging, for nagging closes the hearts where you're trying to plant God's words.

It isn't easy, but it's your job if you're a parent. The next generation will not be better than this one unless you make it so.

# Discovery Learning

*This page contains an alternate lesson plan emphasizing learning activities. Classes desiring such student involvement will find these suggestions helpful. The next page is a reproducible activity page to further enhance discovery learning.*

## LEARNING GOALS

In today's session students should do the following:

1. List specific ways found in 2 Kings 18 that show how Hezekiah held fast to the Lord.

2. Explain what it means to hold fast to the Lord.

3. Decide how they themselves can hold fast to the Lord in at least one specific way.

## INTO THE LESSON

Before class write the following scrambled sentence on your chalkboard:

"Lord the fast He to held."

Cover the scrambled sentence with a piece of shelf paper taped onto your chalkboard. To begin today's class session, tell class members that you want to have a simple contest to see who can unscramble the sentence first. Uncover the sentence, and let class members shout out the answer when they think they have it. Write, "He held fast to the Lord" (2 Kings 18:6) on your chalkboard.

Then ask each class member to find a partner and discuss one of the following ideas together for five minutes:

• *Someone I know who could be described by this sentence.*

or

• *A time in my life when this sentence described me.*

When the five minutes have passed, ask a few volunteers to share their answers. Then discuss some or all of the following questions:

1. What does it mean to hold fast to the Lord?

2. How does a person hold fast to the Lord?

3. When you think of someone's holding fast to the Lord, are you more likely to think of how he or she responds to good times or to bad times? Why?

Tell your group that today's study will look at Hezekiah, the good king described by this sentence. We'll see why the sentence applied to him and how it can apply to us.

## INTO THE WORD

Ask a class member to read aloud 2 Kings 18:1, 2. Briefly present the background for today's lesson and an overview of the studies in this quarter. Tell the class that today's Scripture text shows how Hezekiah was a good king of Judah and what he did to hold fast to the Lord.

Ask another volunteer to read aloud 2 Kings 18:3-6. Then ask each of the pairs of students who discussed the earlier question to find another pair, so that the class members are grouped into fours. These groups should examine verses 3-6 and make a list of all the evidences they find there to show how Hezekiah held fast to the Lord. Allow about six minutes, then ask volunteers to call out items. Write each item on a separate sheet of newsprint. The following items may be included: did what was right in the eyes of the Lord (v. 3); eliminated idolatry (v. 4); trusted God (v. 5); obeyed God's commands (v. 6); enjoyed the Lord's blessings (v. 7); defeated the Lord's enemies (v. 8).

If you have time, you may want to highlight Hezekiah's reign for your class members:

• He stood firm against the king of Assyria, and God gave him a miraculous victory (2 Kings 19:35, 36).

• His nation, Judah, grew in wealth and power under his reign (2 Chronicles 32:27-30).

• He became desperately ill, but God heard his tearful prayer for health and granted him fifteen more years of life (2 Kings 20:1-6).

• He asked for a sign to prove that God would extend his life, and God responded by moving the shadow on the stairway backward (2 Kings 20:8-11).

• The king of Babylon sent messengers and a gift to Hezekiah, to inquire about his recovery (2 Kings 20:12; 2 Chronicles 32:31).

Ask a class member to read 2 Kings 20:13-21. Discuss some or all of the following questions:

1. Why did Hezekiah show the Babylonians everything he owned (2 Chronicles 32:25)?

2. What do you suppose was Hezekiah's tone of voice in verse 15?

3. What do you make of Hezekiah's response to Isaiah's prophecy?

## INTO LIFE

Look again at the class's list of ways that Hezekiah held fast to the Lord. Ask class members, in the same groups of four that researched that list, to answer this question for each item: "How can a Christian today follow the example of Hezekiah in this way?" Give the class several minutes to suggest practical applications for each point. List these on the sheets of newsprint you used earlier.

Close with sentence prayers. Encourage class members to commit themselves to acting out at least one of the application points.

*Option.* Use the reproducible activity, "Hang On!" (page 22) to apply the truth of this lesson to life.

# The Good and the Bad

One of the testimonies to the Bible's truthfulness is its record of the sins and failures of notable people. A description of both good and bad characteristics in human heroes is what we would expect in a true narrative.

On the following chart, write a description or summary of what the cited Scripture reference says about the character's good quality or behavior in the "Good" column. In the "Bad" column, summarize or describe an occasion of wrong actions cited in the text.

| CHARACTER | GOOD | BAD |
|---|---|---|
| Noah | Genesis 6:9 | Genesis 9:20, 21 |
| Abraham | Genesis 15:6; 18:18, 19 | Genesis 12:10-20; 20:1-13 |
| Moses | Hebrews 11:24-29 | Exodus 3:7—4:17 |
| Elijah | James 5:16b-18 | 1 Kings 19:1-3 |
| the apostles | Acts 4:33 | Mark 9:33, 34 |
| Paul (Saul) and Barnabas | Acts 13:46-49; 14:3, 22-26 | Acts 15:36-40 |

# Hang On!

What is the greatest challenge to your faith that you face?

List (a) a Bible passage that encourages you to hold fast to the Lord, (b) someone you can talk to who can help you hold fast, and (c) a prayer of commitment to hold fast to the Lord in the face of this challenge.

a.

b.

c.

# OBEYING GOD'S COMMANDS

**LESSON 2**

## WHY TEACH THIS LESSON?

It seems we can hear the lament over the decay of morality everywhere. Even movie stars and politicians have recently expressed concern. But cries and complaints notwithstanding, the decay continues. We wring our hands and wonder what the world is coming to—and whatever it is that it's coming to, it is coming there faster and faster!

Today's lesson covers a time of decay for the nation of Judah. Evil King Manasseh had led the nation into a downward spiral from which it would never completely recover. But King Josiah was not one to wring his hands and complain. He was a man—well, a boy—of action. And he led the nation in a revival.

Use this lesson to challenge your students to take action. Yes, the moral climate of our society has declined. That just means the need for godly people to act is even greater than before.

## INTRODUCTION

During the 1992 U.S. presidential election, two of the three candidates clamored for change. Some campaign orators even suggested that someone needed to "reinvent government." But no one suggested that the Constitution be abandoned. No one wanted to abolish the presidency or the Congress or the federal court system. The changes recommended were not very radical.

### A. DRASTIC CHANGES

When Hezekiah became king of Judah, a series of drastic changes occurred. He did not change Judah's "constitution"; he simply began to govern according to it. The former king (his father Ahaz) had not done that. But Hezekiah "did what was right in the eyes of the Lord" (2 Kings 18:3). For most of his reign that was the national policy, as we saw in last week's lesson. Both Hezekiah and Judah prospered (2 Chronicles 32:27-30).

The change was no less drastic when Hezekiah died, but it moved in the opposite direction. His son Manasseh was only twelve years old when he became king, so we must suppose his advisers had much to do with the change. But these advisers were not the ones who had helped Hezekiah in his godly rule. They did not abolish the constitution; they simply ignored it. Manasseh "did evil in the eyes of the Lord" (2 Kings 21:2). He encouraged idolatry throughout Judah, even in the courts of the Lord's temple. He "shed so much innocent blood that he filled Jerusalem from end to end" (2 Kings 21:16). His reign is recorded in 2 Kings 21:1-18.

In his later years, Manasseh was captured by the Assyrians. Repentant, he turned to the Lord, who responded by securing the king's his release. Manasseh

DEVOTIONAL READING
**DEUTERONOMY 30:15-20**
LESSON SCRIPTURE
**2 KINGS 22:1—23:20**
PRINTED TEXT
**2 KINGS 23:1-8a**

### LESSON AIMS

*As students participate in today's class session, they should:*

*1. List the evidences in Josiah's society of the generation's ignorance of God's Law.*

*2. Compare this situation with similar trends in our own society.*

*3. Choose at least one way to reemphasize the Bible in their world.*

### KEY VERSE

*The king stood by the pillar and renewed the covenant in the presence of the LORD—to follow the LORD and keep his commands, regulations and decrees with all his heart and all his soul, thus confirming the words of the covenant written in this book. Then all the people pledged themselves to the covenant.*

—2 Kings 23:3

## LESSON 2 NOTES

### HOW TO SAY IT

*Ahaz.  AY-haz.*
*Amon.  AY-mun.*
*Asherah.  Uh-SHE-ruh.*
*Assyria.  Uh-SEER-ee-uh.*
*Assyrians.  Uh-SEER-ee-unz.*
*Auschwitz.  OWSH-vits.*
*Baal.  BAY-ul.*
*Beersheba.  Beer-SHE-buh.*
*Bethel.  BETH-ul.*
*Geba.  GEE-buh (G as in GET).*
*Hezekiah.  Hez-eh-KYE-uh.*
*Hilkiah.  Hil-KYE-uh.*
*Huldah.  HUL-dah.*
*Jeroboam.  Jair-uh-BOE-um.*
*Josiah.  Jo-SYE-uh.*
*Kidron.  KID-ron.*
*Manasseh.  Muh-NASS-uh.*
*Nehemiah.  NEE-huh-MY-uh.*
*Shaphan.  SHAY-fan.*
*Treblinka.  TREB-link-uh.*

### WHAT DO YOU THINK?

*The public reading of Scripture preceded the reforms of King Josiah. Do you think the public reading of Scripture today helps to stir us to renewal of our faith and rededication to service? Why or why not? What can be done to enhance the effectiveness of Scripture reading? Discuss the following:*

*Who should read?*

*When should the reading occur?*

*How do variations like antiphonal readings, responsive readings, or dramatic readings help or hinder the effectiveness?*

*Is the Scripture reading merely a preliminary to a sermon or the Lord's Supper, or can it be a potentially powerful act of worship in itself? Explain.*

came back a changed man. Earnestly he tried to undo the harm he had done (2 Chronicles 33:10-16), but his time was too short. When he died, his son Amon promptly reverted to the earlier evil policy (2 Kings 21:19-22).

By this time Judah was close to anarchy. Amon ruled only two years; then he was killed in his own house by his own servants. This led to a popular uprising. "The people of the land" executed the killers. They put Amon's son Josiah on the throne (2 Kings 21:23, 24).

### B. LESSON BACKGROUND

We are not told who led the uprising that put Josiah on the throne; but we have to suppose those leaders now controlled the government, for the new king was only eight years old. They led well, and the young king "did what was right in the eyes of the Lord" (2 Kings 22:1, 2).

Eighteen years later, at the age of twenty-six, Josiah launched a major project. He planned to repair the temple of the Lord. Manasseh and his evil son had ruled for fifty-seven years, and Josiah himself was in the eighteenth year of his reign before he undertook this project. So for about seventy-five years the temple had been shamefully neglected and polluted by pagan altars and ceremonies. Now it was to be cleaned and repaired (2 Kings 22:3-7).

When the cleanup began, a high priest found in the temple the book of the Law, which God had given to Moses more than seven hundred years before. Quite properly the high priest gave it to Shaphan, who was in charge of the cleanup project. Shaphan took it and read it to the king. When king Josiah heard the Law, he must have realized he and his people were breaking it in dozens of ways. The Law prescribed terrible penalties for such violations.

Was Jerusalem doomed to receive the severe punishment the Law demanded? To find an answer, the king and his counselors decided to consult a prophetess of the Lord in Jerusalem named Huldah. She affirmed that Jerusalem indeed was doomed. But because king Josiah was now doing his best to obey the Law, the punishment would not come during his lifetime (2 Kings 22:15-20). So the young king continued his efforts, as we see in our text.

## I. RENEWING THE COVENANT (2 KINGS 23:1-3)

Repairing the temple had appeared to be the primary task, but now it seemed only a tiny part of what must be done. The whole nation must learn of this Law. Every person must be enlisted in the effort to obey it.

### A. GATHERING THE PEOPLE (vv. 1, 2a)

**1. Then the king called together all the elders of Judah and Jerusalem.**

Each community of *Judah* had some mature citizens who were recognized as leaders. Josiah's first step was to secure their cooperation in bringing all the people together.

**2a. He went up to the temple of the LORD with the men of Judah, the people of Jerusalem, the priests and the prophets—all the people from the least to the greatest.**

This was a mass meeting of the entire nation—officials and common people, rich and poor, *priests* and sinners. The meeting place was *the temple of the Lord*—probably the courtyard through which the temple itself was entered.

### B. READING THE LAW (v. 2b)

**2b. He read in their hearing all the words of the Book of the Covenant, which had been found in the temple of the LORD.**

This must have been a long meeting. Years later Ezra conducted a similar reading, which took half a day (Nehemiah 8:2, 3). On that occasion, however, some time was spent in interpretation or explanation to help the people understand what was read. We are not told whether Josiah paused for explanation.

Obviously *the Book of the Covenant* was "the book of the law" mentioned in 2 Kings 22:8. God's Law constituted a covenant (an agreement or contract) between him and the people who promised to obey it. God agreed to give them peace and prosperity if they kept their promise, but to withhold these if they broke it.

### C. Pledging Obedience (v. 3)

**3. The king stood by the pillar and renewed the covenant in the presence of the Lord—to follow the Lord and keep his commands, regulations and decrees with all his heart and all his soul, thus confirming the words of the covenant written in this book. Then all the people pledged themselves to the covenant.**

*By the pillar* indicates some raised place where the king could be seen by all the assembled people. Some students think the Hebrew phrase means *on the platform* rather than *by the pillar*. The Hebrew word for "pillar" is a noun form of the verb "to stand." The question is whether it refers to something that stood—the pillar —or a standing place, where Josiah stood.

There in the sight and hearing of all the people, and *in the presence of the Lord,* King Josiah *renewed the covenant.* He vowed *to follow the Lord,* to accept his leading. He vowed *to keep his commands* and his *regulations and decrees.* We need not try to distinguish between these terms; all were included in *the words of the covenant written in this book.* Josiah promised to obey them all, with his whole heart and soul.

*Then all the people pledged themselves to the covenant.* Perhaps they had been sitting and now stood up to indicate that they joined the king in his pledge. If not in that way, then in some other manner they demonstrated that all of them were taking the same stand the king was taking.

### Not Enough Room

Empty space! When we think of the heavens, most of us think of an infinity of empty space. But the part of that empty space close to the earth is filling up with satellites. Only thirty years ago, the first communications satellite was launched. Now there are some seven hundred of them in orbit, with dozens more scheduled for launch.

For such satellites to be most effective, there should be only 180 of them, each separated from the next by two degrees of arc—about nine hundred miles at the altitude at which they orbit. More satellites result in radio signal interference among them. So strangely enough, there is not enough room in "empty space" for all our satellites!

When King Josiah began his reforms in Judah, he realized that the temple did not have enough room in it to contain idols as well as the God who had created the heavens and earth. Faith in the true God leaves no room for faith in any other.

The gods that compete today for a place in the temple of our hearts (money, fame, power, selfish pride, among others) may be different from the ones that Josiah eliminated, but the principle is still the same: there is not enough room in our hearts for more than one.

—C. R. B.

## II. CLEANING UP (2 KINGS 23:4-8a)

Places of idol worship were scattered all over the country. Pagan altars were even in the court of the Lord's house. Most of the people in Judah could not remember

### What Do You Think?

King Josiah publicly committed himself to accomplish the will of the Lord. This may call to mind the practice of public rededications in our services of worship—a practice that some Christian leaders view with suspicion. It is true that people who make such rededications often do so from shallow emotionalism and show no real change in their lives after the event. But are there not times for such public recommitments? Under what circumstances would you think a public rededication is appropriate? What should the church do to assist one making such a rededication?

The visual for this lesson is the same one as for lesson 1. It shows a high place (found in what is now western Jordan), perhaps resembling one of those destroyed by King Josiah.

## WHAT DO YOU THINK?

What are some ungodly influences that we may need to get rid of to clean up our community?

What can the church as a whole and/or individual Christians do to rid our community of these things?

(As you discuss this issue, be sure to include things like the sale of pornographic materials, the distribution of illegal drugs, the presence of a pseudo-Christian cult, and any other particular problem in your area.)

## OPTION

Use the reproducible activity "Tearing Down the Idols" on page 30 to facilitate your discussion of this issue.

## NOTE

Some students think the twelve signs of the zodiac are meant by the term constellations. These groups of stars have been recognized from ancient times, but God's Word makes it plain that they are God's creatures, not gods themselves.

a time when idol worship had not been common. Born in the midst of pagan idols, shrines, and ceremonies, how could the people know all of that was wrong? No one had told them about God's Law.

Now that his Law was known, everything pagan was declared abominable, and it was time to purge the entire country.

### A. PAGAN EQUIPMENT (v. 4)

**4. The king ordered Hilkiah the high priest, the priests next in rank and the door-keepers to remove from the temple of the LORD all the articles made for Baal and Asherah and all the starry hosts. He burned them outside Jerusalem in the fields of the Kidron Valley and took the ashes to Bethel.**

In *the temple of the Lord* a cleanup had already begun, during which the book of the Law had been found. Before that, apparently no one had realized that the worst pollution in the temple was the pagan worship occurring there. Now it must stop. Everything that had been used in idolatrous ceremonies had to go. This phase of the cleanup was assigned to the people most closely connected with the temple: *the high priest,* the subordinate priests (*the priests next in rank*), and the temple *door-keepers.*

*Baal* was chief among the imaginary gods worshiped in Palestine. Different communities might represent Baal in different forms, so we often find the plural *Baals,* meaning a number of different idols called Baal. The *Asherah* was a pole representing a goddess connected with Baal. (See the comments on 2 Kings 18:4 on page 16.)

*All the starry hosts* simply means the stars. The pagan Hebrews were among those who "worshiped and served created things rather than the Creator" (Romans 1:25).

All the items used in the worship of these false deities were taken out of the temple court and burned *in the fields of the Kidron Valley* east of Jerusalem. Josiah then *took the ashes to Bethel*. This town was about twelve miles north of Jerusalem. It was one of the places where Jeroboam had introduced idolatry soon after Israel was divided (1 Kings 12:26-30). Already defiled by centuries of idol worship, Bethel was a fitting place for the remains of the idolatry that had defiled God's house. But how tragic it was that Bethel had been so defiled! There Jacob had seen a vision of angels moving between Heaven and earth and had given the place its name—Bethel, meaning "house of God" (Genesis 28:10-22).

### B. PAGAN PRIESTS (v. 5)

**5. He did away with the pagan priests appointed by the kings of Judah to burn incense on the high places of the towns of Judah and on those around Jerusalem—those who burned incense to Baal, to the sun and moon, to the constellations and to all the starry hosts.**

Manasseh and Amon, kings of Judah who were Josiah's grandfather and father, had appointed priests to lead in pagan worship *on the high places* dedicated to such activity. Josiah had these idolatrous priests put to death. (See 2 Kings 23:20.)

To burn incense was an act of worship. The smoke of the incense represented the rising prayers of the worshipers. The *sun* and *moon* and *constellations* were also worshiped, as were *Baal,* the stars, and the Asherah (verse 6).

### C. PAGAN ASHERAH (v. 6)

**6. He took the Asherah pole from the temple of the LORD to the Kidron Valley outside Jerusalem and burned it there. He ground it to powder and scattered the dust over the graves of the common people.**

One might think the *Asherah* would have been among the items destroyed as recorded in verse 4, but now the writer returned to mention it specifically. Possibly only the loose tools and vessels were destroyed before, leaving the Asherah firmly planted in the ground. Now it was cut down or dug up and destroyed. It is thought that the ordinary Asherah was a plain wooden pole, but perhaps this one in the temple was ornamented with metal. This was crushed to powder, as was the golden calf that Aaron had made at Sinai centuries earlier (Exodus 32:20).

When *the common people,* or the poor, died, they were buried in the ground, not in caves or costly chambers hewn in rock. In this *valley outside Jerusalem* was apparently one such graveyard. The ground where they lay was already defiled by their dead bodies, so it was a suitable place to scatter the defiled powder of the Asherah.

### D. PAGAN HOUSES (v. 7)

**7. He also tore down the quarters of the male shrine prostitutes, which were in the temple of the LORD and where women did weaving for Asherah.**

The Hebrew word translated *male shrine prostitutes* literally means "consecrated men," but these men were consecrated to the wrong cause! Various sexual abuses and perversions were frequent parts of pagan worship. Depraved men available for such purposes were housed conveniently inside the *temple* courts. Josiah and his men demolished these structures, perhaps dumping the material in the Kidron Valley where other pagan items had been destroyed.

Some of the houses sheltered *women* who *did weaving for Asherah.* We can easily imagine that devoted pagan women dressed their goddess as a lady, with a clean gown every day. Perhaps that is what they did, but the Hebrew for *did weaving* is literally *wove houses.* Some students therefore conclude that the women made tents or awnings to shelter their idol from sun and rain.

### E. PAGAN HIGH PLACES (v. 8a)

**8a. Josiah brought all the priests from the towns of Judah and desecrated the high places, from Geba to Beersheba.**

Josiah's campaign against idolatry in Samaria (2 Kings 23:19, 20) helps us understand why he *brought the priests* with him and how he *desecrated* their *high places.* He brought these pagan priests so he could have them killed on the very altars they had used to offer sacrifices to their pagan gods. Then he destroyed the places of worship where they had officiated. This he did throughout the land of Judah, *from Geba* in the north *to Beersheba* in the south.

Verses 8b-20 continue the record of Josiah's campaign against idolatry. He carried it beyond the northern border of Judah into the territory that had belonged to Israel. Since 722 B.C. the northern nation had been subject to Assyria, but by Josiah's time Assyria was weakened from revolts elsewhere in its empire. Apparently there was no active resistance to Josiah's campaign against idolatry.

### DESTROYING THE PLACE WHERE EVIL WAS DONE

Just one mile west of a small Polish village lies a reminder of the horrible effects of racial pride. The prison blocks, gas chambers, and crematoria of Auschwitz cover fifteen square miles of Polish countryside. This prison camp was a part of the "solution" to what the Nazis called the "Jewish problem."

Between 1940 and 1945, some two million Jews and Polish citizens were exterminated in Auschwitz and the neighboring camp, Treblinka. These unfortunate souls, caught in the vise of Nazi hatred, were worked to death, killed in medical experiments, or poisoned in the gas chambers.

### WHAT DO YOU THINK?

*Josiah's reforms extended to the house of God, the temple itself. We live in a time when many Christians are substituting personal feelings for the Bible as a standard for belief and behavior. How can we clean up the house of God and get rid of this pagan belief?*

*Another dangerous religious influence affecting many church members is the idea that true believers will achieve material wealth and perfect health (cf. 1 Timothy 6:3-5). How can we combat this view and balance it with the biblical teaching that God allows trials to affect faithful people, too. (See Hebrews 12; James 1.)*

### DAILY BIBLE READINGS

*Monday, Sept. 2—Josiah Orders Repair of the Temple (2 Kings 22:1-7)*

*Tuesday, Sept 3—Josiah Receives the Book of the Law (2 Kings 22:8-13)*

*Wednesday, Sept. 4—Josiah Is Spared From God's Wrath (2 Kings 22:14-20)*

*Thursday, Sept 5—Josiah Orders the Passover Held (2 Kings 23:21-25)*

*Friday, Sept. 6—Josiah's Death (2 Kings 23:26-30)*

*Saturday, Sept. 7—Keep God's Commandments (Psalm 119:1-8)*

*Sunday, Sept. 8—Live Righteously (Psalm 119:9-16)*

## PRAYER

*Almighty Creator, how happy we are that you are also our Father! How good it is to have from you the rules of healthy and happy and honorable living! How graciously you have provided a way of forgiveness when we have failed to follow your rules! As we dedicate our lives to you, we ask for wisdom and grace and power to convey your message in a winsome way to those who need it. May we serve you well for the world's good and your glory. Amen*

## WHAT DO YOU THINK?

*The lesson writer declares "the best thing you and I can do for a better world is to bring people to Jesus. . . ." But the people of the world seem increasingly wary of our efforts to bring them to Jesus. How do the following situations hinder our efforts? What can we do to overcome the obstacles they present?*

*Publicized accounts of Christian leaders' falling prey to sexual temptations.*

*Churches being divided by dissension.*

*Aggressive action by anti-Christian groups.*

*Restrictions on Christian activity in public schools and other public facilities..*

## THOUGHT TO REMEMBER

*Christ is King.*

During the years after the end of the war, museums were erected at both Auschwitz and Treblinka. In establishing these memorials, the Polish parliament wanted to make sure that the world would never forget the possibility for evil that lurks in the human soul.

King Josiah took a different approach concerning the high places of Baal worship and the centers of pagan prostitution in Jerusalem. The king undoubtedly made the right choice for his time and place. There can be no room for a museum of evil in the place where God is worshiped. The same may be said of our hearts, the temple where God is worshiped today.   —C. R. B.

## CONCLUSION

If you leave your garden alone, weeds will take it. They grow faster and more vigorously than petunias and cabbages. You have to be energetic and tireless in weeding.

Your town, your state, or your nation is like a garden. Weeds will take it unless good people are vigilant and vigorous against them.

Weeds seem to be winning in many of our gardens. Moral standards are falling; crime rates are rising. What can we do about it? Hire more police? Build more jails? We have done that until the tax rate appalls us, and look at the weeds! There must be a better way.

### A. CHANGE THE KING

The king set a pattern in Judah. When evil Manasseh was king, he encouraged the weeds, and they multiplied. When Josiah took over, the weeding was a big job, but he did it.

When pleasure is king, the weeds grow. When greed is king, they become monstrous. When comfort is king, we lie in the hammock and ignore them.

What if Jesus were treated as the King he really is? What if all of us would not only pledge allegiance to him, but actually obey him? How beautifully our weedless gardens would bloom!

The best hope—the only hope—of triumphant goodness lies in the kingdom of Christ. The best thing you and I can do for a better world is to bring people to Jesus, make them disciples eager to learn from him, baptize them into him, and teach them to do everything he asks (Matthew 28:19, 20).

### B. CHANGE THE PEOPLE

In order for a society to be changed, people must be changed. This is not done by law or by force; it is done by persuasion and reason. It is done by winsomely presenting the claims of Jesus, by showing the evidence that he is truly the Son of God, and by demonstrating in our living that it is good to follow him. Thus it is that men and women are led to be born again and to flourish as flowers.

Why is this so difficult? Why do we shrink from our task? The gospel is good news, not bad. The King eternal is offering life eternal to people condemned to die. We ought to be telling it freely, enthusiastically, joyously. People ought to be accepting it with delight.

How are we doing? Do we need to reexamine our congregation's program of evangelism? Do we need to examine our own way of living?

# Discovery Learning

*This page contains an alternate lesson plan emphasizing learning activities. Classes desiring such student involvement will find these suggestions helpful. The next page is a reproducible activity page to further enhance discovery learning.*

## LEARNING GOALS

In today's class session, the students will:

1. List the evidences in Josiah's society of the generation's ignorance of God's Law.

2. Compare this situation with similar trends in our own society.

3. Choose at least one way to reemphasize the Bible in their world.

## INTO THE LESSON

Begin today's session by asking, "What would our society be like if we had no Bibles?" Divide the class into four groups. Assign each group one of the following activities to answer the question.

*Newspaper articles.* Write one or several front-page articles describing happenings in your town as a result of no biblical influence on the city.

*Advertisements.* Design ads for products or services that would be sold where the Bible's influence was absent.

*A Day in the Life.* Outline the activities of a typical day in the life of a class member. The outline should show what this person's daily life is like when the Bible's values do not affect it.

*Listing.* Make a list of at least fifteen answers to the question.

After ten minutes let them share with the entire class. Discuss: "How much influence does the Bible have on our society today? How close to our members' descriptions has our world already become?" Tell class members that today's study will look at what happened to the nation of Judah when it had ignored the teachings of God's Word for a generation.

## INTO THE WORD

Present the lesson background under four headings:

The Bad King Manasseh (2 Kings 21:1-18; 2 Chronicles 33:1-16)

The Bad King Amon (2 Kings 21:19-22)

The Boy Josiah Becomes King (2 Kings 21:23, 24; 22:1-7)

Josiah Finds the Book of the Law (2 Kings 22:8-20)

See the Introduction (pages 23, 24) for information.

Write the following questions on your chalkboard: "What did the king do? What did the people do?" Have a volunteer read 2 Kings 23:1-3 and then ask class members to answer the questions.

Regroup the class into the groups that worked together at the beginning of the session. Ask them to skim verses 4-20 and to write a description of what had happened in the society of Judah when the influence of God's Law had been missing. After four to six minutes, ask volunteers to share items as you make a list on your chalkboard. Beside each of these items, write what Josiah and his people did to remedy each of these problems. Your resulting lists should look something like this:

1. Idols were in the temple and throughout the land (Josiah destroyed them).

2. People participated in prostitution as an act of worship (Josiah tore down their quarters).

3. Pagan priests burned incense to Baal, to the sun and moon, and to the stars (Josiah executed them).

4. Places of idol worship had been created (Josiah desecrated and destroyed them).

5. Human sacrifice was a part of pagan worship (Josiah desecrated and destroyed the places where this worship had occurred).

6. Horses and chariots were dedicated to worship of the sun (Josiah removed the horses from their places at the entrance to the temple and burned the chariots).

7. Altars for idol worship had been erected in the temple itself (Josiah pulled them down).

## INTO LIFE

Ask students to try to think of a counterpart in our society to each of the items from the above list. To prod their thinking, ask questions like these:

1. What items or ideas have become almost like idols in the thinking of some of our countrymen?

2. How is sexual immorality central to the value system of some people today?

3. What part does a fascination with the sun, moon, and stars play in the lives of many today? How has this become a form of worship?

Ask class members to decide how a reemphasis on the Bible in our society could counteract some of these trends. What can class members do to place a stronger emphasis on the Bible in their society? In their families? In their congregation? In their own lives?

*Option.* Distribute copies of the reproducible activity, "Tearing Down the Idols," on page 30 to lead this discussion. Be sure to emphasize the Bible's role in "tearing down the idols" (the third column).

# Tearing Down the Idols

On the chart below are listed some popular objects of worship today—although their worshipers would not likely use that term to describe their own activities. How are these things "worshiped"? What can we do to destroy these "idols"—at least as objects of worship?

| ITEM | HOW IS THIS ITEM "WORSHIPED"? | HOW CAN WE STOP THE "WORSHIP" OF THIS ITEM? |
|---|---|---|
| Sun, Moon, and Stars | | |
| Sports, Recreation | | |
| Sexual Pleasures | | |
| Political Power | | |
| Material Possessions | | |
| Other: | | |

# HEARING GOD'S CALL

**LESSON 3**

Sep
15

## WHY TEACH THIS LESSON?

"As a prisoner for the Lord, then, I urge you to live a life worthy of the calling you have received." So wrote Paul to the Ephesians (4:1). He was writing to all the believers in Ephesus—not just to the "preachers." Every Christian has a calling from God—a calling to hope, a calling to life, a calling to service.

Sometimes we are reluctant to heed the call to service. Isn't there someone else who could do that task? Challenge your students to put aside whatever reluctance they may have and to get more involved in service for the Master.

## INTRODUCTION

At the age of eighteen, Carl was appalled when someone asked him to teach a Sunday school class, and doubly appalled when he heard what class it was. The fourteen-year-old boys! Carl knew that class. He had been in it himself only four years earlier. During those four years, no teacher had stayed with that class more than three weeks. Some had fled in tears before the first session was over. Though its membership changed every year, that class was always incorrigible. It was a "treasured" tradition.

At first Carl refused the request. But the lady pleaded so earnestly and tearfully that he gave in. He became a teacher against his will and better judgment.

Carl began his task with more vigor than wisdom. During the first session he literally picked up a defiant student and put him in a chair so forcefully that the chair collapsed in a jumble of sticks.

The boys laughed uproariously. That chair had been broken before. They had pieced it together precariously in the place where they hoped the new teacher would sit. When the joke backfired, even Carl joined in the merriment. The boys accepted him as one of the gang, and the class came under control for the first time in years.

### A. DRAFTED FOR SERVICE

Many Sunday school teachers and other Christian leaders have undertaken their tasks as reluctantly as Carl did. Most of those who have tried earnestly and persistently have become successful.

Reluctant leaders in the Lord's work are not confined to our time. Moses was drafted against his will (Exodus 3:1—4:17), and God made him a magnificent success. Jeremiah likewise was reluctant to take the task assigned to him, but God made him able to do it well.

If we are doing what the Lord wants us to do, we can be sure he will give us the ability.

### B. LESSON BACKGROUND

The historical setting of Jeremiah is described in the first three verses of his book. He was called to prophesy in the thirteenth year of Josiah's reign in Judah. That was five years before Josiah found the book of the Law and set out to reform the nation.

---

**DEVOTIONAL READING**
GALATIANS 1:11-17
**LESSON SCRIPTURE**
JEREMIAH 1
**PRINTED TEXT**
JEREMIAH 1:4-10, 14-17

**LESSON AIMS**

After this lesson a student should be able to do the following:

1. Describe Jeremiah's call, his reluctance, and why he needed to overcome his fears.

2. Compare the situation Jeremiah faced to the situation faced by potential Christian workers today.

3. Resolve to stand firmly for God and to serve in whatever way he calls us to serve.

**KEY VERSE**

The word of the LORD came to me, saying, "Before I formed you in the womb I knew you, before you were born I set you apart; I appointed you as a prophet to the nations." Jeremiah 1:4, 5

*LESSON 3 NOTES*

*The visual for lesson 3 in the visuals packet calls attention to the far-reaching plans the Lord had for Jeremiah.*

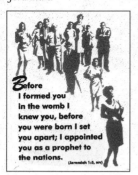

*WHAT DO YOU THINK?*

*The lesson writer says God gave Jeremiah the natural abilities—"the special combination of genes"—that would make him an effective prophet. Do you think God does the same for people today? For example, does the possession of a strong voice and the ability to speak clearly and forcefully demonstrate God's design one to be a preacher? Why or why not?*

*Is there a difference between a spiritual gift and a natural gift if both are used for ministry? Why or why not?*

The teaching of Jeremiah must have been very helpful throughout the period of Josiah's reformation. (See last week's lesson.) But the prophet was not released from service when King Josiah died. Faithfully he proclaimed God's will even when Josiah's evil sons were ignoring it. Courageously he warned that sin would bring disaster, and he kept on doing so while Judah fell under the rule of Egypt, then of Babylon. He continued his warning until his prophecy was fulfilled and most of the people of Judah were driven away to Babylon. Then Jeremiah refused honor and ease in Babylon so he could stay in Judah and help the impoverished few who were left there.

Today's lesson tells of the day when the Lord first "drafted" Jeremiah and called him to the challenging ministry of a prophet.

## I. COMMISSION (JEREMIAH 1:4-8)

Jeremiah was a true priest of God, not one of the spurious ones who worshiped idols. His home was in Anathoth (verse 1), a city of the Levites (Joshua 21:18) only a few miles north of Jerusalem.

### A. THE LORD'S PROPHET (vv. 4, 5)

**4. *The word of the LORD came to me, saying. . . .***

How did *the word* come? Was there an audible voice heard by Jeremiah's ears, or a silent message to his mind? We are not told, but Jeremiah knew who was speaking. It was *the Lord*, Jehovah, and Jeremiah understood the message clearly.

**5. *"Before I formed you in the womb I knew you, before you were born I set you apart; I appointed you as a prophet to the nations."***

The day when the Lord spoke to Jeremiah was not the day when the Lord chose him to be a prophet. That choice was made much earlier. Before he was born, the Lord *set* him *apart* for a special service. Before he was born, the Lord *appointed* him *a prophet to the nations.* The verbs *formed* and *knew* both describe the intimacy of God's design for Jeremiah. The Lord saw that Jeremiah received the special combination of genes that would fit him for the work he was to do. How blessed is any person who finds and does just what he is designed to do!

### B. THE PROPHET'S OBJECTION (v. 6)

**6. *"Ah, Sovereign LORD," I said, "I do not know how to speak; I am only a child."***

Immediately Jeremiah protested that he was not adequate for the task. The Hebrew word translated *child* in our text may be used of a baby, a child of any age, or a young adult. We do not know how old Jeremiah really was at this time, but he was asked to accept an awesome responsibility. Who would not feel inadequate to be a prophet, a spokesman for the Almighty? Perhaps Jeremiah thought a prophet ought to be an older man, a man with more experience, wisdom, and influence.

### C. THE LORD'S INSISTENCE (vv. 7, 8)

**7. *But the LORD said to me, "Do not say, 'I am only a child.' You must go to everyone I send you to and say whatever I command you.***

*The Lord* overruled the prophet's objection and rejected his excuse. Regardless of his youth, the Lord was giving him a job to do. All Jeremiah had to do was to *go* where the Lord would *send* him and *say* what the Lord would tell him to say. Even a child can obey orders.

**8. *"Do not be afraid of them, for I am with you and will rescue you," declares the LORD.***

Opponents would confront Jeremiah. Politicians would oppose him; priests of Baal would condemn him; false prophets would call him a liar. On the side of those opponents would be the power of government, the energy of false religion, and the fury of frustrated men. But the Lord would be with Jeremiah and deliver him. Centuries later, the apostle John would give a similar assurance to Christians: "The one who is in you is greater than the one who is in the world" (1 John 4:4).

## II. INSPIRATION (JEREMIAH 1:9, 10)

Jeremiah soon had convincing proof that God was with him. First, he felt God's touch on his lips, which placed God's words in his mouth. Isaiah was called of God by a similar experience (Isaiah 6:6, 7). Second, God's power accompanied his words. When Jeremiah said something would happen, it did. This proof of God's presence took longer, but it was still very convincing.

### A. THE LORD'S WORDS (v. 9)

**9. Then the LORD reached out his hand and touched my mouth and said to me, "Now, I have put my words in your mouth.**

Did Jeremiah see the Lord's hand? We are not told, and it does not matter. He felt the touch, and he knew what it meant. Jeremiah was inspired like the other prophets and like the apostles of later times. When they were called into court and accused of civil disobedience, they did not have to hire a team of lawyers and plan their defense. In that way the prophets and apostles had an advantage that we do not have as we teach God's Word today. We need to search the Scriptures diligently and deeply. Whether we preach in a pulpit, teach in Sunday school, or talk with a neighbor in the backyard, we need to plan what to say. But we have the inspired Bible to guide us. If we follow it well, our teaching will be true and fruitful.

### B. THE LORD'S POWER (v. 10)

**10. "See, today I appoint you over nations and kingdoms to uproot and tear down, to destroy and overthrow, to build and to plant."**

Thus the prophet's task was made even more awesome. He would dominate *nations* and bring whole *kingdoms* to destruction—not with bow, sword, or battering ram, but with the Lord's word in his mouth. He announced seventy years of subjugation to Babylon (Jeremiah 25:8-11), and it came to pass. He declared God's wrath on the nations surrounding Judah (Jeremiah 25:15-29), and they fell under his judgment. He proclaimed the burning of Jerusalem and the capture of the king (Jeremiah 34:2, 3), and these events occurred.

But Jeremiah's mission was not all destructive. He was empowered also *to build and to plant.* He promised a return from captivity (Jeremiah 30:3), and Judah returned. Looking far into the future, Jeremiah foretold a New Covenant and the forgiveness of sins (Jeremiah 31:31-34). Today Christians rejoice that they are forgiven; they are the people of that New Covenant.

### A HIDDEN POWER

In 1856 an Algerian tribe known as the Marabouts (MAR-uh-boo) rebelled against their French colonial masters. This tribe practiced religious magic, so Napoleon III sent Robert-Houdin (Roe-BEAR Hoo-DEAN), the French magician, to change their mind.

The magician's most impressive trick was the "Light and Heavy Chest." He told the Marabouts, "A baby can pick up this chest, but at my command, even

**WHAT DO YOU THINK?**

*Jeremiah tried to excuse himself from God's call to service on the basis of his youthfulness. What positions or ministries in the church require a certain maturity? At what age would you think one is ready for such ministries or positions? What can the younger people do for the Lord?*

*Are there positions or ministries for which one might be too old? Why or why not—and if so, what?*

**OPTION**

*Use the reproducible matching activity on page 38 to explore how Jeremiah fulfilled each of the six tasks mentioned in verse 10.*

your strongest man cannot do so." He allowed one of their strongest men to pick up the box and then told him, "Now you are weaker than a woman." At that, the man was unable to lift the box from the floor.

The Marabouts were convinced of French strength and gave up their rebellion. What they did not know was that Robert-Houdin's box had a steel plate in the bottom, while the stage floor had an electromagnet under it that was controlled by the magician. In those days, electricity was so new that this unseen power seemed magical.

When Jeremiah received God's call to prophesy, he tried to use his youthfulness as an excuse for not accepting God's assignment. But he was thinking of his own strength, not of the hidden power of God. He did not understand that God's strength could be his if he accepted the prophetic mission. A hidden power is available to us all, greater than we can ever use to its fullest extent. But it works for us only if we trust in God as Jeremiah was called to do.

—C. R. B.

## How to Say It

*Assyria. Uh-SEER-ee-uh.*
*Anathoth. AN-uh-thoth*
  *(O as in ODD).*
*Baal. BAY-ul.*
*Babylon. BAB-uh-lon.*
*Euphrates. U-FRAY-teez.*
*Jeremiah. JAIR-uh-MYE-uh.*

## III. DANGER (JEREMIAH 1:14-17)

The Lord exceeds all experts in the use of visual aids. He needs no blackboard, projector, or object held in his hand. He has a way of showing visual aids that are not really there. They are called visions, one of which is mentioned in Jeremiah 1:13. Jeremiah saw a boiling pot. He observed that it was "tilting away from the north." Thus, the pot's opening was toward the south. This boiling pot was thus tilted toward Jerusalem and Judah, indicating that it was ready to pour out a flood of boiling water over the whole country. The meaning of this extraordinary visual aid is explained in the last part of our text.

### A. ATTACK (vv. 14, 15)

**14. The LORD said to me, "From the north disaster will be poured out on all who live in the land.**

The visionary threat of boiling water symbolized a real evil of a different kind that would come to Judah *from the north.*

**15a. "I am about to summon all the peoples of the northern kingdoms," declares the LORD.**

Elsewhere Babylon is pictured as the great enemy that would destroy Judah (Jeremiah 20:4-6; 34:2, 3), an event that Jeremiah witnessed (Jeremiah 38:28). Babylon was actually east of Judah rather than north, but the Babylonian army would not come from the east because it could not cross the wide and waterless desert east of Judah. It would go up the Euphrates and down through Syria to attack Judah from the north.

The Babylonians would not come alone, for Babylon eventually ruled many of the nations that formerly were ruled by Assyria. Troops from those nations would vastly increase the Babylonian army, so that Judah would be attacked by *all the peoples of the northern kingdoms.*

**15b. "Their kings will come and set up their thrones in the entrance of the gates of Jerusalem; they will come against all her surrounding walls and against all the towns of Judah.**

The *throne* is the symbol of power. The invaders would establish their rule at the very *gates of Jerusalem.* The *walls* were so strong that the city could not be taken by storm, but the troops would surround it on every side so no one could leave without being captured or killed, and no one could bring in food. In time, starvation would force surrender. The invading troops would also move against the other *towns of Judah.*

## B. JUDGMENT (v. 16)

**16. "I will pronounce my judgments on my people because of their wickedness in forsaking me, in burning incense to other gods and in worshiping what their hands have made.**

The destruction of Judah would not be merely the work of the Babylonians and other invaders who would come with them. All of these would be executing God's *judgment* on the people of Judah. The Babylonians did not believe in the Lord and did not intend to serve him; nevertheless, he would use them for his purpose.

### TRASHING THE LANDSCAPE

"Every litter bit hurts," we are constantly reminded, and each "litter bit" in California is adding to a mountain of rubbish. In a recent two-year period, highway cleanup crews in that state collected enough trash from the freeways to cover a football field with nearly sixty feet of rubbish. In the same period they hauled away 120,000 items ranging in size from suitcases to old sofas.

Just one day's collection of debris included a bicycle, a collection of Elvis tapes, magazines, newspapers, various personal hygiene items, a multitude of pieces of clothing, nearly a dozen species of dead animals, discarded diapers, various kinds and amounts of money, political campaign ads, and a lost history report on Teddy Roosevelt. (Imagine the student's excuse: "The freeway ate my homework.")

In Jeremiah's time, Judah had polluted its spiritual landscape with idolatry. The people worshiped other gods and bowed before idols they had made with their own hands. Being surrounded by trash gradually deadens our ability to abhor ugliness in our environment. Judah found the same to be true with its spiritual environment. The kingdom had come to the point where the pollution of idols was readily tolerated.

It is important for us all—especially we who claim to know God—to keep alive our ability to be shocked by evil. Failure to do so will result in the same consequence that Judah suffered: the destruction of our culture and nation.

—C. R. B.

## C. WARNING (v. 17)

**17. "Get yourself ready! Stand up and say to them whatever I command you. Do not be terrified by them, or I will terrify you before them."**

*Get yourself ready.* The Hebrew expression literally speaks of tying the lower part of one's robe up around the waist. It was the usual cutom of one who was about to run or otherwise exert himself. So the expression ("Gird up your loins" in the older translations) became a metaphor for "Get ready for action."

The Lord wanted Jeremiah to strengthen his courage and determination and to get ready mentally for the rigors of giving an unpopular message. The people and their rulers would not be happy to hear that they were vile sinners about to be punished by invaders from the north. They would say that Jeremiah was not patriotic, that he was pessimistic, and that he was on the side of the enemy. They would confront him, threatening him with violence, prison, and even death. He must not be scared. If he would cave in before hostile forces and refuse to give the message that God gave to him, then he would be a faithless prophet. To such a one, the Lord be even more frightening than the people would be.

Verses 18 and 19 tell why Jeremiah had no reason to be afraid. God himself would defend him. God would keep him secure through all the attacks of hostile rulers and people.

### WHAT DO YOU THINK?

God told Jeremiah he was judging his people "because of their wickedness in forsaking him"; yet he pitied them enough to send his prophet to them. Today it is easy to condemn those who build their lives around money and material things to the neglect of spiritual things, or those who desperately try to fill their lives with pleasure and thereby escape facing the weighty questions of death and eternity, and those who turn to alcohol and drugs in a vain attempt to cope with the pressures and stresses they encounter. How can we feel what God feels for these lost people? What would we do about their situations if we did?

### WHAT DO YOU THINK?

God told Jeremiah to get ready for action. He would be opposed by powerful enemies, but the message of the Lord needed to be proclaimed. How is our situation similar, and how can we get ready for action? What kind of opposition will we have to face, and how can we do it?

(See 1 Peter 1:13; Hebrews 12:1.)

## PRAYER

*Almighty God, eternal King, thank you for the truth. Thank you for the honor and privilege and joy of sharing it with others. May we have both wisdom and will to share it well. Amen.*

## THOUGHT TO REMEMBER

*"Preach the Word" (2 Timothy 4:2).*

## WHAT DO YOU THINK?

*How should we respond to the complaint that "Christians are always trying to force their religious views on others"? Why is the idea that we would "force" our view on another inappropriate? (See Revelation 22:17.) How do Acts 4:20; 2 Corinthians 5:11; and 1 Peter 3:15, 16 explain why we must tell others the good news—even if they do not think it is "good"?*

## DAILY BIBLE READINGS

*Monday, Sept. 9—God Creates All People (Psalm 139:13-18)*

*Tuesday, Sept. 10—Israel Forsakes God (Jeremiah 2:4-13)*

*Wednesday, Sept. 11—God Promises Jeremiah Strength (Jeremiah 1:18—2:3)*

*Thursday, Sept. 12—Response of an Obedient Servant (Isaiah 50:4-9)*

*Friday, Sept. 13—Jeremiah Encouraged to Persevere (Jeremiah 15:15-21)*

*Saturday, Sept. 14—Jeremiah Persecuted (Jeremiah 20:7-12)*

*Sunday, Sept. 15—Jeremiah Laments His Birth (Jeremiah 20:13-18)*

## CONCLUSION

Thanks to King Josiah's leadership, Judah returned to God's ways and prospered. After Josiah's death, the nation plunged into evil. Jeremiah's life was often in danger during this period, because he spoke for God.

### A. TAKING THE PLUNGE

Gleaned from newspaper reports, here are a few indications of a similar decline in our country.

To impress older members of his gang, a twelve-year-old boy opened fire on boys of another gang. He missed them, but killed an eleven-year-old girl who just happened to be passing by.

In spite of efforts to teach so-called "safe sex," the number of unwanted pregnancies is growing among schoolgirls.

In 1994, the U.S. Congress passed a highly advertised anti-crime bill, promising billions of dollars for more police and bigger jails. Has crime been conquered?

The 1994 Major League Baseball strike brought financial loss to thousands and generated bitterness that is still present. Some think the strike was caused by the owners' greed, while others think it was caused by the players' greed. Most everyone agrees that greed was the primary factor.

You can add to the list of signs indicating that we are "taking the plunge."

### B. TARGETS FOR TRUTH'S SAKE

Because he repeated God's words, Jeremiah became the target of corrupt politicians, depraved priests, and lying prophets. With increasing frequency, conservative Christians are now being branded as ignorant and intolerant bigots, trying to cram their outmoded standards down everyone's throats.

Has anyone noticed how successfully the atheistic evolutionists are cramming their suspect doctrine down the throats of schoolchildren? Who is wailing because militant homosexuals are trying to make all of us accept their life-style as normal? Aren't all politicians—of whatever party—trying to make all of us accept their policies?

With these and other pressure groups striving earnestly for what they think is right, why are earnest Christians singled out for abusive censure? Jesus knew it would be so, but he did not advise his people to stop their efforts. He said, "Blessed are you when people insult you, persecute you and falsely say all kinds of evil against you because of me. Rejoice and be glad, because great is your reward in heaven, for in the same way they persecuted the prophets who were before you" (Matthew 5:11, 12). Jeremiah was one of those prophets, and he kept on saying what God told him to say. We, too, must keep on teaching the Word of God and doing it with joy.

### C. WHY?

Why was Jeremiah sent to offer God's truth to people who would not accept it, to a nation that would plunge deeper into sin until disaster would come? Why are we sent to offer the gospel of salvation to a world where people throng the way that leads to destruction (Matthew 7:13, 14)? They will keep on doing that until "the elements will be destroyed by fire, and the earth and everything in it will be laid bare" (2 Peter 3:10). So why do we spend time, energy, and money in an effort to avoid what is unavoidable?

The answer is that God is "not wanting anyone to perish, but everyone to come to repentance" (2 Peter 3:9). If we faithfully show the narrow way that leads to life, some precious souls will choose it—and there will be rejoicing in Heaven.

# Discovery Learning

*This page contains an alternate lesson plan emphasizing learning activities. Classes desiring such student involvement will find these suggestions helpful. The next page is a reproducible activity page to further enhance discovery learning.*

## LEARNING GOALS

This lesson will help a student to do the following:

1. Describe Jeremiah's call, his reluctance, and why he needed to overcome his fears.

2. Compare the situation Jeremiah faced to the situation faced by potential Christian workers today.

3. Resolve to stand firmly for God and to serve in whatever way he calls us to serve.

## INTO THE LESSON

Display the following two questions on a poster or an overhead transparency:

**Have you ever felt God was calling you
to do something specific?
If you were God, what would you call
someone to do in this troubled world?**

Read the two questions to the class and ask class members, in groups of two or three, to discuss one of them.

After five minutes tell class members, "Today's lesson looks at how God called one of his prophets to do a difficult task for him. We'll try to see what lessons we can learn about responding to God's call to do something difficult for him today."

## INTO THE WORD

Use material from the Lesson Background to introduce your class members to Jeremiah. Be sure to connect this lesson with the reign of Josiah, which you studied in last week's lesson. Then use one or both of the following activities to lead your group in Bible study:

*Evaluate the Challenge.* Ask class members to write the numbers 4 through 10 and 14 through 19 down one side of a piece of paper. Observe that God's call to Jeremiah was a challenging one. As you or a class member reads Jeremiah 1:4-10, 14-19, have the students write a description of that challenge next to the number of each verse that suggests something of that challenge. (Note that not every verse will have anything to add.) You may want to read the passage aloud two times in order to give class members plenty of time. Then ask them to share their lists in the same groups of two or three that discussed the first assignment.

Here are some possible responses:

6.   Jeremiah was "too young" and not a good speaker.
8.   There seemed to be reason to be "afraid."
10.  Uprooting, tearing down, destroying, and overthrow-

ing nations is no easy task! Neither is the planting and building of them.

14.  Pending disaster from the north.
15.  Invading armies were coming.
16.  God was pronouncing judgment on his people.
17.  Jeremiah needed to be "ready" for opposition.

*Discuss Jeremiah's Response.* Discuss the following questions with the class, or duplicate and distribute them so that the students, in groups of two or three, can discuss them. All of them relate to Jeremiah 1:4-10, 14-19. (The information in parentheses is for the teacher only. Do not add it to what you give the students.)

1. When did Jeremiah feel afraid? Why? (See verse 6.)

2. When might he have felt sad? Why? (See verses 14-16.)

3. What about God's assignment to Jeremiah might have been appealing to him? (The promise of rescue [verse 8]; perhaps the idea of international power [verse 10])

4. What about God's assignment might have made Jeremiah want to run away? (Foreign invaders [verse 15] or the warning that God would terrify him if he gave in to fear of his opponents [verse 19])

5. What response did God demand of Jeremiah? (Courage and faithfulness to the call, verse 19)

## INTO LIFE

Use the activity, "When God Speaks . . ." from the next page to lead your class members to think about the implications of today's study for their own lives. Let class members, in the same groups of two or three as you used before, choose which sentence they want to discuss. Give the small groups at least five minutes, then discuss answers with the entire class.

Next ask your class the following questions. If you have time, you may discuss these questions with the class. If you prefer, use the thoughts in these questions as a prayer guide. Students can pray silently as you read each one:

1. Do you feel God may be calling you to do something that frightens you? How does the experience of Jeremiah affect the answer you will give him?

2. Are you facing opposition because of a stand you are taking for God? How do you feel about this? How could Jeremiah's experience change the way you feel?

3. Have you turned your back on an assignment from God that you ought to reconsider?

# Scripture Matching

In Jeremiah 4:10 God tells Jeremiah he will have a variety of tasks to perform as the Lord's prophet. These are listed below in the left-hand colmn. To the right are references from Jeremiah that describe an occasion when he did each of these tasks. Match the tasks with the proper references.

___ Uproot                a. Jeremiah 25:8-11

___ Tear down          b. Jeremiah 25:17-26

___ Destroy             c. Jeremiah 34:2, 3

___ Overthrow         d. Jeremiah 30:3

___ Build                e. Jeremiah 33:10, 11

___ Plant                f. Jeremiah 31:31-34

# When God Speaks . . .

Read the following statements. For one or more of them, indicate (1) how Jeremiah's life illustrates the truth, and (2) how you have seen that truth in action today.

**The person who speaks for God is often opposed by others.**

1.


2.


**We must listen to God more than people when we are seeking God's will.**

1.


2.


**We must trust God's Word more than our own feelings when we are choosing how to serve him.**

1.


2.

# PROCLAIMING GOD'S WORD
### LESSON 4

## WHY TEACH THIS LESSON?

A vacuum cleaner salesman was trying to make a sale to a preacher. Encountering resistance, the salesman reminded the preacher that "the Good Book says, 'Cleanliness is next to godliness.'" Of course, "the Good Book" says no such thing! But isn't it easy to make assumptions about what the Bible says or about what God wants without making a serious study to find out the truth? Vacuum cleaner salesmen are not the only ones who do so.

Use this lesson to challenge your students to serious Bible study, to know what the Bible says and to act accordingly. Claiming a godly heritage or membership in a faithful church is not enough. Personal knowledge of God's will and a personal commitment to the Lord have no substitute.

## INTRODUCTION

In our elementary school, the first warm days of spring brought an epidemic of truancy. It happened every year. The school board and the principal made a rule mandating a whipping for anyone who played hooky, but the annual epidemic went unchecked. Playing hooky brought a boy a certain prestige among his peers, and rugged lads were willing to take a whipping for that.

Then one spring a new truant officer took over. The first time two students failed to appear after lunch, he went in search of them. Wise to the ways of boys, he found them quickly and brought them back to their punishment. Only half an hour later they appeared in class, subdued and humiliated, with tears on their faces. There was no epidemic that year.

### A. LEARNING FROM THE PAST

People do learn from the past—teachers as well as students. Many of us remember a time when teachers' pay was notoriously low and strikes became popular. In one town a strike resulted in significant raises, and there were three more strikes in five years. In another town, the school board fired the strikers and opened the schools within a week with other teachers. There was no threat of a strike after that.

### B. LESSON BACKGROUND

Judah was in trouble because its people had failed to learn from their past. For nearly eight hundred years, they had prospered when they had lived by God's Law and had suffered when disobedience was widespread. The text of our lesson is not dated, but perhaps it belongs to the time after good King Josiah died. At that time Judah was plunging into idolatry and sin.

The first six chapters of Jeremiah expose Judah's sins; they tell of certain punishment for stubborn sinners; they plead with the people to repent; they promise blessing for obedience. Our text from chapter 7 summarizes of all these points.

## I. KEEP YOUR COUNTRY (JEREMIAH 7:1-7)

The promised land was God's gift to Israel, along with peace and prosperity as long as it remained obedient to him (Deuteronomy 28:1-6, 11, 12). Equally plain

DEVOTIONAL READING
MICAH 6:1-8
LESSON SCRIPTURE
JEREMIAH 7
PRINTED TEXT
JEREMIAH 7:1-15

Sep
22

## LESSON AIMS

After this lesson a student should be able to do the following:

1. Summarize God's message that Jeremiah was to present at the gate of the temple.

2. Compare the sinful condition of Judah in Jeremiah's day with present society.

3. Suggest one specific step that can be taken by the student, the class, or the congregation to help someone obey God better.

## KEY VERSE

This is what the LORD Almighty, the God of Israel, says: Reform your ways and your actions, and I will let you live in this place.    Jeremiah 7:3

*LESSON 4 NOTES*

*The visual for lesson 4 illustrates the need for repentance—in Jeremiah's day and in ours. Display it as you begin the session.*

### WHAT DO YOU THINK?

*Jeremiah was told to stand in the gate of the Lord's house and proclaim his message publicly. How can we gain a public hearing for God's message of sin, righteousness, and judgment to come?*

*How effective might the following be for gaining a public hearing for the gospel message? Why?*

• *The distribution of tracts and other Christian literature.*

• *Using the editorial pages of our local newspaper.*

• *Preaching on a street corner or public square.*

• *Speaking at public meetings such as the Rotary or local businessmen's or business-women's organizations.*

was the promise that Israel would lose that land if it did not obey the Lord (Deuteronomy 28:63). We are looking at a time when the northern kingdom had already lost its part of the promised land (2 Kings 17:1-18). The southern tribe of Judah had survived that disaster because King Hezekiah had led the nation in returning to the Lord (2 Kings 18:1-8). Hezekiah's great-grandson Josiah likewise had promoted godly ways (2 Kings 22:1, 2). But now it appears that Josiah was dead; his sons who succeeded him as king were all evil. Judah was on the brink of losing its part of the promised land, but there was still time to avert that loss.

### A. A PLACE TO PREACH (vv. 1, 2)

**1. *This is the word that came to Jeremiah from the LORD.***

Jeremiah frequently reminds us that he was not the source of the words he spoke. He was writing the words that the Lord gave him. Jeremiah had access to the very counsel of God himself, in contrast to the false prophets (Jeremiah 23:14-22).

**2. *"Stand at the gate of the LORD's house and there proclaim this message:***
   ***"'Hear the word of the LORD, all you people of Judah who come through these gates to worship the LORD***

Jeremiah was not sent to a temple of Baal or to a gathering of pagans; he was sent to give *the word of the Lord* to members of the chosen people who came into the temple (*the Lord's house*) to worship the Lord.

### B. A CALL TO AMEND (v. 3)

**3. *"'This is what the LORD Almighty, the God of Israel, says: Reform your ways and your actions, and I will let you live in this place.***

The Lord did not ask these people merely to *reform* their worship. He wanted them to change their *ways* and their *actions*, meaning their whole way of life. That was what it would take to keep their home *in this place*, which could refer to the temple, the city of Jerusalem, or even to the promised land itself. Otherwise they would lose their home; they would die or be deported.

### C. FALSE SECURITY (v. 4)

**4. *"'Do not trust in deceptive words and say, "This is the temple of the LORD, the temple of the LORD, the temple of the LORD!".***

*The temple of the Lord.* The people of Judah kept saying that over and over. Perhaps the threefold repetition contained a symbolic or even magical significance for them. It was their answer to every warning of coming disaster. This temple was God's own holy house; he would not let any disaster come to it. People who worshiped there would be safe, regardless of what they did elsewhere. But these were *deceptive words,* for the temple of the Lord would not provide safety for those who did not live as the people of the Lord.

### D. HOW TO REFORM (vv. 5, 6)

**5. *"'If you really change your ways and your actions and deal with each other justly. . . .***

No halfway reform would do; God wanted them to *really change* or "thoroughly" (*King James Version*) reform. The first area to be improved was justice. The courts of Judah were so corrupt that Jeremiah was invited to search Jerusalem and see if he could find anyone dispensing justice (Jeremiah 5:1). To *deal with each other justly* was to dispense justice in legal proceedings.

**6. *"'If you do not oppress the alien, the fatherless or the widow and do not shed innocent blood in this place, and if you do not follow other gods to your own harm. . . .***

An *alien* or foreigner in Judah had no friends, no influence, and not much knowledge of local customs. He was easy prey for a crooked merchant, employer, tax collector, or moneylender. Orphans and *widows* were easily victimized because they had no strong man to protect them, no standing with the rulers, and no money to bribe the judges. The Lord wanted fair treatment for all these people who could not secure it for themselves.

Worse than a bit of cheating in business was the shedding of *innocent blood*. A man who had done no wrong might be accused of a terrible crime, convicted by hired perjurers, sentenced by bribed judges, and put to death. Then a creditor could seize his property to pay a debt worth only a fraction of the property's value. This was all easy to arrange when the judges were for sale.

The Lord wanted changes that would put a permanent end to all of these evils. Especially grievous was the worship of *other gods*. The Lord laid the responsibility for the *harm* that would come to the idol worshipers squarely on themselves.

## E. REAL SECURITY (v. 7)

**7. "'Then I will let you live in this place, in the land I gave your forefathers for ever and ever.**

God's promise that the Israelites would inhabit the promised land *for ever and ever* was conditional. They and their descendants could live securely in the promised land as long as they obeyed the Lord. Here God repeats the condition and the promise.

### A JUST SOCIETY

The Oneida (Owe-*nye*-duh) Community of Christian Perfectionists was one of more than three dozen such communities in nineteenth-century America. A goal shared by most of these utopian communes was the establishment of social justice.

John Humphrey Noyes, who founded the Oneida Community, believed in sharing *everything*. Even children were shared—raised by the commune so their mothers would not love them "idolatrously." Monogamy was forbidden, and a "breeding committee" oversaw sexual relationships in a system of what was called "complex marriage."

Jeremiah shows us a very different view of the ideal society: a community where true justice reigns is one in which people do good to one and all because each person is living in covenant relationship with God.

No matter how many utopias are proposed by social visionaries, a truly just society will come only when we live justly in relationship with God. Divine love is both the example and the spirit that empowers us to seek such justice.          —C. R. B.

## II. STOP YOUR SINNING (JEREMIAH 7:8-11)

The security offered in verse 7 could not be realized without the changes demanded in verses 3-6. The Lord proceeded to describe the sins that must be stopped and that would certainly bring destruction if they continued.

## A. SINS (vv. 8, 9)

**8. "'But look, you are trusting in deceptive words that are worthless.**

Already we have seen one example of *deceptive words* in verse 4. Of course, there were other examples. Every promise of benefit from a false god was a lie. Every promise of allegiance to the Lord was a lie unless it was accompanied by actual obedience. Such lies may fool many listeners and even the liars themselves; they cannot fool God.

9. *"Will you steal and murder, commit adultery and perjury, burn incense to Baal and follow other gods you have not known. . . .*

We can see in this cataloging of the people's sins a reflection of those areas of conduct covered in the Ten Commandments. It seems hard to believe that such repulsive sins were common among those who claimed to be God's people and who worshiped him in his temple. Yet, even with the advantages we have now (such as the completed Scripture), sometimes a Christian shocks us by falling into gross sin. In all times and places, "Each one is tempted when, by his own evil desire, he is dragged away and enticed" (James 1:14).

### B. HYPOCRISY (vv. 1O, 11)

10. *"And then come and stand before me in this house, which bears my Name, and say, "We are safe"—safe to do all these detestable things?*

This is the rest of the question that began in verse 9. Can anyone be misled enough to think he is free to indulge in the sins named there, even while he goes through the motions of worshiping in the Lord's temple? Can such a sinner really think his empty words of worship without obedience will cause God to deliver him from his enemies? Will God rescue him from every evil so he can go on doing evil? There is no safety for willful sinners!

11. *"'Has this house, which bears my Name, become a den of robbers to you? But I have been watching! declares the LORD.*

Did the men of Judah think the temple was a bandits' hideout? Did they think they could commit such sins as are described in verse 9 and then escape punishment by taking refuge in the temple and pretending to worship the God they disobeyed? No! This temple was the house of God, the holy God, the just God. Yes, he is merciful and gracious, but he will not acquit the guilty (Exodus 34:6, 7). Sinners who repent can find forgiveness with him, but not those who continue stubbornly in their sins.

**OPTION**

*The reproducible activity, "The Eyes of God," on page 46 is based on verse 11. Use it to discuss this verse.*

### LIVING WITH A LIE

In 1894, French army Captain Alfred Dreyfus was convicted of spying. A cleaning woman hired by the French secret service to work in the German embassy had found some classified French military papers on a desk there. Army officials knew their case against Dreyfus was weak, so they created false evidence to convict him. History has since proved that he was convicted because of prejudice: he was Jewish and came from the German-speaking district of Alsace in France. Twelve years after Dreyfus began his life sentence on Devil's Island, he was exonerated, and his rank was restored. Even though a major in the army was later found to have committed the crime, the Dreyfus affair is still argued in France a century later. Sometimes a lie takes on a life of its own.

For years the people of Judah persisted in living a lie. While claiming to follow God and going through the motions of temple worship, they were liars, thieves, murderers, adulterers, and idol worshipers.

Like Jeremiah's ancient audience and Captain Dreyfus's accusers, we may fool ourselves into thinking we can get away with living a lie. Perhaps, for a while, we can. But eventually the truth will find its way to the surface of the moral swamp we have created for ourselves.

—C. R. B.

**HOW TO SAY IT**

Assyrians. Uh-SEER-ee-unz.
Baal. BAY-ul.
Babylonians. Bab-uh-LOW-
    nee-unz.
Ephraim. EE-fray-im.
Hezekiah. Hez-eh-KYE-uh.
Jeremiah. JAIR-uh-MYE-uh.
Josiah. Jo-SYE-uh.
Judah. JOO-duh.
Shiloh. SHY-lo.

### III. LOOK AT HISTORY (JEREMIAH 7:12-15)

The sinners of Judah could have found ample evidence from their past that God had protected his people when they respected his Law, but there was nothing to support the silly notion that they could find protection in his temple when they were disobedient.

## A. PAST PUNISHMENT (v. 12)

**12. "'Go now to the place in Shiloh where I first made a dwelling for my Name, and see what I did to it because of the wickedness of my people Israel.**

When the people of *Israel* divided the promised land among their tribes, *Shiloh* was the central place of worship. There they set up the tabernacle (Joshua 18:1), which remained there until the Israelites removed the ark of the covenant during a battle with the Philistines (1 Samuel 4:3, 4). The actual destruction of Shiloh is not recorded for us, but from this text it is evident that it had been destroyed, probably by one of the many invaders of the land of Israel. Jeremiah was speaking some time later, but still his hearers could go to Shiloh and see with their own eyes what God had done to that earlier place of worship. From that, they should have known that he would also destroy the place of worship in Jerusalem if the people who pretended to worship there became too wicked to be tolerated. Holy places can never substitute for a holy people.

## B. PRESENT GUILT (v. 13)

**13. "'While you were doing all these things, declares the LORD, I spoke to you again and again, but you did not listen; I called you, but you did not answer.**

The people of Judah had done *all these things*—the wicked things named in verse 9. They could not say they had no way of knowing those acts were wrong. God had given the Law long before, and later he had spoken through Jeremiah and other prophets. *Again and again* God had warned them. But the people preferred their sins and closed their ears and minds to what the prophets were saying.

## C. FUTURE DISASTER (vv. 14, 15)

**14. "'Therefore, what I did to Shiloh I will now do to the house that bears my Name, the temple you trust in, the place I gave to you and your fathers.**

This *house* was the temple. It was called by the Lord's *Name*; it was his house. The people of Judah put their *trust* in it; they said the Lord would take care of them because they worshiped there, in spite of their constant sinning.

*The place* included Jerusalem and the whole land of Judah. God had given it to the ancestors of the present residents, and he had promised that they and their descendants could keep it forever if they would obey him. But now they were disobeying and ignoring the constant pleading of the prophets. Therefore the temple, the city, and the nation were to be destroyed as *Shiloh* had been. Later historians might say the Babylonians had conquered Judah, but they were merely a tool in the Lord's hand.

**15. "'I will thrust you from my presence, just as I did all your brothers, the people of Ephraim.'"**

*Ephraim* was the tribe where Shiloh was located. Its importance in ancient times is seen in the fact that its name—here and elsewhere—represented the entire nation of Israel (the northern kingdom). Before the time of Jeremiah, the Assyrians had defeated Israel and had settled many of its people in foreign lands (2 Kings 17:1-6). That should have been a clear warning to their kinsmen in Judah, the southern nation. But those kinsmen disregarded the warning, and now their nation was about to be destroyed in a similar way.

## CONCLUSION

In urging the people of Judah to think of their past, the Lord cited two examples. He had destroyed the earlier place of worship at Shiloh because of the wickedness of his people (Jeremiah 7:12), and he had destroyed the entire northern nation of Israel because of similar wickedness (v. 15).

*WHAT DO YOU THINK?*

The lesson writer says, "Holy places can never substitute for a holy people." What do modern people attempt to sustitute for holiness? How can the need for holiness be taught to the younger generation in such a way as they will accept it and pursue holiness—without substitute?

*WHAT DO YOU THINK?*

An often-repeated statement notes that "they who will not learn from the past are doomed to repeat it." The residents of Judah should have learned from Israel's history, especially the fall of the northern kingdom. What are some lessons you have learned from history—either biblical or secular history? What mistakes do you think you may have avoided because you learned those lessons?

How can the lessons of the Bible be taught in such a way as to help young people avoid some mistakes in the future? (See 1 Corinthians 10:11, 12.)

What evils in our society do you see as a result of our failing to learn these lessons?

## PRAYER

*Father in Heaven, only you can change sinners into saints. Help us represent you truly as we try to help people be born again and become your children. Amen.*

## THOUGHT TO REMEMBER

*What we do today can change the future.*

## WHAT DO YOU THINK?

*"What we do today can change the future." What are some comparatively small things we can do this week that could change our future?*

*What impact on your future could any of the following have?*
- *Establishing a regular practice of Bible study and prayer, if you have not previously done so.*
- *Eliminating a bad habit.*
- *Taking the first step to heal a broken friendship.*
- *Speaking about Christ to a neighbor or fellow worker.*

## DAILY BIBLE READINGS

*Monday, Sept. 16—People Refuse to Obey God (Jeremiah 7:16-26)*

*Tuesday, Sept. 17—People Will Not Listen to Jeremiah (Jeremiah 7:27-34)*

*Wednesday, Sept. 18—People Are Stubbornly Unrepentant (Jeremiah 8:8-17)*

*Thursday, Sept. 19—Jeremiah Mourns for the People (Jeremiah 8:18-22)*

*Friday, Sept. 20—True Wisdom Is in Knowing the Lord (Jeremiah 9:12-24)*

*Saturday, Sept. 21—People Called to Amend Their Ways (Jeremiah 18:1-11)*

*Sunday, Sept. 22—The Lord Is the True God (Jeremiah 10:1-10)*

Many other examples could have been given. When the people of Israel first approached the promised land, their faithless and fearful rebellion delayed their entrance and made them live as nomads in the desert for forty years (Numbers 13:1—14:35). Led by Joshua, the people then captured the land and settled there. But after Joshua and other faithful leaders died, the people forgot how the Lord had directed their past. Judges 2:6-19 describes a cycle that was repeated throughout the period of the judges. Wickedness brought punishments, poverty, and hardship; these brought repentance; repentance brought deliverance; and then the cycle began again.

The people thought a strong central government could stabilize the nation. They clamored for a king, but that did not solve the problem. David and Solomon brought the kingdom to the peak of its wealth and power; but Solomon in his later years reversed its progress, and his son split it in two. Northern Israel went down to destruction in approximately two hundred years, while southern Judah rotated between good and bad kings until its conquest by Babylon.

For nearly eight hundred years, obeying God had brought good results, and disobeying had brought bad results. How could anyone still choose to disobey?

### A. LOOK AT THE PAST

Schoolchildren used to learn much about the intrepid pilgrims who endured severe hardship in order to obey God as they thought they should. Their example is inspiring, but they were not the only emigrants who believed in obeying God. In Virginia some of the Anglicans doubted that Jesus was divine, but they believed in God and in the virtue of doing his will. Catholics in Maryland, Quakers in Pennsylvania, and Baptists in Rhode Island also believed in God and tried to obey him.

When the British colonies in America declared their independence, they based their declaration on the fact that people are God's creatures, endowed by him with "certain unalienable rights." They closed the Declaration of Independence "with a firm reliance on the protection of divine Providence." The nation grew and prospered.

### B. LOOK AT THE PRESENT

Today the fashion in recounting history seems to be to hide the influence of religion in building the nation. The fashion in education seems to be to twist the separation of church and state into an anti-God policy. In news media the trend seems to be to belittle or ridicule earnest Christians. In entertainment, the tendency is to see no difference between right and wrong. Christians are portrayed as ignorant and bigoted. With increasing frequency, promiscuous sex is presented as normal.

Almost any adult will agree that popular standards of morality have been lowered in his time. Evils once abhorred are now tolerated; evils once tolerated are now accepted.

### C. LOOK AT THE FUTURE

Why did God send Jeremiah to declare that his nation was to be destroyed and its people were to become captives in Babylon? Because that future could be changed! As God's spokesman, Jeremiah told how it could be changed. Simply by obeying God, Judah could outlive Babylon.

Let's be practical. Let's plan one step that we who study this lesson can take this week to help someone become a Christian, or to help someone obey the Lord better. Let's plan it, and let's do it.

# Discovery Learning

*This page contains an alternate lesson plan emphasizing learning activities. Classes desiring such student involvement will find these suggestions helpful. The next page is a reproducible activity page to further enhance discovery learning.*

## LEARNING GOALS

After this lesson a student should be able to do the following:

1. Summarize God's message that Jeremiah was to present at the gate of the temple.

2. Compare the sinful condition of Judah in Jeremiah's day with present society.

3. Suggest one specific step that can be taken by the student, the class, or the congregation to help someone obey God better.

## INTO THE LESSON

Use one of the following activities to begin this session:

*Newspaper search.* Ask students, "How big a problem is sin in our society?" Tell them to search daily newspapers to help them decide on an answer.

They should look at each article or advertisement and decide, "Does this indicate in any way some sin in our society?" After several minutes, allow class members to share their findings.

*Continuum.* Distribute copies of the following diagram:

| | | |
|---|---|---|
| Totally Sinful | Neutral | Pure |

Ask students to indicate on the line the place they think best characterizes society today. Where would they put a mark to describe the society their parents lived in? Where do they think the mark will go twenty or thirty years from now?

Tell students that today's Scripture study looks at a sinful society and what it could do to move itself to the right on this continuum.

## INTO THE WORD

Remind class members that this week's lesson is the second from Jeremiah and the fourth based on the experience of the nation of Judah after the northern kingdom of Israel had fallen to foreign invaders. Remind them that two weeks ago they looked at the reign of the good King Josiah, and that last week's text from Jeremiah was probably written during Josiah's reign. It seems that this week's text looks at a time after Josiah's death, when Judah had once again slipped into sin. Today's text shows the seriousness of the sin in the land.

Ask a volunteer to read Jeremiah 7:1-15, while students listen for clues about the sins of Judah. After the text has been read, ask class members where on the continuum they would put a mark to describe Judah's sinfulness, according to this passage.

Form groups of about five students each. Have each group choose one of the following activities:

*List the sins.* This group makes a list of all the sins plaguing the nation of Judah.

*Write the headlines.* This group thinks of several popular publications: perhaps your local newspaper, *USA Today, National Enquirer, Reader's Digest, Guideposts, Time,* or others. Suppose the publications they have chosen were published in Jeremiah's time. What would be some of the lead articles or stories in the publication, based on what this text tells us about Jeremiah's society? This group should write headlines or titles for those articles or stories. Have them also write a headline that might have appeared over the story of Jeremiah's assignment in today's text.

*Marked Bibles.* Students should use photocopies of this text and colored pencils, pens, or markers. Each student should choose one color to represent the sins of the people, another to represent the warnings of God, and a third to indicate the promises of God. They should mark their text to show where each of these categories appears.

After several minutes, the groups can share with each other the results of their study and the conclusions they have reached. Make sure class members understand the Jews' vain reliance on the safety of the temple (v. 4) and the nature of God's warning to them based on his action at Shiloh (vv. 12-15). (See the lesson commentary.)

## INTO LIFE

If you have listed the sins of Judah, ask class members to decide which of Judah's sins is also present in our society. Beside each sin on your list, students should write evidence or examples of how that sin is present today.

Ask class members to decide what warnings or conditions from God Jeremiah might give if he were speaking to your town or your congregation.

What specific actions could your class members take to move your town to the right on the continuum indicated during "Into the Lesson"? Write these actions on your chalkboard as class members suggest them.

This list will become your prayer request list for the closing activity of your session. Ask a different class member to pray specifically about each of the actions class members have suggested.

# The Eyes of God

"I have been watching," God warned his wayward people (Jeremiah 7:11). The idea of God's watching can be either a comfort or a dread. Look up the Scriptures below and tell whether God's eyes were an encouragement or a warning (or both) in each case. Give a brief explanation for your choice.

Proverbs 5:21

Jeremiah 16:17, 18

Jeremiah 29:23

Hebrews 4:13

Revelation 1:14

Revelation 2:2

Revelation 2:18, 19

Revelation 3:1

Revelation 3:8

Revelation 3:15

When you think about God's eyes on you, are you comfroted or concerned? Why?

# CONTINUING TO TRUST

**LESSON 5**

## WHY TEACH THIS LESSON?

We live in trying times. Almost no one will argue that. If the economy doesn't worry us, the politicians do. If it's not the politicians, it's the moral climate. If it's not one thing, it's another.

Yet we can only imagine how trying were the times for Habakkuk. Troubled by immorality, aware of a growing military menace, harassed by unbelievers, we would have allowed him to plead "burnout" and retire. But he remained faithful because he knew God would remain faithful.

Encourage your students with the same truth. God *is* faithful. Because he is, "the righteous will live by his faith."

## INTRODUCTION

We all have questions, don't we? Some of them are hard to answer, and some of the hardest ones are about good and evil. If God is in charge and if he is just, why do bad things happen to good people? Why do good things happen to bad people? The Bible gives no clear and complete answer. So we say, "I'm going to ask about that when I get to Heaven." We are sure God knows.

Habakkuk's questions were similar to ours, and he got an answer before he went to Heaven. But, as sometimes happens, the answer raised another question as puzzling as the first one.

### A. HABAKKUK

Habakkuk was a prophet, so God spoke to him directly. That was how he got an answer without going to Heaven.

The first verse of Habakkuk's book tells us he was a prophet, and that is about all we know of the man himself. In a little note at the end of his book, he speaks of "my stringed instruments." Some students take this as a hint that he was a Levite who served as a temple musician (cf. 1 Chronicles 23:3-6), but we cannot be sure.

Habakkuk does not say when he received this prophecy, but he gives some clues that help us in fixing the date. To interpret his clues, we need to examine the history of this time. This is recorded in 2 Kings 21—25. Here is a short outline.

**696-642 B.C.** Evil King Manasseh ruled Judah and brought the country deeper and deeper into wrongdoing, but in his later years he reversed his course and tried to undo the harm he had done.

**642-640 B.C.** King Amon promptly revived all the evil of Manasseh's earlier years.

**640-609 B.C.** Good King Josiah restored righteousness and the worship of the Lord, but he was killed in battle with the Egyptian army as it was crossing his country to do battle with the Assyrians.

**609 B.C.** Josiah's son Jehoahaz became king, but he ruled only three months. Egypt then took charge of Judah, put Jehoahaz in prison, and made his brother Jehoiakim king.

DEVOTIONAL READING
PSALM 31:1-10

LESSON SCRIPTURE
HABAKKUK

PRINTED TEXT
HABAKKUK 2:1-4; 3:17-19

Sep
29

LESSON AIMS

After this lesson a student should be able to do the following:

1. Recall two questions of Habakkuk and the answers that came from the Lord.

2. Describe Habakkuk's faith in God in spite of his questions and fears.

3. Express confidence and faith in God in spite of some specific situation or circumstance that troubles him or her.

KEY VERSE

Though the fig tree does not bud and there are no grapes on the vines, though the olive crop fails and the fields produce no food, though there are no sheep in the pen and no cattle in the stalls, yet I will rejoice in the LORD, I will be joyful in God my Savior.
—Habakkuk 3:17, 18

## What Do You Think?

*There are certain questions about God and his dealings with man that no person can answer. Unbelievers may suggest that our inability to answer hard questions about God demonstrates weakness in our religion. How do you answer such a charge?*

*Is this what it means to "live by faith" (2 Corinthians 5:7)? If so, how can the faithless ever appreciate our position? How does such a one come to faith?*

## How to Say It

*Amon.* AY-mun.
*Assyrians.* Uh-SEER-ee-unz.
*Babylon.* BAB-uh-lon.
*Babylonians.* Bab-uh-LOW-nee-unz.
*Habakkuk.* Huh-BAK-kuk.
*Hezekiah.* Hez-eh-KYE-uh.
*Jehoahaz* . Jeh-HOE-uh-haz.
*Jehoiachin.* Jeh-HOY-uh-kin.
*Jehoiakim.* Jeh-HOY-uh-kim.
*Josiah.* Jo-SYE-uh.
*Judah.* JOO-duh.
*Judeans.* Joo-DEE-unz.
*Manasseh.* Muh-NASS-uh.
*Nebuchadnezzar.* NEB-uh-kad-NEZZ-er.
*Wittenberg.* VIT-en-burg.
*Zedekiah.* Zed-uh-KYE-uh.

**609-598 B.C.** Jehoiakim (another son of Josiah) was a very bad king, and the nation sank swiftly into sin. About 605 B.C. Nebuchadnezzar and the Babylonian army conquered Judah and compelled it to pay tribute. Jehoiakim paid for three years and then rebelled. Judah was free for a short time, but was harassed by other smaller nations ruled by Babylon.

**598-597 B.C.** Jehoiachin (Jehoiakim's son) became king, but he ruled only three months. Nebuchadnezzar returned and made him a prisoner along with ten thousand of his people.

**597-586 B.C.** Zedekiah ruled Judah during this period. He was another son of Josiah (an uncle of Jehoiachin). Nebuchadnezzar left him to rule Judah and pay tribute to Babylon. Zedekiah paid for about ten years, then rebelled. Nebuchadnezzar retaliated and besieged Jerusalem for a year and a half.

**586 B.C.** Nebuchadnezzar destroyed Jerusalem and took most of the survivors to Babylon, leaving a few farmers to occupy the land of Judah. This completed the disaster that Habakkuk foretold.

Now we will try to determine where the prophecy of Habakkuk fits into this outline. First, the prophecy came during a time of widespread sin in Judah (Habakkuk 1:2-4). Manasseh was Judah's most notoriously wicked king, so some students think this points to his reign. On the other hand, the Lord told Habakkuk that a terrible disaster was coming to Judah "in your days"—in the lifetime of the people who heard the prophecy (Habakkuk 1:5, 6). This seems to suggest that the prophecy was given at a time later than the evil part of Manasseh's reign. Manasseh died more than half a century before Jerusalem was destroyed.

Second, the Lord said that the prophecy of destruction would be thought incredible (Habakkuk 1:5). This seems to indicate that the prophecy was given before the Babylonians became powerful enough to pose a threat to Judah. This would be some time before 605 B.C. So perhaps Habakkuk gave this prophecy soon after good King Josiah died. The nation by then was plunging swiftly into sin (2 Kings 23:31, 32, 36, 37). Surely a godly prophet such as he would be shocked and alarmed.

### B. Lesson Background

Habakkuk was distressed and grieved by the rampant sin in his country. He was praying for God to do something about it. His question was this: How long would it be before God would answer that prayer? How long would the Lord let such sinning go on (Habakkuk 1:2-4)?

The Lord did not set an exact time, but he said he would do something "in your days"; that is, in the lifetime of Habakkuk and others who heard his promise. The Lord also told what he was going to do. He would bring the Babylonians with a huge army to overwhelm Judah and put an end to its corrupt national life (Habakkuk 1:5-9). The Babylonians were going to rule Judah, and they would be brutal masters.

This answer troubled Habakkuk about as much as the sins of Judah did. The Babylonians were pagans, even more wicked than the people of Judah. How could a just and holy God support them in war, especially when Judah was "more righteous" (Habakkuk 1:13)? Our text begins as Habakkuk was waiting for an answer to that question.

## I. THE LORD'S MESSAGE (HABAKKUK 2:1-4)
### A. Waiting for an Answer (v. 1)

**1. I will stand at my watch and station myself on the ramparts; I will look to see what he will say to me, and what answer I am to give to this complaint.**

Habakkuk pictured himself as a watchman standing on a tower of the city wall, anxiously looking for a runner to come with a message. (See 2 Samuel 18:24-27.) Possibly he found a literal tower (*rampart*) where he could be alone as he waited.

Habakkuk was waiting for more than an answer from God to his own question. He needed to give an answer to some kind of complaint. Perhaps people had complained—or he expected them to complain—about his prophecy of impending doom. Perhaps others shared the same questions he had.

The Hebrew in this verse may also be translated "what I shall answer when I am reproved" (*King James Version*). Again, this is not entirely clear. Is the prophet expecting that people who hear his message will "reprove" him for his unpatriotic talk? Is he perhaps afraid the Lord himself may reprove him for being so outspoken in questioning God's ways? Either is possible from the construction here.

## B. MAKE THE MESSAGE PLAIN (v. 2)

**2. Then the LORD replied: "Write down the revelation and make it plain on tablets so that a herald may run with it.**

Instead of giving the answer immediately, the Lord first told Habakkuk what to do with it. He was to write it plainly *on tablets* or placards so *that a herald may run with it*. Obviously, *the revelation* was not for Habakkuk alone, but was to be published or announced to many.

## C. WAIT FOR THE TIME (v. 3)

**3. "For the revelation awaits an appointed time; it speaks of the end and will not prove false. Though it linger, wait for it; it will certainly come and will not delay.**

The *revelation* told of an event that would not happen immediately, but at *an appointed time* in the future. That time would come in the lifetime of Habakkuk and other hearers (Habakkuk 1:5), but they did not know how long they must wait. No matter how long the event might *linger*, those who heard the prophecy should trust God and *wait for it*. Its *delay* should not be taken by any to be a sign that it would not *come*. Perhaps the wait then was much like our own wait for the Lord Jesus to return. As Peter reminds us, "The Lord is not slow in keeping his promise, as some understand slowness. He is patient with you, not wanting anyone to perish, but everyone to come to repentance" (2 Peter 3:9).

## D. LIFE FOR THE FAITHFUL (v. 4)

**4. "See, he is puffed up; his desires are not upright—but the righteous will live by his faith—**

One whose soul is *puffed up* is a proud man. That described the haughty Babylonians who were about to overrun Judah. These words could also describe the arrogant sinners of Judah. They were proud of their ability to do as they pleased, ignoring the law of God. They certainly were *not upright* either.

Verse 5, however, indicates that the king of the Babylonians was the one whom Habakkuk said was *puffed up*. He was the "arrogant" man who was never at rest, whose desire was unlimited, and who conquered many nations and gathered them into his empire. His soul was not upright; he was an evil man.

In sharp contrast was *the righteous*, the man who trusted God and did right. Many haughty sinners of Judah would die, and others would be driven to Babylon as captives during the fierce onslaught of the Babylonians. But the just could expect his life to be preserved.

The rest of the chapter shows that the proud Babylonians would also in time be destroyed. That was the answer to Habakkuk's second question. The Lord would

*WHAT DO YOU THINK?*

The Lord commanded Habakkuk, "Write down the revelation and make it plain on tablets so that a herald may run with it" (Habakkuk 2:2). What does this suggest about our need to "herald" or proclaim the gospel?

What does it suggest about the scope of our witness? About the urgency of presenting the message?

(See Romans 10:13-15.)

*OPTION*

Explore the New Testament quotations of Habakkuk 2:4 with the reproducible activity, "Living by Faith," on page 54.

*WHAT DO YOU THINK?*

The Lord told Habakkuk his revelation would "certainly come and not delay." Habakkuk was to "wait for it" expectantly. How like the promises of our Lord's second coming this sounds! How might the prophecy of Habakkuk and its fulfillment be used to encourage Christians who may begin to become weary of awaiting the Lord's return? How might it be used to convince the scoffers Peter mentions in 2 Peter 3:3-10?

use the wicked Babylonians for now to punish the Judeans, but in the end all the wicked would meet disaster. Life and peace were possible only by believing, trusting, and obeying the Lord.

*The righteous will live by his faith.* Paul uses this statement to declare that eternal life is granted to those who trust and obey (Romans 1:17; Galatians 3:11). They do not earn eternal life; God gives it to them because of their faith. Therefore we are "continuing to trust," as the title of our lesson puts it. The promise is secure when we are patient in our faith (Hebrews 10:36-39).

### LIVING BY FAITH

Today we are just a month and two days away from the 479th anniversary of the beginning of the Protestant Reformation. Martin Luther, a devout German monk, had been deeply distressed. His soul had found no peace in spite of all his study and training in Catholic theology. His rigorous self-discipline had brought him no joy.

Then he found in Paul's letter to the Romans the key to it all: "The righteous will live by faith" (Romans 1:17)—a quotation by Paul from the prophet Habakkuk. Luther saw that the good works his superiors had told him would bring salvation were hollow and without meaning when faith was absent.

This new understanding of God's Word galvanized Luther into action. To the door of the Castle Church in Wittenberg, Germany, he nailed a list of 95 points in which he challenged the system of works-righteousness from which Scripture and his faith in God had now set him free. The Reformation was born!

God's word to Habakkuk was that *all* we do to make our lives secure, happy, and fulfilling will be useless if we have no faith in God. But if faith inspires our attitudes and prompts our good works, we will find the answer to our souls' deep needs.

When this truth comes alive in our minds, a reformation will be born in our hearts. Living by faith brings freedom and fulfillment!　　　　　　—C. R. B.

## II. JOY IN THE LORD (HABAKKUK 3:17-19)

The last chapter of Habakkuk is the prophet's prayer set to music. In times of trouble it is a splendid prayer for all of the faithful to sing. Facing the invasion of ruthless Babylonians, the prophet confessed his fear. Humbly he prayed to the Lord, "In wrath remember mercy" (v. 2). Through most of the prayer he sang of God's irresistible power (vv. 3-15). In the coming time of distress, that power would be aligned with the Babylonians to punish Judah. Upon hearing this, Habakkuk was filled with fear (v. 16). His prayer concluded, however, with the beautiful assurance found in the last part of our text.

### A. DISASTER (v. 17)

**17. Though the fig tree does not bud and there are no grapes on the vines, though the olive crop fails and the fields produce no food, though there are no sheep in the pen and no cattle in the stalls. . . .**

This verse describes the devastation that was to come. The invading Babylonians would either eat the fruit or destroy the trees. For the people of Judah there would be no *figs,* no *grapes,* and no *olives.* The *fields* would produce *no food.* The crops would be destroyed or stolen by the invaders. The *sheep* and *cattle* would be slaughtered to provide food for the Babylonian army. The people of Judah would become desperately hungry.

### B. JOY (v. 18)

**18. Yet I will rejoice in the LORD, I will be joyful in God my Savior.**

In the midst of utter poverty, close to death from starvation, Habakkuk would still *rejoice in the Lord.* The Lord had said, "The righteous will live by his faith" (2:4).

*The visual for lesson 5 suggests a modern-day application of Habakkuk's call to trust in God (verses 17, 18).*

**WHAT DO YOU THINK?**

*It is popular today to suggest that those who truly have faith in the Lord will never suffer economic problems or even be seriously ill. How does Habakkuk's message in verses 17 and 18 counter such teaching? How would you use this text to comfort or reassure a Christian who was out of work and out of resources? How does it reassure you when you are discouraged about circumstances?*

Habakkuk's faith in God did not depend on his surroundings. The God of his salvation was firmly in control. Thus, Habakkuk found joy in the midst of disaster.

## C. STRENGTH (v. 19)

**19a. The Sovereign LORD is my strength; he makes my feet like the feet of a deer, he enables me to go on the heights.**

Neither the prophet nor the whole nation of Judah had strength enough to resist the overwhelming forces from Babylon. But the Lord had strength enough to do whatever he chose to do, and he would protect the just who lived by faith. Wild *deer* had no fear of invasion. Their *feet* were swift and strong on the mountains where they grazed on leaves and grasses. Destruction of wheat and barley in the valley would not trouble them. In the same way, the faithful would escape danger by the providence of the Almighty and find food to sustain them.

**19b. For the director of music. On my stringed instruments.**

This notation, with which the book of Habakkuk concludes, is viewed by some as evidence that the prophet may have served for a time as a temple musician. As noted earlier in the Introduction, this is one of the few pieces of information we have about Habakkuk himself.

### WHEN "EVERYTHING" GOES WRONG

Pat was a "master teacher," in the words of the elementary school principal who used to supervise her work. In those days, her joy-filled service to God was to introduce children to the wonderful world that opened to them through reading. She had almost completed her doctorate in education. Then "THE BACK" struck.

There had been two back surgeries before, but this time the villain struck in earnest, and there would be no relief. No more classes of kindergartners or first graders. Instead there was the ordeal of three more surgeries. No more getting out to church. Instead there was pain that came, not as an occasional visitor, but as a permanent, grossly unwelcome resident.

So life continues, day after day. But not all is bleak. Pat has taught herself paralegal skills so that when she feels up to it, she can do work at home for some Christian attorneys. She has found release for her teaching instincts by turning every "grandmothering" opportunity into an educational event for her grandchildren.

The pain is bad *every* day, even with heavy, prescribed doses of medication. But on the days when pain invades her life without mercy, the words of Habakkuk (3:18, 19) are among those that help Pat to carry on. Even when almost everything seems to be going wrong, "yet I will rejoice in the Lord, . . . the Sovereign Lord is my strength."

—C. R. B.

## CONCLUSION

The Babylonians' final onslaught is recorded in 2 Kings 25:1-21. They besieged Jerusalem for a year and a half, until there was no strength left to resist. The king of Judah tried to break through the Babylonian lines and escape, but he was pursued and captured. The city was burned, and the stone walls that would not burn were battered down. Many people died by the sword and from hunger. Most of the rest were driven to Babylon. A few were left in Judah, but they soon migrated to Egypt (2 Kings 25:22-26). For half a century Judah lay deserted.

We do not know what happened to Habakkuk, but we do know the fate of his fellow prophet Jeremiah. When Jeremiah predicted defeat by the Babylonians, his own people called him a traitor. The Babylonians were sympathetic to him, so they offered him comfort and ease in Babylon. Jeremiah chose to stay with the remnant in Judah and later accompanied them to Egypt (Jeremiah 40:2-6; 43:5-7; 44:1). Perhaps Habakkuk also was with that group, but we have no record.

## DAILY BIBLE READINGS

**Monday, Sept. 23**—Why Does Evil Go Unpunished? (Habakkuk 1:1-11)

**Tuesday, Sept. 24**—God Will Not Tolerate Wrongs (Habakkuk 1:12-17)

**Wednesday, Sept. 25**—Woes of the Wicked (Habakkuk 2:5-11)

**Thursday, Sept. 26**—Fate of the Wicked (Habakkuk 2:12-20)

**Friday, Sept. 27**—"In Wrath Remember Mercy" (Habakkuk 3:1-8)

**Saturday, Sept. 28**—God Saves His People (Habakkuk 3:9-16)

**Sunday, Sept. 29**—God Is Our Refuge and Strength (Psalm 46)

**What Do You Think?**

The lesson writer demonstrates the many ways fear permeates our society. How can we Christians minister to those who are fearful? What do the following Scripture passages offer to the fearful? Psalm 34; 56:3; Proverbs 29:25; Isaiah 26:3; Hebrews 2:15

**What Do You Think?**

If every person were a Christian, do you think a great many of society's problems would vanish? Why or why not?

Obviously, we would have to say that only if everyone became a truly committed Christian would it make an impact on human woes. Genuine disciples of Christ could bring His love, compassion, righteousness, wisdom, and power to bear on these woes. What would the world be like if everyone were a Christian like you?

**Prayer**

Many things in the world alarm us, our Father, but with David we say, "When I am afraid, I will trust in you" (Psalm 56:3). We know your love is always with us, and your power is enough to meet our every need. Therefore we say, as Isaiah did, "You will keep in perfect peace him whose mind is steadfast, because he trusts in you" (Isaiah 26:3). Thank you, Lord.

**Thought to Remember**

"The righteous will live by his faith."

## A. Fear

Habakkuk became afraid when he learned of the horrible disaster that was coming to his people (Habakkuk 3:2). Unfortunately, the rulers and the people did not share his fear and change their ways, and so disaster came.

Fear is epidemic in some sections of our cities. Elderly citizens are afraid to leave their homes at night. Many citizens think crime ought to be a major concern of the government, and the government responds by spending billions to fight crime. But the root of the problem is beyond the reach of law. Where robbers roam the streets, honest citizens are still afraid to go out at night.

Big companies are "down-sizing" all over the world. As a result, many people are being laid off, and many more are afraid of unemployment and poverty. News media make it plain that cancer and AIDS are frightening many people. Multitudes worry about the accident rate, and some are terrified of old age. And of course, godly people are alarmed by the decay of moral standards.

Within many of our fears looms the same specter that accompanied the fear of a Babylonian invasion. This is the most frightful specter of them all—the fear of death. But this is not so frightful to those who trust in the Lord. Paul expressed a desire to depart and be with Christ, "which is better by far" (Philippians 1:23). Death loses its terror when we know that the price of our transportation to Heaven has already been paid. "Death has been swallowed up in victory!" (1 Corinthians 15:54; see also verses 55-58).

## B. Assurance

Habakkuk was afraid, but he knew where to look for assurance. "I will rejoice in the Lord, I will be joyful in God my Savior" (Habakkuk 3:18). How the fears of the world would fade if people would turn to the Lord!

What if the man-hours and dollars used in seeking the lost were as many as those used in policing and jailing them? Most of our economic problems could be solved by massive doses of the Golden Rule. Sickness would be less and health care would be better if everyone loved his neighbor as himself. The accident rate could be lowered by Christian courtesy, and old age would lose its terror as people came to know the Savior.

We ought to be busy bringing people to Christ. Even if some refuse to come, those who do come and those who bring them will find themselves "safe in the arms of Jesus."

"The righteous will live by his faith."

## C. Faith

Faith is believing. In New Testament Greek, the word *faith* is the noun form of the verb *believe*. Yet faith is more than believing. "Faith is being sure of what we hope for and certain of what we do not see" (Hebrews 11:1).

Faith is trusting. With such trust Habakkuk sang of being like a deer in the mountains when the whole valley below was desolate and barren. With such trust we find security in the Lord when moral standards are falling and crime rates are rising.

Faith is acting, for "faith without deeds is dead" (James 2:26). By faith Abraham packed up his goods and uprooted his family. He did not know where he was going, but he knew the Lord had told him to go (Hebrews 11:8).

Faith is holding on and keeping on. In both Hebrew and Greek, the word can mean either faith or faithfulness. Confidently the inspired writer says, "But we are not of those who shrink back and are destroyed, but of those who believe and are saved" (Hebrews 10:39).

# Discovery Learning

*This page contains an alternate lesson plan emphasizing learning activities. Classes desiring such student involvement will find these suggestions helpful. The next page is a reproducible activity page to further enhance discovery learning.*

## LEARNING GOALS

After this lesson a student should be able to:

1. Recall two questions of Habakkuk and the answers that came from the Lord.

2. Describe Habakkuk's faith in God in spite of his questions and fears.

3. Express confidence and faith in God in spite of some situation or circumstance that troubles him or her.

## INTO THE LESSON

Write one or all of the following open-ended sentences on your chalkboard:

*"The most difficult time for me to trust God is …"*

*"The person I know who trusts God most is …"*

*"Trusting God is easier to talk about than to do because …"*

*"It is easier/harder for me to trust God today than ten years ago because…"*

Ask class members to group themselves into twos or threes, and have each group complete one of the statements. Allow five minutes or less for this; then ask volunteers to share with the class.

Tell the class that today's study looks at a prophet who learned to trust God in the midst of a bleak situation.

## INTO THE WORD

Class members will need your help to understand who Habakkuk was, when he wrote, and how his book is organized. Use the Introduction to the lesson to develop a mini-lecture to deliver before class members do further Bible study. (If you wish, you may ask a class member to present this material.)

Divide your class into four groups or sections. (If your class is larger than about twenty-four, each section could have more than one group.) Write the following assignments on the chalkboard:

1. *Question One (1:1-4)*
2. *Answer One (1:5-11)*
3. *Question Two (1:12—2:1)*
4. *Answer Two (2:2-20)*

Each section in your class will concentrate on the portion of Habakkuk 1 or 2 indicated by the assignment. Ask a class member to read all of chapters 1 and 2 aloud while the rest of the class listens carefully.

After the reading, class members, in their groups, should answer the following questions. (Copy these and give them to the groups.)

*Question 1 Group*—What was the situation in Judah? Summarize Habakkuk's question in a sentence or two.

*Answer 1 Group*—How would God deal with Judah? Summarize God's answer in one or two sentences.

*Question 2 Group*—How did Habakkuk react to God's use of the Babylonians? Summarize Habakkuk's question in one or two sentences.

*Answer 2 Group*—How would God ultimately deal with the Babylonians? Summarize God's answer in one or two sentences.

Give the groups six or eight minutes to complete their assignments. Let each group share its answers with the class. Then discuss: What did Habakkuk fear? What did he have trouble understanding? How did he relate to God in spite of his fear and confusion?

Tell the class that chapter 3 shows a fuller answer to the last question. Ask another reader or pair of readers to read chapter 3 aloud. As class members listen, they should write words that describe Habakkuk's feelings about God.

Allow a few members to tell what words they have written. Discuss: What was Habakkuk's attitude toward God? What was to be the fate of his nation? Why did Habakkuk refuse to give in to despair?

## INTO LIFE

Refer back to the open-ended sentences you used to begin the session. Ask the class to consider the situations named in those statements in light of Habakkuk 3:17-19.

Ask the class members to write their own individual paraphrases of Habakkuk 3:17-19. They should consider what situations or problems from their own lives they would put in the "although" half of their sentences (v. 17). These might be some of the situations from the opening activity or some others. Their completed paraphrases will read something like, "Although my cancer may get worse instead of better, still will I rejoice in the Lord," or, "Even if my son drops out of college instead of finishing his degree, I will trust in God."

Class members may write as many sentences as they wish. Then close the class session by asking volunteers, at random, to read one of their sentences. They should do so with their heads bowed, in an attitude of prayer. After many have been read, close with a prayer expressing faith in God.

*Option.* The reproducible activity, ". . . Not by Sight," on page 54 is similar to the activity above.

# Living by Faith

More than one New Testament passage quotes Habakkuk in order to explain the idea of faith. Read each of the following verses and then find the words in Habakkuk. Then write a one-or two-sentence definition of faith.

**Romans 1:17**

Faith is . . .

**Galatians 3:11**

Faith is . . .

**Hebrews 10:38**

Faith is . . .

# . . . Not by Sight

"We live by faith, not by sight," Paul reminds us (2 Corinthians 5:7). Habakkukl 3:17, 18 provides a good illustration of that principle. List some trying experiences you have faced or are currently facing. Next to each, write how faith in God has sustained you through that situation.

| TRYING CIRCUMSTANCE | VICTORY OF FAITH |
| --- | --- |
|  |  |

# A VAIN SEARCH

**LESSON 6**

## WHY TEACH THIS LESSON?

Who can forget the Susan Smith case? We wept with her as she pleaded on camera for the unknown kidnappers to return her two small children. Then we learned the truth—there were no kidnappers. Mrs. Smith locked the children in her car and then caused it to roll into a lake. She had murdered her own children!

Her act was monstrous, but Susan Smith did not look like a monster. She looked like the lady next door. And so does every sinner. Look up and down the streets—is there a righteous person to be found? We certainly cannot tell by looking.

Use this lesson to remind your class—and yourself—that everyone needs the Lord. There are no "good" people in the sense that they are "good enough" for salvation. Only the grace of God offers that. And only through the name of Jesus is that grace found (Acts 4:12).

## INTRODUCTION

The atheist liked to argue with the preacher. One conversation went like this:

**Atheist:** That God of yours must be a monster, if he really exists. First he made a world full of sinners, and then he's going to burn them all in Hell because they're sinners.

**Preacher:** No, you're off to a bad start. God doesn't make sinners. People who sin make sinners of themselves.

**Atheist:** They all do it, don't they?

**Preacher:** Yes, but that's their choice, not God's.

**Atheist:** And God feels bad about it?

**Preacher:** Yes. He wants everyone to straighten up and do right.

**Atheist:** If he's so smart, why didn't he make people who wouldn't sin? He could have saved himself a lot of grief and them a lot of burning.

**Preacher:** Phil, how are your boys doing in college this year?

**Atheist:** My boys? Oh, I get it. You want to change the subject. I don't blame you. I wouldn't want to defend your God either.

**Preacher:** So tell me about the boys.

**Atheist:** They're doing all right, I guess. Bill's on the football team. Ed hopes to make it in basketball. Both of them are on the dean's list.

**Preacher:** I guess neither of them ever did anything wrong.

**Atheist:** Are you crazy? We used to paddle them nearly every day. Some days we paddled them twice.

**Preacher:** Didn't that make you feel bad?

**Atheist:** Millie cried her eyes out.

**Preacher:** What about you? Weren't you hurting too?

**Atheist:** Yeah. So what?

**Preacher:** Before the children were born, didn't you know they would do wrong sometimes? Didn't you know they would hurt you and make Millie cry?

**Atheist:** Oh, sure. Kids are like that.

**Preacher:** You could have saved yourself a lot of grief and them a lot of paddling just by being childless. Why did you bring children like them into the world?

Oct
6

DEVOTIONAL READING
JEREMIAH 5:20-31
LESSON SCRIPTURE
JEREMIAH 5
PRINTED TEXT
JEREMIAH 5:1-6

### LESSON AIMS

*After this lesson students should be able to do the following:*

*1. List the sins of Judah mentioned in Jeremiah 5.*

*2. Compare these sins with sins in their nation and compare the moral state of Judah with the moral state of their country.*

*3. Choose specific remedies for sins in their country and commit themselves to specific ways to improve the moral fiber of their nation.*

### KEY VERSE

*Go up and down the streets of Jerusalem, look around and consider, search through her squares. If you can find but one person who deals honestly and seeks the truth, I will forgive this city.*

*—Jeremiah 5:1*

*LESSON 6 NOTES*

## WHAT DO YOU THINK?

*Unbelievers ask, "If God exists, why does he allow so much suffering?" The Bible teaches that God has given to all people the gift of free will. We can choose to obey God or to reject his ways. How does the the exercise of this free will to reject God's laws produce much of the suffering we see today? How are such things as poverty, disease, and accidents due in part, at least, to sin? What can we do to erase the blight of sin on our world?*

*The visual for lesson 6 in the visuals packet illustrates verse 1 of the text. Display it as you begin the Bible study.*

**WANTED!**

"Go up and down the streets of Jerusalem, look around and consider, search through her squares. If you can find but one person who deals honestly and seeks the truth, I will forgive this city."

—Jeremiah 5:1, NIV

**Atheist:** Because there isn't any other kind!

**Preacher:** Aw, you could have got a bunch of marionettes—you know, puppets on strings. With less time than you gave to the boys, you could have them putting on a great show, always doing just what you wanted them to do. You could even put little tape players in them, and they would never say a false or mean word. No paddling, no pain, no grief—and no college tuition.

**Atheist:** Nuts! Who wants to play with dolls? We wanted real live children.

**Preacher:** Sure you did—and so did God.

## A. REAL LIVE CHILDREN

We are not told about everything God had in mind when he created man, but it is clear that he wanted a family—children he could love and who could love him. If they had no mind or will of their own, if they could not choose their way, if they were programmed to do always what God wanted them to do, they would be nothing more than puppets, robots, dolls, and toys. God wanted real live children.

So God made people with minds and wills and hearts, people who were capable of thinking and choosing. They could obey him or disobey him, please him or grieve him, love him or hate him.

## B. DISOBEDIENT CHILDREN

Very soon God's children chose to disobey. It brought loss to them and grief to God, but still they chose to disobey. Continued disobedience only worsened man's condition: "The Lord saw how great man's wickedness on the earth had become, and that every inclination of the thoughts of his heart was only evil all the time" (Genesis 6:5). So God destroyed most of humanity and started over with Noah and his family.

Soon disobedience began again, and once more it grew and multiplied. This time God did not destroy all the sinners. He chose one man of faith and obedience to be the father of a nation that would show the rest of the world how good it is to obey God. To Abraham's children God gave the special guidance of his Law, the special protection of his power, and the special encouragement of his love. Still they became disobedient children, bringing disaster upon themselves and grieving their Father in Heaven.

Clearly mankind was not going to make itself obedient, even with the help of God's guidance and protection. Then God revealed the plan that would not fail. He sent the Savior, who was both God and man. Jesus gave his spotless life to redeem the disobedient. By his grace the sinners of earth can be forgiven, cleansed, and made ready to live in God's presence as the obedient children he always wanted.

For this lesson, however, we are still looking at the time before the Savior came—a dark and evil time in Judah.

## C. LESSON BACKGROUND

Jeremiah was God's spokesman for more than forty years. The book called by his name is a collection of prophecies he gave to Judah at different times during those years, along with some historical material. The prophecies are not all arranged in the order in which they were given. Some of them are dated; thus we know when Jeremiah delivered them (for example, see Jeremiah 25:1; 26:1; 32:1; 36:1, 9). The one assigned for this lesson is not dated; it may have come about the same time as Habakkuk's prophecy that we considered last week. From the text itself, we see that it came at a time when Judah was deep in sin.

## I. SEARCHING THE CITY (JEREMIAH 5:1-3)

### A. Search for a Good Person (v. 1)

**1. "Go up and down the streets of Jerusalem, look around and consider, search through her squares. If you can find but one person who deals honestly and seeks the truth, I will forgive this city.**

*Go up and down the streets* suggests a thorough search. *Scour the streets* is the reading in Moffatt's translation. *Look around and consider* also suggests a thorough search: look everywhere and make sure.

Houses in a walled city were crowded closely together to make room for many people, but there were some open places—the public *squares* just inside the gates. These areas were to be searched also. No spot in *Jerusalem* was to be overlooked.

The search was not for a murderer, robber, or other criminal. Any of these could be found easily. This search was for a *person* of a very different kind—a good and honest person. Those who heard Jeremiah's message were invited to search the entire city of Jerusalem and see if they could find even one person who did right and really wanted to find *the truth*. If such a one could be found—just *one*—the Lord said he would *forgive this city.* Jerusalem was nearing destruction because of its wickedness; its only hope was divine pardon.

We are reminded of ancient Sodom. It could have been saved if it had held ten righteous people (Genesis 18:23-32). But ten could not be found; so the one good family was evacuated and Sodom perished (Genesis 19:15-28). We also think of mankind in the time of Noah: "Every inclination of the thoughts of his heart was only evil all the time" (Genesis 6:5). The Lord found eight people worth saving, while all the rest perished (Genesis 6—8). Just one good person could have won pardon for Jerusalem. Where was that one?

In almost any town we can still easily find a good person, or eight or ten of them; but how evil has multiplied in recent years: particularly in our larger cities! Would the search for a righteous person in one of these cities be as desperate as Jeremiah's search in Jerusalem?

### DOES ANYONE SEEK THE TRUTH?

*The Day America Told the Truth* was one of the most revealing books published in 1991. On a chosen day the pollsters fanned out across the nation to question a wide cross section of Americans about a number of significant moral issues.

For example, when questioned whether for $10 million they would abandon their parents, leave their spouses, or become prostitutes for a week, between one-fourth and two-fifths of non-religious people said, "Yes." People who called themselves "religious" said "yes" only about half as often as others. Maybe there is a *little* consolation in that!

Although 90% of those questioned claimed to believe in God, 93% claimed that they were their own final authority on what is moral and immoral! Only 17% defined sin as "going against God's will."

God's challenge to Jeremiah was to survey the city of Jerusalem and see if there was even one person who practiced justice and searched after the truth. The implication was that no such person could be found. Our situation today is probably not quite that serious, but without question the moral foundation of Western society has some large cracks in it. Those of us who claim to know God must set an example of morality for those who do not know him. —C. R. B.

### B. Lying Sinners (v. 2)

**2. "Although they say, 'As surely as the LORD lives,' still they are swearing falsely."**

In modern courtrooms a witness swears to tell "the truth, the whole truth, and nothing but the truth." To make the oath more solemn, the phrase "So help me

## How to Say It

*Abraham.* AY-bruh-ham.

*Babylon.* BAB-uh-lon.

*Babylonians.* Bab-uh-LOW-nee-unz.

*Belshazzar.* Bel-SHAZZ-er.

*Habakkuk.* Huh-BAK-kuk.

*Jeremiah.* JAIR-uh-MYE-uh.

*Judah.* JOO-duh.

*Medes.* Meeds.

*Moffat.* MOFF-ut.

*Nebuchadnezzar.* NEB-uh-kad-NEZZ-er.

*Persians.* PUR-zhuns.

*Zephaniah.* Zef-uh-NYE-uh.

God" used to be included. The oath-taking phrase in ancient Judah was *As surely as the Lord lives.* But sinners in Judah thoughtlessly used that oath even when they were lying. Thus they misused the name of the Lord, violating one of the Ten Commandments (Exodus 20:7). Lying was bad, and using the Lord's name in the process was even worse.

### C. Stubborn Sinners (v. 3)

**3. O Lord, do not your eyes look for truth? You struck them, but they felt no pain; you crushed them, but they refused correction. They made their faces harder than stone and refused to repent.**

*Do not your eyes look for truth?* The obvious answer was yes. The Lord was looking for the truth, expecting his people to speak the truth.

*You struck them.* The Lord had struck the lying sinners of Judah with various kinds of punishment. Probably those punishments were similar to those given to Israel: famine, drought, various types of crop failures, pestilence, and war. (See Amos 4:6-11.) But the sinners of Judah, like those of northern Israel, had not grieved: they were not sorry for their sins, and they continued to do wrong.

*You crushed them.* This is parallel to *you struck them.* By punishments like those named above, the land and nation had been eaten away. Such punishments were meant to make the people see their wrongdoing and correct it, but they had *refused correction.* They had *made their faces harder than stone.* They were stubborn—firm as a limestone ridge, keeping their faces turned toward evil instead of good. Since various punishments had not been effective, God was driven to a more severe one. He was going to bring the Babylonians to devastate Judah, as we have seen in previous lessons.

## II. THE SEARCH CONTINUES (JEREMIAH 5:4-6)

If no good person could be found, there would be no pardon, and the Babylonians would invade and ravage the land. So Jeremiah intensified his search.

### A. Low-down Sinners (v. 4)

**4. I thought, "These are only the poor; they are foolish, for they do not know the way of the Lord, the requirements of their God.**

This sounds like the opinion frequently expressed by modern sociologists—that poverty breeds ignorance, crime, and other social ills. But Jeremiah was not making a general observation on poverty; he was expressing his frustration at trying to carry out the Lord's command to find just one righteous person. He gave the poor the benefit of the doubt and thought that perhaps their status had limited their opportunities to *know the way of the Lord.*

### B. High-class Sinners (v. 5)

**5. "So I will go to the leaders and speak to them; surely they know the way of the Lord, the requirements of their God." But with one accord they too had broken off the yoke and torn off the bonds.**

*The leaders,* such as the elders of the city, the banker and the rich merchant, the priest and the teacher—surely they would be better informed. Surely good men could be found among the wealthy, the rulers, and the scholars.

But these were as bad as the poorer class. They had *torn off the bonds* of God's Law; they had *broken off the yoke* of service to the Lord. Although they thought such an act set them free, they were merely preparing themselves to bear a truly oppressive yoke (a point to be made in next week's lesson). Clearly sin had permeated all of Judah. It has never recognized class distinctions of any kind.

## What Do You Think?

While we dare not let poverty be an excuse for crime and other sin, we cannot deny that it does contribute to these evils. Jesus said, "The poor you will always have with you" (Matthew 26:11). Paul recalled in Galatians 2:10 that the Jerusalem church's leaders asked "that we should continue to remember the poor." What can we do to overcome the effects of poverty? Suggest some specific things our class or our church can do to minister to the physical and spiritual needs of the poor in our community.

### RICH AND POOR ALIKE

Vultures—almost everyone hates them. They have long been associated with death. Monuments from the third millennium before Christ show vultures on a battlefield, attacking the corpses of slain soldiers. The vultures that still visit Gettysburg National Military Park are thought to be descendants of those that feasted on horses killed in the Civil War battle. Their history as carrion eaters makes them unwelcome guests.

But vultures are "equal opportunity scavengers." In recent years, large flocks of vultures have been moving to suburbia! They find suburban dumps to be very pleasant sources of food. They damage boat seats and lawn furniture and tear roofs from houses. They seem not to care whether they are eating carrion or cars. They are happy with either poor people's garbage or the contents of rich people's garages.

The sin that Jeremiah found in Jerusalem also affected rich and poor alike. He thought to excuse the poor for their sin because their poverty might have limited their opportunity to know God. But then he saw that the rich were sinners also. The truth he discovered is the same today: disobedience and lack of faith know no social or economic boundaries. Righteousness has far more to do with the contents of our hearts than with the contents of our pocketbooks or bank accounts.

### C. PUNISHMENT FOR ALL SINNERS (v. 6)

**6. Therefore a lion from the forest will attack them, a wolf from the desert will ravage them, a leopard will lie in wait near their towns to tear to pieces any who venture out, for their rebellion is great and their backslidings many.**

*A lion* is much bigger than a man and armed with frightful claws and teeth. *A wolf from the desert* is a hungry wolf. He has left the deserted areas where there is no food, and now he is ravenously looking for prey. *A leopard* is also a fearsome beast of prey.

Some students believe this is to be taken literally, as a promise that actual wild beasts would kill the people of Judah. But it was more likely that Jeremiah was speaking figuratively at this point. These savage beasts were symbols of the savage Babylonians. Their coming is foretold in verses 15-17 of this chapter and in Jeremiah 1:14-16. For other examples of this symbolism, see Jeremiah 4:7; Hosea 13:7, 8; Habakkuk 1:6-8; and Zephaniah 3:3.

Eventually these foes would surround the city of Jerusalem, guarding it on every side so no food could be taken to the people inside. Anyone going out would not be torn in pieces by wild animals, but would be captured or killed by the enemy. After a year and a half of such treatment, the Babylonians would break through the walls of Jerusalem and capture the entire city (2 Kings 25:1-12).

In the rest of Jeremiah 5, the prophet elaborates on the wickedness of Judah and the punishment that was to come because the prophets (other than the Lord's prophets) were false, the priests were no better, and "my people love it this way" (v. 31).

### CONCLUSION

Boarding a bus in a strange city, a lady asked the driver about her destination.

"It's easy to find," he explained. "You'll see a big Sears store on the right. You want to get off at the next stop after that one."

"Shall I come back to this door to get off?"

"Well, a lot of people will be getting on at that stop. It will be easier to leave by the rear door."

The lady took a seat near the rear door of the bus. At the proper stop she rose and stood at that door while the front door opened and people poured on. Finally she called to the driver, "Will you please open the back door?"

*DAILY BIBLE READINGS*

*Monday, Sept. 30—All Classes Indicted (Ezekiel 22: 23-31)*

*Tuesday, Oct. 1—False Teachers (Titus 1:10-16)*

*Wednesday, Oct. 2—Judah's Ingratitude (Isaiah 1:2-9)*

*Thursday, Oct. 3—God Unable to Pardon (Jeremiah 5: 7-17)*

*Friday, Oct. 4—God Judges Stubborn People (Jeremiah 5:18-31)*

*Saturday, Oct. 5—God Will Destroy Israel (Hosea 13:4-11)*

*Sunday, Oct. 6—God's Punishment for Falsehood (Jeremiah 6:11-15)*

## WHAT DO YOU THINK?

*This attitude of "Let the government do it" is still prevalent. Yet history has proved that governments do not accomplish many tasks well. Many government programs designed to help the poor have failed. Governments often stumble in their efforts to fight crime and protect the innocent. Government-controlled education for our children is frequently inadequate.*

*Why do you think the government has so often failed in these areas? Are these not the legitimate concerns of government? Why or why not? What is needed—either to replace the government programs or to supplement them—so that the genuine needs they attempt to meet are met adequately?*

## PRAYER

*Heavenly Father, how grateful we are for your Word! You yourself have told us what to do. More than that, you have given your only begotten Son to bear our sins and give us pardon and life. In gratitude we pledge ourselves to follow where he leads. By your grace and power may we be as faithful as Jeremiah was, and as safe for eternity. Amen.*

## THOUGHT TO REMEMBER

*A charge to keep I have,*
*A God to glorify;*
*A never-dying soul to save,*
*And fit it for the sky.*
    *—Charles Wesley*

"Lady," he called back, "you have to do it yourself."

At the touch of her hand the door opened easily, and she went on her way.

## A. YOU HAVE TO DO IT YOURSELF

The Lord gave careful and adequate information to his people. The instructions provided in his Law were marvelously thorough and detailed. He ordered that the Law be read to the nation every seven years (Deuteronomy 31:10-13). He laid on every parent the responsibility of keeping the Law in his heart and passing it on to the next generation (Deuteronomy 6:6, 7). The door was unlocked, and the way was open for everyone to do right; but still each person had to "do it himself."

The nation got into trouble because the people did not do what the Law said to do. When there was no strong national government, the citizens did as they pleased (Judges 21:25)—and what they pleased did not please God!

The Israelites then thought that a strong central government would keep them out of trouble. They wanted a king to lead them and fight their battles for them (1 Samuel 8:19, 20). But did they want the king to help them do right, or did they want him to protect them while they went on doing wrong?

After all, kings were only people. Many of them did evil in God's sight. The people followed them, selfishly seeking profit and pleasure rather than righteousness. They wanted the government to assure peace and prosperity; they did not want to "do it themselves."

## B. ANY NATION CAN DO IT

Some students object to any comparison of our nation with Israel or Judah. Those nations were in a unique position, they say. We are not God's chosen people; our laws are not made by him. He has not promised to bless us above all the other nations. This is true, but the Scripture says, "Things happened to them as examples and were written down as warnings for us" (1 Corinthians 10:11). The verses before that list several sins Israel committed that we must avoid (vv. 6-10).

Israel and Judah were not the only nations that rose by integrity and fell by corruption. Consider the Babylonians who conquered Judah. Pagan though they were, Nebuchadnezzar's troops were strong, dedicated, and well-disciplined. Half a century later, Belshazzar and his nobles were drinking themselves drunk when the alert Medes and Persians took over Babylon and its empire (Daniel 5:1-4, 30, 31). The empire of the Medes and Persians grew corrupt in its turn, and fell before the vigorous forces of Alexander the Great. Alexander's empire was split four ways, then these sections grew tyrannical and corrupt before they were conquered by the armies of Rome. The Roman Empire lasted for centuries, but its end was also due to rottenness within as well as to assault from without.

Having no inspired prophet to instruct us now, we cannot predict when a great nation will fall or when another will rise. But nations still rise through integrity and devotion, and fall through greed and corruption. Any nation can do it.

## C. YOU CAN BE SAFE WITH THE LORD

Jeremiah was a lonely voice crying in the wilderness of Judah's sin. His pleading went unheeded, and he himself was persecuted. But Jeremiah was faithful, and he was safe when Judah was crushed.

Today we hold the good news of the pardon before a world that does not welcome it. We may be ignored, we may be scorned, we may be persecuted; but if we are faithful, we will be safe when the world is on fire. You can be safe for eternity without a human companion, but you cannot be safe without God.

# Discovery Learning

*This page contains an alternate lesson plan emphasizing learning activities. Classes desiring such student involvement will find these suggestions helpful. The next page is a reproducible activity page to further enhance discovery learning.*

## LEARNING GOALS

After this lesson students should be able to:

1. List the sins of Judah mentioned in Jeremiah 5.

2. Compare these sins with sins in their nation and compare the moral state of Judah with the moral state of their country.

3. Choose specific remedies for sins in their country and commit themselves to specific ways to improve the moral fiber of their nation.

## INTO THE LESSON

Ask class members to divide themselves into pairs and tell each other about "the most righteous person I know." Class members may mention anyone they wish, but he or she must be a person the class member actually knows or knew; not a person from history or someone the class member has read about. They ought not to reveal the peoples' identities, just their righteous character.

After three or four minutes, ask several volunteers to tell some of the characteristics of the righteous people who were described to them. List these characteristics on the board. Then read Jeremiah 5:1 to the class. Explain that this was God's challenge to Jeremiah and his condition for saving the city of Jerusalem.

Ask class members to think about your city or town. Suppose God issued the same challenge to you about your community. Whom would you suggest as a person who meets these standards? Can you think of people who are not members of your congregation to suggest?

Tell the class that the nation of Judah and the city of Jerusalem had sunk into such paganism that God had no choice but to destroy them. We might consider if the spiritual decay in our country will bring a similar judgment.

## INTO THE WORD

Give the class a brief summary of Jeremiah's life and ministry. Then lead them into one or both of the following Bible study activities.

**Question and Answer.** Write the following questions on your chalkboard. Challenge students, in groups of three, to write a one-sentence answer to each question:

1. What did God seek (v. 1)?

2. What did the people proclaim (v. 2)?

3. What was the people's attitude (v. 3)?

4. Where did Jeremiah find sinners (vv. 4, 5)?

5. What would be the people's fate (v. 6)?

After a few minutes, discuss with your class the situation in Judah as it is described in our text. What words would your members use to describe that society? How hopeful were the prospects for its future?

**Marked Bibles.** Class members should use their own Bibles, or photocopies of all of Jeremiah 5. Students should read through the chapter (or you can ask a volunteer to read it aloud) and mark the sections in this way: circle the words of God; put a box around the words of Jeremiah; put an exclamation point in the margin beside descriptions of the sins of the people; draw an arrow pointing at sections that describe the punishment of God. (Note that some sections will be marked twice.)

After a few minutes, class members may compare their papers with each other in pairs, then with the whole class, as you lead the discussion. What general impressions of Judah have the class members gathered? How would they describe the ministry of Jeremiah? The attitude of God? What surprises them about this passage? What frightens them? What encourages them?

## INTO LIFE

Work with the class to list on the board all the sins of Judah from Jeremiah 5. Ask the class, "How do you react to the list? Do you find it surprising or not? Why?"

Beside each sin write an example of how it exists in our society. Ask, "How would this list have looked different if we had written it twenty years ago? Fifty years ago?"

Read or summarize the material under "B. Any Nation Can Do It" in the lesson commentary (page 60). Read this sentence or write it on your chalkboard: "Nations rise through integrity and devotion, and fall through greed and corruption." Ask the class, "Is our nation better characterized by the words *integrity and devotion* or *greed and corruption*? Is our nation 'rising' or 'falling'? Why?" Have them give evidence to support their answers.

What can Christians do to help their nation rise through integrity rather than fall through corruption? Your class has already mentioned several righteous people in your town. What can they do to build on that trend?

Make a list of specific actions class members can take. Ask class members to raise their hands to indicate their willingness to work on the items mentioned. Then ask a volunteer to pray about each item on the list. End your session with these prayers, making sure each item on your list is mentioned specifically.

# Word Search

Jeremiah was told to search the streets of Jerusalem for one righteous person. Search the grid below for words from Jeremiah 5:1-6. Then check the box below to see how many of the hidden words you found.

```
U O T R U T H R E P E N T A E Y E S
O C J S A O D B R I N W A H N H E E
E B O U E F N S T O N E O T V O R A
F H S R S A D D E S E R T L G T E E
H O D E R C A C C O R D D N F S F E
L N N L U E M F S B F L I T T Y U O
O E L Y F S C D A C R R E N X O S U
J S E F A N T D L A O E A E K E R
E T O O U O A R I E S M K V D E D R
R L P O B D U E W O E E I E K E N T
U Y A L S N A S R R N G L C N G R A
S E R I H S S E I N R S A Y U E E S
A S D S T T D U O O R T I S D O E D
L C E H E R Q I F T T E R I E T P E
E I N E A E L E A A N H S P N E I A
M N R H R S E A R C H N A N O A K L
E T A V E N T U R E O P E R S O N S
S S Q U A R E S E C S T R U C K R A
```

# FALSE HOPES FOR PEACE
## LESSON 7

## WHY TEACH THIS LESSON?

It is easy to study the history of God's people and shake our heads at the Is-raelites. "Why were they so foolish and stubborn," we wonder. We turn to the Gospels and wonder the same thing about the disciples. But our Bible study is missing the point we only observe the people of the past. What about us today?

Do not allow your class simply to see how the residents of Judah were deceived by Hananiah. Challenge them to know their Bibles so well that they will not be similarly deceived. Push them to add to their knowledge action—to be doers of the Word and not hearers only.

## INTRODUCTION

### A. SUNNY FORECASTS

We all like sunny forecasts, don't we? Politicians win elections by promising a change for the better, but sometimes the improvement is hard to see. Scientists win fame by proclaiming that we have risen from brutes to human beings, and now are rising to heights not yet imagined. Such rosy forecasts do little to slow the crime rate. Preachers fill their auditoriums by means of glowing sermons picturing grow-ing godliness and the brotherhood of man, but neither of these is seen in the dingy streets on the other side of town.

No one likes the "doomsayer." He becomes the object of derision, contempt, and anger. But doom is as real as triumph.

### B. TRUE FORECASTS

God's prophets had sunny forecasts too, but such promises were tied to obedi-ence to the law of God (Deuteronomy 28:1-6). Disobedience was linked to promises of terror (Deuteronomy 28:15-19). Even Jeremiah promised blessing and joy in the future (Jeremiah 31:1-14); but that future lay beyond a time of punish-ment, for the actions Jeremiah saw in his day demanded punishment.

Without the gift of prophecy, we should be cautious about predicting the future. But on the basis of thousands of years of history, we can declare with all confidence that disobeying God has bad consequences, though in God's mercy those conse-quences may be long delayed. With equal confidence we can declare that doing God's will brings happiness, though in a sinful world that happiness also may be delayed.

### C. DISASTER IN THREE PHASES

In the first chapter of Jeremiah and again in the first chapter of Habakkuk, we see a gloomy forecast of Judah's disastrous defeat by the Babylonians (Jeremiah 1:15,16; Habakkuk 1:6-9). That event was in the future when those prophets wrote about it. Now, as we look back on the events, we see that the disaster came in three phases, each one more severe than the one before it. Mercifully God brought minor disaster first, giving his people time to repent and avoid the greater calamity. But the people did not repent. Stubbornly they continued their evil ways until the destruction was complete.

DEVOTIONAL READING
JEREMIAH 30:13-24
LESSON SCRIPTURE
JEREMIAH 28, 29
PRINTED TEXT
JEREMIAH 28:5-14

Oct
13

### LESSON AIMS

*After this lesson students should be able to:*

*1. Tell about the conflicting prophecies of Hananiah and Jere-miah.*

*2. Recognize the Bible as their best help in distinguishing truth from falsehood.*

*3. Resolve to follow the Bible in their own living.*

### KEY VERSE

*Then you will call upon me and come and pray to me, and I will listen to you. You will seek me and find me when you seek me with all your heart.*

*Jeremiah 29:12, 13*

*First phase.* About 605 B.C. the Babylonians first subdued Judah. They took a few captives (Daniel 1:1-7). King Jehoiakim was left to rule Judah and pay tribute to Babylon. After three years he rebelled and stopped paying. The Babylonians sent other satellite nations to harass Judah until Nebuchadnezzar was ready to come back (2 Kings 24:1, 2).

*Second phase.* About 597 B.C. the Babylonians returned to Jerusalem. By then Jehoiachin was king. He quickly surrendered, and the Babylonians took him captive along with ten thousand leading citizens and craftsmen. Zedekiah was made king of Judah and forced to pay tribute to Babylon (2 Kings 24:8-17).

*Third phase.* About nine years later, Zedekiah rebelled. The Babylonians came to subdue Jerusalem for the third time. Entering the city after a siege of eighteen months, they destroyed it and took most of the survivors to Babylon (2 Kings 24:18—25:21). Thus the disaster was complete about 586 B.C.

### D. LESSON BACKGROUND

The events in this lesson took place during the second phase of disaster. Jehoiachin and ten thousand citizens had been taken to Babylon. Although a bit of confusion exists as to the exact time indicated in Jeremiah 28:1, most students believe that the events recorded there occurred in Zedekiah's fourth year (approximately 593 B.C.).

Hananiah was a false prophet who cheerfully said what the people wanted to hear. He claimed his message came from God, but that was a lie. His false message was that the power of Babylon would be broken within two years. King Jehoiachin would return along with all the captives and spoil taken from Jerusalem. Judah and the other subject nations would be freed. That message was popular, but it was not true. Our text begins with Jeremiah's response to it.

### I. VAIN HOPE (JEREMIAH 28:5-9)

Jeremiah was in a difficult spot. A lie had been told by one who claimed to speak for God. As God's real spokesman, Jeremiah had to expose it. But the lie was popular; king, officials, and people loved it. A denial would be dangerous, but those who proclaim God's message cannot choose the easy, popular way. They have to say what God says.

### A. PUBLIC PLACE (v. 5)

**5. Then the prophet Jeremiah replied to the prophet Hananiah before the priests and all the people who were standing in the house of the LORD.**

The lie had been told in a public meeting (vv. 1-4); thus, the denial could not be whispered in secret. *Priests* and *people* might be angered by the truth, but the truth must be told.

### B. EARNEST WISH (v. 6)

**6. He said, "Amen! May the LORD do so! May the LORD fulfill the words you have prophesied by bringing the articles of the LORD's house and all the exiles back to this place from Babylon.**

Jeremiah took no pleasure in foretelling the coming disaster! His attitude was like that of Jesus, who wept as he foretold the destruction of Jerusalem (Luke 19:41-44). So, before denouncing the lie that had been told, Jeremiah voiced his earnest wish that the Lord might indeed bring back all the captives and all the spoil that had been taken to Babylon. That spoil included the royal treasury as well as the temple treasury (2 Kings 24:13). The captives included military and civic leaders, along with the blacksmiths who made swords and spears (2 Kings 24:14).

### WHAT DO YOU THINK?

*"Those who proclaim God's message cannot choose the easy, popular way. They have to say what God says." Can you think of a time when you or someone you know had to take an unpopular public stand in the name of the Lord? If so, describe the event. What was the result? Has it strengthened your resolve to take a stand for the Lord? Why or why not?*

### NOTE

*Another way to view verse 6 is that Jeremiah was using sarcasm. The people, hearing his tone of voice, would quickly identify whether Jeremiah were expressing a wish or sarcastically "agreeing" (amen) with Hananiah.*

Without leaders and without weapons, the men of Judah would not rebel again—or so the Babylonians hoped. Like the rest of the people in Judah, Jeremiah wished that both captives and treasures might return; but he knew they would not. The Lord had told him that.

## C. THE LORD'S TRUTH (vv. 7-9)

**7. "Nevertheless, listen to what I have to say in your hearing and in the hearing of all the people.**

Even though Jeremiah, Hananiah, all the priests, and all the people fervently wished the captives would return, they needed to hear what the Lord had to say.

**8. "From early times the prophets who preceded you and me have prophesied war, disaster and plague against many countries and great kingdoms.**

It was nothing new for a prophet to say that disobedience would bring *disaster.* Moses had given a lengthy warning on the subject (Deuteronomy 28:15-68). Numerous prophets since that time had brought variations of the same message, each speaking as God had directed him. After such warnings, anyone in Judah should have been suspicious when a man like Hananiah announced an end to the people's punishment without an end to their sin.

**9. "But the prophet who prophesies peace will be recognized as one truly sent by the LORD only if his prediction comes true."**

*Peace* was more than the end of war. In the Hebrew way of thinking, it included health, happiness, prosperity, and welfare in general. As noted in verse 8, most of the prophets foretold increasing trouble, not peace, for sinners. When one promised peace for sinners, as Hananiah did, it would be wise to wait and see if the promise was fulfilled. If it was, then the one who made it could be accepted as God's prophet. Hananiah promised that Babylon would lose its power and that the captives would be home within two years (vv. 2-4). Thus, in two years everyone would know whether or not he was a real prophet.

## II. POPULAR PROPHECY (JEREMIAH 28:10, 11)

Jeremiah had illustrated his prophecy of judgment by wearing on his neck a yoke such as an ox or donkey might wear when it was pulling a plow or cart. This was a symbol of Judah's subjection to Babylon. The whole nation was "yoked" and compelled to work for Babylon. Though the people were living in their own country and tilling their own soil, a part of their produce had to go to pay tribute to Babylon as punishment for their sins. Jeremiah advised them to accept this yoke, for resistance would only bring more severe punishment. Jeremiah also sent yokes to the kings of surrounding countries with the same advice, for the Lord had delivered all those countries into the hand of Babylon. (See Jeremiah 27:1-11.)

## A. SYMBOLIC ACT (v. 10)

**10. Then the prophet Hananiah took the yoke off the neck of the prophet Jeremiah and broke it.**

The *yoke* was merely a symbol to illustrate Jeremiah's messages. Probably it was lighter than a real yoke, so Hananiah was able to break it. Thus the false prophet illustrated his false message in a manner that simultaneously cast doubts on Jeremiah's message.

## B. INTERPRETATION (v. 11)

**11. And he said before all the people, "This is what the LORD says: 'In the same way will I break the yoke of Nebuchadnezzar king of Babylon off the neck of all the nations within two years.'" At this, the prophet Jeremiah went on his way.**

### WHAT DO YOU THINK?

*Jeremiah gave the people a good test for checking the credentials of a prophet who predicted what would happen in the future: see whether it comes true. Not all false teachers make predictions, however. How can we evaluate the credentials of those who claim to speak the truth? How are we to decide who is right when two teachers explain a Bible text differently?*

### HOW TO SAY IT

*Habakkuk.* Huh-BAK-kuk.
*Hananiah.* Han-uh-NYE-uh.
*Jehoiachin.* Jeh-HOY-uh-kin.
*Jehoiakim.* Jeh-HOY-uh-kim.
*Nebuchadnezzar.* NEB-uh-kad-NEZZ-er.

*Writers of self-help books assure us that a more optimistic outlook and a commitment to positive thinking would solve many of our problems. And the Bible endorses certain forms of optimistic, positive thinking. We can be legitimately positive about God's existence, his love for us, his provisions of salvation, and his willingness to hear our prayers. But many "positive thinking" experts are like Hananiah, making promises that cannot be substantiated. It sounds good, but it ignores the reality of sin and fails to make room for repentance and holiness. How should a Christian respond when confronted with such advice?*

WHAT DO YOU THINK?

*Hananiah is described in Jeremiah 28:12 as a "prophet." That is a reminder of how deceptive a person's title may be. What's wrong with the titles worn by such people as the following?*

*A "doctor" who performs abortions.*

*A "minister" who seeks only his own glory and profit (cf. Mark 10:45).*

*A "teacher" whose aim is to destroy students' faith.*

*What other examples of people whose actions are opposed to the legitimate use of their titles can you think of?*

Hananiah's act needed no explanation, but he provided one anyway. He repeated his former prediction (vv. 1-4): Babylon's *yoke* would be broken *within two years*, and Judah and the other "yoked" *nations* would be free.

While this false prophet made use of the true prophet's illustration and copied his language (*This is what the Lord says*), his prophecy was still false. In two years everyone would know this. In fact, within two months they would witness the sudden death of Hananiah as punishment for having preached "rebellion against the Lord" (Jeremiah 28:15-17). This was predicted by Jeremiah, thus validating in a most compelling manner his claim to be a true prophet.

For the present, however, the false prophet had the advantage of the last word. Jeremiah left the scene and *went on his way.* No doubt the crowd was pleased to have it so, for the false prophecy was the popular one.

### FALSE PREDICTIONS

Early in 1988, a false prophet proclaimed the Lord's return later that year. Thousands of copies of his book were distributed. After the Lord failed to come as expected, the teacher said the return would be in 1989. But the "prophet" learned his lesson. After his second failure he said he would not be prophesying anymore.

A similar prediction occurred in 1994. A Bible prophecy teacher said Christ would return within a two-week period in September, 1994. Many Christians were taken in by the hoax. In a radio interview on the first day of his two-week "window" of return, the "prophet" announced that the "Great Tribulation" had just ended. More than one Christian was heard to remark that the suffering was not nearly as bad as many prophecy preachers had led them to believe it would be!

False prophets are nothing new. In spite of Jesus' words to the contrary, many have claimed to know the day of Christ's return, sometimes using spectacular means to get people's attention. There were false prophets before Christ also. Hananiah fits the classic pattern. Using a vivid method of illustrating his "truth," he misled the people of God. We should search the Scriptures carefully and be wary of those who claim to know too much.

—C. R. B.

## III. TRUE PROPHECY (JEREMIAH 28:12-14)
### A. THE LORD'S WORD (v. 12)
**12. Shortly after the prophet Hananiah had broken the yoke off the neck of the prophet Jeremiah, the word of the LORD came to Jeremiah.**

It is startling to see false *Hananiah* called *the prophet* exactly as *Jeremiah* is. One may be called teacher, preacher, professor, or doctor; but if he teaches falsehood, no title of honor can make what he says true. *The word of the Lord* came to Jeremiah. Hananiah spoke his own word, a word chosen to please the crowd.

### B. FROM BAD TO WORSE (v. 13)
**13. "Go and tell Hananiah, 'This is what the LORD says: You have broken a wooden yoke, but in its place you will get a yoke of iron.**

The light *wooden yoke* that *Hananiah* broke was a symbol of the tribute Judah was already paying to Babylon. Hananiah promised an end of that, but in so doing he was actually preparing a heavier yoke for the people of Judah. The eventual captivity of the people in Babylon would be the *yoke of iron,* heavier than the tribute they were paying while they were in their own country. That harsher bondage would be due in part to Hananiah's misleading prophecy.

### C. DEFEAT AND BONDAGE (v. 14)
**14. "'This is what the LORD Almighty, the God of Israel, says: I will put an iron yoke on the necks of all these nations to make them serve Nebuchadnezzar king**

*of Babylon, and they will serve him. I will even give him control over the wild animals.'"*

Although *Nebuchadnezzar* and his army had placed the yoke of tribute on Judah and would impose the heavier *yoke* of captivity, a higher power was involved. *The Lord Almighty,* Jehovah, said, *I will put an iron yoke on the necks of all these nations.* He was responsible for what the Babylonians were doing. He had sentenced Judah and other nations to defeat and captivity because of their sins. (Some of the other nations are named in Jeremiah 27:1-7.) All of them were wicked, but the people of Judah were most accountable, because Jehovah had given them his special care and help. (See Amos 3:2.) They had received his Law but had chosen to ignore it.

The Babylonians did not believe in Jehovah; they did not intend to serve him. Nevertheless, they were his agents to execute the sentence he had pronounced. Into the power of Babylon, the Lord of Heaven and earth was delivering not only all the people of Judah, but even the *wild animals.* The rule of Babylon was to be complete.

### TRADING ONE YOKE FOR ANOTHER

Many of us adults can remember when the only kind of bread we wanted to eat was that fluffy white stuff that you could compress in your hands into a ball of unappetizing dough. Our parents preached the value of whole wheat bread (ugh!), which seemed to take far too much effort to chew.

Not long ago, *Science* magazine reported that whole wheat toast and some other "healthy" foods had caused cancer in laboratory rats. Natural carcinogens in our food may actually be more dangerous than the artificial chemicals that we have learned to hate in this health-conscious age.

Wouldn't it be ironic if we were to find that "natural" ingredients may be as harmful as the ones we manufacture? While seeking to avoid one evil, we may have unwittingly opened ourselves to another! But this would not be anything new.

Hananiah, the false prophet of Judah, viewed Jeremiah as an enemy of his people. Jeremiah had worn a wooden yoke around his neck as a symbol of the Babylonian bondage that the people had suffered because of their sin. Hananiah removed Jeremiah's yoke and broke it to illustrate his prophecy that Babylon's power would soon be broken.

But Hananiah had only made a bad situation worse. Jeremiah declared that Hananiah's false prophecy had not broken a yoke of wood; it had created a yoke of iron for his people. It is better to listen to the facts than to assume what we want to believe.

—C. R. B.

## CONCLUSION

"Relax." said Hananiah. "Take it easy. Go on with your business and your fun. In a couple of years our troubles will be over. Babylon will be out of the picture, and our captive friends will be back home."

"Reform." said Jeremiah. "Quit your greedy, cheating life-style. Stop your immoral fun. Otherwise Babylon will be back, and our trouble will be twice as bad as it is now."

How could the people know who was telling the truth? Jeremiah suggested two ways.

1. Wait and see. In two years everyone would know Hananiah was wrong In seven or eight years everybody would know Jeremiah was right—but by then most of them would be either captives in Babylon or corpses in the ashes of Jerusalem.

2. Look at the record. True prophets have always foretold disaster as punishment for sin, and disaster has come. Why should this time be different?

"Within two full years . . . I will break the yoke of the king of Babylon."
(Jeremiah 28:3, 4)

"After seventy years be accomplished at Babylon I will visit you, . . . causing you to return to this place."
(Jeremiah 25:10)

*Use the visual for lesson 7 in the visuals packet to dramatize the difference between the false message of Hananiah and the true Word of God. Discuss how false teachers today attack the truth of God's Word. The reproducible activity, "Tell the Truth," on page 70 can assist you in leading this discussion.*

### DAILY BIBLE READINGS

*Monday, Oct. 7—Do Not Listen to False Prophets (Jeremiah 23:16-22)*

*Tuesday, Oct. 8—False Prophets Against God (Deuteronomy 13:1-5)*

*Wednesday, Oct. 9—Do Not Fear False Prophets (Deuteronomy 18:15-22)*

*Thursday, Oct. 10—False Prophets Speak to Exiles (Jeremiah 29:1-9)*

*Friday, Oct. 11—God Promises to Hear Prayers (Jeremiah 29:10-14)*

*Saturday, Oct. 12—Prophets Are the Lord's Servants (Jeremiah 29:15-19)*

*Sunday, Oct. 13—God Punishes False Prophets (Jeremiah 29:20-32)*

## WHAT DO YOU THINK?

*If the people of Judah had been more familiar with the Scriptures, they would not have been deceived by Hananiah. What deceptions have been foisted on Christians because they did not know the Bible well enough? What can we do to make sure we know the Bible well enough to avoid being deceived by false teaching?*

*Why do so many Christians ignore opportunities to study the Bible by failing to attend Sunday school or having a personal time of Bible study? What can be done to encourage these practices?*

## PRAYER

*How good you are to give us the Bible, our Father; and how far we are from making it as useful as you have made it to be! Forgive our neglect, we pray, and help us as we try to give your Word a bigger place in our daily living. Amen.*

## THOUGHT TO REMEMBER

*"Your word is a lamp to my feet" (Psalm 119:105).*

The people of Judah chose the first way. They waited, they saw, and they became captives in Babylon and corpses in the ashes of Jerusalem.

### A. BACK TO THE BIBLE

The people of Jerusalem could have known which prophet was right. They should have recalled the Law that king Josiah had read to them some twenty-five years earlier. According to that law, sin would lead to disaster. But disaster was always somewhere in the future. There was profit that very day in a crooked business deal; there was fun that very night in an immoral pagan feast.

There are many kinds of voices in our world. There is the voice of optimism: "Things are bound to get better. We don't have any problems that can't be solved with a few billion dollars." There is the voice of pessimism: "We're on the slippery slope, plunging to our doom." There is the voice of God: "Seek me and live" (Amos 5:4). Do we want to live?

### B. KNOWING

The people of Jerusalem were without excuse, though several years had passed since the Law had been taken seriously by their leaders. How shall we be excused if we have a Bible in the living room, but choose to give more time to trash on TV?

A tennis player needs to know the rule book; a Christian needs to know the Bible. This takes time. We need to read large portions, not swiftly to get it done, but thoughtfully to see what teaching or example we can find for our lives today. We need to study the Bible in groups as well as alone. A Sunday school class is great, if we make it so by doing our homework and being ready to contribute a thought or ask a pertinent question. Also great are half a dozen neighbors with open Bibles in someone's living room. It may be greater still if there is a Bible concordance, a Bible dictionary, a Bible commentary, and someone who knows how to use them. It helps if some quiet person thoroughly familiar with the Bible is there, not to lecture, not even to teach, but to help the others with their learning.

### C. TALKING

How long has it been since you heard someone talking about the Bible on a bus, in a car pool, at a baseball game, at a party, over lunch, in a barber- shop, or at home? If the Bible is so vital in our lives, why do we talk about it less than about baseball scores, the crime rate, the political campaign, or the latest styles? When do you talk about it? See a suggestion in Deuteronomy 6:7.

### D. DOING

Jesus said, "Everyone who hears these words of mine and puts them into practice is like a wise man who built his house on the rock" (Matthew 7:24). Perhaps not many people know the Bible very well, but many *know* more than they *do*. A recent television program did a story on honesty. The investigator took short rides in ten taxis. In each cab he left a billfold with a hundred dollars and enough identification so the owner could easily be reached by phone, by mail, or in person. Probably all ten drivers knew the Bible says, "You shall not steal," but only two of them returned the billfolds.

Doesn't most every liar know the Bible says, "You shall not give false testimony"? Doesn't nearly every adulterer know it says, "You shall not commit adultery"? Doesn't almost everyone know the Golden Rule, and the commandment to "love your neighbor as yourself"? Don't you and I both know the Bible says, "You shall not covet"?

Are we building our houses "on the rock"? Are we doing as much as we know?

# Discovery Learning

*This page contains an alternate lesson plan emphasizing learning activities. Classes desiring such student involvement will find these suggestions helpful. The next page is a reproducible activity page to further enhance discovery learning.*

## LEARNING GOALS

After this lesson students should be able to:

1. Describe the conflict between Hananiah and Jeremiah.

2. List situations in our society where people choose pleasant lies instead of hard truths.

3. Choose one specific way they can help keep their own congregation or community from making the same error.

## INTO THE LESSON

Before class write the following three sentences on your chalkboard or on a poster:

"He told a popular lie."

"I wanted to believe it, but it wasn't true."

"I was afraid the news would be bad."

To begin today's session, each class member should find a partner. Tell the class you want each person to "tell a story" beginning with one of the above sentences.

Give them five minutes to talk with each other. Then take about five minutes more to hear several of the stories.

Tell the class that each of these sentences could have been spoken by or about someone in the story that is in today's Scripture text. Challenge them to find the person or persons characterized by these sentences as they hear Jeremiah 28 read aloud.

## INTO THE WORD

Use the Introduction (pages 63, 64) to remind class members of the background to this lesson. Then choose some or all of the following activities to help them explore Jeremiah 28. (If you have time for all the activities, they should be completed in the order indicated here.)

**Dramatic Reading.** Choose four class members to read Jeremiah 28 aloud: a narrator, someone to read the words of the Lord, someone to read the words of Hananiah, and someone to read the words of Jeremiah.

For something different, tell class members to respond out loud, as if they are watching a melodrama. This means they should cheer the hero and boo the villain—even hiss if they want. For a more "reserved" approach to the same idea, have class members make "Cheer" and "Boo" flash cards to hold up at the appropriate times as the Scripture is read.

**Outline.** Write on your chalkboard the following verse divisions of Jeremiah 28:1-4; 5-9; 10,11; 12-14; 15-17.

In groups of three to five, class members should write a heading and a one-sentence summary for each section.

Allow eight minutes; then let each group report. Write an all-class version on your chalkboard if you have time.

**Scriptures and Sentences.** Write the following sentences on the board, or distribute them on a handout:

• Being popular is usually easier than being unpopular.

• Many people would rather believe a pleasant lie than a hard truth.

• Sooner or later, disobeying God always brings disaster.

Ask class members, in groups of about five, to decide how today's Bible lesson teaches each of these truths. Let them work in groups for several minutes before you discuss all the sentences with the class.

**Discussion.** Consider these questions with the class:

1. Why did Hananiah lie to the people?

2. Why did Jeremiah risk his reputation to tell the truth?

3. When Jeremiah exposed Hananiah's lie, Hananiah became abusive toward Jeremiah. What lessons can we learn from Jeremiah's response at that point? (He simply walked away; v. 11.)

4. Why didn't Jeremiah just wait until they could see for themselves what God would do?

5. Later Jeremiah repeated and intensified his warning, but still the people chose to believe the lie. Why do you think they did that?

## INTO LIFE

Discuss these questions with the class:

1. What does this lesson teach you about God?

2. What does this lesson teach you about life?

3. What does this lesson teach you about yourself?

Challenge class members to look again at the sentences that were found under "Scriptures and sentences." Discuss with them: "How have you seen each of these sentences proven true in our world?"

Discuss with the class: How can we keep our church from making the same mistake Jeremiah's people made? What actions can one person take to protect his church or his city from falling into this kind of error?

Write specific suggestions on the chalkboard. Ask class members to look at the list and to tell which of the ideas they are willing to pursue. You may want to write their names beside the items they choose. Close with a prayer time, mentioning these commitments as you pray.

# Symbols of Bondage

Jeremiah used a yoke to illustrate his prophecy regarding subjection to Babylon. What are kind of bondage might each of the symbols below illustrate?

"They promise them freedom, while they themselves are slaves of depravity—
for a man is a slave to whatever has mastered him" (2 Peter 2:19).

"Then you will know the truth, and the truth will set you free" (John 8:32).

# Tell the Truth

Hananiah lied to the people. It was a pleasant lie, so the people chose to believe it. Jeremiah delivered the true Word of God.

How is the Word of God challenged today? Write below what you believe is the most popular lie being circulated today. Then write some suggestions of what you, your class, or your church can do to taker a stand with God's Word to counter this lie.

Today's Most Popular Lie:

What we can do about it:

# A REBELLIOUS PEOPLE

**LESSON 8**

## WHY TEACH THIS LESSON?

"God did not give us a spirit of timidity, but a spirit of power, of love and of self-discipline" (2 Timothy 1:7). Well, if God did not give us such a spirit, who did? Why are so many Christians timid about sharing their faith?

The hero of today's lesson is Ezekiel. God would not allow for timidity on Ezekiel's part—and it's a safe guess he does not allow it on ours either. Ezekiel was told to be faithful, whether his audience listened or not. Whether they accepted the message or refused it. Whether they honored the Lord's prophet or persecuted him. Faithfulness is what the Lord required, not results. God knew most of the exiles would not listen. Still, he wanted to give them every opportunity to repent. And there were a few who *would* listen. Those few were precious to the Lord.

Many people have closed their ears and their hearts to God's message. We know that, and often that means we quit telling the good news. God knows it, too, but still he wants the message told. The few who will listen are still precious to him.

Challenge your class to pursue faithfulness and not to be overly concerned about "results."

## INTRODUCTION

Susan was an enthusiastic sleeper, hard to awaken in the morning. When her husband shook her gently and spoke to her, she answered sleepily without opening her eyes. Then the husband said, "Honey, your brother has been killed in an accident."

Instantly Susan sat up, wide awake and horrified. "No!" she shouted.

The newspaper reports that a teen-age boy has been sentenced to life imprisonment for killing his father and mother. It seems impossible to doubt his guilt. He admits it freely; reporters say he brags about it. Still his aunt insists, "I know that boy. He didn't kill anybody."

### A. DENIAL

Very often, denial is the first response to unwelcome news: "No! That can't be true!" But denial is futile if the news is true. More than that, denial may stand in the way of what needs to be done.

This was illustrated in our lesson last week. Jeremiah told his people they would be captives in Babylon if they did not change their ways. If they had accepted the truth and changed their ways, they could have remained in Jerusalem. But they chose to deny the truth, and so they became captives.

### B. LESSON BACKGROUND

Review the three phases of Judah's disaster as they are described in the Introduction to last week's lesson. That lesson fell in the second phase, and so does this one. King Jehoiachin and ten thousand citizens of Judah were captives in Babylon already; other thousands still lived in Judah. Jeremiah was one of those.

Ezekiel was one of the captives who had been taken along with the ten thousand. He gave God's message to the other exiles in Babylon. Last week's lesson was dated in the fourth year of king Zedekiah (Jeremiah 28:1). This week's lesson is

DEVOTIONAL READING
EZEKIEL 3:16-21
LESSON SCRIPTURE
EZEKIEL 2:1—3:21
PRINTED TEXT
EZEKIEL 2:3-7; 3:4-11

LESSON AIMS

After this lesson a student should be able to:

1. Briefly review the instructions God gave to Ezekiel.

2. Accept the responsibility of sharing God's Word with others.

3. Describe some way to share God's Word this week.

Oct
20

KEY VERSE

*You must speak my words to them, whether they listen or fail to listen, for they are rebellious.*

*Ezekiel 2:7*

WHAT DO YOU THINK?

In our lesson text we see God repeatedly referring to his people as "rebellious." In what ways is this an appropriate description for our modern society? To what extent does people's desire for "freedoms" actually represent a desire to be free of the constraint of law or a moral code?

To what extent do you think Christians exhibit the same rebellious tendency? What can be done to help us remain submissive to the Lord and not be rebellious?

WHAT DO YOU THINK?

A prophet is one who speaks for God. In that sense, we might say the church itself is a "prophet" in the community. What can we do to be sure that, even if people in our town do not accept the biblical message taught in our church, yet "they will know that a prophet has been among them"?

dated nearly a year later. By then, the captives had been in Babylon nearly five years (Ezekiel 1:1-3).

## I. COMMISSION (EZEKIEL 2:3-7)

From the opening verses of Ezekiel, we learn that he was nearly thirty years old when the Lord called him to be a prophet. With other captives he was settled "by the Kebar River" (Ezekiel 1:1). It is thought that this was actually one of the large irrigation canals in the land of Babylon. The captives may have worked in grain fields, vineyards, and date orchards similar to those in Judah; but the flat plain of Babylon was certainly different from the hills of home. See how their grief was expressed in Psalm 137:1-6.

### A. HARD JOB (vv. 3-5)

**3. He said: "Son of man, I am sending you to the Israelites, to a rebellious nation that has rebelled against me; they and their fathers have been in revolt against me to this very day.**

The Lord called Ezekiel to be a prophet, a special messenger of the Almighty. That did not mean he was exalted to a position of divinity. He was a *son of man*, a human being like the men to whom he was sent.

Immediately the Lord made it clear that his prophet's job would not be easy. He must take God's message to *a rebellious nation*. The Hebrew text reads "nations" here, perhaps alluding to the disunited status of the people. Through generation after generation *the Israelites* had been breaking God's Law. Ezekiel could not expect them to welcome the Lord's message and obey it. It was more probable that they would viciously persecute him.

**4. "The people to whom I am sending you are obstinate and stubborn. Say to them, 'This is what the Sovereign LORD says.'**

The captives in Babylon were accustomed to doing wrong. It would be difficult to turn their hearts to the Lord.

**5. "And whether they listen or fail to listen—for they are a rebellious house—they will know that a prophet has been among them.**

Even if Ezekiel's listeners would reject the message and go on stubbornly in their evil way, yet *they will know that a prophet has been among them*. Ezekiel's words about future events would prove to be true. He predicted the continued desolation of Judah at the hands of the Babylonians and the eventual fall of Jerusalem (Ezekiel 11:1-12; 12:17-20; 22:17-31; 24:20-27). This came to pass (33:21), so Ezekiel's credentials as a prophet were verified.

But Ezekiel was also a prophet of hope, who sought to comfort the discouraged exiles with promises of restoration (11:16-20; 34:20-31; 36:22-38; 37). Those who were alive when the captives were allowed to go home would see yet another validation of Ezekiel's claim to speak as the Lord's prophet. Hopefully they would be ready to obey God and go back to Jerusalem with a firm trust in him and an earnest desire to do his will.

### B. ENCOURAGEMENT (vv. 6, 7) ⟶ Key Verse 7.

**6. "And you, son of man, do not be afraid of them or their words. Do not be afraid, though briers and thorns are all around you and you live among scorpions. Do not be afraid of what they say or terrified by them, though they are a rebellious house.**

The captives had proved themselves to be a rebellious house. They would not cease their rebellion and become obedient to the Lord at Ezekiel's call. Rather, they would attack God's prophet with words as sharp as *briers and thorns*, and with hearts as venomous as *scorpions*. Still the prophet must go on fearlessly with his assigned work.

7. *"You must speak my words to them, whether they listen or fail to listen, for they are rebellious."*

The rebels in Babylon would close their ears to Ezekiel's message. At the same time, their counterparts in Jerusalem would close their ears to Jeremiah's call and continue in their sin. In a few years they, too, would be deported to Babylon, where they would stay for several years. Perhaps Ezekiel wondered why he should keep on giving people a message that they would not accept.

The answer is that the Lord was looking far ahead. In a few years he would indeed send the rest of Judah's rebels to captivity in Babylon; but some fifty years later he would open a way for them to go back to Jerusalem. When that way was opened, close to fifty thousand people would make the long trip home to rebuild Jerusalem and the temple (Ezra 2:64-69). If we faithfully hold forth the gospel of our Lord even when it is rejected, who knows what results may appear in fifty years?

Four times in five verses Ezekiel's hearers are branded as *rebellious*. Twice comes the warning that they are likely to refuse to listen to Ezekiel's message. Still the Lord insists, *You must speak my words to them.* Do we sometimes give up too soon?

### A NEEDED REMINDER

Atop the U. S. Capitol building in Washington, D.C., stands the figure of a robed goddess bearing a sword and shield. The symbolic "protector of Congress," it is called the "Statue of Freedom."

This statue stood atop the Capitol for 130 years until it was removed for repairs in 1993. Weighing seven and a half tons, the statue is nineteen feet tall and stands 287 feet above the street. It was originally designed wearing the likeness of a liberty cap worn by freed Roman slaves. But many people in 1863 (when the statue was first erected) thought the "freedom cap" was inappropriate for a nation that still practiced slavery. So the cap was changed to a helmet, with an eagle's head and feathers.

Skeptics of government might say the goddess has not protected Congress from very much, in light of the political scandals and moral hijinks that have so often made Congress a poor example of what freedom is supposed to be about. Nevertheless, the statue is a continuing reminder of the noble ideals on which the nation was founded.

The nation of Israel had drifted from the moral ideals upon which God had founded it. The people had become rebellious and wayward when Ezekiel spoke God's word to them. However, even though they did not heed his message, they could not escape the ideals he preached and their own accountability to them.

—C. R. B.

## II. COMMISSION REPEATED (EZEKIEL 3:4-11)

With a touch of his hand, the Lord put his words in Jeremiah's mouth (Jeremiah 1:9). When Jeremiah thought about giving up his hard and thankless mission, those words were in him as a fire; he could not hold them in (Jeremiah 20:9).

The Lord chose another way to implant his words in Ezekiel, but it was no less effective. The Lord gave Ezekiel a scroll to eat, a scroll inscribed with mournful messages and promises of punishment yet to come. The prophet ate the scroll (Ezekiel 2:8—3:3). Thus God's message became a part of his very being. He could no more abandon it than he could abandon his stomach or his liver. He could only treasure and proclaim it as the Lord directed.

As we see in the next portion of our text, the Lord then repeated the commission that we have studied in the earlier verses of our text.

---

**WHAT DO YOU THINK?**

God wanted Ezekiel to be persistent in delivering his message—in spite of rejection, living among "briers" and "thorns" and "scorpions." How can we be as faithful and persistent in spite of opposition as Ezekiel was called to be?

How would you answer a Christian who did not want to share the gospel because he or she did not want to appear "pushy"? What if the person said he or she was afraid of rejection or ridicule?

**WHAT DO YOU THINK?**

The gospel is the most precious thing that we can share. We have no reason to be apologetic in doing so. Do you agree or disagree? Do you think an impartial observer would answer for you the same way you answered for yourself? Why or why not?

**WHAT DO YOU THINK?**

The lesson writer describes how Ezekiel ate the scroll, and "God's message became a part of his very being." How can we make God's Word a part of our own being? How important are each of the following? What advice would you give for practicing each?
- Cultivate our appetite (appreciation) for the Bible.
- Plan a balanced diet (a good variety of doctrines, commands, warnings, promises, exhortations, and assurances).
- Finding a suitable time and place for study.
- Follow our eating with exercise.

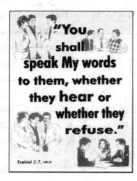

"You shall speak My words to them, whether they hear or whether they refuse."

Ezekiel 2:7, NKJV

*The visual for lesson 8 in the visuals packet illustrates the importance of being a faithful witness for the Lord.*

OPTION

*Explore the issue of what to do "When No One Will Listen" with the reproducible activity on page 78.*

### A. EASY JOB MADE HARD (vv. 4-7)

**4. He then said to me: "Son of man, go now to the house of Israel and speak my words to them.**

The prophet's preparation was complete. God's message was in him and was a part of him. Now it was time to get to work—to *go . . . to the house of Israel,* as much of it as was in Babylon, and proclaim these words that had filled him.

**5. "You are not being sent to a people of obscure speech and difficult language, but to the house of Israel.**

Ezekiel was in the land of Babylon, but his mission was not to the Babylonians. He did not have the *language* problem that many missionaries have—the problem of learning a language before he could deliver his message effectively. He was sent to *the house of Israel,* to his own people who had come to Babylon with him. He was not going to a people with an *obscure speech* (the Hebrew reads "deep of lip") or a *difficult language* (the Hebrew reads "heavy of tongue"). His native language was their native language. It should have been easy to give God's message to them.

**6. ". . . not to many peoples of obscure speech and difficult language, whose words you cannot understand. Surely if I had sent you to them, they would have listened to you.**

In the reports of missionaries, we read of dozens of new Christians in Burma and India, and of new congregations meeting in homes in China. Meanwhile our home churches rejoice with the addition of just one person or two. Likewise, Ezekiel might have found a better reception if he had been sent to the Babylonians with their *obscure speech* and *difficult language*. But he was sent to the captives from Judah. They had no difficulty in understanding what he was saying, but they were not happy to hear it.

**7. "But the house of Israel is not willing to listen to you because they are not willing to listen to me, for the whole house of Israel is hardened and obstinate.**

Thus the job that should have been easy was very hard. The problem was not in the language; it was in the people. They were impudent and hard-hearted. We are reminded of Jesus' words to the Jews of his day: "You refuse to come to me to have life" (John 5:40).

### GETTING OUR TANGUES ALL TONGULED UP

William Archibald Spooner is one of those unfortunate people whose name has become a household word on the basis of his mistakes rather than his noble accomplishments. The term *spoonerism* refers to Spooner's habit of transposing sounds within words.

For example, a student who was not performing well academically was rebuffed by Spooner: "You have tasted a whole worm. You have hissed my mystery lectures." [*You have wasted a whole term. You have missed my history lectures.*] In a sermon he once said, "The Lord is a shoving leopard." [*The Lord is a loving shepherd.*] He is reputed to have told a woman looking for a seat in church, "Mardon me, padam, this pie is occupued; allow me to sew you to another sheet." [*Pardon me, madam, this pew is occupied; allow me to show you to another seat.*] However, Spooner scholars think this one may be fictitious.

Most of us get our "tangues all tonguled up" from time to time, but find that we usually can communicate satisfactorily in our native language. We have more difficulty when trying to converse with someone who speaks a different language from our own.

But at times communication difficulties are caused by other problems, such as a stubborn heart. So it was in Ezekiel's day: Israel failed to hear his message from God, not because of a foreign language or any speech impediments, but because of the impediment of an obstinate heart.

—C. R. B.

HOW TO SAY IT

*Kebar.* KEE-bar.

*Ezekiel.* Ee-ZEEK-yul or Ee-ZEEK-ee-ul.

*Jehoiachin.* Jeh-HOY-uh-kin.

## B. ENCOURAGEMENT REPEATED (vv. 8, 9)

**8. "But I will make you as unyielding and hardened as they are.**

Many of Ezekiel's hearers would glower at God's prophet—their faces hard, bitter, and hostile. To counter this, God had made Ezekiel as strong as any of these. Ezekiel would still need to exert himself, to do his best to be strong, courageous, and determined; but if he did, God guaranteed that his best would be good enough. He would be able to endure all the opposition and go on with his work.

**9. "I will make your forehead like the hardest stone, harder than flint. Do not be afraid of them or terrified by them, though they are a rebellious house."**

Among all ten thousand Israelites then in captivity with him, Ezekiel would find few sympathizers. Few stalwart souls would stand by his side to give him courage and support in his stand for truth and right. He would seem to stand alone. Therefore God repeated his encouragement with emphasis. Unseen but Almighty, the Lord would be at Ezekiel's side. The prophet need not be *afraid* or *terrified*. He and the Lord could not be overcome by ten thousand or ten million hostile rebels.

## C. SUMMARY (vv. 10, 11)

**10. And he said to me, "Son of man, listen carefully and take to heart all the words I speak to you.**

In this verse and the next one, we see the Lord's summary of the responsibility he was giving his prophet. It was not enough just to hear the message with his ears; Ezekiel was told to receive it in his *heart*, with willing submission.. Whatever the Lord said would be true and whatever he did would be right. Ezekiel's words would reflect these convictions.

**11. "Go now to your countrymen in exile and speak to them. Say to them, 'This is what the Sovereign LORD says,' whether they listen or fail to listen."**

Briefly the Lord repeated Ezekiel's commission. Several points are emphasized in these few words. First, it was time to *go*; Ezekiel must be about his mission. Second, his mission was not to the ruling Babylonians; it was to his own *countrymen*, the ten thousand captives of Judah who were with him in Babylon. Third, he was to make it clear that he was speaking for the *Lord* God—not for himself, for any of his countrymen, or for the Babylonians. Fourth, he was to keep on faithfully with his work, whether his countrymen would *listen* or not.

## CONCLUSION

Did you ever watch a boy smoke his first cigarette? The first puff starts him coughing. Why does he ever take a second puff?

Because it is forbidden. He wants to prove that he can do as he pleases. So he smokes, though it gives him a quick cough, nausea in half an hour, and lung cancer in fifty years.

Isn't it amazing the way we human beings insist on hurting ourselves?

## A. WE HURT OURSELVES

"You will be like God," promised the snake. With that in mind, Eve ate the one fruit in all the world that would hurt her.

To the people of Israel, God gave a detailed Law with specific instructions about what was good for them. They chose to do what was bad for them, and they continued until disaster came.

Ask your doctor how many of his patients have hurt themselves with self-imposed overwork, stress, or anxiety. Ask how many pleasure seekers have hurt themselves with wild carousing, or how many sober, respectable people have hurt themselves by overeating. Visit an emergency room and ask how many bones have

---

### WHAT DO YOU THINK?

God's promise to make Ezekiel's face and forehead strong suggests that we Christians may have to be a bit hardheaded and thick-skinned at times. But stubbornness and being "intolerant" are usually considered negative character traits. What are some issues about which stubbornness is a positive trait? When is stubbornness a negative trait? Can one who is stubborn in a positive sense at the same time be stubborn in a negative way? How can we be sure to be positively stubborn and not negatively stubborn?

### WHAT DO YOU THINK?

In their quest for fun and excitement, people engage in all kinds of self-destructive behavior. How can we show them that the greatest enjoyment and excitement comes from following Christ?

Do you agree that Christians have more genuine fun than anyone? Why or why not?

What is it about being a Christian that gives you the most joy and satisfaction? How could you share that information with an unbeliever?

## PRAYER

*How patient you have been, our Father, holding forth the Word of life through long centuries! With joy we accept it and treasure it, and we pray for help in sharing it. Amen.*

## THOUGHT TO REMEMBER

*Someone is following you.*

## DAILY BIBLE READINGS

**Monday, Oct. 14**—*Ezekiel Hears a Voice (Ezekiel 1:22-28)*

**Tuesday, Oct. 15**—*Ezekiel to Speak for God (Ezekiel 3:12-21)*

**Wednesday, Oct. 16**—*Wait for God's Timing to Speak (Ezekiel 3:22-27)*

**Thursday, Oct. 17**—*God Gave Ordinances in the Wilderness (Ezekiel 20:1-13a)*

**Friday, Oct. 18**—*People Disobeyed Ordinances (Ezekiel 20:18-24)*

**Saturday, Oct. 19**—*Look to the Lord (Micah 7:1-7)*

**Sunday, Oct. 20**—*Prophets Without Honor in Own Land (Matthew 13:53-58)*

---

been broken by their owners' reckless driving. Ask Alcoholics Anonymous how many people have damaged their abilities and ruined their reputations by drinking. Ask the counselors how many people have ruined their marriages and their happiness by carelessness. Search the statistics for the number of people who have destroyed themselves with illegal drugs. The daily papers tell of innocent children who have inherited the HIV virus through no fault of their own, but how many adults are dying of AIDS because of their own misconduct?

Search your church roll for the names of people who have hurt themselves by dropping out of church. Search the faces of your friends for the frowns of those who have hurt themselves by holding a grudge. Search your heart. How have you been hurting yourself?

Jesus gave his life to redeem us from our sins and to give us life instead of death, but most of mankind rejects his offer and chooses the way that leads to destruction (Matthew 7:13, 14).

Why?

### B. GOD HELPS US

God gave specific instructions to Adam and Eve: "Leave that fruit alone. It will harm you." To the people of Israel he gave more extensive instructions in the Law, and added the inspired teaching of prophets like Jeremiah and Ezekiel. To people of later ages, including us, he gave Jesus and the apostles. The way of life has never been hidden from human sight. Why do so many people choose to die?

God helps us not only by his Word; he helps us also by his presence. Jesus is there when we meet together in his name (Matthew 18:20). When one of us has no Christian friend with him, he is not alone. The Holy Spirit is with him (1 Corinthians 6:19). And God is one: the Father and the Son also abide with us when we love them and obey them. Jesus said, "If anyone loves me, he will obey my teaching. My Father will love him, and we will come to him and make our home with him" (John 14:23). So we are never alone, and we do not make decisions for ourselves alone. Planning calls for consultation. As I think of what I would like to do today, I ask, "Will Jesus and his Father go along with that?" If they will not, neither will I.

How does God help us? He gives us wisdom if we value it and ask for it (James 1: 5). Do we sometimes fail to ask, because we want to do something foolish?

How does God help us? He gives us protection, if we are willing to use it. He will not let any temptation be too strong for us to resist (1 Corinthians 10:13). If we give in to temptation, it is because we do not do our best. The devil never makes us do anything we really do not want to do.

How does God help us? Praise his name, he forgives us if we honestly confess our sin and beg for mercy (1 John 1:9). If I am burdened with a load of guilt, I have no one but myself to blame.

### C. WHO IS ON THE LORD'S SIDE?

The Lord put his words in Jeremiah's mouth and Ezekiel's stomach (Jeremiah 1:9; Ezekiel 2:8—3:3). As Christians, most of us do not claim any such extraordinary experience; but we do have in our hands the Word of God, the Holy Bible. Are we too quiet about it?

Many people do not want to know God's Word. Does that excuse our silence? Christian teaching may be ridiculed by our fellow workers and slandered by people high in education and government. Does that intimidate us? Or do we speak up at every opportunity, trusting the Lord to make us as strong as Ezekiel?

# Discovery Learning

*This page contains an alternate lesson plan emphasizing learning activities. Classes desiring such student involvement will find these suggestions helpful. The next page is a reproducible activity page to further enhance discovery learning.*

## LEARNING GOALS

After this lesson a student should be able to:

1. Summarize the instructions God gave to Ezekiel.

2. Tell why faithfulness is more important than "results."

3. Make a commitment to share God's Word with someone this week.

## INTO THE LESSON

Read the following sentences and ask your class members to raise their hands to indicate whether they agree or disagree with each one.

• When a person is doing God's will, he will be successful.

• I can determine God's will by deciding what I most enjoy.

• A preacher knows he is preaching the truth when his listeners respond positively to his message.

• Since God's Word is a source of truth and joy, men and women who truly understand it are happy to obey it.

Class members may discuss each sentence briefly, if you wish. Stop any involved discussion by telling the class that the study of today's Scripture story will shed light on the issues raised by these sentences.

## INTO THE WORD

Before class, copy the following Bible study questions to use as a handout in today's session.

Use the Lesson Background of the lesson commentary to connect this week's study with last week's. Then distribute the Bible study questions to class members. The questions are based on Ezekiel 2:1—3:11.

Class members may answer the questions alone or in groups of between five and seven. After several minutes, discuss answers with the class.

1. List all the words you can find in Ezekiel 2 to describe the Israelites who would receive Ezekiel's message.

2. How would they respond to Ezekiel's preaching?

3. What one word would you use to describe the kind of audience the Israelites would be for Ezekiel?

4. How was Ezekiel supposed to feel about his mission and his audience?

5. What did God tell Ezekiel to do with the document that contained his words? What is the significance of this command?

6. How did Ezekiel come to feel about God's Word? What choice did Ezekiel have about sharing it?

7. Who does God say might have received his message more readily than the Israelites? What does this tell you about the Israelites?

8. How would God help Ezekiel with his difficult task?

## OPTION

Ask class members to prepare a first person essay, diary entry, or letter, that might have been written by Ezekiel. The assignment should describe what God called Ezekiel to do, what Ezekiel expected to happen as a result, and why he obeyed God anyway. Class members may write the assignment individually, or groups may cooperate to write the assignments. Allow several minutes for these to be written, before volunteers share them with the whole class.

## INTO LIFE

Continue your discussion of this passage by considering the following application questions with your class members:

1. How do you suppose Ezekiel may have felt about his orders from God? How do you think you would have reacted?

2. Have you ever felt called by God to do something difficult or distasteful? Did you do it? Why or why not? How did you feel afterward?

3. Have you ever tried to share the message of God with someone who rejected the message and hated you for sharing it? What happened? What did you learn from the experience? How does today's Scripture study shed light on this experience?

4. Was Ezekiel "successful"? Some Christians today have a tendency to measure their effectiveness for God by how others respond. What does Ezekiel's experience say about that? Have you ever wanted to quit some service for God because your "audience" did not seem to receive your message or service as you expected they would? How do we decide that such a decision on our part is legitimate?

Ask class members to share something they are trying to do for God that is very difficult. Perhaps some will share something they have considered doing, but have hesitated because it seems so hard. Remind them that God demands faithfulness more than "success." Close with sentence prayers, asking God for courage to follow the example of Ezekiel.

# When No One Will Listen

Ezekiel was told to preach the message, whether the captives listened or not (Ezekiel 2:7). Read the following passages. What do they state or imply about the evangelist's response when his or her hearers refuse to listen?

Isaiah 53:1

Ezekiel 33:7-9

Matthew 7:6

Matthew 10:5-16

Luke 10:1-12; 16

Acts 13:45, 46

Acts 18:9-11

Based on today's text and these Scriptures, what would you advise a fellow believer who has been trying to share Christ with a neighbor, but the neighbor has been stubbornly refusing to pay any attention?

What would you advise a missionary who is frustrated with the lack of results in the mission field where he or she is serving?

# PERSONAL RESPONSIBILITY

**LESSON 9**

## WHY TEACH THIS LESSON?

A farmer bought a new tractor equipped with a roll bar designed to protect the driver in case the tractor turned over. Unfortunately, the opening into this farmer's barn was not high enough to accomodate the roll bar, so he removed it. Later, he was injured when the tractor rolled over on him. So he sued the manufacturer of the tractor and won a substantial settlement!

Stories like that are common today. Even responsible people might easily be tempted to take advantage of a system that so easily grants victim status to people whose own behavior has caused harm. Personal responsibility is not popular.

This lesson is a sober reminder that God judges by a different standard from that employed in our legal system. It's not so easy to plead victimization. The farmer should have known: "A man reaps what he sows" (Galatians 6:7).

## INTRODUCTION

Two-year-old Annie was very interested in the daffodils that grew in a box under a sunny window. When the first flower opened, she was delighted. Seeing that it came from a bud, she hastened to help another bud open and display its glory.

Daddy interrupted her effort, explaining that some processes of nature are not to be hurried. The bud must be allowed to open in its own good time.

Annie stayed away for a while, but she was not convinced. Soon she came back to pick a bud apart with her tiny fingers. This time Daddy did not try to explain, but spoke with the voice of authority: "I'll spank you if you do that again."

Annie tried to take an interest in other things; but Daddy was hidden behind a newspaper, and the lure of unopened buds was irresistible.

Daddy's face was invisible, but his voice was stern: "Are you picking at those buds again?"

"Yes."

"Didn't I tell you I would spank you?"

"Yes."

"So do I have to spank you?"

"I guess so." The tot trotted over to Daddy and bent her little form over his knee.

### A. RESPONSIBILITY

Annie was an intelligent child. She learned early that actions have consequences. She was an honest child. She acknowledged her guilt and accepted the consequences. Some older wrongdoers are not so honest. They deny the facts; or, if that is impossible, they deny their responsibility.

This week we have a message from God about actions and consequences, and about responsibility.

### B. LESSON BACKGROUND

In 597 B.C. Nebuchadnezzar of Babylon subdued Judah for the second time. He took king Jehoiachin and ten thousand citizens of Judah back to Babylon with him. (See the outline of those times in the Introduction to Lesson 7, pages 63, 64.)

DEVOTIONAL READING

PSALM 5:1-12

LESSON SCRIPTURE

EZEKIEL 18

PRINTED TEXT

EZEKIEL 18:1-13, 19, 20

LESSON AIMS

After this lesson a student should be able to:

1. Describe the mistaken belief of the captives in Babylon.

2. State the true principle that corrected that mistaken belief.

3. Accept responsibility for his or her own actions.

Oct
27

KEY VERSE

The son will not share the guilt of the father, nor will the father share the guilt of the son.

Ezekiel 18:20

## WHAT DO YOU THINK?

*Actions have consequences, yet it seems that many people fail to recognize this simple fact. How would the number of cases of sexually transmitted diseases be affected if people considered the consequences of their actions before doing anything? How would the number of abortions be affected if people generally took responsibility for their actions instead of trying to escape the consequences? How, then, can we teach people to think ahead and to take responsibility? Do you think our church is effectively teaching that to our young people? Why or why not? Are the adults in our church modeling that? What can we do to improve?*

## OPTION

*Use the reproducible activity, "Popular Lies," on page 86 to explore how our society has its own false proverbs. Make copies of the activity or simply discuss the expressions together.*

One of those ten thousand captives was Ezekiel the prophet. He gave God's word to his fellow exiles in Babylon (Ezekiel 1:1-3), while Jeremiah was continuing to speak for God in the homeland of Judah. Today's lesson looks at one of God's messages to the captives in Babylon.

## I. PROVERB AND PRINCIPLE (EZEKIEL 18:1-4)

The Lord's message began by quoting a proverb. It was not one of the proverbs of Solomon, but an uninspired saying often repeated by the people of Judah. Apparently the people held such sayings in higher esteem than the Word of God. On other occasions, Ezekiel's messages consisted of responses to the conventional wisdom expressed by these proverbs (Ezekiel 11:2, 3; 12:21-28). Ironically, one of the criticisms leveled against Ezekiel was that his own messages consisted of nothing more than proverbs or "parables" (Ezekiel 20:49).

Such popular sayings appear in any society. "Time and tide wait for no man" is one of ours. "A stitch in time saves nine" is another. Such sayings are often repeated because they are true and because they can be applied in many situations. But some of these sayings are not completely accurate. An example is "Clothes make the man." We know this is not really so, but the clothes a man wears do help us shape our opinion of him, and thus the saying remains popular.

### A. GOD'S WORD (v. 1)

**1. The word of the LORD came to me.**

This indicates the beginning of a new revelation from the Lord, not a continuation of the one recorded in chapter 17.

### B. USELESS PROVERB (vv. 2, 3)

**2. "What do you people mean by quoting this proverb about the land of Israel:**
**"'The fathers eat sour grapes, and the children's teeth are set on edge'?**

*What do you people mean?* The question seems to ask for an explanation, but it really means that no explanation or excuse is sufficient for what has been done. This proverb was apparently well known in Judah (Jeremiah 31:29). The captives in Babylon had been using it in a way that was wrong.

*Sour grapes* (or anything sour) can produce a peculiar and unpleasant sensation that is described in the phrase, *teeth are set on edge.* As the captives in Babylon were using the proverb, that painful sensation represented the pain and shame of their captivity. The sour grapes that caused it were the sins of Judah. The captives claimed, however, that they were being punished for the sins of former generations, not for their own sins. Like many modern wrongdoers, they wanted to avoid responsibility when circumstances worsened. They were saying, "It's not our fault."

It was true that Judah's punishment had come "because of the sins of Manasseh" (2 Kings: 24:3), and Manasseh had died forty-five years before these captives were taken. But these captives were not punished just because Manasseh and others of his generation committed those sins; they were punished because they themselves continued to commit those sins.

**3. "As surely as I live, declares the Sovereign LORD, you will no longer quote this proverb in Israel.**

*You will no longer quote this proverb in Israel.* Here the Hebrew idiom is so different from ours that it is hard to put into our language. Translating some of the words more literally, we read, *It will not be for you anymore to use this proverb.* The meaning seems to be that it will not be right or proper for you to keep on using this proverb as you have been using it. In the next few verses the Lord will show that such use is mistaken.

## C. USEFUL PRINCIPLE (v. 4)

**4. "For every living soul belongs to me, the father as well as the son—both alike belong to me. The soul who sins is the one who will die.**

The word *soul* means person. Each person *belongs* to God, the Creator. Each is accountable to him, and each must take responsibility for what he himself does.

This principle calls for some careful thinking. At an earlier time, God clearly described himself as "punishing the children for the sin of the fathers to the third and fourth generation of those who hate me" (Exodus 20:5). The message we see in Ezekiel seems so different that some students suggest that God now was amending his older law. But we need not see either a contradiction or an amendment.

The sins of parents do affect their children. Many innocent babies died when God destroyed most of the world's population with a flood, when he destroyed Sodom with fire, and when he destroyed Jericho with the swords of the Israelites. In today's world, children also suffer for the sins of their parents. A sinner is put in jail, leaving his family in poverty. Sinful parents neglect their children; the children grow up in the streets and become thieves and murderers. A drunken father takes the wheel to drive home with his family, and all of them are killed in an accident. Obviously, *the soul who sins* does not always die alone. What then does it mean to say, *The soul who sins is the one who will die?* Two thoughts emerge.

First, while children share some of the results of their parents' sins, they do not share the guilt. Therefore, they share only the earthly results of their parents' sins, not the eternal results A criminal act by a father may cause him to be imprisoned, and the subsequent loss of his provision for the family will have consequences that last for years, even generations. But the guilt belongs to the father alone..

Second, children often adopt the ways of the parents. In one sense, then, a sinful parent is responsible for the sin of the child because he taught the child to sin. At the same time, every person at some point becomes accountable for his own actions. If those actions are sinful, the punishment meted out is for those sins, not the sins of the parent. This was the situation of the exiles. Their ancestors had sinned and caused the captivity. They had continued the sin of their ancestors and thus shared the guilt. Their punishment was just. In Judah's history, the warnings of judgments and the delays that came because a good king brought reform are ample evidence of this truth.

### IT'S NOT MY FAULT!

For many years now, it seems that some people have excused almost every lapse from standards of decent or moral behavior by saying that the sinner is a victim of something. Everything from graffiti vandalism to thievery to drug abuse to random violence has been accounted for by claiming the perpetrator was the victim of some unfortunate circumstance in the past.

This folly has been satirized nicely by a newspaper comic strip. "Modern Ethics 101" was written on the door of a college classroom. Inside, the professor pointed to the blackboard, which read, "DON'T BLAME ME, IT'S: my victim's fault, society's fault, television's fault, the government's fault, the school system's fault, my parents' fault, my victim's parent's fault, my religion's fault, your religion's fault, your race's fault." The bottom line on the blackboard read, "Choose one for misdemeanors, any combination of two for felonies."

We started down this slippery path in an attempt to save every person's dignity. But by ignoring the truth of personal responsibility, we have not dignified people; we have dehumanized them. The Israelites of Ezekiel's day had a proverb, "The fathers eat sour grapes, and the children's teeth are set on edge," and they were paying the price for forgetting about personal responsibility. History seems to repeat itself, doesn't it? By now, we should have learned!      —C. R. B.

### WHAT DO YOU THINK?

"The soul who sins is the one who will die" (Ezekiel 18:4). Perhaps no previous generation has marshaled more excuses for sin than ours has. We blame it on our parents, our society, the little quirks in our personality, and the terrible pressures we face. God here emphasizes each person's responsibility for his own sin. In the New Testament we read a similar truth: "The wages of sin is death" (Romans 6:23).

Why has this message of personal responsibility and accountability become so lost in our culture? What will it take to re-emphasize the biblical truth in our secular society?

## II. ONE WHO SHALL LIVE (EZEKIEL 18:5-9)

God then gave to Ezekiel a description of one who would not die but "surely live"—a description drawn from the Law and the Prophets.

### A. JUSTICE (v. 5)

**5. "Suppose there is a righteous man who does what is just and right.**

The way of life was not a secret. The Law of God had been before Israel for centuries. Plainly it set forth the regulations and promised, "the man who obeys them will live by them" (Leviticus 18:5; Galatians 3:12).

### B. NO IDOLATRY OR IMMORALITY (v. 6)

**6. "He does not eat at the mountain shrines or look to the idols of the house of Israel. He does not defile his neighbor's wife or lie with a woman during her period.**

To *eat at the mountain shrines* was to join in a pagan feast, eating the meat of animals sacrificed to Baal or some other imaginary god. To *look to the idols* was to worship them. The reference to *his neighbor's wife* indicates adultery. The last portion of the verse calls attention to a requirement stated in Leviticus 18:19 and 20:18.

### B. HONESTY AND GENEROSITY (vv. 7, 8)

**7. "He does not oppress anyone, but returns what he took in pledge for a loan. He does not commit robbery but gives his food to the hungry and provides clothing for the naked.**

"Mistreat" would be a good synonym for *oppress*. One hoping to receive life should be careful not to take unfair advantage of anyone in any way.

He *returns what he took in pledge for a loan*. To buy food for his family, a poor man might pawn his outer garment, hoping to earn enough that day to redeem it. The Law said that the garment must be returned at night, even if the debt was not paid, for the borrower would need it to keep him warm as he slept (Exodus 22:26, 27).

He *does not commit robbery*. It seems that greedy men sometimes simply took the property of defenseless victims (Micah 2:1, 2). They could escape punishment by bribing corrupt judges, but they would still die for their sin.

He *gives his food to the hungry and provides clothing for the naked*. One seeking life should be more than fair; he should be generous in sharing food and clothing with the needy. Certainly Christians, who have experienced God's love in Jesus, should demonstrate this same kind of compassion (Matthew 25:31-46; 1 John 3:17, 18).

**8. "He does not lend at usury or take excessive interest. He withholds his hand from doing wrong and judges fairly between man and man.**

According to God's Law, his people were to make loans to the needy without charging interest (Exodus 22:25). *Excessive interest* is literally "increase" and may have included profit made by selling produce at a price above the cost of production. The Law seems to have regarded the nation of Israel as a family in which the members generously helped each other instead of trying to make a profit.

The man hoping for life should avoid any kind of wrongdoing. He is not to exploit the needy in any way. If called on to mediate a dispute between others, he must *judge fairly*, and not with favoritism.

### C. OBEDIENCE TO GOD (v. 9)

**9. "He follows my decrees and faithfully keeps my laws. That man is righteous; he will surely live, declares the Sovereign LORD.**

*My decrees and my laws* both refer to living by God's laws. That is the way *to deal truly*, to do right, to be just. According to the Law, that is the way to *live* and escape the sinner's punishment of death.

---

**WHAT DO YOU THINK?**

According to God's Law, his people were to make loans to the needy without charging interest (Exodus 22:25). Do you think Christians who loan money should charge any interest?

What about lending to the poor? Should Christians follow the Old Testament mandate? Why or why not?

What about lending to fellow Christians? If Israel was a family in which no one endeavored to make a profit from another, as the lesson writer suggests, how much more should that be true of the church? What do you think?

See Matthew 5:42. How does that speak to this issue?

## III. ONE WHO SHALL DIE (EZEKIEL 18:10-13)

### A. CROOKED AND VIOLENT (v. 10)

**10. "Suppose he has a violent son, who sheds blood or does any of these other things. . . .**

It was quite possible for the good man described in verses 5-9 to have a son who was very different. Consider Manasseh, the evil son of good King Hezekiah.

### B. IDOLATROUS AND IMMORAL (v. 11)

**11. . . . (though the father has done none of them): "He eats at the mountain shrines. He defiles his neighbor's wife.**

The bad son of a good father might neglect all the duties to God and man that his father had done so well. He might join in riotous pagan feasts *at the mountain shrines*, and indulge in the adultery that often accompanied such feasts.

### C. GREEDY AND OPPRESSIVE (vv. 12, 13a)

**12, 13a. "He oppresses the poor and needy. He commits robbery. He does not return what he took in pledge. He looks to the idols. He does detestable things. He lends at usury and takes excessive interest.**

The father described in verses 5-9 was not only honest—he was kind, generous, and helpful to people in need. The son now being described was greedy for gain. For his own profit he was utterly heartless in mistreating and exploiting those who had no way of resisting. Worshiping idols instead of God, he forsook all the moral standards of divine law in his pursuit of profit and pleasure.

### D. DOOMED TO DIE (v. 13b)

**13b. "Will such a man live? He will not! Because he has done all these detestable things, he will surely be put to death and his blood will be on his own head.**

Certainly this cruel, vicious, and wicked man would not be allowed to escape punishment because his father was good. Probably those who heard this message would have agreed with that. It would be unthinkable for a father's goodness to excuse the badness of his son. Nor would it be fair or just for a righteous son to be punished on account of his father's evil deeds (as verses 14-18 teach). Still, Ezekiel's hearers wanted to believe they were suffering because of their fathers' sins, not their own. This convenient belief enabled them to deny their own sin and claim that God's ways were unjust. God responded to this claim in verses 25-32.

### MAKING LEMONADE

George F. Will, the political commentator, wrote a column about his son Jonathan on Jon's twenty-first birthday. Jon has Down's syndrome, a defect in one's chromosomes that causes physical abnormalities and mental retardation in varying degrees of severity.

Jon could make excuses about his inability to function at a normal level, but he does not. As his father writes, "He does not 'suffer from' Down's syndrome. It is an affliction, but he is happy. . . . Although Jon would be forgiven for shaking his fist at the universe, he has been equable. I believe his serenity is grounded in his sense that he is a complete Jon and that is that."

In other words, instead of complaining about his lot in life, Jonathan Will has gone about being the best person he can be, given the chromosomal limitations with which he was born. He is a good example of the old proverb, "When life gives you lemons, make lemonade."

The Israelites of old seemed to delight in excusing their moral failures and violations of God's Law by blaming their parents. But Ezekiel held up the Law as the

## HOW TO SAY IT

Baal. BAY-ul.
Babylon. BAB-uh-lon.
Ezekiel. Ee-ZEEK-yul or Ee-ZEEK-ee-ul.
Hezekiah. Hez-eh-KYE-uh.
Jehoiachin. Jeh-HOY-uh-kin.
Jeremiah. JAIR-uh-MYE-uh.
Judah. JOO-duh.
Manasseh. Muh-NASS-uh.
Nebuchadnezzar. NEB-uh-kad-NEZZ-er.

## DAILY BIBLE READINGS

**Monday, Oct. 21**—*Ezekiel Made Watchman (Ezekiel 33:1-9)*

**Tuesday, Oct. 22**—*Promise of a Righteous Branch (Jeremiah 33:10-16)*

**Wednesday, Oct. 23**—*The Righteous Shall Live (Ezekiel 33:17-22)*

**Thursday, Oct. 24**—*Righteousness Is Rewarded (Psalm 18:17-22)*

**Friday, Oct. 25**—*Trust in God (Psalm 3)*

**Saturday, Oct. 26**—*Turn From Sinful Ways Ezekiel 18: 21-28)*

**Sunday, Oct. 27**—*Each Person Must Test Own Work (Galatians 6:1-5)*

*The visual for lesson 9 in the visuals packet illustrates the principle of verse 20.*

The son shall not bear the guilt of the father, nor the father bear the guilt of the son.

## WHAT DO YOU THINK?

*"The soul who sins is the one who will die." In light of the New Testament revelation, we could alter the statement to read, "The soul who follows Jesus is the one who will live." Some people think we have taught the former message too much and have not adequately communicated the good news of the latter. Others say we have only talked of the good news and have failed to communicate the serious reality of the bad news.*

*What do you think? How well is our church balancing these two messages? What would you suggest to make sure we keep them in proper balance?*

## PRAYER

*Almighty God, Father of mercies and God of all comfort, we are thankful for Your Word that shows us the way to live. We are thankful for the Savior who opens that way for us. Dedicating our lives to You, we beg for wisdom and strength and courage to walk always in the way everlasting. Amen.*

## THOUGHT TO REMEMBER

*I am responsible.*

moral norm and said that each person has the responsibility to live up to it, regardless of the heritage he has received at birth. The principle still stands: accept what you have been given and then do your best to please God by the way you live. By the grace of God, make some nice, sweet lemonade!

—C. R. B.

## IV. PRINCIPLE REEMPHASIZED (EZEKIEL 18:19, 20)

### A. QUESTION AND ANSWER (v. 19)

**19. "Yet you ask, 'Why does the son not share the guilt of his father?' Since the son has done what is just and right and has been careful to keep all my decrees, he will surely live.**

The Lord's declaration in verses 4-18 was plain. Each person is judged by what he himself does, regardless of what his father did. Still the captives clung to their opinion: their captivity was due to their ancestors' sins, and they themselves were not responsible for it.

The answer of God remained unmistakably clear. None of the people's arguments could nullify the principle of personal responsibility. Regardless of what his father did, if a son obeys God and does right, *he will surely live.*

### B. SUMMARY (v. 20)

**20. "The soul who sins is the one who will die. The son will not share the guilt of the father, nor will the father share the guilt of the son. The righteousness of the righteous man will be credited to him, and the wickedness of the wicked will be charged against him."**

Thus the principle from verse 4 is repeated, and the point of the illustrations in verses 5-19 is reemphasized. A father's sins may bring loss and grief to his son, but they bring the son no guilt. Likewise, a son's sins may disturb his father greatly, but they do not make the father guilty. There is no way for anyone to escape responsibility for what he or she does.

## CONCLUSION

"The soul who sins is the one who will die." If a soul is just and right, keeping the Law of God, that soul shall live. All this is clear, isn't it? But there is a catch.

### A. THE CATCH

No one is just and righteous enough to merit life—no one at all. No one has kept God's Law so well that he deserves no punishment—not Moses the lawgiver, not David, the man after God's own heart, not Hezekiah, the best of Judah's kings.

This was known even in Old Testament times: "There is no one who does good, not even one" (Psalm 53:3). It is also stated emphatically in the New Testament: "All have sinned and fall short of the glory of God" (Romans 3:23).

### B. THE SOLUTION

In ancient times God promised a New Covenant by which sins can be forgiven (Jeremiah 31:31-34). In later times he sent his Son to establish that covenant. The one sinless man in all history offered his life to atone for all the sins of the world (1 John 2:1, 2). Those who accept his offer become truly righteous, not by doing no wrong, but by being forgiven. Their righteousness is not attained by their own efforts; God gives them his righteousness because of their faith (Philippians 3:8-11). Thus, even sinners can live, if they renounce their sins and follow Jesus. Eternal life is a free gift (Romans 6:23). Even so we do not escape our own responsibility. We must decide to follow Jesus, and we must do it. We must trust and obey.

# Discovery Learning

*This page contains an alternate lesson plan emphasizing learning activities. Classes desiring such student involvement will find these suggestions helpful. The next page is a reproducible activity page to further enhance discovery learning.*

## LEARNING GOALS

After this lesson a student should be able to:

1. Describe the mistaken belief of the captives in Babylon.

2. State the true principle that corrected that mistaken belief.

3. Accept responsibility for his or her own actions.

## INTO THE LESSON

Ask each class member to write a three-sentence description of his father, and then a three-sentence description of his mother. When they have finished, each should find a partner (not one's spouse), and the partners should share the descriptions with each other.

Next, the partners should talk with each other about how each is like the parents he has just described. Either a person can volunteer how he is like one or both of his parents, or his partner can tell him some way he resembles the description he has written.

Discuss with the class: "Are you aware of how you resemble your parents? Was anyone surprised by his partner's assessment of his similarity to his parents? How do you feel about being like your parents? How many are pleased to be like their parents? How many deliberately try to be different from their parents?"

Tell the class that today's Scripture challenges us to consider the relationship of our parents' strengths and weaknesses to our own.

## INTO THE WORD

Remind the class of the historical setting for this passage of Scripture. (See "B. Lesson Background.") Tell the class that one way to analyze today's text is to see it as a series of questions and answers. Tell the class to listen for the questions and answers as class members read aloud from Ezekiel 18.

Divide the reading into the following sections:

Question 1 (vv. 1, 2); Answer 1 (vv. 3, 4); Question 2 (vv. 5-13a); Answer 2 (v. 13b); Question 3 (implied, vv. 14-17a); Answer 3 (vv. 17b, 18); Question 4 (v. 19a); Answer 4 (vv. 19b, 20).

Now ask class members, in groups of three or four, to paraphrase each question and answer on a sheet of scrap paper.

Give the groups at least five minutes to discuss and write, then ask for some members to share what they have written. Write the questions and answers on your chalkboard.

Ask the class, "Why do you suppose Ezekiel delivered this message to the Israelites? What lesson did they need to learn? What misconception about themselves and their captivity were they holding?"

Ask class members to tell you what the proverb (not an inspired proverb of God, but a popular saying of the time) in Ezekiel 18:2 means. (See the discussion in the lesson commentary. See also the reproducible activity, "Popular Lies," on the next page.)

## INTO LIFE

Ask class members to return to their small groups and to suggest situations where one generation has felt the effects of the previous generation's sins. They may share general examples ("Children of smokers are more likely to become smokers") or personal stories ("My father was an alcoholic; now my brother has a drinking problem").

Let several members share their examples. Then discuss: "Is it inevitable that we will repeat the mistakes and the sins of our parents? Why or why not? What does Ezekiel's teaching tell us about personal responsibility for our own sins?" Can they cite examples where a person intentionally avoided the sin of his parents or his ancestors?

Observe that the same mistaken proverb is popular in our own day, with some revision. Instead of blaming "our fathers," we blame "the sixties." Ask the class to suggest a number of problems that can be traced to the sixties. List these on the chalkboard.

Now ask each class member to choose one of these problems and to write his or her response to the following questions about that problem.

1. How have you been tempted by this problem situation?

2. How have you sometimes avoided a sin related to this situation?

3. What one thing can you do today to best help you overcome temptation in regard to this situation?

These responses are meant to be kept private. But as class members return to their small groups one last time for sentence prayers, they may share what they have written, if they wish.

After a brief time of prayer in the groups, close with a prayer that all your class members will be able to take responsibility for their own actions.

# Popular Lies

"The fathers eat sour grapes, and the children's teeth are set on edge" (Ezekiel 18:2). This popular proverb of Ezekiel's time was not true. Consider the following popular expressions of our day. What wrong actions do they suggest or seem to endorse? What is the proper Christian way to act instead?

| EXPRESSION | WRONG BEHAVIOR SUGGESTED OR ENDORSED | PROPER CHRISTIAN RESPONSE |
|---|---|---|
| "Nice guys finish last" | In order to get ahead we must cheat, lie, and otherwise take advantage of others. | Honesty, consideration for others, fairness. |
| "It's not what you know, but who you know." | | |
| "You have to grab for all the gusto you can." | | |
| "You can't legislate morality." | | |
| "It doesn't matter what you believe as long as you are sincere." | | |

What are some other expressions that are commonly believed but not true? What can the church do to help people understand and believe the truth?

Whose responsibility is it to tell people the truth about these expressions? (See Ezekiel 33:1-9.) What are *you* doing about that responsibility? What can you do this week?

---

# A PORTRAYAL OF DOOM

**LESSON 10**

## WHY TEACH THIS LESSON?

Today's lesson includes a dramatic visualization of God's coming judgment on Jerusalem. Unwelcome in its own time, it may offend the sensitivities of polite society today. But the coming disaster would overshadow the symbol to a degree none of those who first witnessed it could imagine.

What's more, there is a coming judgment for our generation as well. We don't know when, but a day is coming when eternal punishment will come on the faithless. That judgment will overshadow the fall of Jerusalem even more than that event overshadowed its predictions. Your students' only appropriate response is repentance for sin and commitment to God's ways.

## INTRODUCTION

### A. VISUAL AIDS

In Lesson 7 we saw a yoke used as a visual aid by the prophet Jeremiah and by the false prophet Hananiah. This week we will consider some visual aids that were used by Ezekiel the prophet. These were highly unusual visual aids; probably those who saw them were both surprised and puzzled.

### B. LESSON BACKGROUND

In Babylon many of the captives from Judah lived in a settlement called Tel Aviv, meaning "hill (or heap) of grain ears." It may have received its name from the fertility of the area. One of the major cities of modern Israel goes by the same name. The town in Babylon was by a "river" called Kebar, which was actually a large irrigation canal. There Ezekiel came with God's message (Ezekiel 3:15).

## I. PICTURE OF SIEGE (EZEKIEL 4:1-3)

The Lord had taken away Ezekiel's voice, promising to restore it when it was time for him to speak (Ezekiel 3:26, 27). Apparently the message in verses 1-3 was given without a word, using only visual aids. Not all the information in our text was communicated this way. Certainly the command in verse 7 is for verbal preaching.

### A. THE CITY (v. 1)

**1. Now, son of man, take a clay tablet, put it in front of you and draw the city of Jerusalem on it.**

A *clay tablet* was the most frequently used writing material in Babylon. A stylus was used to inscribe a message on a slab of soft clay, and the writing became permanent when the clay dried. Ezekiel could take such a tablet and *draw the city* on it by drawing a map with a stylus, or he could shape the soft clay into a more elaborate relief map. This would quickly be recognized by captives who had lived in Jerusalem only five years before (Ezekiel 1:2, 3).

### B. THE ENEMY (v. 2)

**2. Then lay siege to it: Erect siege works against it, build a ramp up to it, set up camps against it and put battering rams around it.**

DEVOTIONAL READING
ACTS 10:9-16
LESSON SCRIPTURE
EZEKIEL 3:22—5:17
PRINTED TEXT
EZEKIEL 4:1-13

### LESSON AIMS

As students participate in today's class session, they should:

1. Describe the teaching helps used by Ezekiel and tell what he taught by means of them.

2. Evaluate how open they are to the challenge to repent when serious Bible study exposes a need to repent.

3. Commit to a personal Bible study plan that encourages repentance for sin.

Nov
3

### KEY VERSE

Turn your face toward the siege of Jerusalem and with bared arm prophesy against her.
Ezekiel 4:7

## WHAT DO YOU THINK?

*Some people do not like talk of "doom" and "judgment." Preferring to focus on the positive, they ignore virtually any mention of punishment or judgment. But the Scriptures were inspired by God not only for the positive, like "teaching" and "training in righteousness." They were also given for "rebuking" and "correcting" (2 Timothy 3:16). Ezekiel's message in today's text was certainly one of "doom." How much "doom" do you think is appropriate in this gospel age when we are trying to tell the "good news" of Jesus Christ? Explain.*

## WHAT DO YOU THINK?

*Ezekiel 4 is an interesting chapter with its description of the "visual aids" God told the prophet to use. Jeremiah's belt (Jeremiah 13:1-11) and his yoke (27:1-15; 28:10, 11) are two other examples of the prophets' use of visual aids. What does this suggest about our use of visuals today?*

*Does it endorse Christian-message T-shirts and bumper stickers? Why or why not?*

*Does it suggest preachers and/or teachers should use visual aids? Why or why not?*

*Does it suggest a need for Christians with artistic talents— music, visual arts, writing, drama, etc.—to produce works that will glorify God and attract people to hear the gospel? Why or why not?*

Thus Ezekiel was to build a prophecy in clay. Probably using sticks along with the soft clay, he was to construct little models of the items that the Babylonians would use about five years later to besiege Jerusalem. They would *erect siege works*. These were a system of towers used to besiege a city and to protect the soldiers from a surprise attack by men from the city. This same word is used in 2 Kings 25:1 during the actual siege of Jerusalem.

The Babylonians would also *build a ramp* to the top of the city wall. They would *set up camp*, pitching their tents on all sides of the city to be sure no one from inside would escape and no one from outside would bring in provisions. They would then prepare *battering rams* to break down the gates after the defenders were weakened by starvation.

### C. THE IRON PAN (v. 3)

**3. Then take an iron pan, place it as an iron wall between you and the city and turn your face toward it. It will be under siege, and you shall besiege it. This will be a sign to the house of Israel.**

*An iron pan* might be found in someone's kitchen. It was the object on which loaves of dough were placed before they were shoved into an oven. (See Leviticus 2:5.) This was to symbolize *an iron wall*.

A number of views exist as to what this *wall* represented. Some see it as a symbol of Jerusalem's wall in which the people were trusting. Others see it as depicting the severity (like iron) of the Babylonian siege. Still another view is that the wall stood for the barrier that the people's sins had erected between themselves and God. The separation of the model city from God's prophet indicated that the real Jerusalem was cut off from God's help. The coming destruction by the Babylonians would be punishment by the Lord himself.

Apparently the model of Jerusalem *under siege* was to be built in a public place, perhaps in the marketplace of Tel-abib. There it would be seen by members of *the house of Israel* who were captives in that area. They would tell others about it, and thus what Ezekiel was doing would become *a sign* to the whole nation.

## II. PICTURES OF PUNISHMENT (EZEKIEL 4:4-8)

Ezekiel had just represented himself as an enemy besieging the city of Jerusalem and its sinful people. Now he was to represent the sinful people.

### A. ISRAEL'S PUNISHMENT (vv. 4, 5)

**4. Then lie on your left side and put the sin of the house of Israel upon yourself. You are to bear their sin for the number of days you lie on your side.**

The sun rising in the east provided the basis for the Israelites' sense of direction. "East" was considered the "front," thus "north" was the direction on their *left side*. Here *the house of Israel* meant the northern kingdom, separated from the southern nation of Judah. The prophet was to lie on his left side, facing north, as if crushed by the weight of Israel's sin laid upon him. He must continue to lie in that position for the number of days specified in the next verse.

**5. I have assigned you the same number of days as the years of their sin. So for 390 days you will bear the sin of the house of Israel.**

For *390 days* (about thirteen months) Ezekiel was to lie prone, bearing *the sin of the house of Israel*. Each day meant a year in which Israel would have to bear her sin, or be borne down by the weight of her sin. Apparently this meant the number of years that Israel sinned plus the number of years she would be punished by captivity. Ezekiel was to lie helpless on the ground as a symbol of Israel's lying helpless in sin and captivity.

The northern nation had become separated from the south around 931 B.C. Almost immediately its *sin* had begun, with King Jeroboam's introduction of pagan worship and practices (1 Kings 12:25-33). Moving forward 390 years from that point brings us to 541 B.C., very close to the time when the captives in Babylon were liberated by the Persian emperor Cyrus (Ezra 1:1-4). These captives likely included people of both northern and southern kingdoms.

## B. JUDAH'S PUNISHMENT (v. 6)

**6. After you have finished this, lie down again, this time on your right side, and bear the sin of the house of Judah. I have assigned you 40 days, a day for each year.**

After picturing the punishment of Israel by lying on his left side, Ezekiel was to picture the punishment of Judah by lying on his *right side*, facing the south. This he must do for *40 days*, indicating that Judah's punishment would continue for forty years.

How should this forty-year period be understood? What time does it cover? It is difficult to speak with certainty. If we count from the final stage of Judah's captivity, which occurred in 582 B.C. (Jeremiah 52:30), then forty years later brings us to 542 B.C., which once again is very close to the time of the release of the captives by Cyrus.

Others have observed that the two numbers given, 390 and 40, total 430. This was the number of years Israel spent in bondage in Egypt, according to Exodus 12:40, 41. The longer period of punishment allotted to the north would seem to reflect its greater guilt, due to its quicker acceptance of pagan ways.

## C. PICTURE OF POWER (v. 7)

**7. Turn your face toward the siege of Jerusalem and with bared arm prophesy against her.**

In this verse, Ezekiel returned to the role of a warrior coming to destroy Jerusalem. Just as we roll up our sleeves to undertake a hard or dirty job, the prophet's uncovered arm represented strength at work. (See Isaiah 52:10.) It was the Lord's strength that was coming against Jerusalem, though the army of Babylon was the weapon in his hand. The prophet's *face toward the siege of Jerusalem* represented the Lord's face turned in anger toward the sinful city.

## D. PICTURE OF PERSISTENCE (v. 8)

**8. I will tie you up with ropes so that you cannot turn from one side to the other until you have finished the days of your siege.**

In some way, the Lord was going to restrain his prophet and keep him lying in the assigned position, first on the left side and then on the right, for the required number of days. Did this restraint indicate the bondage of sin, as Ezekiel was to "bear the sin" first of Israel and then of Judah? Or did it symbolize the bondage of the besieged city? Either position is possible.

As for the restraint itself, a literal understanding is, obviously, that Ezekiel was actually tied up *with ropes*. Some students think that the prophet was physically paralyzed, unable to move. If the Lord chose, however, he could control the man's mind and muscles without actually paralyzing or tying him.

It does not seem necessary to suppose that Ezekiel lay bound and motionless through twenty-four hours of every day. His mission could be accomplished and his prophecy given even if he were there in position only a part of each day. He must have risen for the activities ordered in the following verses of our text. He may have been free to engage in normal activities at night, when there would be no one

*The visual for lesson 10 in the visuals packet is a chart that helps summarize and explain what God commanded Ezekiel to do in today's text.*

## WHAT DO YOU THINK?

*We can only imagine how much weight Ezekiel must have lost eating only bread and water for fourteen months! We have to admire the devotion to his ministry that his acceptance of such a hard assignment illustrates. How many modern Christians display the same kind of commitment to the Lord's work? Why do you think it is not more common than it is?*

*What can you do to renew your commitment to the Lord's work? What can you do to encourage others to be more committed?*

to see his visualized prophecies. But the daily picture had to be continued without fail through the allotted time periods.

### No Escape

For sheer emotional involvement with his audiences, Harry Houdini has never been equaled as a magician. Houdini perfected the skill of extricating himself from apparently impossible situations. He toured the world, upsetting authorities in many cities with his ability to escape from their most secure prisons. In what was perhaps his most spectacular stunt, he allowed himself to be bound with ropes, locked in a packing case secured with steel tape, and then dropped into New York City's harbor. Only fifty-nine seconds later the great Houdini was free, swimming safely at the surface.

To portray the coming captivity of Israel and Judah, Ezekiel lay on his left side for 390 days and then on his right side for 40 days, perhaps bound with ropes so he could not turn. In this graphic manner, he showed the effect of sin on Israel and Judah. Its effect is the same on us. No sleight of hand can free us from sin's bondage. In the moral realm, there is no magic. Only God can break sin's cords that bind us.

—C. R. B.

## III. PICTURE OF HUNGER (EZEKIEL 4:9-13)

The last part of our text presents a visualized prophecy that pointed to both of the events already pictured—the siege and the captivity.

### A. Mixed Bread (v. 9)

**9. Take wheat and barley, beans and lentils, millet and spelt; put them in a storage jar and use them to make bread for yourself. You are to eat it during the 390 days you lie on your side.**

Usually *wheat* was ground and sifted to make a fine flour with which *bread* was baked. *Barley* could also be used, but it provided a much coarser bread. Ezekiel was told to picture a time when food would be so scarce that all kinds of grain and seed would be mixed with wheat and barley to make an inferior kind of bread. *Spelt,* for example, is a lesser quality kind of wheat.

This act suggested the severity of existence during the siege pictured in verses 1-3. Ezekiel was to eat this inferior bread for *390 days*—the time of punishment pictured in verses 4 and 5. Why the forty days of verse 6 (representing the punishment of Judah) were not included in this set of commands is difficult to ascertain. It may have been another way to show that the treatment of the northern kingdom would be more severe than that of the south.

### B. Small Rations (vv. 10, 11)

**10. Weigh out twenty shekels of food to eat each day and eat it at set times.**

It seems that the only kind of *food* that Ezekiel was to eat was the inferior bread made of mixed grains. He was to allow himself only a limited amount of that—*twenty shekels for each day*. A footnote in our text estimates twenty shekels to be "about eight ounces (about 0.2 kilogram)." Ezekiel was not to eat the daily ration all at once, but *at set times,* probably at the usual meal times. Thus Ezekiel was to picture conditions during the coming siege of Jerusalem.

**11. Also measure out a sixth of a hin of water and drink it at set times.**

According to another footnote, *a sixth of a hin* is "about 2/3 quart (about 0.6 liter)." That would be less than an eight-ounce glass of *water* with each meal, with none between meals. Such rationing would add to the suffering of the people in Jerusalem during the coming siege and would be especially harmful during hot weather. When the people were living on such inadequate amounts of food and

---

### How to Say It

*Babylon.* BAB-uh-lon.

*Babylonian.* Bab-uh-LOW-nee-un.

*Cyrus.* SIGH-russ.

*Ezekiel.* Ee-ZEEK-yul or Ee-ZEEK-ee-ul.

*Ezra.* EZ-ruh.

*Hananiah.* Han-uh-NYE-uh.

*Jehoiachin.* Jeh-HOY-uh-kin.

*Jeremiah.* JAIR-uh-MYE-uh.

*Jeroboam.* Jair-uh-BOE-um.

*Judah.* JOO-duh.

*Kebar.* KEE-bar.

*Persian.* PUR-zhun.

*Tel Aviv.* Tell-Ah-VEEV.

water, each one would be "appalled" to see how he and his companions were wasting away (vv. 16, 17).

## C. DEFILED FOOD (vv. 12, 13)

**12. Eat the food as you would a barley cake; bake it in the sight of the people, using human excrement for fuel.**

The bread of mixed grains was to be prepared and eaten as a *barley cake* was; that is, in a small flat loaf more like a hamburger bun than what we think of as a "loaf" of bread.

During a long siege, lack of fuel frequently became a serious problem. Ezekiel was to illustrate this by using dried *human excrement* for fuel to bake his bread. At Ezekiel's horrified protest he was allowed to use cow manure instead (vv. 14, 15). That was a little less revolting (cow manure was often used for fuel in the ancient Near East), but still the bread was defiled.

**13. The LORD said, "In this way the people of Israel will eat defiled food among the nations where I will drive them.**

Not only during the siege, but all through the long captivity the people of Israel would have to eat *defiled food*. It would not always be defiled in the same way Ezekiel's bread was, but in various ways it would not comply with the strict regulations of God's Law. The people of Judah had ignored that Law so long and so flagrantly that he was going to drive them into captivity among pagan *nations* where food approved by the Law would not always be available.

### AN EPIDEMIC OF MORAL DEFILEMENT

Cholera is a plague that still haunts vast areas of the world. Outbreaks of the disease remain common in those countries where proper sanitation of food and water supplies does not exist. The disease is acquired by consuming food or water contaminated by human waste. Without prompt treatment by antibiotics and intravenous infusion of fluids, death comes rapidly to the victim because of massive dehydration.

During the period of 430 days that Ezekiel lay bound on his side as a demonstration of the moral pollution and bondage of Israel and Judah, he survived on bread and water. That was bad enough, but the circumstance that was calculated to draw the attention of the people to their sins was the fact that his bread was baked over human waste!

Although Ezekiel was permitted to use cow manure instead of human waste, the picture is still an unpleasant one. Yet wasn't that just the point? Somehow, Israel and Judah had to be shocked into seeing that their spiritual pollution had reached the epidemic stage. May God's warnings about their moral defilement not be lost on us.

—C. R. B.

## CONCLUSION

### A. OPTIMIST AND PESSIMIST

When ten thousand captives of Judah were marched away to Babylon, Hananiah remained in Jerusalem with a cheery assurance. Babylon would be crushed and the captives would be back home in less than two years (Jeremiah 28:2-4). Perhaps Hananiah became the most popular prophet in Jerusalem.

On the other hand, Jeremiah advised the captives to settle down for a long stay in Babylon. Judah would be subject to that nation for a total of seventy years, he wrote in a letter to the exiles (Jeremiah 29:4-10). Furthermore, Jerusalem would be burned and the rest of its people would become captives (Jeremiah 34:1-3). That was not a popular message. Powerful men in Jerusalem wanted the king to have Jeremiah killed; but when the king told them to kill him themselves, they decided to put him in a dungeon to silence his voice (Jeremiah 38:1-6).

*DAILY BIBLE READING*

**Monday, Oct. 28**—*Ezekiel Ordered to Shave Hair (Ezekiel 5:1-4)*

**Tuesday, Oct. 29**—*Jerusalem's Fate for Sinning (Ezekiel 5:5-9)*

**Wednesday, Oct. 30**—*The Lord Speaks in Anger (Ezekiel 5:13-17)*

**Thursday, Oct. 31**—*High Places to Be Destroyed (Ezekiel 6:1-10)*

**Friday, Nov. 1**—*The Lord Known by His Judgments (Ezekiel 6:11-14)*

**Saturday, Nov. 2**—*Days of Punishment (Hosea 9:1-9)*

**Sunday, Nov. 3**—*God Rejects Israel (Hosea 9:10-17)*

## What Do You Think?

*What kind of Bible study do we need, so that we can test the claims that some preachers, teachers, and writers make today?*

*In Ephesians 4:14 Paul expresses his vision that Christians "will no longer be infants, tossed back and forth by the waves, and blown here and there by every wind of teaching and by the cunning and craftiness of men in their deceitful scheming" (New International Version). Paul indicates that only a Christ-centered kind of spiritual growth will bring that vision to reality. Our Bible study should be concerned with who Jesus Christ is, the details of his life on earth, the realities and results of his death and resurrection, his headship over the church, and the certainty of his coming again. When we study the Old Testament, we should aim to see it as Jesus did. When we study the New Testament, we should aim to see Jesus as his disciples saw him.*

## Prayer

*In a time when dozens of voices are calling us to dozens of ways, how good it is to know that one voice is always calling to the way that leads to life! Dear Father, we thank you for your Word, for we know we can depend on it. Help us to find in our busy lives the time to know it better, and help us to find in our selfish hearts the will to follow it better. Amen.*

## Thought to Remember

*God's Word is truth.*

### B. Getting Attention

Ezekiel was one of the ten thousand captives in Babylon. There he gave the same message Jeremiah was giving in Jerusalem. He must have been as unpopular as Jeremiah was. The other captives had no authority to put him in a dungeon, but they could walk away instead of listening.

God told Ezekiel how to get attention. Can't you imagine some of the comments? "Hey, that's a little map of Jerusalem. What's the idea of that?" Soon the little battering rams around the miniature city gave the answer.

"Why is he lying out there on the ground day after day?"

"It's a symbol of our lying here in captivity."

"Why does he cook that outlandish bread and nibble such a little bit of it?"

"It's a picture of the hunger when Jerusalem will be under siege."

Some faithful Christians are suspicious of a preacher who recruits a band, gathers a crowd in a tent, and shouts his message. We are no less suspicious of one who stages a spectacular show on national TV. In some cases our suspicion has been justified. But a preacher is not to be judged by how noisy he is. A better question is this: Is his message true? Truth deserves respect, whether the telling of it is loud or soft, modest or spectacular, conventional or unconventional.

### C. Testing for Truth

Hananiah said he was speaking for God, but that was a lie. Jeremiah and Ezekiel made the same claim, and it was true. How could the hearers tell truth from falsehood?

An earlier prophet in Jerusalem told where to go for an answer: "To the law and to the testimony: if they do not speak according to this word, they have no light of dawn" (Isaiah 8:20). Plainly the Law told what was right and what was wrong. Powerfully it promised blessing for doing right and disaster for doing wrong. Anyone should have known Hananiah was a liar when he promised blessing to open and unrepentant sinners. Anyone should have known Jeremiah and Ezekiel were truthful when they preached what the Law said.

We Christians are not under the Law, but the Christian teaching recorded in the New Testament is the standard by which teachers are tested. If we do not know that standard well enough to conduct a test, we are in danger of being duped by teachers who teach their own word, not the Word of God. If their teaching does not agree with that of Jesus, Peter, John, and Paul, it is because they have no light.

### D. Turning from Error

Sometimes choosing the true instead of the false is as much a decision of the will as it is a matter of knowing which is which. Those who followed prophets like Hananiah probably did know he was telling a lie. But they liked the lie. It made no demands of repentance on them.

Paul told Timothy there would be people like that. "They will gather around them a great number of teachers to say what their itching ears want to hear. They will turn their ears away from the truth and turn aside to myths" (2 Timothy 4:3, 4).

When the Word of God exposes sin in our lives, we can repent of the sin and seek to do right. That is what God wants. Or we can find some teacher to explain away the sin, tell us that what the Bible "seems to say" is not really what it says. Our "itching ears" may want to hear that, but what we really need is to face the truth, turn from the error, and enjoy the blessings of serving God and walking in the truth.

# Discovery Learning

*This page contains an alternate lesson plan emphasizing learning activities. Classes
desiring such student involvement will find these suggestions helpful. The next page
is a reproducible activity page to further enhance discovery learning.*

## LEARNING GOALS

As students participate in today's session, they will:

1. Describe the teaching helps used by Ezekiel and tell what he taught by means of them.

2. Evaluate how open they are to the challenge to repent when serious Bible study exposes a need to repent.

3. Commit to a personal Bible study plan that encourages repentance for sin.

## INTO THE LESSON

Begin today's class session with a word association game. Give class members slips of paper, and ask them to write down the first word that comes to mind as you read each of the following words: *defeat, repentance, change, error, punishment, disaster.* Or ask class members to write a sentence using at least two of these words.

This activity is meant to point out the importance of change in order to avert the negative consequences of certain acts. Tell the class that today's Scripture text contains some dramatic visualized prophecies that showed the Israelites the dire consequences that would come to them because of their sin. They ignored these warnings. Would we ignore such prophecies if they came to us today?

## INTO THE WORD

Deliver a brief lecture to your class to explain the visual aids God told Ezekiel to use to portray his message to the exiles in Babylon. (The visual for lesson 10 in the visual packet would be a good help in presenting this lecture.) Use the following outline:

1. The clay tablet (vv. 1-3)
2. Lying on the left side (vv. 4, 5)
3. Lying on the right side (vv. 6-8)
4. Unclean bread (vv. 9-13)

As class members listen to the lecture, they should make notes under the following headings, which they write across the top of a paper:

Ezekiel's actions

Ezekiel's words

What they symbolized

The lesson they taught

If you prefer, you can make this a small-group activity. Students study the text and complete the chart without input from you. Then, after about six or eight minutes, the groups report to each other. During this time you answer questions and help students complete their charts.

Discuss: How do you think the Israelites reacted to this prophecy? What was offensive or outrageous about it? What was intimidating or convicting about it? Do you believe it stimulated repentance? Why or why not?

## INTO LIFE

Before class prepare a poster or overhead projector transparency with the following discussion starters (or write them on your chalkboard ahead of time):

Think of a time when . . .

• Someone did something dramatic to get my attention.
• I was wrong, and I did something to make it right.
• Someone corrected me, and I took it to heart.
• I lost, but I learned an important lesson.
• I was defeated by defeat.
• I refused to take good advice.
• A sermon or Bible study challenged my behavior.

In groups of two or three, class members should talk with each other about these sentences. Each person should choose one of them to discuss with his or her small group.

After six or eight minutes, allow volunteers to share responses. Then discuss with the class:

1. How do these relate to today's Bible study?

2. Do you know someone with an obvious character or temperament flaw? Do you know someone who makes the same error again and again in his life? Why is it so difficult for some adults to change?

3. Do you believe it is difficult or easy to repent of sin? Why?

Remind the class that God allowed Jerusalem to fall because the Jews would not repent of their obvious sins. Ask each class member to consider: What sin in my life would cause God to challenge me to repent?

Comment on the availability of several plans for Bible reading. (For example, every December *The Lookout* magazine from Standard Publishing prints a plan for reading the Bible through in a year.) Ask for volunteers to share some of the features of their own Bible study plans. Ask, "How many of these plans focus on repentance?" (Most only give references to read; what the reader does from there is up to him or her.)

Distribute copies of "Making a Difference," page 94. Ask the students to commit to using this or some other plan that helps them take seriously the challenges to repent that they discover in their personal Bible study.

# Making a Difference

There are numerous plans available for reading the Bible. Many take you through the Bible in a year. Others take you through the Old Testament once and the New Testament twice. Some incorporate the Psalms and Proverbs every day, as well as assigning portions of other books.

Whatever plan you use, the important thing is allowing the reading to make a difference in your life. God has given us the Scriptures "for teaching, rebuking, correcting and training in righteousness, so that the man [or woman] of God may be thoroughly equipped for every good work" (2 Timothy 3:16, 17).

Use the following chart along with your regular reading plan each day. Use it to guide you to allow the Scriptures to make a difference in your life.

| |
|---|
| PASSAGE: _____ |
| Summary of the passage. |
| What does this passage "teach" me? |
| For what does this passage "rebuke" me? |
| What "correction" does this passage require of me? |
| For what ministry does this passage provide "training"? |
| What is the most important thing I could do in the next five to ten days to incorporate the message of this passage in my life? |

# God's People Face Judgment

# JERUSALEM FALLS

**LESSON 11**

## WHY TEACH THIS LESSON?

We've read the warnings. We've seen it coming. Today we see it happen: Jerusalem is destroyed. We don't have to hear a prophet's declaration today. The point is clear. God takes sin seriously, and punishment is certain. It may be delayed for one reason or another, but it is sure.

The people of Judah had heard the warnings. They should have seen it coming. They could have stopped it with sincere repentance. But they ignored the warnings and suffered the consequences.

It should not take much explanation for your students to get the message. The stark image of a smoldering city surrounded by rubble where once stood a wall is a warning to us yet today: "the wages of sin is death" (Romans 6:23).

At the same time, we dare not miss the fact—also stated in Romans 6:23—that "the gift of God is eternal life in Christ Jesus our Lord." Offer the warning, but give the promise as well. The God of judgment is also the God of grace. Your class needs to hear both messages today.

## INTRODUCTION

It's called by some the "universal law of seedtime and harvest": a man reaps what he sows. It is a biblical principle. Paul states it twice, in 2 Corinthians 9:6 and in Galatians 6:7. More often than it is stated, it is illustrated—as in our lesson for today.

### A. GETTING WHAT WE DESERVE

Although prophets such as Jeremiah, Habakkuk, and Ezekiel had been warning their audiences repeatedly that the destruction of Jerusalem was imminent, these men did not rejoice to see the city fall. They took no "I told you so" attitude as they watched Jerusalem's residents leaving their homes in tears.

No type of discipline, whether coming from parents, judges, church elders, or prophets, is easy to administer. But in a fallen world, such discipline is necessary to maintain order in a home, a church, and a society. Those who fail to heed the clear warnings they have been given should expect no other treatment except punishment.

Perhaps we should pause at this point to consider how unparalleled the message of the cross continues to be. The Son of God, who did nothing to deserve punishment, took upon himself the treatment that we had coming to us. In mercy God has provided a way for sinful man to be saved. A way was also provided for the people of Judah. They simply refused to accept it.

### B. LESSON BACKGROUND

It will be helpful to refer once again to the material provided in the Introduction to Lesson 7 on pages 63, 64 (under the heading "C. Disaster in Three Phases"). This is a summary of the significant events leading up to the fall of Jerusalem in 586 B.C.

During October we read how Jeremiah continued to give God's word to the people who stayed in Judah, and how Ezekiel did the same for the captives in

DEVOTIONAL READING
PSALM 74:1-12
LESSON SCRIPTURE
2 KINGS 24, 25
PRINTED TEXT
2 KINGS 24:20b—25:12

LESSON AIMS

After this lesson a student should be able to:

1. Describe the terrible consequences that finally came to Jerusalem because of the sins of the Jews.

2. Explain that God is a God of both mercy and wrath.

3. Pursue the way of mercy and truth.

Nov
10

KEY VERSE

But if you do not listen
I will weep in secret
because of your pride;
my eyes will weep bitterly,
overflowing with tears,
because the Lord's flock will be
taken captive.
—Jeremiah 13:17

**Lesson 11 Notes**

*The visual for lesson 11 in the visuals pack is a time line that will help students understand the chronology of events concerning Jerusalem's fall. Display it at the beginning of the session.*

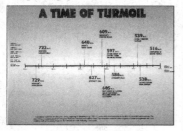

## What Do You Think?

*For Jerusalem the long-prophesied judgment finally came when the Babylonian armies laid siege to the city. Do you think this suggests judgment upon our own society is likely—a judgment other than the final judgment? Why or why not?*

*Read 2 Peter 3:3, 4. How similar do you think modern people's attitude about God's final judgment is to the Jews' attitude about the fall of Jerusalem? What can we learn from their experience?*

Babylon. In last week's lesson we read that Ezekiel built a model city in clay to foretell the end of Jerusalem. Now we are to see how that prophecy was fulfilled.

## I. DEFEAT (2 KINGS 24:20B—25:4)

We can understand why Nebuchadnezzar's patience was wearing thin when King Zedekiah rebelled against Babylonian rule. Nebuchadnezzar's army was having to march against Jerusalem for the third time. He realized that the only way to deal with this problem was to eliminate it.

### A. Rebellion (v. 20b)

**20b. Now Zedekiah rebelled against the king of Babylon.**

Zedekiah was the native king whom Nebuchadnezzar had left to rule Judah after the ten thousand captives had been removed in 597 B.C. He was an uncle of the king (Jehoiachin) who had been taken to Babylon (v. 15).

Zedekiah had been made to swear allegiance to Nebuchadnezzar (2 Chronicles 36:13), but now he *rebelled*. Perhaps it distressed him to pay the heavy tribute to Babylon year after year. He may have thought Nebuchadnezzar and his army were busy with troubles elsewhere in the empire. He may have hoped for an alliance with other small kingdoms, which would be strong enough to break off the yoke of Babylon. It is also possible that he thought that Egypt would come to help him, especially since a new, more aggressive pharaoh had recently assumed power there. Whatever his reasons were, and in spite of the warnings of Jeremiah, Zedekiah broke his oath and rebelled.

### B. Siege (vv. 1, 2)

**1. So in the ninth year of Zedekiah's reign, on the tenth day of the tenth month, Nebuchadnezzar king of Babylon marched against Jerusalem with his whole army. He encamped outside the city and built siege works all around it.**

The *ninth year of Zedekiah's reign* places the beginning of the siege around 588 B.C. Nebuchadnezzar's *whole army* was involved in this campaign. Of course, he had other troops in other parts of his empire. We are not told how many soldiers came against *Jerusalem*, but surely the number was so overwhelming that the men of Judah would not dare to meet them in open battle. The people of Judah could only take refuge behind the strong walls of Jerusalem.

The Babylonians surrounded *the city* on every side so that no one could sneak in with food for the hungry defenders or escape from the besieged city. They also *built siege works all around it*. These were assault towers manned by archers by which a besieged city was attacked. These towers were impressive and intimidating, sometimes as much as twenty stories high. In Ezekiel 4:2, which was part of last week's lesson text, Ezekiel visualized the coming siege of Jerusalem, including these siege works. Here his prophecy came to fulfillment.

**2. The city was kept under siege until the eleventh year of King Zedekiah.**

From the exact dates given in verses 1 and 3, we see that the siege continued about a year and a half.

### C. Crisis (v. 3)

**3. By the ninth day of the fourth month the famine in the city had become so severe that there was no food for the people to eat.**

Within a year and a half, the siege reached a critical stage. The *food* stored in the city was all gone. The starving people had no strength or will to resist the invaders. Inside their strong walls they were safe from Babylonian swords, but they were about to die of starvation.

## D. Attack and Flight (v. 4)

**4. Then the city wall was broken through, and the whole army fled at night through the gate between the two walls near the king's garden, though the Babylonians were surrounding the city. They fled toward the Arabah.**

Some of the starving people had already "gone over to the king of Babylon" (v. 11); that is, they had slipped out of the city and had surrendered to the Babylonians. From such defectors the Babylonians knew how terrible the famine was becoming. When they determined that the people were probably too weak to resist, they brought up a battering ram and broke into the city. It is likely that they smashed a gate on the north side, where the ground was nearly level. The other three sides of the city were protected by ravines outside the walls. Officers of the Babylonian army then came in and established their headquarters at "the Middle Gate" (Jeremiah 39:3).

Judah's *army*, the soldiers who were there to defend the city, thought resistance was useless. They tried to escape by night through the other side of the city at the southeastern corner, near which was located *the king's garden*. The king went with them (Jeremiah 39:4), likely accompanied by the other officials of Judah.

When the Babylonians, who had surrounded the city, joined in the effort to break through the walls, they left some unprotected sections through which Zedekiah and those with him could escape. The compact body of Judah's soldiers found such an opening and fled eastward, down the mountain road *toward the Arabah,* the narrow plain beside the Jordan River.

### COURAGE AND COWARDICE

The annals of warfare are filled with stories of unbelievable courage as well as unspeakable cowardice. Out of World War II came the story of the bravery of Corrie Ten Boom and her family, who risked their lives in saving countless Jews from extermination by the Nazis.

Other names live on in infamy from that terrible time. Marshal Philippe Petain was a World War I hero who disgraced his name by leading the Nazi puppet government in France. On a single day in 1942, Petain's forces arrested thirteen thousand Jews to be sent to the Nazi death camps.

Vidkun Quisling was a Norwegian politician who sympathized with Nazi principles. He returned home from Germany just three days before the Nazis invaded Norway in 1940. Quisling's aid to the German occupational forces gained him a dishonorable distinction in history: his name is now used to describe a traitor.

Judah had its cowards, too. When Babylon laid siege to Jerusalem, King Zedekiah and his soldiers found a way to escape, leaving behind those whom they should have protected. No doubt they had a good rationale; cowards usually do.

Sometimes it is difficult to determine whether an act is true bravery or mere bravado. But our tendency to look for the easy way out of difficult situations should make us wary of the temptation and cause us to honor true courage when we find it.

—C. R. B.

## II. CAPTURE (2 KINGS 25:5-7)

At the point of escape, the Babylonians were too few to stop the fugitives, but they knew which way they went. Quickly they assembled a force strong enough to go in pursuit.

## A. Pursuit (v. 5)

**5. But the Babylonian army pursued the king and overtook him in the plains of Jericho. All his soldiers were separated from him and scattered.**

---

### How to Say It

*Arabah.* AR-uh-buh.

*Babylon.* BAB-uh-lon.

*Babylonian.* Bab-uh-LOW-nee-un.

*Baroque.* Buh-ROKE.

*Ezekiel.* Ee-ZEEK-yul or Ee-ZEEK-ee-ul.

*Frauenkirche (German).* Frow-un-KEER-kih.

*Gedaliah.* GED-uh-LYE-uh (G as in get).

*Habakkuk.* Huh-BAK-kuk.

*Jehoiachin.* Jeh-HOY-uh-kin.

*Jeremiah.* JAIR-uh-MYE-uh.

*Jericho.* JAIR-ih-ko.

*Judah.* JOO-duh.

*Mediterranean.* MED-uh-te-RAY-nee-un.

*Nebuchadnezzar.* NEB-uh-kad-NEZZ-er.

*Nebuzaradan.* Neb-uh-zar-AY-dun.

*Petain (French).* Pay-TAN.

*Riblah.* RIB-luh.

*Zedekiah.* Zed-uh-KYE-uh.

Those who escaped had a head start while the pursuers were gathering their forces. The pursuers, however, were well fed; the fugitives were weak from hunger.

It was about twenty miles to *the plains of Jericho.* Possibly dawn had come by the time the men of Judah reached this territory, so they could see the Babylonians gaining on them. It is likely that the morale of the army was so low at this point that the soldiers simply deserted their king and *scattered,* with every man looking out for himself. It was easy for the Babylonians to round up the king and the other important men.

## B. JUDGMENT (v. 6)

**6. And he was captured. He was taken to the king of Babylon at Riblah, where sentence was pronounced on him.**

By this time in history, Nebuchadnezzar dominated all the countries at the east end of the Mediterranean Sea. It seems that he began the siege of Jerusalem (v. 1), then left his generals to conduct it while he made his headquarters at *Riblah,* two hundred miles to the north in what is now Syria. From there he directed the affairs of all these western territories in his empire. King Zedekiah was taken there as a prisoner, and there he was tried, judged, and condemned. Having broken his oath of allegiance to Nebuchadnezzar, he was considered a traitor.

## C. PUNISHMENT (v. 7)

**7. They killed the sons of Zedekiah before his eyes. Then they put out his eyes, bound him with bronze shackles and took him to Babylon.**

Nebuchadnezzar and his officers saw no reason to be merciful to this petty rebel who had caused them so much trouble. The punishment was severe. First, Zedekiah had to watch while his *sons* were *killed.* Jeremiah 39:6 adds that the other leading men ("nobles") of Judah were also killed. Apparently all these had been captured along with the king. Then Zedekiah's eyes were gouged out, and he was taken to Babylon in chains—a dismal journey of approximately five hundred miles.

### BEASTLY BEHAVIOR

For years, the decrepit old cannery of Monterey, California, was an eyesore to the community. Then about a decade ago, the structure was turned into a world-class marine aquarium and study center. One of the startling findings of a research team at the Monterey Bay Aquarium is that sea otters can be extremely vicious.

Most of us think of otters as charming creatures that lie on their backs on the surface of the sea and crack mussel shells on rocks they have brought up from the ocean floor. But scientists at Monterey have discovered that male otters will sometimes kill prospective mates by biting them or drowning them. Researchers have also observed male otters kidnapping otter pups, holding them for "ransom" until the mother gives up the food she has found for her offspring.

If this behavior shocks us, how much more ought such behavior by humans be repugnant! Yet we know that violence is an all-too-common phenomenon of human life also. We see this in the way Zedekiah was treated by his captors. They forced him to watch as they murdered his sons, and then humiliated him by putting out his eyes. The last sight he would remember for the rest of his days would be the violent death of his sons. Today, with increasing frequency, we see such beastly behavior in those who neither honor God nor respect his creation. —C. R. B.

## III. DESTRUCTION (2 KINGS 25:8-10)

Having thus disposed of the rebels, the Babylonians proceeded to make sure that Jerusalem would not be a place of refuge for any future troublemakers.

*WHAT DO YOU THINK?*

We may wince as we read of the punishment king Zedekiah received from the Babylonians. We might wonder why God allowed him to be treated so cruelly. But he had rejected God and God's prophets. His rebellion against Nebuchadnezzar was foolish and presumptuous, since he had ignored prophetic counsel in the matter. We might say he was already blind since he had closed his mind to God's truth. (See John 9:39-41.)

What lessons does this have for our time? Does it speak to the issue of tough sentencing for violent criminals? If so, how? Does it address our need to avoid spiritual blindness? If so, how? What other lessons can you suggest?

*OPTION*

Explore the balance between God's wrath and his mercy with the reproducible activity, "Wrath and Mercy," on page 102

## A. FIRE (vv. 8, 9)

**8. On the seventh day of the fifth month, in the nineteenth year of Nebuchadnezzar king of Babylon, Nebuzaradan commander of the imperial guard, an official of the king of Babylon, came to Jerusalem.**

This was nearly a month after the end of the siege (v. 3). Apparently the people of Judah had been living under Babylonian military government for that month. Now came a special envoy, probably from Riblah, to direct the destruction of Jerusalem.

**9. He set fire to the temple of the LORD, the royal palace and all the houses of Jerusalem. Every important building he burned down.**

Verses 13-17 tell of the valuable items that were removed from *the temple* and taken as spoil by the Babylonians. When all of this had been removed, the temple itself, which had taken seven years to build (1 Kings 6:37, 38), was torched. Such was also the fate of *the royal palace,* which had taken thirteen years to build (1 Kings 7:1), and all the other houses and *every important building* in Jerusalem.

## B. DEMOLITION (v. 10)

**10. The whole Babylonian army, under the commander of the imperial guard, broke down the walls around Jerusalem.**

When the fire had burned itself out, all the *Babylonian* soldiers had the arduous task of tearing down the massive stone walls. By such drastic measures, Nebuchadnezzar was determined to insure that the city of Jerusalem would never again pose a serious threat.

### UTTERLY DESTROYED

Dresden was once known as "the Florence of Germany," in reference to the Italian city's famous architecture. But then, on the night of February 13, 1945, Allied bombers dropped thousands of tons of incendiary bombs on Dresden in retribution for Nazi Germany's devastation of Europe. For a week the city was an inferno.

Estimates of fatalities in the bombings ranged from thirty-five thousand to two hundred thousand people. Most of the city, including the marvelous *Frauenkirche,* was utterly destroyed. This Protestant church had been one of northern Europe's finest examples of baroque architecture. For nearly fifty years, the pile of debris and a couple of standing portions of the walls were left as silent reminders of the horrors of war. Then, in 1993, city officials began rebuilding the church, hoping to have it completed by 2006, sixty-one years after it was destroyed.

Modern weapons of warfare devastated Dresden and decimated its populace, but the primitive weapons of the Babylonians destroyed Jerusalem just as completely. The temple, the palace, and all the houses were burned, and the city walls were leveled. And so they would remain until the Jews returned and possessed the means and the leadership necessary to rebuild them. The destruction of Jerusalem was God's retribution on Judah for generations of unfaithfulness. The testimony of the Bible stands as a witness of the wages of sin to all who will see.

—C. R. B.

## IV. CAPTIVITY (2 KINGS 25:11,12)

The people of Judah had lost their homes; now they were to lose their homeland as well.

## A. TAKEN TO BABYLON (v. 11)

**11. Nebuzaradan the commander of the guard carried into exile the people who remained in the city, along with the rest of the populace and those who had gone over to the king of Babylon.**

### PRAYER

Father in Heaven, King eternal, Ruler of Heaven and earth, we give you thanks for your faultless Word. In its perfect light we see and confess our sins. For these we beg forgiveness as we dedicate anew our lives to your service. May we be guided by your wisdom and strengthened by your power to do your will. Amen.

### WHAT DO YOU THINK?

Imagine the horror of exile! Psalm 137 gives us a glimpse into the hearts of these captives. We see the weeping, the desolation, the longing for home, and the bitterness toward the Babylonians that they experienced. Aside from what the Bible shows us, we know from experience how painful homesickness can be. Remembering that experience and then imagining our separation from home as a permanent, irrevocable act can aid us in understanding the exiles' suffering. If we have lost our home or valuable possessions in a disaster, we also have a hint of the exiles' desolation.

What lessons does this teach us? Many Christians have had to endure the same treatment (Hebrews 10:34). Could you? What does it take to be able to remain faithful in spite of such treatment?

How might identifying with the misery of the Jewish exiles help us communicate the warning of an eternity without God?

## Daily Bible Reading

**Monday, Nov. 4**—*The Reign of Jehoiakim (2 Kings 24:1-7)*

**Tuesday, Nov. 5**—*Second Capture of Jerusalem (2 Kings 24:8-19)*

**Wednesday, Nov. 6**—*The Destruction of the Temple (2 Kings 25:13-17)*

**Thursday, Nov. 7**—*The Leaders Taken to Babylon (2 Kings 25:18-24)*

**Friday, Nov. 8**—*King Jehoiachin Set Free (2 Kings 25:25-30)*

**Saturday, Nov. 9**—*Appeal to God for Help (Psalm 74:1-11)*

**Sunday, Nov. 10**—*God's Sovereign Power (Psalm 74:12-17)*

## What Do You Think?

*Given the experience of Israel and Judah—denying God in times of prosperity and returning to him in times of need—do you think poverty is perhaps better than wealth? Why or why not?*

*Consider Proverbs 30:8, 9; 1 Timothy 6:10; Matthew 19:23, 24.*

## What Do You Think?

*How can we effectively warn against presuming on God's mercy? How can we help people see his delay in giving us the punishment we deserve should lead us instead to repentance?*

*See Romans 2:4; 2 Peter 3:10-13.*

## Thought to Remember

*God lives; God knows; God rules.*

Now began the long, dreary march of some five hundred miles to *Babylon*. The same official who had supervised the demolition took charge of the deportation. He assembled the people who were still alive in Jerusalem after the siege, those who had gone out and surrendered during the siege, and *the rest of the populace*. This last phrase may include some people of Judah who had not been in Jerusalem during the siege, but had stayed out in the hills or down in the Jordan Valley.

### B. Left Behind (v. 12)

**12. But the commander left behind some of the poorest people of the land to work the vineyards and fields.**

The Babylonians did not want the land of Judah to be entirely uninhabited. They left some people to till the ground and to produce some revenue for Babylon. Those left behind were some of *the poorest people of the land*. Without wealth, influence, or leadership, they would not be likely to stage another rebellion. Nebuzaradan "gave them vineyards and fields" (Jeremiah 39:10), hoping that they would peacefully till their farms and pay whatever taxes they were asked to pay. A man named Gedaliah was put in charge of the remnant, with the title of governor rather than king (Jeremiah 40:7) .

### CONCLUSION

"Everything that was written in the past was written to teach us, so that through endurance and the encouragement of the Scriptures we might have hope" (Romans 15:4). So what does the history of Israel teach us?

### A. Prosperity Can Be Dangerous

With rare exceptions, the people of Israel were loyal and obedient to God when they were fighting their way into the promised land and risking their lives every day. God gave them victory. Then they became prosperous, at ease, and comfortable. Soon the more prosperous ones found that they could become even more prosperous by cheating poorer neighbors. They found pleasure in the pagan feasts of their godless neighbors. In prosperity they drifted away from God, but then their prosperity began to vanish. Crops failed, or bandits invaded the land and stole harvests and livestock. This brought poverty and misery. In their suffering the people turned to God again and begged him for help. Prosperity came back—and then they drifted away from God again.

Such was the history of Israel for some eight hundred years. What does it teach us? It teaches us to put obedience to God and helpfulness to others above our own profit and pleasure. Have we learned?

### B. Misinterpreting Mercy

God did not destroy his people as soon as they began to drift away from him. In mercy he gave them time to turn back to him in worship and obedience. But they misinterpreted his mercy. They took it as permission to keep drifting away.

How many are drifting away from God now? In mercy God delays punishment, yet drifters continue in their path.

We are warned that some will doubt Jesus' promise that he will come again. "He's not coming," they say. "We can forget about him and do as we please." But he is coming, and so is disaster to those who disobey him (2 Peter 3:3-10)

What does Israel's history teach us that pertains to this? It teaches us that God always keeps his promises. It teaches that he lives and rules. It teaches that our ultimate success depends on doing his will. Have we learned?

# Discovery Learning

*This page contains an alternate lesson plan emphasizing learning activities. Classes desiring such student involvement will find these suggestions helpful. The next page is a reproducible activity page to further enhance discovery learning.*

## LEARNING GOALS

After this lesson a student should be able to:

1. Describe the terrible consequences that came to Jerusalem because of the sins of the Jews.

2. Explain that God is a God of both mercy and wrath.

3. Pursue the way of mercy and truth.

## INTO THE LESSON

Ask the class to make a list of "Everyday Warnings": a speed limit sign, a railroad crossing flasher, or a warning light on an automobile dashboard—warning signals that anyone might hear or see in a normal week. As class members suggest ideas, write them on your chalkboard.

After you have completed as long a list as possible in a few minutes, ask the class, "What happens when each of these warnings is ignored?" If you wish, you may jot down the consequences in a column beside the first list. If you have time, you may ask members to tell what happened to them when they ignored one of the warnings.

Tell the class that today's lesson shows the terrible consequences of ignoring God's warnings.

## INTO THE WORD

Use material from the Introduction to the lesson commentary to set the historical context for today's lesson. Remind your group that last week's study looked at Ezekiel's dramatic prophecies of the fall of Jerusalem. This week's study examines the fall itself.

Prepare a handout by listing the following sentences in random order. Ask class members, in groups of two or three, to examine 2 Kings 25:1-21 and to put the sentences in order. (If your class uses *NIV® Bible Student,* you may use the activity page there for this purpose.)

(1) Nebuchadnezzar marched against Jerusalem.

(2) Nebuchadnezzar's army kept Jerusalem under siege..

(3) Famine in Jerusalem left the people with nothing to eat.

(4) The Babylonians broke the wall and entered the city.

(5) Zedekiah, king of Judah, fled Jerusalem with his army, because they decided resistance against the Babylonians was useless.

(6) Zedekiah, king of Judah, was captured by Babylonian forces in the plains of Jericho.

(7) Zedekiah watched as his own sons were killed.

(8) Zedekiah was blinded by the Babylonians, put into shackles, and taken to Babylon.

(9) A Babylonian official burned the temple, the palace, and every other important building in Jerusalem.

(10) All the walls surrounding Jerusalem were destroyed.

(11) All but the poorest residents of Jerusalem were taken into exile in Babylon.

(12) The Babylonians looted the temple, transporting valuable gold, silver, and bronze items to Babylon.

(13) The king of Babylon executed the chief priest, as well as other priests and officials from the land of Judah.

After several minutes, review the sentences with the class, making sure everyone has the order correct. Ask the class to brainstorm a list of words that describe how they feel after reading this story, or a list of words to describe this story.

*Option.* After the above activity, or instead of it, ask your group to pretend they are movie producers. They will plan an epic film called "The Fall of Jerusalem," based on 2 Kings 25:1-21. In groups of five to eight, they should decide: (1) What will we call our movie? (2) What scenes will it include? (3) What parts do we need to cast for it? (4) Who should play each of these parts? (5) What will be the film's climax? (6) What should be the background music?

Give the groups eight minutes to answer these questions and to decide anything else they wish about their movies; then discuss the ideas with the entire class. (This will help class members reflect on the bitter realities associated with this sad story of Jerusalem's fall.)

## INTO LIFE

Write these two sentences on your chalkboard: "God is a God of mercy." "God is a God of wrath." Ask the class to decide how our study this quarter, and especially this week, illustrates each of these truths. If you have time, let half of the class, in groups, discuss the first sentence while the other half discusses the second sentence. (Distribute copies of the next page for a variation on this activity.)

Let several members share their thoughts. You may want to add some of the material from the Conclusion to the lesson commentary.

Ask class members to make a list for your chalkboard under the heading, "Our Country Needs God's Mercy Because. . . ." As members suggest items, write them under the heading.

End with sentence prayers for God's mercy on our country.

# Wrath and Mercy

God is a God of Wrath. We see that in his judgment on Jerusalem. God is a God of Mercy. We see that in his keeping a remnant alive and in bringing home the exiles at the end of their period of captivity.

Look up the following Scriptures. Write a brief note next to each reference about what it teaches us concerning either God's wrath or his mercy. How are wrath and mercy exhibited? What moves God to act with wrath or to extend his mercy?

THE WRATH
OF GOD

THE MERCY
OF GOD

| | |
|---|---|
| Numbers 11:1-10 | Exodus 34:6, 7 |
| Deuteronomy 29:27 | Deuteronomy 4:31 |
| 2 Samuel 6:7 | 1 Kings 8:23 |
| Psalm 2:2-5 | 1 Chronicles 16:34 |
| Psalm 79:6 | Psalm 62:12 |
| Isaiah 5:25 | Psalm 145:8, 9 |
| Isaiah 47:6 | Micah 7:18-20 |
| Jeremiah 44:3-6 | Luke 1:50-53 |
| Romans 2:5-9 | Romans 2:4 |
| 1 Thessalonians 2:16 | Romans 11:32 |
| Hebrews 3:18, 19 | 2 Corinthians 1:3 |
| Hebrews 12:29 | Ephesians 2:4, 5 |
| 2 Peter 3:10-13 | 1 Timothy 1:13-16 |
| Revelation 6:15-17 | James 5:11 |

# A CRY OF ANGUISH

**LESSON 12**

## WHY TEACH THIS LESSON?

Human suffering. Nothing touches us more profoundly. We see pictures of starving children on the news, and we weep. Pictures of Nazi death camps with their gas chambers and mass graves send chills down our spines. Reports of abortions numbering in the millions, some by extremely cruel and painful procedures, horrify us. We might begin to wonder whether God cares about us at all.

This lesson answers in the affirmative. Its pictures of the poor and desperate remnant left in Jerusalem after everyone else was deported is as mournful as any we have seen. "Why do you always forget us? Why do you forsake us so long?" Some in your class may easily identify with the prophet's feelings. If so, be sure they hear the hope found in the next verse: "Restore us to yourself O LORD, that we may return; renew our days as of old."

## INTRODUCTION

When was the last time you studied a Sunday school lesson from Lamentations? The last time the International Lessons took a text from this book was July 13, 1980. Obviously this is not the most popular part of the Bible; but it is nonetheless a wonderful book. It is deeply emotional and filled with human sorrow, but it is also filled with trust in the Lord and brightened with gleams of hope.

### A. LAMENTATIONS

Lamentations is a collection of five sad lyric poems mourning the downfall of Judah and the destruction of Jerusalem. There are graphic pictures of horror. There is frank confession of sin. There are calls to turn from sin to God. There is a recognition of God's mercy. Occasionally, there is even bright hope of a better day.

### B. LESSON BACKGROUND

It was late in July when the Babylonian troops came to destroy Jerusalem (2 Kings 25:8, 9). It must have taken a month or two to demolish the massive walls and organize the captives for the long march to Babylon. So we may suppose it was around September when at last the poor of Judah were left alone.

While these people had been given fields and vineyards (Jeremiah 39:10), food does not spring instantly from the ground. The grapes of that year's crop had been devoured; the farmers would have to wait a year for another crop. It was time to start planting the wheat and barley, but there would be no harvest of these until May. And what would they use for seed?

If some had managed to preserve scanty amounts of silver, they could have bought both food and seed in Egypt or Mesopotamia; but that meant a long trip. A few sheep and cattle may have been hidden from the Babylonians, so perhaps there was a small supply of milk and meat. There may have been a few donkeys to bring home the seed purchased abroad, and to pull the plows. In any case, it is likely that the farmers left in Judah suffered months of hunger.

Our text includes a bit of the mournful poetry of that tragic time of poverty and desperation.

DEVOTIONAL READING
PSALM 13:1-6
LESSON SCRIPTURE
LAMENTATIONS
PRINTED TEXT
LAMENTATIONS 5:1-10, 19-22

LESSON AIMS

After this lesson a student should be able to:

1. Describe the condition of the people of Judah who were left there after Jerusalem was destroyed and explain what brought them to that sad condition.

2. Write a contemporary lamentation describing the effect of sin on our society.

3. Decide to be involved in some effort to restore our society to God's favor.

KEY VERSE

Restore us to yourself O LORD, that we may return; renew our days as of old.
Lamentations 5:21

Nov
17

*LESSON 12 NOTES*

## OPTION

*If your class usually begins with an oral reading of the Scripture text, try the choral reading activity on page 110.*

## WHAT DO YOU THINK?

*It seems presumptuous for anyone to ask God to "remember," as Jeremiah did in Lamentations 5:1. (See also Psalms 25:6; 74:2; and 119:49.) Even more so is Jeremiah's concern that God had forgotten his people (v. 20). Is this simply a weakness in Jeremiah's faith, or is it okay to be "presumptuous" in our prayers? When our prayers go unanswered and we encounter problems and look in vain for divine guidance; when from our earthly standpoint, it seems that God has forgotten us, how should we pray?*

*The practice of assigning human characteristics to God is called anthropomorphism. To what extent is it okay to assign such human qualities as forgetfulness to God, and at what point does that become blasphemous—denying the essence of God's deity?*

## I. LOSS (LAMENTATIONS 5:1-4)

### A. PLEA FOR ATTENTION (v. 1)

**1. Remember, O LORD, what has happened to us; look, and see our disgrace.**

The prophet began by asking God to *remember* the terrible disaster that had come upon the people of Judah. This does not mean that Jeremiah thought God was unaware of anything that had happened. Even in our time, when someone leads in public prayer, a critic may scoff that a person would try to give some information to God. In prayer a Christian says one of our number is seriously sick and needs a special blessing, or he notes that the roof of our meetinghouse leaks and we need funds to fix it, or he points out that one of our missionaries needs protection because of a civil war in the district where he or she serves. Such a statement is not made to inform God; it is made to introduce a subject of prayer. One who prays aloud in a meeting is not voicing his own private prayer; he is leading the group in prayer. A statement like one of those above brings the thoughts of the whole congregation together so all may join in the prayer. The opening verse of our text served the same purpose. Probably this carefully worded poem (as well as the other portions of Lamentations) was not written to be the writer's private prayer, but to be the united prayer of a group.

### B. LOSS OF HOME (v. 2)

**2. Our inheritance has been turned over to aliens, our homes to foreigners.**

The land where these people lived had been given to the tribe of Judah nearly eight hundred years earlier, when Israel had come from Egypt to the promised land. Through the centuries each family's homestead had been passed on from generation to generation. A farmer might sell his property if he was deep in debt, but every fifty years during the year of Jubilee there was a redistribution of real estate. Each tract was then restored to the original owner or his heirs, so that a family's inheritance could not be lost forever.

Now the inherited land no longer belonged to the people of Judah. It had been turned over to pagan foreigners. People of Judah were allowed to live on the land and cultivate it, but they were not the owners. They were renters or sharecroppers. The "tax man" would be around at harvest time to collect the owners' share, and the Babylonians did not intend to give the property back in the year of Jubilee.

### C. LOSS OF FAMILY (v. 3)

**3. We have become orphans and fatherless, our mothers like widows.**

Probably every person now living in Judah was bereaved. Countless people had died of starvation during the long siege. Brave men had died in feeble and futile resistance when the enemy had broken into Jerusalem. Leaders of the nation had been slaughtered after being captured. Most of the survivors had been taken to Babylon. Those who remained were stricken with grief.

### D. LOSS OF PRODUCE (v. 4)

**4. We must buy the water we drink; our wood can be had only at a price.**

When the Israelites were about to inherit the land of Canaan, God promised them prosperity if they would "carefully follow the terms of [his] covenant." Included in that prosperity would be the ease of having "aliens" (foreigners) among them who would "chop your wood and carry your water" (Deuteronomy 29:9-11). This verse presents a stark contrast to that promise. Because they had not followed the covenant, now they themselves were the "aliens," at the mercy of another people for their own wood and water.

It is not necessary to suppose that the Babylonians set up a store and sold these items over the counter. More likely the people of Judah still gathered wood from the forests and drew water from the springs and wells. They could use these products of the land, but they would pay a price assessed through some kind of taxation.

## II. ANGUISH (LAMENTATIONS 5:5-7)

"Every cloud has a silver lining," says a popular maxim; but when clouds are darkest, it is hard to see the lining. The people living in Judah had many reasons to be thankful. They were alive. They were still in their homeland. Water and firewood were available. They could plant seed and reap harvests. They could increase their flocks of sheep and herds of cattle. For a time, however, their blessings were hidden under their tremendous loss. The people were so deep in misery that they could see nothing else clearly.

### A. OVERWORK (v. 5)

**5. Those who pursue us are at our heels; we are weary and find no rest.**

The picture here is of relentless work. *At our heels* is a modern idiom that suggests being pressured, especially when combined with the term *pursue*. When the pursuers are at one's heels, the runner is desperately trying to stay ahead. But the word translated "heels" is better rendered "necks," and *pursue* might just as well be translated "drive." The people of Judah were no longer being pursued; they had been caught! The mention of "necks" suggests a yoke of hard labor. By stern necessity the people of Judah were driven to continual hard work—the way a farmer would drive a yoke of oxen. Seed for planting must be brought from far away, and quickly. Fields must be plowed and planted; that too must be done without delay. Perhaps plows must be made, along with yokes for the oxen (since the Babylonians may have used such necessities for firewood). Neglected grapevines and fruit trees must be pruned. Cattle and sheep must be taken to pasture. Perhaps every family had lost some of its members, so those who were left had to work longer hours, without the benefit of needed *rest*.

### B. SUBMISSION (v. 6).

**6. We submitted to Egypt and Assyria to get enough bread.**

Is this a confession of past sin or a statement of the conditions at hand? It could be either or both. The past sin was relying on foreign nations instead of God to deliver them in the period preceding Jerusalem's fall. The term *submitted* might literally be rendered "gave the hand." It is used in Jeremiah 50:15 ("surrenders"), describing the collapse and surrender of Babylon. Today, for someone to "come out with his hands up" would be the likely equivalent. Judah had surrendered to these nations in a vain attempt to be saved from another enemy.

As for the current situation, the people of Judah had little or no money with which to buy grain for food or seed. Perhaps they had to "give their hands" to work for the Assyrians (which could be a generic reference to any of the Mesopotamian people) and Egyptians in exchange for grain. Or perhaps the idea of surrender is still appropriate, as the people had to humble themselves before these other nations and admit their distress in order to get *bread*.

### HISTORY REPEATING ITSELF

Some twelve hundred years before the text of today's lesson was written, the ancestors of Jeremiah's audience experienced severe famine in Canaan. Jacob sent his sons to Egypt to buy grain so they would not starve. The family moved to Egypt and

HOW TO SAY IT
Assyria. Uh-SEER-ee-uh.
Babylon. BAB-uh-lon.
Babylonian. Bab-uh-
  LOW-nee-un.
Canaan. KAY-nun.
Ezekiel. Ee-ZEEK-yul or
  Ee-ZEEK-ee-ul.
Hezekiah. Hez-eh-KYE-uh.
Jehoahaz. Jeh-HOE-uh-haz.
Jehoiakim. Jeh-HOY-uh-kim.
Jeremiah. JAIR-uh-MYE-uh.
Josiah. Jo-SYE-uh.
Judah. JOO-duh.
Lamentations. Lam-un-TAY-
  shunz.
Manasseh. Muh-NASS-uh.
Mesopotamia. Mes-uh-puh-TAY-
  me-uh.

later became enslaved there. They became so accustomed to living in an idol-worshiping culture that after God miraculously delivered them from slavery, they fashioned a golden calf to worship at Sinai while Moses was on the mountain speaking with God. Their life in the promised land would turn out to be a tragic tale of continuing flirtation with idolatry.

And now, because they had forgotten God, the people of Judah were looking again to Egypt for their bread (Lamentations 5:6). Many actually migrated there, seeking a more peaceful existence, in spite of the warnings of the prophet Jeremiah (Jeremiah 42:7—43:7).

What causes us to repeat the past? George Santayana, the twentieth-century American philosopher, has said, "Those who will not learn from history are destined to repeat it."

We have much more of the past to learn from than did the people of Israel and Judah (including the inspired lessons of Scripture to instruct us). Nevertheless, "each generation has to learn for itself that the stove is hot," as someone has said. Modern idolatries of many sorts would lure us away from God, and we have our own spiritual famines with which to contend. We should hear again the lessons of the children of Israel.     —C. R. B.

### C. SIN (v. 7)

**7. Our fathers sinned and are no more, and we bear their punishment.**

Jeremiah knew that the misery of the people was caused by sin. He had urged the people to turn from their sins, but had met with only stubborn resistance. The sins of the *fathers* included those of evil king Manasseh. Years after he died, the Scripture says, Judah was destroyed for his sins (2 Kings 24:1-4). Now, in poverty, grief, and misery, the people were bearing the punishment for the sins of their fathers.

We should, however, consider our lesson for October 27. There we read that some of the captives in Babylon were saying they were innocent, but were suffering for the sins of former generations. Ezekiel set them straight in no uncertain terms. They were not suffering because their fathers had sinned, but because they themselves had continued in the sins of their fathers (Ezekiel 18).

This was equally true of the people of Judah who were left in their homeland. They were in poverty and misery, not because their fathers had sinned, but because of their own sins. Jeremiah stated this in no uncertain terms: "The crown has fallen from our head. Woe to us, for we have sinned!" (Lamentations 5:16).

At the same time, the tragic consequences of the destruction of Jerusalem and the collapse of the nation were being felt particularly by those who remained in the land. Certainly they were suffering the effects of the nation's sins in a way their fathers had not.

### III. MISERY (LAMENTATIONS 5:8-10)

After acknowledging that the misery of his people was due to sin, Jeremiah went on to describe some other aspects of that misery.

### A. HELPLESSNESS (v. 8)

**8. Slaves rule over us, and there is none to free us from their hands.**

God's people should have been masters of the pagans, not their servants. They should have dominated the ungodly nations as they had done in the days of David and Solomon. But their sins had caused them to lose their high standing. They had no power to resist the Babylonians, and no other nation was able and willing to help them. In bygone times God had delivered them from all enemies, but now he had delivered them to the Babylonians.

## B. DANGER (v . 9 )

**9. We get our bread at the risk of our lives because of the sword in the desert.**

*The sword in the desert* may refer to the sword of nomad tribes living in the desert. People going to Assyria or Egypt to get food were in danger of being killed and robbed by such bandits. Another danger was that such tribes would invade Judah to steal food left by the Babylonians, brought from abroad, or produced in Judah. The men in Judah were few in number, and surely the Babylonians had not left them well armed.

## C. HUNGER (v. 10)

**10. Our skin is hot as an oven, feverish from hunger.**

This may look back to the terrible famine during the siege of Jerusalem, or perhaps it describes some of the people who were starving in the aftermath of the siege. Verses 11-18 continue to portray the dark cloud of anguish over the people left in Judah. The last part of our text, which is also the conclusion of the book of Lamentations, offers a glimpse of the silver lining.

## IV. HOPE (LAMENTATIONS 5:19-22)

The lament we have been reading provides the background for the main points of the prayer. They are two: a declaration of steadfast faith, and a plea for restoration.

## A. STATEMENT OF FAITH (v. 19)

**19. You, O LORD, reign forever; your throne endures from generation to generation.**

Even though the temple, which had symbolized God's presence, was demolished, God still lived and ruled. He would continue to do so forever. He had brought affliction to his people because they had not acted as his people ought to act. For centuries they had chosen to do wrong rather than right, and now they were paying the price for their choice.

But hope was not dead. God had brought anguish to unrepentant sinners; he could bring restoration if they would repent. He still had power to bless his righteous people. Such was Jeremiah's faith, and such was his message of encouragement for his countrymen.

## B. PLEA FOR RESTORATION (vv. 20, 21)

**20. Why do you always forget us? Why do you forsake us so long?**

In view of God's unchanging sovereignty, recognized in verse 19, Jeremiah then expressed his continued anguish at the condition of his people. In the midst of trying circumstances, the question is often raised, "If God is in control, why are we suffering as we are?" Jeremiah pleaded that God in mercy put an end to the *long* time of the people's affliction. Such an anguished cry also appears in Psalms 10:1; 13:1, 2; 22:1; 74:1; 88:14.

**21. Restore us to yourself O LORD, that we may return; renew our days as of old.**

Now came the main plea of the prayer. Jeremiah was asking the Lord to bring back the "good old days"—the days of peace, prosperity, and blessing that his people had enjoyed when they had been loyal to him and his Law. Obviously there could be no such restoration unless the people who had turned away from God would turn back to him. Here the writer prayed that the Lord himself would do this. But these people had a will of their own. They had turned away from God by their own will, not his. How could the Lord turn them back? There are two possible answers.

*Restore us to yourself, O Lord.*

*Visual 12 of the visuals packet illustrates the anguish of one who would pray the prayer of verse 21. The Lord is still the source of renewal even as he was for the remnant left in Judah.*

## WHAT DO YOU THINK?

*The lesson writer points out that Jeremiah's preaching was designed in part to turn people back to God. How can the preaching of the Word accomplish that in our time?*

*Some preachers are very entertaining, and their sermons are full of humor. How can such preaching help turn people to the Lord? Others are stern and denouncing, calling for repentance with virtually every breath. Is this better? Why or why not?*

*Some preachers are very scholarly; their sermons are logical and full of information. Others are very emotional—intense and moving. Which, if either, do you prefer and why? Which do you think is more likely to turn people to the Lord? Why?*

## WHAT DO YOU THINK?

*To be rejected by God—surely there is no prospect more frightening than that. God has shown us in many places in the Scripture that he will reject those who reject him and his Son. (See Hosea 4:6.) Many people do not have that kind of picture of God. They are aware of his love, but they have no concept of his holiness; they know God is merciful, but they give no thought to his judgment. These same people think of themselves as decent, honest individuals worthy of a place in Heaven.*

*How can we communicate the idea of God's rejection of sinners in a way that will enhance our evangelistic efforts? How can we convince people that only by grace can they be saved—and that without grace their only prospect is rejection?*

## PRAYER

*How good you are, our Father! How deeply you have loved us, how mercifully you have called us, and how greatly you have blessed us! "We all like sheep have gone astray," but the Savior has paid the debt of sin for us all. Forgive our repeated straying, we pray, and strengthen our resolve to stray no more. Amen.*

## THOUGHT TO REMEMBER

*Restore us to yourself, O Lord.*

First, he could turn them by means of the inspired preaching of Jeremiah. Jeremiah would point out their continuing sin. He would remind them that it was the cause of their present agony. He would tell them that God was eager to bless them with peace and joy, but must wait for them to trust and obey.

Second, if such pleading would not turn the people back to God, he could allow the present agony to continue until their stubborn spirit would be broken and they would turn to God for relief. He is praying for the same thing Paul promises in Romans 8:28, for God to work for the good of his chosen people even through the trial of bad times.

### C. THE LAST WORD (v. 22)

**22. . . . unless you have utterly rejected us and are angry with us beyond measure.**

God *utterly rejected* most of humanity in the days of Noah. He utterly rejected the sinners of Sodom in the days of Abraham. He utterly rejected the depraved tribes of Canaan and sent Israel to wipe them out. Jeremiah recognizes the possibility of God's acting in such a way. Certainly God had no obligation to the people of Judah who were suffering as they were. He would be entirely within his rights if he would utterly reject them and leave them to die in their sorrow. And if they continued to be unrepentant and ignored the prophetic warnings as the residents of Jerusalem before the fall had done, utter rejection is precisely what they could expect.

But the man of God dared to pray that it would not be so. He prayed that the people of Judah would indeed be turned back to God and would be restored to the former days of peace and joy. There was a silver lining. There was hope. There could be restoration.

### CONCLUSION

Though they were deeply saddened, the people of Judah were still blessed. God was taking vigorous action to turn them back to him. Once he had blessed them with prosperity and comfort, and they had turned away from him. Now he had taken away their prosperity and comfort, so that they would see their need for him and come back to him. If they utterly refused to return, they would be utterly rejected. The choice was theirs.

### A. BACK TO THE LORD!

The people of Judah are typical of all mankind. In paradise Adam and Eve turned away from God, and paradise was lost. The rest of us have followed their example. Blessed with sunshine and rain, with a fruitful earth and a loving God, "all have sinned, and come short of the glory of God" (Romans 3:23). Some have seen their mistakes and turned back quickly; others have waited for affliction to prod them. In prison, in sickness, in poverty, or in grief, they have seen their need and have turned back to the loving Father—and have given thanks for the agony that turned them back.

### B. A GREATER BLESSING

The people of Judah were blessed to have been prodded by anguish, but now we have a greater blessing. We are called by the glad gospel of salvation. We are informed that God sent his only begotten Son to redeem us. We know that Jesus died in our place, paid the penalty for our sin, and opened wide the way for us to turn back to God. We can walk through all our days on earth with our Father's unseen presence beside us, and we can know that we will see his face forever in Heaven. The choice is ours. Why will anyone choose to be utterly rejected?

# Discovery Learning

*This page contains an alternate lesson plan emphasizing learning activities. Classes*
*desiring such student involvement will find these suggestions helpful. The next page*
*is a reproducible activity page to further enhance discovery learning.*

## LEARNING GOALS

After this lesson a student should be able to:

1. Describe the condition of the people of Judah who were left there after Jerusalem was destroyed and explain what brought them to that sad condition.

2. Write a contemporary lamentation describing the effect of sin on our society.

3. Decide to be involved in some effort to restore our society to God's favor.

## INTO THE LESSON

Choose one of the following activities to get a discussion started in this session. (Each activity is meant to be completed by a group of between four and six.) If you prefer, suggest all the options to your class and let groups choose the activity they want to do.

*Acrostic.* Students should write the word *sorry* vertically down a sheet of paper. Then for each letter in the word, they should write a word they associate with *sorry.*

*Newspaper search.* Give a stack of newspapers to the class and ask members to find examples of situations where people were sorry for their sin. When they are ready to report, ask them if they found instances where people were not sorry for their sin.

*Sentence writing.* Put these words on the chalkboard: SIN, SORRY, PUNISHMENT. Students are to write sentences that contain at least two of the words. Each small group should produce at least four sentences, and each of these words should be used in at least one of the sentences.

After any or all of these activities, discuss the following questions with your group: "What is the attitude toward sin in our society? Does sin always lead to sorrow? Give examples to support your answer. How would our society change if more people were more sorry about sin?"

Tell the class that today's lesson looks at the situation in Judah after the fall of Jerusalem. Our text shows a society devastated by the results of its sinfulness. Could such a document be written by anyone in our day?

## INTO THE WORD

Begin with a bit of background about the book of Lamentations itself (see Lesson Background, page 103). Read all of Lamentations 5 aloud. Because of its poetic nature, this text lends itself to some sort of "creative" reading. You could read it responsively (alternate reading the verses between the men, the women, and yourself).

Or prepare a choral reading before class. Photocopy the Scripture and mark phrases for different readers, following the thought patterns of the text instead of just the verse divisions. (See the next page for a suggestion.)

Next, ask class members to analyze the text. Have them categorize the punishments of the people under these headings: Emotional Suffering; Physical Suffering. Have them work in pairs for several minutes before you discuss as a class.

If you have time, ask students to answer individually the following questions, all based on Lamentations 5:

1 What is the saddest verse in this chapter?

2. What is the most serious punishment the people are suffering?

3. What is the climax of the chapter?

4. What is hopeful about the chapter?

5. What verse most reminds you of a modern situation?

After a few minutes, let several class members share their answers to each question. Discuss with the class: "Who suffered in Jerusalem (see verses 11-18)? Who was responsible for the suffering of the Jews? How can we reconcile verse 7 with verse 16? Why is the confession of verse 16 important?"

Ask the class to decide how this chapter would be different if it were not for verses 19-22.

## INTO LIFE

Lamentations 5 contains the anguished cries of Jeremiah in behalf of the people of Judah suffering for their sin. Ask the class: "Are people in our society suffering because of their sin? Suppose we were to compile a 'lamentation' for a contemporary sufferer in our society. How would it read? What would it contain?"

Ask the class to work in groups of four to six to compile some "lamentations." After they have listed ways in which people today suffer because of their sin, perhaps they will have time to write a more poetic version, in the style of Lamentations 5.

Ask each group to read its "lamentation." Observe that Jeremiah's role was to call the people to repentance (v. 21). Ask, "What can we do together, to call our society to return to God and be renewed?"

Close your class session with prayers concerning the sinfulness of our society. Prayers should both express repentance for society's sins and vow to take steps to make our society more holy.

# Choral Reading

Use the following in a group to perform a choral reading of Lamentations 5.

**LEADER**
[1]Remember, O LORD, what has happened to
 us;
  look, and see our disgrace.

**MEN**
[2]Our inheritance has been turned over to
 aliens,
  our homes to foreigners.
[3]We have become orphans and fatherless,
  our mothers like widows.

**WOMEN**
[4]We must buy the water we drink;
  our wood can be had only at a price.
[5]Those who pursue us are at our heels;
  we are weary and find no rest.

**LEADER**
[6]We submitted to Egypt and Assyria
  to get enough bread.

**MEN**
[7]Our fathers sinned and are no more,
  and we bear their punishment.
[8]Slaves rule over us,
  and there is none to free us from their
   hands.

**WOMEN**
[9]We get our bread at the risk of our lives
  because of the sword in the desert.
[10]Our skin is hot as an oven,
  feverish from hunger.

**MEN**
[11]Women have been ravished in Zion,
  and virgins in the towns of Judah.

**WOMEN**
[12]Princes have been hung up by their hands;
  elders are shown no respect.

**MEN**
[13]Young men toil at the millstones;
  boys stagger under loads of wood.

**WOMEN**
[14]The elders are gone from the city gate;
  the young men have stopped their music.

**MEN**
[15]Joy is gone from our hearts;
  our dancing has turned to mourning.
[16]The crown has fallen from our head.
  Woe to us, for we have sinned!

**WOMEN**
[17]Because of this our hearts are faint,
  because of these things our eyes grow
   dim
[18]for Mount Zion, which lies desolate,
  with jackals prowling over it.

**LEADER**
[19]You, O LORD, reign forever;
  your throne endures from generation to
   generation.
[20]Why do you always forget us?
  Why do you forsake us so long?

**ALL**
[21]Restore us to yourself, O LORD, that we may
  return;
  renew our days as of old
[22]unless you have utterly rejected us
  and are angry with us beyond measure.

# GOD'S POWER TO RESTORE

**LESSON 13**

## WHY TEACH THIS LESSON?

Probably no one will deny that we live in trying times. Some of your class members may be getting pessimistic about the church's influence in society. Others may be facing severe trial in their personal lives. For one reason or another, any number of your students may find their hope waning. This lesson reminds us that "with God all things are possible" (Matthew 19:26). No matter how desperate the situation for you, your church, or any of your students, the God who made dry bones come to life can bring new life today.

## INTRODUCTION

The Old Testament gives us accurate records of important events, but sometimes it is hard to learn exactly when those events happened. The following dates help provide an outline of the time we have been studying. The dates printed in bold-face type are those that apply to our lessons for the past three months.

*1407 B.C.* The people of Israel arrived in the promised land after forty years of nomadic life in the desert. The Lord guaranteed peace and prosperity if they would obey his law, but their frequent disobedience brought punishment instead. Finally they decided they needed a king. The Lord consented, though he warned that a king would not solve their problems (1 Samuel 8:10-22).

*1051 B.C.* Saul became Israel's first king. He was followed by David, then Solomon, and Israel built a magnificent empire. While David was a man after God's heart (Acts 13:22), Solomon eventually strayed from the Lord. God promised him that the kingdom would be divided. The reigns of these three kings are covered in 1 Samuel 10:1—1 Kings 11:43.

*931 B.C.* After Solomon died, Israel was split into two kingdoms (1 Kings 12:1-17). The northern part was still called Israel; the southern part was called Judah. Most of the nation's power was lost, and so was much of its devotion to the Lord.

**722 B.C.** The Assyrians conquered northern Israel and scattered most of its people in foreign countries (2 Kings 17:1-6).

**605 B.C.** Nebuchadnezzar of Babylon conquered Judah and took a few captives to Babylon (Daniel 1:1-7). The rest of the people were left in Judah with a native king (Jehoiakim) to rule them and pay tribute to Babylon (2 Kings 24:1-7).

**597 B.C.** Judah rebelled and stopped paying tribute. Nebuchadnezzar's army returned and took king Jehoiachin and ten thousand captives to Babylon. Another native king (Zedekiah) was left to resume paying tribute (2 Kings 24:8-17).

**586 B.C.** After Judah rebelled again, the Babylonians destroyed Jerusalem and took most of the survivors to Babylon (2 Kings 24:18—25:12).

*538 B.C.* An alliance of Medes and Persians conquered the Babylonian empire (Daniel 5:28-31). The captives were liberated (Ezra 1:1-4), and about 50,000 of them went home to rebuild Jerusalem and the temple (Ezra 1:5-8; 2:64, 65).

## A. QUICK REVIEW

In September our lessons focused on efforts by both kings and prophets to stem the rising tide of evil in Judah. Two great kings (Hezekiah and Josiah) led Judah in

---

**DEVOTIONAL READING**
HOSEA 14:1-9

**LESSON SCRIPTURE**
EZEKIEL 37

**PRINTED TEXT**
EZEKIEL 37:1-14

**LESSON AIMS**

After this lesson a student should be able to:

1. Describe Ezekiel's vision of dry bones and tell the meaning of it.

2. Compare Israel's need for restoration with his or her own situation.

3. Pray that God will give new spiritual vitality to his or her life or ministry.

**OPTION**

Use the visual for lesson 11 (see page 96) to assist you in reviewing this chronology.

**KEY VERSE**

I will put my Spirit in you and you will live, and I will settle you in your own land. Then you will know that I the Lord have spoken, and I have done it, declares the Lord.                Ezekiel 37:14

## LESSON 13 NOTES

### HOW TO SAY IT

*Assyrians. Uh-SEER-ee-unz.*
*Edom. EE-dum.*
*Ezekiel. Ee-ZEEK-yul or*
   *Ee-ZEEK-ee-ul.*
*Ezra. EZ-ruh.*
*Habakkuk. Huh-BAK-kuk.*
*Hananiah. Han-uh-NYE-uh.*
*Hezekiah. Hez-eh-KYE-uh.*
*Jehoiachin. Jeh-HOY-uh-kin.*
*Jehoiakim. Jeh-HOY-uh-kim.*
*Jeremiah. JAIR-uh-MYE-uh.*
*Josiah. Jo-SYE-uh.*
*Judah. JOO-duh.*
*Medes. Meeds.*
*Nebuchadnezzar. NEB-uh-kad-*
   *NEZZ-er.*
*Persians. PUR-zhunz.*
*Zedekiah. Zed-uh-KYE-uh.*

### WHAT DO YOU THINK?

*At first glance it may seem to us that Ezekiel was evasive. We may feel he should at least have expressed his opinion. Instead we have here a demonstration of the man's humility and teachableness. It is wise for us to admit that we are still ignorant about God and His Word, and that we have a great deal yet to learn.*

*When should we speak up and give an opinion, and when should we say, "Only God knows"? What happens when we try to speak authoritatively about questions to which God alone has the answer? What happens when we don't say enough about questions to which God has given us the answer?*

doing right; but when these monarchs died, their successors quickly turned to evil, and the people followed. Jeremiah gave warning to the nation, but the nation did not repent. Habakkuk revealed that while Judah was to be destroyed, its punisher (the Babylonians) would also be destroyed. God was still in control.

The October lessons showed Jeremiah faithfully continuing to preach God's message, in spite of opposition. Ezekiel was called to serve as God's spokesman to those already exiled.

Thus far in November, the lessons have told how Ezekiel used a clay model to foretell the siege of Jerusalem. We have seen that Jerusalem was captured and destroyed, and we have read from Jeremiah's poetic cry of anguish in Lamentations. Now the closing lesson of the series tells of "God's Power to Restore."

### B. LESSON BACKGROUND

Ezekiel 33:21 records how news came to Ezekiel that Jerusalem had been destroyed. Chapter 34 blames this disaster on the "shepherds" (leaders) of Israel, but it adds that the Lord would still care for his sheep. Chapter 35 proclaims woe upon a long-time enemy of Israel (Edom); then chapter 36 declares that Israel will be restored. Our text illustrates this restoration with a dramatic vision.

## I. VALLEY OF DRY BONES (EZEKIEL 37:1-6)

Instructed by the Lord, Ezekiel sometimes used visual aids in his teaching. We saw some examples in an earlier lesson (November 3). In similar fashion, the Lord sometimes used visions to give his messages to Ezekiel. Chapter 1 records an impressive vision to emphasize the Lord's glory. Chapters 8-11 tell of a series of visions concerning the temple and the abuses going on there. Now we come to a dramatic vision illustrating the restoration of Israel and Judah after their captivity.

### A. VISION (vv. 1, 2)

**1. The hand of the LORD was upon me, and he brought me out by the Spirit of the LORD and set me in the middle of a valley; it was full of bones.**

*The hand of the Lord* seems to mean the power of the Lord, which took possession of Ezekiel to give him a message. The phrase is also used in Ezekiel 1:3; 3:22; 8:1; and 40:1. Each time it introduces a visionary experience.

*The Spirit of the Lord* was also involved in this. Several times in Ezekiel, the Spirit "raised," "lifted," "took," or "brought" Ezekiel to another place (2:2; 3:12, 14, 24; 8:3; 11:1, 24; 43:5). In our text Ezekiel was *brought* to *a valley* that *was full of bones.* Perhaps this was the same location where Ezekiel had earlier seen a vision (3:22, 23), although there the word used is translated "plain." The Hebrew word, however, is the same as the one here rendered "valley."

**2. He led me back and forth among them, and I saw a great many bones on the floor of the valley, bones that were very dry.**

The Lord, by his hand and Spirit, *led* Ezekiel about the *valley* so he could inspect the bones thoroughly. Two facts were notable: there were a *great many bones,* and they were *very dry.* It was as if a tremendous battle had been fought in the valley long before, as if countless thousands of men had been slain (v. 9). It appeared that the bodies had not been buried, but left until lions, jackals, and vultures had stripped all the flesh from the bones. The bones had then been dried and bleached by the sun.

### B. QUESTION (v. 3)

**3. He asked me, "Son of man, can these bones live?" I said, "O Sovereign LORD, you alone know."**

An ordinary *son of man*, an ordinary human being, might have answered quickly, "Of course not!" But God's prophet knew that God's power was unlimited. He would not try to answer the question that God alone could answer.

## C. ANSWER (vv. 4-6)

**4. Then he said to me, "Prophesy to these bones and say to them, 'Dry bones, hear the word of the LORD!**

The prophet was to speak to the bones as if they could hear. He was to give them the *word of the Lord,* just as he had been giving it to his fellow captives in Babylon.

**5. "'This is what the Sovereign LORD says to these bones: I will make breath enter you, and you will come to life.**

This answered the question that the Lord had raised in verse 3. Although receiving the *breath* of life would be the final step in the process of restoring the bones (v. 10), it was probably mentioned here to emphasize God's primary intention.

**6. "'I will attach tendons to you and make flesh come upon you and cover you with skin; I will put breath in you, and you will come to life. Then you will know that I am the LORD.'"**

The bones would live, but not as bare bones or skeletons. God would provide them with the ligaments that hold bone to bone and the *tendons* that attach bone to muscle. He would provide *flesh.* Here this term refers to the muscles and various internal organs of the human body. God would then supply *skin* to cover the assembled bodies. To these completed bodies he would give *breath,* and they would become alive. Their restoration to *life* would prove to them and everyone else that the one who restored them was *the Lord,* Jehovah, the one true and living God, and the creator and giver of life.

### HOPE FOR LIFE

Colma, California, is the town that has been called "more dead than alive." The city got this unusual claim to fame in 1937, when San Francisco found itself running out of building room and moved all its cemeteries to Colma.

This little town, ten miles south of San Francisco, has no schools, churches, or grocery stores, but it has more than a dozen cemeteries (including Pet's Rest, a pet cemetery with its own "nondenominational" chapel!). The cemeteries cover eighty percent of the two square miles of land within the town limits. The 1,100 living residents are outnumbered by some two to three million deceased ones. The official tongue-in-cheek slogan for the town is, "It's great to be alive in Colma."

It may be great to be alive in Colma, but that is no consolation for the millions who lie buried there. No slogan, however catchy, can bring them back to life.

When God showed Ezekiel the valley of dry bones, he said to the prophet, "Can these bones live? . . . Prophesy to these bones and say to them, 'Dry bones, hear the word of the LORD! . . . You will come to life. Then you will know that I am the Lord'" (Ezekiel 37:3, 4, 6).

To a world that is dead in its sin the message is still the same: "Hear the word of the Lord, and live!" Today we do not have to receive in a vision to know that God can raise the dead; God has spoken to us through the risen Christ, confirming our faith and giving hope to the world.        —C. R. B.

## II. LIFE FOR DRY BONES (EZEKIEL 37:7-10)

At this point, the dry bones had no ears and no minds, but Ezekiel was to speak to them as if they could hear and understand. That seemed absurd, but Ezekiel trusted God and spoke the message God gave him.

### WHAT DO YOU THINK?

God could have simply told Ezekiel to watch as he assembled the dry bones into living bodies. Instead, Ezekiel was told to prophesy to the bones to initiate the process. Why do you suppose Ezekiel was to play a part in this, even though God was obviously the cause of bringing the bones to life?

In the book of Acts, divine intervention is clear in the conversion of the Ethiopian Eunuch (chapter 8), Saul of Tarsus (chapter 9), and Cornelius (chapter 10). Yet in each case God used a human messenger to deliver the message and provide baptism. How is this similar to Ezekiel's role in the valley of dry bones? What does it suggest about our role in the work of the Lord?

## A. BODIES FOR THE BONES (vv. 7, 8)

**7. So I prophesied as I was commanded. And as I was prophesying, there was a noise, a rattling sound, and the bones came together, bone to bone.**

The prophet's word brought quick results. Even before he finished his message, the bones were in motion.

From our text, it appears that the *noise* and the *rattling sound* were one and the same. While that is certainly a possible understanding, the Hebrew is not quite so clear. The noise and the rattling (literally, "shaking") may have been two separate phenomena. The noise may have been a dramatic sound like a great clap of thunder or the loud blast of a trumpet. Some think a "voice" (also a valid translation instead of "noise") may have shouted something like, "Bones, get up!" Others suppose there was only the sound of bones moving on the ground and clicking against each other as each bone found those that must be joined to it to form a skeleton.

The shaking, if it were not the rattling of the bones coming together, is not easy to define. Some students think this was an earthquake; others think it was merely the multitude of bones shaking themselves free from the earth and moving to find and join other bones.

The translation here in the *New International Version* is probably as good an explanation as any. But whatever the noise sounded like, and whatever the shaking looked or sounded like, the bones came together. Each one joined a neighbor so that complete skeletons were formed.

**8. I looked, and tendons and flesh appeared on them and skin covered them, but there was no breath in them.**

Perhaps what Ezekiel witnessed was like watching a movie with impressive special effects. Ligaments fastened the bones together, and muscles appeared on them along with all the necessary glands and organs of human bodies. Then skin appeared on the bodies. We wonder whether the bodies were clothed, but we are not told. Clothed or naked, they were like corpses, breathless bodies lying on the ground.

## B. LIFE FOR THE BODIES (vv. 9, 10)

**9. Then he said to me, "Prophesy to the breath; prophesy, son of man, and say to it, 'This is what the Sovereign LORD says: Come from the four winds, O breath, and breathe into these slain, that they may live.'"**

Translators have difficulty with this verse because the same Hebrew word can mean either *wind, breath,* or *spirit*. If we translate "Prophesy unto the wind," as in the *King James Version*, then it is proper to translate, "Come from the four winds, O wind, and blow upon these slain." Another possible translation is, "Prophesy unto the Spirit" and "Come from the four winds, O Spirit, and breathe upon these slain."

With any of these translations, including the one followed here in our *New International Version* text, the intent of the order is clear. The spirit or *breath* of life was to enter the lungs of the lifeless bodies; they were to become alive and start breathing. The breath, wind, or spirit was to *come from the four winds*, or from all directions. This suggests that there was to be an abundant supply of it, enough for all the uncounted thousands of bodies in the valley.

**10. So I prophesied as he commanded me, and breath entered them; they came to life and stood up on their feet—a vast army.**

God's order given through his prophet was obeyed promptly. The *breath* or spirit of life came into the lifeless bodies, and the valley of dry bones was filled with living human beings standing upright.

*WHAT DO YOU THINK?*

The lesson writer points out, "Sometimes a visual aid is so captivating that the watchers lose sight of the truth it teaches." Can you remember some story told in a sermon but not the point the story was supposed to illustrate? How can we make sure we get the point? What responsibility does this suggest for teachers and preachers? What responsibility does it suggest for learners and hearers? (Consider Luke 8:18; Matthew 13:11-15.)


*WHAT DO YOU THINK?*

Some churches or individual members may identify with the exiled Israelites' feelings of being dead and dried up. What should leaders do when members of the church complain that the congregation is dead?

How might leaders determine whether the complaint is legitimate? In other words, how does one know whether the church or the one complaining has a problem? What might cause a member to think wrongly that the church is "dead"? What might be the cause if there really is a problem? What are some possible solutions?

## III. MEANING (EZEKIEL 37:11-14)

Sometimes a visual aid is so captivating that the watchers lose sight of the truth it teaches. Even a story told to illustrate a point may so fascinate the hearers that they forget the point it illustrates. So the Lord promptly and clearly explained the meaning of the dramatic vision of dry bones that came to life.

### A. DRY BONES REPRESENT PEOPLE (v. 11)

**11. Then he said to me: "Son of man, these bones are the whole house of Israel. They say, 'Our bones are dried up and our hope is gone; we are cut off.'**

The dead and dried bones represented *the whole house of Israel*. This included the people of Judah who recently had been taken to Babylon, the ten thousand who had been taken with Ezekiel a few years earlier, and the people of northern Israel who had been scattered among foreign lands for more than a century. At this point in history, both parts of the divided nation had been destroyed and scattered; but they would be restored to life and be united again (vv. 15-23).

As individuals, the captives in Babylon were living and active, but as a nation they were as dead as bare bones bleached by time. They realized this and expressed their desperation through the statement quoted in the last half of this verse. The expression *cut off* is more literally rendered "cut off to ourselves." The captives in Babylon still had one another, but the holy temple and the holy city no longer existed. The people were separated from their homeland by some five hundred miles of desert. They also felt themselves separated from the holy God, and they thought the separation was permanent—as permanent as it would be if they were dead and buried.

### B. PEOPLE TO BE RESTORED (v. 12)

**12. "Therefore prophesy and say to them: 'This is what the Sovereign LORD says: O my people, I am going to open your graves and bring you up from them; I will bring you back to the land of Israel.**

To the captives, Babylon was their grave. They could no more escape than a dead man could dig his way out of the ground. But the Lord knew better. As usual, the word LORD (written with small capitals) represents the Hebrew word that has come into English as "Jehovah." It means the One who is, the only God who really exists, the One who always has lived and always will live. He was the One who promised to break the grip of Babylon, set his people free, and bring them again into the land of Israel.

### C. KNOWLEDGE TO BE RESTORED (vv. 13, 14)

**13. "'Then you, my people, will know that I am the LORD, when I open your graves and bring you up from them.**

After a time *the Lord* was going to rescue his people from their captivity and take them back to their homeland. Then they would realize who he was—the only true God, who can foretell the future and do wonders.

**14. "'I will put my Spirit in you and you will live, and I will settle you in your own land. Then you will know that I the LORD have spoken, and I have done it, declares the LORD.'"**

Again we see the Hebrew word that can mean either spirit or breath. By his *Spirit* or by his breath, Jehovah was going to restore life to the dead nation of Israel. Israel again would possess the ancient homeland.

The history of later centuries shows that the Israelites learned well from their captivity. They learned who their God was, and they were far less prone to the worship of idols. They fell into sins of other kinds; for example, some of them married

*The visual for lesson 13 in the visuals packet tries to capture the joy of having experienced restoration in the Lord.*

*I will put my Spirit in you and you will live.*

### DAILY BIBLE READING

**Monday, Nov. 18**—*Israel and Judah Reunited (Ezekiel 37:15-22)*

**Tuesday, Nov. 19**—*They Will Worship One God (Ezekiel 37:23-28)*

**Wednesday, Nov. 20**—*Israel Delivered From Captivity (Zechariah 9:11-17)*

**Thursday, Nov. 21**—*Restoration of Davidic Kingdom (Amos 9:11-15)*

**Friday, Nov. 22**—*God Redeems His People (Zechariah 10:1-12)*

**Saturday, Nov. 23**—*God Comforts His People (Isaiah 49:8-15)*

**Sunday, Nov. 24**—*Sing Praise to the Righteous Lord (Psalm 98)*

## PRAYER

*Father in Heaven, by marvelous grace you have saved us from the greatest of all troubles, the torment of Hell. Help us then to find joy in the lesser troubles that come our way, and by them to grow into what you want us to be. Give us also clear sight to see and eliminate those things in our lives that need your forgiveness; and until they are eliminated, continue to forgive them in Jesus' name. Amen.*

## WHAT DO YOU THINK?

*How often do we hear someone say when caught in an error, "It was my own fault"? People almost always find something else or someone else to blame. But on certain rare occasions an individual faces up to his responsibility. What good can come to an individual who admits his or her responsibility? What good can come to others as a result of such an admission?*

*What are some of the bad results when one refuses to admit responsibility?*

*Are there people who admit to fault when they are innocent? If so, with what result? How can we determine when to admit blame and when it is justifiable to shun it?*

## THOUGHT TO REMEMBER

*Find your own fault first.*

pagan women (Malachi 2:11), some of them mistreated their wives (Malachi 2:14), and some of them robbed God by withholding the tithes and offerings required by the Law (Malachi 3:8-10). But they did not fall into idolatry as they had done before the captivity. They knew who their God was, but they faltered in obeying him. Don't we all? All the people of the world, ancient and modern, need the Savior.

### BRINGING THE DEAD TO LIFE

No one knows what killed the dinosaurs. The fossil remains of these great creatures seem to indicate that at some point in the distant past, they disappeared within a very short period of time. In recent years, scientists have speculated that the dinosaurs died either when many volcanoes erupted within a short span of time or when a giant meteorite crashed into the earth.

However it happened, just a few years ago Hollywood found a way to capitalize on the popular interest in dinosaurs. *Jurassic Park* was a Tyrannosaurus-size hit movie. The premise of the film was that scientists had discovered a way to extract the genetic stuff of dinosaur DNA trapped in the dinosaur blood they had found in the remains of prehistoric mosquitoes. From this DNA, scientists recreated several races of dinosaurs in frightening form. With the help of some amazingly realistic computerized special effects, the filmmakers created an exciting film, even though the premise was farfetched.

The message of Ezekiel was that God would restore to life the "dead bones" of Israel—a nation whose faith had long been dead. God *still* has that power: he needs no cinematic sleight of hand to bring the dead to life. His Spirit is a life-giving power that can revive the souls of all who, in faith, place themselves in the hands of their Creator and Redeemer.

—C. R. B.

## CONCLUSION

### A. OUR OWN FAULT

When the ten thousand captives were taken to Babylon along with Ezekiel, they were quick to say, "It's not our fault" (see the lesson for October 27). They claimed they were suffering unfairly for the sins of their ancestors. Only when disaster was complete, only when Judah had fallen, and only when hope was gone were they ready to acknowledge the bitter truth: "It's our own fault."

How quickly we all blame someone else when something goes wrong! How hard it is to say, "It's my own fault"! But one vital step toward better times is to see our own mistakes and correct them.

### B. LOOK AT RESULTS

Some of our troubles are not our own fault. A crippling accident may be entirely the fault of someone else. Sickness comes to good people as well as to bad. A hurricane or a drought afflicts the innocent as well as the guilty.

It then becomes important to think about results. For example, read the story of the blind man in John 9. This man was blind from birth, and Jesus' disciples asked about the cause. Was he blind because his parents sinned? Could he be blind from birth because of his own sins?

Jesus turned their thinking from cause to effect. As a result of this man's blindness, the work of God was seen in his healing.

The Bible often encourages us to look at the results of our trials rather than the cause of them. James writes, "Consider it pure joy, my brothers, whenever you face trials of many kinds" (James 1:2). Joy in trouble? Why? Because we know that keeping on in spite of trouble will develop perseverance, and with perseverance we can grow spiritually and become what a Christian ought to be. (Read James 1:3, 4 as well.) So be faithful through your trials! But correct your faults.

# Discovery Learning

*This page contains an alternate lesson plan emphasizing learning activities. Classes desiring such student involvement will find these suggestions helpful. The next page is a reproducible activity page to further enhance discovery learning.*

## LEARNING GOALS

After this lesson a student should be able to:

1. Describe and explain Ezekiel's vision of dry bones.

2. Compare Israel's need for restoration with his or her own situation.

3. Pray that God will give new spiritual vitality.

## INTO THE LESSON

If you can find a recording of the well-known spiritual that recounts Ezekiel 37, play it for the class. (Maybe you have class members who would sing it for the group!) Ask class members if they know where the spiritual came from and what it means. How many class members have read the biblical account that is the basis for the spiritual?

*Option.* Bring a skull or a skeleton (or a picture of one) to class. Ask class members what ideas or words they would associate with it.

After either activity, tell the class that today's study, after looking at the Jews' failure because of sin, looks at the promise of hope and new life that God offered them. His promise to them reminds us of the spiritual life he makes available to all of us.

## INTO THE WORD

Ask a class member to summarize or read the chronology in the Introduction (page 111) of the lesson commentary. Then use the material under "A. Quick Review" on pages 111 and 112 to summarize this quarter's lessons. When you have finished, have the class discuss these questions:

1. What have we learned this quarter about sin?

2. What have we learned about God's patience and mercy?

3. What have we learned about his wrath?

4. What have you decided about everyday life today in light of what we have learned from these studies?

Before class members open their Bibles for this week's study, explain to them the context of Ezekiel 37 (use "B. Lesson Background," page 112). Then distribute the following list of statements. Class members are to decide whether each statement is true or false and to cite a verse to prove their conclusion. (Answers, for the teacher's reference, are included here.)

1. Ezekiel lived in the valley of dry bones (false, vv. 1, 2).

2. Ezekiel knew at once that the bones would be transformed into living bodies (false, v. 3).

3. God told Ezekiel to take his message to the bones (true, vv. 4-6).

4. God prophesied that the bones would be destroyed because of their sin (false , vv. 5, 6).

5. Ezekiel did not want to take God's message to the bones (false, v. 7).

6. The bones immediately became bodies, with voices that prophesied and praised God (false, vv. 7-9).

7. The bones represented the twelve apostles and the church (false, vv. 11, 12).

8. The revived bones represented a restored nation in Israel (true, vv. 11-14).

Give students a few minutes to answer the statements. Then they should each find a partner and compare answers. Next, discuss each statement with the class, explaining why it is true or false if necessary.

## INTO LIFE

Distribute copies of the reproducible activity on the next page. (Or write on your chalkboard the headings from the left-hand column of the chart and give each group a sheet of newsprint to list their ideas.) Ask class members, in groups of four each, to choose at least one of these topics—except the last one—and to decide, "What 'dry bones' do we see in this area?" They are to discuss how spiritual vitality has dried up because people have forsaken God. After six or eight minutes, ask them to report.

Next, ask class members to return to their groups and consider the last topic. After some brief personal reflection, ask individuals in the groups to discuss a time in their lives when they felt very dry spiritually. After a few minutes, without reporting back to the class, group members should then consider how God brought them "back to life." After they have discussed this second topic for several minutes, ask for volunteers to share their responses.

In your closing prayer time, ask different class members to pray, with each using one of the following prayers as the basis for his or her thoughts:

"God, help us to avoid the willful sinfulness of the Israelites."

"God, help us to see the dry bones in our country, our congregation, and our lives."

"God, thank you for breathing spiritual vitality into our lives, just when we needed it."

"God help us to 'come alive' for you in this place right now!"

# The Valley of Dry Bones

Ezekiel saw a valley full of dry bones, bleached by the sun. But God was able to put flesh on the bones and breathe his Spirit into the bodies, bringing them back to life. Today we see several valleys of dry bones—places and situations that need a breath of life from God's Spirit. Consider the following "valleys": what "dry bones" do you see in this area? How can God's Spirit be made to breathe new life into these situations?

| VALLEY | DRY BONES | HOW TO BREATHE GOD'S SPIRIT INTO IT |
|---|---|---|
| The Church in Our Society | | |
| Families | | |
| Education | | |
| The Media | | |
| Government | | |
| The Court System | | |
| Our Local Congregation | | |
| My Own Life | | |

# Winter Quarter, 1996-97

## Theme: New Testament Personalities

### Special Features

### Lessons

*ABOUT THESE LESSONS*

This series of lessons highlights individuals who appear within the pages of the New Testament record. Some are quite prominent; others may appear for only a short time. Some exhibit a strength of spiritual character; others illustrate the heartache of failure. All remind us of how important it is to follow Jesus and to make his cause our cause.

Dec 1
Dec 8
Dec 15
Dec 22
Dec 29
Jan 5
Jan 12
Jan 19
Jan 26
Feb 2
Feb 9
Feb 16
Feb 23

# Learning From
# People of the Past

*by David Morley*

Most Christians would love to visit the lands of the Bible and walk where the great Bible heroes walked. What a thrill it would be to visit Nazareth and recall Gabriel's visit to Mary, announcing the coming birth of Jesus the Messiah! How moving to sit in the Garden of Gethsemane and visualize Jesus praying, the disciples sleeping, and the betrayer approaching the gate! How interesting to walk the streets of Corinth and imagine walking with Paul, Timothy, Aquila, and Priscilla! What a flood of emotion would sweep over us as we approached Calvary, where our Savior died in our place!

Many Christians actually do visit such places and are greatly inspired by their visits. But wouldn't it be even more exciting if somehow we could travel back through time and actually walk and talk with Jesus? What a thrill that would be! What would we ask the Lord? What lessons would he teach us? How could we minister to him and help in the work of his kingdom?

Of course, time travel will remain forever in the realm of science fiction. None of us will ever have the chance to go back to those days—except, that is, in our imaginations. And that is exactly what we are invited to do in the lessons for this quarter. We will participate in sort of a "time travel of the mind," as we study "New Testament Personalities."

SURVEY OF THE QUARTER

Each lesson in this series is about one or more persons who were associated with Jesus or with the early church. The lessons are divided into three units. Each unit includes characters from a specific historical period. The first unit is entitled, "Persons of Jesus' Nativity and Early Life." The people who are studied include Elizabeth and Zechariah, Mary, the shepherds, the wise men and Herod, and Simeon and Anna. These people were privileged to live during the time when God fulfilled the words of the prophets and sent his promised Deliverer and Messiah into the world as a baby. Most of them were filled with joy to witness such an event. Herod, in contrast, saw this child as a threat to his power and attempted to kill him.

The second unit, "Persons in Jesus' Ministry," includes lessons on John the Baptizer, Mary and Martha, Peter, and Judas Iscariot. These people all had close contact with Jesus during his adult years. To them was granted the privilege of seeing Jesus work miracles and hearing him teach and preach. They found Jesus to be so much more than they expected, and also so much different from what they expected the Messiah to be. All but Judas learned valuable lessons from the Lord.

The third unit highlights "Persons of the New Testament Church." The characters studied are Barnabas, Stephen, Priscilla and Aquila, and Timothy. Each of these played an important role in the early church. They possessed varied talents and were called to various works, but each made a significant contribution to the kingdom of the Lord.

## LEARNING FROM BIBLE CHARACTERS

The idea of time travel is certainly intriguing, and it has provided a wealth of material for fiction writers and movie producers. Even imaginary time travel can occupy our minds and entertain us for hours at a time. But there needs to be more than entertainment here. We dare not be content to walk with these Bible characters as mere spectators. Many of those who actually walked with them did not profit from the journey. Their minds were closed to the lessons that were there. As you and your class take this imaginary journey back in time, pay close attention. There are lessons to be learned here—lessons that will make your lives in the here and now to be much more fruitful in the Lord's service.

Some of the characters you will meet provide examples of good (to be imitated); others give examples of evil (to be avoided). But we can learn lessons from them all because spiritual principles never change. Actions that brought spiritual growth and God's blessing then do the same today. Actions that led to spiritual disaster then cause spiritual disaster today as well. The key to learning from the lives of Bible characters is to see how we are like them and how our situations parallel theirs. Then we can learn from their experiences and decisions. Several comparisons are useful as we seek to identify with these people of long ago.

With the exception of Herod, the people associated with Jesus' birth displayed an *attitude* of spiritual sensitivity and of joy and wonder at the workings of God. Perhaps it was because they had such an attitude that they received special guidance from angels, dreams, and a star.

*ATTITUDE*

As you teach these lessons, challenge your students to evaluate their attitudes. Try to get them to feel the excitement of Zechariah, Elizabeth, Mary, and the others. Do they ever feel excited about God's works? Do they have eyes to see God's working in the lives of people today? Do they have ears to hear when God calls them? Do you have such spiritually sensitive eyes and ears? Do you get excited about what God is doing in your church and community? We all need to feel excitement over what God has done in the past and what he continues to do today. When we are filled with wonder at God's works, the natural response is worship and obedience, just as in the case of the shepherds and wise men.

Several of the individuals in these lessons were faced with daunting *challenges*. Mary was challenged to allow her entire world to be turned upside down. Peter was challenged to leave all to follow Jesus. Stephen was challenged to keep preaching in the face of persecution. They all knew the costs, and they were willing to make the sacrifices. When they accepted the challenges, God walked with them and cared for them. It is only because they accepted their challenges that they were used of God.

*CHALLENGE*

Try to lead your students to identify with these characters in their moments of decision, as they weighed the cost of God's call and chose to follow him. Every Christian faces challenges to his faith and dedication—some with far-reaching or long-term consequences. It is likely that some of your class members are facing such challenges now. We are strengthened to respond to God's call when we remember those who have answered his call before us. It may be a call to teach a class, serve as a leader, call on visitors, or go to a foreign field as a missionary. God did not desert any of these people in our lessons when they answered his call, and he will not desert anyone who answers his call today.

Just as we do, these New Testament personalities possessed both *strengths and weaknesses*. Peter was bold, but he was impulsive. Martha was industrious and generous, but she could get some of her priorities out of order. Judas had zeal, but he also had the fatal flaw of greed. Jesus worked with these people, taught them, and helped them build on their strengths and overcome their weaknesses. When we compare Peter and Judas, we see how important it is to overcome our weaknesses lest they overcome us.

*STRENGTHS & WEAKNESSES*

As you study these lessons, help your students look for similarities between themselves and the Bible characters. Encourage them to identify and develop their own individual strengths. Warn them to be aware of their weaknesses and to work very hard to overcome them. God still works with us, one by one, to guide us and refine us. However, we must submit to his leading, teaching, and discipline.

*TALENT*

These people had a variety of *talents*. Several were powerful preachers. Barnabas had a real talent for encouragement. Martha was an organizer and hostess. Priscilla and Aquila could make tents, but they also could teach effectively. Whatever talents these individuals had, they gladly used them in the Lord's service. As they did so, their talents became even more refined and powerful. These people made very important contributions to the work of the kingdom.

Each person in your class possesses some talent or talents that can be used for the Lord. Whether they are the same talents as those of the Bible characters is not important. (You are not likely to have any tentmakers in your class!) What matters is that the people in our lessons enthusiastically used their talents. As your students see the joy that these people felt in using their talents for the Lord, they will be encouraged to use their talents as well. As they understand that God can use ordinary people and talents to do his work, they will be more confident to volunteer to serve. The people in your class can make a difference. They can make valuable contributions to the work of the church.

## GROWING IN FAITH

The character studies that make up our lessons this quarter are much different from lessons in history or doctrine. The specific goal of studying people is to grow as a person. Remember to make this your emphasis in each lesson. Ask yourself what each person did and what characteristics each person possessed that are worthy of imitation. On the other hand, you should also identify mistakes and negative characteristics that we must avoid.

Challenge each of your class members to make personal Christian growth a goal for this lesson series. Perhaps a student will pick one of the Bible characters and say, "I want to be like that." Another may want to identify one strong trait in each person and work to build those traits in himself. Still another can analyze a lesson that the Bible character learned and apply that lesson to herself.

*CHANGE FOR THE BETTER*

However you and your students approach the lessons, do not forget that the goal is growth—change for the better. If you or your students are just the same at the end of the quarter as you were at the beginning, then you have not really learned the lessons, no matter how well you can recite the facts and tell the stories. At the same time, do not expect to reach perfection in three months. Zechariah, Elizabeth, Simeon, and Anna did not reach their high levels of devotion without many years of discipline. Barnabas did not become a wonderful encourager overnight. Priscilla and Aquila did not become effective teachers until they had spent long hours being taught by Paul.

Keep in mind that the people you will study this quarter were not supermen or superwomen. They were just ordinary people who (except for Herod and Judas) put spiritual interests first and who submitted their lives to the Lord. Ordinary people like us can grow as well if we do the same.

# ELIZABETH AND ZECHARIAH

**LESSON 1**

## WHY TEACH THIS LESSON?

During this quarter, the theme of each lesson will not be apparent from the lesson title. Atop each lesson will be a designation of an individual, a couple, or a group who will be the focus for the lesson. The question each time will be, "What can we learn from this person or these people?"

From Elizabeth and Zechariah we learn that God is faithful. Even when it seems his people have missed out, he often has some special blessing reserved, to be given in his own time. Encourage your class to be faithful and to wait for the special blessing God has in store for them. This will be especially seen in their prayer lives. Let this lesson be a reminder "that they should always pray and not give up" (Luke 18:1).

## INTRODUCTION

### A. A WELL-RUN KINDERGARTEN?

In his book *Your God is Too Small*, J. B. Phillips observes that some people are disappointed with God because he doesn't run his world as the ideal kindergarten teacher runs her classroom: the diligent and cooperative student receives immediate praise and reward while the uncooperative and rowdy child is scolded and quickly sent to the corner. Perhaps the analogy is somewhat dated—discipline isn't what it used to be—but it is true that we humans frequently want God to give immediate reward for goodness (especially if it's ours) and swift punishment for badness (if it's somebody else's).

But God doesn't usually work that way. He often reserves his best blessings and opportunities for those believers who have faithfully endured long periods of trial and testing. God allows painful times in our lives, not because he is punishing us, but because it is the hardships that build our character. On God's part these are allowances of love.

Nor can we think that God no longer loves us when he doesn't with haste answer our prayers. Whether it's Joseph in Egypt, or Job, or the sisters of Lazarus, or Paul, pleas to God for deliverance are often denied so that God can give an even greater blessing in his due time. Someone has said, "We ask for silver, and God sends his denials wrapped in gold."

### B. LESSON BACKGROUND

Luke's Gospel account serves as an excellent bridge between the Old and New Testaments. The last writer of the Old Testament, Malachi, had recorded the Lord's promises that he would send someone to "prepare the way" before him (3:1) and—in the last two verses of the Old Testament—that he would send Elijah before the "day of the Lord" (4:5, 6). Both these prophecies were fulfilled by John the Baptizer (Mark 1:2-4; Matthew 11:14), so with his birth the methodical historian Luke logically begins.

God had been silent for four hundred years. As the time came for the birth of the Savior, God broke his silence, sending a heavenly messenger to a humble and righteous old priest named Zechariah.

---

DEVOTIONAL READING
**LUKE 1:18-24**
LESSON SCRIPTURE
**LUKE 1:5-25, 57-80**
PRINTED TEXT
**LUKE 1:5-13, 24, 25, 59-64**

LESSON AIMS

*As a result of this lesson the student should:*

*1. Tell how God answered the prayers of the godly couple Elizabeth and Zechariah.*

*2. Explain that godliness is not always immediately rewarded.*

*3. Make a commitment to persevere in prayer, trusting in God's timing for his answer.*

VISUALS FOR THESE LESSONS

*The Adult Visuals packet contains classroom-size visuals designed for use with the lessons in the Winter Quarter. The packet is available from your supplier. Order No. 292.*

KEY VERSE

*Both of them were upright in the sight of God, observing all the Lord's commandments and regulations blamelessly.*
                    *Luke 1:6*

**LESSON 1 NOTES**

*The visual for lesson 1 in the visuals packet shows a map of Palestine highlighting most of the places covered in lessons 1-9. Display it as you begin the lesson.*

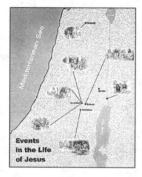

**OPTION**

*Elizabeth and Zechariah must have prayed long and hard for a child, but they were not blessed in the manner they had expected. Use the reproducible activity "Blessings to the Faithful," on page 130 to discuss how God's blessings are sometimes different from what we expect.*

## I. PROMISE TO A RIGHTEOUS COUPLE (LUKE 1:5-13)
### A. GOOD CHARACTER (vv. 5-7)

**5. In the time of Herod king of Judea there was a priest named Zechariah, who belonged to the priestly division of Abijah; his wife Elizabeth was also a descendant of Aaron.**

*Herod,* the Idumean (Edomite), was the founder of the Herodian dynasty in Palestine. That this man came to be called "the Great" by no means reflects anyone's estimate of his character or morals, but only that he was a shrewd politician who, despite his cruelty, was able to bring prosperity and order to Palestine. Though he was an energetic builder of cities and of buildings (including the majestic temple in Jerusalem), most Jews hated him. *Judea* here probably means all of Palestine, the entire land of the Jews, and is not limited to the province south of Samaria that bore that name. Herod ruled from 37 to 4 B.C.; the events of this lesson should probably be dated about 6 B.C.

Both Zechariah and Elizabeth were of priestly lineage, able to trace their ancestry back to Aaron. Since the days of David there had been twenty-four courses, or *divisions,* of priests (see 1 Chronicles 24) that took turns, a week at a time, performing the required priestly duties in the temple (preparing the sacrifices, offerings, altars, candlesticks, consecrated bread, etc.). Only four of these divisions returned from Babylonian captivity, but they were re-divided into twenty-four courses again, and renamed according to the old names. Zechariah belonged to the eighth course, Abia, or Abijah, which took its turn about two weeks a year, but which also joined all the priestly courses for service during the great annual feasts of Passover, Pentecost, and Tabernacles.

Although Hebrew law demanded only that a priest marry a woman of pure Hebrew blood, priests who married into another family of the priestly line were particularly honored. Such was the case with Zechariah. Elizabeth, too, was a *descendent* of Aaron, with the same name, in fact, as Aaron's wife (Exodus 6:23; "Elisheba" is transliterated from the Hebrew; "Elizabeth," from the Greek, represents the same name).

**6. Both of them were upright in the sight of God, observing all the Lord's commandments and regulations blamelessly.**

Certainly this couple was not morally perfect in every aspect of their lives (Romans 3:23), but over the years they had done their best to keep the stated commands of God's laws. Thus, they were "blameless" in the same sense as other righteous but less-than-perfect biblical figures, such as Noah (Genesis 6:9), Abraham (Genesis 17:1), and Job (Job 1:1). This dedicated pair certainly deserved God's best, but it appeared that God had overlooked them.

**7. But they had no children, because Elizabeth was barren; and they were both well along in years.**

Sadly, *Elizabeth* had been unable to give her husband a child. Her barrenness was more than disappointing: most Jews considered childlessness a disgrace for a woman, and usually saw it as a sign of God's displeasure with her. After all, Scripture taught that children were blessings from God to the obedient (Deuteronomy 7:14; Psalm 113:9; 127:3), and childlessness was a fate that the wicked could expect (Leviticus 20:20, 21). Rachel's "Give me children, or I'll die!" (Genesis 30:1) poignantly expresses the shame and desperation Elizabeth must have felt. (See verse 25.)

Though verse 6 above shows that Elizabeth was not *barren* because of some wickedness, her neighbors might naturally suspect that she was not as devout as she seemed. Legally, barrenness was grounds for divorce if her husband so chose. Of course, all those neighbors had to do was to look in the Scriptures for examples of godly barren women—Sarah, Rebekah, Hannah, and others—and they would have known that barrenness is not always a punishment for evil. In a fallen world, innocent people sometimes suffer along with the guilty.

## B. PROVIDENTIAL FORTUNE (vv 8-10)

**8, 9. Once when Zechariah's division was on duty and he was serving as priest before God, he was chosen by lot, according to the custom of the priesthood, to go into the temple of the Lord and burn incense.**

The week came for the Abijah *division* to do its tour of service in the temple, so Zechariah headed up to Jerusalem.

Except on the Sabbath—when all the priests in a division would serve—there was only a handful of tasks to be performed daily in the temple. However, there were hundreds of priests (estimates vary from about 330 to about a thousand) in each division. Therefore, each division of priests would cast lots each day to see which of them would be privileged to carry out the sacred duties that day.

Both priests and people considered the preparing and burning of the incense on the golden altar the most solemn and honorable duty of the daily service. This altar was located near the veil of entrance into the Holy of Holies, so the incense service would bring an ordinary priest the closest to the Holy of Holies that he could ever come. All other priests were to leave the Holy Place when he began his work, which was associated with the morning and evening sacrifices, when a lamb was sacrificed to God on behalf of the nation. But just before the morning sacrifice and just after the evening sacrifice the designated *priest* would carry fire from the altar of burnt offering to the golden altar in the Holy Place and *burn incense* with it. The sweet-smelling aroma was to accompany the smell of the sacrifices upward to God. At the same time, the ascent of the incense also symbolized God's reception of the prayers of Israel that were being offered up simultaneously in the courts of the temple (cf. Revelation 5:8; 8:3, 4).

Selection for this incense ministry was a once-in-a-lifetime opportunity. A priest could be so honored only once, after which he was considered "rich and holy." Many priests were never chosen, and those who were considered it the highlight of their lives. And the *lot* had finally fallen, after years of waiting, to Zechariah. More than "good luck," the providential hand of God was at work putting the man where God wanted him.

**10. And when the time for the burning of incense came, all the assembled worshipers were praying outside.**

According to some, when the priest entered the Holy Place with the fire and *incense,* a little bell was rung in the courts of the temple to signal the people to begin their prayers. So, as the old priest offered the incense inside, the people outside in the courts prayed, awaiting the priest to come out and dismiss them with a benediction. This normally happened rather quickly, but today's priest would be delayed. Old Zechariah had been selected for an honor far greater than even incense-burning.

## C. GOOD NEWS (vv. 11-13)

**11. Then an angel of the Lord appeared to him, standing at the right side of the altar of incense.**

The *right side of the altar of incense* would be just in front of the veil that led into the Holy of Holies. This *angel,* who later identifies himself as Gabriel, had come from the presence of God (verse 19) with a divine message.

**12. When Zechariah saw him, he was startled and was gripped with fear.**

*HOW TO SAY IT*

Abijah. Uh-BYE-juh.
Deuteronomy. Due-ter-
   AHN-uh-me.
Edomite. EE-duh-mite.
Elisheba. Eh-LISH-eh-buh.
Elizabeth. Ee-LIZ-uh-beth.
Gabriel. GAY-bree-ul.
Idumean. Id-you-ME-un.
Jehohanan. Jeh-hoe-HAY-nun.
Malachi. MAL-uh-kye.
ouchi (Greek). oo-KEE.
Zechariah. Zek-uh-RYE-uh.

*Fear* is the usual response in the Bible to the sudden appearance of angels. Angels were no doubt quite unlike the soft, effeminate, or baby-like forms often created by artists' imaginations. As God's mighty warriors they were likely imposing and intimidating figures. Adding the surprise factor—no angel had been seen for over four hundred years, as far as we know—it is understandable that *Zechariah* was overcome with fear.

**13. But the angel said to him: "Do not be afraid, Zechariah; your prayer has been heard. Your wife Elizabeth will bear you a son, and you are to give him the name John.**

What *prayer* had Zechariah been praying? For a son? Perhaps; and if so, what a lesson for Christians to persevere in prayer, even when everything looks as if the prayer will not be answered. Or perhaps this prayer had not been prayed since many years earlier, but only now answered. Interestingly, Zechariah's own name means "The Lord remembers." God sometimes answers our prayers not with "No," but with "Wait." We can be assured that he will not forget to answer when the right time comes.

Or had he been praying, along with other righteous Jews, for the coming of the Messiah and his kingdom? Or had he just now as a priest interceded for Israel, that her sins would be forgiven? The birth of Zechariah's son would be the first in a series of redemptive events that would, in fact, grant all these requests.

God-given names seem to always have etymological significance. The name *John,* a shortened form of "Jehohanan," means "Jehovah's Gift," or "Jehovah is Gracious." The coming of John—and even more, the coming of his greater Kinsman—showed just how gracious God really is, not only to this godly couple but to the entire world.

Gabriel went on to tell Zechariah that his son would become a great prophet who would prepare people for the coming of the Lord. The old priest, in a moment of doubt, asked Gabriel for a sign that this unbelievable news was true. The sign that he got was his own inability to speak (and perhaps to hear, as well) until the prophecy was fulfilled. After his week's duty at the temple, Zechariah went back home.

## II. BLESSINGS ON THE OLD COUPLE (LUKE 1:24, 25)
### A. CONCEPTION (v. 24a)
**24a. After this his wife Elizabeth became pregnant.**

Before long, the impossible happened. Just as God through Gabriel had promised, Elizabeth did become pregnant, thus illustrating the meaning of her own name, "God is an oath" (i.e., absolutely faithful to keep his word).

### B. JOYFUL SECLUSION (vv. 24b, 25)
**24b, 25. And for five months [she] remained in seclusion. "The Lord has done this for me," she said. "In these days he has shown his favor and taken away my disgrace among the people."**

Luke doesn't say why Elizabeth stayed out of sight for such a long time, but suggests that it was a time of excitement and joy. Perhaps she wanted to enjoy this time privately with her husband for as long as possible, the two of them offering up unhindered praise to God for a while before they created a stir with their happy news. And, perhaps she knew that no one would believe her anyway until she started to "show," and that a premature announcement would only intensify her own humiliation and her neighbors' suspicion of her. Instead, she would savor these private moments until the time when all could recognize that God himself had taken away from her the undeserved stigma of barrenness.

---

### WHAT DO YOU THINK?

*If our prayers are not answered immediately, how can we know God hears us?*

*See Exodus 2:24; Psalms 6:9; 34:4; 66:19; 118:21; Luke 1:13; 18:1; 2 Corinthians 5:7.*

### WHAT DO YOU THINK?

*Zechariah was disciplined when he asked the angel for a sign (Luke 1:18-20). At what point do you think honest doubt becomes unbelief?*

*See Deuteronomy 6:16; Isaiah 1:18; Matthew 11:2-6; 16:1-4.*

*Zechariah was a priest, and most of the priests were Sadducees. Read Acts 23:8. If he was a Sadducee, and if he believed what the party as a whole believed, how might this have affected the Lord's dealing with his doubt?*

God had not overlooked the faithful service of this faithful pair after all. Displaying an evident knowledge of the Scriptures Elizabeth recited the words of Rachel after God had opened her barren womb with the birth of Joseph: "God has taken away my disgrace" (Genesis 30:23).

### WHOSE DISGRACE?

William J. Bennett's book, *The Index of Leading Cultural Indicators,* contains some disturbing statistics about the state of American society. In 1990, for example, more than two-thirds of all births to teens were to unmarried girls, compared with less than one-third in 1970. In 1991 some thirty percent of all births in the U.S. were illegitimate. In 1994 it was estimated that nearly twenty-five percent of all pregnancies ended in abortion.

Elizabeth thought her barrenness was a disgrace. Our present disgrace is fertility without responsibility. Elizabeth was ashamed that she had borne no children, a condition that was hardly a sin. Yet millions today commit fornication, adultery, and the murder of abortion with little trace of remorse, let alone guilt. The public conscience has been seared by years of permissiveness, promiscuity, and perversion.

If "godly sorrow brings repentance" (2 Corinthians 7:10), America is not likely to repent soon. Too many have lost their capacity for shame. They sense no disgrace in sinful behavior, so they exhibit no contrition. Until our national disgrace is acknowledged, we will continue to degrade ourselves, plummeting into ultimate dissipation and self-destruction. "Righteousness exalts a nation, but sin is a disgrace to any people" (Proverbs 14:34).         —R. W. B.

## III. OBEDIENCE FROM THE BLESSED COUPLE (LUKE 1:59-64)

### A. THE FALSE ASSUMPTION (v. 59)

**59. On the eighth day they came to circumcise the child, and they were going to name him after his father Zechariah.**

After nine months Elizabeth gave birth to her son, and celebration was held by her family and friends. The Law commanded (Leviticus 12:3) that boys be circumcised *on the eighth day* after their births. It would be hard to overemphasize the importance to the Jewish people of this rite of circumcision. It was a solemn ceremony by which a male became part of the covenant people of God as his parents pledged to rear him in accord with the law of God. This eighth-day circumcision was part of a Jewish man's "faultless" pedigree (Philippians 3:5-6). At that time it appears that the fathers usually performed the surgery, which took place in the home. Some commentators refer to an ancient Jewish custom in which the baby boy was circumcised while propped up on a chair that was called "the throne of Elijah," in hopes that he might be the long-awaited forerunner of the Lord prophesied by Malachi. Whether or not the custom was followed in John's circumcision, surely this was the only occasion it would ever have been appropriate.

It had also become the custom to give a boy his name on the day of his circumcision, perhaps because Abram had received his new name, Abraham, on the day of his circumcision. It was rather common to name a son after his grandfather, or sometimes his father (cf. Joseph's son Joseph, Matthew 13:55), and the family and friends assumed Zechariah and Elizabeth would want to perpetuate the elderly father's name by naming the boy Zechariah.

### B. ELIZABETH'S CORRECTION (vv. 60, 61)

**60. But his mother spoke up and said, "No! He is to be called John."**

Zechariah celebrated silently, still mute, and probably wondering how long he would remain so, but Elizabeth informed the celebrants what the boy's

### WHAT DO YOU THINK?

*Zechariah and Elizabeth's relatives wanted to follow tradition and name the newborn child Zechariah, after his father. Tradition can be either positive or negative, beneficial or harmful, depending on our point of view and how tradition is used.*

*What are some benefits of following tradition? What are some problems that come from following tradition?*

*Why are some Christians often reluctant to break tradition and try something new?*

## PRAYER

*Father, teach us to trust you more. Let us never forget that someday we will be glad for each deprivation and each trial, when we can see how you used them to accomplish your will, and how they were always for our ultimate good.*

## THOUGHT TO REMEMBER

*"Sometimes [God's] providences, like Hebrew letters, must be read backwards" (John Flavel).*

## WHAT DO YOU THINK?

*Zechariah "began to speak, praising God" (Luke 1:64). Besides speaking, we can praise God through music, through giving gifts and offerings, and through acts of service. However, God is praised most by a life lived daily and consistently according to the teachings of Jesus.*

*What do you think of the place of praise in the life of the church? Is enough attention paid to it? Why or why not? How can Christians be taught and encouraged to praise God not only in worship services, but in their daily lives as well?*

name would be. In the original Greek, the answer of Elizabeth begins with the strong negative *ouchi*, "No indeed!" God had commanded that the name be *John*, and so the matter was settled for this obedient couple. Zechariah had evidently made regular use of his writing tablet (v. 63) over the past nine or ten months, communicating to his wife the temple events and the revelations of Gabriel.

**61. They said to her, "There is no one among your relatives who has that name."**

The family and friends questioned Elizabeth's name selection unaware of any *relatives* by *that name,* and perhaps thinking that she had not consulted the silent Zechariah. The father, after all, had the final say in all such matters.

### C. ZECHARIAH'S CONFIRMATION (vv. 62-64)

**62 Then they made signs to his father, to find out what he would like to name the child.**

It is possible that the friends just forgot that Zechariah was not deaf but only mute, but it is more likely that he was deaf as well as dumb. (The Greek word for "unable to speak" in verse 22 of this chapter literally means "blunt" or "dull," and is the regular word for both "deaf" and "mute" in the Gospels; it can mean either or both.) By *sign* language the friends asked him his choice of a *name* for his son.

**63. He asked for a writing tablet, and to everyone's astonishment he wrote, "His name is John."**

His tablet was probably a wooden board covered with wax that could be written on with a sharp stylus and then smoothed out after each message. Zechariah confirmed the name *John,* but evidently neither he nor Elizabeth explained the reason for their choice, so their friends were left astonished by the unexpected development.

**64. Immediately his mouth was opened and his tongue was loosed, and he began to speak, praising God.**

What praise must have been bound up in this old-man-new-father! How he must have radiated a joy and excitement uncharacteristic of a man his age. The curse on his speech now withdrawn, he immediately proceeded to give glory to his miracle-working God. Perhaps the "Benedictus" prayer of verses 68-79 is part of his praise offered here. The friends considered the loosing of his tongue a miracle, and the whole affair became the talk of the town as folks formed high expectations for this divinely-sent little baby boy (vv. 65, 66). How Christians today need to loosen their tongues and praise God for his gracious answers to our prayers!

## CONCLUSION

Someone once said, "If I could have the power of God for just one day, I'd sure do things much differently; but, if I could have his wisdom, too, I suppose I'd do things just as he does." During the difficult times of our lives we often wonder why God doesn't do things differently. Why does he not remove those burdens and trials from us if he really does love us? Why does he not answer when we pray? Doesn't he know how hard we have it? Doesn't he know how faithful we've been?

Yes, he knows. And, he knows what we most need. But he cares for our character more than for our comfort. And our character needs the refining of fire (1 Peter 1:7). Painful as it might be for the moment, God is preparing us for glory to come (2 Corinthians 4:17; Romans 8:18). "The refiner is never very far from the mouth of the furnace when it's his gold in the fire" (Charles Spurgeon).

# Discovery Learning

*This page contains an alternate lesson plan emphasizing learning activities. Classes desiring such student involvement will find these suggestions helpful. The next page is a reproducible activity page to further enhance discovery learning.*

## LEARNING GOALS

As a result of this lesson the student should:

1. Tell how God answered the prayers of the godly couple Elizabeth and Zechariah.

2. Explain that godliness is not always immediately rewarded.

3. Make a commitment to persevere in prayer, trusting in God's timing for his answer.

## INTO THE LESSON

Open today's session by asking for prayer requests. List these requests on a poster board or the chalkboard.

Review the list, asking, "When would it be best for these requests to be answered?" Ask, but don't discuss: "Is it appropriate for us to put suggestions for timing into our prayer requests? Why isn't God's timing the same as ours?"

Observe that in this lesson you will share in the life of another couple who had made repeated prayer requests but had to wait on the Lord's timing for an answer.

Assure the class that we will share in a prayer time for these listed needs a bit later in the lesson.

## INTO THE WORD

Early in the week, ask one person to prepare a brief oral report for the class on the organization and function of the temple priests. Have the student include information about the responsibility of preparing and burning incense on the golden altar. Resources for the report are included in this week's commentary (see page 125) and in most Bible dictionaries. Displaying a picture of the temple or of a priest will add interest to this report.

Begin this portion of study with the student's presentation.

After the report, display a poster with the words "Evidence of Zechariah and Elizabeth's Godliness." Ask the students to watch for descriptive words or phrases that tell of this couple's godliness.

Read today's Scripture text aloud. Allow students to share their findings for the poster. Their answers should include at least the following:

"Upright in the sight of God" (v. 6).
"Observing all the Lord's commandments" (v. 6).
"Blameless" (v. 6).
Elizabeth gave credit to the Lord (v. 25).
Zechariah praised God (v. 64).

From verse 6, ask "What does *blameless* mean? Is *blameless* the same as *sinless*? Does this mean they were morally perfect?" Refer to the lesson commentary, page 124, for information to guide this discussion.

Remind the students that here was a godly couple who had had to wait patiently for God's blessing. They even experienced personal grief and cultural hardship as they waited for God's blessing. It wasn't until they had reached an advanced age that God finally answered their prayer. Here is a lesson about perseverance in prayer. The fact that our prayer is not answered immediately does not necessarily mean God has rejected our prayer (even though that is his option).

## INTO LIFE

Ask "Do you sometimes wonder about God's timing? There have been other Bible couples who have had to wait until their later years for children." Ask the class to name a few (i.e., Abraham and Sarah waited for Isaac; Elkanah and Hannah waited for Samuel). Use the reproducible activity "Barren But Not Forgotten" on the next page to facilitate this.

Repeat the question "Why does God sometimes wait to answer our prayers?" Allow the class to discuss the question. Remember, there may be numerous or different reasons for different situations. God knows what timing is best for us. He knows what timing is best for history.

Ask: "May our relationship with the Lord sometimes affect the timing of his answers to our prayers?" Yes. Sometimes he may want our character to be refined. See the conclusion in the lesson commentary for a discussion of this concept.

There are so many instances when we ask for God's help. Ask the class to resolve to be patient while waiting for God's answers. We must continually trust his wisdom. Our lesson commentary writer quotes: "If I could have the power of God for just one day, I'd sure do things much differently; but, if I could have his wisdom, too, I suppose I'd do things just as he does."

Conclude with group prayer. Have the groups pray for a portion of the list made at the beginning of the class. Assign as many of the requests as you can to specific individuals in the class. Ask each one who will accept the assignment to make a commitment to pray daily for each concern until an answer is clear.

# Barren But Not Forgotten

Elizabeth was not the only woman in the Bible who was barren—at least for a while. Look up the following Scriptures. Identify who was barren, describe her character, and tell how her prayers for a child were finally answered.

Genesis 16:1-16; 17:15-19; 18:9-15; 21:1-7

Genesis 25:21-23

Genesis 29:31—30:24

1 Samuel 1:1-28

# Blessings to the Faithful

Whether we admit it or not, we are influenced by the values of a secular society. So we tend to think of God's rewards in terms of money, success, and happiness, almost as if they were bonuses for a job well-done. So we are puzzled when devout Christians struggle with disappointments and failures, when faithful saints experience almost continual suffering and grief or live on the ragged edge of poverty. "Why doesn't God reward righteousness with material benefits?" we wonder.

However, while God always rewards righteousness, his rewards are not always what we expect. Look up the passages cited below. What does God promise to the faithful?

Romans 2:6, 7

Romans 15:5

1 Corinthians 10:13

2 Thessalonians 3:16

2 Timothy 2:7

Revelation 2:10

Revelation 3:21

# MARY, MOTHER OF JESUS

**LESSON 2**

Dec
8

## WHY TEACH THIS LESSON?

"I am the Lord's servant," Mary answered. "May it be to me as you have said" (Luke 1:38). Where could we find a better statement of submission to the will of God than here? This is the challenge of today's lesson, to lead students to the same level of commitment.

Of course, Mary was a unique individual. Some may use that to suggest her level of submission is not attainable. But Mary's favor was through the grace of God, and that is available to all. Encourage your students to see commitment like Mary's to be a natural response to the grace of God.

## INTRODUCTION

### A. REFLECTIONS

**Current Concerns.** A recent survey of young people from evangelical homes revealed these statistics: 66% lied to their parents in the last three months; 36% cheated during the same time interval; 57% will not affirm moral absolutes to govern behavior.

Approximately one-third of the high school students at a Christian service camp saw nothing wrong with pre-marital sex. The teacher was able to show them that the Bible has moral absolutes. One student later expressed gratitude for this instruction. It was completely new to him!

**Constant Commands.** In every generation there have been troubles and tribulations, apprehensions and anxieties, and dreads and distresses. It is in these times that the Christian takes advantage of the opportunity to demonstrate his faith. The mature Christian recognizes that he and the Lord together can handle any challenge.

Today's lesson is about the Lord's announcement to Mary that she had been chosen to be the mother of the Messiah. She lived at a time in which the ruling Romans were hostile to her religion, and immorality was an accepted lifestyle in the Mediterranean world. Her fears of the future may have been similar to today's concerns.

### B. REVIEW

Elizabeth, one of the two personalities in last week's lesson, is a part of today's lesson. She was a relative of Mary, the subject for today.

The lesson text is again from Luke 1. Luke was more than a physician. He was a careful historian who investigated "everything from the beginning" (Luke 1:3). We, as well as Theophilus, can "know the certainty of the things you have been taught" (Luke 1:4).

## I. GABRIEL VISITS MARY (LUKE 1:26-38)

### A. THE ANGEL'S ASSIGNMENT (vv . 26, 27)

**26. In the sixth month, God sent the angel Gabriel to Nazareth, a town in Galilee.**

It was the *sixth month* of the pregnancy of Elizabeth (see last week's lesson), but it was much more than that. It was the beginning of the time the world had

DEVOTIONAL READING
LUKE 1:24-56

LESSON SCRIPTURE
LUKE 1:26-56

PRINTED TEXT
LUKE 1:26-42

LESSON AIMS

*As a result of this lesson each student should be able to:*

*1. Describe Mary's reaction to the message of the angel.*

*2. Explain the nature of total submission to God's will.*

*3. State his or her personal commitment to the will of God.*

KEY VERSE

"I am the Lord's servant," Mary answered. "May it be to me as you have said."
— Luke 1:38

## LESSON 2 NOTES

*Use the visual for lesson 1 to note the places mentioned in this lesson and to trace Mary's journey to see Elizabeth.*

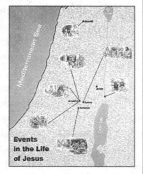

**Events in the Life of Jesus**

### WHAT DO YOU THINK?

*Extraordinary angelic activity marked the transition from the Old Testament era based on the Law to the New Testament era based on faith in Christ. An angel broke a four-hundred-year prophetic silence by bringing prophetic messages to Zechariah and Mary. An angel also announced the birth of Jesus to lowly Bethlehem shepherds.*

*Passages such as Hebrews 1:14 and 13:2 indicate that angels still function in a special way on behalf of believers. What do you think is the role of angels today? Support your answer.*

*How does our possession of the Scriptures (see 2 Timothy 3:15-17) and the indwelling of the Holy Spirit (see Acts 2:38) affect our need for angelic messengers?*

awaited since Adam and Eve were banished from Eden. Paul says, "When the time had fully come, God sent his Son, born of a woman" (Galatians 4:4).

"The time had fully come" because the world order was on the verge of moral collapse. The Roman and Greek gods were recognized by many people for what they were—false gods. Religion had become just a tradition, and spiritual apathy was the result. Roman oppression created a negative outlook on life. Slaves had no status, and women were often considered to be mere chattels.

Because "the time had fully come," the angel *Gabriel* had one more mission. In the past he had been sent to Babylon to provide understanding for the prophet Daniel (Daniel 8:16; 9:21, 22). He had appeared to Zechariah at the temple in Jerusalem. Now he was sent from God one more time—not to a capital city, but to *a town in Galilee,* named *Nazareth.*

Galilee was in the northern third of Palestine. The common thought in Judea was that nothing "good" would ever come from Nazareth (John 1:46). That was about to change!

**27. . . . to a virgin pledged to be married to a man named Joseph, a descendant of David. The virgin's name was Mary.**

Gabriel's assignment was not to the town, however, but to a *virgin* whose name was *Mary.* Isaiah had prophesied that the Messiah be born of a virgin (Isaiah 7:14). The fact that Luke, a physician, gives such unequivocal testimony about Mary's virginity is especially valuable.

Through the centuries Mary's purity of character has been attacked by those who will not accept the reality of miracles. The unfounded, absurd speculations are less credible than the testimony of eyewitnesses given in the Gospels.

*Mary* was a frequent name both then and now. Other forms of the name are Marie and Miriam. "When the time had fully come" she became engaged to *Joseph.* Each of them was a *descendant of David,* but it is Joseph's ancestry that is noted here. It is never stated directly that Mary was a descendant of David. It is strongly implied in verse 32, and it is believed that the genealogy of Luke 3:23 ff. is Mary's. It was necessary that an actual descendant of David be the Messiah who would sit on David's throne (Psalm 132:11; see also 2 Samuel 7:12-14a; Matthew 1:1; 22:42).

### B. THE ANGEL'S ACKNOWLEDGMENT (v. 28)

**28. The angel went to her and said, "Greetings, you who are highly favored! The Lord is with you."**

Gabriel appeared to Mary directly as he had done to Zechariah. This was not a dream or a vision. In both instances, however, the angel's manifestations were in private, not in public.

The angel said Mary was *highly favored.* This expression was much more than just a courteous greeting. Though she may well have been an attractive young woman, this was not a compliment on her physical appearance. (David's family was known for physical beauty; see 1 Samuel 16:12 for David himself and 2 Samuel 14:25 for Absalom, his son.)

Mary could be said to be highly favored because she had been chosen to give birth to the Messiah. The Lord was selecting her to have the task of rearing the Son of God during his early years. It was through Mary's Son that "all peoples on earth" would "be blessed" (Genesis 12:3).

The word for *favored* here is a form of the word Greek word for *grace.* The angel was not suggesting Mary had earned the right to the great honor about to be bestowed on her. This was an act of God's grace. In that sense, we might say all Christians are *highly favored*—the Lord is with us, as well!

## C. MARY'S APPREHENSION (v. 29)

**29. Mary was greatly troubled at his words and wondered what kind of greeting this might be.**

Mary was an intelligent young woman. She knew that a messenger from God always had a message with meaning. Something important was about to be communicated, but she did not have enough information to understand her role in it. She said nothing outwardly, but her mind was racing with a variety of thoughts: wonder and marvel, curiosity and concern. The comforting phrases helped her to remain calm, but she was still *troubled*.

## D. THE ANGEL'S ANNOUNCEMENT (vv . 30-33)

**30. But the angel said to her, "Do not be afraid, Mary, you have found favor with God.**

The angel was aware of Mary's apprehension, and he provided comfort to her mind in three ways. (1) *Do not be afraid*. These words were often used when heavenly beings spoke to humans (Genesis 15:1; 21:17; Luke 1:13).

(2) He called her by name, and this can be done in a compassionate way that brings assurance. It is interesting that her name was known in Heaven. It is also fascinating that our Lord said that he would acknowledge before the "Father and his angels" the name of each person who overcomes (Revelation 3:5).

(3) The thought that Mary had *found favor* or grace was repeated. This brought further reassurance, for God's messengers, whether angels or prophets, often pronounced judgment on those who were disobedient to God's commands. This was a message of grace, however, not judgment.

**31. "You will be with child and give birth to a son, and you are to give him the name Jesus.**

This is the announcement that the angel was commissioned to give. It is a progressive statement in that each part offers increasingly specific information: Mary would conceive a *child*; the baby would be a *son*; and his *name* would be *Jesus*.

As a girl Mary had probably thrilled at the accounts of the women in the Scriptures who had been blessed with sons in special ways: Sarah (Genesis 18:10), the unnamed mother of Samson (Judges 13:3), Hannah (1 Samuel 1:11ff.), and the woman of Shunem (2 Kings 4:16). In each case, however, the woman involved already had a husband.

She may have assumed that these promises involved Joseph as the actual father, and that these things would happen after their marriage. It is possible that she thought of the prophecy of Isaiah 7:14, or that the Lord prompted her to think of that verse: "The virgin will be with child and will give birth to a son, and will call him Immanuel." It is true that the Romans controlled Israel at that time, but the Greeks had thrust their language on the world at the time of Alexander the Great. In all likelihood Mary understood the Scriptures in that language also, and she knew that the Greek word for "virgin" must mean that and nothing else.

The name *Jesus* in Greek is the same as *Joshua* in Hebrew. It means "the Lord is salvation," or "salvation is of the Lord." Two things combined to give it special significance: its meaning and the fact that it was specifically chosen by God for the Messiah.

**32. "He will be great and will be called the Son of the Most High. The Lord God will give him the throne of his father David.**

The descriptive phrases of the promised Son continue to build. The adjective *great* was associated with kings such as Darius, Alexander, or Antiochus, each of whom had ruled over Palestine in the past. Now it is applied to the promised Son of Mary!

### WHAT DO YOU THINK?

Mary was told she was highly favored by God (verse 28), and that she had "found favor with God" (verse 30). No doubt, Mary was a devout and righteous person. A similar expression is used of Noah in Genesis 6:8, and the next verse describes Noah's righteous character.

But favor *means* grace, and grace is something that cannot be earned. What, then, do you think is the relationship between righteous behavior and grace?

Certainly we can do nothing to earn our salvation, but can those who are saved by grace secure "more grace" by means of righteous behavior. Why or why not?

See Acts 4:33; 6:8; 13:43; 2 Corinthians 8:1, 6; Hebrews 4:16; James 4:6; 1 Peter 5:5.

### HOW TO SAY IT

*Absalom.* AB-suh-lum.
*Antiochus.* An-TIE-uh-kus.
*Baal.* BAY-ul.
*Cyrus.* SIGH-russ.
*Darius.* Duh-RYE-us.
*Elijah.* Ee-LYE-juh.
*Elisha.* Ee-LYE-shuh.
*Gabriel.* GAY-bree-ul.
*Immanuel.* Ih-MAN-you-el.
*Joshua.* JOSH-oo-uh.
*Judah.* JOO-duh.
*Judea.* Joo-DEE-uh.
*Magnificat (Latin).* Mag-NIF-ih-COT.
*Miriam.* MEER-ee-um.
*Shephelah.* SHEF-ih-lah.
*Shunem.* SHOO-nem.
*Simeon.* SIM-ee-un.
*Theophilus.* Thee-AHF-ih-luss.
*Zechariah.* Zek-uh-RYE-uh.

## WHAT DO YOU THINK?

*God chose for special honor a humble peasant maiden from a culturally backward area of the world. It seems God delights in using "the foolish things of the world to shame the wise" (1 Corinthians 1:27). God looks for people who are willing and responsive, someone who is humble enough to recognize that any success he has is only because God is working through him and using him (1 Corinthians 1:26-29).*

*Then what qualifications—if any—should we look for when we need someone to perform some ministry in the church? Is it possible to put too much emphasis on ability? Why or why not? Do you think we put enough emphasis on humility and other spiritual factors? Why or why not? How can we avoid the trap of recruiting just about anyone to fill a gap in our program instead of looking for gifted persons whom God has called to ministry?*

*Son of the Most High* is a descriptive phrase that suggests a special association with deity. This is confirmed in the angel's words in verse 35.

Mary's Son would occupy *the throne of his father David*. This phrase documents three facts: it implies that Mary is a descendant of David; it promises that her son would be a king; and it shows a further fulfillment of the promise made to David in 2 Samuel 7:12-14.

**33. "And he will reign over the house of Jacob forever; his kingdom will never end."**

The kingdom of the Messiah has three distinctive characteristics: it is spiritual (John 18:36), universal (Daniel 7:14), and eternal (Daniel 2:44; 7:14). The *house of Jacob* (or Israel) must therefore refer to all people everywhere who worship and serve the Christ, regardless of physical ancestry (Galatians 3:29).

### E. MARY'S APPEAL (v. 34)

**34. "How will this be," Mary asked the angel, "since I am a virgin?"**

Mary's response was different from Zechariah's unbelief (Luke 1:20), or Sarah's doubting laughter (Genesis 18:12). Her question indicates acceptance, but she was puzzled and perplexed with a natural bewilderment. The universal experience of mankind was that a woman must have been sexually intimate with a man in order to conceive a child. *How* would a *virgin* conceive a child?

### F. THE ANGEL'S ANSWER (vv. 35-37)

**35. The angel answered, "The Holy Spirit will come upon you, and the power of the Most High will overshadow you. So the holy one to be born will be called the Son of God.**

The angel's answer involved two parts: the creative power of God, and the nature of the child that was to be born. As the Spirit of God was active in the original creation (Genesis 1:2), so he would be the agent in Mary's conception. We are not informed how the Holy Ghost (Spirit) accomplished this. If the angel's explanation had been phrased according to our present understanding of genetics, it would have baffled men in the intervening centuries. It was not essential for Mary (or for us) to understand completely the ways of God. Her task and ours is simply this: "The righteous will live by faith" (Romans 1:17).

The use of the term *Most High* in other places indicates that this was a term for God (see v. 32).

The child is given two designations: *holy* and *the Son of God*. Holiness is the supreme attribute of God. It is frequently stated that God is "holy" (Leviticus 11:44, 45). The entire account of Jesus' birth is sacred.

During December it is appropriate to emphasize Jesus' birth and Mary's role in it, but it is his resurrection that confirms for all honest seekers that the testimonies about him are true.

### ACCIDENT OR SURPRISE?

Too often, parents speak of unplanned pregnancies as "accidents." Sometimes they do so even in the presence of their children. Despite the teasing tone, youngsters hardly like to think of their conception as some sort of mishap. Such "accidents" are much better called "surprises." If a child has to know at all, his self-esteem will suffer less if he is referred to as a "surprise."

Mary's pregnancy was a surprise—most certainly *not* an accident. The conception was planned by God and effected by the Holy Spirit. It was "on purpose"— God's purpose, "when the time had fully come" (Galatians 4:4). Those connected with the circumstances surrounding the birth of Christ were surprised, but generally they were surprised and pleased. The ones who were well acquainted with Messianic prophecies were more pleased than surprised. For people such as Simeon and

Anna, the birth of the long-expected Jesus in their lifetime was a most joyous turn of events.

This same observation can be made concerning the second coming of Christ. His return certainly will not be an accident. Though the timing will be a surprise, the faithful will be pleasantly surprised. What a joy it will be if this blessed event should occur in our lifetime!           —R. W. B.

**36. "Even Elizabeth your relative is going to have a child in her old age, and she who was said to be barren is in her sixth month.**

Gabriel provided confirmation for his message. It was in the form of astounding news about *Elizabeth*, a *relative* who had been childless. These personal details were new and exciting to Mary.

**37. "For nothing is impossible with God."**

God can do more than the "laws" of nature allow us to do. He is the one who established the laws, and he can set them aside to accomplish his purposes. In the context the angel's final remark refers primarily to Elizabeth, and it gave further assurance to Mary.

The history of God's redemptive plan often has miracles occurring at critical times: various events from the lives of Moses and Joshua, the encounters of Elijah and Elisha with the worshipers of Baal, the ministry of Jesus, and the early years of the church.

### G. MARY'S AFFIRMATION (v. 38)

**38. "I am the Lord's servant," Mary answered. "May it be to me as you have said." Then the angel left her.**

Mary's affirmation of acceptance is an outstanding declaration of faith, trust, and devotion. The verbal exchange between her and the angel shows that she was not naive. She had the ability to assess the immediate future, and certain matters would be difficult: Joseph's reaction, the lack of acceptance of her explanation of her pregnancy, and the resultant remarks that were certain to come from others in Nazareth. She understood the embarrassing situations that she would encounter, and she expressed her unqualified acquiescence to God's plan.

### II. MARY VISITS ELIZABETH (LUKE 1:39-42)

### A. MARY'S SOJOURN (v. 39)

**39. At that time Mary got ready and hurried to a town in the hill country of Judea,**

The timing of some of the events which followed is not recorded. Did Mary share her news with Joseph immediately, and is that the reason "he had in mind to divorce her quietly" (Matthew 1:19)? Or did she defer informing him until she returned from her journey into the hill country? The divine record does not tell us, for such matters are not really important.

It was not customary for women, especially engaged women, to travel alone. It is assumed that Mary journeyed with others. Her inner joy about Elizabeth's news prompted her to make her trip with haste. There is something distinctive about the way women react to babies.

The town in Judea is not identified. The *hill country of Judea* was the hilly part between the Shephelah (foothills) to the west and the Judean desert to the east.

### B. MARY'S SALUTATION (v. 40)

**40. where she entered Zechariah's home and greeted Elizabeth.**

When Mary greeted Elizabeth, it was surely more than a formal greeting such as was used by Gabriel. It must have been a joyous salutation between the young

**WHAT DO YOU THINK?**

God is omnipotent (all-powerful); we know that. We agree that "nothing is impossible with God." Yet, while the spiritual side of our nature reaches out to God in faith, our human side wants to keep one foot firmly on the ground. Thus, in practice, we sometimes act as if God is limited to our own understanding and our own abilities.

How can we practically demonstrate our faith in a God who does the impossible? What would this church attempt if we all had a firm faith in God's omnipotent power? What objections would never be heard when a new ministry is proposed?

**WHAT DO YOU THINK?**

Gabriel spoke the message of God. He did not need to "prove" what he said was true, yet he offered Mary confirmation his by telling Mary of her relative Elizabeth.

How is God's message today confirmed? Some Christians say, "God's Word says it; I believe it; that settles it." What of those who are not yet believers—is it proper to offer them confirmation of the Bible's truth? If so, how? What obligation does the Christian have to be knowledgeable about history and science and other disciplines to be able to harmonize what we know from them with the truth found in the Bible?

## LET US PRAY

*God in the highest, lead me today into paths of righteousness that also include paths of service. May my eyes be opened to see the opportunities that I have avoided in the past.*

## THOUGHT TO REMEMBER

*It was not essential for Mary (or for us) to understand completely the ways of God. Her task and ours is simply this: "The righteous will live by faith" (Romans 1:17).*

## DAILY BIBLE READINGS

**Monday Dec. 2**—Accepting God's Plan (Psalm 138:1-8)

**Tuesday, Dec. 3**—Joseph Accepted Mary (Matthew 1:18-25)

**Wednesday, Dec. 4**—Mary's Song of Praise (Luke 1:46-56)

**Thursday, Dec. 5**—Mary and Joseph Go to Bethlehem (Luke 2:1-7)

**Friday, Dec. 6**—Mary and Joseph Go to Egypt (Matthew 2:13-18)

**Saturday, Dec. 7**—Mary and Joseph Go to Nazareth (Matthew 2:19-23)

**Sunday, Dec. 8**—Jesus Provides for Mary's Care (John 19:23-27)

virgin and an aged woman, each of whom was carrying a son who fulfilled prophecies given hundreds of years before. Mary was surely eager to hear a confirmation of the details that Gabriel had given her, but that had to wait. Her salutation was a stimulus for dramatic reactions.

### C. ELIZABETH'S STATEMENT (vv. 41, 42)

**41. When Elizabeth heard Mary's greeting, the baby leaped in her womb, and Elizabeth was filled with the Holy Spirit.**

Mary's salutation caused three things to happen immediately. John, though still unborn, *leaped* in his mother's *womb* in such a way that she knew something unusual had transpired. Some have proposed that John was already giving homage to the Son of God, but that seems to suppose a developed intellect that is beyond normal. It is better to think that God prompted the movement as a sign to *Elizabeth*.

Second, Elizabeth was filled with the Holy Spirit, prior to making an inspired utterance. It is interesting that such inspiration is ascribed to the statements of Zechariah (1:67) and Elizabeth, but not to Mary's magnificent response (vv. 46-55).

**42. In a loud voice she exclaimed: "Blessed are you among women, and blessed is the child you will bear!"**

The third reaction is Elizabeth's pronouncement of blessings on Mary and Jesus. Chronologically these are the first beatitudes of the New Testament, and the very first one is upon Mary.

There is also a contrast between the faith of Mary and that of Zechariah. Her faith enabled her to enter into the home with a salutation. Because of Zechariah's unbelief, he entered the same house some six months earlier not able to speak at all.

## CONCLUSION

### A. THE PLACE OF MARY

It has been well said that Mary was blessed *among* women, not *above* women. Through the centuries, however, men have added much to the simple teaching of the New Testament. Mary has been declared sinless along with Jesus, and said to have been a perpetual virgin. It has been declared that her body did not decay, for it experienced an "assumption" into Heaven at her death. Some have supposedly heard "prophetic" utterances from her, and a recent headline in a newspaper read: "Book compiles the prophecies of Mary."

Some have gone to the opposite extreme and ignored the one who was declared blessed. As today's lesson indicates, she should be accorded the honor that Scripture says she deserves. She was favored by God, the recipient of his grace. She shines as an example of submission to the will of God—not just when it is comfortable and convenient, but complete and sacrificial submission.

### B. ACCEPTING THE CHALLENGE

Believers of today need to move beyond being just "Sunday Christians," and to accept the challenges and invitations for special service and sacrifice. It is time for many to move from always being fed, to feeding others—by teaching a class, serving as a youth sponsor, increasing financial stewardship, leading a Bible study, participating in a calling program, supporting a missionary, becoming a missionary, or being a foster parent. There will be some heartaches, rejections, and disappointments—just as there were for Mary. The determined Christian understands this, and he continues faithfully in the service of Christ.

# Discovery Learning

*This page contains an alternate lesson plan emphasizing learning activities. Classes desiring such student involvement will find these suggestions helpful. The next page is a reproducible activity page to further enhance discovery learning.*

## LEARNING GOALS

As a result of this lesson each student should be able to do the following:

1. Describe Mary's reaction to the message of the angel.

2. Explain the nature of total submission to God's will.

3. State his or her personal commitment to the will of God.

## INTO THE LESSON

Before class begins, prepare a large poster board with the following events from the Christmas story listed. (List each event on a separate line with plenty of space between each event. You may need to use two sheets of poster board.)

An angel's visit to Mary or Joseph
Mary's visit to Elizabeth
The virgin birth
The Bethlehem nativity scene
The shepherds
The impact of Jesus' birth

Open today's lesson by asking the class to name Christmas carols or cite phrases from Christmas carols that reflect each of these events from the Christmas story. Have a class member write each song title or phrase by the corresponding event.

After the activity is completed, point out that few or no songs or phrases refer to Gabriel's announcement to Mary, or to Mary's visit with Elizabeth. These important scenes in the Christmas story get little attention in music, Christmas cards, and nativity scenes. Yet God has recorded them for us.

## INTO THE WORD

Divide the class into groups of 4-6 people. Each group is to work on one of the two following tasks. Give each group an instruction sheet for its task and a large piece of poster board to record answers. Note: you may have more than one group working on the same task.

**Task #1:** Read today's text. Then 1) list all the descriptive words or phrases of the promised Son that would be given to Mary. 2) List one or two phrases in songs (preferably, Christmas songs) that describe or reflect these descriptions of Jesus; e.g.: Verse 35 calls him "Son of God." The last stanza of a familiar carol uses

that description: "Silent night, holy night, Son of God, love's pure light . . ."

Other descriptions include "great," "Son of the Most High," "the throne of his father David," "he will reign," "his kingdom will never end," "the holy one." As the class lists these and their songs, mention the significance of these descriptions as cited in today's commentary.

Mention that the name *Jesus* is the same as the Hebrew name *Joshua*, which means "The Lord is Salvation."

**Task #2:** Read today's text. 1) On poster board, list phrases or words from it that are clues about Mary's character and godliness. Be ready to share the significance of these characteristics with the class. 2) Discuss verse 38 and the implications of Mary's model for women today.

Ask the groups to report their findings. If more than one group has been working on a task, compare their answers. After the reports on task #2, share the concepts and remarks from the lesson commentary called "The Place of Mary" on page 136.

## INTO LIFE

Ask the class: "If you had to record Mary's reaction to Gabriel's announcement in just one word, what word would you use." Probably someone will mention "submissive" or "willing" (verse 38). Focus on that attitude as the key word for application into life. Mary wasn't naive. Remind the class that Mary knew the implications her becoming pregnant without being married. She knew the questions people would raise. She knew people would have trouble believing her claim to be still a virgin. Yet she yielded herself to God's will and plan. Her willing submission to God's will is a model for us.

Have the small groups write a brief prayer expressing desire to be submissive to the will of God. They are to write a prayer in the form of an acrostic. Those groups who did task #1 should write their prayer on the word "Yield." The other groups write theirs on the word "Trust." You may display this acrostic/prayer as a model on a transparency or poster board.

Lord, I often find life challenging.
Over and over I must give myself to your will.
Very often I need your wisdom.
Encourage me to stay close to you.

# A Puzzling Message

Mary received a puzzling message from an angel that first disturbed her and then filled her with joy. Read Luke 1:26-42 and then see how many words you can get in the crossword puzzle below.

## DOWN

1. Mary's first response to the angel's words (v. 29)
2. The angel's first word to Mary (v. 28)
5. What Mary had "found" with God (v. 30)
6. The name to be given to Mary's son (v. 31)
8. The angel's name (v. 26)
11. The town where this message was delivered (v. 26)
12. Mary's relative who was also to have a child (v. 36)
14. How Mary thought about the angel's greeting (v. 29)
16. The _____ of the Most High would overshadow Mary (v. 35)
17. Jesus was to receive the _____ of David (v. 32)
19. The title Mary gave herself (v. 38)
20. "You will . . . give _____ to a son" (v. 31)
21. ". . . and you will give him the _____ Jesus" (v. 31)
23. Jesus' royal ancestor (v. 32)

## ACROSS

3. The name of the virgin Gabriel visited (v. 27)
4. This was never to end (v. 33)
7. What God cannot do (v. 37)
9. The region where Nazareth was located (v. 26)
10. Mary would give birth to a _____ (v. 31)
13. Greek for "messenger," this is the kind of being who delivered the message to Mary (v. 26)
15. This One would "come upon" Mary and the power of the Most High overshadow her (v. 35)
18. Jesus' Father (v. 35)
20. An adjective that could no longer be used of Elizabeth (v. 36)
22. The region where Mary went to the hill country (v. 39)
24. This word is used three times to describe Mary (vv. 27, 34)
25. How the power of God would come on Mary (v. 35)

# THE SHEPHERDS

**LESSON 3**

## WHY TEACH THIS LESSON?

"No more of it!" the leaders demanded. "You must never again speak or teach in the name of Jesus." The response of Peter and John to this demand is well known to many Christians: "We cannot help speaking about what we have seen and heard" (Acts 4:20).

They weren't the first. Years before a band of shepherd could not help speaking about what they had seen and heard. What they had seen were angels and then a baby in a manger. What they had heard was good news of God's grace.

This lesson should challenge your students, who have also heard good news of God's grace, to tell that good news to others.

## INTRODUCTION

### A. BELOVED CHARACTERS

The story is told of a kindergarten teacher who asked her students to tell the class what their fathers did for a living. One young girl said that she thought her father was a shepherd. When asked why she thought this, she responded, "Because he usually walks around the house in his bathrobe."

Most of us have little knowledge of the shepherd's life beyond the impressions we receive from our Christmas pageants and live nativity scenes. Shepherding is not a vocation we teach in school or that many of us see in our daily lives. Even those who raise sheep today, or live near those who do, have difficulty identifying with people who used to live in open fields "keeping watch over their flocks."

Nevertheless, the shepherds of Luke 2 are a favorite part of the Christmas story. We enjoy visualizing a quiet night, gentle sheep, an angelic visit, and a trip to the manger. We may know few facts regarding shepherds, but we know that we like these shepherds. As we study the biblical text, let us learn from these shepherds.

### B. LESSON BACKGROUND

Last week's lesson focused upon Gabriel's announcement to Mary that she would give birth to the promised Messiah. This week's lesson moves approximately nine months forward to the events surrounding that birth.

The birth of Jesus in Bethlehem was about ninety miles south of Nazareth, the hometown of Joseph and Mary. The couple was away from home at this awkward time because a decree by the Roman emperor Augustus required that they, along with everyone else, return to their family place of origin long enough to register for a new census. For Joseph and Mary that meant a trip to Bethlehem (Luke 2:1-5).

The lack of housing in Bethlehem was likely due to a large influx of visitors from all over the Roman empire who like Joseph had come to register. The result of this overcrowding was that the Son of God was born in an animal stable (Luke 2:6, 7).

## I. A DAY OF GRACE (LUKE 2:8-12)

### A. A GIFT FOR ALL MEN (vv. 8-10)

**8. And there were shepherds living out in the fields nearby, keeping watch over their flocks at night.**

**DEVOTIONAL READING**
MICAH 5:2-9

**LESSON SCRIPTURE**
LUKE 2:1-20

**PRINTED TEXT**
LUKE 2:8-20

Dec
15

**LESSON AIMS**

As a result of studying this lesson, the students will be able to:

1. Tell how the shepherds learned about the birth of the Messiah and how they responded to the news.

2. Compare the shepherds' response to the "gospel" to their own.

3. Suggest one way they can "spread the word" about Jesus this week.

**KEY VERSE**

The shepherds returned, glorifying and praising God for all the things they had heard and seen, which were just as they had been told. *Luke 2:20*

## LESSON 3 NOTES

*The visual for lesson 3 in the visuals packet is appropriate for the Christmas season, showing a traditional nativity scene. Have it on display when the class arrives. Or post it when you begin to discuss verse 16, as it illustrates what the shepherds found.*

## WHAT DO YOU THINK?

*While their menial occupation put them near the bottom of the social ladder, the Bethlehem shepherds were important to God. His announcement was a gracious gesture showing that he values the condition of the heart more than social status.*

*How can we—as a church and individually—demonstrate that we accept people of all races and social levels? How well are we communicating that? Is our church truly open to all people, or do its people look very much alike? How can we be more open?*

On the day Jesus was born a band of shepherds was in the vicinity of Bethlehem. For the most part shepherds were nomadic people. They often had a permanent home base, as the shepherd David had in his father's house in Bethlehem (1 Samuel 16:10-13). The laws regarding possession of land, including the rights of redemption and the year of jubilee, were designed to ensure each family in Israel a permanent place of their own. But sheep need grass and tend to eat it right down to the ground, so much of the shepherds' time was spent moving their flock of sheep and goats throughout the open countryside in search of grass. At night shepherds would herd their animals together, usually into a make-shift pen or "fold," temporarily constructed from pieces of wood and/or the sides of natural rock formations. Once the flock was secure, the shepherds could take turns sleeping while one remained on guard.

Some have suggested that the birth of Jesus could not have occurred in December based on the assumption that shepherds would not be sleeping outdoors in fields during the winter. However, the work of a shepherd is a year-round duty. Sheep must still be led to pasture for feeding even in winter. On a Christmas tour of Bethlehem today it is still possible to see some shepherds tending sheep in the nearby fields.

God's decision to make the first announcement of the birth of his Son to shepherds well illustrates the gracious nature of God. In biblical times shepherds were on the low end of the social scale. Their living and working conditions did not measure up to urban standards. But God is no such respecter of persons. The privilege of first hearing of the long-awaited birth of the Messiah was given to some lowly shepherds.

**9. An angel of the Lord appeared to them, and the glory of the Lord shone around them, and they were terrified.**

The text does not identify this *angel* by name, but it may very well have been Gabriel, the same angel who appeared to Zechariah in the temple (Luke 1:11, 19) and later to Mary in Nazareth (Luke 1:26, 27). *The glory of the Lord* was apparently a radiant light shining forth from the angel, probably symbolizing the fact that he had just come from the glorious presence of God with a divine message to deliver.

It was a natural response for the shepherds to be *terrified* of the angel. Under normal circumstances, shepherds were accustomed to facing dangerous situations. David, for example, dealt with a lion and a bear even as a boy (1 Samuel 17:34-36). But these anticipated dangers would not fully prepare one for confronting in the dark of night an unearthly being who radiated a heavenly glory. The picture of fear touching Zechariah (Luke 1:12, 13), Mary (Luke 1:29, 30), and the shepherds makes them seem like common people with whom we can easily identify.

**10. But the angel said to them, "Do not be afraid. I bring you good news of great joy that will be for all the people.**

The phrase *good news* is a translation of a Greek word that in other passages is often translated by the Old English word *gospel,* derived from *god* (good) and *spel* (tale). Thus we could speak of the angel's proclaiming the "gospel" of Jesus Christ when he announced the good news of Jesus' birth.

The grace of God is emphasized again when the angel declared that the birth of Jesus is good news *for all the people.* When mankind sinned, God was under no obligation to save anyone, and certainly not at so great a cost as the suffering experienced by his Son at Calvary. To save even one sinner by this means would be a great act of grace. Consider the boundless measure of God's grace in that he sent his Son to provide a means of salvation for every person who has ever lived on this earth. (See John 3:16; 1 John 2:2.) That is truly *good news of great joy . . . for all the people.*

### COMMUNICATION BARRIERS

Nearly all missionaries experience the frustration of communication barriers. Language and cultural differences erect huge hurdles to anyone ministering on foreign soil. Often, suspicion and other forms of fear must be overcome.

The Judean shepherds, not surprisingly, were "terrified" at the unexpected visit of the Lord's angel. Their reaction to the supernatural sights and sounds accompanying the event could have short-circuited their reception of the vital message. Thus, the first words from the divine messenger were, "Do not be afraid" (Luke 2:10).

In a sense, every Christian faces similar challenges in personal evangelism. Prospects may be "fearful" of Christians because of an unfortunate personal experience in the past, the questionable actions of some "televangelists," or some other negative impression of the church that they have received.

Whatever the cause, such fears are real to unbelievers and must be overcome by modern messengers of God. Our words, attitudes, and actions should communicate the message: "Do not be afraid."       —R. W. B.

## B. A REMEDY FOR OUR SIN (vv. 11, 12)

**11. *"Today in the town of David a Savior has been born to you; he is Christ the Lord.***

Three of our most popular titles for Jesus are introduced in this passage. The Gospel of John and the New Testament epistles often refer to Jesus as *Savior.* But Luke 2:11 is the only verse in the Synoptic Gospels (Matthew, Mark, and Luke) to use this title in reference to Jesus. However, the concept of Jesus as our Savior pervades the Synoptics, notably in the angel's message to Joseph: "you are to give him the name Jesus, because he will save his people from their sins" (Matthew 1:21).

The title *Christ* is the Greek equivalent of the Hebrew word *Messiah.* Both terms mean "the anointed one," that is, the one God has chosen to perform a certain task. In biblical times prophets, priests, and kings were typically installed into their office with a ceremony in which a small amount of oil was placed upon their heads. This symbolized their selection and calling by God for the task at hand. Jesus is the ultimate "anointed one." He is the ultimate prophet, being himself the Word of God incarnate (John 1:1, 14; Hebrews 1:1, 2). He is the ultimate priest, who offered the ultimate sacrifice at Calvary (Hebrews 9:11-14). He is the ultimate king—"King of Kings" (Revelation 19:16). Thus he wears the title *Christ* or Messiah in a way that is unique.

The title *Savior* implies the work of Jesus. The title *Christ* implies God's appointment of Jesus. But it is the title *Lord* that particularly implies our obligation to Jesus. We owe him a complete submission to his revealed will. By virtue of his victory over the forces of Satan and death, Jesus now lays claim to "all authority in heaven and on earth" (Matthew 28:18). "God exalted him to the highest place," so much so that "every knee should bow . . . and every tongue confess that Jesus Christ is Lord" (Philippians 2:9-11). If we want the child who was born in Bethlehem to be our Savior and Christ, we must also acknowledge him as our Lord.

**12. *"This will be a sign to you: You will find a baby wrapped in cloths and lying in a manger."***

The baby was wrapped in strips of cloth somewhat comparable to our cloth diapers or baby blankets. Apparently Mary was prepared for the possibility of a birth during her trip south. These cloths in and of themselves would not serve

### HOW TO SAY IT

*Augustus.* Aw-GUST-us.
*Gabriel.* GAY-bree-ul.
*Goshen.* GO-shen.
*Judean.* Joo-DEE-un.
*Samaria.* Suh-MEH-ree-uh.
*Synoptic.* Sin-OP-tick.
*Syria.* SEER-ee-uh.
*Zechariah.* Zek-uh-RYE-uh.

### WHAT DO YOU THINK?

Should Christians expect to receive messages from angels today? Why or why not?

Use the reproducible activity, "Angels Watching Over Me," on page 146 to assist you with this discussion. Note that aside from their role connected with the birth, resurrection, and second coming of Jesus, we are told very little about the role of angels. A few appearances are recorded in Acts, but beyond that our information is very sparse. We need to be careful when it comes to speculating about angels today.

as an indicator of the Messiah, for such would be the appropriate care for any baby the shepherds would find in crowded Bethlehem. The sign was the oddity of finding a child being loved and cared for (as indicated by the *cloths*) in a *manger* or feed trough. Not only did this clue narrow the shepherd's search to places where animals would be fed, but it also provided a unique indicator that could not be missed.

Though the angel's words did not explicitly say "go seek the child," that assignment was clearly implied in the giving of a sign. A heart that is eager to serve the Lord does not require much more than just a suggestion from the Lord that there is work to be done.

## II. A NIGHT OF GLORY (LUKE 2:13-16)

### A. A SOUND OF PRAISE (vv. 13, 14)

**13, 14. Suddenly a great company of the heavenly host appeared with the angel, praising God and saying, "Glory to God in the highest, and on earth peace to men on whom his favor rests."**

As *suddenly* as the first *angel* had appeared, a large number of angels joined him. Perhaps the timing is an indication of the kindness of God toward the shepherds. To begin this encounter with one glorious angel was very frightening. To have begun with a great company of angels would have been dreadful. The arrival of the angels in stages was a good thing for the shepherds.

Our Christmas carols typically picture the angels as singing their praise to God. The terms *praising* and *saying* are consistent with this idea, though they do not necessarily indicate a musical expression of praise. However, there is a metrical balance to their words. *Glory to God* is balanced against *peace to men*. *Glory in the highest* matches *on earth peace*. This feels like a song.

This passage illustrates the double use of the word *glory* in Scripture. The angels radiate the glory *of* God (v. 9), and say "glory *to* God," to praise him. God is worthy of having both kinds of glory attributed to him.

*On earth peace to men of whom his favor rests* sounds quite different from the "Peace on earth; goodwill to men" of the familiar carol and numerous Christmas cards. It is based on the *King James Version*. Other translations render it still differently because (1) the available Greek manuscripts are not exactly alike and (2) the Greek text can be understood in more than one way. But every translation conveys the key idea here: that mankind is under God's good will and grace through Jesus Christ.

### B. A SCENE OF PROMISE (vv. 15, 16)

**15. When the angels had left them and gone into heaven, the shepherds said to one another, "Let's go to Bethlehem and see this thing that has happened, which the Lord has told us about."**

We can only imagine the excitement that must have filled the souls of the *shepherds* as they reflected on their heavenly experience. For them there is no question but that they must *go* immediately *to Bethlehem* and search for the Messiah child. This is the kind of enthusiasm we associate with people when they first come into contact with Jesus Christ. It is an enthusiasm we would do well to rekindle afresh during this Christmas season.

We need not worry about their losing their sheep while they were gone to town. The sheep could remain in their field pen under the watch of a single shepherd, as is the case each evening when they take turns sleeping.

**16. So they hurried off and found Mary and Joseph, and the baby, who was lying in the manger.**

## WHAT DO YOU THINK?

The traditional wording (based on the King James Version) of "Peace on earth; goodwill to men" seems out of place in a world torn by violence and bloodshed at every hand. How does the wording here, "On earth peace to men of whom his favor rests," offer hope in such a world? How does this "favor" or grace come to "rest" on people? Does this mean Christians have no problems? Why or why not? What kind of peace has knowing the Lord brought to your life? How can we spread that peace and hope to others more effectively?

The description is so basic and simple. It is perhaps much less than we might have anticipated, given the angelic build-up. And yet, what else would the shepherds have expected to find in a stable? Surely not a throne with royal attendants, much less the radiant glory of God they had seen displayed by the angels. They were not seeking a man ready to lead them, but a *baby* in a *manger*.

But that was enough. For with that seemingly helpless baby God's salvation had finally arrived on earth. The wait was almost over. As is still the case today with so many of us, that first nativity scene filled their hearts with hope and promise for the future.

## III. A TIME OF GOOD NEWS (LUKE 2:17-20)
### A. A MESSAGE WORTH RETELLING (vv. 17, 18)
**17. When they had seen him, they spread the word concerning what had been told them about this child.**

The shepherds had seen too much of the working of God to keep it all to themselves. They became "evangelists," for the basic definition of "evangelist" is one who "proclaims good news to others." The angel had delivered good news to the shepherds (v. 10), and they in turn felt compelled to share that good news with others.

Here is an example that should challenge each one of us. The shepherds knew very little about the Messiah. They had not yet witnessed his ministry, his death, his resurrection. They had not had the opportunity to enjoy the benefits of Jesus' work, to mature within the fellowship of his church, to read the New Testament Scripture. But they were ready to tell about what they did know regarding Jesus. They knew *what* they *had been told* and what they had seen; they knew enough. *They spread the word.*

We have a great number of advantages over the shepherds, and yet we are often so quiet among non-Christians that no one would know that we have good news to share. We can learn much from these simple shepherds. We, too, can spread the word simply by telling what we know. If we know enough to have accepted Christ, then we know enough to tell others about him so that they, too, can accept him.

### UNLIKELY PROSPECTS

An outreach tool used by increasing numbers of churches today is the demographic report. Developed primarily for salespeople, this set of statistics defines the average person in a church's market territory. Such information guides churches in designing strategies for evangelism. Programming, publications, and promotions are aimed at the statistical composite of the average constituent in a given geographical radius.

If pollsters in New Testament times had surveyed the Bethlehem area, the demographics would not have suggested that the shepherds on the Judean hillside were the ideal market for the angelic promotion of the news of Jesus' birth. Shepherds were uneducated, unsophisticated, with little disposable income. Consumer-conscious marketers would have considered them to be unlikely prospects. The preliminary announcement of the good news would have been made to people of position, power, and substance.

Evangelistic outreach is a major concern of the church. To whom should we go with the truth of God? How can we most efficiently and effectively use our time and resources to help the kingdom grow? We must be wise as we determine our strategy, but we must not compromise the gospel to accommodate our culture. And we must not ignore "unlikely prospects," for, as the angel said, the good news is for all the people.                    —R. W. B.

### WHAT DO YOU THINK?

*The shepherds were enthusiastic witnesses to what they had seen and heard concerning Jesus. This is the kind of zeal new converts often have. But when the newness wears off, we settle into a more normal routine of living the day-to-day Christian life. Some give in and return to the old life. The challenge we face as Christians is similar to that which married couples face: to keep the daily routine from becoming mundane and boring.*

*What can this church do to help people keep their zeal for sharing Christ? Suggest two or three positive actions we can take.*

### WHAT DO YOU THINK?

*The shepherds could easily have rationalized that they could not go to Bethlehem—they had work to do. Or later, they could have said, "No one will believe this story; let's just keep quiet about what we have seen and heard." Why didn't they? How can we imitate their example? Many times we are afraid we will be rejected or ridiculed if we speak of our faith—how can we appreciate the glory of God enough to do as the shepherds did? Do we need angels to appear to us!? How can we be motivated to tell the news as the shepherds were?*

## PRAYER

*Father, help us to see more clearly the fullness of the grace you have bestowed upon us through our Lord and Savior Jesus Christ. May we then be faithful witnesses of what we have seen and heard in your Word and in our lives. In Jesus' name, amen.*

## THOUGHT TO REMEMBER

*This Christmas season is once again a day of "good news of great joy . . . for all the people." Let us share this good news with all who need our Savior and Christ and Lord.*

## DAILY BIBLE READINGS

**Monday, Dec. 9**—*Don't Be Afraid of Adversaries (Isaiah 41:11-16)*

**Tuesday, Dec. 10**—*Don't Be Afraid of Criticism (Isaiah 51:4-8)*

**Wednesday, Dec. 11**—*Don't Be Afraid of Changes (Isaiah 54:4-8)*

**Thursday, Dec. 12**—*Don't Be Afraid of Adversities (Haggai 2:4-9)*

**Friday, Dec. 13**—*God Can Free Us From Fear (Luke 12: 22-31)*

**Saturday, Dec. 14**—*God Is Our Shield (Genesis 15:1-6)*

**Sunday, Dec. 15**—*Everything Praise the Lord! (Psalm 150:1-6)*

**18. And all who heard it were amazed at what the shepherds said to them.**

Is it any surprise that people were filled with wonder and puzzlement over this strange story told by *the shepherds*. A typical reaction was probably to write off this message just as they would normally write off the shepherds themselves. And yet they would still have to wonder about the possibilities.

It is not likely that the shepherds revealed the name of the young Messiah and his parents, since there is no indication in the Gospels that Jesus' identity was known prior to his revealing himself at his baptism. What is more likely is that the shepherds simply reported what they had seen and heard in the field and by the manger. This story that the Messiah had been born in Bethlehem, though mostly dismissed as unfounded rumor, would then serve to stir up a messianic expectation that both John the Baptist and Jesus could later tap into when they began their ministries.

### B. A STORY WORTH REMEMBERING (vv. 19, 20)
**19. But Mary treasured up all these things and pondered them in her heart.**

For most parents the birth of their first child is a precious and memorable experience. But imagine being in Mary's place, participating in a miraculous conception of the Son of God, a providential move to the city of David for the birth, a humble setting at a manger, and visits by angels and shepherds. These memories were certainly among her most *treasured* ones. No wonder she frequently recalled them and reflected on them.

That she *pondered* or "reflected on" these memories is also not surprising. Any new mother would reflect on the events surrounding the birth of her first child. But perhaps it suggests even more. After all, Mary had been told this child had a special future. No doubt she thought about his mission and marveled at the evidence of God at work already in preparing him for that mission.

**20. The shepherds returned, glorifying and praising God for all the things they had heard and seen, which were just as they had been told.**

The *shepherds*, likewise, did not soon forget this experience. They had a story worth remembering and retelling for the rest of their lives.

## CONCLUSION

In 2 Kings :14—7:20 the city of Samaria was under siege by an army from Aram (Syria). The people within were starving to death because their food supply had been cut off. Outside the walls of the city were four lepers with little prospects for surviving. If they entered the city, they would starve to death with those inside. If they surrendered to the enemy, they would likely be killed. And yet the latter option at least held the prospect that they might be taken captive and fed. One night they ventured into the enemy camp.

It was then that they discovered that God had already frightened off the Arameans with the sound of an approaching army. The lepers began to enjoy a bounty of food and supplies that had been left behind. However, in the midst of their celebration they realized that they should have been sharing their good fortune with the people starving within the city. "We're not doing right. This is a day of good news and we are keeping it to ourselves" (2 Kings 7:9).

Is it not amazing that those whom society casts off, such as lepers and shepherds, can sometimes teach us great lessons regarding our spiritual duty to God. Perhaps it is their lowly status that helps them more fully appreciate the depths of the grace of God and their duty to witness to his grace through Jesus Christ. As we reflect upon the nativity story, let us humble ourselves with a spirit akin to these shepherds.

# Discovery Learning

*This page contains an alternate lesson plan emphasizing learning activities. Classes desiring such student involvement will find these suggestions helpful. The next page is a reproducible activity page to further enhance discovery learning.*

## LEARNING GOALS

As a result of this lesson, the students will be able to:

1. Tell how the shepherds learned about the birth of the Messiah and how they responded to the news.

2. Compare the shepherds' response to the "gospel" to their own.

3. Suggest one way they can "spread the word" about Jesus this week.

## INTO THE LESSON

Open the lesson by reminding the class that last week we listed songs and choruses that told about various events surrounding the birth of Jesus. There were very few that told about the angel's announcement to Mary, but many songs and lines in songs that are about the shepherds. Ask the class to recall some of the songs or lines in the songs that tell about the shepherds. Then ask the class why they think so many songs have been written that focus on the shepherds.

Ask, "Of all the references to shepherds in the Christmas carols you know, how many mention the shepherds' telling others what they had seen?" Probably there will be only a few. Observe that it's more comfortable to identify with the shepherds at worship (at the manger) than in service (telling others). Today we will try to see the latter and challenge ourselves to follow their example.

## INTO THE WORD

Read Luke 2:1-20 aloud. (Or have a student read it.) Point out that this is the third lesson in as many weeks that has included a message from an angel. Note that angelic appearances were actually rare; that we have several connected with the birth of Jesus points out the fact that this was a unique event. There is a danger that we will begin to think of these visits by angels as commonplace because of their frequency in the nativity accounts. This is dangerous, as it leads to a misunderstanding of the biblical role of angels. (*Option:* Use the activity, "Angels Watchin' Over Me," on page 146 to explore the New Testament's teaching about angels.)

Put the following information on index cards, one paragraph per card. Distribute the cards and have the students work to arrange the cards in order, according to the text. If you have a large class, prepare more than one set of cards and divide the class into sections, with each section taking a set of cards. (The verse numbers in paren-theses are for the teacher's use and should not be included on the cards.)

- The good news is not only for a certain social class. It is for the lowly shepherd as well as for the wealthy king. It is not only for a certain race. The gospel is for the Jew and for the Gentile. (v. 10)
- Jesus is the ultimate "anointed one" or Christ. He is the ultimate prophet, priest, and king. (v. 11)
- The "sign" was not that the baby was wrapped in cloths, but that such a well-cared-for baby was in a manger. (v. 12)
- Jesus brings peace to those who accept God's offer of grace through him. (vv. 13, 14)
- True believers need only a suggestion, not a command, to stir them to action. (vv. 15, 16)
- An evangelist merely tells what he himself knows about the Christ. Whether he knows little or much, he is eager to share. (v. 17, 18)
- A mother's pride is understandable, but Mary's heart must have been full of even more than a typical mother's. Her son was the Son of God! (v. 19)

After a few minutes, check on their progress. Make sure they get the statements arranged according to the verse order. Comment on any paragraph as needed, using information in the commentary.

## INTO LIFE

The coming of the Savior is always "good news!" The prophets foretold it. The shepherds shared it. The Gospels record it. The apostles preached it. And we must share it.

Allow class members to apply this important concept by giving them prepared self-evaluation and commitment sheets shown below. Ask them to complete the sheets to determine their willingness to share the good news.

1. I am alert to opportunities to share my faith in my Lord.    Always    Usually    Seldom
2. I am confident talking about my faith and God's grace to non-Christians.    Always    Usually    Seldom
3. I am comfortable in inviting people to worship with me at our church.    Always    Usually    Seldom
4. The names of some people I have influenced for Jesus include:
5. I am determined to be the witness that God wants me to be.    Always    Usually    Seldom

Ask the class members to complete the sheets. Close with prayer for strength to complete their commitments.

# Angels Watchin' Over Me

There is great interest in angels today. Angels are the subject of popular books and television programs. They occupy the minds and conversations of many. Unfortunately, much of the information being distributed cannot be substantiated, and often it contradicts what the Scriptures tell us about angels.

Use the following chart to see what the New Testament says about angels.

SUMMARIZE THE ROLE OF ANGELS IN THE OLD TESTAMENT

Acts 7:53; Galatians 3:19;
Hebrews 2:2

WHAT ROLE DID ANGELS PLAY IN THE EVENTS OF THE BIRTH OF JESUS

Matthew 1:20-24
Matthew 2:13-19
Luke 1:11-19, 26-38
Luke 2:9-15

WHAT ROLE DID ANGELS PLAY IN THE MINISTRY OF JESUS?

Matthew 4:11
Luke 22:43

WHAT ROLE DID ANGELS PLAY AT THE RESURRECTION OF JESUS?

Matthew 28:1-7
John 20:10-13

WHAT ROLE DID ANGELS PLAY IN THE LIFE OF THE EARLY CHURCH?

Acts 5:18, 19; 12:5-11
Acts 8:26
Acts 10:1-8, 22, 30-32
Acts 27:23-25

WHAT ROLE WILL ANGELS PLAY AT CHRIST'S SECOND COMING AND THE JUDGMENT?

Matthew 13:36-43; 16:27
Matthew 24:30, 31, 36
Matthew 25:31-33
Luke 12:8, 9
2 Thessalonians 1:6-8

WHAT GENERAL ROLE OR ROLES ARE INDICATED FOR ANGELS?

Matthew 18:10
Matthew 26:53
Luke 15:10
Luke 16:22
Acts 12:21-23
1 Corinthians 4:9
Hebrews 1:4-7, 14
Hebrews 12:22-24
Hebrews 13:2
1 Peter 3:22

# THE WISE MEN AND HEROD

**LESSON 4**

## WHY TEACH THIS LESSON?

"God is in control!" So sings a contemporary Christian vocalist, and so affirms the Scripture. But sometimes, even if for just a fleeting moment, most of us wonder about that. A dad loses his job, a child is killed in an accident, a mother is disabled by sickness. Romans 8:28 sticks in our throats.

One of the most tragic events in Scripture climaxes our study today. Herod, jealous for his throne and eager to eliminate all rivals, had the children of Bethlehem murdered! Where was God? How could he have allowed it? Why did he ever let those wise men tell Herod of the Christ child in the first place?

Challenge your students to see the good that came even through this tragic event. Romans 8:28 is true indeed, and a source of comfort if they will believe it!

## INTRODUCTION

### A. TREASURE HUNT

Is there anything so exciting as a treasure hunt? The idea has fostered great imaginations and classic literature for centuries. For some it is a game, as the "treasure" is not of any real value, but the hunt itself becomes a challenge requiring imagination and creativity. The treasure is soon discarded after it is found.

For others, it is serious business. Salvage crews plumb the ocean depths for treasure-laden ships; archaeologists sift through the dust and rubble of centuries for artifacts of a civilization long since gone. Others search for treasure of different sorts. Thousands of dollars are spent in hope of finding treasure worth many times more. It is a test of skill and knowledge and endurance.

When the Magi (popularly referred to as wise men) of Matthew 2 searched for the new-born King, they faced a challenge that tested their skill and knowledge. Their "treasure" was no party favor or even a cache of gold and jewels. It was a baby—a newborn king to be worshiped and adored. It was their Savior and Lord.

### B. LESSON BACKGROUND

Matthew's account of the birth of Jesus contains different information from what we have learned from the Gospel of Luke. Whereas Luke focuses on the mother Mary and her kinsmen Zechariah and Elizabeth, Matthew keys in on Joseph. While Luke describes a visit by nearby shepherds, Matthew is interested in a visit by foreign wise men. Together these two different accounts give us a fuller picture of the birth of Jesus.

Even the genealogies presented in these two Gospels exhibit a difference in focus. Luke does not present his genealogy until Jesus begins his messianic ministry in the third chapter. Then Luke traces Jesus' lineage back to Adam, perhaps to emphasize the relationship all people have with this Savior. Matthew, on the other hand, puts his genealogy up front as he opens both his Gospel and his nativity account. Matthew's purpose becomes clear as his story unfolds. He wants to establish Jesus' regal descent from David (Matthew 1:1) as a prelude to his account of the wise men seeking the "king of the Jews" (Matthew 2:2). Jesus' royal lineage in chapter 1 lays the groundwork for his royal treatment in chapter 2.

**DEVOTIONAL READING**
**MATTHEW 2:13-23**
**LESSON SCRIPTURE**
**MATTHEW 2**
**PRINTED TEXT**
**MATTHEW 2:1-12, 16**

Dec
22

**LESSON AIMS**

*After participating in this lesson, the student will be able to:*

*1. Tell the biblical account of the visit of the Magi and Herod's attempt to kill the Christ child.*

*2. Relate how God's providence was at work in the visit of the wise men and the plotting of Herod.*

*3. Praise God for his providential care.*

**KEY VERSES**

*On coming to the house, they saw the child with his mother Mary, and they bowed down and worshiped him. Then they opened their treasures and presented him with gifts of gold and of incense and of myrrh.* Matthew 2:11

## WHAT DO YOU THINK?

*Since the wise men apparently were astrologers, some people say that God's communicating with them validates astrology for today. Yet the Bible condemn astrology. How would you answer someone who believed practicing astrology was okay?*

*See Isaiah 47:13-15; Deuteronomy 4:19; 17:2-7; 2 Kings 17:16-20; 21:1-5; Daniel 2:1-11.*

*Some have observed that the fact that God communicated directly with these men suggests they were more than mere astrologers. What do you think that may suggest about the validity of astrology? Others point out that the Bible nowhere specifically says they were astrologers—just that God used a star to guide them. Daniel was called a "wise man" (Daniel 2:13), but he was not an astrologer. What does that suggest about this issue?*

## OPTION

*Some people believe that the star of Bethlehem was a miracle. Others believe it was a natural phenomenon. Use the reproducible activity, "Providential Star," on page 154 to explore that issue.*

## I. THE SEARCH FOR CHRIST (MATTHEW 2:1-8)

### A. VISITORS FROM THE EAST (vv. 1-3)

**1. After Jesus was born in Bethlehem in Judea, during the time of King Herod, Magi from the east came to Jerusalem**

The identity of the *Magi* is quite a mystery for us today. The name *Magi* is from the Latin; in Greek it is *magoi*. They are literally "the mighty ones," not in physical strength or political authority, but in knowledge. Thus our popular designation, "the wise men."

Their specific origin in *the east* is not certain. The ancient Medes and Persians (modern-day Iran) had their wise men who specialized in several scholarly disciplines including astronomy and astrology. Likewise the ancient Babylonians (modern-day Iraq) also had wise men who studied astronomy and developed charts for planetary and stellar orbits as well as accurate astral calendars. These and other areas east of Palestine could have produced the wise men of Matthew 2.

Their knowledge and interest in the Jewish hope for a coming Messiah can be attributed to the dispersion of the Jews in both the Assyrian conquest of Israel and the Babylonian conquest of Judah. The Assyrians relocated many Jews to the cities of the Medes (2 Kings 17:6) while the Babylonians later took back to their home the finest among the young Jewish men, such as Daniel and his three friends. The eastern wise men may not have practiced Judaism, but they at least had an awareness of and appreciation for Jewish messianic prophecies.

Many of our modern-day assumptions regarding the wise men cannot be confirmed by the biblical text or by historical resources. For example, we often sing about "the three kings." Matthew, however, does not indicate the number of these men, nor does he suggest that they possessed any royal status. In fact, in most of the eastern cultures the wise men were not kings but, rather, served as counselors to kings. It is only a church tradition that supplies the names Melchior, Balthasar, and Caspar, and their separate origins from India, Egypt, and Greece (two of which are not even east of Palestine). No more credible than this is the claim of several cathedrals throughout church history to possess the bones of the wise men.

**2. . . . and asked, "Where is the one who has been born king of the Jews? We saw his star in the east and have come to worship him."**

The nature of this *star* is not explained in our text. Some astronomers suggest there was an alignment of certain stars and planets. Some have suggested an alignment of Jupiter, the "king planet," with another planet or a star was interpreted as signaling the birth of a new king. Or it is suggested that there may have been an unusual amount of meteor activity. Others prefer a supernatural explanation in which God created an unusual phenomenon in the sky to guide the wise men to Israel. Whatever the origin of the star, the timing of its appearance and its behavior (see comments on verse 9, page 150) are sure signs that God was at work here.

But if the wise men were following a divinely sent star, why did they stop in Jerusalem? Perhaps they were not following the star at this point. The Bible does not say the wise men followed the star all the way to Judea. It simply tells us they *saw his star in the east* and that later "the star they had seen in the east [not "the star they had followed from the east"] went ahead of them until it stopped over the place where the child was" (verse 9). There may have been two appearances of the star: one to initiate their journey and a second to guide them to the journey's end. In that case, a stop in Jerusalem would be logical for those looking for a Jewish king. The joy they felt at seeing the star (verse 10) does suggest the star was at least a temporarily out of their sight.

Our curious natures want to know more about this star. Not the least of our questions is why it provided precise guidance only after the wise men had alerted

Herod to the new king's birth! But Matthew's interest is not in the mechanics of the star, but in the intent of the wise men: they had *come to worship him*. We must satisfy ourselves that God was in control in leading the wise men, and his care for his Son was in no way compromised by Herod's learning of his birth.

### 3. When King Herod heard this he was disturbed, and all Jerusalem with him.

Matthew introduces us to *King Herod* the Great, who ruled Israel from 37 B.C. to 4 B.C. There were other members of his family who wore the name "Herod," but none with accomplishments worthy of the title "the Great." Herod is known as a clever political strategist and a patron of great art and architecture. In Jerusalem alone Herod built a theater, an amphitheater, a hippodrome, and a palace, as well as a major enlargement of the Jewish temple.

This reference to Herod gives us a historical peg for dating the birth of Jesus. Herod died in March or April of 4 B.C. Jesus' birth was obviously sometime before that, probably in 5 B.C.

The words of the wise men troubled Herod. The Greek literally says he was "shaken" by what he heard. The problem was his constant insecurity regarding his position as king of Israel. Herod's family was not of Jewish descent. They were Edomites. He somewhat practiced the Jewish religion, but he was not a true Jew. Throughout his reign, Herod feared that the people would revolt against him, and thus he tried to maintain his position with generous favors, such as his building projects. When that tactic seemed ineffective, he resorted to physical force and deadly intimidation.

And thus all Jerusalem was also shaken when the wise men came asking about a new "king of the Jews." They knew Herod's likely response. He had already killed several of his own family members, including sons, because he suspected they wanted his throne. In fact, shortly after this episode, and only five days before his death, Herod killed one more son out of fear and suspicion. What the people feared when they heard mention of a new king was soon realized in the killing of the babies in Bethlehem.

### B. Prophecy of a Birth (vv. 4-6)

### 4. When he had called together all the people's chief priests and teachers of the law, he asked them where the Christ was to be born.

Herod's minimal ties with the Jewish heritage made him ill-equipped to handle the kind of messianic question posed by the wise men. He had to seek an answer from the leaders of the Jewish religion. Note that *Christ* is used here according to the biblical pattern, not as the last name of Jesus, but as the Greek title for *Messiah*.

### 5, 6. "In Bethlehem in Judea," they replied, "for this is what the prophet has written: 'But you, Bethlehem, in the land of Judah, are by no means least among the rulers of Judah; for out of you will come a ruler who will be the shepherd of my people Israel.'"

The chief priests and scribes refer to Micah 5:2 for the location of the birthplace of the Messiah. Though Herod was ignorant of the significance of this passage, the average Jew understood. One of the reasons so many Jews rejected Jesus' claims was their mistaken assumption that he had been born in Nazareth rather than in Bethlehem (John 7:42). But God in his providence had arranged for the fulfillment of Old Testament prophecy. Consider the appropriateness of the birth of the messianic successor to King David in Bethlehem, the "city of David."

### C. Deception by the King (vv. 7, 8)

### 7. Then Herod called the Magi secretly and found out from them the exact time the star had appeared.

## What Do You Think?

The Bible gives neither the day nor the year of Jesus' birth. Christmas was first celebrated on December 25 in the middle of the fourth century A.D. Thus, many believe the likelihood that Jesus' birth actually occurred on December 25 is rather slim. In fact, some believe there we should not observe a "Christmas holiday" at all since it is not biblical.

What do you think? Are there good reasons for celebrating on December 25—or any day? What might be gained by not celebrating? Which has greater potential for evangelism—celebrating or not celebrating? Why? What abuses should be guarded against by those who do celebrate?

## How to Say It

*Assyrians.* Uh-SEER-ee-unz.
*Babylonians.* Bab-uh-LOW-nee-unz.
*Balthasar.* Ball-TAY-sar.
*Caspar.* KASS-par.
*Edomites.* EE-duh-mites.
*Herod.* HAIR-ud.
*Judah.* JOO-duh.
*Judea.* Joo-DEE-uh.
*Magi.* MADGE-eye.
*magoi (Greek).* MAH-goy.
*Medes.* Meeds.
*Melchior.* MEL-key-or.
*Micah.* MY-kuh.
*Simeon.* SIM-ee-un.
*Zechariah.* Zek-uh-RYE-uh.

## WHAT DO YOU THINK?

*The wise men traveled over a thousand miles to find Jesus, while the priests and scribes refused to go just a few miles—from Jerusalem to Bethlehem. Why are some people more willing to seek Jesus than others?*

*Which are most people in our society like today, the wise men or the Jewish religious leaders? Why?*

*How much like the wise men are most of our church members today? How many of us would expend similar time and energy to worship the Lord? How can we be more like the wise men?*

The devious nature of *Herod* is well portrayed in this passage. What Herod actually wanted was to find out as much as he could about this child so he could send his soldiers to kill him. But to get this information he feigned an interest in their investigation of the new king's star. By knowing the date when the *star* first *appeared,* Herod could estimate the age of his rival.

This discussion with the wise men had to be conducted in secret so that Herod would not appear to have too much interest to their news of another king. The Jews, eager to have their Messiah and suspicious of Herod, might guess his true intentions and try to rescue the child. And if anyone did suspect Herod's intentions, the private meeting ensured that he had information the Jews did not. They would have a hard time rescuing their Messiah if they did not know who it was they hoped to save.

**8. He sent them to Bethlehem and said, "Go and make a careful search for the child. As soon as you find him, report to me, so that I too may go and worship him."**

Knowing the location of the child's birth and guessing the age of the child would not automatically lead to a discovery of the child. There would be many families to interview in Bethlehem in order to locate the child in question. And it was possible that the family was no longer in Bethlehem. Thus Herod could not send in his soldiers yet. The best plan for now would be to persuade the wise men to do the searching for him and inform him of the results. His craftiness and guile were worthy of the devil himself: *that I too may go and worship him.*

## II. THE DISCOVERY OF CHRIST (MATTHEW 2:9-11)

### A. LIGHT FROM THE STAR (vv. 9, 10)

**9. After they had heard the king, they went on their way, and the star they had seen in the east went ahead of them until it stopped over the place where the child was.**

This is the first time that Matthew mentions any unusual movement related to the *star.* But once again he provides no explanation. The star apparently gave the appearance of moving toward Bethlehem and of stopping over a specific building. Artists have typically portrayed this scene with a ray of light emanating from the star to *the place where the child was.* However all this happened, it is clear that at this point something supernatural was occurring. It is possible that when the wise men first began their search they were applying their interpretation theories to natural movements in the sky. But forward movement and standing still over a location is not natural for stars and planets. The biblical language makes it clear that this was a miraculous work of God.

**10. When they saw the star, they were overjoyed.**

Their joy was not so much at seeing an "old friend," but in having God provide supernatural assistance and confirmation for their search. What could have been a lengthy process was completed in short order. Now at last they had reached the goal of their searching.

This assistance was for a greater purpose than they could have guessed. Herod would expect the search to take some time. The wise men—as well as Mary and Joseph and the child—could be out of Bethlehem long before Herod would begin to suspect they had concluded their search without coming to report to him.

### B. GIFTS FOR A KING (v. 11)

**11. On coming to the house, they saw the child with his mother Mary, and they bowed down and worshiped him. Then they opened their treasures and presented him with gifts of gold and of incense and of myrrh.**

The shepherds found Jesus lying in a manger, apparently in some kind of animal stable. But the wise men found him in a *house*. Obviously Joseph had moved his family to more appropriate quarters just as soon as something had become available. Our modern nativity scenes with both shepherds and wise men surrounding the manger are historically inaccurate, but are usually done for the sake of convenience in telling the story.

The wise men honored the newborn king with three valuable gifts. The value of *gold* requires no explanation. *Incense* ("frankincense" in the *King James* and in Revelation 18:13) refers to an expensive incense derived from a milky white tree resin, usually burned in a bowl to release a sweet aroma in a room. *Myrrh* was also made from a tree resin and was quite expensive. It was not used as an incense, but as a pain reliever or anesthetic. It was also used in embalming the dead.

Consider the actions of the wise men toward Jesus. They presented him with expensive gifts and the actions of *worship* and homage, and all of this before Jesus had actually done anything for them. He was just a baby, the promise of a King and a Savior. But already they were grateful for his work on their behalf and ready to express their appreciation and allegiance to his will.

We get to see Jesus' work from a different perspective—as already completed. Yet with this advantage, do we seek him and honor him with the same diligence and eagerness of these men? Truly they deserve the title "wise men."

### GIFTS FOR GOD

What do you give to someone who has everything? Many of us resort to giving gift certificates from stores, restaurants, and theaters. No matter what we give, gracious recipients are pleased and thankful. They recognize that "it's the thought that counts." Thus, we who give are blessed as much as or more than the receivers.

The toddler Jesus could hardly appreciate the fine gifts of the wise men, though his parents surely were grateful for such valuable treasures. God Incarnate did not need gold, incense, and myrrh. He owns "the wealth in every mine." But the thought that prompted the giving was what was meaningful. The Magi expressed reverence, worship, and submission, and they were blessed more than Jesus.

God does not need our paltry tithes and offerings. "He owns the cattle on a thousand hills." But he knows how blessed we will be by giving. In his eyes, our thoughts count supremely. When we share our resources with thoughts of love, loyalty, and worship, God is pleased. —R. W. B.

## III. THE ATTACK AGAINST CHRIST (MATTHEW 2:12, 16)

### A. WARNING FROM A DREAM (v. 12)

**12. And having been warned in a dream not to go back to Herod, they returned to their country by another route.**

This is the first indication of God's actual speaking to the wise men. He had been guiding them before, but in a manner that required them to seek out additional information from the Jewish leaders in Jerusalem. This time clear instructions were needed. God could not allow the wise men unwittingly to assist Herod in his murderous plot. Thus God spoke through a dream to move the wise men away from Herod.

Verses 13-15 are not included in our printed text, but here we have some of the best evidence of God's providence at work. Not only were the wise men directed not to report to Herod, at about the same time God used a dream to instruct Joseph to flee with his family to Egypt (Matthew 2:13). Were the gold, incense, and myrrh sold to finance the trip and to provide living expenses while they were out of Judea? It is likely that at least part of the items were so used. We

*The visual for lesson 4 challenges us to honor Jesus as our King by crowning him Lord of all.*

## WHAT DO YOU THINK?

God's providence is evident all through this story. The wise men are providentially guided to find Jesus. Their gifts likely become God's providence to finance the flight to Egypt. Herod's plot is thwarted by God's warnings to the wise men and Joseph. Jesus' future safety is assured by Herod's probable belief that his murderous plan succeeded.

How aware are most Christians today of God's providence? Why do you think so? How can we be more alert to his providence? What blessings would such an awareness give?

## PRAYER

Father, rekindle within us the spirit of enthusiasm we felt when we first encountered our Lord and Savior Jesus Christ. May we honor the newborn King with the worship and offerings and devotion he so richly deserves. May we serve him secure in your providence to give what we need to do so. In the name of Jesus we pray, amen.

## THOUGHT TO REMEMBER

Wisdom is not to be measured in the amount of knowledge one has, but in the manner in which one uses his knowledge. The truly wise person is the one who uses his knowledge to serve the Lord.

have no record of how long the family spent in Egypt, but the implication is that it was a short time.

### B. VIOLENCE AGAINST THE YOUNG (v. 16)

**16. When Herod realized that he had been outwitted by the Magi, he was furious, and he gave orders to kill all the boys in Bethlehem and its vicinity who were two years old and under, in accordance with the time he had learned from the Magi.**

Jewish history has recorded several occasions of enemy assault on the Jews, from the various invasions in the Old Testament to the Roman siege in A.D. 70 to the holocaust under Nazi Germany. All of these are tragic. But this episode is notable because it involves an assault from within, by the King of Israel against his own citizens, and even worse, an assault on innocent children.

The order to kill all children two years old and under does not necessarily imply that Jesus was now about two years old. It is more likely that Herod was minimizing the margin for error by using a figure higher than the actual case. Matthew does not say how many children were killed. Without knowing more about the size of Bethlehem, we can hardly even guess. Perhaps a dozen children died.

The end result of Herod's mad scheme: innocent lives were wasted, the messianic plan continued unhindered, and Herod died shortly thereafter.

### CONCLUSION

A popular slogan for Christmas cards, bumper stickers, and songs is the phrase "wise men still seek him." It is ironic that these men from afar have become a symbol of the Christmas spirit. And yet that sentiment is understandable. Matthew presents these men as genuine seekers of truth and God. They were willing to expend great effort and expense to find the Messiah of Jewish prophecy and to honor him. And when they did find him, they treated him in the royal manner he deserved, giving him a rich measure of homage and worship.

The wise men disappear from the pages of the Bible, but not from our reflections on Christmas. They symbolize the best in human nature. They challenge us to follow their example, to be "wise" in our relationship with Jesus Christ.

They also picture for us the providence of God. Certainly we see God's providence in the rescue of Jesus. Even before Herod began his pursuit, the Lord's family was already on the way to Egypt, financed by the gifts of the wise men. And suppose Herod had found out about the Christ child from someone other than the wise men and at a different time. What if one who had heard the shepherds' report passed along the information to Jerusalem? Or what if one who had been at the temple when Simeon declared Jesus to be the God's "salvation" had reported to the king?

Knowing Herod's character, we can be sure there would have been an assault against the Christ child. By bringing the wise men in when he did, God made sure the assault failed, his Son's escape was financed, and Herod was—no doubt—satisfied that he had succeeded in his miserable plan. As for the dozen or so children who died, we grieve for them as we grieve for the countless other innocent victims of a sin-torn world. We comfort ourselves with the knowledge that there were not more, as there would have been if Herod had attempted repeated unsuccessful assaults against the holy child. As for those children themselves, what could have been better for them than to go to be with the Lord?

While we are left with many questions, we can be sure God's purposes do not fail. And when we align ourselves with those purposes, we will receive the blessings of his providence!

# Discovery Learning

*This page contains an alternate lesson plan emphasizing learning activities. Classes desiring such student involvement will find these suggestions helpful. The next page is a reproducible activity page to further enhance discovery learning.*

## LEARNING GOALS

After participating in this lesson, the student will be able to:

1. Tell the biblical account of the visit of the Magi and Herod's attempt to kill the Christ child.

2. Relate how God's providence was at work in the visit of the wise men and the plotting of Herod.

3. Praise God for his providential care.

## INTO THE LESSON

To prepare for this lesson, spell out the words "GOD IS IN CONTROL" in all capital letters, one letter per sheet of paper. (Use half-sheets of typing paper, 5 1/2 by 8 1/2 inches.) Post these in the front of the class with the letters turned to the wall.

Tell the class you're going to play a game like TV's "Wheel of Fortune." Make two or three teams; then have the teams take turns choosing one letter at a time. If the letter chosen is in the puzzle, turn over every sheet with that letter. After each correct guess, the team that made the guess may try to solve the puzzle.

Provide some small prize for the team that solves the puzzle; then point out that our lesson text today illustrates this truth.

## INTO THE WORD

Early in the week, ask two persons to make brief reports to the class on the following assignments. One person should identify the wise men from the east. The other person should prepare a report on the star that appeared to the wise men. Give each person copies of the appropriate material from the lesson commentary and a copy of a Bible Dictionary as resource material.

Open this part of the lesson with the reports on wise men and the star. Then read the text for today's lesson with the class.

Follow this with a mini-lecture laced with appropriate questions. An outline and questions for the lecture follow. Fill in the outline with information gleaned from the lesson commentary.

### A. HEROD THE GREAT

1. His title and family background.

2. The dating of Jesus' birthday.

*Questions:* Why was Herod "troubled?" Why was all of Jerusalem "troubled?"

### B. HEROD'S INQUIRY

1. Bethlehem: a fulfillment of Micah's prophecy.

2. Herod's devious trickery.

*Question:* Why did Herod ask when the star appeared?

3. Herod's lie: "That I too may go and worship him."

### C. FINDING THE CHRIST CHILD

1. The star's movement as a supernatural event.

*Option:* Use the reproducible activity, "Providential Star," from the next page at this point.

2. Finding Jesus at the house.

*Questions:* Why do so many nativity scenes include the wise men at the stable? What are incense and myrrh?

3. The return home and disappearance from biblical history.

### D. THE SLAUGHTER OF INFANTS

1. Other times this has happened in biblical history.

*Question:* How is God's control seen in this event?

## INTO LIFE

Display a poster or show a Christmas card with the often-used saying, "Wise men still seek him."

Use the following discussion questions to help class members make this lesson personal:

Why did the Magi or wise men seek Jesus? (To worship him and bring gifts.)

What indications in our text are there of sacrifice and possible discomfort these important men endured in order to worship Jesus? (Traveled a long distance, expensive gifts, carefully chosen gifts.)

It is clear that these men held their worship as something important and made a great sacrifice to do it. Perhaps part of the reason is that they were sure the hand of God was in their journey. They knew—somehow—that this star meant the Messiah had been born.

We can see God's providence in this event. Ask the class to cite examples; list them on the board as they do. (Use the material in the commentary section to assist you and supplement their answers.)

What can we do to be more aware of God's work in our own lives? What effect will it have on our worship if we do? On our service? On our outreach?

Close with prayer that your students will be alert to God's working in their lives and will respond to him with worship, commitment, and service.

# Providential Star

Some believe the star of Bethlehem was a miracle. Others believe it was a natural phenomenon. It could have been either in origin, but it was clearly used by God for his purpose. In this it is like the great fish that swallowed Jonah. Was it specially created for the purpose of rescuing Jonah (a miracle) or was it a naturally occurring fish or whale such as others that have been known to swallow humans who survived (natural)?

The star and the fish were each controlled by God so that the event—leading the wise men or rescuing Jonah—becomes a clear sign of God at work, and that is a miracle! This is God's providence, the way he provides for his own. Sometimes he uses miraculous means; sometimes he simply exercises his control of natural phenomena. Look up the following Scriptures and see how God has provided for his people through the ages. Write "M" in the final column if you think the event was miraculous; "N" if you think it was natural.

| SCRIPTURE | EVENT | M OR N |
|---|---|---|
| Genesis 6:8—8:19 | | |
| Genesis 19:15-23 | | |
| Genesis 21:14-20 | | |
| Genesis 31:4-9 | | |
| Genesis 45:4-11 | | |
| Exodus 2:1-10 | | |
| Exodus 14:5-31 | | |
| Exodus 40:36-38 | | |
| Joshua 11:16-23; 24:11-13 | | |
| Judges 7:8-22 | | |
| 1 Samuel 7:7-12 | | |
| 1 Samuel 17:40-51 | | |
| 2 Kings 13:1-5 | | |
| 2 Kings 19:14-19; 35, 36 | | |
| Daniel 3:1-30 | | |
| Matthew 2:13-23 | | |
| Acts 23:12-33 | | |

# SIMEON AND ANNA

## LESSON 5

## WHY TEACH THIS LESSON?

Youth. How it is praised and envied today! It has not always been that way. Earlier generations valued the elderly, especially for their wisdom. It's a lesson we need to have repeated.

Today's text gives us a message from two senior saints. Their message is needed if we are to understand and appreciate the role of the Christ. And if we gain a better appreciation for our older saints along the way—so much the better.

## INTRODUCTION

### A. FIFTEEN MINUTES OF FAME

In a critique of our modern western culture, with its orientation toward high tech and mass media, one of our artists is reported to have said that we now live in an age in which anyone can have "fifteen minutes of fame." Ordinary people become overnight news sensations because of heroic acts, scandalous crimes, and unusual stunts. But the notice is short-lived. For just as quickly as the attention comes, it shifts to other interesting people, and former news stories fade away, never to be heard again.

These cultural dynamics of our day have little to do with biblical times. And yet there is one interesting parallel. The Bible often gives readers a brief glimpse of fascinating characters, with no prelude or follow-up. We can read the entire stories of many of them in far less than fifteen minutes! The classic example in the Old Testament is Melchizedek, for whom we have three brief verses of information (Genesis 14:18-20) and many questions. The same could be said regarding various characters in the Christmas story: Zechariah and Elizabeth, the shepherds, the wise men, Simeon, and Anna. We are intrigued by the brief descriptions given by Matthew and Luke, and wish we knew more of their stories. As it is we have to content ourselves with the verses we are given and simply appreciate the good things we do know about these people.

### B. LESSON BACKGROUND

After the Gospel of Luke describes the birth of Jesus and the visit by the shepherds, the story jumps ahead to a visit to the temple in Jerusalem by Joseph, Mary, and the baby Jesus. We know nothing about the intervening month and a half, except to guess that Joseph moved his family to more appropriate quarters than a stable just as soon as possible. Why they had not already headed back home to Nazareth becomes clear in today's lesson. The parents had a duty under Mosaic Law to show up in the temple at this time with their newborn child.

## I. THE PARENTS' DUTY (LUKE 2:22)

### A. MARY'S PURIFICATION (v. 22a)

**22a. When the time of their purification according to the Law of Moses had been completed. . . .**

The *Law of Moses* stipulated a period of uncleanness of forty days after a woman gave birth to a boy and eighty days after the birth of a girl (Leviticus 12:1-5). Thus

DEVOTIONAL READING
PSALM 42:1-11
LESSON SCRIPTURE
LUKE 2:21-40
PRINTED TEXT
LUKE 2:22, 25-38

Dec
29

### LESSON AIMS

As a result of participating in this lesson, the student should be able to:

1. Know and understand the descriptions of Jesus given by Simeon and Anna.

2. Explain the significance of these descriptions.

3. Praise and worship Jesus specifically for one of the characteristics mentioned.

### KEY VERSES

It had been revealed to him by the Holy Spirit that he would not die before he had seen the Lord's Christ.

Coming up to them at that very moment, she (Anna) gave thanks to God and spoke about the child to all who were looking forward to the redemption of Jerusalem.          Luke 2:26, 38

## WHAT DO YOU THINK?

Joseph and Mary followed the prescribed ritual when they brought the infant Jesus to the temple in Jerusalem. The dictionary defines a ritual as "the established form for a ceremony." Religious rituals link us to the past and with the faith of the previous generation. Rituals can provide a sense of stability and continuity in a world that often is anything but stable. On the other hand, rituals can make worship stale and routine, mere forms without substance.

What rituals does your church practice? How meaningful are these to you? Why? Which would you like to replace? Why? How can rituals be kept meaningful and significant?

we can date Mary and Joseph's temple visit in verse 22 by knowing that the time of Mary's purification was *completed* forty days after Jesus' birth.

During this time the mother was not to participate in public worship services or other activities outside the home. This period of being "unclean" was not intended to be a negative reflection on women nor on childbearing, but was essentially a time of recuperation.

After this time of uncleanness the couple was expected to take an offering of *purification* to the temple. Ideally, it was done immedaitely after the period of uncleanness was ended, but it could be delayed until a major feast. (The mother did not even have to be present!) Since Jesus had been born in Bethlehem, just five miles from Jerusalem, it was not difficult to make this trip to the temple.

Verse 24 indicates that Joseph and Mary offered two birds for Mary's purification, either two turtledoves or two pigeons. Mosaic Law actually preferred a lamb and one bird, but allowed the substitution of a second bird if a couple could not afford a lamb (Leviticus 12:6-8). Apparently Joseph and Mary could not afford a lamb. This suggests that the visit of the wise men occurred shortly after this purification ceremony; Joseph could have certainly afforded a lamb had they already received the wise men's gifts. If so, then Joseph returned to Bethlehem after this presentation, probably intending to make that the family home. After the trip to Egypt and the return, he changed that plan because Herod's son was as bad as Herod (Matthew 2:19-23). Luke makes a long story short and immediately refers to the family's return to Nazareth (verse 39), agreeing with Matthew 2:22, 23.

### B. JESUS' PRESENTATION (v. 22b)

**22b. Joseph and Mary took him to Jerusalem to present him to the Lord**

The purification ceremony for the mother also took on an additional significance when she had given birth to her firstborn son. In the last of the ten plagues on Egypt in the book of Exodus, God killed every firstborn male of man and beast except in those families in which the blood of a slaughtered lamb had been smeared on their front door frame. From that point on God laid claim to every firstborn male among the Jews. Every firstborn makle animal suitable for sacrifice was sacrificed. One not suitable for sacrifice was either redeemed with one that was or was killed (Exodus 13:2, 12, 13). Children, of course, were not killed. Every Jewish couple was required to present their firstborn son to the Lord in the presence of a priest and redeem him with a lamb (Exodus 13:13). The redemption price, which Joseph no doubt paid, was five shekels of silver (Numbers 18:15, 16).

### TRUST AND OBEY

Marriage has fallen into disrepute in our culture. An alarming number of couples are opting for "unholy matrimony" (living together without marriage), with no regard for whether such a decision is right or wrong.

Why are so many choosing to live in sin? Millions flaunt God's absolutes to conform to adulterous life-styles. They may be ignorant of God's Word; more likely, they feel that the biblical teaching is irrelevant to modern culture.

Perhaps Mary and Joseph wondered if God's Law applied to their special child. After all, should the Messiah be bound by Mosaic statutes? Presenting God's Son to God might have seemed like a trivial formality. How could a religious ceremony consecrate Jesus any more than his unique conception and miraculous birth had done? In spite of whatever questions and doubts they might have had, Joseph and Mary "took him to Jerusalem to present him to the Lord" (Luke 2:22).

Trusting God, even when his way fails to make sense to us, requires hard-core faith. It means submitting to his authority and obeying his absolutes, despite the popularity and acceptance of more permissive behavior.

There is still "no other way to be happy in Jesus, but to trust and obey" (John H. Sammis).
—R. W. B.

## II. SIMEON'S FAITH (LUKE 2:25-35)

### A. GOD'S PROMISE (vv. 25, 26)

**25. Now there was man in Jerusalem called Simeon, who was righteous and devout. He was waiting for the consolation of Israel, and the Holy Spirit was upon him.**

From this sketchy description we get almost no biographical details regarding *Simeon*, but we learn much about his moral and spiritual character. He was a *righteous* man, that is, one who was committed to doing what was right and fair in all of his dealings with both man and God. Simeon was *devout*. The basic idea of the Greek word used here is one who has a religious attitude at all times, even when he is not doing something religious. This is not a fanatic who is always talking religion but a person who is comfortable discussing religious things in any situation in which they naturally arise.

Simeon was awaiting *the consolation of Israel*. For centuries the Jews had been looking for their Messiah to come and take the throne of David, restoring Israel to a place of prominence (Acts 1:6). For some reason near the end of the first century B.C. there was an unusual number of Jews who believed that the arrival of the Messiah was no longer in the distant future, but was actually going to happen in their day. Both John the Baptist and Jesus were able to take advantage of this messianic enthusiasm and draw large crowds to them as they preached that the kingdom of heaven was near.

Simeon was one of those eagerly anticipating the Messiah. His hope was not unfounded—*the Holy Spirit was upon him*. The significance of that is seen in verse 26.

**26. It had been revealed to him by the Holy Spirit that he would not die before he had seen the Lord's Christ.**

Simeon enjoyed a privilege unparalleled among the saints of old. God had guaranteed him that he would live long enough to see the Messiah. We do not know at what point in his life Simeon received this revelation. Was it a promise he had lived with for many years, or had it been given in his old age? Did people take him seriously, or was he passed off as an eccentric? Were there others who had received similar revelations? Were such revelations the cause of the intense messianic expectancy at this point in history? These are questions that cannot be answered, but they cannot be easily dismissed either.

### B. SIMEON'S SONG (vv. 27-32)

**27. Moved by the Spirit, he went into the temple courts. When the parents brought in the child Jesus to do for him what the custom of the Law required. . . .**

It was no coincidence that Simeon arrived in the *temple* at the same time Jesus' *parents* were there. Of course, this devout man may have made a regular practice of visiting the temple and watching for the Messiah. But on this occasion, he was specifically led *by the Spirit* into the temple.

**28. Simeon took him in his arms and praised God, saying. . . .**

Imagine the shock of having a stranger approach you and request to hold your child. Luke's simple telling of the story does not indicate how much persuasion it took (if any) for Simeon to convince Jesus' parents to trust him. But with all of the unusual things that had already occurred to them related to Jesus' birth, Joseph and Mary were apparently open to considering this unusual request.

On the other hand, perhaps they knew Simeon's character and were not alarmed. They may have seen him before when they were in Jerusalem for the

---

**WHAT DO YOU THINK?**

*Expectancy and anticipation are important themes in the story of Simeon and Anna. Both of them had a confident expectation of God's working out his purposes. That confident expectation is what the Bible calls "hope." How can we have the same kind of hope in regard to prayer? In regard to the second coming? In regard to our eternal reward in Heaven?*

**WHAT DO YOU THINK?**

*Luke points out the devout and faithful character of Simeon and Anna. Faithfulness puts us, like Simeon and Anna, in positions where we can be chosen and used by God.*

*What are some of the keys to long-term faithfulness like that of Simeon and Anna? What can the church do to assist those who are struggling to remain faithful?*

Passover. Perhaps others had pointed him out as a righteous and devout man of God. Even if they were not personally acquainted with Simeon, it is easy to imagine that his reputation was known to virtually everyone in the temple courts. Their response may have been more of wonder than of fear.

**29-31. "Sovereign Lord, as you have promised, you now dismiss your servant in peace. For my eyes have seen your salvation, which you have prepared in the sight of all people.**

These words suggest the possibility that Simeon was an old man nearing death, though it should be acknowledged that no description of his age is actually given. Simeon looked at the baby and saw salvation for all people. Perhaps we should take a lesson and view young people today with the eyes of faith in what they can accomplish for the Lord. What would be the response if children regularly heard that they had potential for bringing God's salvation to others? We need to look beyond the external appearances of people we meet and imagine the possibilities and potential they possess. With the appropriate encouragement and support, some young person in your congregation may become an outstanding Christian leader.

Of course, this was more than the blessing of an elder saint on a young child. Simeon was no doubt speaking by inspiration. God had *promised* Simeon that he would see the Messiah, and we believe the Lord also let Simeon know that the promise had been fulfilled. By the time we read verses 34 and 35, we know for sure Simeon is prophesying—that is, speaking by inspiration. There is no way he could know the things he spoke about there except by inspiration.

**32. . . . a light for revelation to the Gentiles and for glory to your people Israel."**

Simeon exhibited an insight into God's plan of salvation that was uncommon among the Jews. (This is to be expected of a prophet.) The Jewish people were not an evangelistic people, sending missionaries among the Gentiles. Even the early church had difficulty understanding the full significance of Jesus' Great Commission. They took the gospel to all nations, but only to the Jews who were dispersed throughout the nations. It took Peter's experience with Cornelius (Acts 10) to help the church see the broad scope of God's salvation through Jesus Christ.

Simeon, however, spoke like the Old Testament prophets (e.g., Isaiah 42:6, 7; Micah 4:1, 2), who anticipated the salvation of Gentiles as well as Jews. Even the words *light* and *glory* are appropriate for these two categories of people. Since the Gentiles had lived for ages in darkness, outside the knowledge of Jehovah God, the Messiah would bring them *light*. But the Jews had known the true God and had even witnessed his glory in the mighty works of God, the pillar of cloud and fire, and the imagery within the tabernacle and temple. For them, the Messiah would bring an even greater view of the *glory* of God.

## C. JESUS' DESTINY (vv. 33-35)

**33. The child's father and mother marveled at what was said about him.**

Why should this incident amaze Jesus' parents? Not being native to Jerusalem, they had probably been blending in anonymously with the temple crowd. They would not expect a stranger—even a stranger with a sterling reputation—to pick them out of the crowd or to know the true identity of their son. But the truly amazing thing was Simeon's appreciation of their son's messianic mission, especially his exceptional grasp of the broad extent of God's plan of salvation.

Manuscript differences produce some differences among English versions here. For *the child's father and mother* the *King James* has "Joseph and his mother." Of course, the term *father* is not being used in the biological sense here, but in the legal sense. Joseph had assumed the role of father for Jesus even though he was not the child's biological father.

---

### WHAT DO YOU THINK?

In Simeon's words we see both aspects of biblical prophecy: foretelling future events and forthtelling a message from God. The Old Testament prophets spent more time telling the people God's messages directed toward them than they did predicting the future. In the first-century church, prophets also declared God's messages. But on some occasions they also predicted future events (Acts 11:27, 28; 21:10, 11).

Many people believe the prophetic function in the church is continued in the role of the preacher today. What do you think? What do 1 Corinthians 13:8-10; Ephesians 2:20; and Hebrews 1:1-3 suggest about that? What problems might result if a preacher begins to assume he has prophetic authority instead of preaching strictly by the authority of God's Word?

### OPTION

Use the reproducible activity, "Title Search," on page 162 to explore the significance of some of the titles used for Jesus in this passage.

Perhaps some copyist, zealous for maintaining the doctrine of the virgin birth, changed the wording to "Joseph and his mother" as we find in some texts. This produces a grammatical problem, as it sounds like the "mother" here is Joseph's. Of course it is not. Elsewhere Joseph is referred to as Jesus' "father" or "parent" in Luke 2:27, 41, 43, and 48. As long as we understand the term in a legal sense and not a biological one, there is no problem with the word *father.*

**34. Then Simeon blessed them and said to Mary, his mother: "This child is destined to cause the falling and rising of many in Israel, and to be a sign that will be spoken against.**

Simeon picked up on the Old Testament prophecies that speak of the Messiah's rejection by his own people. For example, the prophet Isaiah portrays the Messiah as a stone on which the faithful will climb up and be saved, while for those who kick at it the stone becomes a "stumbling block" (Isaiah 8:13-15; 28:16). Isaiah also pictures the Messiah as a sign or visible object lesson from God that will be understood by the faithful but rejected as meaningless by most (Isaiah 8:18; 53:1-3).

**35. . . . so that the thoughts of many hearts will be revealed. And a sword will pierce your own soul too."**

For the first time in the nativity narrative, Simeon introduced a sobering thought of suffering and death. Joseph and Mary's son was to be rejected by his own people and pierced. The Jews of that day could not imagine a Messiah who, rather than killing his enemies, was in fact killed by the enemy. They had rejected all references to the Messiah's suffering, such as Isaiah's "suffering servant" passages, and had interpreted them as applying to some other servant of God. This bias was still evident many years later when Paul spoke of the cross as a "stumbling block" to most Jews (1 Corinthians 1:23).

With the benefit of the New Testament witness we understand how suffering figured into God's plan for Jesus. It was through Jesus' death that atonement and forgiveness of our sins were accomplished. The promised victory over our enemy occurred shortly thereafter in his resurrection. We do not know if Joseph and Mary understood this aspect of the messianic plan any better than the rest of their countrymen. Now through Simeon they were given a glimpse of their son's ultimate mission, and incidentally, the hurt that Mary would experience as she watched her son die on the cross. The faithful commitment of Joseph and Mary to the will of God has been evident throughout the Christmas story, but perhaps even more so now as, from this point on, they raised up and prepared their son for a ministry they knew would bring personal pain at least to Mary. Could they even yet, however, have imagined the horrors of Calvary—or the victory of the empty tomb?

## III. ANNA'S WITNESS (LUKE 2:36-38)

### A. ANNA'S DEVOTION (vv. 36, 37)

**36. There was also a prophetess, Anna, the daughter of Phanuel, of the tribe of Asher. She was very old; she had lived with her husband seven years after her marriage.**

The second person to approach Joseph and Mary in the temple on this occasion was also operating under a special influence by the Holy Spirit. *Anna* was a member of the ancient *tribe of Asher,* one of the original twelve tribes of Israel. We know nothing of her father *Phanuel,* but his mention implies that he had some prestige in that day. Anna had been married *seven years* before her husband died.

**37. . . . and then was a widow until she was eighty-four. She never left the temple but worshiped night and day, fasting and praying.**

To say that Anna *never left the temple* could mean that she had made some kind of arrangements for living in an apartment on the temple grounds. But since that

**WHAT DO YOU THINK?**

Simeon and Anna are not among the best-known characters of the Bible, yet they fill an important role. What behind-the-scenes supporting roles are filled by faithful saints in our congregation that help others to communicate the gospel? Can you identify some of these helpers? How can we express appreciation for their ministries? How can we be more involved in such supportive ministries?

The visual for lesson 5 in the visuals packet is an artist's depiction of Simeon and Anna in the temple.

## PRAYER

*Father, help us to humbly commit ourselves to your service in whatever capacity you present to us. And help us to be ever expectant for the work our Messiah Jesus Christ has yet to do in our lives. In Jesus name we pray, amen.*

## THOUGHT TO REMEMBER

*God has a service for all of us to perform when we are ready to yield ourselves completely to the leading of his Spirit and his Word.*

## DAILY BIBLE READINGS

*Monday, Dec. 23—Our Hope Is in God (Psalm 42:1-11)*

*Tuesday, Dec. 24—Honor Older Widows (1 Timothy 5:3-10)*

*Wednesday, Dec. 25—First-born Son Redeemed (Exodus 13:11-16)*

*Thursday, Dec. 26—The Mission of the Servant (Isaiah 42:1-9)*

*Friday, Dec. 27—The Hope of Salvation (1 Thessalonians 5:1-11)*

*Saturday, Dec. 28—Salvation Through Jesus Christ (Acts 4:5-12)*

*Sunday, Dec. 29—A Sure Salvation (Romans 8:31-39)*

was not usually done for single women, it may simply mean that she made long visits to the temple each day. Whatever the case, it is clear from the description that Anna possesses a spiritual character comparable to Simeon's.

### B. JESUS' MISSION (v. 38)

**38. Coming up to them at that very moment, she gave thanks to God and spoke about the child to all who were looking forward to the redemption of Jerusalem.**

Luke does not specifically indicate what prompted Anna to approach Joseph and Mary and begin speaking about their special child. Perhaps she heard what Simeon said. Perhaps the Holy Spirit was pointing her toward the Messiah child just as he had done for Simeon. In either event, Anna's devotion to God shines through as from that point on she began testifying to visitors that the Messiah had finally arrived, for she had seen him with her own eyes.

It is not likely that either Simeon or Anna revealed the names of Jesus and his parents, since Herod's only clue for finding Jesus was a location and approximate age. What these two people did was initiate a "rumor" like that of the shepherds that would stir up a messianic expectation that would prepare people for the preaching of John the Baptist and Jesus that would come later.

### HOW LONG, LORD?

For several years I ministered to a Christian man who was incurably ill. His lungs were almost "burned up" due to occupational hazards of chemical dust and smoke fumes. He had to be hospitalized every few months, sometimes for a week or so, sometimes longer.

Toward the end of his life, he would frequently ask in his misery, "Why doesn't the Lord take me?" As his minister and shepherd, I frankly was stymied. I dreaded the question because I had no answer. His desire was not only for death; he was also longing for life, for deliverance, and for the Lord's promised "consolation."

Anna herself must have wondered, "How long must we wait, Lord? How long?" Her temple vigil is a classic model of patient perseverance. For years she had faithfully pursued her single purpose of prayer and preparation. When the Lord arrived, she immediately recognized him as the long-awaited Redeemer.

Why is Christ delaying his return? He promised: "I will come back and take you to be with me" (John 14:3). Especially when we are sick, sad or lonely, we wonder, "How long, Lord?" But just as surely as Anna's faith was finally rewarded, so will ours be, for Jesus' second coming is as certain as was his first. My deceased friend has been ushered already into his presence.                —R. W. B.

## CONCLUSION

Sometimes we wonder why we are given a long list of credits at the end of theater and concert guidebooks, television programs, movies, and music tapes and CDs. Why not just list the main performers and singers? Because as important as the main characters are, there would be no production if it were not for the labor of those who work behind the scenes. They deserve some recognition for the finished product.

Simeon and Anna are minor characters in the drama of Jesus Christ. Their names are not as prominent in our minds as people like Joseph, Mary, Peter, James, and John. And yet a careful look at their story reminds us that the true significance of our labors is not in the size of our tasks but in the size of the faith that performs those tasks.

They also help us to understand the mission of the Messiah. As Israel was sometimes short-sighted, so are we. The descriptions of the Messiah by Simeon and Anna will help us take the longer, more loving view.

# Discovery Learning

*This page contains an alternate lesson plan emphasizing learning activities. Classes desiring such student involvement will find these suggestions helpful. The next page is a reproducible activity page to further enhance discovery learning.*

## LEARNING GOALS

As a result of participating in this lesson, the student should be able to:

1. Know and understand the descriptions of Jesus given by Simeon and Anna.

2. Explain the significance of these descriptions.

3. Praise and worship Jesus specifically for one of the characteristics mentioned.

## INTO THE LESSON

Before class, write "The Name of Jesus" on the chalkboard or on a poster. If your class enjoys Scripture choruses, begin the session by singing "Praise the Name of Jesus," "His Name Is Wonderful," or "Jesus, Name Above All Names"—or a medley of all three.

After you sing (or to begin the session if you choose not to sing the choruses), ask the class to call out every word or phrase in Scripture they can recall that describes Jesus. Have two people ready to list these on the board or poster as people "rapid fire" their answers. Have lots of space available for writing these many answers. Mention that we will discover the richness of some of these descriptions as cited by Simeon and Anna when they saw the baby Jesus.

## INTO THE WORD

Begin the Bible Study by appointing two "listening teams." Team #1 is to listen for anything that will help us to get to know Simeon and Anna (age, occupation, hopes, or other information). Team #2 is to listen for words that describe the purpose and life of Jesus. Then read Luke 2:21-40.

After reading the text, present a brief lecture on the purpose and length of the days of purification for Mary, the purification ceremony, and the presentation of the firstborn son. Notes in the lesson commentary will be helpful.

Ask listening team #1 to report what they have discovered about Simeon and Anna. Record these on a poster board, flip chart, transparency, or some other means of display. (Ask a class member to do the writing.) Things this team might note about Simeon could include the following: he was righteous and devout, the Holy Spirit was upon him, he was waiting for the consolation of Israel, he was probably elderly, he held a special promise from God that he would not die before he had

seen the Messiah, he was able to prophecy about the future of Jesus and Mary.

Remarks about Anna should include that she was a prophetess, a daughter of Phanuel of the tribe of Asher, she was 84 years old, she had been a widow after being married only seven years, and she spent much time in the temple fasting and praying.

While we know a few things about these two characters from Jesus' early childhood, it really is only a brief glimpse. Yet God has chosen to record their response to seeing the baby Jesus. There must be a reason for this. The clue lies in what they said about Jesus.

Ask listening team #2 to report the words and phrases they have found that describe the purpose and life of Jesus. Ask another class member to write their findings on a large visual. Their report should include: The consolation of Israel (verse 25), The Lord's Christ (verse 26), God's salvation (verse 30), a light for revelation to the Gentiles (verse 32), glory to Israel (verse 32), destined to cause the falling and rising of many (verse 34), a sign that would be spoken against (verse 34), and redemption (verse 38).

After the list is completed, discuss the significance of each of these descriptions of Jesus. Use the lesson commentary to help understand the sayings in these verses. Questions you might ask of the class include: "What does 'consolation of Israel' mean?" "What is the significance of the description, 'the Lord's Christ'?" "Why the special mention of the Gentiles in verse 32?" "What is the 'glory of Israel'?" Be sure to mention the notes on the "suffering servant" concept from the commentary on verse 35. You may want to use the reproducible activity, "Title Search," on the next page to assist with this discussion.

## INTO LIFE

Form groups of three or four and have the students discuss the personal significance they find in the various titles. For example, one who came to Christ late in life, after living a life of "darkness," may especially appreciate the title "Light . . . to the Gentiles" (verse 32). One who has been ridiculed for his or her faith may take comfort in observing Jesus also was "spoken against" (verse 34).

Have the groups conclude with sentence prayers praising and worshiping Jesus particularly for the qualities they have discussed. When they finish, close the class by singing "Jesus, Name Above All Names."

# Title Search

Many titles or descriptions of Jesus are included in today's text. Listed below are several of them. Use a concordance to look up additional Scripture references where the same titles or descriptions are used. Then write a brief description or definition of the title.

The "consolation" of Israel (v. 25)

The Lord's "Christ" (v. 26)

God's "salvation" (v. 30)

"Light" for revelation to the Gentiles (v. 32)

"Glory" to Israel (v. 32)

A "sign" to be spoken against (v. 34)

"Redemption" (v. 38)

# Wear the Name

As Christians, we wear the name of Christ, both as co-heirs with him (Romans 8:17) and as his ambassadors (2 Corinthians 5:20). With that in mind, which title above is most significant to you and why?

# JOHN THE BAPTIZER

**LESSON 6**

## WHY TEACH THIS LESSON?

John the Baptist is one of the best-known characters in the Bible. Bold and unconventional, he appears larger than life on the Gospel pages. Jesus himself commended John as the greatest among "those born of women" (Luke 7:28).

And just when it seems we are unable to identify with such a stellar saint, we learn John had doubts even as we. Even the great may doubt. The great, when they doubt, get answers. Comfort your students with the idea that doubt does not diminish the faithfulness of God's servant. Honest doubt, carefully investigated, may become the staunchest of faith!

## INTRODUCTION

### A. DOUBT AND FAITH

Lew Wallace was a "doubter." Though an accomplished lawyer, Civil War hero, and former governor and ambassador, in the late nineteenth century he started research on a historical novel to be set in the first century. He believed Jesus Christ to be no more than a mere man. But, because he intended to incorporate some material about Jesus into his book, he began for the first time to read the Bible accounts of his life. When his Bible reading and his historical research were complete, Wallace was a believer. His novel, *Ben Hur: A Tale of the Christ*, reflects his firm conviction that Jesus was, in fact, the Son of God and Savior of the world.

Neither Christ nor Christianity has anything to fear from honest doubt. Philip told Nathanael, a skeptic about Christ, to "Come and see" (John 1:46). Having done so, Nathanael proclaimed Jesus the Son of God and the King of Israel.

Today's study shows a wavering faith in John the Baptist. But Jesus knew that John's were honest misgivings, and he simply bade him, "Look at the evidence."

### B. LESSON BACKGROUND

The lesson today moves us forward about three decades from the first five in this series, as we begin a look at four key personalities during the ministry of Jesus. We start with Jesus' powerful forerunner, John, who began to broadcast the Messianic kingdom's arrival in about A.D. 26.

It is important to see that John's brief ministry was actually the transition period between the law and the gospel. Jesus said, "The Law and the Prophets were proclaimed until John. Since that time, the good news of the kingdom of God is being preached" (Luke 16:16; cf. Matthew 11:13; Luke 3:18; Acts 10:37). Mark (1:1) says that John's preaching was "the beginning of the gospel." That John would prepare the way for the Lord had, of course, been appointed by God centuries earlier (Isaiah 40:3; Malachi 3:1) and had been reaffirmed at his birth just three decades earlier (Luke 1:17, 76, 77).

## I. JOHN'S MINISTRY TO THE MULTITUDES (MARK 1:4-8)

### A. JOHN'S MESSAGE (vv. 4, 5)

**4. And so John came, baptizing in the desert region and preaching a baptism of repentance for the forgiveness of sins.**

DEVOTIONAL READING
MATTHEW 11:7-17

LESSON SCRIPTURE
MARK 1:1-15; LUKE 7:18-30

PRINTED TEXT
MARK 1:4-11, 14, 15; LUKE 7:18-23

**LESSON AIMS**

As a result of today's lesson, the student will:

1. Compare John's ministry announcing Christ to the world with his later doubts about Jesus.

2. Explain why even faithful people may sometimes have doubts.

3. Suggest some ways to resolve doubts about one's faith.

Jan 5

**KEY VERSE**

I baptize you with water, but he will baptize you with the Holy Spirit. Mark 1:8

## LESSON 6 NOTES

### WHAT DO YOU THINK?

We can learn a lot about effective ministry by looking at John the Baptizer. People listened to John because he lived his message. He was genuine and authentic. He preached the truth even when it was not popular. He was bold and yet humble.

Why do some preachers and teachers have a problem with that? What is the temptation to try to appear more than one is? Why is it so damaging when one who preaches the truth is found out to be a fraud in his personal life?

How can the church minister to its leaders to help them be open and honest?

### WHAT DO YOU THINK?

We often feel uncomfortable around people (like John the Baptizer) whose life-style differs from the norm. Sometimes it is difficult to see beneath the exterior of such a one and to see the person underneath. John proves that "different" does not always equal "bad." Beneath John's unconventional and nonconformist exterior was a man of unflinching courage, deep conviction, and great piety.

What can we do to be sure we do not judge people by appearances, but to share with each one equally the love of God? How well does our church do this? Where could we improve?

*John* did not carry on his work in the sacred city, Jerusalem. He roamed the uninhabited, uncultivated, and mostly desolate areas of the *desert* of Judea (the place is identified in Matthew 3:1), which extended from the area just west of the Dead Sea northward to the southern parts of the Jordan River valley. Luke indicates that John especially ministered in the regions around the Jordan River (3:3; cf. John 1:28; 3:23), where there would be abundant water for baptisms.

John's sermon themes show why his *preaching* was the beginning of the gospel. He proclaimed the arrival of the kingdom of heaven (Matthew 3:2), belief in the coming Messiah Mark 1:7, 8; Acts 19:4), *repentance* (a genuine change of mind and heart, leading to a change of life), *baptism,* and righteous living as a demonstration of real repentance and of a preparedness for the judgment to come (Luke 3:7-14). All these themes would be stressed by Jesus and, in the Christian age, by the apostles.

John baptized men and women who would commit themselves to repentance. Baptism seems to be a totally new rite introduced by John. There is no convincing evidence to link baptism to the ceremonial washings and baths of the Jews, of the Essenes, or of the Qumran community. Nor can it be shown that Jewish proselyte baptism was practiced this early. John was "*the* baptizer."

John's baptism promised a *forgiveness of sins.* The same Greek structure is used here (literally, "into a forgiveness of sins") as is used in Acts 2:38 of Christian baptism and in Matthew 26:28 of the death of Jesus. Just as Christ's blood was poured out to produce, or result in, forgiveness of sins, so did John's baptism, and now Christian baptism, produce, or result in, forgiveness. Evidently submission in faith to John's baptism produced forgiveness in the same manner as the Old Testament sacrificial system did. Neither remained adequate in the New Covenant age (Acts 19:1-5; Hebrews 9:15).

**5. The whole Judean countryside and all the people of Jerusalem went out to him. Confessing their sins, they were baptized by him in the Jordan River.**

John certainly fulfilled his appointed task of arousing the nation of Israel to righteousness. His unique personality, his powerful preaching of the coming Messiah and coming judgment, his blazing denunciation of the hypocritical Jewish leaders (Matthew 3:7-10), and his unique rite of baptism combined with the expectant atmosphere in Palestine (Luke 2:25, 38; 3:15) to set the whole region ablaze with excitement. The Jewish historian Josephus validates this verse; he asserts that it was John's popularity and influence with the people that alarmed Herod Antipas and led him to put John to death (*Antiquities*, 18.5.2).

Two figures of speech common to the Bible are found in this verse. A metonymy occurs when one set of words (*countryside* in this case) is used as a substitute for another set of words that is closely connected to it ("the *people* of the countryside" is meant). And the uses of *whole* and *all* in the verse are no doubt examples of hyperbole, which is an obvious exaggeration for the sake of emphasis. The imperfect tense (indicating repeated action) of the verb *were baptized* suggests a constant flow of penitent Israelites turning to obey God, acknowledging and renouncing *their sins.*

### B. JOHN'S DRESS AND DIET (v. 6)

**6. John wore clothing made of camel's hair, with a leather belt around his waist, and he ate locusts and wild honey.**

John's appearance reflected the poor but rugged wilderness man that he was. Even Jesus once commented that John was not noted for his "fine clothes" (Matthew 11:8). Dressing like his prototype Elijah (2 Kings 1:8), he wore a coarse, itchy robe woven from *camel's hair,* and a *leather belt* around his *waist.* This strip of leather kept the robe from flowing or blowing too loosely, and the robe could be tucked up under it for ease of walking, running, or working.

The *locusts* here were not, as is sometimes said, carob pods. They were large grasshoppers, which have always been a part of the diet of the East. Leviticus 11:22 declares locusts "clean," or permissible to eat, and the Jews were known to eat several varieties of them, roasting or frying them after removing the legs and wings. For dessert John searched the clefts of the rocks and the hollow trees and took what the wild bees of Judea had so generously provided.

### WOULD YOU HIRE THIS PREACHER?

Sometimes pulpit committees look for ministers who possess a pleasant if not handsome appearance, a ready smile, and the ability to dress for success. They want a leader who is up-to-date, fashionable, and non-controversial. After all, preachers must appeal to the baby boomer crowd.

John the Baptizer would have failed to qualify in nearly every one of these areas. He seemed rather eccentric with his strange style of dress and his even stranger eating habits. His preaching was often controversial and rarely accommodating to prevailing political philosophy. His demeanor and tone were austere and dogmatic. Not many of today's pulpits would be available to him.

The surprise is that so many ("the whole Judean countryside") came to to hear John—and scores of those who came and heard were baptized. Who would have guessed? John seems to have been all wrong for the part. But his convictions, his passion, and his guileless humility shone through the rough facade of his exterior.

Is it possible that pulpit committees tend to look for the wrong qualifications in leadership? —R. W. B.

### C. JOHN'S MESSIANIC PREDICTIONS (vv. 7, 8)

**7. And this was his message: "After me will come one more powerful than I, the thongs of whose sandals I am not worthy to stoop down and untie.**

A faithful minister will always exalt Christ. John humbly confessed that he was not the Christ (many were wondering) and pointed to a greater *one* who would *come* after him. This one was so great that John wasn't even fit to be his slave. It was the slave's job to remove the sandals of his master or of an honored guest after travel and to clean them for wearing again later. In Palestine these sandals would invariably be layered with dust or with mud, depending on the weather. It is said that in several cultures of the time a "disciple" of some great man was willing to do any service for his master except untie his sandals—this was the one task too low for anyone but a slave. Yet John felt unworthy even to do that for the coming Messiah.

**8. I baptize you with water, but he will baptize you with the Holy Spirit."**

Some students believe this promise was fulfilled in the miraculous outpouring of the Spirit on the apostles on the day of Pentecost (Acts 2). To others the promise seems to be broader, made to the multitudes here, not just the few who would later become apostles. The New Testament does promise an indwelling of the Spirit for all believers (Acts 2:38; 1 Corinthians 3:16). However, Jesus himself reserved the term *baptized with the Holy Spirit* for the fulfillment of the promised "gift" from the Father (Acts 1:4, 5), which came on Pentecost. This is not to negate the Spirit's role in Christian baptism (John 3:5; 1 Corinthians 6:11; 12, 13; Titus 3:5, 6), but to distinguish between two separate manifestations of the Spirit's work.

### II. JOHN'S MINISTRY TO JESUS (MARK 1:9-11)

### A. JESUS' BAPTISM (v. 9)

**9. At that time Jesus came from Nazareth in Galilee and was baptized by John in the Jordan.**

### WHAT DO YOU THINK?

John was an outspoken and outstanding leader, and yet he was humble. Why is humility often difficult—especially for those in leadership or who tend to be outspoken? How can we minister to each other and help one another to remain humble?

Is there a tactful way to tell a person he or she needs to be more humble? If so, how? If not, what should you do when a Christian brother or sister is not displaying humility?

## HOW TO SAY IT

*Antipas. AN-tuh-pas.*

*baptizo (Greek). bap-TIDZ-owe.*

*Elijah. Ee-LYE-juh.*

*Essenes. ESS-eenz.*

*Galilean. Gal-uh-LEE-un.*

*Herod. HAIR-ud.*

*Herodias. Heh-ROE-dee-us.*

*Josephus. Joe-SEE-fuss.*

*Judea. Joo-DEE-uh.*

*Judean. Joo-DEE-un.*

*Machaerus. Muh-KEER-us.*

*Malachi. MAL-uh-kye.*

*Nathanael. Nuh-THAN-a-el or
   Nuh-THAN-yul (th as in
   thin).*

*Nicodemus. NICK-uh-DEE-mus.*

*Perea. Pur-EE-uh.*

*proselyte. PRAHS-uh-light.*

*Qumran. Koom-RAHN.*

*schizo (Greek). SKIDZ-owe.*

This occasion marks the climax of John's ministry and the beginning of Jesus'. After thirty years of obscurity *Jesus* was ready to introduce himself to the public. Leaving his family and his carpentry work in *Nazareth,* he traveled down to the *Jordan* River valley to find *John.* He did not come to hear John, but to be *baptized* by him (Matthew 3:13). He did not need to be convinced of his duty; he already knew that it was time for him to begin his work.

*In the Jordan* is literally, in the Greek, **into** *the Jordan.* Since Jesus was not liquefied (the only way he could be "poured" or "sprinkled" into the Jordan), it is obvious that baptism in the New Testament was by immersion. This fact is further shown by the etymology of the Greek word *baptizo,* as well as the "coming up out of the water" in verse 10.

It is not completely clear why Jesus submitted to John's baptism. Jesus was sinless, so he did not need a "baptism of repentance for the forgiveness of sins." Matthew quotes Jesus himself that he did it "to fulfill all righteousness" (3:15), which perhaps means that he wanted to identify himself with what were the right things for all other humans to do even though he might formally be exempt from those requirements. (Compare the temple-tax incident in Matthew 17:24-27.)

### B. HEAVEN'S RESPONSE (vv. 10, 11)

*10. As Jesus was coming up out of the water, he saw heaven being torn open and the Spirit descending on him like a dove.*

We see the diverse personalities of the Godhead here. God the Spirit and God the Father were in full agreement with this action by God the Son. The sky was *torn open* (Greek *schizo*), and the Holy *Spirit,* who is essentially bodiless, took upon himself the bodily form of a *dove* (see Luke 3:22) and descended on Jesus.

What the dove form represents is hard to tell for sure. The common suggestions are gentleness, innocence, hope, peace, love, or sacrifice. Regardless, John recognized this as the sign that Jesus was actually the Messiah and the Son of God (John 1:33, 34).

*11. And a voice came from heaven: "You are my Son, whom I love; with you I am well pleased."*

The Father's words of approval recall two Messianic prophecies; Psalm 2:7 says, *"You are my Son,"* and Isaiah 42:1 calls God's suffering servant "my chosen one, in whom I delight." We are not sure whether John, or any others present, heard or understood the *voice,* but Matthew's wording, in the third person ("This is my Son, whom I love"), suggests John probably both heard and understood. It is likely that any other bystanders heard but did not understand the voice (cf. John 12:28, 29 and Acts 9:7 with 22:9).

### III. JOHN'S MINISTRY GIVING WAY TO JESUS' (MARK 1:14, 15)

#### A. JOHN'S ARREST (v. 14a)

*14a. After John was put in prison. . . .*

Mark later provides the details of John's arrest and subsequent murder (6:17-29) at the hands of Herod Antipas and his wife Herodias. The Jewish historian Josephus also speaks of this arrest and locates the place of the imprisonment to be in Herod's castle at Machaerus, which was in Perea, just east of the Dead Sea.

*Muh KEER us*

#### B. JESUS' ARRIVAL IN GALILEE (vv. 14b, 15)

*14b, 15. Jesus went into Galilee, proclaiming the good news of God. "The time has come," he said. "The kingdom of God is near. Repent and believe the good news!"*

The first eight months of Jesus' ministry had been conducted in Judea, and he had begun to draw more crowds and make more disciples than John. A

**IS HE THE ONE?**

*The visual for lesson 6 in the visuals packet shows how John's doubts about Jesus were answered. Display it as you begin to discuss point IV.*

combination of three factors now led him to leave Judea: First, he knew that the Pharisees had learned of his successes and would be increasing their opposition to him (John 4:1-3). Second, he received the news that John had been arrested (Matthew 4:12). Finally, he was following the lead of the Holy Spirit (Luke 4:14).

John's arrest, then, can be dated about December of A.D. 27, as it coincides with the start of Jesus' long and productive Galilean Ministry, which lasted nearly two years.

Notice that Jesus preached the same gospel that John had, though he no doubt added many of his own details to the themes his forerunner had first introduced. The messianic *kingdom* of God was *near*, and these Galilean hearers needed to commit their lives to the gospel he was announcing to them. Jesus' fame soon spread all over Galilee (Luke 4:14).

## IV . JOHN'S LAST MESSAGE (LUKE 7:18-23)
### A. JOHN'S DOUBTS (vv. 18-20)
**18a. John's disciples told him about all these things.**

*John's disciples,* who apparently were permitted to visit him in prison, reported to him about the great miracles Jesus had been performing and about the great reception he had received among the Galileans. John's response is somewhat surprising.
**18b, 19. Calling two of them, he sent them to the Lord to ask, "Are you the one who was to come, or should we expect someone else?"**

Many interpreters think that John was not showing signs of doubt, as it might appear, but was rather asking this question for his disciples' sake—he wanted them to hear it straight from Jesus that he was the Messiah. Some think John was impatient and was just prodding Jesus to hurry up and publicly declare himself as Messiah and eliminate all doubts among the Jews.

However, it is probable that John's faith was actually starting to waver (see verse 23). He probably expected the sort of Messiah most other Jews, including the Twelve, were expecting. Where was the powerful political deliverer whom John himself had preached, who would baptize the obedient in the Spirit and would burn the wicked like chaff (Luke 3:17)? From his dark dungeon cell, where he had been for more than six months by this time, John's discouragement with Jesus' long delay seems to have led him to have misgivings. If Jesus really were the Christ, why had he not vindicated John's preaching and shown himself plainly to the world?
**20. When the men came to Jesus, they said, "John the Baptist sent us to you to ask, 'Are you the one who was to come, or should we expect someone else?'"**

John's two disciples traveled the seventy or so miles to Galilee and faithfully carried out their assigned task.

### B. JESUS' REASSURANCE (vv. 21-23)
**21. At that very time Jesus cured many who had diseases, sicknesses and evil spirits, and gave sight to many who were blind.**

Jesus prefaced his verbal answer to the two men by working a series of miracles. The evidential value of the miracles is clear here; the two were to go tell John everything they had witnessed and let John decide if Jesus was indeed the Christ.
**22. So he replied to the messengers, "Go back and report to John what you have seen and heard: The blind receive sight, the lame walk, those who have leprosy are cured, the deaf hear, the dead are raised, and the good news is preached to the poor.**

## WHAT DO YOU THINK?

Jesus and John both preached repentance. Essentially, repentance means a turning around. We are walking in one direction, and then we turn around and begin walking in the opposite direction.

What do you think of the emphasis on repentance in the church today, is it too little, about right, or too much? Why?

Obviously those who are outside of Christ need to repent, but that concept is foreign to many. How can we make sinners aware of their need to repent and submit to Jesus for salvation (Acts 2:38)?

Is repentance only for those outside of Christ, or do Christians continue to need to repent? Why or why not? (See 1 John 1:8—2:2.)

## WHAT DO YOU THINK?

It seems amazing one so bold as John may have wrestled with doubt. Doubt suggests unbelief or an unwillingness to believe. But such is not always the case. We can have doubts even when we want to believe and actually do believe. Honest doubt asks questions that need to be resolved. (See Mark 9:24.)

How can we determine whether one has honest doubt or is deliberately refusing to believe? How should we respond to either situation?

Jesus answered John's doubts with evidence, not arguments. What evidence would you offer an inquisitive doubter to lead him or her to faith in Jesus Christ?

Jesus was calling attention to the Old Testament prophecies about the coming Messiah's ministry of miracles (see Isaiah 29:18, 19; 35:4-6; 42:7; 61:1-3). "I am doing the Messiah's work. Yes, I am he." John had perhaps misapplied the prophecies of judgment to Christ's first coming, whereas they properly describe his second. He appeared the first time to be, in John's own words, "the Lamb of God, who takes away the sin of the world" (John 1:29). He will come a second time to judge and to destroy the wicked.

### OF PUDDING AND FRUIT

Do you know a good cook when you see one? Skilled chefs are not recognizable by their appearance. Anyone can wear a chef's hat and an apron.

Good cooks are identified by the food they prepare. "The proof is in the pudding," as the saying goes. The same principle applies to carpenters, car manufacturers, seamstresses, and Messiahs. All are evaluated by the product of their labors. Uniforms, vocabulary—even diplomas and degrees—are not necessarily proofs of competence. Until one tastes the pudding, he or she cannot be certain that a person who calls himself "cook" deserves the title. "By their fruit you will recognize them," Jesus said (Matthew 7:20).

When John asked for proof of Jesus' messiahship, the Lord invited him to inspect the fruit of his labor. His many miraculous deeds and his preaching were the proof of his pudding (see also John 10:37, 38).

We believe Christ's claims because we have inspected the fruit of his ministry and have determined, like Nicodemus, that he is "from God. For no one could perform the miraculous signs you are doing if God were not with him" (John 3:2).

—R. W. B.

### 23. Blessed is the man who does not fall away on account of me."

Jesus sent the disciples back to John with words that were at the same time both a gentle rebuke and a firm encouragement. "John, keep your faith no matter what the circumstances; it is well-founded. Don't stumble now. Be assured that your message about me is true, no matter how little you understand my program of things." No doubt, John's faith was renewed and firmly settled for the final days of his life.

## CONCLUSION

John's doubts were honest doubts. Jesus, after John's two disciples had left him, proceeded to defend John's character and commend him to the multitudes (Luke 7:24-28). John was not "a reed swayed by the wind," in spite of his apparent wavering. His confusion caused him to doubt, but he addressed his doubts. It was, in fact, his integrity that had forced him to send the two to Jesus. He had to be sure that he was preaching the truth about Jesus; he would not compromise his message, but he must be sure that it was correct.

Most Christians—even church leaders—at times have tinges of doubt. Is what I believe really true? Does it deserve my life's devotion? Am I leading others astray? Such doubts are nothing to be ashamed of if they are followed by a renewed looking at the evidence. Lazy, dishonest doubt is content to be unsure; sometimes it even prefers the darkness. Honest doubt, healthy doubt, seeks more light. And its reward is a firmer conviction about what it believes. When we have doubts, may we respond as John did, with integrity and honesty, diligent to turn the doubt into firm conviction.

Jesus' challenge to John must also challenge us: look at the evidence. In light of what Jesus did and spoke, is it not much easier to believe than to disbelieve that he is the Christ, the Son of God and the Savior of the world?

# Discovery Learning

*This page contains an alternate lesson plan emphasizing learning activities. Classes desiring such student involvement will find these suggestions helpful. The next page is a reproducible activity page to further enhance discovery learning.*

## LEARNING GOALS

As a result of today's lesson, the student will:

1. Compare John's ministry announcing Christ to the world with his later doubts about Jesus.

2. Explain why even faithful people may sometimes have doubts.

3. Suggest ways to resolve doubts about one's faith.

## INTO THE LESSON

Before the class begins, have a large poster prepared that reads: "What do these four persons have in common: Thomas, John the Baptist, Nathanael, and Lew Wallace?" Answer: They all shared a healthy skepticism about Jesus.(You may need to help by revealing the identity of each of these persons or noted characteristics of each.)

Nathanael was a skeptic who was told "Come and see." Having done so, he proclaimed Jesus as the Son of God. Thomas was known as "doubting Thomas," who after seeing Jesus' wounds proclaimed him as "My Lord and my God." Lew Wallace was the author of *Ben Hur: A Tale of the Christ.* He began his novel doubting that Jesus was anything more than mere man. But as he began to do research, he became convinced him that Jesus was the Son of God. His classic novel reflects his new conviction.

Remind the class that it is not uncommon for people to have doubts about Jesus. How we handle those doubts, however, will make a great deal of difference in what happens to our faith. Today, we will discover that John the Baptist had some similar doubts about Jesus, even after he had baptized Jesus and had witnessed God's Spirit descending upon him.

## INTO THE WORD

Divide the class into small groups of four to six pupils and assign each group one of the sets of questions, Scriptures and materials listed below. Mark an article on John the Baptist in a Bible Dictionary for Group 1. Group 2 should be given a copy of the lesson commentary on verse 8 and an article from a Bible Dictionary on John's baptism. Group 3 should be given a copy of the lesson commentary on Luke 7:18-23.

Group 1: Read the article about John the Baptist from the Bible Dictionary. Summarize his life for the class by having one person report on his birth and early life, another person report on his personal life and ministry, and a third person report on his imprisonment and death.

Group 2: Your task is to report on the purpose of John's baptism and the reason for Jesus submitting himself to baptism. Read Mark 1:7-11 and the marked article on John's Baptism from the Bible Dictionary.

Group 3: Read Luke 7:18-23. What are the indications of doubts that are surfacing in John or his disciples? Can you define the doubts they are experiencing? How did Jesus offer reassurance to John and his disciples? The notes from the lesson commentary will be helpful in preparing your report.

Allow 8-10 minutes for the groups to prepare their reports. Then call the groups together to share their findings. Permit others outside the groups to ask questions or make relevant comments. Compare the results of Group 1 with those of Group 3. Discuss, "Do you find doubt like these in a man like John the Baptizer to be surprising? Why or why not?"

## INTO LIFE

Make the transition from Bible study to the life application by using the following discussion questions (see the lesson commentary conclusion for assistance):

Our lesson writer says, "Most Christians—even church leaders—at times have tinges of doubt. Is what I believe really true? Does it deserve my life's devotion? Am I leading others astray?"

1. Why do faithful people sometimes doubt?

2. What will determine if these doubts are *helpful* in their faith or if they will be *destructive*?

3. What are some of the common "doubts" or questions adults raise about their faith today, or may have unanswered from their teen years?

4. How can we help people make their questions "healthy" skepticism rather than destructive doubt?

(We must encourage them to inquire, to find answers. Lazy doubt will result in no answers and increasing skepticism. Healthy inquiry will find answers and reward us with firmer convictions.)

Encourage each class member to resolve whatever doubts he or she may have. By study and inquiry they may discover a depth to their faith they have never enjoyed before.

*Option:* Use the reproducible activities on the next page to explore how to respond to doubt.

Conclude with prayer that God will bless the faith of each student and will help dismiss any doubts.

# A Case of Doubt

Even the faithful can have doubts. If those doubts are faced honestly, they can usually be answered if a person is willing to spend the time and to take the effort required. One of the best ways to relieve doubt is to seek the counsel of a trusted Christian friend. How would you answer if someone from our church confessed to you the following doubt?

I just don't know any more. I thought God promised to answer prayers. When Mom died last spring, don't you think we prayed for her like we'd never prayed before? She was only 57! Why couldn't God heal her? If God couldn't heal her, then can he do any of the other things he promised in the Bible?

# Don't Doubt It!

Many of our doubts can be answered by a careful search of the Scriptures. Consider the doubts in the left-hand column below. Then look up the Scriptures in the right-hand column. Draw a line from each doubt to the Scripture reference that best answers the doubt.

| | |
|---|---|
| How do I know the Bible is true? | John 16:33 |
| How do I know I'm saved? | 1 Corinthians 1:18-25 |
| How do I know God hears my prayers? | 1 Corinthians 10:13 |
| I'm not sure I can handle temptation. | 2 Corinthians 12:8-10 |
| But I'm not good enough to be saved! | Ephesians 2:8-10 |
| If I sin after I'm saved, will God still forgive me? | 2 Timothy 3:16, 17 |
| But sometimes I don't *feel* forgiven! | Hebrews 4:16 |
| I'm having so much trouble; I must be doing something wrong. | 1 John 1:8, 9 |
| My professor says intelligent people don't believe the Bible. | 1 John 3:19, 20 |
| I've prayed and prayed for relief. Doesn't God care? | 1 John 5:13 |

How do I know the Bible is true? (2 Timothy 3:16, 17); How do I know I'm saved? (1 John 5:13); How do I know God hears my prayers? (Hebrews 4:16); I'm not sure I can handle temptation. (1 Corinthians 10:13); But I'm not good enough to be saved! (Ephesians 2:8-10); If I sin after I'm saved, will God still forgive me? (1 John 1:8, 9); But sometimes I don't *feel* forgiven! (1 John 3:19, 20); I'm having so much trouble; I must be doing something wrong. (John 16:33); My professor says intelligent people don't believe the Bible. (1 Corinthians 1:18-25); I've prayed and prayed for relief. Doesn't God care? (2 Corinthians 12:8-10).

# MARY AND MARTHA

**LESSON 7**

## WHY TEACH THIS LESSON?

First things first. The principle seems so basic it ought not need to be stated. But how frequently have we ignored this principle!

Today's lesson is a call to re-establish priorities. Challenge your students to evaluate their activities with eternity in mind. Even good must sometimes wait for what is better. Feed the spirit; worship the Lord. These are the "better" things.

## INTRODUCTION

### A. FIRST GIVE YOURSELF

We all have heard of parents who work very hard to give their children the very best clothes, toys, or education but neglect to give the children the most needed things of all: their time and love. Even though the gifts the parents give may well be motivated by their love for the children, such things are less than useless if the parents do not first give themselves to talk to the children, to listen to them, and to play with them.

Today's lesson is about two sisters and the gifts they gave Jesus. In the end they both learned that the most important thing to give was their love.

### B. LESSON BACKGROUND

Mary and Martha, along with their brother Lazarus, were some of Jesus' closest friends (John 11:5). The sisters are mentioned only three times in the Gospels, and two of the accounts comprise this lesson's printed text. The other instance is in John 11, which tells of the raising of Lazarus.

The first event likely occurred during the fall of the year preceding Jesus' death. The occasion was a visit by Jesus and the disciples. Jesus used the opportunity to teach Martha a valuable lesson in priorities.

The second event in today's text took place the day before the triumphal entry and six days before the Passover at which Jesus was crucified (John 12:1, 12). The setting was a supper that had been prepared for Jesus and the disciples. Here Mary presented Jesus a valuable gift in a very dramatic way.

The experiences and actions of these two sisters teach us valuable lessons about the place the Lord should have in our hearts and lives and how we should express our love to him.

## I. A LESSON IN PRIORITIES (LUKE 10:38-42)

### A. MARTHA'S GRACIOUS HOSPITALITY (v. 38)

**38. As Jesus and his disciples were on their way, he came to a village where a woman named Martha opened her home to him.**

The twelve *disciples,* and perhaps others, were traveling with *Jesus* as he went about preaching and teaching. Their journey brought them to the *village* of Bethany, which is located less than two miles east of Jerusalem on the eastern slope of the Mount of Olives. *Martha* graciously welcomed them into her house. The fact that the house belonged to Martha placed on her the responsibility of being hostess to the group. As we shall see, she took this responsibility very seriously.

DEVOTIONAL READING
PSALM 27:1-6
LESSON SCRIPTURE
LUKE 10:38-42; JOHN 12:1-8
PRINTED TEXT
LUKE 10:38-42; JOHN 12:1-8

LESSON AIMS

As students participate in today's class session, they should:

1. Compare the gifts of Mary with the service of Martha and the criticism of Judas.

2. Suggest principles for acceptable service.

3. Get involved in a ministry, or evaluate their participation in a current ministry, so that they pursue what is best.

Jan
12

KEY VERSES

"Martha, Martha," the Lord answered, "you are worried and upset about many things, but only one thing is needed. Mary has chosen what is better, and it will not be taken away from her."
Luke 10:41, 42

**LESSON 7 NOTES**

*Have you chosen the better way?*

*The visual for lesson 7 in the visuals packet is an artist's portrayal of the incident in today's lesson text. Have it on display as students arrive.*

## WHAT DO YOU THINK?

*Martha opened her home to Jesus. Are our homes open to him? Would he be comfortable with the conversation around our dinner table? Could we invite him to read the magazines in our homes or to watch the television shows we watch? Would he be grieved by the way we talk to other family members or by the vocabulary we use?*

*How can we make sure our homes are open to Jesus? Why is it important that we do so?*

## OPTION

*Explore this text by using the reproducible activity page, 186.*

Martha did well to welcome Jesus and his followers into her *home*. Her hospitality revealed a good heart and a sincere interest in the kingdom of God. She followed in the train of many other Bible characters who welcomed the Lord and his prophets. What a blessing gracious hospitality is to those who receive it!

### B. MARY AT JESUS' FEET (v. 39)
**39. She had a sister called Mary, who sat at the Lord's feet listening to what he said.**

It appears that *Mary* lived with Martha, and she was present for this very special occasion. Mary stayed in Jesus' presence because she wanted to hear what he said. Perhaps he was taking this leisure time to teach the disciples or to answer questions people had.

How we would like to sit at Mary's side! Couldn't we all sit *at the Lord's feet* and listen to him for hours? Or could we? In our day our churches are blessed with thousands of godly preachers who have invested a lifetime studying God's Word and walking with the Lord, yet we sometimes have a hard time listening to them for half an hour while they open the Word to us. We have available all kinds of books and magazines to help us grow in our faith and understanding, but we seldom find the time to read them. We all need to imitate Mary, who put everything else aside to take advantage of the opportunity to learn from the Lord.

### C. THE EXASPERATED HOSTESS (v. 40)
**40. But Martha was distracted by all the preparations that had to be made. She came to him and asked, "Lord, don't you care that my sister has left me to do the work by myself? Tell her to help me!"**

Making *preparations* for thirteen or more guests required a lot of work. This problem would have been aggravated if the group had come unexpectedly—after all, they couldn't phone ahead! It all got to be too much for Martha.

*Don't you care?* Martha must have been very upset indeed to make such an accusation against Jesus. Apparently she felt that Jesus should have excused Mary and told her to help instead of leaving Martha to *do the work* by herself. This is the heart of the matter. Martha did not mind the preparations so much as she resented the fact that Mary was not helping.

We can learn many lessons from Martha. She was willing to work hard to do the necessary but unglamorous tasks involved in caring for her guests. She was indeed rendering a good and important ministry to the Lord. How refreshing a good supper would have been after walking all day!

The operation of the church today requires all sorts of workers, too. We need people to clean, stuff envelopes, water plants, maintain vehicles, mow yards, remove snow, repair facilities, move chairs, cook and deliver meals, and perform countless other jobs. The ministry of the church suffers when Christians are not willing to do these things. We need many Marthas today.

Martha got upset because Mary did not share her priorities, and the same conflict haunts us today. It is natural for each person to feel that the ministry he or she works in is a high priority and that it should be a priority for everyone else as well. If others do not place the same importance on it, hard feelings and anger sometimes result. We must recognize that the church has need of many different ministries and learn to value them all.

Martha's gift of service to the Lord was soured because of her angry attitude. Surely she rejoiced when she saw Jesus approaching her home and looked forward to ministering to him. If she had kept that attitude, she would have kept her joy. However, Martha's anger took the joy out of her labor.

Again we can learn from Martha's error. If we decide to perform some service for the Lord, then let us do it with joy. If others join us in the work, well and good. But even if no one else helps and we begin to weary from the load, let us still rejoice. The Lord sees our work and appreciates it. That is sufficient. Anger or resentment only ruins the gift.

### D. CHOOSE WHAT IS NEEDED (vv. 41,42)

**41. "Martha, Martha," the Lord answered, "you are worried and upset about many things.**

As we would expect, Jesus remained calm and composed in the face of this onslaught. The repeating of Martha's name served to emphasize Jesus' affection for her and soften the rebuke that followed. What was it that *worried and upset* Martha? Cooking in the first-century was not the efficient process that cooking is today. It would take more time and effort than we can imagine to pull together a large meal. Preparing bread began with grinding the grain to flour. If she served meat, she had to slaughter and dress the animal. (See Genesis 18:7.)

**42. "But only one thing is needed. Mary has chosen what is better, and it will not be taken away from her."**

Martha was worried about many things, but *only one* was *needed,* and Martha was giving no attention to it. She was concerned with food and preparations, and had thus missed the more important opportunity to hear the word of God. Mary, on the other hand, had chosen that good part when she sat to listen to Jesus.

Even though they were delivered tenderly, Jesus' words were nonetheless a rebuke. It was not that the things Martha was doing were unimportant or unappreciated. The men did need life's necessities. Perhaps Martha was too obsessed with time. Would it really have mattered if they had eaten two or three hours later? Perhaps she was going overboard and making needlessly elaborate preparations. In some way she was placing much too much importance on the things she was doing. Physical concerns are important, but the one thing that is truly necessary is to feed the spirit.

We all have responsibilities like Martha's that press on us every day. We do our jobs, work at home, run the kids around, work overtime, and do a thousand other seemingly endless chores. To a certain extent they are necessary, but they must not be allowed to take over our lives. Specifically, we must not allow such things to crowd the spiritual out of our lives.

All Christians face this challenge. It is not that we don't love Jesus. We promise ourselves that as soon as we get everything done, we will pray or read the Bible or start going to that new midweek class. But somehow we never get caught up. We need to learn that routine chores can wait so we can feed ourselves spiritually.

Christians can even become so obsessed with their work for the Lord that they lose sight of the Lord himself. People who lead some aspect of the worship service can become so distracted that they fail to worship. Teachers can study for hours but fail to learn the lesson themselves. People burn out on all kinds of church work when they fail to keep themselves close to Jesus. If we keep our relationship with him strong and vital, he gives us strength to do more than we can do on our own. However, if we fail to provide for our spiritual nourishment, our love for the Lord and our spiritual vigor eventually weaken and grow cold.

It is unlikely that Mary was a slacker who never helped with the work, but at this time the work would have to wait. She chose to be with Jesus. Martha could have made the same choice. Even though the management of the home was her responsibility, she could have taken time to be with Jesus. We all must learn to choose the *better* part.

### WHAT DO YOU THINK?

*Martha wanted Jesus to tell Mary to get to work and stop loafing. Sometimes we are tempted to be critical of those in our congregation who do not appear to be shouldering their part of the responsibilities. Jesus may want to talk to us about our critical attitude, just as he wanted to speak to Martha.*

*When should we speak to someone about his or her failure to serve? After all, studies indicate that in most churches, 80% of the work is done by 20% of the people. Are the 80% loafing or "sitting at Jesus' feet"? How can we tell? Who should speak to those who are not serving? What should he or she say?*

### WHAT DO YOU THINK?

*Mary literally sat at Jesus' feet to learn from him. We can sit at his feet when we make time to read and study the Bible and then meditate on what the Word says. We sit at Jesus' feet when we pray. We sit at Jesus' feet when we listen to a sermon or a Sunday school lesson that increases our understanding of the Scripture and challenges us to apply it. We sit at Jesus' feet when we worship him with other believers in Christian fellowship.*

*How often do we act like Martha—ignoring the chance to sit at Jesus' feet because we are distracted by other things? How do we know when we ought to "sit at his feet" and when we ought to do the other things?*

## THE NEED FOR MARTHAS

Jesus' comments to Martha in our lesson text were not meant to disparage Martha's value, nor the value of her worthwhile contribution to his visit. He simply and softly rebuked her judgmental attitude toward her sister and gave her the divine perspective on what seemed to be an unfair circumstance.

This needs to be kept in mind in today's world, where cultural forces have seemingly reduced the rank of any woman without a career to second-class citizen. Stay-at-home wives and mothers should not be ashamed to declare the worthiness of their vocation. Someone should be demonstrating on behalf of those who cook, clean, counsel, encourage, administrate, schedule, train, comfort, discipline, transport, and carry out scores of other tasks. These women who do necessary household chores, superintend their homes, hold together their families, and successfully rear children are involved in perhaps the most demanding and least appreciated of careers.

Martha's spiritual descendants, for whom we should be eternally grateful, are legion. Their leadership may be hardly noticed by the church; just as it is often taken for granted in the home. The cooks, the flower arrangers, the Communion preparers, the nursery attendants—these are vital though unsung heroes and heroines in God's family. Their ministries are invaluable to the success of kingdom enterprises. God bless them every one!         —R. W. B.

## II. AN ACT OF DEVOTION (JOHN 12:1-8)

### A. A SUPPER WITH FRIENDS (vv. 1, 2)

**1. Six days before the Passover, Jesus arrived at Bethany, where Lazarus lived, whom Jesus had raised from the dead.**

Jesus was coming to Jerusalem for a final confrontation with his enemies. He would die *six days* later. Indeed, his conscious purpose for coming to Jerusalem at this time was so that he might die in fulfillment of prophecy and of God's will.

Before entering Jerusalem, Jesus stopped and stayed in *Bethany*, the same village as in the previous event. Sometime between that earlier visit and this one he had come to Bethany and raised *Lazarus* from the dead.

**2. Here a dinner was given in Jesus' honor. Martha served, while Lazarus was among those reclining at the table with him.**

Jesus' friends made him a *dinner*. Matthew mentions that this was in the house of a man called Simon the Leper (Matthew 26:6). Even though it was not at her house, *Martha served*. The fact that she served even at someone else's home indicates that she was prominent in the village and among Jesus' followers. It also shows that she had a heart and talent for serving. *Lazarus* is mentioned among the invited guests, but Mary is not. Did she come uninvited (verse 3), or did John mention only Lazarus here since he was gong to refer to Mary immediately after?

### B. MARY'S EXTRAORDINARY ANOINTING (v. 3)

**3. Then Mary took about a pint of pure nard, an expensive perfume; she poured it on Jesus' feet and wiped his feet with her hair. And the house was filled with the fragrance of the perfume.**

This was not an impulsive act by Mary. Since this was not her home, she had to have come prepared with the *perfume*. Mary had planned this offering in advance.

Matthew and Mark say that Mary anointed Jesus' head; here John notes she anointed his *feet*. Evidently she did both, starting with his head and finishing with his feet. It was usual to wash and anoint a guest's feet, but it was very unusual to use such expensive ointment. Mary concluded by wiping Jesus' feet *with her hair*. This exceedingly humble and tender action showed her extreme humility in the Lord's presence. Her compelling desire to minister to the Lord and show her love to him overrode any feelings of pride or embarrassment.

*The house was filled with the fragrance.* This is the comment of an eyewitness, one who actually smelled the sweet perfume.

Mary's actions were extraordinary. The great cost of the gift did not matter to her. She did not care that all eyes were on her as she knelt at Jesus' feet and wiped them with her hair, if she thought about that at all. The only thing that mattered to her then was Jesus. Her only thought was to minister to him, to do as much for him as she could.

It is only when we focus on Jesus that we do extraordinary things for him. If we dwell too much on the cost or sacrifice, we may become unwilling to pay it. But if we remember the One to whom we offer the gift or service, and if we remember what he has done for us at what cost to himself, then we dedicate everything we have and everything we are to his service.

When we focus on Jesus, we do not hear or care what others say. They may call us foolish, extravagant, or even dangerous, but we care only about Jesus' approval.

## C. JUDAS'S OUTRAGE (vv. 4-6)

**4, 5. But one of his disciples, Judas Iscariot, who was later to betray him, objected, "Why wasn't this perfume sold and the money given to the poor? It was worth a year's wages."**

Far from being moved by Mary's beautiful act, *Judas* was outraged and railed at what he considered a blatant waste of such a valuable commodity. In his view, scented oil would have done just as well. He estimated that the ointment was worth almost *a year's wages* for a common laborer. A great deal of money indeed! Judas suggested that the *money* could have been *given to the poor.*

**6. He did not say this because he cared about the poor but because he was a thief; as keeper of the money bag, he used to help himself to what was put into it.**

With the advantage of hindsight John put the lie to Judas' professed concern for the poor. *He was a thief* who cared nothing for the suffering of the unfortunate. His rage came from the thought of how much money had slipped through his fingers when Mary used the ointment for such a foolish thing as anointing Jesus' feet. Money that was given to Jesus and the disciples was kept in a single *bag,* and Judas was in charge of it. He carried it, but often used it for his own purposes.

Judas is the subject of lesson nine, and so he will be discussed in more detail there. However, we see in this text one of Judas's main problems was the sin he had let into his heart. His greed made it impossible for him to appreciate Mary's gift to the Lord. The jaundiced viewpoint of his avaricious heart twisted and perverted his outlook on everything.

So it is with every sin that finds a home in man's heart. The heart filled with prejudice cannot recognize the value of individuals. The heart filled with envy cannot rejoice when others are blessed. The heart filled with lust cannot appreciate beauty and innocence. Sin always twists and perverts the eyes of the mind.

## D. JESUS JUSTIFIES MARY (vv. 7, 8)

**7. "Leave her alone," Jesus replied. "It was intended that she should save this perfume for the day of my burial.**

Jesus rebuked Judas and anyone else who thought Mary's actions foolish and extravagant. By defending her, he revealed his appreciation and approval.

The rest of the verse is difficult to understand. Modern translators suggest several different variations. The main idea seems to be this: Jesus knew that his death and *burial* were only a few days away. With this in mind, he considered Mary's anointing to be a true burial anointing. He may have meant that the Father intended the ointment to be used in this way.

### WHAT DO YOU THINK?

*Throughout history, there have been a variety of methods to express religious devotion. Some have been extreme, such as total isolation from the world, self-mutilation, and vows of celibacy. In most cases, these were attempts to substitute acts of devotion for genuine, heartfelt devotion. The act of devotion that Jesus desires most is the sacrifice of ourselves (Romans 12:1). In what ways might the sacrifice of oneself be expressed? Is it obvious to others when one has sacrificed himself to the Lord? If so, how?*

### WHAT DO YOU THINK?

*Judas criticized Mary's action. Of course, we know his motives. Do you think similar motives are behind criticisms of those who give devoted service today? Why or why not? How should we handle it when someone criticizes our devotion or our service? How do you respond to an act of worship that seems extravagant—as Mary's act did to Judas and the other disciples (cf. Matthew 26:8, 9)? How do we balance the demands of stewardship and of wholesale devotion on the order of Mary's act?*

## WHAT DO YOU THINK?

Jesus said we would always have the poor among us. What are we doing for these poor among us? Do you think we are doing enough? Why or why not? How much of the church's resources do you think ought to go toward benevolence?

## PRAYER

Father above, from whom comes every good and perfect gift, help us to give our best to you. As we spend time in worship and in prayer, increase our faith and understanding. When we labor for you, help us do it with a cheerful heart even when we grow weary. Accept our gifts. In the name of your perfect Gift, who rendered the ultimate labor of love, we pray. Amen.

## THOUGHT TO REMEMBER

The best gift we can give to the Lord is ourselves.

## DAILY BIBLE READINGS

Monday, Jan. 6—Mary and Martha Send for Jesus (John 11: 1-16)

Tuesday, Jan. 7—Martha Believes in the Resurrection (John 11:17-27)

Wednesday, Jan. 8—Mary Believes in Jesus' Power (John 11:28-32)

Thursday, Jan. 9—Jesus Raises Lazarus From the Dead (John 11:33-44)

Friday, Jan. 10—Jesus Anointed in Simon's Home (Mark 14:3-9)

Saturday, Jan. 11—Women Minister to Jesus' Body (Mark 15:42-47)

Sunday, Jan. 12—Be Confident in the Lord (Psalm 27:1-6)

**8. You will always have the poor among you, but you will not always have me.**

Jesus was not callous toward the *poor.* He often ministered to them and always treated them with kindness. However, poverty will exist until the end of the world, and so Jesus' disciples always will have opportunity to minister to the poor. Jesus, on the other hand, would be among his followers only a short time longer. The opportunity to minister to him was soon to end.

### GOOD, BETTER, BEST

"Enter to worship; depart to serve." This is often seen on church bulletins and outdoor signs. Whether worship or service is more important is not subject to debate. For the church, it is not an either/or option; it is a both/and obligation. We are commanded to worship, and we are compelled to serve.

In this lesson's texts, Martha served while Mary worshiped. Generalities, however, should not be concluded from one or two instances. It surely must not be assumed that Martha never worshiped, nor that Mary never served. Both did what seemed best to them at the time.

Jesus favored the choice of worship on these occasions. But remember the profound lesson he taught while celebrating his last Passover with his disciples? Under those particular circumstances (where feet needed washing), the Lord emphasized humble service as a key to his kingdom. After he had washed the feet of his followers, he instructed them to do likewise. We should follow Christ's example.

Occasionally we must choose, from good things to do, the best thing to do. Sometimes that will be worship, sometimes service, sometimes both—but never will it be neither.

—R. W. B.

## CONCLUSION

Mary and Martha demonstrate an important lesson: we ought always to give Jesus our best. Both women truly loved the Lord, but they showed their love in different ways.

Martha wanted to give to Jesus, and she set about to render a useful and pleasant service to him by ministering to his physical needs. She did not realize that this was not her best. What Jesus wanted most was Martha herself. He would have been delighted for her to sit at his feet, too. This was not an either/or situation. Martha could have done both things. Perhaps after Jesus' rebuke, she did take time to sit down with him.

We must learn to give the Lord the things that are best. True, it is important that we give him our money and our physical labors. But in addition to these things, and before these things, we must give him ourselves. We must spend time with him, and not just spend time working for him. Prayer, worship, meditation, Bible study—these are the necessary things. Even though we sometimes feel that there is so much of the Lord's work to do that we cannot take much time to spend in these ways, we must remember what Jesus said is truly necessary.

Teacher, do your students give their best time to spend with the Lord? Challenge them to evaluate their priorities in light of what Jesus told Martha.

When she wanted to give Jesus a gift, Mary gave him the very best that she had. This was a unique situation, but it demonstrates that we do not give the Lord our leftovers or things that no longer have any value to us. The Lord does not want us to impoverish ourselves to give him gifts, but it is a poor gift that is not valuable to the one who gives it. When we joyfully give a gift that costs us something, then we have given an acceptable gift; we have performed an act of devotion.

Teacher, ask your students what kinds of gifts they give the Lord. Do they truly sacrifice to give to him?

# Discovery Learning

*This page contains an alternate lesson plan emphasizing learning activities. Classes desiring such student involvement will find these suggestions helpful. The next page is a reproducible activity page to further enhance discovery learning.*

## LEARNING GOALS

As students participate in today's class session, they should:

1. Compare the gifts of Mary with the service of Martha and the criticism of Judas.

2. Suggest principles for acceptable service.

3. Get involved in a ministry, or evaluate their participation in a current ministry, so that they pursue what is best.

## INTO THE LESSON

Before class, write the following words on the chalkboard: *fuel, lubrication, spark plugs, tires*. When you call the class to order, ask, "Which of these is most important for operating an automobile? Why?" In your discussion, observe that each item is essential. Timing is usually what makes one item more important than the others. When the tank is nearly empty, fuel is the most important; when the tires have the minimum legal tread depth, tires become the priority.

Sometimes we compare ministries in the church. We have a tendency to believe what *we* do for the Lord is especially important. We may even believe our gift is more important than another's. We need to see that each gift is important. When we do that, we can better appreciate each other's service and more humbly evaluate our own.

## INTO THE WORD

Ask the class to form two groups. Ask one group to study Luke 10:38-42. As the group examines the passage, the following questions should be answered:

1. What was Martha's gift to Jesus on this occasion?

2. What was Mary's gift to Jesus?

3. What was Martha's complaint?

4. Had Martha realized Mary had chosen "what is better," what would she have done?

The second group is to study John 12:1-8 and answer the following questions:

1. What was Martha's gift to Jesus on this occasion?

2. What was Mary's gift?

3. What was Judas's complaint?

4. Why did Jesus not agree with Judas?

5. If Mary had sold the ointment and bought a cheaper anointing oil to use and had given the remainder of the sale price to the poor, would that have been

an acceptable gift? Why or why not? What if she had kept the balance for herself—she still gave more than anyone else—would that have been acceptable? Why or why not?

Allow about ten minutes for the two groups to work; then ask for reports from each group. Discuss the last question from each group in the larger group: What should Martha have done, sit with Jesus or serve with joy? Why? What about Mary's gift; could she have given less and still been commended? Why or why not?

## INTO LIFE

Mary gave herself completely to Jesus. She would not miss an opportunity to hear the words of eternal life (John 6:68) from his lips. She could give no less than her best—and all of it—in anointing him.

How can we give our best? To consider this with the class, distribute the following list of "complaints." Ask each student to suggest how he or she would answer each complaint in light of today's Scriptures.

1. I work in the church nursery during every Sunday school session. None of the other mothers ever helps out; they just go to class every week and enjoy themselves. I'm tired of it!

2. Why should we give all the money we got from the Hendersons' estate to missions? Don't the elders know there are things we need right here in our own church? Our kitchen looks like it was designed in the fifties! Let's get up to date!

3. Every time we have a work night at church, just a few of us show up and work our hearts out! And where are the elders? Where is the preacher? Where are the deacons? If the leaders won't participate, then why should we?

As you discuss each situation, list some general principles about service that can form a set of guidelines for acceptable service. Write these on the chalkboard.

Ask the students to call out the names of ministries in which they participate. Write these on the chalkboard. Note the variety of ministries represented just by the people in your class. Say something about the importance of each one. Observe how people can follow the principles on the chalkboard as they participate in these ministries. Challenge class members to get involved in ministry if they are not already, and to follow the principles for acceptable service if they are.

# Mary and Martha

Mary and Martha both gave gifts to Jesus (Luke 10:38-42). Martha's problem was she could not appreciate Mary's gift. In complaining, she cheapened her own gift of service to the Lord.

Martha's contribution was important, and there were surely times when Mary served with her. There are still many "Martha" jobs needed in the church. What Mary did was also important, and surely Martha must have sat at Jesus' feet on occasion. There are many times we need to imitate "Mary" in the church today.

List some activities or ministries that are important in our church today. Then check whether this task imitates Martha or Mary.

| ACTIVITY OR MINISTRY | MARTHA | MARY |
|---|---|---|
| | | |
| | | |
| | | |
| | | |
| | | |
| | | |

Now review your list. Put a star (☆) next to each activity your regularly participate in. Do you more often imitate Martha or Mary?

If you said Martha, do you ever resent the Marys? If so, how do you deal with that resentment? How can you better appreciate their gift and, thus, make your own gift more meaningful.

If you said Mary, are you careful to express appreciation to the Marthas who serve, usually behind the scenes, to make your times with the Master more meaningful?

# New Testament Personalities

# PETER

## LESSON 8

## WHY TEACH THIS LESSON?

Peter is a fascinating character. Often quick to speak and slow to think, he is easily identified with by many. Today we will see him at his best and at his worst. At his best, he declares Jesus to be the Christ, the Son of the living God. At his worst, he tries to tell Jesus what to do. Through it all, he is loved by the Lord. And, of course, he becomes the outstanding Christian leader we recognize in the book of Acts.

Use this lesson to remind your students that a mistake—even a big, foolish, sinful mistake—does not take us outside the sphere of God's love and service for him. Challenge them to serve even as Peter served in the faith expressed in the "Good Confession."

## INTRODUCTION

### A. THE MASTER SCULPTOR

Michelangelo was one of the greatest artists of all time. Though he lived and worked four centuries ago, his creations still stun us with their beauty and power. Two of his most famous works are sculptures. The *Pietà* depicts Mary holding Jesus' lifeless body on her knees after he was taken down from the cross. *David* is a figure of the ancient king, standing tall and proud, displaying perfect physique. Both of these pieces are so lifelike that they look almost as if the real people were frozen and turned to marble.

Like all other sculptures, these two works began as large blocks of stone. In his mind's eye, the great artist saw Mary, Jesus, and David in the stone. Carefully he chiseled and polished until only the magnificent figures remained.

Jesus gave Simon the name Cephas (Hebrew) or Peter (Greek), both of which mean "Rock." When Jesus first met Peter he was much like one of the large blocks of stone that Michelangelo began with. But Jesus, like the artist, was able to see what this rock of a man could become. Slowly, patiently, masterfully, Jesus chiseled and polished Peter until he became the great leader and apostle of the early church. The Lord continues to work on people's hearts and lives today to transform us into creations of beauty and strength.

### B. LESSON BACKGROUND

Today's text consists of two selections from Matthew. The first portion records Peter's call to become Jesus' full-time follower and disciple. Peter had met Jesus earlier and doubtless had spent many hours and days with the Lord, listening to him teach and watching him perform miracles. See John 1:40ff. Now, however, Jesus called him to a new level of discipleship. This event took place rather early in Jesus' public ministry.

The second portion of text records an event that happened as much as two years later in Jesus' ministry, after the disciples had walked with him for many months. The Lord asked them who they believed him to be. Peter, speaking for the group, declared that they believed Jesus to be the Christ. We call this Peter's "Great Confession."

DEVOTIONAL READING
LUKE 22:54-62
LESSON SCRIPTURE
MATTHEW 4:18-20; 16:13-23
PRINTED TEXT
MATTHEW 4:18-20; 16:13-23

Jan
19

LESSON AIMS

As students participate in today's class session, they will be able to:

1. Describe Peter's call to discipleship and his confession of Jesus' identity.

2. Explain why knowing Jesus' true identity is essential to participating in his work of "fishing" for men.

3. Suggest some specific ways we can help bring people to believe in "the Christ, the Son of the living God."

KEY VERSE

Simon Peter answered, "You are the Christ, the Son of the living God."          Matthew 16:16

LESSON 8 NOTES

## I. A FISHER OF MEN (MATTHEW 4:18-20)

**18. As Jesus was walking beside the Sea of Galilee, he saw two brothers, Simon called Peter and his brother Andrew. They were casting a net into the lake, for they were fishermen.**

The *Sea of Galilee* is located in the northern part of Israel. It is really a large lake on the Jordan River. Jesus walked on the waters of this lake and stilled a storm on its surface. On the surrounding hills he preached the Sermon on the Mount and fed the multitudes. He lived for a time in Capernaum on its northern shore.

Jesus was not out for a casual stroll. This was a momentous day, a day of decision. It marked the beginning of a new phase in Jesus' ministry. He was *walking by the Sea* because he was looking for the men he was about to find. It would be the beginning of a new phase of ministry for them, too!

*Simon* was *called Peter* by Jesus himself (John 1:42). He and *his brother Andrew* were at work when Jesus found them.

**19. "Come, follow me," Jesus said, "and I will make you fishers of men."**

*Follow me.* This was a call to a life-changing commitment. Peter and some of the other disciples had followed Jesus on many occasions before this. They even may have been with him for months, but they had gone back home and back to work. Now, Jesus invited them to make a break with their old lives. He asked them to leave their businesses, their homes, and their families to follow him (Mark 10:28). Following Jesus meant more than physically trailing along beside him. It meant sharing his life as an itinerant preacher. It meant learning and accepting his teachings. Though they could not know it then, it meant that they eventually would share his fate by being killed at the hands of their enemies. Their lives would never be the same if they accepted the Lord's call.

What would they do if they followed Jesus? He said he would make them *fishers of men.* This powerful figure is easily understood. Peter knew about fishing. He knew it involved hard work, long hours, uncertain results, and even danger. It would be the same for a fisher of men.

**20. At once they left their nets and followed him.**

Momentous decision or not, Peter and Andrew did not hesitate, but left their nets *at once.* They had seen and heard enough of Jesus to convince them that he was from God and that following him was the most important thing they could do. The impression we get is that the fishermen left their nets where they lay and went with Jesus immediately. Mark assures us there were others there to care for the equipment and, we suppose, to continue the business (1:20).

Jesus demands the same commitment from every one of his followers. The decision to become a Christian is the decision to follow Jesus wherever he leads. Jesus says, "Follow me wherever I lead you and do whatever I tell you to do."

In the same way that Peter was required to leave his career, home, and family to follow Jesus, the Lord warns that every Christian must be willing to sacrifice family or anything else to follow him (Matthew 10:32-39). At the same time, Jesus promises that whoever leaves house or family or lands to follow him will receive "a hundred times as much" in this life and eternal life as well (Mark 10:29, 30).

### CHANGING CAREERS

A generation ago, people expected to begin a career with a company and stay until retirement. Several recessions and "downsizings" later, that expectation changed. A person may have to change companies to remain employed in his or her field of expertise. Current college graduates face the prospects of changing, not just companies, but careers at least twice in their working lives.

Surveys also reveal that a sobering percentage of today's workers are dissatisfied with their jobs. Only a fortunate few work at something truly fulfilling. All the coffee

**OPTION**

*Pursue the fishing analogy for evangelism with the reproducible activity, "Fishers of Men," on page 186.*

**WHAT DO YOU THINK?**

*What does it mean to leave everything to follow Jesus? Does he demand that we, like Peter and Andrew, leave our secular businesses to follow him? Why or why not?*

*How can one who owns a home and a car and a full wardrobe say he has "left everything" to follow Jesus? How can you tell one who has "left everything" from one who hasn't?*

breaks, profit sharing, and other perks in the world will not suffice if you are unhappy with what you do to earn a living.

Peter may have liked his fishing career, but it did not take long for him to leave the nets behind when Christ called. He changed abruptly from fisherman to fisher of men and subsequently found true fulfillment.

Jesus still calls all of us to some kind of personal ministry. Some heed the call to a vocational career of Christian service, but all disciples, no matter how they earn their living, can be fishers of men.                                                —R. W. B.

## II. KEEPER OF THE KEYS OF THE KINGDOM (MATTHEW 16:13-23)
### A. PETER'S GREAT CONFESSION (vv. 13-17)

**13. When Jesus came to the region of Caesarea Philippi, he asked his disciples, "Who do people say the Son of Man is?"**

At this time the disciples had been with Jesus for about two years. They had traveled the length of the country with him. Now Jesus led them to *Caesarea Philippi*, which was at the extreme north of the country, about twenty-five miles north of the sea of Galilee. He appears to have led them away from the center of his popularity so that he could have some privacy with the group. They did not enter the city, at least not at once, but remained in the general *region.*

When he had the disciples alone, Jesus asked them what the masses thought of him. Jesus frequently referred to himself as *the Son of Man.* It seems to have been his favorite self-designation. It emphasized his humanity and, at the same time, conveyed the idea that Jesus was the greatest of all men and the representative of all mankind. Paul compared Jesus to a kind of second Adam, one who brought life rather than death (Romans 5:12-21).

**14. They replied, "Some say John the Baptist; others say Elijah; and still others, Jeremiah or one of the prophets."**

The apostles had heard many speculations about Jesus' identity. The people were confused. They guessed that Jesus was *John the Baptist* come back from the dead after being beheaded by Herod, or that he was *Elijah, Jeremiah,* or some other *prophet* come back to the earth. Of course all these guesses were wrong, but they show that the common people regarded Jesus as someone sent by God and on a par with the greatest prophets. In contrast to these popular notions, most of the Jewish leaders rejected Jesus as a fraud and a troublemaker.

Today as well as then, people have many opinions as to Jesus' identity. Some call him a great teacher or prophet. Some call him a good man. Some call him a fool or a fraud.

**15. "But what about you?" he asked. "Who do you say I am?"**

Jesus next asked the disciples to give voice to their own convictions about his identity. Did they share the popular ideas or did they have greater faith? More than anyone else, the disciples had had ample opportunity to observe Jesus and form an accurate idea about who he was.

**16. Simon Peter answered, "You are the Christ, the Son of the living God."**

Jesus addressed the whole group, but in typical fashion *Peter* spoke out first and *answered* for the group. Without hesitating he declared Jesus to be the *Christ,* or Messiah, a title that refers to the great deliverer and king who was promised throughout the Old Testament. (For more on *Christ,* see comments on Luke 2:11, 12, page 141.)

Peter went on. He said that he believed Jesus to be God's *Son.* This meant that Peter considered Jesus to be more than any mere human: he was divine. This was a dramatic confession. The Jews did not expect the Messiah to be God himself come to deliver them, but Peter and the others had heard and seen enough of Jesus to

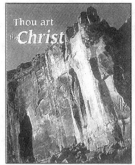

*The visual for lesson 8 in the visuals packet calls attention to the "rock" on which the church is built: "You are the Christ." Display it as you discuss verse 16.*

## HOW TO SAY IT

Aramaic.  Air-uh-MAY-ick.
Augustus.  Aw-GUST-us.
Caesarea.  Sess-uh-REE-uh.
Capernaum.  Kuh-PURR-nee-um.
Cephas.  SEE-fus.
Hades.  HAY-deez.
Michelangelo.  MIKE-uh-LAN-
 jell-owe.
Philippi.  Fuh-LIP-pie.

## WHAT DO YOU THINK?

Jesus promised the gates of Hades could not overcome the church. If we picture an army beating on the gates of a city, then this pictures the church on the offensive. What offensives has our church launched recently to attack Satan's kingdom? What offensives can we launch?

The word for overcome suggests more than the strength of a gate, however. It suggests Satan's kingdom is on the offensive—charging out through "the gates of Hades" to engage the church in battle. On what fronts do we see this battle today? Where do we need reinforcements to battle the devil and his forces?

reach this radical but correct conclusion. *Living God* means the true, active, personal God of creation as opposed to the false gods and dead idols worshiped by the pagans.

"Who do you believe Jesus is?" is the most important question in the world. Everyone who has heard of Christ must answer it. To those who believe with Peter that Jesus is the divine Son of God and the Savior of the world, to those who acknowledge him as Lord and submit their lives to him, to those who obey him, he gives eternal life. All who reject him are rejected by him.

**17. Jesus replied, "Blessed are you, Simon son of Jonah, for this was not revealed to you by man, but by my Father in heaven.**

Jesus' blessing of sounds like an exclamation of joy bursting out of Jesus' heart. Peter understood what God was revealing through him! He believed! Jesus' mission depended on the belief, on the unshakable faith of Peter and the others, and that faith indeed lived in their hearts. Peter had not learned this spiritual truth through human wisdom or agency, but from the *Father*. Probably this does not mean that Peter was directly and miraculously filled with the knowledge of Jesus. More likely Jesus meant that God revealed his identity and nature through his words and miracles. Other men and women had seen and heard much of the same things as Peter and the other disciples, yet they did not believe as Peter did.

### B. THE KEYS OF THE KINGDOM (vv. 18, 19)

**18. And I tell you that you are Peter, and on this rock I will build my church, and the gates of Hades will not overcome it.**

Jesus had given Simon the name *Peter* at an earlier time, and now he repeats it. The name means "rock," but not the same *rock* as in the next clause. In the Greek language this second word for *rock* is feminine, while the word for *Peter* is masculine. Jesus was making a play on words to emphasize his point: "You're a rock, Peter, and on the great rock that you have confessed, the truth of who I am, I will build my church."

*The gates of Hades* refers to the realm of death and the dead. Hebrews describes the devil as holding the power of death (2:14). Thus, Hades is the kingdom of Satan, the kingdom that is directly opposed to the Lord's kingdom. In ancient times, when cities relied on walls for protection, gates were crucial. If a gate failed to withstand the attacks of the enemy, the city was lost. Jesus promised that the gates of Satan's kingdom could not prevail against the kingdom of heaven. In the mighty struggle that would ensue, the Lord's armies and the his kingdom would prevail. Notice that the kingdom of heaven is on the offensive, attacking Satan's kingdom. Christ himself shattered the gates of the devil's kingdom. He opened the way for sinners to return to the family and fellowship of God. The Lord's soldiers plunder Satan's kingdom every time a person is brought to believe in Jesus and accept him as Lord.

**19. I will give you the keys of the kingdom of heaven; whatever you bind on earth will be bound in heaven, and whatever you loose on earth will be loosed in heaven."**

Peter had a natural ability for leadership, and the Lord had been sculpting and polishing that ability. Jesus now said explicitly that he would *give* Peter, as the leader of the disciples, *the keys of the kingdom of heaven*. Peter used the key of the gospel message to open the doors of the kingdom to the Jews on the day of Pentecost when he preached the first gospel sermon (Acts 2). Several years later he used the same key when he opened the kingdom to the Gentiles (Acts 10).

*Bind* and *loose* refer to the commandments and rules of the kingdom. We must not think that Peter and the other apostles had the authority to make up any rules they wanted and these would be enforced in heaven. Rather, as spokesmen filled and inspired with the Holy Spirit, they proclaimed the Lord's own message, his rules and commandments.

## C. A STINGING REBUKE (vv. 20-23)

**20. Then he warned his disciples not to tell anyone that he was the Christ.**

For the time being it was sufficient that only the disciples know that Jesus *was the Christ.* They needed to believe it beyond doubt so that Jesus could proceed to explain his mission to them. Jesus did not want the crowds to be told, and so he strictly instructed the disciples *not to tell anyone.* The disciples were to have a hard enough time understanding what Jesus would tell them; the multitudes would not understand at all.

**21. From that time on Jesus began to explain to his disciples that he must go to Jerusalem and suffer many things at the hands of the elders, chief priests and teachers of the law, and that he must be killed and on the third day be raised to life.**

Up to this time Jesus had worked to convince the disciples to believe in him and trust him. Now Jesus began to tell them things that were hard to believe and hard to trust.

*Jerusalem* was the center of Jewish life and religion, the site of the temple, so it was not unusual for a Jew to go to Jerusalem. But it also was the center of opposition to Jesus. Going there would soon mean that he would *suffer many things.* The Gospel accounts portray his horrible sufferings, and we shudder at them even today. *The elders, chief priests and teachers of the law* formed the ruling political power of the nation, subject only to the Romans. They also formed a powerful coalition against Jesus. By their efforts he would *be killed.* However, *on the third day* he would *be raised* again. This was not in the plan of the elders and priests, but it was in God's plan, and it would come about.

**22. Peter took him aside and began to rebuke him. "Never, Lord!" he said. "This shall never happen to you!"**

*Peter took him aside.* We can just see Peter pulling Jesus away from the group, speaking in hushed tones but barely able to keep from shouting, *Never, Lord!* The very thought of Jesus suffering and dying was so shocking, so incomprehensible, so abhorrent to the disciples that they recoiled from it in horror and disbelief. How could these things happen to the Christ, the Son of God? How and why would the Father permit it?

Boldly, rashly, Peter *began to rebuke him.* In doing so, Peter overstepped his bounds. He may have been emboldened by Jesus' earlier praise, but he left his place as a disciple and presumed to instruct the Master. Did Peter not think that Jesus knew the Father's will? As if the force of his will were sufficient to guarantee it, Peter proclaimed *This shall never happen to you!* Did he really think that he knew better than Christ what must be done?

**23. Jesus turned and said to Peter, "Get behind me, Satan! You are a stumbling block to me; you do not have in mind the things of God, but the things of men."**

*Peter* was not *Satan,* nor was he possessed by Satan, but his words were the words of Satan. In the wilderness Satan had tempted Jesus to avoid suffering, and that was the temptation urged now by Peter. If Jesus followed Peter's way, he would stumble on the path the Father had set for him. This was because Peter did *not have in mind the things of God.* He was not in tune with God's will; his thoughts were those of men. The Jews thought of casting off the Roman rule and of rebuilding their kingdom to be even more glorious than in the days of David and Solomon. The disciples argued about which of them would hold the most prominent places

## WHAT DO YOU THINK?

We may be shocked that Jesus called Peter "Satan." The word Satan means "adversary." Peter became Christ's adversary by putting human desires and interests above God's desires and interests. We can be guilty of the same and thus become Satan's tools without even realizing it! We do it when we put our opinions over God's Word. We do it when our attitude belies the truth we hold even when we are correct on an issue.

What are some other ways we may put "the things of men" over "the things of God"? More importantly, how can we be sure we do not?

## PRAYER

*Dear Father, we place ourselves in your hands to do with as you wish. Shape us and change us into what you would have us to be. Make us instruments to be used in your service. Perfect the image of your Son in us. Amen.*

## THOUGHT TO REMEMBER

*If we submit ourselves to his hands, God will fashion us into individual masterpieces.*

## DAILY BIBLE READINGS

*Monday, Jan. 13—The Calling of Simon Peter (Mark 1:14-18)*

*Tuesday, Jan. 14—Peter's Pentecost Sermon (Acts 2:14-21)*

*Wednesday, Jan. 15—Peter Confirms Jesus' Resurrection (Acts 2:22-36)*

*Thursday, Jan. 16—Peter Works Two Miracles (Acts 9: 32-42)*

*Friday, Jan. 17—Peter's Vision of Food (Acts 10:9-16)*

*Saturday, Jan. 18—Peter Visits Cornelius (Acts 10:23-33)*

*Sunday, Jan. 19—Peter's Sermon to Cornelius (Acts 10:34-43)*

in such a kingdom, sitting at Jesus' right and left hands on a throne in Jerusalem. These were their thoughts, human thoughts, but they were not the thoughts of God.

Peter surely had a lot to think about. Jesus had verified that he was indeed the Messiah. What joy and excitement! He promised that Peter would have an important place in the work of his kingdom. What honor and privilege! But then came the stinging rebuke. What hurt and humiliation! Jesus was not yet through chiseling and shaping Peter.

### CARING YET TOUGH

"Tough love" is recommended for parents, spouses, teachers, and others who want to demonstrate genuine concern for the objects of their affection. It means caring enough for people that you will confront them with their unacceptable words or behavior, that you will clearly communicate your disagreements with them, that you will discipline them when appropriate, and that you will intervene when they engage in self-destructive activities.

Tough love always affirms with positive reinforcement when possible, but it never sidesteps confrontation when conflict occurs. A child gains a sense of security when parents both praise and punish appropriately. Neither abuse nor permissiveness produces wholesome attitudes and behavior. Tough love balances actions and reactions for the total good of any relationship.

Peter's emotions must have soared when he was pronounced "blessed" by Jesus (Matthew 16:17-19). They plummeted just as quickly when, moments later, he was strongly reprimanded by Jesus (v. 23). Yet Jesus loved Peter—unconditionally. He praised him when his thinking and speaking demonstrated maturity. He rebuked him when his attitude and counsel were carnal and offensive. Jesus' love is a tough love, and he still chastens those whom he loves (Revelation 3:19).    —R. W. B.

## CONCLUSION

Michelangelo did not go to the quarry to sculpt. First the piece of marble was cut loose from the ground so that it could be fashioned. Then the great artist could begin the work of chiseling away the unwanted stone until only the final sculpture remained.

In a similar way, when Jesus called Peter to leave his home and job to follow him, the Lord cut the disciple loose so that he could begin the work of sculpting him. If Peter had been unwilling to leave the comfort, familiarity, and security of these things, he could not have been shaped by Jesus into the great leader of the apostles. Of course, Peter was willing, so day by day Jesus worked to sculpt him. He chiseled away wrong ideas and wrong attitudes. He cut away Peter's pride. He taught Peter to bring himself under control. He gave him responsibilities. He encouraged him. The Lord rebuked Peter when he got out of bounds. Some of Peter's training and teaching must have been exhilarating, and some of it was surely excruciating.

In the end, when Jesus was finished with Peter, he was a masterpiece. The great apostle was strong and courageous. He was a true leader. He was a rock.

Peter is not the Lord's only masterpiece. Through the centuries he has sculpted multitudes of men and women into spiritual works of art, and he continues to do so today. The process is the same as with Peter. Jesus cannot begin to sculpt and shape us until we leave the world behind and place ourselves in his hands. Then he begins the work of cutting off wrong beliefs and attitudes, sinful habits, selfishness, pride, and all such things until he shapes us into his own glorious image.

Teacher, challenge your students to submit consciously and deliberately to the sculpting of the Master's hands.

# Discovery Learning

*This page contains an alternate lesson plan emphasizing learning activities. Classes desiring such student involvement will find these suggestions helpful. The next page is a reproducible activity page to further enhance discovery learning.*

## LESSON GOALS

As students share in today's class session, they will:

1. Describe Peter's call to discipleship and his confession of Jesus' identity.

2. Explain why knowing Jesus' true identity is essential to participating in his work of "fishing" for men.

3. Suggest some specific ways we can help bring people to believe in "the Christ, the Son of the living God."

## INTO THE LESSON

Write the following open-ended sentence on a chalkboard or poster board before your students arrive.

**The kind of leader I am most willing to follow is . . .**

Divide the class into groups of three or four each to work on ways to complete this sentence.

After a few minutes, ask the groups to report their ideas about the qualities of a good leader while you record them on the chalkboard or poster board. Then ask, "How does Jesus demonstrate these leadership qualities?"

Move into the Bible study by saying, "Today we will look at Peter, who became a great leader in the church. We cannot understand Peter's acceptance of Jesus' call, however, unless we understand who Jesus is. When we see Jesus as Peter saw him, we, too, will want to follow wherever he leads us."

## INTO THE WORD

Keep the class in small groups. Give half the groups Assignment 1 below. Give the other half Assignment 2. (The groups working on Assignment 2 may need additional resources like information from the lesson commentary or other reference books to assist them.)

## ASSIGNMENT 1

Read Matthew 4:18-22; Mark 1:16-20; Luke 5:1-11. From these accounts of the calling of Jesus' first disciples, write several "newspaper stories" that might have appeared the following day in the local paper of Peter's hometown. The stories should address the "who, what, when, where, why, and how" of this event.

**Who?** Who left a business to start a new "career"? Who called them to this new position?

**What?** What amazing thing happened? What do we know of this one who is calling disciples? What was the response of Peter and others to him?

**When?** When did this take place?

**Where?** Where did it happen?

**Why?** Why would a successful team of fishermen abandon their business? Why is Jesus calling people to follow him?

**How?** How will the business survive without them? How will they provide for themselves? How will they accomplish the new mission they are setting out on?

## OPTION

If your students would rather not write "newspaper stories," simply give them the questions to answer.

## ASSIGNMENT 2

Read Matthew 16:13-23; Mark 8:27-33; Luke 9:18-22. Have this group answer the following questions:

1. What wrong ideas about Jesus' identity were circulating? What wrong ideas about him circulate today?

2. How did Peter identify Jesus? Why is this the only basis for our following him?

3. What is the significance of Jesus' promise that his church would not be overcome by the gates of Hades?

4. How did Peter's action after Jesus began to tell of danger ahead show he did not fully understand the confession he had made? How do we sometimes make the same mistake?

Give the groups about ten to fifteen minutes to work; then ask for reports. Not every group needs to report on every point, but make sure each point is discussed.

Refer the class to Matthew 16:24, 25. After Peter tried to tell the Lord how things should be, Jesus reminded them all of the role of a disciple. The decision they had made to follow him was a costly one, but it would be well rewarded. But they had to *follow*.

## INTO LIFE

Observe that the call to us remains to "follow," to be "fishers of men," to exalt Jesus as "the Christ, the Son of the living God." Brainstorm some ways to do that. Include what your church is already doing, but try to get the class to be creative and to come up with new ideas.

Is there some specific plan your class can implement together? Are there some new ideas individuals can try this week? Encourage each member of the class to get more involved in bringing others to know Jesus for who he really is.

# Fishers of Men

Jesus promised to make Peter and Andrew "fishers of men." Of course, he was talking about evangelism, a role we must continue today. What can we learn from fishing that may help us win lost souls to Christ?

| FISHING | EVANGELISM |
|---|---|
| A good fisherman uses a good lure or bait. | How can we attract people to hear the gospel? What are some inappropriate "lures" we should avoid? |
| A good fisherman uses different lures for different fish. | Different methods attract different people. How can we determine the appropriate methods to reach the people in our immediate area? |
| A good fisherman knows what time of day and what weather conditions produce the best likelihood of catching fish. | What kind of "timing" issues may affect the effectiveness of our evangelistic efforts? |
| A good fisherman must respond appropriately to the "nibble" on his bait. | Why is sensitivity important in dealing with people who need to accept the Lord Jesus? |
| A good fisherman is patient. | What problems can result if we get impatient in our evangelistic efforts? |
| A good fisherman knows he will not always be "successful." | Some people will not accept the gospel. How can we keep that in perspective and not take their rejection personally when someone refuses our message? |
| A good fisherman takes pride in his sport. | We give God the glory for the salvation of lost souls, but isn't being part of his grand work of redemption something to take pride in? How can we appreciate the blessings of being part of this without becoming proud as if we had done something by our own power or cleverness? What is the danger of such pride? (Write your answer on the back of this sheet.) |

# JUDAS ISCARIOT

**LESSON 9**

## WHY TEACH THIS LESSON?

Caution! The story of Judas is so tragic we can scarcely comprehend it. How could one who had followed Jesus so closely for three years turn on him and betray him? We are tempted to speculate rather than stick with known facts.

The truth is we don't know why. The Bible does not tell us that—only that he did it. He is called a betrayer and a thief, but nothing else is revealed about his character. Remind your students that some questions cannot be answered; we simply have to renew our own commitment to the Lord. Betray him? "Surely, not I, Lord!"

## INTRODUCTION

### A. WHAT WENT WRONG?

The "unsinkable" *Titanic* proudly set out for New York on its maiden voyage. But just before midnight on April 14, 1912, the ship struck an iceberg and sank two and a-half hours later. "What went wrong?"

The "roaring twenties" seemed so carefree. Through 1928 and 1929 the New York Stock Exchange was bullish. But on October 29, 1929, the market crashed. "What went wrong?"

A young person grows up in a Christian home with plenty of love and good Bible teaching. But he goes to college, abandons his faith, moves in with his girl-friend, and leaves his broken parents asking, "What went wrong?"

In the life of Judas we are faced with the ultimate question of "What went wrong?" How could one who had walked for so long as a close friend of Jesus could end by betraying the Lord?

One step at a time, through a series of wrong choices, Judas separated himself from the Lord and hardened his heart. Finally he passed the point of no return. The same process continues in the lives of many people today, and it could happen to any of us. A chain of wrong choices may lead to disaster, and sometimes this chain is very short. If we are not careful, we may destroy our own lives by making a series of bad choices.

### B. DID JUDAS HAVE A CHOICE?

Did Judas have a choice, or was he powerless to prevent his betrayal of Jesus? Clearly it was known beforehand that the Lord would be betrayed and who the betrayer would be. Long before it happened, even before it entered Judas's heart to do so, Jesus knew that Judas would betray him, and called the traitor a devil, although without naming him explicitly (John 6:64, 70, 71). In today's lesson text Jesus revealed to Judas that he knew what he intended to do (Matthew 26:25). But knowing what a person will do is not the same as causing him to do it.

Judas was not always a betrayer. There is no hint in the Gospel accounts that he had any less faith and zeal than the other apostles at first. But Satan was at work trying to get to Jesus through his apostles. All of them seemed to wrestle with the temptation of pride. (See Mark 9:33-37; Luke 9:46; 22:24.) But Satan scored a victory in the case of Judas, apparently through the temptation of greed. (See John 12:4-6.)

**DEVOTIONAL READING**
MATTHEW 27:1-10

**LESSON SCRIPTURE**
MATTHEW 26:14-16, 20-25, 47-50; 27:1-5

**PRINTED TEXT**
MATTHEW 26:14-16, 20-25, 47-50; 27:1-5

## LESSON AIMS

As students participate in today's class session, they should:

1. Describe how Judas plotted and executed his plan to betray Jesus.

2. Identify factors that likely contributed to leading Judas to betray Jesus.

3. Examine their own lives to see if any of these factors exist and ask God for help in removing them.

Jan 26

## KEY VERSE

Then Judas, the one who would betray him, said, "Surely not I, Rabbi?" Jesus answered, "Yes, it is you."

*Matthew 26:25*

LESSON 9 NOTES

## HOW TO SAY IT

*Gethsemane. Geth-SEM-uh-nee*
*(G as in get).*
*Iscariot. Iss-CARE-ee-ut.*
*Kerioth. CARE-ee-awth.*
*Pilate. PIE-lut.*
*Tiberius. Tie-BEER-ee-us.*
*Zechariah. Zek-uh-RYE-uh.*

## WHAT DO YOU THINK?

*Since God is sovereign, all-knowing, and all-powerful, he could have stopped Judas from betraying the Lord. Just the same, he could perform a miracle every time he sees us heading for trouble, making a wrong decision, or yielding to temptation. He could protect us from every sin, error, blunder, and mistake, but he does not. Instead, he allows us to act as we choose—either for good or for bad.*

*Do you ever wish God would override your free will and keep you from making mistakes? If so, why? What would happen to your acts of devotion if your could not choose to do them yourself?*

*How might God sometimes try to block us from sin without violating our free will? (See 1 Corinthians 10:11-13; Philippians 4:8, 9; James 1:5)*

Judas did not set out to become a traitor, but step-by-step, making his own choices, he reached that terrible decision.

### C. LESSON BACKGROUND

Today's lesson text covers four events in the life of Judas. They all occur in the last few days before Jesus' death. Soon after Jesus rebuked Judas because he criticized Mary for anointing him with the expensive perfume (see lesson 7), Judas went to the chief priests and plotted to betray Jesus. This is recorded in the first passage of our text.

The second portion of text relates an event that took place in the upper room when Jesus ate the Passover with the disciples on the night he was betrayed. Jesus revealed to Judas that he knew what he was plotting to do. The third event, the actual betrayal, took place later the same night in the Garden of Gethsemane.

The final portion of the lesson text tells of Judas's remorse and suicide. This happened on the morning of the day Jesus was crucified.

### I. JUDAS'S HEINOUS PLOT (MATTHEW 26:14-16, 20-25, 47-50)
### A. THE PLOT CONCEIVED (vv. 14-16)

**14. Then one of the Twelve—the one called Judas Iscariot—went to the chief priests.**

*Then* sets the time for this event. Matthew's account of the anointing at Bethany (see lesson 7) comes immediately before the telling of this event, so this must have come soon after. Bethany was just two miles from Jerusalem. Perhaps *Judas* sneaked off that very night when everyone else was asleep and *went to the chief priests*. Perhaps he waited until the group was in Jerusalem and an opportunity to slip away came his way.

Matthew does not mention either Mary or Judas by name in the earlier incident. Apparently, he wanted to focus on the event, not the people involved. But from John's Gospel we know it was Judas who took the lead in criticizing Mary. Was he frustrated because he didn't get his hands on such a large amount of money? Was he angry and resentful, stinging from Jesus' rebuke?

The name *Iscariot* probably means "man of Kerioth," thus designating his home town. He was *one of the Twelve,* and just as the rest of them, he was commissioned to preach the arrival of the kingdom of Heaven and given power to heal the sick, raise the dead, cleanse lepers, and drive out demons (Matthew 10:7, 8). What wonderful and exciting days those must have been! But those days were gone.

It is impossible for us to know exactly what happened in Judas's heart to change him from one of the loyal Twelve to a betrayer. Students have made many suggestions, including disillusionment with Jesus when he did not set up an earthly kingdom as Judas might have expected. Others believe that Judas may have been attempting to "force the hand" of Jesus. In other words, by putting Jesus in a life-threatening situation, Judas may have hoped that Jesus would move with more urgency to establish his kingdom. It is quite clear, from Judas's response to Mary's anointing of Jesus, and from John's additional comment about Judas's stealing (John 12:6), that he was a man often driven by selfishness and greed. Perhaps Judas's dissatisfaction with Jesus had been building for some time prior to that point; the incident with Mary was the proverbial "last straw."

From the standpoint of the chief priests, Judas's timing could not have been better. It should be noted that we cannot be certain when Judas approached the chief priests with his scheme, whether late on the Saturday after the anointing by Mary or after Jesus' last day of teaching (probably Tuesday of the final week). During this day of teaching, the priests and their cohorts had tried to embarrass Jesus in public through a series of supposedly "hard" questions. Instead, on each occasion Jesus had given an answer that left his critics silenced and the multitudes even more enthralled with him.

It became apparent to the chief priests that they and their companions would succeed in arresting Jesus only "in some sly way" (Matthew 26:4). When one of Jesus' own followers approached them with an offer, they must have been quite surprised, but pleased nonetheless.

**15. . . . and asked, "What are you willing to give me if I hand him over to you?" So they counted out for him thirty silver coins.**

*Thirty silver coins* did not represent a great amount of money. It was about the price of a slave. Greedy though he was, Judas sold out the Lord for a pittance. Does this meager sum suggest Judas was acting out of anger and resentment? Jesus' enemies surely would have paid much more than this to be rid of their nemesis!

**16. From then on Judas watched for an opportunity to hand him over.**

The cold-blooded nature of the plot is evident in this verse. Judas diligently looked for a way to betray Jesus to the chief priests.

### IS YOUR PRICE RIGHT?

From time to time, we are provided with new evidence that our world is becoming increasingly warped and weird. In one recent survey respondents were asked to select from a list of possible answers to the question, "What would you do for $100,000?" The reported results were sobering, even frightening. Several women indicated that they would become prostitutes for a day. Some parents answered that they would put their children up for adoption. A few participants even said they would kill a stranger for $100,000!

Cynical criminal types in movie and TV dramas often say, "Everyone has his price; what's yours?" Are they right? Will people really do *anything* for money? If that is the rule, then Judas was certainly no exception. Apparently his relationship with Jesus had become superficial and hypocritical. He actually sold out to the enemies of the Lord for a few coins—the equivalent of the price of a slave.

Does your love for and loyalty to Christ carry a price tag? Sometimes professed disciples sell him out for far less than Judas's blood money. Nominal Christians have betrayed the Lord for as little as a few moments of carnal pleasure, a few winks of sleep on Sunday morning, or a part of a tithe withheld for personal use.

No price is right when one is trying to bargain over eternal matters. In fact, it is futile to do so. "What can a man give in exchange for his soul?" (Matthew 16:26).

—R. W. B.

### B. THE PLOT EXPOSED (vv. 20-25)

**20. When evening came, Jesus was reclining at the table with the Twelve.**

This was the *evening* of the Passover, the evening in which Jesus was betrayed and arrested. The location was the upper room. All of *the Twelve* were present, including Judas. Had he already arranged with the chief priests to meet them later and escort them to the garden, or was he still looking for an opportunity? If so, he must have been filled with anticipation and anxiety.

**21. And while they were eating, he said, "I tell you the truth, one of you will betray me."**

The disciples had been shocked on other occasions when Jesus spoke about dying or being killed (as in Matthew 16:21, 22). Now came the unbelievable news that one of them would be the instrument of making this happen. The atmosphere must have been extremely tense.

---

*WHAT DO YOU THINK?*

*Jesus' other disciples apparently had no idea that Judas was dipping his hand into the group's "treasury." In the same way, some secret sins today can be kept secret for a long time. Sometimes even those who know us best (husband, wife, family member, co-worker, close friend) have no idea of what is going on.*

*What is the danger of carrying a "secret sin"? What happens when such sin finally becomes public—as it so often does? Why do we sometimes think we can "get away with it" as long as no one else knows?*

*(See Luke 12:2.)*

*WHAT DO YOU THINK?*

*While they were at Oxford University, John and Charles Wesley were leaders of a support group for Christians, called the Holy Club. At meetings of the Holy Club, the members examined each other with penetrating and probing questions about their personal lives—not to embarrass or humiliate or ridicule anyone, but to provide mutual accountability. If there was a problem, it could be confessed in a safe, non-threatening, and supportive environment of fellow believers. Then they could all pray about the problem.*

*Would you join a "holy club" today? Why or why not? How can we be encouraged to confess and repent of secret sin? What kind of accountability would be appropriate to help people feel they have a way out when carrying secret sin?*

*(See James 5:13-16.)*

*The visual for lesson 9 focuses on the question that each disciple asked of Jesus in the upper room: "Lord, is it I?" (King James Version).*

**WHAT DO YOU THINK?**

*Everyone agrees Judas's betrayal of Jesus was a heinous offense. It is possible, however, that many people repeat the crime every day. Some would say we betray Jesus by failing to say we are Christians because we fear the ridicule of those around us. Do you agree or disagree? Why?*

*Some would say we betray Jesus by remaining silent when others are taking his name in vain. Do you agree or disagree? Why?*

*Some would say we betray Jesus by saying we love and serve him at church, but then carelessly violating his teachings during the week. Do you agree or disagree? Why?*

*Some would say we betray Jesus by willfully and repeatedly sinning. Do you agree or disagree? Why?*

*What is the solution for these situations?*

**22. They were very sad and began to say to him one after the other, "Surely not I, Lord?"**

*Very sad* strikes us as the understatement of the century! How could words express how crushed in spirit they were? Yet even in their grief they did not point fingers and accuse one another. Rather, each wondered if he himself would do this unthinkable deed: *Surely not I, Lord?*

**23. Jesus replied, "The one who has dipped his hand into the bowl with me will betray me.**

Sharing a meal together was considered an act of friendship in the ancient near east, so much so that to dip one's *hand* in the *bowl* with another became an idiom for sharing a close friendship. This was part of the heinous nature of Judas's betrayal. It is reflected in the somber words of Psalm 41:9: "Even my close friend, whom I trusted, he who shared my bread, has lifted up his heel against me."

John, who gives a more detailed account of this portion of the meal, adds that Jesus took some bread, dipped it in the dish (which contained a sauce or gravy), and handed it to Judas (John 13:25, 26). When we read that, we wonder how the other disciples could have missed such a clear sign of the betrayer's identity. But the act was so natural in their culture, and the expression so idiomatic, that it never occurred to them. Its literal significance was surely not lost on Judas, however!

**24. The Son of Man will go just as it is written about him. But woe to that man who betrays the Son of Man! It would be better for him if he had not been born."**

*The Son of Man* is Jesus. His sacrificial death was *written* throughout the Old Testament, even though the Jews did not recognize it. One purpose of the book of Matthew is to point out many of the ways in which Jesus fulfilled prophecy.

Although Jesus' death on the cross fulfilled God's plan for mankind's salvation, this did not excuse Judas from responsibility for his actions. Jesus still pronounced *woe to that man who betrays the Son of Man!*

**25. Then Judas, the one who would betray him, said, "Surely not I, Rabbi?" Jesus answered, "Yes, it is you."**

*Judas*, who knew full well that he was the guilty party, must have been reluctant to ask the fateful question, *Surely not I?* But the others had, and he no doubt felt compelled to ask it as well and to continue his pretense. Jesus, however, knew exactly what Judas was doing. His answer, literally "You have said it," was an expression of affirmation, *Yes, it is you.* We wonder whether Jesus whispered it so only Judas heard it—it's hard to imagine the other disciples allowing him to leave if they knew he was the betrayer! Or was this whole terrible matter simply beyond the disciples' comprehension at this point, each of them so stunned he simply could not assimilate any new information for a few painful moments?

The others had said, "Lord"; Judas called Jesus *Rabbi,* "Teacher." Some have suggested this shows that Judas no longer regarded Jesus as his Lord. That may be stretching things a bit. "Rabbi" was a common title for Jesus' followers to use of him. If there were that much significance to the difference of terms, Judas probably would have lied about his allegiance to Jesus' lordship just so the other apostles would not suspect him.

**C. THE PLOT EXECUTED (vv. 47-50)**

**47. While he was still speaking, Judas, one of the Twelve, arrived. With him was a large crowd armed with swords and clubs, sent from the chief priests and the elders of the people.**

The setting has now shifted to the Garden of Gethsemane. Jesus had just returned from praying for the third time and had found Peter, James, and John asleep. Just then *Judas* came into the garden with a *large crowd* with *swords and clubs.* Jesus' enemies were taking no chances. They didn't know what Jesus would do, and they couldn't be sure that a large crowd of people would not be alerted and try to rescue Jesus.

**48. Now the betrayer had arranged a signal with them: "The one I kiss is the man; arrest him."**

The *kiss* was another act of despicable hypocrisy. Judas's kiss identified Jesus for the soldiers, who may not have known him by sight. Fearful that he might escape, they wanted quick and positive identification.

**49. Going at once to Jesus, Judas said, "Greetings, Rabbi!" and kissed him.**

Quickly, brazenly, Judas performed the most infamous action in all of history. To say *Greetings, Rabbi* was yet another hypocritical gesture. Judas had rejected all that Jesus was, all that he taught, and all that he stood for.

**50. Jesus replied, "Friend, do what you came for."**
**Then the men stepped forward, seized Jesus and arrested him.**

Only the Son of God could have addressed Judas in such a kind manner as *Friend.* Jesus and Judas both knew why Judas was there. Jesus did not need to rebuke Judas; his actions were rebuke enough.

When Jesus was *arrested,* it appeared that Judas and his fellow conspirators had succeeded. The other disciples, who had earlier pledged unswerving loyalty to Jesus, fled in panic (Matthew 26:56).

## II. JUDAS'S WRETCHED END (MATTHEW 27:1-5)

**1, 2. Early in the morning, all the chief priests and the elders of the people came to the decision to put Jesus to death. They bound him, led him away and handed him over to Pilate, the governor.**

By *morning* the Jewish leaders had begun to implement their plan to kill Jesus. They could not do this without Roman approval (John 18:31), so they took Jesus to *Pilate the governor.*

**3. When Judas, who had betrayed him, saw that Jesus was condemned, he was seized with remorse and returned the thirty silver coins to the chief priests and the elders.**

It is on the basis of this verse that some have speculated *Judas* was merely trying to force Jesus into action, that having him arrested would cause him to unleash his power, destroy his enemies, and set up his kingdom. Instead Jesus *was condemned*—the plan had backfired. Judas was now grief-stricken.

More likely this was simply a matter of the full import of one's actions finally dawning on him. Judas knew Jesus would be condemned, but he thought he could handle it. He had rationalized the act in his mind, but his heart was still condemning him. When it all became actual, Judas was seized with remorse. This is not the remorse that moves a person to reform his life, such as when one becomes a Christian. Rather it is the grief that arises from a searing hot guilty conscience. Its end is self-loathing and self-destruction.

*The thirty silver coins* that Judas formerly had coveted so much now became utterly detestable to him. He could not wait to be rid of them.

**4. "I have sinned," he said, "for I have betrayed innocent blood."**
**"What is that to us?" they replied. "That's your responsibility."**

It was a long time coming, too long, but Judas finally acknowledged his sin. He had *betrayed innocent blood.* Jesus had never done anything wrong—certainly he had never done any harm to Judas. The horribleness of Judas's sin shattered the hardness of his heart and caused him to see himself as he really was.

The chief priests, on the other hand, felt no such remorse and no sympathy for the one who did. To the contrary, their perverse hearts were delighted.

### WHAT DO YOU THINK?

*Judas experienced deep sorrow and regret for what he did, but that did not address his real need. He could have been forgiven if he had genuinely confessed and repented.*

*Peter went out and "wept bitterly" after he denied the Lord (Luke 22:62). Later he told Simon, the sorcerer of Samaria who had become a Christian, to repent and pray when he reverted to his old way of greed (Acts 8:22). What should we do today when we know we have sinned? To whom should we confess it? Under what circumstances should we make a public statement of repentance?*

### WHAT DO YOU THINK?

*If you had been one of the other apostles and Judas returned with pleas of repentance, how would you have handled it? Could you have forgiven him? Why or why not? How forgiving are we of people in the church who fail? How can we be more forgiving— as Jesus forgave Peter for his denials?*

*What kind of influence do you think Judas could have had if he had repented? What kind of testimony can people today have who have sinned and then come back to the Lord?*

## PRAYER

*Dear Father, we tremble to think of Judas's destruction. We tremble even more when we realize that each of us could follow in his path. Help us discern the sins in our hearts and cast them out with your help. Refine and increase our faith. Help us to accept your discipline. In his name, Amen.*

## THOUGHT TO REMEMBER

*Destruction is only a few steps away from each of us.*

## DAILY BIBLE READINGS

**5. So Judas threw the money into the temple and left. Then he went away and hanged himself.**

Judas could not undo what he had done. In utter blackness of soul, he went and *hanged himself.* He could not live with his guilt and remorse. Thus ends one of the world's great tragedies. Judas's story could have been so much different.

### SORRY IS NOT ENOUGH

In a made-for-television movie that reprised the characters of the once-popular series, *The Waltons,* John Walton was running for the public office of county supervisor. He left his son Ben in charge of operations at the family sawmill. Ben and a helper took the opportunity to bid on a large lumber contract for a new residential development that was pending approval by the county commissioners. This, of course, posed a conflict of interest for John and seemed to compromise his personal integrity.

When father confronted son with the dilemma, the dialogue was heated. John Walton was disappointed, frustrated, and angry. Ben was contrite and said, "I'm sorry, Daddy." But the conflict was not that easily resolved. John's fiery retort was: "*Sorry* is not enough, Ben. You have made me and our family look bad. You have disgraced our name in the community. This kind of reputation doesn't go away quickly."

Judas wanted desperately to undo his deed. Though "seized with remorse" (Matthew 27:3), his attempt to reverse the outcome of his betrayal was unsuccessful. Sometimes *sorry* is not enough. Even the "godly sorrow" that leads to repentance and forgiveness can leave lasting temporal damage. Not every consequence of human error can be fixed. How much better to walk with the Lord and simply avoid the need for sorrow, remorse, or repentance.     —R. W. B.

## CONCLUSION

Judas made several choices that led him step-by-step down the path to his own destruction. We must study his actions closely so that we can avoid his mistakes and his fate.

First, Judas let a habitual sin—stealing from the disciples' treasury—take over his life. Sin forms a barrier between the sinner and God. Habitual sin, sin that we have welcomed and made a part of our lives, hardens the heart and silences the conscience. We ought to take a serious look at our lives on a regular basis, scrutinizing everything that we do to see whether any sin is finding a permanent home in our lives and do whatever it takes to cast out that sin before it controls us.

Second, Judas allowed his faith in the Lord to weaken, crumble, and fail. In the end he had no faith nor love for Jesus. Sin and faith cannot live together in a person's heart. If sin grows, faith dies. Jesus warned, "Because of the increase of wickedness, the love of most will grow cold" (Matthew 24:12).

At the end, Judas was so far gone that he did not respond even when Jesus revealed that he knew what he planned to do. Jesus was making one final appeal to Judas, but Judas did not grasp his last chance. God does not let his children go back to the world without seeking to rescue and restore them. The writer of Hebrews tells us that God disciplines those whom he loves, and he urges us to accept the Lord's discipline. Sometimes the Lord's discipline comes from a Christian brother or sister who speaks a word of concern and warning. If we are wise, we will listen to the concerns of those who love us and are concerned about our souls.

One poet has said that the saddest of all words are "It might have been." This is certainly true in Judas's case. His life might have been, indeed should have been, so much different. But his is not the only life that could have been different. Many people follow the road to destruction and ruin. It does not have to be that way for anyone. Guard your ways every day, and preserve your life.

# Discovery Learning

*This page contains an alternate lesson plan emphasizing learning activities. Classes desiring such student involvement will find these suggestions helpful. The next page is a reproducible activity page to further enhance discovery learning.*

## LESSON GOALS

As students participate in today's class session, they should:

1. Describe how Judas plotted and executed his plan to betray Jesus.

2. Identify factors that likely contributed to leading Judas to betray Jesus.

3. Examine their own lives to see if any of these factors exist and ask God for help in removing them.

## INTO THE LESSON

Before your class session begins, write on the chalkboard or on a poster that can be displayed for the class to see: "Why did Judas do it?"

As you begin, ask the question this way: "Many explanations have been offered to explain why Judas betrayed Jesus. What are some of them?"

Some of the answers you may receive are as follows:

1. He saw the resistance mounting and decided he wanted to be on the "winning" side.

2. He was trying to force Jesus to take action and set up his earthly kingdom.

3. He was disillusioned with Jesus' ministry since it was not leading to an earthly kingdom.

4. He wanted to get even with Jesus for embarrassing him when he criticized Mary's use of the ointment.

Discuss very briefly the relative merit of each suggestion. Is there any Scriptural support for the ideas? Any Scriptural contradictions?

Make your transition into the Bible study portion of the lesson by explaining that though we would like to know the answer to this question, the Bible gives us none. What we will see in this lesson is that Judas—one of the Twelve and unsuspected by the others—turned out to be a betrayer. It is a tragedy that should draw us closer to the Lord and compel us to renew our allegiance to him.

## INTO THE WORD

For the Bible study activity you will need four groups to work independently. Or, if your class is not too large, you may complete this portion of the Bible study as one large group. Assign each group the following passages of Scripture (or, if the whole class is working on this together, ask someone to read each passage so that everyone can hear).

Group One:     Matthew 26:6-16; John 12:1-6
Group Two:     Matthew 26:20-25

Group Three:    Matthew 26:47-50
Group Four:     Matthew 27:1-5

Ask the groups to summarize what they learn of Judas from each assigned passage. Give them ten or twelve minutes to work, and then ask for reports. Supplement their reports with information from the lesson commentary.

You might prepare an overhead transparency to use here. On the transparency, have the following four headings. Reveal each one as the appropriate group finishes. This will serve to sum up the reports and leave an outline in the students' minds as the Bible study is concluded.

  I.   Judas is rebuked; offers to betray Jesus to the chief priests
 II.   Judas learns Jesus knows what he is planning.
III.   Judas betrays Jesus.
IV.   Judas, filled with remorse, commits suicide.

## OPTION

Use the reproducible activity, "The Judas Factor," on the next page for Bible study and application.

## INTO LIFE

Remind the students we do not know why Judas did what he did. Only God knows that. But we know what he did, and we know some of what was going on in his life before the betrayal.

One thing was secret sin. He was stealing from the apostles' treasury and, apparently, getting away with it. Another issue in Judas's life is a hardness of heart. When Jesus revealed he knew what was in Judas's heart, Judas continued in the plan as before. A softer heart would have broken and begged forgiveness. Also, Judas obviously let silver become more valuable to him than the Lord.

Assign three small groups to discuss these issues. What causes similar problems today? How can it be recognized? How can the church provide an atmosphere for dealing with it positively and lovingly?

After a few minutes, ask for reports from each group. If there are some practical suggestions for what the church can do in each case, discuss how your class might be instrumental in initiating such ministries.

At the heart of the matter, however, is personal responsibility. Judas and Judas alone was responsible for his drifting away from the Lord. Close with a time of prayer that each student would recommit himself or herself to follow the Lord.

# The Judas Factor

We don't know exactly why Judas betrayed Christ. Several theories have been proposed, but it is best to stick with what the Scripture tells us and avoid excessive speculation.

Listed on the chart below are some Scripture references that will lead you to the facts we know about Judas, facts that may provide insight into what led him to betray his Lord. Look up each Scripture and summarize what is said about Judas there. Consider also each statement under "Introspection." Based on Judas's life, examine yourself and see whether there is any hint of this attitude in your own life. What can you do to be sure your heart is pure in each regard?

| FACTS AND REFERENCES | INTROSPECTION |
|---|---|
| Mark 3:13-19; Luke 6:12-16 | When Judas was chosen, there was no reason to suspect him of any treachery. A good start is not enough. |
| Matthew 10:1ff | Judas seemed just like each of the others, faithful, active, involved in ministry. Activity is no substitute for faithfulness. |
| John 6:70, 71 | Jesus knows even before it happens what someone will do. |
| John 12:4-6 | Secret sin poisons the mind against the service of others. |
| Matthew 26:14-16; Mark 14:10; Luke 22:1-5 | "The love of money is a root of all kinds of evil" (1 Timothy 6:10). |
| John 13:1-5 | What shameless hypocrisy! Fellowship with the Lord and with Satan are not compatible. |
| Matthew 26:20-25; John 13:24-30 | Crisis. The truth is known. Repent or harden the heart? It was, indeed, "night"! |
| Matthew 26:47-50; Mark 13:43-46; Luke 22:47, 48; John 18:1-5 | Things are not always what they appear to be. A friendly greeting? A sign of love? |
| Matthew 27:3-5; Acts 1:18 | "Sorry" is not good enough. |

# BARNABAS

**LESSON 10**

## WHY TEACH THIS LESSON?

Nearly every church has one, though many of its members are not aware of the fact. There is usually one faithful saint who takes more pleasure in seeing others succeed than in pursuing personal acclaim. This one is quick to give praise for a job well done—or even a job not so well done if it is done in the right spirit. Handshakes are usually not enough; this one prefers to hug. Generosity is common, though frequently anonymous.

We might name this person Barnabas. The apostles did when they found such a person in their congregation in Jerusalem. Today's lesson highlights some of his contributions to the early church. Not surprisingly, we remember a young man he encouraged much more than we remember Barnabas. Who has not heard of the apostle Paul? God used Barnabas to give us Paul.

Challenge your students to be encouragers. Encouragers put the good of the kingdom ahead of personal interests. Encouragers look for people who have potential and get them into ministry. Encouragers make a difference!

## INTRODUCTION

### A. THE POWER OF ONE

Among the maxims prefixed to Poor Richard's Almanac, Benjamin Franklin included this one, adapted from the writings of George Herbert: "For the want of a nail the shoe was lost; for the want of a shoe the horse was lost; for the want of a horse the rider was lost." Someone has since added: "For the want of a rider, a message was lost; for the want of a message, a battle was lost; for the want of a battle, a kingdom was lost; and all for the want of a nail!"

Little details can make a big difference. We might say: "For want of a Christian, a kind word was lost; for want of a kind word, an influence was lost; for want of an influence, a soul was lost—and all for the want of one Christian!"

### B. LESSON BACKGROUND

Today's lesson begins the final unit of our study of New Testament personalities. This unit looks at people who made a difference in the early church by their faithful service for Christ.

The first of these individuals is Barnabas. His contribution to the early church was substantial. The three passages from Acts 4, 9, and 11 in today's lesson text all show how he provided needed encouragement at critical times in the life of the early church. As we study these examples, we should give serious consideration to how we can follow his example by being encouragers of others. This is a ministry in which every Christian can participate, Like Barnabas, every believer can make a significant difference through encouragement.

## I. ENCOURAGEMENT BY GENEROSITY (ACTS 4:32, 36, 37)

### A. A GENEROUS CHURCH (v. 32)

**32. All the believers were one in heart and mind. No one claimed that any of his possessions was his own, but they shared everything they had.**

**DEVOTIONAL READING**
ACTS 15:1-11

**LESSON SCRIPTURE**
ACTS 4:32-37; 9:23-31; 11:19-30

**PRINTED TEXT**
ACTS 4:32, 36, 37; 9:26, 27; 11:22-30

## LESSON AIMS

*As a result of this lesson the student should:*

*1. List some ways Barnabas encouraged the early church.*

*2. Tell why encouragement is important to a church or an individual.*

*3. Suggest a specific way he or she can encourage someone this week.*

Feb
2

## KEY VERSES

*When he arrived and saw the evidence of the grace of God, he was glad and encouraged them all to remain true to the Lord with all their hears. He was a good man, full of the Holy Spirit and faith.*
— Acts 11:23, 24

## LESSON 10 NOTES

*The visual for lesson 10 challenges each Christian to "be a Barnabas." Have it on display as your students arrive.*

### WHAT DO YOU THINK?

*Barnabas became well known for his compassion for the needy. Who in our church is known for such compassion? Is our church as a whole seen as compassionate toward those in need? Why or why not? What can we do to be sure we treat those in need with respect, thoughtful attention, genuine caring, and Christian compassion?*

### WHAT DO YOU THINK?

*Barnabas was not the only one who sold a field. Acts 4:34 and 35 tell us this was a frequent event, so that "there were no needy persons among [the disciples]." Can it be said of our church that we share so generously that there are no needy persons among us? Why or why not? Should there be this same level of sharing? If not, why not? If so, how can we get there?*

Verse 31 mentions that the believers "were all filled with the Holy Spirit and they spoke the word of God boldly." Their bold preaching was one result of the Spirit's presence. Their unity was a second sign of the Spirit in their lives. And their willingness to share their possessions was a third sign of their spiritual fullness. They appreciated the Lord's ownership of all things (Psalm 24:1), so while they still possessed or owned their property, they considered themselves mere stewards. When another of God's people had a need that could be met by using their property, they sold it to provide for that need (verse 34).

### B. A GENEROUS INDIVIDUAL (vv. 36, 37)

**36. Joseph, a Levite from Cyprus, whom the apostles called Barnabas (which means Son of Encouragement). . . .**

We know *Joseph* exclusively by his nickname. *Barnabas* is Aramaic for *Son of Encouragement.* (*Bar* is Aramaic for "son." *Nabas* appears to be a shortened or colloquial term for "consolation" or "encouragement.") The phrase *son of* is a Hebrew idiom used to describe a person's character or characteristics. How different must Barnabas have been in temperament than two other followers of Jesus who earned the nickname "Sons of Thunder" (Mark 3:17).

The Greek word for *encouragement* is instructive. It comes from two words that mean "call alongside." A form of the word, translated "Counselor" ("Comforter" in the *King James Version*), refers to the Holy Spirit (John 14:16); in 1 John 2:1 it refers to Jesus, who "speaks . . . in our defense" (*KJV*: "advocate"). It has, thus, a wide range of meaning. The encourager may give a pat on the back, a word of instruction, a rebuke, or a legal defense. Picture a coach pulling the athlete aside, putting his arm around him, and then telling him what he needs to hear—whether praise or criticism. This is the encourager.

As a Levite, Barnabas would likely have been well trained in the Mosaic law. In addition, Barnabas had been living outside of Judea on the island of *Cyprus.* Here he would have been influenced by—or, at least, acquainted with—the Greek culture more than in Judea. These background factors helped to prepare Barnabas for the important role he would play in encouraging and aiding the church's spread throughout the Mediterranean basin.

**37. . . . sold a field he owned and brought the money and put it at the apostles' feet.**

Such sale of property and giving the *money* to the church funded the church's benevolence program, administrated by *the apostles.* (Acts 6 tells of how the apostles came to delegate this ministry to another group of men, so that they could give themselves more fully "to prayer and the ministry of the word," Acts 6:4.) The selling and giving were entirely voluntary in the early church. Thus, Peter told Ananias in Acts 5:4, "Didn't it belong to you before it was sold? And after it was sold, wasn't the money at your disposal?" This was no Marxist-style "Communism." Marx attempted to enforce the "sharing" of resources by government force. The early church's giving and receiving was a voluntary cooperation based on a common love for the Lord Jesus Christ, who himself taught and modeled self-sacrifice.

Barnabas's gift to the church was a practical expression of his encouraging character. If he had not acted as he did, the early church would have lost the inspiration of his example. If Barnabas had not acted, the church would have had less means with which to provide for those in need. Barnabas's act of encouragement made a difference in the early church.

## II. ENCOURAGEMENT BY SUPPORTIVE WORDS (ACTS 9:26, 27)

Barnabas's most important role in the early church was that of companion to Saul or Paul.

**26. When he came to Jerusalem, he tried to join the disciples, but they were all afraid of him, not believing that he really was a disciple.**

The subject of this verse is Saul of Tarsus. Earlier verses of Acts 9 tell how he started for Damascus with orders from the high priest, authorizing him to persecute any *disciples* (the usual term for Christians) he found there. Along the way, he was confronted by Jesus, who gave him new marching orders. In Damascus he was baptized and began preaching Jesus.

Galatians 1:8 tells us Paul made this trip to *Jerusalem* three years after he had started out for Damascus. Still, his role in Stephen's murder and his persecution of the church continued to weigh on the disciples' hearts. The believers were skeptical and *afraid*.

**27. But Barnabas took him and brought him to the apostles. He told them how Saul on his journey had seen the Lord and that the Lord had spoken to him, and how in Damascus he had preached fearlessly in the name of Jesus.**

*Barnabas* courageously stood up for *Saul* and encouraged the *apostles* to accept Saul. The term *apostles* is here used in a generic sense, as Luke sometimes uses it (cf. Acts 14:4, 14). Peter is the only one of the Twelve that Saul saw (Galatians 1:18, 19), but he also saw James, an outstanding leader, and perhaps some others.

We do not know why or how Barnabas recognized Saul as a genuine disciple or why the others at first did not. And how did Barnabas find out that Saul *had seen the Lord* and that he had *preached* Christ *in Damascus*? Did he have more than Saul's word on those things? What risk did Barnabas take in standing up for Saul? Was there any fear on his part that Saul might turn out to be a pretender? We only know he did accept Saul and encouraged others to do the same.

Barnabas's action of encouragement affected the entire history of the church. We are sure God would somehow have made known to the apostles that Saul was a genuine disciple even if Barnabas had not been there. But Barnabas was there, and he was the instrument God used to win Saul's acceptance. Barnabas's action of encouragement made a big difference in the life of the church.

### "A FRIEND IN NEED"

*Shadowlands* is the moving story of well-known Christian author C. S. Lewis, and his double marriage to Joy Gresham. Their first ceremony was merely a legal formality for convenience. Joy Gresham was in London on a visitor's visa, and Mr. Lewis consented to marry her so that she and her son could stay in England by virtue of Lewis's citizenship. It was an act of genuine friendship: she was a "friend in need," and he was a "friend indeed." Later, these two friends married again, this time for love and commitment, until they were separated by Joy's untimely death.

*Shadowlands* is a poignant love story, but it is much more than mere romance. It is the true account of a beautiful friendship that finally, and almost incidentally, was consummated in marriage. Such true and loving relationships are so rare that they become unforgettable.

Joseph possessed such a capacity for brotherly love that the apostles called him by a new name—Barnabas, the "son of encouragement." When a new Christian named Saul confronted the suspicious resistance of believers in Jerusalem, Barnabas came to his defense, vouching for his integrity. Later, when Saul had retreated to Tarsus, Barnabas coaxed him back to active ministry in Antioch. Saul was a friend in need; Barnabas was a friend, both "indeed" and "in deed." —R. W. B.

## III. ENCOURAGEMENT BY TEACHING (ACTS 11:22-26)

Acts 8:1 informs us that persecution scattered many of the believers out of Jerusalem after Stephen's death. That event is recalled in Acts 11:19, 20, with the additional note that some of these scattered believers settled in Antioch, a

---

**WHAT DO YOU THINK?**

When it comes to assisting those with material and financial needs, some people say the church has no business in such matters; let the government provide for such persons while the church provides spiritual help. Others say the government has no business in such matters—the church should care for the poor and needy. Of course, a variety of other opinions fall in between. What do you think? How much should the church do? How much should government do? What makes the difference?

**WHAT DO YOU THINK?**

Imagine a person who has been a flagrant sinner and an outspoken enemy of the church. Suddenly this person claims to have found Christ. Would he be accepted into our church fellowship? Why or why not? Would you be concerned that he might be just pretending and that he has his own agenda? What would you do with such fears? How quickly would you consider the person ready for the church's leadership or ministry programs like teaching a Sunday school class? Why?

**WHAT DO YOU THINK?**

New believers need love and unconditional acceptance. They need to feel that they belong and that they are part of the church fellowship. They need friends. How good is our church at providing these things? What can we do to ensure that these needs are being met?

*The visual for lesson 11 is a map that may assist you in telling of these places.*

## WHAT DO YOU THINK?

IF YOUR CHURCH IS MORE THAN FIVE YEARS OLD, USE THIS QUESTION:

*The church at Antioch was a new congregation with great potential. New churches are exciting! A new church is not bound to the past. No one can say, "This is the way we've always done it." How can older churches like ours catch the excitement common to new churches? How can we break free of tradition and make a new start for the Lord?*

IF YOUR CHURCH IS LESS THAN FIVE YEARS OLD, USE THIS QUESTION:

*The church at Antioch was a new congregation with great potential. New churches are exciting! A new church is not bound to the past but free to move into the future. Of course, an older church can often draw strength and inspiration from its history and tradition. It may have an established reputation that is respected by the community. How can newer churches like ours draw strength from the past? Without an established reputation, how can we be sure people in our community do not look on us as just the latest fad—or worse, some cult group?*

cosmopolitan city whose population included many Jews and Gentiles. We do not know how much time passed before the scattered disciples reached Antioch, but we know they took the gospel with them (Acts 11:19).

The dramatic way in which the church at Jerusalem was led to include Gentiles (Acts 10:1—11:18) leads us to believe that the conversion of Cornelius and his house represents the first time Gentiles were included. Perhaps, then, it was word of that event that reached Antioch and prompted the change from telling the good news "only to Jews" (Acts 11:19) and, instead, preaching "to Greeks also" (verse 20). Whatever prompted the change, it seems at that point that church growth exploded (verse 21), so much so that the news traveled south to Jerusalem.

### A. BARNABAS COMES TO ANTIOCH (vv. 22-24)

**22. News of this reached the ears of the church at Jerusalem, and they sent Barnabas to Antioch.**

*Antioch* was located fifteen miles inland from the Mediterranean Sea on the Orontes River. Ancient cities were often built a few miles inland up a navigable river to protect them from pirate attack or from enemy fleets. Antioch's position near the northern border of modern Lebanon placed it at an intersection between the routes to Greece, Persia, and Egypt.

When *the church at Jerusalem* heard about the growing church in Antioch, *Barnabas* was sent to visit the new community of believers. We are not told why Barnabas was sent, but the most likely reason, judging by what he did after he arrived (verses 25, 26), was to assess their need for additional help, perhaps from specially gifted teachers or prophets. The new believers in Antioch needed encouragement in maintaining their new faith, and Barnabas was just the person to provide this.

**23. When he arrived and saw the evidence of the grace of God, he was glad and encouraged them all to remain true to the Lord with all their hearts.**

Barnabas *encouraged* the church in Antioch. He recognized the *grace of God* at work, and he encouraged the church to continue holding *true to the Lord*. He also recognized a need for more work to be done (verses 25, 26).

**24. He was a good man, full of the Holy Spirit and faith, and a great number of people were brought to the Lord.**

This description of Barnabas parallels Luke's description of Stephen in Acts 6:5. The ministry of Barnabas made a recognizable difference in church at Antioch.

### B. BARNABAS BRINGS SAUL TO ANTIOCH (vv. 25, 26)

Barnabas's encouragement of the church at Antioch continued in another form; he recruited Saul of Tarsus to come to Antioch and help build up the church.

**25. Then Barnabas went to Tarsus to look for Saul.**

*Tarsus,* Saul's home town, lay north and west of Antioch, less than one hundred miles by boat. A Jewish community had thrived in Tarsus for hundreds of years. (Jews are noted in Tarsus in 171 B.C. in the Apocrypha's 2 Maccabees 4:30ff.) Saul returned to his home town after the believers helped him escape death threats in Jerusalem (see Acts 9:29, 30). What had Saul been doing during this period? Having no record, we assume Saul must have been preaching Jesus as the Son of God just as he had done at Damascus and Jerusalem (see Acts 9: 20, 28, 29).

**26. And when he found him, he brought him to Antioch. So for a whole year Barnabas and Saul met with the church and taught great numbers of people. The disciples were called Christians first at Antioch.**

It seems Barnabas came to *Antioch* not to inspect—as some have suggested—but to work. He saw the field was ripe for harvest (John 4:35), so he recruited another laborer and spent a full *year* in fruitful ministry.

Here is the *first* occasion of the name *Christians*. Up to this time the Lord's followers had been called "disciples" (Acts 9:26), "believers" (Acts 5:12), or "brothers" (Acts 6:3). These names continued even after this, along with others, like "saints" (Romans 1:7), or "the faithful" (Ephesians 1:1).

The origin of the term *Christian* is disputed. Some believe it was a term of ridicule based on the common slave name "Chrestos," meaning "useful." This is pure speculation; the text does not indicate it. Peter writes of being "insulted because of the name of Christ" and of suffering "as a Christian" (1 Peter 4:14, 16), but he does not say the name itself is the insult. The apostles were "suffering disgrace for the Name" of Jesus even before they were called *Christians* (Acts 5:41).

Others believe that *Christian* was a name given by God to the followers of Jesus. The Greek word translated *called* in this verse is used elsewhere in the New Testament of God's calling, warning, or speaking to someone (cf. Acts 10:22; Hebrews 8:5). Many who hold to this view also see this new name as the fulfillment of a prophecy found in Isaiah 62:2: "The nations [Gentiles] will see your righteousness, and all kings your glory; and you will be called by a new name that the mouth of the Lord will bestow." One wonders, however, why the inspired writings do not make more use of the name if it came from God. It appears only twice after this (Acts 26:28; 1 Peter 4:16).

Still others suggest that the disciples themselves coined the term. Again, as with each suggestion, this is speculative. All we know is that the term began to be used here. *Christian* describes one as a follower of Christ, so the title thus recognizes the change that sets the Lord's followers apart from non-followers.

### SAFETY NET

The National Church Growth Research Center in Washington, D.C., has developed a program to restore "ministerial dropouts" to the pulpit. The "Safety Net," as it is named, encourages preachers who have resorted to secular work (or are about to), to reconsider their decision. The program works through a network of Barnabas-type Christian counselors who are committed to rescuing God's servants from the deep despair that has resulted in too many quitting the cause.

Apparently Barnabas had caught this concept, even in the first century. He threw a "safety net" beneath Saul by involving him in a congregation where his talents could be used fruitfully. Saul's call to ministry was honed and polished through the friendship and encouragement of Barnabas. Barnabas was not content just to *send* for Saul or to *invite* him to serve at Antioch; he personally went to Tarsus, found Saul, and brought him back. Later, these fast friends became a most effective missionary team.

The gift of encouragement is one worth developing. This can be done through prayer and practice. Speak a word, send a card, or make a call today to some Christian servant who may be discouraged. Perhaps you hold the "safety net" that could rescue a ministry.                                                                    —R. W. B.

## III. ENCOURAGEMENT BY SHARING (ACTS 11:27-30)

Barnabas's character and familiarity with the Jerusalem church made him a natural choice for another traveling ministry of encouragement.

### A. A NEED FORETOLD (vv. 27, 28)
**27. During this time some prophets came down from Jerusalem to Antioch.**

The communication between the church at Jerusalem and the church at Antioch continued in the form of *prophets* who traveled *from Jerusalem to Antioch*. As Ephesians 4:11, 12 notes, God gifted some to be prophets for the building up of the church. These prophets were especially important at that time because the New Testament Scriptures were not in any completed written form.

---

**HOW TO SAY IT**

*Agabus.* AG-uh-bus.
*Ananias.* An-uh-NYE-us.
*Antioch.* ANN-tee-ock.
*Apocrypha.* Uh-POCK-ruh-fuh.
*Aramaic.* Air-uh-MAY-ick.
*Barnabas.* BAR-nuh-bus.
*Chrestos.* CREST-awss.
*Claudius.* CLAW-dee-us.
*Cyprus.* SIGH-prus.
*Cyrene.* Sigh-REE-nee or Sigh-REEN.
*Josephus.* Joe-SEE-fus.
*Judea.* Joo-DEE-uh.
*Levite.* LEE-vite.
*nabas (Aramaic).* nah-BAHS.
*Orontes.* Or-AHN-teez.
*Suetonius.* Soo-TOE-nee-us.

## THOUGHT TO REMEMBER

*You can make a difference if you try; encourage at least one person every day.*

**28. One of them, named Agabus, stood up and through the Spirit predicted that a severe famine would spread over the entire Roman world. (This happened during the reign of Claudius.)**

The prophet *Agabus* appears again in Acts 21:10, 11, where he warns Paul of his coming arrest. Here Agabus forewarns the church of an impending shortage of food. The Roman historian Suetonius reports that "a series of droughts had caused a scarcity of grain" during the reign of *Claudius*, who ruled Rome from A.D. 41 to A.D. 54. The Jewish historian Josephus refers to a famine in Judea that occurred in the year A.D. 46.

### B. A NEED ANSWERED (vv. 29, 30)

**29. The disciples, each according to his ability, decided to provide help for the brothers living in Judea.**

The relatively new Christians in Antioch showed that they were genuine followers of Christ by responding to Agabus's message with action. It is noteworthy that the first benevolent offering sent away from home was sent from a mission church to its "mother church." The Gentile-Jewish congregation at Antioch obviously felt an indebtedness to the Jerusalem church. (See Romans 15:27.)

**30. This they did, sending their gift to the elders by Barnabas and Saul.**

By this time, *the elders,* not the apostles, received money given to the church. *Barnabas*, mentioned first, appears to lead the delegation. Involving *Saul* in taking the offering to Judea may have been another effort by Barnabas to encourage Saul's acceptance by the Jerusalem church. Again, Barnabas appears in the role of encourager for both a church and an individual.

## CONCLUSION

Joseph was his given name. But because of his encouraging ways, he is known universally as Barnabas, the Son of Encouragement. Barnabas is a marvelous example of how one person can make an enormous difference. One wonders what the early church might have been like without Barnabas. The church in Jerusalem might have had a more difficult time caring for its needy members; perhaps morale among the believers would have been lower. Who would have stood up for Saul? Who would have assisted the church in Antioch? Who would have accompanied Paul on the missionary journey recorded in Acts 13 and 14?

Of course, God is not limited. We feel certain he would have raised up *someone* for these tasks if Barnabas had not been there. But the fact is, Barnabas *was* there and it is he whom God used. Barnabas is the one who made such a difference in the life of the early church because he allowed God to use him as an encourager.

Everyone makes some difference. Every Christian can have a significant impact on his church and on his community by following Barnabas's example.

What are some of the ministries of encouragement available to church members? Here are some suggestions: writing notes of encouragement, asking people about circumstances in their lives that need prayer, giving small gifts of food or money, sending care packages to missionaries, greeting people each Sunday, writing poetry about others, inviting others home for a meal, visiting residents in the nursing home, calling people on the phone, taking pictures of new members or of members at work for Christ, spending time with children who have no father or mother at home, and making craft items to give to people.

Every congregation has its own needs and circumstances that must be addressed, but perhaps these suggestions have given you some ideas. Like Barnabas, every believer can have a positive influence for Christ through the encouragement of others.

# Discovery Learning

*This page contains an alternate lesson plan emphasizing learning activities. Classes desiring such student involvement will find these suggestions helpful. The next page is a reproducible activity page to further enhance discovery learning.*

## LEARNING GOALS

As a result of this lesson the student should:

1. List some ways Barnabas encouraged the early church.

2. Tell why encouragement is important to a church or an individual.

3. Suggest a specific way he or she can encourage someone this week.

## INTO THE LESSON

Before class, write on the board, "Men need encouragement more than women." Ask the class whether they agree or disagree with this statement. However the class generally feels about the differences between men and women, at some point you should reach a consensus that *everyone* needs encouragement. Next, point out that encouragement means "to give courage, hope, or confidence." (Note the explanation of the Greek word and the coach-athlete illustration on page 196.) Encouraging others is one of the most dominant themes in the New Testament. It is a concept presented over one hundred times in the book of Acts and the epistles.

Then lead a brainstorming session during which class members create a list of encouraging acts that they have observed recently. Record the responses on the board.

## INTO THE WORD

Barnabas made a number of significant contributions to the life of the early church. In order to measure his influence, we will observe Barnabas in action, according to the record in Acts. Each time we read about Barnabas, we will find him busy providing needed encouragement.

Divide the class into four smaller groups. Assign each group a section of Scripture from Acts that features Barnabas (or you can divide the Scriptures differently, depending on the size of your class). The sections that should be studied are as follows:

| Group | Scripture | Subject |
|-------|-----------|---------|
| 1 | Acts 4:32, 36, 37 | Barnabas encourages the Jerusalem church |
| 2 | Acts 9:26-28 | Barnabas encourages Saul |
| 3 | Acts 11:22-30 | Barnabas encourages the church at Antioch |
| 4 | Acts 15:36-41 | Barnabas encourages Mark |

Instruct each groups to read the Scripture text and then discuss the following questions:

1. What did Barnabas do in this scene?

2. Why were Barnabas's actions encouraging?

3. How could we today encourage someone in the same way Barnabas encouraged another in this text?

Each group should appoint a reporter who will summarize the group's findings for the whole class later.

Allow approximately ten minutes for the groups to do their assignments. Then have the reporter from each group summarize its group's discussion. You may want to keep track of the answers to question three to suggest to students when you challenge them to put the idea of encouragement into practice.

If time permits, after the groups have completed their reports, you may want to ask the class to try and imagine the early church without Barnabas. What would have been missing? (See the comments in the Conclusion, page 200, for some ideas.)

## OPTION

Use the first reproducible activity, "Barnabas: A Man Who Earned His Nickname," on page 202.

## INTO LIFE

Barnabas's encouraging words and actions were very significant in the life of the early church. Like Barnabas, every Christian can have a similar impact in his or her congregation. Ask the class to consider how they can be like Barnabas this week. Challenge each student to choose at least one encouraging act learned from the life of Barnabas and put it into practice. Remind them that it takes approximately twenty-one days to form a habit, so they will need to repeat this act at least twenty-one times to make it a good habit. How about doing an encouraging act once a day for the next three weeks?

## OPTION

Use the second reproducible activity, "Be a Barnabas," on page 202.

Close the class with prayer for class members and situations they may encounter where encouragement is needed. Pray that God will help each student to be sensitive to people's needs for encouragement in the upcoming weeks.

# Barnabas: A Man Who Earned His Nickname

Joseph, nicknamed Barnabas by the apostles, made a big difference in the life of the early church. Each time we read about Barnabas in the book of Acts, we find him providing encouragement to someone who needed it. Examine the following Scriptures and summarize your findings.

| SCRIPTURE | BARNABAS'S ACTIONS<br>Describe what Barnabas did and how it encouraged someone. |
| --- | --- |
| Acts 4:32, 36, 37 | |
| Acts 9:26-28 | |
| Acts 11:22-30 | |
| Acts 15:36-41 | |

# Be a Barnabas

Everyone needs encouragement! Encouragement means giving hope, courage, or confidence. Think of some ways you can be like Barnabas by giving hope, courage, or confidence to those around you. List your ideas below; then choose one from each category to put into practice.

What can I do to encourage my family?

What can I do to encourage my church?

What can I do to encourage my neighbor?

# STEPHEN

### LESSON 11

## WHY TEACH THIS LESSON?

"Be faithful, even to the point of death, and I will give you the crown of life" (Revelation 2:10). Christians have taken comfort in that verse for centuries—and many have received their crown at the end of that kind of faithfulness.

The Greek word for "crown" in that verse is *stephanos*. We see the same word used today in the name *Stephen*. The subject of today's study wore the same name, and he received the same crown. He was the first faithful witness to lay down his life for the Lord Jesus Christ. "Stephanos" received the "stephanos" of life!

Use this lesson to challenge your students to be courageous witnesses for the Lord. Stephen is our model, and his very name becomes a reminder of the reward that awaits us!

## INTRODUCTION

### A. THE COURAGE TO SPEAK UP

When Nikita Khrushchev was invited to the United States nearly thirty-five years ago, he gave a press conference at the Washington Press Club. The first question was directed to Mr. Khrushchev by the interpreter: "Today you talked about the hideous rule of your predecessor, Stalin. You were one of his closest aides and colleagues during those years. What were *you* doing all that time?"

Khrushchev's face turned red. "Who asked that?" he roared. Five hundred reporters peered down into their notepads. "Who asked that?" he shouted again. No one spoke or moved.

"That's what I was doing," Khrushchev concluded.

To do what is right when everyone around you chooses wrong demands courage. To stand up and speak up for what you believe when an angry crowd disagrees with you demands courage. It is the kind of courage that our Lord requires from those who are his witnesses. "'Do not fear what they fear; do not be frightened.' But . . . always be prepared to give an answer to everyone who asks you to give the reason for the hope that you have" (1 Peter 3:14, 15). "For God did not give us a spirit of timidity; but a spirit of power" (2 Timothy 1:7).

Stephen courageously witnessed for Christ to a hostile crowd. He did not change his message to please his listeners; he spoke the truth with courage even though it cost him his life. His witness is a powerful example for us.

### B. LESSON BACKGROUND

The church of Jesus Christ was established with the words of Jesus still ringing in the apostles' ears: "You will be my witnesses in Jerusalem, and in all Judea and Samaria, and to the ends of the earth" (Acts 1:8). Peter declared the "promise" to be "for all who are far off—for all whom the Lord our God will call" (Acts 2:39). Nevertheless, during the time covered by the first seven chapters of the book of Acts, there is no record of any but Jews in Jerusalem having heard the good news of Jesus. That was about to change!

Luke introduces Stephen to us as the first of seven men chosen by the Jerusalem church to administer the distribution of food to needy widows. All of the seven

DEVOTIONAL READING
MATTHEW 5:43-48
LESSON SCRIPTURE
ACTS 6:1—8:3
PRINTED TEXT
ACTS 6:8-15; 7:54-60

## LESSON AIMS

As students participate in today's session, they will:

1. Describe Stephen's courageous witness in the face of lethal opposition.

2. List some reasons Christians today need to be courageous witnesses.

3. Identify situations in which they plan to be a more courageous witness for Jesus Christ.

Feb
9

## KEY VERSE

*Now Stephen, a man full of God's grace and power, did great wonders and miraculous signs among the people.* Acts 6:8

*The visual for lesson 11 in the visuals packet is a map. Use it to locate some of the places mentioned in today's lesson.*

**WHAT DO YOU THINK?**

*Stephen was described as "a man full of God's grace and power." He "did great wonders and miraculous signs." Are these the credentials for being effective witnesses for Jesus? Why or why not? How can we who have no miraculous sign gifts give effective testimony for Jesus?*

**WHAT DO YOU THINK?**

*Witnessing to hostile people can easily develop into a confrontation. Maybe we should avoid such people. Jesus did say we are not to give what is sacred to "dogs" (Matthew 7:6). Is this a valid course of action? Why or why not? If so, why didn't Stephen avoid the situation in our text?*

*The gospel goes against the grain of contemporary culture and values, which is sure to make some people angry. Sometimes we must follow Stephen's example and speak up for Christ. How do we know when to confront and when to keep quiet?*

were chosen because they were "known to be full of the Spirit and wisdom" (Acts 6:3). Stephen is especially noted as "a man full of faith and of the Holy Spirit" (v. 5). All seven men had Greek names, a factor that probably helped to reassure the Grecian widows who had been neglected (v. 1). These men took over the daily food distribution, providing more time for the apostles to engage in prayer and the ministry of the word. As a result, "the word of God spread. The number of disciples in Jerusalem increased rapidly, and a large number of priests became obedient to the faith" (Acts 6:7).

The apostles, however, were not the only ones responsible for the increase of the word of God. Although he was one of those who had been designated to oversee the ministry to the widows, Stephen certainly did his part to spread the gospel.

## I. COURAGE AMONG THE PEOPLE (ACTS 6:8-11)
### A. WONDERS AND MIRACLES (v. 8)
Stephen explained to his fellow Jews how Jesus' death and resurrection fulfilled their nation's role and their people's hopes. Many of the Jews refused to accept this testimony, but Stephen courageously continued to witness for his Lord.

**8. Now Stephen, a man full of God's grace and power, did great wonders and miraculous signs among the people.**

G. Campbell Morgan described Stephen as a man "full of sweetness and strength." Stephen's *power* was demonstrated in his ability to work *great wonders and miraculous signs among the people*. This ability evidently came from the laying on of the apostles' hands (see verse 6 and compare with Acts 8:18).

### B. WISDOM IN SPEAKING (vv. 9-11)
**9. Opposition arose, however, from members of the Synagogue of the Freedmen (as it was called)—Jews of Cyrene and Alexandria as well as the provinces of Cilicia and Asia. These men began to argue with Stephen.**

This *synagogue* was evidently made up of Jews from several different countries. Since Stephen's name was Greek rather than Hebrew, it is not surprising to find him speaking to Jews whose homes or ancestors were from lands outside of Palestine.

The *Freedmen* were either freed slaves or the descendants of freed slaves. The Roman general Pompey took many Jewish prisoners when he invaded Judea in 63 B.C. He released them all when he reached Rome. They may then have settled in *Cyrene* (in northern Africa), *Alexandria* (in northern Egypt), *Cilicia and Asia*. The latter two territories were provinces in Asia Minor. Cilicia was the province in which Saul's hometown of Tarsus was located; thus, he may have been a member of this particular synagogue.

**10. . . . but they could not stand up against his wisdom or the Spirit by whom he spoke.**

The Freedmen's dispute with Stephen probably led to a formal public debate. Stephen knew he faced strong opposition. But he courageously witnessed about Christ, and God's *Spirit* helped him. Stephen's courageous witness calls to mind the assurance Jesus gave his disciples: "I will give you words and wisdom that none of your adversaries will be able to resist or contradict" (Luke 21:15).

**11. Then they secretly persuaded some men to say, "We have heard Stephen speak words of blasphemy against Moses and against God."**

Those who had taken part in the debate with Stephen had no argument that could successfully answer his witness about Jesus, but still they refused to accept his testimony. Instead, they recruited—or bribed—*some men* to accuse Stephen of *blasphemy*. If they could not refute his message, they would make the messenger look bad. By this they hoped to win the support of the public even though they clearly had not refuted anything Stephen had said.

## II. COURAGE BEFORE THE COUNCIL (ACTS 6:12-15)

### A. STEPHEN ARRESTED (v. 12)

**12. So they stirred up the people and the elders and the teachers of the law. They seized Stephen and brought him before the Sanhedrin.**

The *people and the elders and the teachers of the law* are mentioned as part of this crowd, but not the priests. Luke earlier noted that "a large number of priests became obedient to the faith" (Acts 6:7). Did that "large number" represent a majority of the priests? Were there not enough unbelieving priests to make them a significant body of opposition?

This crowd dragged Stephen before the *Sanhedrin,* the highest ruling body of the Jewish nation. This council was composed of seventy members plus the high priest, who served as its president. This was the group that had condemned Jesus to death. Anyone claiming to act in his name would not likely be well received by this group! A fair hearing was out of the question. Stephen must have known his life was in danger.

It is significant to note that Stephen's preaching resulted in the loss of public favor through the agitation of *the people.* The Christians had previously enjoyed "the favor of all the people" (Acts 2:47; see also 4:21; 5:13, 26).

### B. STEPHEN ACCUSED (vv. 13-15)

**13. They produced false witnesses, who testified, "This fellow never stops speaking against this holy place and against the law.**

Stephen's enemies used the same tactics against him that the priests and council members had used against Jesus: "And the chief priests and the whole Sanhedrin were looking for evidence against Jesus so that they could put him to death; but they did not find any. Many testified falsely against him, but their statements did not agree" (Mark 14:55, 56). Stephen's accusers, however, appeared more united. These *false witnesses,* probably the same ones mentioned in verse 11, twisted Stephen's words to make him appear to speak *against this holy place* (the temple), *and against the law.* These charges, if they could be substantiated, would mean Stephen was guilty of blasphemy.

**14. For we have heard him say that this Jesus of Nazareth will destroy this place and change the customs Moses handed down to us."**

The assertion that *Jesus of Nazareth will destroy this place* (the temple) was similar to the charge made against Jesus himself: "We heard him say, 'I will destroy this man-made temple and in three days will build another, not made by man'" (Mark 14:58). John records Jesus' actual words: "'Destroy this temple, and I will raise it again in three days.' . . . But the temple he had spoken of was his body" (John 2:19, 21). Stephen may have quoted Jesus in order to prove Jesus' messiahship by his resurrection. Stephen may also have suggested that the Jerusalem temple was not God's true dwelling place, a point that he made quite clear in his later defense (Acts 7:48-50). Or perhaps the witnesses had remembered the similar charges against Jesus and were attempting to tie Stephen to the charges that had condemned Jesus.

The charge that Jesus had come to *change the customs Moses handed down to us* may have had some truth to it. If Stephen had told that Jesus came to fulfill the law (Matthew 5:17), then he may have suggested that some practices mandated by the law were no longer necessary. The writer of Hebrews notes that Jesus' once-for-all-sacrifice for sin put an end to the need of offering sacrifices "endlessly year after

### WHAT DO YOU THINK?

When it comes to religion, many people are not willing to consider other views. They do not even want to think about the possibility that they may have invested a good portion of their lives in a belief that is wrong. Others maintain that religion is a highly personal matter and that it is no one else's business what they believe. Such a view is commonly expressed in the erroneous maxim: "We are all going to Heaven—just by different roads."

What steps can be taken to develop a relationship with a person that will allow such matters to be discussed openly and honestly? Why are so few Christians apparently willing to take the time and make the effort to develop such a relationship? What happens when we try to witness to our Lord without laying such a foundation?

### OPTION

Use the reproducible activity, "Courage Needed Then," on page 210 to explore how serious were the charges against Stephen and the charges he leveled at the Sanhedrin.

## WHAT DO YOU THINK?

*Stephen's position was, in a nutshell, that Jesus fulfilled the Old Testament law. This, of course, rendered the ceremonial aspects of the law superfluous. The Jewish leaders, who made their living by observing these ceremonial rituals, were unwilling to accept this truth. Financial considerations, as well as love for the traditional forms, no doubt played a part in their opposition.*

*How do such concerns prompt people to oppose the truth today? How do Christians sometimes put financial issues and tradition ahead of the truth? How can we be sure to allow the truth to direct our thinking about money and tradition instead of the other way around?*

## HOW TO SAY IT

*Caesarea.* Sess-uh-REE-uh.
*Cilicia.* Suh-LISH-ee-uh.
*Cyrene.* Sigh-REE-nee
  or Sigh-REEN.
*Cyrenians.* Sigh-REE-nee-uns.
*Judea.* Joo-DEE-uh.
*Khrushchev.* KROOSH-shef.
*Pilate.* PIE-lut.
*Pompey.* PAHM-pee.
*Samaria.* Suh-MEH-ree-uh.
*Sanhedrin.* San-HEED-run
  or SAN-heh-drun.
*stephanos (Greek).* STEF-
  uh-noss.

year" (Hebrews 10:1). Even so, *change* would have been a misleading term; *fulfill* would have been more accurate, and it would not have suggested anything illegal.

The Jerusalem temple and the Law of Moses were the pillars of the Jewish faith. To speak about changing or destroying them was, in traditional Jewish thought, to speak against God's will. This was considered blasphemy, a capital crime.

**15. All who were sitting in the Sanhedrin looked intently at Stephen, and they saw that his face was like the face of an angel.**

Saul of Tarsus was may well have been Luke's source for this particular detail. It reminds us of the glory of Moses' face when he descended from Mount Sinai (Exodus 34:29, 30).

### HUNTING FOR LITTLE BEARS

Excusing an unproductive life on the basis of small or inadequate resources is always a temptation. "I could have accomplished that much too, if I had had his money, his charisma, his good looks, etc." One of my favorite stories comes from a "Mutt and Jeff" cartoon, in which the two friends are camping by a forest in grizzly country. Jeff (the little guy) says, "Man, if I was as big as you are, I'd go into the woods, find the biggest bear in there, and kill him with my bare hands!" Mutt (the big guy) replies, "Well, there's a lot of *little bears* in there!"

Stephen's record shows a man who was respected by his peers and who experienced success in whatever he undertook. As the adage says, "Cream rises to the top." From among thousands of disciples in Jerusalem, Stephen was selected as one of only seven men to administer the first "food pantry" of the church. Shortly thereafter, we find him preaching and debating in the local synagogue. He rose from waiter to witness overnight, it seems. He performed "great wonders and miraculous signs among the people" (Acts 6:8).

When we contrast our puny personal evangelistic efforts with Stephen's, we may be tempted to excuse ourselves on the basis of his apostolic blessing and his resulting possession of the special powers of the Holy Spirit. Truthfully, however, Stephen's biggest advantage is described by the phrase *full of faith*. Besides, we should never forget that a lot of "little bears" live in our neck of the woods.    —R. W. B.

## III. COURAGE IN THE FACE OF DEATH (ACTS 7:54-60)

The next portion of our lesson text is preceded by Stephen's defense before the Sanhedrin (Acts 7:1-53). Stephen traced the history of Israel from the time of Abraham, pointing out that the people had resisted God's will again and again. The learned ones among them knew this was true. Stephen then brought his speech to a climax by declaring that the Jews before him had also resisted the will of God: the had killed "the Righteous One" (Acts 7:52), the Messiah. They had accused him of blasphemy; now he accused them of blasphemy (resisting the Holy Spirit, v. 51) and murder. To this accusation they reacted with fury.

### A. A VICIOUS CROWD (v. 54)

**54. When they heard this, they were furious and gnashed their teeth at him.**

Stephen had traced the history of his people accurately. Up to this point the hearers made no protest. They knew what they were hearing was true. But their attitude changed when Stephen accused them of killing "the Righteous One." They knew he meant Jesus, and they were determined to cling to their opinion that Jesus was a blasphemer. They snarled at Stephen like a pack of wild animals.

### B. STEPHEN'S VISION (vv. 55, 56)

**55. But Stephen, full of the Holy Spirit, looked up to heaven and saw the glory of God, and Jesus standing at the right hand of God.**

The *Holy Spirit* had been guiding Stephen thus far (Acts 6:5, 8), and *Stephen* continued to follow his leading. He *looked up* and *saw the glory of God, and Jesus standing at the right hand of God*. This confirmed Jesus' resurrection and ascension, and demonstrated that the *glory of God* was not to be associated with the temple, but with the person of Jesus.

**56. "Look," he said, "I see heaven open and the Son of Man standing at the right hand of God."**

The title *Son of Man* has clear messianic import in prophetic passages like Daniel 7:13, 14, which tells of such a one vested with tremendous power and coming with the clouds of heaven. Perhaps some of the members of the Sanhedrin recalled Jesus' use of the same title in a similar context: "You will see the Son of man sitting at the right hand of the Mighty One and coming on the clouds of heaven" (Mark 14:62). The anger and jealousy that had driven them to condemn Jesus was now rekindled in their hearts and leveled full-force against Stephen.

That Stephen saw Jesus *standing* may be of some significance, since the words of Jesus quoted above refer to his *sitting*. Some propose that Jesus stood as a witness on Stephen's behalf. Because Stephen had faithfully and unashamedly acknowledged Christ before men, Jesus was now acknowledging his servant before the Father (Matthew 10:32). Others believe that Jesus was standing to greet this brave disciple, who was about to join him in glory.

## C. A VENGEFUL CROWD (vv. 57, 58)

**57, 58. At this they covered their ears and, yelling at the top of their voices, they all rushed at him, dragged him out of the city and began to stone him. Meanwhile, the witnesses laid their clothes at the feet of a young man named Saul.**

The Jews *covered their ears* so that they would not hear such "blasphemy" as this. The Sanhedrin now ceased from being a court of law and turned into an enraged mob.

This was clearly not a legal action; it had turned into a riot. Still, in accordance with Deuteronomy 17:7, the *witnesses* took part in Stephen's execution. Stephen was also taken *out of the city* (Leviticus 24:13, 14; Numbers 15:32-36) to be stoned. Roman law did not allow the Jews to execute anyone. But Pilate, the Roman governor of Judea, usually lived in Caesarea, which was nearly sixty miles from Jerusalem. The unruly mob was in no mood to go through proper channels.

In this verse, Luke introduces *Saul*, who had just heard Stephen's defense. Saul stood watching and approving of the stoning. He never forgot this scene: "And when the blood of your martyr Stephen was shed, I stood there giving my approval and guarding the clothes of those who were killing him" (Acts 22:20). The *clothes* that were laid at Saul's feet were the heavier outer garments that might have hampered the throwing of stones.

On the surface, Saul's role seems minor—watching the clothes of the murderers. But he himself indicates he gave his "approval" to the act. Some have suggested he actually assumed responsibility for Stephen's death. After all, in a riot, it is difficult to point out who did what. But Saul made himself conspicuous by guarding the clothes. If Pilate did decide to hold the Jews responsible for this illegal act, Saul was one conspirator who could be singled out and charged.

## D. STEPHEN'S VICTORY (vv. 59, 60)

**59. While they were stoning him, Stephen prayed, "Lord Jesus, receive my spirit."**

In the face of death, *Stephen* did not waver in his allegiance to Christ. How could he think of retreat when Jesus was standing there above him in glory? Earnestly he appealed to the living Lord to receive Stephen's own spirit into that heavenly scene.

**WHAT DO YOU THINK?**

*On one hand, the story of Stephen seems a tragic one. Why doesn't God protect his witnesses when their testimony exposes them to harm and danger? The fact is, the Greek word for witness is the source of our English word martyr. (See Acts 22:20 and observe the footnote; Revelation 2:13.) There is something in the very nature of being a witness that exposes one to risk and danger.*

*How does one's willingness to put his life on the line—or to endure lesser ridicule or persecution—validate his message? What good have you seen come from suffering for what one believes?*

*(See Acts 5:41; James 1:2-4; 1 Peter 4:12-17.)*

**WHAT DO YOU THINK?**

*Courage in the face of danger comes from a firm conviction that we are right and that what we are doing is God's will. The source of our courage is Christ himself. As we lean on him, he supports and encourages us. Such a view sustained Stephen as he was being martyred for his witness.*

*How can we instill such conviction in believers today?*

*Why do cult believers seem to have this kind of conviction about their wrong views? How can we give conviction without brainwashing?*

*How effective are our Bible studies and worship services in doing this? What changes would you suggest to improve our programs in that regard?*

## PRAYER

*Lord, when I am afraid to speak up for you, remind me of Stephen's courageous witness. Remind me that you will be with me just as you were with Stephen, that you are standing by the throne of God looking out for me. And I will try courageously to stand up and to speak up for you. Amen.*

## THOUGHT TO REMEMBER

*The Lord wants you to make a difference for him.*

## DAILY BIBLE READINGS

**Monday, Feb. 3**—*Stephen Chosen to Be Deacon (Acts 6:1-8)*

**Tuesday, Feb. 4**—*Stephen's Testimony Before the High Priest (Acts 7:1-10)*

**Wednesday, Feb. 5**—*Stiff-necked People Resist the Holy Spirit (Acts 7:54-60)*

**Thursday, Feb. 6**—*Gain True Life by Enduring Persecution (Luke 21:12-19)*

**Friday, Feb. 7**—*Take Refuge in God (Psalm 57:1-11)*

**Saturday, Feb. 8**—*Pray for Those Who Persecute You (Matthew 5:43-48)*

**Sunday, Feb. 9**—*Acknowledge God Before People (Luke 12:4-12)*

This was similar to Jesus' prayer from the cross: "Father, into your hands I commit my spirit" (Luke 23:46).

**60. Then he fell on his knees and cried out, "Lord, do not hold this sin against them." When he had said this, he fell asleep.**

Like Jesus, *Stephen* prayed for the forgiveness of those who murdered him. Then he became the first Christian to die for the sake of Jesus. In one sense, Stephen lost his life; but by virtue of Jesus' resurrection, he gained it. The victory belonged to him, not to his accusers. He did not die; he simply *fell asleep*. Such language testifies to the impact of Christ's resurrection.

### MESSIANIC MARTYRDOM

Psychoanalysts were the first, I suppose, to coin the term *messianic complex*. It has been used to describe the obsession of certain charismatic leaders, particularly religious leaders, who have assumed the speech and behavior of a messianic figure or who have presumed to possess his authority and power. "Father Divine," Jim Jones, and David Koresh are examples.

Stephen, the first Christian martyr mentioned in Acts, spoke words as he was dying that resembled some of the words Jesus uttered from the cross. Did Stephen purposely provoke the stoning to draw attention to himself? Was he deluded as to his own identity? Did Stephen suffer from a messianic complex?

The more likely explanation is that just as Jesus quoted Scripture on the cross, Stephen quoted his Lord. He felt privileged to share the sufferings of Christ. His dying words matched the Lord's because he was spiritually linked by love and commitment to the Savior. As he honored him in life, he desired to honor him in death.

Paul possessed this outlook and described it in these words: "I want to know Christ and the power of his resurrection and the fellowship of sharing in his sufferings, becoming like him in his death, and so, somehow, to attain to the resurrection from the dead" (Philippians 3:10, 11).      —R. W. B.

## CONCLUSION

Inspired by the Holy Spirit, Stephen proclaimed the message of Jesus and was faithful even to death. It is significant that Saul of Tarsus was present to hear Stephen's courageous testimony. In years to come, Saul would become Paul the apostle. He would take up Stephen's message and carry it far and wide. He too would be faithful even to the point of death.

Although Stephen could not have realized it, his death resulted in the expansion of the church's witness beyond Jerusalem. Following Stephen's death, Luke records that "a great persecution broke out against the church at Jerusalem, and . . . [believers] were scattered throughout Judea and Samaria" (Acts 8:1). He then adds, "Those who had been scattered preached the word wherever they went" (v. 4). In this way, Stephen helped fulfill Jesus' commission to send "witnesses . . . in all Judea and Samaria" (Acts 1:8). What was said of Abel in Hebrews 11:4 could be applied to Stephen: "He still speaks, even though he is dead."

We can see what a pivotal role Stephen played in the early church because of his courageous witness. What about us today? What courageous role does God want us to play?

Ask each class member to think of at least one person to whom he needs to witness. What message does that person need to hear? What fears or apprehensions arise when thinking about witnessing to this person? Ask your class members to pray specifically for a courageous witness to those they have in mind. Also ask them to share examples of courageous Christian witnessing that they have observed or in which they have participated. These examples will encourage you and other members of the class.

# Discovery Learning

*This page contains an alternate lesson plan emphasizing learning activities. Classes desiring such student involvement will find these suggestions helpful. The next page is a reproducible activity page to further enhance discovery learning.*

## LESSON GOALS

As students participate in today's session, they will:

1. Describe Stephen's courageous witness in the face of lethal opposition.

2. List some reasons Christians today need to be courageous witnesses.

3. Identify e situations in which they plan to be a more courageous witness for Jesus Christ.

## INTO THE LESSON

As you begin your class session, divide the students into two groups, and give the following assignments:

Group 1. Think of a time in your life when someone told a terrible lie about you. Tell the others in your group what effect the lie had on your life and your relationships. Was the lie ever exposed? What happened? Did you ever forgive the person who told the lie? If so, how?

Group 2. Think about someone in your life who makes you desire to serve Christ more faithfully. Tell your group who this person is and why he or she encourages you in this way.

Allow the groups plenty of time to tell their own stories. When you think everyone has had an opportunity to share, ask each group to elect someone to tell his or her story to the whole class.

Ask the students how they would feel if a terrible lie were told about a person whom they admired as a great example of faith. Would they believe it? How would they refute it? How might it hurt the church? Do they know of a time when this has happened?

Make the transition into the lesson by telling the class that Stephen was one of the most courageous believers in the first-century church. The Jewish leaders, unnerved by his powerful testimony about Jesus, found it necessary to fabricate a lie about him to try to rid themselves of his witness.

## INTO THE WORD

As you move into the Bible story portion of the lesson, use the lesson background provided to create a mini-lecture to introduce Stephen. Observe that Stephen's name means "crown," but don't elaborate.

Next, distribute copies of the reproducible page (210). Ask the students to work in groups or alone to complete the first activity, "Courage Needed Then." (Answers are provided below for your convenience.)

Acts 6:11: Stephen was accused of "speaking against Moses and against God."

Acts 6:13: Stephen was accused of speaking against the temple and the law.

Acts 6:14: Stephen was accused of claiming Jesus would destroy the temple.

Acts 7:35-37: As the Israelites had rejected their first "deliverer," Moses, Stephen implied they had rejected God's ultimate deliverer, Jesus, who was the "prophet" like Moses.

Acts 7:44-50: God cannot be housed in a building made by human hands—not even the temple.

Acts 7:51-53: They were guilty of resisting the Spirit, killing the Messiah (just as their fathers had killed the prophets who predicted the Messiah's coming), and not obeying the law they accused Stephen of blaspheming.

Acts 7:56: Jesus, "the Son of Man," was in Heaven next to God.

With such charges being made against Stephen and by Stephen, it took great courage and confidence in the Lord Jesus to continue.

## INTO LIFE

Ask the class whether any of them have ever been persecuted for trying to give accurate testimony about who Jesus Christ is. If some in the class have experienced ridicule or other forms of persecution for their courageous witness about Jesus, allow them to share the circumstances briefly.

Refer the class to the second activity on page 210: "Courage Needed Now." Allow about eight minutes for students to complete the activity; then discuss briefly.

Ask each class member to choose one of the situations on his or her chart, or to think of one person to whom he or she needs to make a bold witness about Jesus Christ, and make a commitment to act with courage this week to testify for Jesus in that situation.

Remind the class that *Stephen* means "crown." Then have someone read that last half of Revelation 2:10. Observe that the word for *crown* in that verse is *stephanos*—the same as the name "Stephen." Stephen becomes both our model of faithfulness and a reminder of its reward! Lead the class in a time of prayer in which everyone has opportunity to commit himself to be more courageous in witnessing about the lordship of Christ, to be faithful to the point of death—looking forward to the crown of life.

# Courage Needed Then

Look up the following Scriptures to see either what charges Stephen made or what charges were brought against him. Compare each with the traditional Jewish thinking of the time, and you will see why Stephen needed courage to give his testimony.

| CHARGES | TRADITIONAL JEWISH THOUGHT |
|---|---|
| Acts 6:11 | Any statement that diminishes the importance of God or the Law of Moses is blasphemy, punishable by death. |
| Acts 6:13 | The temple and the rituals performed there were to last forever. To suggest otherwise was to deny God's Word. |
| Acts 6:14 | Moses gave the law by God's authority. Anyone who claims to change that claims to be superior to God. That is blasphemy. |
| Acts 7:35-37 | The prophet "like Moses" would be accepted as the Messiah, not rejected. |
| Acts 7:44-50 | The temple was God's dwelling place. |
| Acts 7:51-53 | The Sanhedrin ensured compliance with the law. |
| Acts 7:56 | Jesus was a pretender who was dead and buried—somewhere! |

# Courage Needed Now

Stephen's courageous witness is a model for us all. On the chart below, list some situations that especially need courage on the part of the Lord's witness. Next to each, write one specific act that would demonstrate courage and give a positive testimony for the Lord Jesus Christ.

| SITUATION | COURAGEOUS ACT OF TESTIMONY |
|---|---|
|  |  |
| I will act with courage this week to | |

# PRISCILLA AND AQUILA

**LESSON 12**

## WHY TEACH THIS LESSON?

"If someone forces you to go one mile, go with him two miles. Give to the one who asks you, and do not turn away from the one who wants to borrow from you" (Matthew 5:41, 42). It's called going the extra mile. It might also be called rare.

The subjects of our study knew about miles. They may be the most mobile couple in the New Testament. From Rome, to Corinth, to Ephesus, and finally back to Rome, this couple got around! They knew about "second miles," too. Wherever they were, they gave of themselves for the Lord's service. Their house was his house; their lives were his.

Use this lesson to challenge your students to be more open to being used by God, at home or elsewhere. How are we using our homes? How open are we to allowing the Lord to use *us* in whatever way will glorify him? If we follow the example of Priscilla and Aquila, we'll see our homes and our very selves as tools for God's use.

## INTRODUCTION

### A. FAITHFUL SERVANTS

The book of Acts is full of accounts of men and women of faith who refused to be silenced concerning the gospel of Christ. Because of the willing and sacrificial spirits of such faithful saints, the early church grew at an amazing rate. Three thousand were baptized on Pentecost (Acts 2:41). Daily the Lord added to that number (v. 47) until soon there were 5,000 (Acts 4:4). "More and more men and women believed in the Lord and were added to their number" (5:14); still "the number . . . increased rapidly" (6:7)—so much so that Luke stopped giving estimates.

Barnabas and Stephen, subjects of our previous two lessons, contributed to that explosive growth in the church at Jerusalem. Today's lesson focuses on a godly couple, Priscilla and Aquila, who demonstrated that same spirit on the frontier of the church. In Corinth, in Ephesus, in Rome—wherever they found themselves, they were a blessing to the church by their generous spirit and positive witness. It was the presence of such committed saints that "turned the world upside down" for Christ (Acts 17:6, *KJV*) within just a couple of decades.

### B. LESSON BACKGROUND

Priscilla and Aquila are mentioned (always together, never separately) six times in the New Testament (three times in Acts and three times in Paul's letters). Priscilla's name occurs first in four of the six instances—perhaps an indication that she enjoyed a higher social status than her husband or that she was more well known in the church. Aquila was originally from the Roman province of Pontus in Asia Minor, located along the southern shore of the Black Sea.

## I. ASSISTING PAUL (ACTS 18:1-4)

Paul's second missionary journey was an eventful one. He traveled with Silas after he and Barnabas disagreed over whether to take John Mark along (Acts 15:36-40). At Lystra, Timothy joined the team (Acts 16:1-3), and at Troas Luke signed on

**DEVOTIONAL READING**
1 THESSALONIANS 5:12-22

**LESSON SCRIPTURE**
ACTS 18:1-4, 18, 19, 24-26; ROMANS 16:3-5a

**PRINTED TEXT**
ACTS 18:1-4, 18, 19, 24-26; ROMANS 16:3-5a

## LESSON AIMS

As students participate in today's class session, they should:

1. List some of the contributions of Priscilla and Aquila to the cause of Christ.

2. Identify the attitude that seems to have motivated their service.

3. State some ways Christians today can imitate the faithfulness of Priscilla and Aquila.

Feb
16

The visual for lesson 12 in the visuals packet (see page 216) challenges every Christian to use his home for Christ, as Priscilla and Aquila did. Have it on display as you begin the lesson.

## KEY VERSES

Greet Priscilla and Aquila, my fellow workers in Christ Jesus. They risked their lives for me. Not only I but all the churches of the Gentiles are grateful to them.
—Romans 16:3, 4

(Acts 16:10). From there the team went into into Macedonia and Achaia (territories located in modern Greece). In Philippi, he and Silas were illegally beaten and imprisoned (Acts 16:22-24). No mention is made of what happened to Luke or Timothy, however. The team faced rioting mobs in Thessalonica (Acts 17:5) and Berea (Acts 17:13), and ridicule in Athens (Acts 17:32).

## A. ARRIVING IN CORINTH (vv. 1, 2)

**1. After this, Paul left Athens and went to Corinth.**

The city of *Corinth* was one of the commercial giants of the Roman world. By the first century it had become a thoroughly pagan city, housing temples dedicated to such deities as Aphrodite, the Roman goddess of love. The worship of this goddess included acts of prostitution and gave rise to Corinth's reputation as a center of immorality. Making inroads in such an atmosphere would be difficult.

*Paul* had come to Corinth from *Athens*, where he had been "greatly distressed" over the predominance of idolatry (17:16) and where some had mocked his preaching of the resurrection (17:32). He also came alone. Silas and Timothy had been left behind at Berea (Acts 17:13, 14) and did not catch up with Paul until he was in Corinth (Acts 17:15; 18:5)*. Luke appears to have remained at Philippi; his first person (*we*) narrative ends there, and he returns to third person (*he, they*). It was a period in Paul's ministry when he might have become quite discouraged.

**2. There he met a Jew named Aquila, a native of Pontus, who had recently come from Italy with his wife Priscilla, because Claudius had ordered all the Jews to leave Rome. Paul went to see them.**

It is commonly held that *Priscilla* and *Aquila* were already believers when Paul *met* them in Corinth. The word *met* is more properly *found,* the same term used of his meeting the twelve disciples of John in Ephesus in Acts 19:1. In addition, there is no mention of Priscilla and Aquila's believing Paul's message and being baptized as there is for Lydia in Philippi (Acts 16:14, 15). Jews form *Pontus* as well as *Rome* were in Jerusalem on Pentecost (Acts 2:9-11). Aquila could have been among them, or the couple could have been converted by one of them after they had returned home.

The evidence is not conclusive, however. Aquila is called a *Jew,* not a "believer" or a "disciple." There were many conversions not recorded in Acts—that of Priscilla and Aquila may be among them. Paul's immediate attachment to this couple seems to have been for financial reasons rather than for Christian fellowship.

This couple had previously lived in Rome, but an edict from Emperor *Claudius* had forced them to leave. This edict, dated at about A.D. 49, is mentioned by the Roman historian Suetonius, who says that Claudius (who ruled A.D. 41-54) took this action because of riots in Rome that were instigated because of one "Chrestus." This name may be a corrupted form of the name "Christ," written by a historian who knew very little about Christianity. Apparently Jewish resistance to the preaching of Christ caused no small stir in the city of Rome. The emperor, seeing the matter as a strictly Jewish affair, simply expelled all the Jews.

The timing of this event was surely providential. Whether Priscilla and Aquila were already Christian or were converted by Paul, their presence in Corinth at just this time is evidence of God at work. From here on, this couple would be instrumental in the work of Paul and of the kingdom of God.

## B. SUPPORTING PAUL (vv. 3, 4)

**3. And because he was a tentmaker as they were, he stayed and worked with them.**

Priscilla and Aquila's occupation was tentmaking, which usually amounted to leather working. This trade involved long hours of punching holes in pieces of

### *NOTE

Timothy appears to have joined Paul in Athens, but then he was sent back to Macedonia, to Thessalonica (1 Thessalonians 3:1-6). Whether Timothy and Silas then came to Corinth together or separately is not known.

### WHAT DO YOU THINK?

We do not know whether Priscilla and Aquila were already Christians when Paul met them or not. If they were not Christians, then Paul joined them in their work and witnessed to them on the job. How much witnessing is appropriate on the job today? Are there situations at work where it would be inappropriate to witness? If so, why?

If they were already Christians, then imagine how much they must have encouraged each other. How much do you encourage your leaders? How could you improve? What especially do you find encouraging from them? When did you last thank them for that?

leather with an awl, and then stitching the materials together to serve as awnings or tents. These could then be sold to merchants for their booths in the market-place. Priscilla and Aquila may have rented a two-story structure in the market-place of Corinth, using the lower level for a workshop and the upper level for living quarters.

**4. Every Sabbath he reasoned in the synagogue, trying to persuade Jews and Greeks.**

Though somewhat limited by his hours spent in making tents, Paul's efforts to preach the gospel of Christ continued uninterrupted. He did not fail to take every opportunity to go to the *synagogue*. True to his "custom" (see Acts 17:2), Paul focused on persuading the *Jews* that Jesus is the Christ (18:5).

Paul's presence in the synagogue also brought him into contact with *Greeks*. These were the "God-fearers"—Gentiles who had not been circumcised, but had become participants in synagogue worship and instruction (see the example of Cornelius in Acts 10:1, 2).

## II. TEACHING IN EPHESUS (ACTS 18:18, 19, 24-26)

Eventually, opposition against Paul reached a fever pitch in Corinth (as it often did elsewhere). His eighteen-month ministry (Acts 18:11) came to a turning point. Jewish opponents tried to force a hearing before Gallio, proconsul of Achaia. Priscilla and Aquila's loyalty to the cause of Christ may have been severely tested during this time. Gallio ruled, however, that the issues raised by the Jews had nothing to do with maintaining law and order. Paul did not even have to say a word in his own defense. Gallio threw out the case, claiming it was a Jewish matter, involving "questions about words and names and your own law" (Acts 18:12-17).

### A. BEGINNING AGAIN (vv. 18, 19)

**18. Paul stayed on in Corinth for some time. Then he left the brothers and sailed for Syria, accompanied by Priscilla and Aquila. Before he sailed, he had his hair cut off at Cenchrea because of a vow he had taken.**

After remaining in Corinth *for some time,* Paul decided to travel back to the Roman province of *Syria,* to Antioch from which he had started (verse 22). Paul had reported back to Antioch at the conclusion of his first missionary journey, also (Acts 14:26).

Paul did not go alone on this trip; he invited *Priscilla and Aquila* to go with him. They had become his partners in the work of the gospel. Paul's tentmaking with them had ceased when Silas and Timothy arrived in Corinth with additional operating funds (Acts 18:5). But they remained co-workers for the sake of the cross. Now they would assist in planting a new church.

We do not know how difficult a move this might have been for them. If their business was doing well, it would have been a challenge to relocate and try to establish themselves in a new city. If, however, the Jews' opposition to Paul also affected them and their business, relocation might have been a good business decision to move. Whatever the case, it is apparent they went in faith, ready to contribute to the kingdom in whatever way they could.

Paul's *vow* has caused some confusion among Bible students. First, it seems to be a part of the Old Covenant, and some wonder why a Christian would observe Jewish law. Jewish Christians, however, saw no conflict between many of the features of the Jewish faith and their new Christian faith. The law had been intended to "lead us to Christ" (Galatians 3:24). Its pictures of Christ were no less valid once the Christ had come. Rather, they were more clear. Paul opposed the observance of the law for the sake of justification (Galatians 2:16), but not for worship.

### WHAT DO YOU THINK?

*When an unexpected blessing comes our way, it is easy to thank God. What about when difficulties come—why do we not always follow James's advice and "consider it pure joy" (James 1:2)? Priscilla and Aquila were in Corinth because they were expelled from Rome. Paul was there after some discouragement in Athens. Yet God used their meeting to bless all three. How can we be more faithful about praising God for the good he works even through difficult times? (See Romans 8:28.)*

### WHAT DO YOU THINK?

*Today, many countries disapprove of missionaries entering their borders. One of the most creative and fruitful responses to that has been through "tentmakers"—people who enter the country to work at a specific job or industry and seek to influence others for Christ while engaged in such work. How can Christians who travel abroad use their work to influence others for Christ today? What about those who travel widely in their own country—how might they use their work as a "tentmaking ministry," influencing people for Christ while working and traveling?*

### WHAT DO YOU THINK?

*It is quite possible that Priscilla and Aquila closed their business in Corinth and moved Ephesus for the purpose of assisting Paul in establishing the church in that city. What kind of risks do you suppose went along with such a move? What risks have you taken for the gospel? With what result?*

## HOW TO SAY IT

*Achaia.* Uh-KAY-uh.

*Aphrodite.* Aff-roe-DYE-tee.

*Apollos.* Uh-PAHL-us.

*Aquila.* ACK-will-uh.

*Berea.* Buh-REE-uh.

*Cenchrea.* SEN-kree-uh.

*Chrestus.* CREST-us.

*Claudius.* CLAW-dee-us.

*Ephesus.* EFF-uh-sus.

*Gallio.* GAL-lee-owe.

*Macedonia.* Mass-uh-DOE-
   nee-uh.

*Nazirite.* NAZ-uh-rite.

*Philippi.* Fuh-LIP-pie
   or FIL-uh-pie.

*Priscilla.* Prih-SILL-uh.

*Septuagint.* Sep-TOO-ih-jent.

*Suetonius.* Soo-TOE-nee-us.

*Thessalonica.* THESS-uh-low-
   NYE-kuh.

## WHAT DO YOU THINK?

*When Priscilla and Aquila hear Apollos preaching and realized his doctrine was deficient, they took him aside privately and talked to him kindly. They did not confront him or embarrass him, but they also did not ignore his error. How can we follow their example when we disagree with a neighbor or family member about what the Bible says? How should we respond if a teacher or preacher in our church is in error?*

*Are there some "mistakes" you would not bother to correct? Why or why not?*

*Suppose the situation was reversed. What if Apollos had heard Aquila preach and had mistakenly attempted to point out his error? How should Aquila have handled that? How should we respond if we are challenged for teaching what we know is true?*

The second matter is the vow itself. The Nazirite vow was a vow of separation, and it involved letting one's hair grow until the time specified in the vow was over. (Samson was a Nazirite for life, so his hair was never to be cut.) Ordinarily, the hair was to be cut in the temple at the end of the period of separation and offered on the altar along with a burnt offering. Jewish custom had by this time allowed the hair to be cut elsewhere, but it had to be offered on the altar in Jerusalem within thirty days. If this is the vow Paul had taken, it would explain his urgency to leave (verse 21), assuming he was on his way to Jerusalem. (Some manuscripts include a note in verse 21 that Paul hoped to be in Jerusalem for an upcoming feast.) Acts 18:22 says Paul "went up and greeted the church." The expression "went up" is frequently used in reference to Jerusalem, so it is assumed by most that Paul went there before returning to Antioch.

Others suggest the vow was not the Nazirite vow but one similar to it. In that case, a trip to Jerusalem would be unnecessary. The church Paul "went up" to greet in verse 22 may simply have been the one at Caesarea, the harbor city at which he had landed. Luke does say at the outset that Paul "sailed for Syria" (Acts 18:16) and not Judea. Still, he stopped in Ephesus (verse 19) on that same trip; a stop in Jerusalem would not change the fact that his ultimate destination was Antioch of Syria.

**19. They arrived at Ephesus, where Paul left Priscilla and Aquila. He himself went into the synagogue and reasoned with the Jews.**

Always prepared to seize new opportunities for service, Priscilla and Aquila began a ministry in *Ephesus*, the most important city of the province of Asia (located in what is today western Turkey). This commercial city was dominated by the worship of the goddess Diana (Artemis was her Greek name), and proudly displayed a temple to her, which was considered one of the seven wonders of the ancient world. The Ephesians adored Diana; evangelizing this city would not be easy.

The word *left* suggests that Paul had plans for Priscilla and Aquila in Ephesus. He was going on to Antioch, but he left them in Ephesus to prepare for his return. But before he left, he did some groundbreaking. In his usual manner, he first made contact with the *Jews* in the *synagogue*. Priscilla and Aquila proceeded to use their home to further the gospel, as 1 Corinthians 16:19 shows.

### B. INSTRUCTING APOLLOS (vv. 24-26)

**24. Meanwhile a Jew named Apollos, a native of Alexandria, came to Ephesus. He was a learned man, with a thorough knowledge of the Scriptures.**

Paul had already left *Ephesus* when *Apollos* arrived. He was from *Alexandria*, the capital city of Egypt, and may have traveled to Ephesus for business purposes. Alexandria was a city that placed a strong emphasis on learning, so we are not surprised that Apollos was *a learned man*. One should keep in mind that Alexandria was also the city in which the Greek translation of the Old Testament (called the Septuagint) was made. This may have contributed to Apollos's familiarity with the *Scriptures*.

**25. He had been instructed in the way of the Lord, and he spoke with great fervor and taught about Jesus accurately, though he knew only the baptism of John.**

Not only did Apollos have training in the Old Testament Scriptures, but he had also been taught certain truths of the gospel. He knew *the way of the Lord*, and he could teach many of the truths that *Jesus* had spoken. But his knowledge was imperfect. Like the disciples Paul would later meet (Acts 19:1-7), he did not know about *baptism* into the Lord Jesus or about the gift of the Holy Spirit (Acts 2:38). Nevertheless, Apollos was devoted to proclaiming *the things of the Lord*. If only his grasp of God's plan of salvation could be improved, his presence in Ephesus would be of great value in advancing the gospel.

**26. He began to speak boldly in the synagogue. When Priscilla and Aquila heard him, they invited him to their home and explained to him the way of God more adequately.**

Soon after Apollos arrived at Ephesus, *Priscilla and Aquila heard him* speaking in the *synagogue*. They immediately saw the potential in him. They took him aside privately, inviting him *to their home*. This approach would protect the dignity of this promising preacher of the gospel.

The remarkable sensitivity of Aquila and Priscilla in handling this matter with Apollos is an example that modern Christians should not overlook. Unfortunately, some today react to any type of doctrinal difference with an attitude of hostility toward the person who espouses the other viewpoint. To consider speaking with someone who may hold a different teaching is taken as compromise. Speaking *about* the doctrinal position of others is much more convenient than actually speaking *to* those who hold that position. In refusing to address such individuals directly, we may be missing the opportunity to mold another Apollos—a preacher with powerful skills for advancing the cause every believer holds dear.

Aquila and Priscilla focused on the potential of Apollos, rather than on his inadequate doctrinal views. They arranged for a meeting that would produce the best results. They carried out their mission in such a way that Apollos, far from being offended, was convinced of the truth of what they presented. Later he traveled to Corinth and became a powerful influence for Christ in that city (Acts 18:27, 28).

In this way, the providential work of God came full circle. Paul instructed Aquila and Priscilla at Corinth, they instructed Apollos at Ephesus, and then Apollos went to Corinth to "water" where Paul had planted (1 Corinthians 3:6).

## III. MINISTERING IN ROME (ROMANS 16:3-5a)

When Paul returned to Ephesus from Syria (during his third missionary journey), he spent more time there (three years) than in any of the other cities that Acts says he visited (Acts 20:17, 31). Aquila and Priscilla worked by his side through many dangerous circumstances during these years.

At some point Aquila and Priscilla returned to Rome, probably after the death of Claudius (the emperor who had expelled the Jews from Rome) in A.D. 54. Perhaps once again Paul had asked them to do some preliminary work, as he hoped to visit Rome in the near future. When he wrote to the Romans, he sent greetings to his faithful friends.

### A. RISKING THEIR NECKS (vv. 3, 4)

**3. Greet Priscilla and Aquila, my fellow workers in Christ Jesus.**

Romans 16 concludes a letter that Paul wrote to a church he had never visited. By the time of its writing, he was ministering in Corinth once again. Coming to Rome, however, was something he earnestly hoped to do after a visit to Jerusalem (Acts 19:21; Romans 1:8-17; 15:23-32).

In bringing the letter to the Romans to a close, Paul's mind turned to familiar faces of believers he had met in other cities of the Roman empire. Some twenty-six names are included in this list of greetings. Near the top of the list are the names of *Priscilla and Aquila*.

**4. They risked their lives for me. Not only I but all the churches of the Gentiles are grateful to them.**

Perhaps Paul was recalling incidents such as the riot in Ephesus (Acts 19:23-41), which had jeopardized the whole missionary team.

*DAILY BIBLE READINGS*

**Monday, Feb. 10**—*Priscilla and Aquila Host a Church (1 Corinthians 16:15-24)*

**Tuesday, Feb. 11**—*Priscilla and Aquila Support Paul's Teachings (Acts 18:1-11)*

**Wednesday, Feb. 12**—*Each Person Has a Special Duty (1 Corinthians 3:5-9)*

**Thursday, Feb. 13**—*Support Others' Christian Work (Romans 12:1-8)*

**Friday, Feb. 14**—*Share Christian Life-styles (Romans 12:9-21)*

**Saturday, Feb. 15**—*Fulfill the Law of Love (Romans 13:8-14)*

**Sunday, Feb. 16**—*Respect Your Leaders (1 Thessalonians 5:12-22)*

*WHAT DO YOU THINK?*

The churches of the Gentiles would owe Priscilla and Aquila much if by risking their lives for Paul they had saved his. Beyond that, Paul seems to say their own labors for the church were something for which the Gentiles were grateful.

Who are some people we could say that about in our church? Cite some of their contributions to the life and ministry of our congregation. How can we get more people involved to such a degree?

*OPTION*

This is not a question people will likely want to answer aloud, but suggest your students spend some time reflecting on it: Would Paul cite your name as someone to whom the church should be grateful? How noticeable would your absence be if you moved away from our area?

*All the churches of the Gentiles* owed a great debt to this couple. Aquila was first introduced as a Jew (Acts 18:2), but he and his wife had caught the vision of the Great Commission—that the gospel was for all people. Their labors, like Paul's, had been mostly among Gentiles.

## B. HOSTING A CHURCH (v. 5a)

**5a. Greet also the church that meets at their house.**

Here we see another illustration of Priscilla and Aquila's intense commitment to spreading the gospel and building the *church*. Once again they had opened *their house* to the believers to use for a meeting place.

### MOVERS AND SHAKERS

Contemporary society is characterized by mobility. People move much more frequently than in former years. Often church directories become outdated even before they are distributed. Those in the business world who want to be "upwardly mobile" usually must be geographically mobile as well. A sad sequel to this story is that many Christian "movers" do not continue to be Christian "shakers."

Aquila and Priscilla led a rather nomadic life, moving from Rome to Corinth, then to Ephesus, and finally back to Rome. Through it all, the biblical record reveals that they maintained their faith, their witness, and their service. Their support of Paul, their efforts in teaching Apollos, and their ministry in Rome all testify to their consistent commitment to Christ.

When Christians move, their first priority should be finding, or beginning, a fellowship of believers with whom to worship and serve. We are promised that if we give the kingdom of God priority, all other necessities will be supplied (Matthew 6:33). If we are to be the "salt of the earth," we must be "shakers" as well as "movers." —R. W. B.

## CONCLUSION

### A. SERVICE AND STEWARDSHIP

Priscilla and Aquila found in their business and in the use of their home opportunities to participate in the proclamation of the gospel. They used their business to support the spread of the gospel. They used their home to support and encourage devoted workers in the kingdom. What they had was the Lord's, and they would use it for him.

In many cases, our homes have become entertainment centers in which we have invested thousands of dollars in equipment and resources. If our homes are considered a gift from the Lord, then using them for his service will be a natural result.

### B. COOPERATION AND COMMUNICATION

The sensitivity that Aquila and Priscilla demonstrated in their counseling of Apollos shows modern believers that doctrinal differences can be handled in a positive manner, without having to resort to mutual accusations. Because the issue of baptism could not be ignored, Aquila and Priscilla knew that action had to be taken. Their handling of the matter shows their maturity and their ability to see the larger good of the kingdom.

### C. COURAGE AND HOSPITALITY

Priscilla and Aquila also made hospitality a cornerstone of their faith. At a time when opening their home to Christians was not only inconvenient but also dangerous, they repeatedly placed themselves in the position of hosts. Not only their home, but their lives were at the Lord's disposal. They "risked their lives" for Paul and the gospel. What have we risked for the sake of the kingdom?

# Discovery Learning

*This page contains an alternate lesson plan emphasizing learning activities. Classes desiring such student involvement will find these suggestions helpful. The next page is a reproducible activity page to further enhance discovery learning.*

## LEARNING GOALS

In today's class session, students should:

1. List some of the contributions of Priscilla and Aquila to the cause of Christ.

2. Identify the attitude that seems to have motivated their service.

3. State some ways Christians today can imitate the faithfulness of Priscilla and Aquila.

## INTO THE LESSON

As students arrive, give each a piece of paper on which is written, "The worst thing about moving is. . . ." Ask the students to think about how they would complete that sentence. They may discuss the idea with others as more people come to class, or you may have them think about it individually.

Call the class to order and ask for some answers. List the responses on the chalkboard or on a poster so everyone can see them. You should get answers like "Finding a new doctor," "Getting the kids enrolled in a new school," "Packing," "Unpacking," "Finding a good church." If no one mentions church, bring up the subject yourself. Discuss the problems of finding a church: doctrine, location, programming, worship styles, and other things you might consider. Ask, "What if you moved to a city that had no church at all?" After a brief discussion, point out that the New Testament characters you will be studying today faced that challenge.

## INTO THE WORD

Position three posters around the room, one labeled Corinth, one Ephesus, and one Rome. Ask the students to form three groups, one near each poster. Have a good reader from the Corinth group to read Acts 18:1-11 aloud. Someone from the Ephesus group should then read Acts 18:18, 19, 24-26 aloud. Finally, ask a reader from the Rome group to read Romans 16:3-5 aloud. Ask each group to write on its poster the contributions of Priscilla and Aquila to the church in that city. Assist each group with background information from the commentary section of this book or from other research as needed.

## CORINTH

Giving Paul a place to work and support his preaching in Corinth is all that is mentioned, so that, we must assume, was their major contribution. Another Christian,

Justus, provided a place for the church to meet (18:7). We can be sure that this couple was also active in the life of the church since Paul wanted them to come with him to Ephesus (18:18, 19).

Corinth may be where the couple was converted. If it was, their conversion was dramatic, as their whole lives were obviously dedicated to the Lord from this point on.

## EPHESUS

Helping to establish the church there is certainly notable, and must have been the reason Paul left them there. But the greater work may have been their teaching of Apollos, who would go on to touch many more lives than they could probably have imagined. This is what Scripture specifically mentions of their work, so it cannot be discounted. Who knows what far-reaching influence we may have today when we touch the life of even one individual for Christ?

## ROME

Paul says a church met in their home, and that is all we know for sure about their role. This, of course, became more and more risky as time went on. Within six years of the writing of this letter, Rome would be burned and the Christians blamed. Those who stood out as Christian leaders would be especially vulnerable to retribution. If Priscilla and Aquila had risked their lives before, they may have yielded their lives to the Roman executioner after that.

## INTO LIFE

Ask the class to suggest one-word descriptions of Priscilla and Aquila. Words such as *courageous, dedicated, hospitable,* and *selfless* should be mentioned. Make a list of all the descriptions offered. Ask, "How did these qualities advance the cause of Christ in their day?" After a bit of discussion, ask, "How can our practice of the same qualities advance the cause of Christ today?"

Ask the class to form groups of three or four. Ask each group to think of one specific way we can imitate the faithfulness of Priscilla and Aquila. The group should suggest a plan of action, not just a character trait or attitude. After four or five minutes, ask for reports.

Close with a challenge for the students to act with the same faithfulness and courage for the cause of Christ as did this fine Christian couple.

# Map It Out

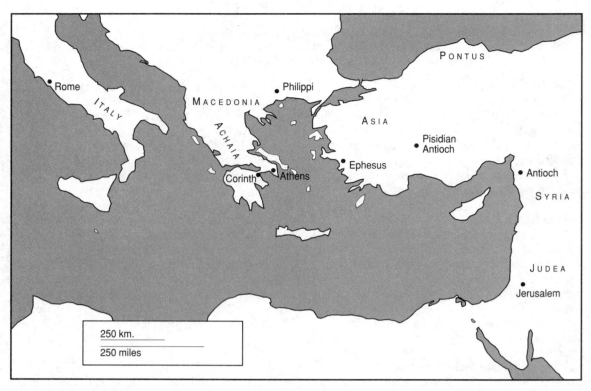

Locate the following places on the map above. Tell what you know of Priscilla and/or Aquilla's activities in each.

Pontus (Acts 18:2)


Corinth (Acts 18:1-4)


Ephesus (Acts 18:18-20; 24-26)


Rome (Acts 18:2; Romans 16:3-5)



What one act of Priscilla and Aquila seems most like something you could do to serve the Lord today? Plan how you will do that. Write your plan below.

# New Testament Personalities

### Unit 3. Persons of the New Testament Church
(Lessons 10-13)

# TIMOTHY

**LESSON 13**

## WHY TEACH THIS LESSON?

This could be a lesson for the teenagers. Its subject is hardly more than a teen himself in the first scene we will view. But he became a dynamic witness for the Lord Jesus Christ under the mentoring of the apostle Paul.

This lesson challenges young and old alike to serve the Lord with faithfulness and sincerity. The elderly Paul, nearing death in our final Scripture passage, was still serving. Young Timothy, in a variety of ways, served with and for the apostle.

Challenge your students to "fan into flame" whatever spiritual gift or ability for ministry they possess.

## INTRODUCTION

### A. THE TRUTH ABOUT YOUTH

What can we say about the younger generation? Do they seem too restless, too lazy, too frivolous, too wasteful, too superficial, too worldly? All of these charges have been made against today's youth.

The irony of this is that almost every younger generation has received the same criticism. Older Christians have expressed these concerns for years. Yet God has always raised up faithful believers to guarantee that the church would advance. Among these believers have been younger disciples such as Timothy, the subject of our final lesson in this unit and in this quarter. His example should encourage us to believe that God will raise up young people from this present generation as well, who will faithfully uphold the cause of Christ.

### B. LESSON BACKGROUND

Timothy became one of Paul's most beloved co-workers. His name means "one who honors God," and his ministry with Paul lived up to this description. The two were partners on most of Paul's second and third missionary journeys recorded in Acts.

The frequency with which Timothy is mentioned in the letters of Paul illustrates the important role he played in the apostle's life and ministry. Timothy was with Paul when he wrote the following epistles (as indicated in the opening verse of each): 2 Corinthians, Philippians, Colossians, 1 Thessalonians, 2 Thessalonians, and Philemon.

That an intimate friendship developed between Timothy and Paul is obvious from the terminology the apostle uses of his younger companion. Paul describes Timothy as his "true son in the faith" in 1 Timothy 1:2, and as his "dear son" in 2 Timothy 1:2. In Romans 16:21, Paul uses the term "fellow worker" of Timothy, and in 1 Thessalonians 3:2 he calls Timothy "our brother and God's fellow worker in spreading the gospel of Christ."

## I. TIMOTHY'S REPUTATION (ACTS 16:1-5)

Paul had visited Timothy's hometown of Lystra on his first missionary journey. No doubt it was at that time that he became acquainted with Timothy's family and that Timothy became a Christian.

DEVOTIONAL READING
1 TIMOTHY 4:6-16

LESSON SCRIPTURE
ACTS 16:1-5; 1 CORINTHIANS
4:14-17; PHILIPPIANS 2:19-24; 2
TIMOTHY 1:3-7; 3:14, 15

PRINTED TEXT
ACTS 16:1-5; 1 CORINTHIANS
4:14-17; PHILIPPIANS 2:19-22; 2
TIMOTHY 1:3-7

## LESSON AIMS

As a result of this study, a student will be able to:

1. List qualities evident in Timothy's life that are key to an active faith in the Lord.

2. Describe how such qualities can be developed today.

3. Either choose one person to encourage and help to develop such faith qualities or choose one faith quality and work on developing it to a greater degree in his or her own life.

Feb
23

## KEY VERSE

For this reason I am sending to you Timothy, my son whom I love, who is faithful in the Lord. He will remind you of my way of life in Christ Jesus, which agrees with what I teach everywhere in every church.

—1 Corinthians 4:17

## WHAT DO YOU THINK?

Every Christian has at least one gift, talent, or skill. What we are able to do for Christ depends on whatever gift, talent, or skill we possess. Some gifts equip a person for vocational service (they derive their living from their ministry). Other gifts may enable one to serve Christ and to work in the church on a volunteer basis while working in a secular vocation. Both types of gifts are necessary for the church to have an impact on its surroundings.

How can we determine whether one has gifts suited for vocational ministry or not? How much do you think young people should be challenged to choose ministry as their vocations?

## WHAT DO YOU THINK?

How can the church support a young person who believes God has called him to vocational Christian service? Should the local church seek to validate his call to the ministry by examining his life and gifts? Why or why not? Should the church support his training financially? Why or why not? If so, how much should be spent? Should the support be conditional, and if so what conditions should be imposed? Why? What other support and encouragement might be appropriate?

When Paul began to plan his second trip, he wanted to visit the churches he and Barnabas had established on the first (Acts 15:36). The dispute over whether or not to take John Mark divided the missionary team. Paul and Silas started out through Syria and Cilicia; Barnabas and John Mark sailed for Cyprus (vs. 37-41). This put Paul on a course that would lead him to his next co-worker.

### A. CREDENTIALS FOR SERVICE (vv. 1, 2)
**1. He came to Derbe and then to Lystra, where a disciple named Timothy lived, whose mother was a Jewess and a believer, but whose father was a Greek.**

*Derbe and Lystra* were located in southern Galatia (what is today south central Turkey). *Timothy*, a native of Lystra, was already a *disciple* of Jesus when Paul arrived. Timothy's mother, *a Jewess*, had married a *Greek*, or Gentile. The fact that Timothy's father is not described as a proselyte or "God-fearer" probably means that he had little personal interest in promoting the worship of the one true God—much less this recent interest of his wife and son in the Jewish "Messiah" or "Christ."

We do not know what difficulties this difference of faith caused for Timothy or his mother. Most Gentiles were polytheists—that is, they believed in many gods. Most did not object to the Jews' worship of their own God, but they found it strange that they limited themselves to only one God.

### JUMPING THE HURDLES
Children of "unequally yoked" parents generally must leap high hurdles to find and keep personal faith. Their circumstances can be confusing and inhibiting. They may love both parents, yet their parents do not serve the same Master. The believing parent (often the mother) may be a strong influence during early childhood years, but too often a child in a spiritually divided home will make no personal commitment to Christ. He sees his decision as favoring one parent or the other. The dilemma immobilizes him.

Timothy's Jewish mother and Greek father created a potentially paralyzing situation for him. But somehow, perhaps through the additional influence of a believing grandmother, Timothy survived the odds and developed not only *saving* faith, but *serving* faith as well.

Christians must take very seriously the biblical cautions against marrying unbelievers. Spiritually divided homes jeopardize marital harmony, and raise additional hurdles their offspring must jump in order to make and keep personal vows to God.
—R. W. B.

**2. The brothers at Lystra and Iconium spoke well of him.**

Timothy's reputation as a young man who was serious about his faith had spread throughout the church at *Lystra*, and even to *Iconium* some twenty miles away. Believers in these cities considered his spiritual development to be quite impressive.

### B. INVITATION FROM PAUL (vv. 3-5)
**3. Paul wanted to take him along on the journey, so he circumcised him because of the Jews who lived in that area, for they all knew that his father was a Greek.**

So interested was Paul in this promising young man that he wanted him to become a permanent member of the missionary team. But Paul usually began his evangelistic work in any city by going to the synagogue and preaching to the Jews there (Acts 17:1, 2). This posed a potential problem with *the Jews who lived in that area* who knew of Timothy's background and upbringing. They were aware of the fact that *his father was a Greek*, and that he apparently had refused to have Timothy *circumcised* as an infant. This could constitute a significant stumbling block in their minds and give them reason to oppose Paul's efforts (no doubt many of them would be quite pleased to have such grounds). In order to keep this from becoming a barrier to his evangelistic work, Paul had Timothy *circumcised* in accordance with the Old Testament regulation.

It is important to note the distinction between this situation and that involving Titus, to whom Paul refers in Galatians 2:3-5. There Paul was contending that circumcision should not be imposed on Gentiles who accepted Christ (5:6-12). Timothy was Jewish, at least in part. For that reason, and because he would be working with Jews, it was prudent for him to conform to Jewish law. Titus, on the other hand, was Gentile. There was no reason for him to be circumcised. In neither case was circumcision related to salvation.

**4. As they traveled from town to town, they delivered the decisions reached by the apostles and elders in Jerusalem for the people to obey.**

The cities visited by Paul, Silas, and their new companion included those locations visited during the first missionary journey. Within these predominantly Gentile churches, the question of whether Gentile Christians were required to be circumcised and keep the Law of Moses had arisen. This issue had been addressed by the Jerusalem conference (Acts 15:22-29). The *decisions reached by the apostles and elders* attending that conference were now *delivered* by the missionaries as they traveled. Timothy's presence, and how circumcision had been handled in his case, probably helped clarify additional questions that were raised.

**5. So the churches were strengthened in the faith and grew daily in numbers.**

Paul's choice of Timothy to accompany the missionary team and his handling of the sensitive question of circumcision contributed to the continued growth of the *churches*.

## II. TIMOTHY'S UNSELFISH SPIRIT (1 CORINTHIANS 4:14-17; PHILIPPIANS 2:19-22)

One of Paul's most critical needs was for missionary companions who would be able to travel to churches needing help with special problems. Not only did this require workers with a sterling reputation; it also required individuals with a servant's heart, who were willing to suffer inconvenience for the good of the church.

Both the Corinthian and the Philippian churches were congregations founded by Paul during his second missionary journey with the help of Timothy. Over the next few years of Paul's ministry, these churches faced severe challenges. Paul needed the help of his trusted companion to address these situations.

### A. MINISTRY TO A TROUBLED CHURCH (1 CORINTHIANS 4:14-17)

Paul wrote 1 Corinthians from Ephesus during his three-year ministry there on his third missionary journey. Serious problems had arisen in Corinth just a short time after he had left. Timothy was dispatched with the letter to address these problems.

**14. I am not writing this to shame you, but to warn you, as my dear children.**

With these words, Paul concluded the first section of his first letter to the Corinthian church. Four segments of the congregation were in conflict. (See 1 Corinthians 1:12.) The Corinthians were showing more loyalty to favorite preachers and the factions that had been built around them than they were to Jesus alone.

Although Paul's tone may have seemed sharp and severe, he did not consider the Corinthians his enemies, but his *dear children.* He wanted *to warn* them of the consequences of their divisive spirit.

**15. Even though you have ten thousand guardians in Christ, you do not have many fathers, for in Christ Jesus I became your father through the gospel.**

*HOW TO SAY IT*

Apollos. Uh-PAHL-us.
Barnabas. BAR-nuh-bus.
Cilicia. Suh-LISH-ee-uh.
Corinth. KOR-inth.
Corinthian. Koe-RIN-thee-un (th as in thin).
Derbe. DER-bee.
Ephesian. Ee-FEE-zhun.
Ephesus. EFF-uh-sus.
Eunice. YOU-niss.
Galatia. Guh-LAY-shuh.
Iconium. Eye-KOE-nee-um.
Lystra. LISS-truh.
Philemon. Fih-LEE-mun or Fie-LEE-mun.
Philippi. Fuh-LIP-pie or FIL-uh-pie.
Philippian. Fih-LIP-pee-un.
proselyte. PRAHS-uh-light.
Samaria. Suh-MEH-ree-uh.
Silas. SIGH-lus.

*WHAT DO YOU THINK?*

Paul appealed to the Corinthians on the basis of his being their "father" in the faith. What responsibility do you think we have to those who led us to faith in Christ? Why? What responsibility does one have for people whom he has led to the Lord? Should he keep in touch and continue to monitor their spiritual growth? Why or why not?

## WHAT DO YOU THINK?

*Paul sent Timothy to Corinth to help the church work through some serious problems. Do churches today have a responsibility to try to help sister churches in trouble? Why or why not? If so, how?*

*If a sister congregation was having serious problems and asked our church to send some leaders to serve as elders for a limited time, until the problems were solved, what do you think the church would do? Why? What do you think the church should do? Why?*

## WHAT DO YOU THINK?

*When calling a minister, how can a congregation be sure to get someone like Timothy, who will take a genuine interest in their welfare and not just his own? What kind of questions should be asked? What kind of background check should be made? Of course, Timothy got a good recommendation from Paul. How many recommendations should be required of a ministry candidate? From whom should these come?*

The Corinthians were choosing sides, identifying with different preachers. Paul had a message for all of them, not just the ones who said, "I follow Paul" (1 Corinthians 1:12). So he reminded them he was *father* to them all; he had introduced them to the gospel. These other teachers, whom he here calls *guardians* to contrast with the father figure he uses for himself, did not number *ten thousand*. The exaggeration heightened the urgency of his appeal to listen to him. Nor did he disparage the role of any of these guardians. It was the Corinthians who had improperly exalted these others. The teachers were co-workers in the same pursuit.

**16. Therefore I urge you to imitate me.**

If Paul was the Corinthians' "father" in the faith, this should constitute sufficient grounds for them to accept his counsel. He urged them to be *followers* of his by seeking unity among themselves and putting to rest their contentions.

**17. For this reason I am sending to you Timothy, my son whom I love, who is faithful in the Lord. He will remind you of my way of life in Christ Jesus, which agrees with what I teach everywhere in every church.**

Paul knew that *Timothy* could provide the leadership necessary to heal the divisions in the Corinthian church. Though he was sending Timothy with some reservations about how he would be received (see 1 Corinthians 16:10, 11), Paul was confident in his beloved *son*.

### B. MINISTRY FOR THE WELFARE OF OTHERS (PHILIPPIANS 2:19-22)

The book of Acts concludes with Paul living under house arrest in Rome (Acts 28:16, 30, 31). During this time, Paul was able to preach the gospel to "the whole palace guard" (Philippians 1:12, 13).

Despite the limitations that he faced during his imprisonment, Paul did his best to keep in contact with the churches. The "prison epistles" of Ephesians, Philippians, Colossians, and Philemon represent Paul's communications during this period. Timothy's name appears with Paul's in the opening verse of each of these letters except Ephesians. Paul was able to use his trusted companion to travel to places where he could not go.

The Philippian church held a special place in Paul's heart. These saints had aided him financially at some difficult moments (Philippians 4:10-19). News had come, however, that false teachers were making inroads among the believers (3:2), and that friction had developed between some prominent church members (4:2, 3). The church needed the encouragement that someone like Timothy could offer.

**19. I hope in the Lord Jesus to send Timothy to you soon, that I also may be cheered when I receive news about you.**

Paul's sense of responsibility for the welfare of the churches did not end with his imprisonment. He felt a burden for all congregations wherever he was. (See 2 Corinthians 11:28.) Timothy's journey to Philippi would give him the opportunity to learn about the current state of the believers and to return the *news* to Paul.

**20, 21. I have no one else like him, who takes a genuine interest in your welfare. For everyone looks out for his own interests, not those of Jesus Christ.**

Here Paul expressed the highest level of confidence in Timothy. This confidence was based on Timothy's unselfish character. Such a spirit was just the kind of influence the Philippians needed to solve their problems.

### GENUINE FRIENDSHIP

Dale Carnegie lists "six ways to make friends" in his classic book, *How To Win Friends and Influence People*. One of his suggestions is, "Become genuinely interested in other people." Perhaps he borrowed that principle from Philippians 2:19, 20, found in today's lesson text (many of Carnegie's concepts are biblical).

Timothy was a standout among Paul's companions and co-workers, because he took a genuine interest in the welfare of those he served. His priority was to act in the interest of Christ and all Christians. His giving was without guile; his ministry was free of ulterior motives.

If we want to win friends to Christ and influence people for God, we too must demonstrate a genuine interest in others. We must become "people persons." We must add to our faith those qualities listed in 2 Peter 1:5-7. These virtues will open many doors of opportunity, and will help us to be effective and productive in every ministry. They must, however, be real. The world already has been disillusioned by too many hypocrites.                                                —R. W. B.

**22. But you know that Timothy has proved himself, because as a son with his father he has served with me in the work of the gospel.**

Paul illustrated Timothy's qualification for service with terminology appropriate to a family business. Timothy had learned to serve with Paul much as a *son* learns the family business while his *father* supervises him. Timothy had submitted himself in such a way that he could faithfully carry out the wishes of the apostle.

If great things are to be accomplished in the church today, then believers will need to imitate the unselfishness of Timothy. This means that believers will not be concerned with getting due recognition or proper rewards for their efforts. Through such a spirit, unity in the church will be preserved, and the gospel will never be hampered by embarrassing church quarrels.

## III. TIMOTHY'S FOUNDATIONS OF FAITH (2 TIMOTHY 1:3-7)

Timothy's trademark of unselfishness was no accident. Paul's words in this portion of our text make clear that Timothy's character was formed in the early years of his life.

Paul and Timothy had been serving the Lord together for some fifteen years, sometimes side by side, sometimes in coordinated efforts in different locations. Now, Paul was a prisoner in Rome. He knew he was nearing the end of his earthly life; he was "ready to be offered" and prepared for his "departure" (2 Timothy 4:6, *King James Version*). He wrote this final letter to Timothy, hoping that his young friend would come to visit him one last time in his prison cell. His words offer a number of personal reflections on Timothy's life and service.

### A. CHILDHOOD TRAINING (vv. 3-5)
**3. I thank God, whom I serve, as my forefathers did, with a clear conscience, as night and day I constantly remember you in my prayers.**

Imprisonment may have kept Paul from staying in touch with various congregations, but it never kept him out of touch with God. Despite his surroundings, Paul's *prayers* for Timothy continued *night and day*. His reference to his *forefathers* included Abraham, Moses, and other outstanding men of faith from Israel's history. Paul recognized that his faith in Christ had its roots in their faith in the promises of God.

**4. Recalling your tears, I long to see you, so that I may be filled with joy.**

Paul's longing for Timothy sprang from the apostle's awareness that his opportunities to see his young friend were quickly vanishing. Timothy's *tears* were probably shed the last time the two had parted. Perhaps on that occasion they feared it would be their last meeting. (Compare Paul's farewell to the Ephesian elders in Acts 20:36-38).

**5. I have been reminded of your sincere faith, which first lived in your grandmother Lois and in your mother Eunice and, I am persuaded, now lives in you also.**

### WHAT DO YOU THINK?

*Paul credits the faith of Timothy's mother and grandmother for playing a key role in his developing a sincere faith. How seriously do you think Christian parents today think about their role in passing on their faith to their children? Why? How can the church assist and encourage parents in rearing faithful kids?*

*Eunice's role in passing on the faith to Timothy was complicated by the fact that her husband was not a believer. What special challenges does having unbelieving spouses present to Christian parents? What can the church do especially for them?*

*Use the visual for lesson 13 in the visuals packet to highlight Paul's challenge to Timothy in 2 Timothy 1:7.*

"God hath not given us the spirit of fear; but of power, and of love, and of a sound mind."

## WHAT DO YOU THINK?

*"God did not give us a spirit of timidity, but a spirit of power, of love and of self-discipline." What causes timidity for Christians today? What kind of duties are we often timid about performing? Why? How can we better follow the leading of the "spirit of power, of love and of self-discipline"?*

## PRAYER

*Father, how thankful we are for those who cared enough for us to assist and encourage us in our spiritual growth! Help us to make a difference in the life of another, as Paul did in the life of young Timothy. In Jesus' name, amen.*

## THOUGHT TO REMEMBER

Good vision includes the ability to see what another believer can be.

## DAILY BIBLE READINGS

*Monday, Feb. 17—Timothy's Work in Corinth (1 Corinthians 16:5-11)*

*Tuesday, Feb. 18—Timothy to Teach Sound Doctrine (1 Timothy 1:3-11)*

*Wednesday, Feb. 19—Speak Out for the Lord (2 Timothy 1: 8-14)*

*Thursday, Feb. 20—Be Strong for the Lord (Ephesians 6:10-20)*

*Friday, Feb. 21—Be True to God's Call (1 Corinthians 1: 26-31)*

*Saturday, Feb. 22—Timothy's Mission (2 Timothy 4:1-5)*

*Sunday, Feb. 23—Defend the Faith (2 Timothy 3:10-17)*

Paul proceeded to reflect on Timothy's roots in the faith. *Lois* (his *grandmother*) and *Eunice* (his *mother*) were given credit for implanting within Timothy the knowledge of the truth that led him to his faith in Christ. This knowledge began with instruction in the Old Testament Scriptures (2 Timothy 3:15). It was solidified by the *unfeigned,* or sincere, *faith* of Lois and Eunice themselves.

### B. USING A SPIRITUAL GIFT (vv. 6, 7)

**6. For this reason I remind you to fan into flame the gift of God, which is in you through the laying on of my hands.**

Paul reminded Timothy to use the *gift* he had been given by *God.* This was probably a spiritual gift passed on to Timothy by Paul's *laying* his *hands* on him. (See the example of the disciples in Samaria in Acts 8:17 and in Ephesus in Acts 19:6.) The use and fruitfulness of such gifts depended on the eagerness of the believer. Timothy had to stir up the coals of this gift so that it might be useful in his ministry.

**7. For God did not give us a spirit of timidity, but a spirit of power, of love and of self-discipline.**

As a young man, Timothy surely drew strength from the older apostle. With Paul's death imminent, Timothy would have to find that strength on his own. But it wasn't his own, it was the *spirit of power* supplied by *God* himself. Paul's words to Timothy have much to offer today's believer, who often finds himself encountering intimidating situations. Believers have nothing to fear when God's *power* and *love* energize them, whatever the trial or difficulty.

## CONCLUSION

### A. UNSELFISH LEADERSHIP

Timothy's example speaks volumes concerning the qualities needed for effective spiritual service. His unselfish concern for the welfare of other believers set him apart in the church. Skill, creativity, and intelligence are all important ingredients for leaders in the church, but nothing is as crucial as the kind of mature Christian temperament possessed by Timothy.

Leaders who hope to build the church on a lasting foundation will turn their attention to the spiritual qualities exhibited by Timothy. Such a leader will build with materials that will stand the test of public scrutiny and of God's judgment as well.

### B. BRIDGING THE GAP

Frequently people of the older generation question whether they can relate to youth or help them become mature Christians. Paul's acceptance of Timothy and his constant encouragement of this young soldier for Christ point out how older church members can make a difference in the lives of younger followers of Jesus. In many cases, we who are more experienced in the faith cannot know the influence we might have when we put our effort into building the youth. They will not be the "church of tomorrow" unless we teach them the faith today.

### C. DEVELOPING LEADERS AT HOME

Just as Timothy's upbringing equipped him to become an exceptional minister of the gospel, so the homes of young people today can provide the motivation that enables them to answer the call of God. Parents should never underestimate the role they play in lighting the spark of spiritual interest in young people. This mission can be accomplished in spite of conditions at home, which may be less than perfect.

May God give us the foresight to see every young person as a potential leader who could one day be used by God.

# Discovery Learning

*This page contains an alternate lesson plan emphasizing learning activities. Classes desiring such student involvement will find these suggestions helpful. The next page is a reproducible activity page to further enhance discovery learning.*

## LEARNING GOALS

As a result of this study, a student will be able to:

1. List qualities evident in Timothy's life that are key to an active faith in the Lord.

2. Describe how such qualities can be developed today.

3. Choose one person to encourage and help to develop such faith qualities, or choose one faith quality and work on developing it to a greater degree in his or her own life.

## INTO THE LESSON

Write the word *FAITH* vertically on the chalkboard or on a large poster. Divide the class into two to four groups. (Each group should have at least four members. Large groups are okay.) Ask each group to suggest a word or phrase that begins with each letter of the word *faith*. Each word should describe a quality that is key to an active faith in the Lord. Listed below are some possibilities.

**F:** fervent
**A:** alert to possibilities
**I:** independent
**T:** trustworthy
**H:** holy

Allow about five minutes; then ask for a report from each group. Having more than one group should give you some variety so that you have several qualities listed.

Once all the ideas have been posted, ask the class how such qualities can be developed. What role does the Christian home play? How about the church? How important are individual Christian leaders, and how do such individuals become significant in a person's life? How important is it to begin this process in one's youth? (These questions are listed on page 226 under the heading "Developing Faith"; copy and distribute the page if you wish.)

These are weighty questions, and you will be tempted to take a long time discussing them. Try to move quickly and just get the issues stated. Encourage the class to think about these questions as you move into the Bible study.

## INTO THE WORD

Divide the class into three, six, or nine small groups of not more than four members each. (If your class is very large, add more groups in multiples of three.) Each group will be given a Scripture text and asked to (1) describe the faith of Timothy, (2) list factors suggested by the text that helped Timothy to develop such faith, and (3) tell how he exhibited his faith in ministry.

Instruct each group to appoint a reader, a recorder, and a reporter. The reader will read the Scriptures aloud. The recorder will take notes on the group's discussion of the Scripture and questions. The reporter will summarize the group's discussion when called on by the teacher.

Assign the groups these Scriptures: Group One, Acts 16:1-5; Group Two, 1 Corinthians 4:14-17; Philippians 2:19-22; Group Three, 2 Timothy 1:3-7.

Allow twelve to fifteen minutes for this activity. Provide help from the commentary section of this book, or from other references, as needed. At the end of the time allowed, ask for brief reports from the groups. (Groups with duplicate assignments should report only information that was not included in the reports already given.)

Now return to the questions raised earlier ("Developing Faith" on the next page). Encourage class members to draw on their small-group discussions to provide insight as you discuss these issues.

## INTO LIFE

The need for developing an active ministering faith makes two demands on each of us. First, it demands that our own faith be developed to the highest level it can, and demonstrated in a life of service for the Lord. Second, it demands we look for ways to develop faith in others, such as our children, other young people around us, or other adults who are perhaps newer to the faith than we.

Distribute index cards to the class. Mention that you cannot know what is the greatest need in each of the students' lives right now. They will have to examine that for themselves. Ask for a time of quiet prayer, in which each student will pray about his or her greatest need regarding developing faith. What quality that is seen in Timothy's life is absent from the student's life and needs to be developed? Is there some young "Timothy" that the student could mentor and lead to a greater level of faith and service? Ask each member of the class to write one of the following on his or her index card.

(1) One quality of Timothy's life and faith that needs to be developed more fully in the student's life.

(2) The name of a person whom the student can influence and help to develop a more active, ministering faith.

*Option:* Use the second activity, "Positive Faith Influences," for application.

# Developing Faith

Helping others to develop an active, ministering faith is crucial to the ministry of the church into the next generation.

What role does the Christian home play in that?

What role does the church play?

How important are individual Christian leaders to developing faith in a person?

How do such individuals become significant in a person's life?

How important is it to begin this process in one's youth?

# Positive Faith Influences

In a recent *Effective Christian Education* study young people were asked to choose the top five positive influences on their faith. Here are their top ten choices, ranked in order of perceived influence.

| | | | |
|---|---|---|---|
| My mother | 73% | My father | 53% |
| My pastor | 45% | My youth group | 37% |
| My Sunday school | 28% | My friends | 27% |
| A youth group leader | 24% | Retreats | 23% |
| Church camp | 23% | A grandparent | 23% |

The study found the three following elements have the greatest influence on young people's faith maturity:
• talking about faith.
• participating in devotions, prayer, or Bible reading.
• being involved in service projects.

1. Which of these do you need to make a more regular part of your own experience?

2. Name one other person you can work with to help that person develop a greater faith. (One practice that many find helpful is meeting regularly with one other Christian to help each other develop a greater faith. Perhaps the person you name will be one with whom you could share such a relationship.)

3. How can you and this other person begin?

# Spring Quarter, 1997

## Theme: Hope for the Future

### Special Features

### Lessons

#### Unit 1. Stand Fast in the Lord

#### Unit 2. Letters to Churches

#### Unit 3. A Message of Hope

## ABOUT THESE LESSONS

The lessons for the Spring Quarter challenge Christians to acknowledge God's control of the future and their need to prepare for that future by living faithfully for him in the present. The Scripture texts are taken from Paul's two letters to the Thessalonians and from the book of Revelation. They remind us that the second coming of Jesus is a doctrine that should thrill, motivate, and encourage Christians to live each day in anticipation of the day!

Mar 2

Mar 9

Mar 16

Mar 23

Mar 30

Apr 6

Apr 13

Apr 20

Apr 27

May 4

May 11

May 18

May 25

# A Season and a Reason for Hope

*by Edwin V. Hayden*

Spring is an appropriate season for a lesson series entitled, "Hope for the Future." For those who have had to endure a long, cold winter, the warmth and beauty of springtime have been anticipated with great hope. More important, however, spring carries both the promise and the provisions of fruitful harvests yet to come. The blossoms of springtime are the beginnings of the fruit to be harvested during summer. The spring sun that soothes winter-stiffened joints also warms the soil, preparing it to receive the seed that will one day supply a variety of grains and vegetables. This bounty will sustain us through another winter season, until spring again arrives to pave the way for another harvest.

## BEYOND WHAT IS SEEN

Hope looks beyond the range of present vision, for "hope that is seen is no hope at all. Who hopes for what he already has? But if we hope for what we do not yet have, we wait for it patiently" (Romans 8:24, 25). Patient waiting distinguishes the confidence of Christian hope from the vague wishfulness that is commonly called hope but may be nothing more than postponed frustration. Hope's value depends on *what* one hopes for and *why* he hopes for it. James compares this attitude with a farmer's patient expectation of the "autumn and spring rains" that will aid in producing his crops, thus providing a living for himself and his family (James 5:7). Paul makes such patience a matter of thanksgiving in his prayers for the Christians in Thessalonica: "We continually remember before our God and Father your work produced by faith, your labor prompted by love, and your endurance [patience] inspired by hope in our Lord Jesus Christ" (1 Thessalonians 1:3).

Hope—the expectation of future and unseen benefits—is strong motivation. The motivation may lie in the *certainty* of the coming good, as in the assurance of tomorrow's sunrise or next week's paycheck. Equally strong may be the *value* of the expected benefit, though the fulfillment is somewhat less certain. Thus we invest our lives and possessions in the upbringing and education of our children, expecting them to "turn out well" and prove to be the best of all investments.

Then there is the lottery, which entraps millions of victims with the lure of great wealth, although the basis of expectation is virtually nonexistent. The "hope" lies solely in the size of the bait. Let us consider, in contrast, the Christian's hope—as sure as the reality of God and as vast as the treasures of Heaven.

## MANY ARE HOPELESS

Tragically, much of the modern world lives in a state of hopelessness. Many act as though life carried the inscription found above the gates of Dante's *Inferno*: "Abandon hope, all ye who enter here." Increasing numbers of young people, who can find no purpose in life and see no relief from its meaninglessness, are committing suicide. Many others are throwing their lives away in small pieces.

If there is no God, no resurrection, and no life beyond the physical and the material, what real hope is there? For even those with aspirations to leave the world a better place for their having lived here, what ultimate hope exists? Many geologists agree with Scripture in the conviction that the material world is headed (some believe very slowly) to ultimate disintegration. Perhaps, then, we can improve the conditions of people while the world lasts. But what is the ultimate value of that, if those people have nothing beyond material existence? Hear the triumphant cry of Paul at the conclusion of his seemingly "hopeless" imprisonment: "The time has come for my departure. I have fought the good fight, I have finished the race, I have kept the faith. Now there is in store for me the crown of righteousness, which the Lord, the righteous Judge, will award to me on that day—and not only to me, but also to all who have longed for his appearing" (2 Timothy 4:6-8).

## FAITH AND HOPE

Hope depends on faith, and both rest ultimately in God and what he has revealed through his Son. Since God "raised him from the dead," writes Peter, "your faith and hope are in God" (1 Peter 1:21). John Ruskin, the nineteenth-century essayist and reformer, referred to hope as the child of faith and as the most distinctive Christian virtue. In fact, he said, hope is a proof that faith exists. He went on to say that faith makes the *present* visible, but hope makes the *future* visible. Faith *inspects,* but hope *expects.* Faith looks *at,* but hope looks *up.* Faith *sees,* and hope *foresees.* Faith *realizes,* but hope *idealizes.* Faith is quiet in *possession,* but hope trembles with *expectation.* Faith *holds on* to what *is,* but hope *leaps out* to what *shall be.* Faith is a *conviction;* hope is a *dream* of the very highest kind.

This dream, based on the works and the words of Almighty God, focuses on life beyond death—specifically on resurrection from the dead and eternal life with God in Heaven. Glad anticipation of that reality is the essence of Christian hope.

The circumstances during which much of the New Testament was written were extremely perilous for Christians. Our lessons for this quarter, dealing with the theme of "Hope for the Future," come from the writings of Paul to the Thessalonians and from the visions delivered to John that are found in the book of Revelation. The Thessalonian letters are among the earliest of the New Testament writings, while Revelation may well have been the last of the New Testament books written. Yet both Paul and John were emboldened by the same hope, and attempted to empower their readers with that hope. Of course, those readers include us.

## IMPLEMENTING HOPE

The five lessons in March speak of Jesus as the basis of our hope, and they point the way toward building a life of hope securely on him. All of the lesson texts in this unit are taken from Paul's letters to the Thessalonians. These Scriptures reflect the Thessalonians' need for additional instruction concerning the second coming of Christ so that they could live in proper preparation for that day.

**Lesson 1. "Proclaim the Gospel."** The proclamation of Christ requires conviction, character, and caring on the part of the proclaimers. Paul and his partners demonstrated these qualities as they established the church in Thessalonica.

**Lesson 2. "Live in Love and Holiness."** If the hearers of the gospel are to realize their hope in Christ and convey that hope to others, they must reflect the Christian character and love that the Lord commanded and the apostles demonstrated.

**Lesson 3. "Pray for Others."** The believer's hope in Christ sustains him through difficulties, including persecutions. Members of God's family are to pray for one another so that their faith may be adequate for such testings.

**Lesson 4. "Do What Is Right."** The Christian's hope of Heaven does not exempt him from the responsibility to be a good and productive citizen on earth. If anything, his commitment to Christ gives him a greater capacity to live as such a citizen. It also lays on him a greater responsibility to honor his Lord by representing him well.

**Lesson 5. "The Resurrection Hope."** Our Easter lesson focuses on the basis of our hope in Jesus himself, and on the promise of resurrection to all who believe

MARCH

and follow him. Jesus' resurrection is recounted from Matthew's Gospel; the promise of the saints' resurrection at Jesus' return comes from 1 Thessalonians 4:13-18.

## ASSURANCE TO THE FAITHFUL

Our April lessons, "Letters to Churches," revolve around the Lord's promise, "Be faithful, even to the point of death, and I will give you the crown of life" (Revelation 2:10). They are taken from five of the seven letters to churches, which John was commanded to write from his exile on the island of Patmos.

*APRIL*

**Lesson 6. "Commanded to Write."** John's vision of the glorified Christ includes Jesus' command for him to write letters as dictated to "the seven churches in the province of Asia" (Revelation 1:4).

**Lesson 7. "To Smyrna and Pergamum."** The church at Smyrna was spiritually rich, though materially poor. The congregation at Pergamum was a more affluent church, endangered by false teaching. To both groups of saints, the Lord promises glory with him on the condition that they faithfully overcome their present difficulties.

**Lesson 8. "To Thyatira."** The rewards of victory are promised to a church seriously threatened by vicious and seductive leadership. Jesus challenges these believers to remain faithful to what they already possess in him.

**Lesson 9. "To Philadelphia and Laodicea."** A church with limited strength (Philadelphia) is promised a reward for its faithfulness, while a proud and self-satisfied church (Laodicea) is rebuked, warned, and tenderly invited to repent.

## VISIONS OF HEAVEN

Our lessons for May develop "A Message of Hope," using passages from the book of Revelation that depict the Lamb of God in all his glory, and the city of God in all its unparalleled magnificence.

*MAY*

**Lesson 10. "The Redeeming Lamb."** Jesus Christ, glorified after his sacrificial death, is found to be the only One worthy to receive and open the sealed record of divine mysteries.

**Lesson 11. "Provision for the Redeemed."** Protection from the "wrath of the Lamb" (Revelation 6:16) is provided for multitudes who have come faithfully through great tribulation, having washed their robes white in the blood of the Lamb.

**Lesson 12. "The Victorious Christ."** The Lamb of God is presented as a triumphant warrior, having conquered all the enemies of God, and as the judge of all the earth, meting out eternal reward and punishment according to everyone's doing.

**Lesson 13. "A New Heaven and Earth."** The Holy City, new Jerusalem, is depicted in terms of glorious and immeasurable grandeur. It is a place free from evil and all its consequences, providing tender intimacy with God forever.

May these lessons give us renewed confidence to sing Edward Mote's familiar words:

My hope is built on nothing less
Than Jesus' blood and righteousness;
I dare not trust the sweetest frame,
But wholly lean on Jesus' name.
On Christ, the solid Rock, I stand;
All other ground is sinking sand,
All other ground is sinking sand.

*Hope for the Future*
**Unit 1. Stand Fast in the Lord**
(Lessons 1-5)

Mar
2

# PROCLAIM THE GOSPEL

**LESSON 1**

DEVOTIONAL READING:
*1 THESSALONIANS 1:1-10*
LESSON SCRIPTURE:
*1 THESSALONIANS 2:1-13.*
PRINTED TEXT:
*1 THESSALONIANS 2:1-13.*

## WHY TEACH THIS LESSON?

"Image is everything!" Such is the conventional wisdom of our day. To a large extent, the expression is true. We live in an age of images. Our perception of the truth is developed from the images given us by the media and others.

Unfortunately, those images can be distorted. Many Christians have learned how painfully true that is. Those who try to make a difference in the name of the Lord are portrayed as power mongers, trying to "impose" an arbitrary set of standards on others. The more public the person is, the more bitter and personal the attacks against him or her become. And if a Christian leader should turn out to be less than he has claimed, the media seem to delight in exposing him.

Today's lesson is especially appropriate. Paul and his companions had been accused of being swindlers, trying to con the Thessalonians out of their hard-earned money. Paul's defense was his own character. His behavior spoke for itself. Encourage your students to live in such a way that their behavior and character speak in defense of the gospel.

## INTRODUCTION

### A. DEFENSE OF THE GOSPEL

The young church at Thessalonica was under attack (1 Thessalonians 1:6). Apparently its members were being ridiculed as deluded followers of crafty and deceptive foreigners who had brought ridiculous tales of a Jewish cult leader called Jesus. These so-called preachers, the scoffers alleged, had then skipped town when the pressure became too much for them. The Roman world was full of such wandering "philosophers," who were in reality swindlers. Thus, the implication, if not a flat-out accusation, was that these men had also taken considerable cash from their followers when they left.

What would happen to the cause of Christ in and around Thessalonica if such charges were left unanswered? For the sake of Christians young and mature, in Thessalonica and elsewhere, it was necessary to cite the testimony of the Thessalonian people and the integrity of Paul and his companions to establish the fact that the church in that city was not a band of deluded fools following after self-serving con men. The Christians constituted a company of substantial believers in an established gospel. They were the recipients of a priceless heritage, as seen in the behavior of those who had brought the message. "For we do not preach ourselves, but Jesus Christ as Lord, and ourselves as your servants for Jesus' sake" (2 Corinthians 4:5).

### B. A CLOSER LOOK AT THE WORK SITE

Thessalonica (modern Salonika) was a city of some two hundred thousand residents, located about one hundred miles west of Philippi in the Roman province of Macedonia. It was the capital of the province and thus a strategic center from which to spread the gospel (1 Thessalonians 1:8). Paul, Silas, and Timothy arrived there on Paul's second missionary journey after their tumultuous experience in Philippi. They had established a church in Philippi, but in the process, Paul and

LESSON AIMS

*This lesson should prepare the student to:*

*1. Name several ways in which Paul and his companions exemplified the spirit of Christ in their teaching ministry at Thessalonica.*

*2. Show how the character of a teacher affects the students' acceptance of his teaching.*

*3. Put into action a plan to improve his own influence for Christ among the people around him.*

KEY VERSE

*But with the help of our God we dared to tell you his gospel in spite of strong opposition.*
1 Thessalonians 2:2

LESSON 1 NOTES

*The visual for lesson 1 in the visuals packet is a map of the Mediterranean area, including Philippi, Thessalonica, and other cities mentioned. Have it on display as you begin the session, and refer to it as you discuss the movements of Paul and his associates from city to city.*

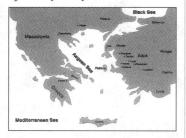

**\*NOTE**

*Earlier, Silas and Timothy had both remained at Berea (in Macedonia) when Paul went to Athens (Acts 17:14, 15). Only Timothy is mentioned with Paul in Athens (1 Thessalonians 3:1, 2), so we cannot say for certain whether Silas was with Timothy there and returned with him to Macedonia or stayed in Macedonia when Timothy went to Athens. Either way, they could both have come from Macedonia to join Paul in Corinth (Acts 18:5)*

**VISUALS FOR THESE LESSONS**

The Adult Visuals/Learning Resources *packet contains classroom-size visuals designed for use with the lessons in the Spring Quarter. Order No. 392 from your supplier.*

Silas had been arrested, flogged, and imprisoned (all unlawfully) for healing a demon-possessed girl (Acts 16:16-40).

In Thessalonica, the missionaries found a Jewish synagogue. There Paul taught on three successive Sabbaths and won some converts among the Jews and some of the Gentiles who had come to respect the Old Testament Scriptures but were not full proselytes to Judaism. At the same time he made some bitter foes among the Jews. They were especially incensed that Paul was telling the Gentiles they did not need to submit to the Jewish law. Paul's antagonists finally stirred up a mob and stormed the house of a man named Jason, with whom Paul and his companions had lodged. The Jews brought charges before the city rulers that the apostles had "caused trouble all over the world," teaching against the decrees of Caesar and promoting another king called Jesus. For the safety of all persons involved, the Christians sent Paul and Silas on to Berea, where they received a far more positive response (Acts 17:1-12).

How long were the apostles in Thessalonica? It is hard to arrive at a specific length of time, but they were there long enough to accomplish the following: (1) they established a viable church and built some lasting friendships (1 Thessalonians 1:2-4); (2) Paul established himself in a self-sustaining occupation (1 Thessalonians 2:9); and (3) Paul received financial gifts at least twice from the saints at Philippi (Philippians 4:16).

## C. LESSON BACKGROUND

Paul was deeply concerned for the welfare of the Thessalonian church and expressed that concern in making plans to visit it (1 Thessalonians 2:17, 18). When those plans did not materialize, he sent Timothy so that he could encourage the believers and then report to Paul on their condition (1 Thessalonians 3:1-8). Paul was in Athens when he dispatched Timothy on this mission (3:1, 2). Apparently Silas accompanied Timothy, because Acts 18:5 records that both Timothy and Silas rejoined Paul in Corinth, having come from Macedonia.\* Their good news concerning the Thessalonians' continued faithfulness in the face of persecution (1 Thessalonians 3:6-8) was most encouraging to Paul. The report also seems to have included bad news of the disbelieving Jews' ongoing campaign to discredit the church by slandering the apostles who had brought it into being. So Paul—joined by Silas and Timothy (1 Thessalonians 1:1)—wrote one of the earliest pieces of written material in the New Testament, to strengthen and encourage the beleaguered young church in Thessalonica. The year was apparently A.D. 52, and the place of writing was Corinth.

## I. WORKERS WITH THE WORD (1 THESSALONIANS 2:1-12)

The Thessalonian Christians were committed to Christ, in keeping with the gospel preached by Paul and his partners. To protect these saints from the slanderous attacks of Paul's opponents, the gospel had to be firmly defended and established. One way of doing this was to demonstrate that the teachers of that gospel were men of integrity, known to be speakers of truth.

### A. IN THE FACE OF OPPOSITION (vv. 1-3)
**1. You know, brothers, that our visit to you was not a failure.**

The readers were able to draw from their own experience and memory the facts that would establish confidence in their teachers and what they had been taught. Paul, Silas, and Timothy's *visit to* Thessalonica had been as a team of servants. They had come into the city investing themselves and becoming involved in the lives and experiences of the people they taught. This whole procedure had not been *a failure;* it was not a waste of time. It had resulted in the establishment of a growing and influential church in an essentially pagan city.

The phrase *was not a failure* is literally "was not empty" or "was not in vain." (See the *King James Version*.) The word for *empty* or *vain* is translated "empty-handed" in Mark 12:3, leading some Bible students to believe Paul is making a very different point here, that the missionaries did not come with hands outstretched to receive material benefits; they came bearing gifts of themselves and the gospel. The context better supports the former interpretation, however.

**2. We had previously suffered and been insulted in Philippi, as you know, but with the help of our God we dared to tell you his gospel in spite of strong opposition.**

The wounds from Paul and Silas's flogging at *Philippi* (Acts 16:22, 23) may not have been fully healed when they arrived at Thessalonica. In any case, their embarrassing treatment by the authorities in Philippi was well known (Acts 16:35-40).

Also well known in Thessalonica was the way in which Paul and his partners had plunged into their work, making themselves just as vulnerable as they had in Philippi. Their Christ-like example was most evident in their endurance of affliction. Such circumstances served to strip away any veneer of piety, so that the real substance of their faith appeared.

*With the help of our God,* with full confidence in the divine source of their message, they *dared* to preach the *gospel* without hesitation, *in spite of strong opposition* similar to what they had faced previously in other cities. The Greek term for *opposition* in this verse is *agonia,* from which we get our English word *agony.* It implies a strenuous effort or struggle. The phrase might literally be rendered, "we dared to preach . . . in much agony." Its real focus is on the efforts of the one laboring instead of the opposition, but resistance is assumed because of the struggle.

**3. For the appeal we make does not spring from error or impure motives, nor are we trying to trick you.**

This suggests the kind of charges being brought against the missionaries and their teaching. Accustomed to the kind of roaming charlatans and swindlers who victimized the Roman world (Acts 8:9; 13:6-10), Jewish opponents could easily accuse Paul and his partners of being "cut from the same cloth." Nothing could be farther from the truth.

Instead, the *appeal* (literally, urging, exhortation, or admonition) of the gospel message was to a higher way of life. It did not spring from *error.* It was not motivated by desires rooted in *impure motives.* Here the word *trick* translates a word that originally described a fisherman's method of enticing his catch. Paul and his companions did not "bait" their appeal with promises to potential converts of health, wealth, and happiness. Instead they preached Christ in plain terms, relying for success on the power of the Holy Spirit rather than the wisdom of men (1 Corinthians 2:1-5). They did not try to hide some of the harsher aspects of following Jesus, such as the fact that the believers would suffer persecution (1 Thessalonians 3:4).

## B. IN THE SIGHT OF GOD (vv. 4-6)

Here Paul outlined the basic motivation that compelled him and his companions to serve as they did.

**4. On the contrary, we speak as men approved by God to be entrusted with the gospel. We are not trying to please men but God, who tests our hearts.**

*Approved* means proved by testing. Thus, Paul and others like him were *entrusted* to deliver the *gospel* to the Gentiles, much as a bank representative is commissioned to deliver items of great value only after being subjected to close scrutiny. Paul acknowledged his commission as a solemn trust, so he spoke with a constant awareness of his accountability before *God.*

---

### WHAT DO YOU THINK?

Paul may have been able to show the Thessalonians the wounds he had received at Philippi for his faithfulness to the gospel. While we probably have no physical wounds we can attribute to people's reaction to our faith and witness, what wounds may we bear in our spirits?

Have you ever experienced rejection and ridicule because of your stand for Christ? If so, how did you respond? How would you respond now in light of this passage?

Might we sometimes confuse wounds received for Christ and those that result from efforts to protect or promote ourselves? How can we be sure we suffer for Christ and not because we provoked an assault?

### HOW TO SAY IT

*agonia.* ag-owe-NEE-uh.
*Berea.* Buh-REE-uh.
*Caesarea.* Sess-uh-REE-uh.
*Ephesus.* EFF-uh-suss.
*Macedonia.* Mass-uh-DOE-nee-uh.
*Philippi.* Fuh-LIP-pie or FILL-uh-pie.
*Salonika.* Suh-LAHN-ik-uh or Sal-uh-NEE-kuh.
*Silas.* SIGH-lus.
*Thessalonica.* THESS-uh-loe-NYE-kuh.

This did not mean that he acted without regard to the feelings of those about him. After all, "Love your neighbor" is commanded by him who claims our first devotion. In fact, Paul made clear in a letter to another church that he would go out of his way to please those to whom he preached if it would result in their salvation (1 Corinthians 9:19-23), but he would not compromise his message. That was not his to alter. He was merely an ambassador (2 Corinthians 5:20); his first duty was to be faithful to the King whom he represented. He would please God first and men only as it was consistent with that.

### WHOM ARE YOU TRYING TO PLEASE?

It is a characteristic of our age that we eagerly seek to please others. Commercially, this is obvious. When an automobile is advertised by its manufacturers, great pains are taken to show how "pleasing" it is. The seats are comfortable and adjustable, the ride is very smooth, and the brakes stop the car quickly but without grabbing. One will be happy with the many miles it will run on a gallon of gas. The appearance of the car in your driveway will make all your neighbors envious.

It is also true that many churches publicize how "user friendly" they are. They feature services at different hours to make them more convenient to attend, facilities so children (or even babies) can be cared for during worship or study periods, and ample parking close at hand. Some even advertise that one can dress informally and feel more relaxed and comfortable while in worship.

Of course, it is not necessary to stress that a church has uncomfortable seats, long, boring services, or inadequate parking space in order to show that it is not being influenced by "worldly" distractions. But we must be concerned in all our decisions that our primary motive is the desire to please *God*. We must find a way to emphasize consecration rather than comfort; God's way, not the easy way; and eternal ends instead of merely temporal means. After all, we are following the way of the cross, not the way of the cushion.     —J. G. V. B.

**5.** *You know we never used flattery, nor did we put on a mask to cover up greed— God is our witness.*

The Thessalonian Christians were fully aware that Paul was not among those who "by smooth talk and flattery . . . deceive the minds of naive people" (Romans 16:18). He was not given to *flattery,* seeking the favor of persons by extravagant praise. On the other hand, he was generous with words of real appreciation, as in the first chapter of this epistle, where he begins with the typical Pauline prayer: "We always thank God for all of you" (v. 2). He to whom the prayer was addressed knew its sincerity. He was *witness* to the fact that the apostles did not use words as a *mask* to hide greedy purposes.

**6.** *We were not looking for praise from men, not from you or anyone else. As apostles of Christ we could have been a burden to you.*

Although the term *apostle* is usually applied to one of Jesus' twelve disciples, it is used of others outside that group (see Acts 14:14) and even of Jesus (Hebrews 3:1). In such passages (as well as in the verse before us), the word carries its basic meaning of "one who is sent out."

Paul, Silas, and Timothy, working together in the apostolic task of evangelism, could have trumpeted their right to respect and honor. Paul, an "apostle" in the official sense (cf. 1 Corinthians 9:1, 2) could have demanded unquestioned obedience (2 Corinthians 10:8), but he preferred the way of self-forgetful service and gentle persuasion. The group, as "apostles" in the general sense (ones sent out), had the right to be supported, but that would have been a *burden* on the Thessalonians (1 Corinthians 9:7-14).

---

### WHAT DO YOU THINK?

*What is the difference between flattery and genuine praise? Can the same words be either, depending on other factors? If so, what factors?*

*See Romans 14:19.*

### NOTE

*Acts 1:15-26 tells of the choosing of Matthias to replace Judas as an apostle. There the qualifications for the office of apostle are given: one who was "with us . . . from John's baptism to the time when Jesus was taken up from us," and "a witness . . . of his resurrection" (vv. 21, 22). Paul said his having "seen the risen Lord" qualified him as well (1 Corinthians 9:1).*

## C. WITH LOVING CARE (vv. 7-9)

Paul had just explained how his ministry was *not* conducted; he now turned from this negative perspective to a more positive one.

**7, 8. But we were gentle among you, like a mother caring for her little children. We loved you so much that we were delighted to share with you not only the gospel of God but our lives as well, because you had become so dear to us.**

The apostles' ministry resembled a family relationship more than it did a business or form of government. The fact that a *mother* is *gentle* does not mean that her influence is substandard. She pours herself into the life of her *children* without thought of advantage to herself. She directs that life by her constant care and consistent teaching. This was the kind of self-investment practiced by the missionaries, because the people among whom they labored *had become so dear* to them.

### GENTLENESS

How many times is the soft touch the means by which change, growth, and blessing are furthered! We know that one cannot cause plants to grow by pulling them up in impatient haste. They must be gently placed in the earth, carefully nurtured, and tenderly cultivated. Sometimes a child will be given a puppy for a present and will want to maul and pinch and pummel it. This only scares and alienates the new pet. The child must be taught to pat the dog softly and be "nice" to it, not rough and harsh.

Surely in spiritual matters, Paul's example of gentleness has much to teach us. Some have used a "fire and brimstone" approach in the teaching of Christian truth. This usually includes a fierce denunciation of certain sins, a stern warning about the consequences of disobedience, and a vehement cry that all such conduct is cursed, doomed, and well-nigh unforgivable. The calm, considerate, and concerned attitude with which Jesus treated the woman caught in adultery should encourage us to show the gentleness characteristic of Paul's treatment of the Thessalonians.

Such gentleness does not imply indifference to sin, but confidence in the truth and a loving desire to encourage and build up others in a teaching situation. As Paul observed, "Speaking the truth in love, we will in all things grow up into him who is the Head, that is, Christ" (Ephesians 4:15).                        —J. G. V. B.

**9. Surely you remember, brothers, our toil and hardship; we worked night and day in order not to be a burden to anyone while we preached the gospel of God to you.**

The missionaries' self-giving included manual labor by which they supported themselves while preaching in Thessalonica, as Paul also did in Corinth (Acts 18:1-3; 1 Corinthians 9:14-19) and in Ephesus (Acts 20:34). Paul did not hold to the Greek and Roman disdain for manual labor and laborers. Instead he accepted the God-ordained respect for work and workers (Exodus 20:9; 31:1-5; Proverbs 6:6-11; 31:10-31), and he urged the same upon his converts (Ephesians 4:28). This was true especially in Thessalonica, where he cited more than once his own example and declared, "If a man will not work, he shall not eat" (2 Thessalonians 3:10).

Paul insisted that those who preach the gospel have a right to live of the gospel (1 Corinthians 9:4-14), for "the worker deserves his wages" (Luke 10:7). As for himself, however, he chose to work a double shift, *night and day,* in order to provide an example for others and to deprive his critics of any excuse for charging him or his companions with mercenary motives (1 Corinthians 9:15-19).

## D. WITH PARENTAL PATIENCE (vv. 10-12)

**10. You are witnesses, and so is God, of how holy, righteous and blameless we were among you who believed.**

### WHAT DO YOU THINK? *Note*

As an apostle, Paul could have been very authoritarian. Instead, he was gentle and compassionate. Interestingly, we often see the authoritarian approach used in cults. What are some contrasts we can note between Paul's relationship to the churches and the kind of leadership exercised in cults?

Cult leaders usually seek to dominate their followers and exercise control over their behavior. What was Paul's approach? (See 2 Corinthians 1:24).

Cult leaders engage in self-glorification. What was Paul's approach? (See Philippians 1:20).

Most cult leaders live in luxury while their followers sacrifice for them. What was Paul's approach? (See 2 Corinthians 11:23-29). *Note*

### WHAT DO YOU THINK?

Paul was determined to make clear that he was not after financial gain. In keeping with that spirit, some churches include a note in their Sunday bulletins that visitors are in no way obligated to contribute to the offering. Some people say this emphasizes that the church's ministries are supported by the faithful giving of its members. Others argue it robs visitors of the joy of giving. What do you think?

Many churches (and parachurch ministries) make monthly statements of income and expenditures available to anyone on request. How might such a statement demonstrate that the money received is being used responsibly? Can you think of any reason it would not be appropriate to publicize such information? If so, what?

Again the writers cited the testimony from their readers, who were *witnesses* in matters observable to all, and from *God,* who knew what was not evident to human eyes. The apostles' integrity and generosity were evident in their daily dealings with those about them. No fault could be reasonably charged or proved against them. They were careful to do right in the eyes of everybody (Romans 12:17; 2 Corinthians 8:20, 21). This is the course that every Christian—especially every parent, leader, and teacher—would do well to follow.

**11, 12. For you know that we dealt with each of you as a father deals with his own children, encouraging, comforting and urging you to live lives worthy of God, who calls you into his kingdom and glory.**

With motherly tenderness (v. 7), the apostles had met the immediate needs of the infant church. With the teaching, exhortation, and supportive encouragement of a *father,* they had pointed the developing church toward maturity in Christ.

## II. WORKING OF THE WORD (1 THESSALONIANS 2:13)

**13. And we also thank God continually because, when you received the word of God, which you heard from us, you accepted it not as the word of men, but as it actually is, the word of God, which is at work in you who believe.**

Paul's constant prayerful concern for his Christian friends is again evident. The epistle began with an expression of thanks for the people's response to the ministry rendered among them (1:2-10). A second cause for thanks was now introduced: their understanding and attitude toward the message itself—*the word of God.* The Thessalonians had *heard* and *accepted* the spoken word of God, telling of the living Word of God—the Lord Jesus Christ. The spoken word was respected for its divine source and *received* as something that possessed the power to *work* in those *who believe.* Thus received, it did its work in the Thessalonians, changing their lives, giving them purpose and hope, and radiating out to their neighbors, both near and far (1 Thessalonians 1:5-10).

The Word of God still works when it is presented, accepted, and followed as such, in spite of imperfections in the messengers. "We have this treasure in jars of clay," Paul said, "to show that this all-surpassing power is from God and not from us" (2 Corinthians 4:7). This is not an excuse for carelessness or irresponsibility in the Christian leader or follower. One's "jar of clay", or body, should be a tool to magnify the message, not cheapen it. The Word of God is a word of life and a word for living. In Thessalonica it was lived by both messengers and hearers.

## CONCLUSION

What did the apostle Paul accomplish by penning the passage we have just reviewed? If it was meant to protect himself from criticism and mistreatment, it failed badly. He was haled before the authorities in Corinth, mobbed in Ephesus, attacked in Jerusalem, imprisoned in Caesarea and Rome, and (if we may believe the strongest of implications) was finally executed as a criminal.

If, however, this passage was written to protect the church and the gospel, setting an example and precedent for Christian ministry in ages to come, it succeeded mightily indeed. The church at Thessalonica was strengthened to overcome its obstacles, and succeeding generations of churches have partaken of that comfort. Succeeding generations of gospel messengers also have been strengthened to overcome difficulties and to share in the ultimate victory won by Paul.

Sadly, all too many messengers have placed self-protection and self-promotion ahead of protecting the gospel and the church. May each of us be willing, like Paul and his companions, to pay any price to keep the gospel pure and untarnished.

# Discovery Learning

*This page contains an alternate lesson plan emphasizing learning activities. Classes desiring such student involvement will find these suggestions helpful. The next page is a reproducible activity page to further enhance discovery learning.*

## LEARNING GOALS

As a result of participating in today's lesson, a student will be able to:

1. Name several ways in which Paul and his companions exemplified the spirit of Christ in their teaching ministry at Thessalonica.

2. Show how the character of a teacher affects the students' acceptance of his teaching.

3. Put in action a plan to improve his own influence for Christ among those around him.

## INTO THE LESSON

Begin the class by asking students to name a preacher, teacher, or other Christian leader whom they think was or is especially effective in sharing the Word of God with others. This should be someone who had (or is still having) significant influence on their lives. Ask, "What made that person so effective?" Ask each person to share with one other person why a particular leader is significant in his or her life. Then ask volunteers to share some of the influential characteristics they heard as you write them on the chalkboard. Make the transition into the lesson by pointing out that the positive influence and example of mature Christians is absolutely necessary for the growth of individuals and the church.

## INTO THE WORD

Divide the class into several groups and ask them to read 1 Thessalonians 2:1-13. Give each group a sheet of paper and a pen or pencil. Have the group designate a reporter to take notes and to report the group's conclusions. Ask each group to write down a list of as many of the positive characteristics and qualities of Paul, Silas, and Timothy (1 Thessalonians 1:1) as they can find stated or implied in this passage. After *one minute,* stop the writing and see which group has the longest list, giving small prizes (such as a bag of candy) to the group with the most items. Answers might include: bold (v. 2), truthful and honest (vv. 3, 5), trustworthy (v. 4), focused on pleasing God (v. 4), gentle and loving (vv. 7, 8), hard-working (v. 9), holy (v. 10), righteous (v. 10), blameless (v. 10), encouraging (vv. 11, 12), and thankful (v. 13). Allowing each group to contribute, write a complete list of all their responses on a chalkboard or on poster board.

*Option:* Use the word search puzzle on the next page to introduce several positive characteristics from the text.

Now ask the class members to name some of the stated and implied characteristics in this passage that are the opposite of the ones just listed. Some answers would be: contentious (v. 2), deceitful, unclean, and tricky (v. 3), focused on pleasing men (vv. 4, 6), flattering and covetous (v. 5), and burdensome (v. 6).

Next, write the words "mother" and "father" on the chalkboard. Ask the women to suggest reasons a preacher, teacher, or church leader would be much more effective by demonstrating the positive characteristics of a "nursing mother" (vv. 7-9). Then ask the men to suggest reasons a leader would be more effective by demonstrating the positive qualities of a father (vv. 10-12). List these under the appropriate headings.

## INTO LIFE

The character of a teacher often determines whether others listen to and accept what is being taught. Ask the class to give one or two illustrations of people who have led others with "ulterior motives" or selfish ambitions. Keep it brief, and avoid any gossip or unkind words. The idea is to note that people of this type are still around. In contrast, our goal should be to influence *positively* those around us. This means that we must purposefully conduct ourselves in ways that increase our influence for Christ, avoiding any behavior that sours that influence. Ask the class to name three or four leaders who lead in this way.

Review the list of positive characteristics and qualities listed earlier. Ask each class member to identify two or three on which he or she is "doing well" and one or two on which he or she "needs work." Remind the class that accountability to others is helpful and ask each person to share his or her conclusions with another person. Give them a few minutes to do this.

Now ask the students to identify specific people with whom they have influence. This could include children, neighbors, fellow employees, and relatives, among others. Have them share this with the same person as before. Ask this final question: "What one thing will you do this week to improve your influence with the people you named?" Encourage them to be specific.

Close with prayer for God's help in becoming people who are committed to living blameless and positive lives, so that we can have the greatest possible influence for our Lord.

# Searching for a Man Like Paul

Paul shared his heart with the Thessalonians as he described the qualities he and his associates brought with them to their ministry in Thessalonica. In the heart below find fifteen qualities stated or implied in 1 Thessalonians 2 that describe Paul's attitude among those to whom he ministered. Write the words you find in the puzzle grid on the blank lines below. Next to each, write the verse number that suggests this adjective of Paul and his co-workers.

```
        E H R                  O C S
      A E A E E            B R A V E
    R G E D L A S      O C L O E T G
  T P F E R N I U P C E R I D E N U A
  R I G H T E O U S O M E N E I N O L
C R E N C O U R A G I N G A V E E T E Y
D S H D O A I S E E H R S O H A A G E X
E D T I N M H H H F E O L I F E N I O W
F L R H A R D W O R K I N G B I N S H V
  H N O W O E O K P A H R E T L S H U
  A C E A H E N H U U R O R S E E D A
  T I R E L E S S O R O L L T E H
    F A I T H F U L F E E Y V T
      G E N T L E M N M E O D
        H A O R O M A O R N
        O O C M L T P S
          O A B D P Y
          N L A E
          H I
```

_____    _____    _____

_____    _____    _____

_____    _____    _____

_____    _____    _____

_____    _____    _____

brave (v. 2), pure (v. 3), approved (v. 4), faithful (v. 4), honest (v. 4), responsible (v. 4), gentle (v. 5), loving (v. 7), hardworking (v. 9), tireless (v. 9), holy (v. 10), righteous (v. 10), blameless (v. 10), encouraging (v. 12), comforting (v. 12)

# LIVE IN LOVE AND HOLINESS

**LESSON 2**

## WHY TEACH THIS LESSON?

Last week's lesson made a strong point of the importance of purity and right-eousness in the lives of Christian leaders. This lesson makes the same point for Christian followers. Integrity is not just for leaders; purity is not just for special "saints." Each of us who has put on Christ is a saint and is called to a holy life-style.

Do not assume that everyone in your class either understands or consistently practices that. A person's presence in a church building is no guarantee of moral purity. Challenge your students to take Paul's words to heart. Someone in your class probably needs that challenge.

## INTRODUCTION

### A. CHRISTIANS IN THE WORLD

An ancient Greek writing entitled "Address to Diognetus," apparently from the third century A.D., provides a vivid description of how Christians lived and behaved among their fellowmen at that time. Here are some of its contents:

"[Christians] live in their native lands, but like foreigners. They take part in everything like citizens, and endure everything like aliens. Like everyone else they marry, they have children, but they do not expose their infants. They set a common table, but not a common bed. They find themselves in the flesh, but they do not live after the flesh . . . They obey the established laws, and in their own lives they surpass the laws. They love all men and are persecuted by all men . . . are insulted, and they do honor."

Here were people who had taken seriously the instructions of Christ and the apostles concerning love and purity!

### B. LESSON BACKGROUND

The opening of Christian gatherings with a word of prayer is more than a good habit; it is an expression of our basic faith and character. Our study today begins with a word *on* prayer from 1 Thessalonians 3.

The opening verses of 1 Thessalonians 3 record Paul's concern for his friends in Thessalonica, his sending of Timothy to encourage them (since he could not go himself), and his rejoicing at Timothy's return, with good news of their steadfast-ness. "Now we really live," he exults, "since you are standing firm in the Lord" (v. 8). With verse 9 comes the mention of specific prayer. Paul gives thanks to God for the Thessalonian Christians and for the joy they have brought him, and he contin-ues with a petition that he may revisit them and supply what is still lacking in their faith and life (vv. 10, 11).

This shift from thanks to petition, and from rejoicing in his friends' accomplish-ments to concern for their maturity in Christ, reflects an attitude that is critically im-portant in kingdom labors. Is God's messenger never satisfied and always asking for more? Yes, he is never satisfied! Pleased with the good—certainly! Satisfied with an

DEVOTIONAL READING:
1 PETER 1:13-22.

LESSON SCRIPTURE:
1 THESSALONIANS 3:6—4:12.

PRINTED TEXT:
1 THESSALONIANS 3:12—4:12.

LESSON AIMS

*After this study, the student should:*

*1. Summarize Paul's explana-tion of the importance of personal purity and of brotherly love in the Christian life.*

*2. Explain how a person may rejoice in present spiritual accom-plishments and yet still see the need for ongoing development in Christian maturity.*

*3. Set and pursue specific goals for personal purity and Christian love.*

KEY VERSE

*May the Lord make your love increase and overflow for each other and for everyone else. . . . May he strengthen your hearts so that you will be blameless and holy in the presence of our God and Father when our Lord Jesus comes with all his holy ones.*

—1 Thessalonians 3:12, 13

unchanging level in that good—certainly not! One might as well expect a proud parent to be satisfied with two-year-old behavior in a four-year-old child.

There is a difference, however, between our children on the one hand and God's children on the other. In this world we reach physical maturity and virtually quit growing. Our minds slow down, and we find learning new things to be increasingly difficult. But in Christ we never reach the end of opportunity for development, and we always have eternity to anticipate. Our text this week deals with carrying out our earthly responsibilities while looking past them to Heaven.

## I. PRAYER FOR GROWTH (1 THESSALONIANS 3:12, 13)

The apostle was thankful to hear of his friends' faithfulness to the gospel. Yet there was still room for growth.

### A. GROWTH IN LOVE (v. 12)

**12. May the Lord make your love increase and overflow for each other and for everyone else, just as ours does for you.**

Paul's prayer for the believers at Thessalonica was that their love, both among themselves and toward all other persons, should *increase and overflow.* As love was the identifying badge of Jesus' disciples (John 13:35), so the ongoing development of that love became the central element in growth toward the likeness of Christ (Ephesians 4:15). The missionaries' Christ-like devotion to the Thessalonians (*just as ours does for you*) constituted an example of the love they recommended.

#### LOVE: INCREASING AND OVERFLOWING

For centuries the Nile River has flowed north from the mountains of Africa through the desert regions of the Sahara and emptied into the Mediterranean Sea. Each year the river has overflowed its banks, depositing rich, fertile soil on its flood plain. This soil has in turn produced an abundance of crops and vegetation. Here wheat and cotton, and palm and date trees have flourished and brought prosperity to Egypt. Winding like a long green serpent across the reddish brown dullness of the desert, the Nile has made possible continued civilization for thousands of years.

Paul urged the Thessalonian Christians to allow God to make them "increase and overflow for each other." The love that God has manifested to us in Jesus is to stimulate us not only to love him in return, but to love all our brothers and sisters who are in him.

But this is not the whole story. Verse 12 adds that this love is to abound not just "for each other," but "for everyone else" as well. Thus, our love is to overflow like the Nile to refresh and renew all the lives we touch in the process. Christian living should not be constricted and directed as if being forced through a concrete sluiceway. Rather, it must be allowed to expand and to enrich art, literature, civic concerns, commerce, medicine, political life—indeed, everything we touch as Christians.

—J. G. V. B.

### B. GROWTH IN HOLINESS (v. 13)

**13. May he strengthen your hearts so that you will be blameless and holy in the presence of our God and Father when our Lord Jesus comes with all his holy ones.**

The Christian's love for others will lead toward increasing holiness. Thus, the monastic life, in which one withdraws from social contacts, is not the way to godliness. While holiness must affect our *hearts,* it must be expressed with our hands and our feet. A key to one's acceptance before Jesus will be the practical expression of love to the sick, the sorrowing, the hungry, and the homeless (Matthew 25:31-46).

---

### WHAT DO YOU THINK?

*As Christians we are not only to love one another, our love is to "increase and overflow . . . for everyone else" (1 Thessalonians 3:12). See also Galatians 6:10. What are some practical ways we demonstrate that love?*

---

The Lord make you to **increase** and abound in love one toward another, and toward **all men, even as we do** toward you: to the end he may stablish your hearts unblamable in holiness before God, even our Father, at the coming of our **Lord Jesus Christ** with all his saints.

——1 Thessalonians 3:12, 13

*The visual for lesson 2 in the visuals packet illustrates 1 Thessalonians 3:12, 13. Display it as you discuss these verses.*

The final judgment on holiness will take place *when our Lord Jesus comes* in his glory. Accompanying Jesus at his appearing will be a vast retinue of *holy ones.* Who are these "holy ones"? Mark 8:38 makes it clear that Jesus will be accompanied by his "holy angels" when he returns, so surely they are included here. (See also Matthew 13:41; 25:31; 2 Thessalonians 1:7.) Frequently, however, the word for *holy ones\** is translated "saints" (e.g., Philippians 1:1) or "holy people" (2 Thessalonians 1:10). Paul later tells the Thessalonians that "God will bring with Jesus those who have fallen asleep in him" (1 Thessalonians 4:14). Perhaps we should understand the reference to *holy ones* here to include both saints and angels.

## II. PLEA FOR PURITY (1 THESSALONIANS 4:1-8)

The apostle now began to exhort the Thessalonians concerning the subjects about which he had been praying.

### A. LIVE TO PLEASE GOD (vv. 1, 2)

**1, 2. Finally, brothers, we instructed you how to live in order to please God, as in fact you are living. Now we ask you and urge you in the Lord Jesus to do this more and more. For you know what instructions we gave you by the authority of the Lord Jesus.**

Paul gave the Thessalonians instructions on *how to live* so that they would grow spiritually, so that their lives would be pleasing to *God.* He and his partners would *ask* and *urge,* but they would not compel. Once again they pointed to their on-site teaching, by word and by example, which had dealt with the kind of everyday living that will prepare one for the day when Jesus returns.

### B. GOD COMMANDS SEXUAL PURITY (vv. 3-5)

Paul then turned his attention to a crucial element of the God-pleasing life—one that was of great concern in the first-century world and is extremely relevant to our time.

**3. It is God's will that you should be sanctified: that you should avoid sexual immorality.**

*God's will* may be seen at two levels: what he determines and what he desires. We cannot change what he *determines,* but we can thwart his *desires* for us by our own rebellious choices. God earnestly desires our sanctification—that we be set apart and steadfastly committed to him and his way. Many acts, attitudes, and principles are included under sanctification. Perhaps the most significant one is the avoidance of *sexual immorality.* One Christian educator summed up his own teaching on this matter in these words: "Purity before marriage; faithfulness in marriage."

The opposite viewpoint is captured in the Greek word, *porneia,* rendered in this verse as *sexual immorality.* The word is the basis for our term *pornography,* which depicts and promotes *porneia,* both mentally and physically. Such *porneia* was a major component of pagan religion in Corinth, the city from which Paul wrote the Thessalonian letters. He did not for a moment compromise with this immoral life-style but brought up his heaviest spiritual artillery to establish God's position on this sensitive personal matter. The Thessalonians were to *avoid sexual immorality.* This is similar to the counsel given to the Corinthians: "Flee from sexual immorality" (1 Corinthians 6:18), for it is a particularly destructive sin against the body, and it defiles the very temple of God (vv. 18-20).

### AVOID SEXUAL IMMORALITY

Solomon is revealed to us in Scripture as one of the wisest men who ever lived. The range of his understanding was remarkable. The writer of 1 Kings says of him,

---

*\*NOTE*

*Literally the word for "holy ones" is simply the adjective* holy, *but it is clearly being used as a noun here, so it is translated "holy ones."*

---

WHAT DO YOU THINK?

*Sexual immorality is rampant today. It is not only tolerated; it is glamorized and defended—and this in spite of the clear health risks. Thus, the pressure on those who would "avoid sexual immorality" can be intense.*

*What do you think is the most important thing a single Christian can do to "avoid sexual immorality"? What is the most important thing a married Christian can do?*

---

WHAT DO YOU THINK?

*While there is a growing movement toward sexual abstinence among teenagers, some influential people still suggest that it is unrealistic to expect young people to resist sexual urges. The content of most movies and television programs seems to accept this latter viewpoint, with heroes and heroines almost invariably ending up in bed together.*

*What are some effective ways the church is assisting our young people to control their bodies and resist the pressures of the media and others who encourage immorality? What more can the church do to encourage the young people in this?*

## HOW TO SAY IT

*Achaia.* Uh-KAY-uh.
*Berea.* Buh-REE-uh.
*Corinth.* KOR-inth.
*Diognetus.* Dye-ahg-NEE-tus.
*Judea.* Joo-DEE-uh.
*Macedonia.* Mass-uh-DOE-nee-uh.
*Philippi.* Fuh-LIP-pie or FIL-uh-pie.
*porneia (Greek).* pore-NAY-uh.
*Silas.* SIGH-lus.
*Thessalonica.* THESS-uh-loe-NYE-kuh.

"He spoke three thousand proverbs and his songs numbered a thousand and five. He described plant life [botany]. . . . He also taught about animals [zoology] and birds [ornithology], reptiles [herpetology] and fish [ichthyology]. Men of all nations came to listen to Solomon's wisdom" (1 Kings 4:32-34).

While all this is true, it is also recorded that "he had seven hundred wives of royal birth and three hundred concubines, and his wives led him astray" (1 Kings 11:3)

How similar is Solomon's position to that in which modern society finds itself. We exalt wisdom in the study of nature and in the creation of literary and cultural productions. We have beautiful buildings and all sorts of mechanical and electronic devices. Yet, as in the case of Solomon, all of the remarkable accomplishments of our lives tend to be foiled and soiled by our sexual profligacy. A chaste, controlled, wholesome married life would have crowned Solomon's career with beauty and blessing. His tragic example has much to say to our times. We must not let the temptations and trends of modern life drown out the words of Paul's solemn warning: "Avoid sexual immorality."

—J. G. V. B.

**4, 5. . . . that each of you should learn to control his own body in a way that is holy and honorable, not in passionate lust like the heathen, who do not know God.**

Every Christian is to accept and use the gift of sex responsibly, as a gift from God. One is to possess and *control*—not be possessed and controlled by—the physical *body*. The victim of sensual passion ceases to be master of his own person. (See Romans 1:24-27.)

The word for *body* here appears twenty-three times in the New Testament, but this is the only place it is translated "body." Ordinarily it is used to refer to an inanimate object like a jar (Luke 8:16; John 19:29) or merchandise (Mark 11:16). Frequently it is some kind of container, like the "sheet" Peter saw in his vision (Acts 10:16), "pottery" (Romans 9:21; Revelation 2:27), or "jars of clay" (2 Corinthians 4:7). This last reference is instructive, for it clearly refers to human bodies as "jars of clay," which contain our abilities and emotions, becoming the instruments through which we serve God in the world. The word is elsewhere used to personify inanimate "objects" (Romans 9:22, 23) or an "instrument" (Acts 9:15; 2 Timothy 2:21) for God's purposes. So there is good reason to accept the translation "body" here as giving the correct understanding.

On the other hand, some commentators and even translators (as in the *Revised Standard Version*) consider the word to be a reference to be a man's wife (as in 1 Peter 3:7). Thus, what Paul is telling the Thessalonians would be similar to his teaching in 1 Corinthians 7:2: "Since there is so much immorality, each man should have his own wife, and each woman her own husband."

Either way, one's goal is to live honorably to the glory of God, *not in passionate lust*. In a society filled with various abuses of God's precious gift of sex, the gospel called men and women to lives of purity and faithfulness, both to God and to one's spouse. Needless to say, this teaching possesses great relevance to modern society, which seems obsessed at times with *passionate lust*. It is an area where Christians must determine to live differently from those who *do not know God*.

### C. GOD PUNISHES THE IMPURE (v. 6)

**6. . . . and that in this matter no one should wrong his brother or take advantage of him. The Lord will punish men for all such sins, as we have already told you and warned you.**

Whoever commits sexual *sins* is trespassing in areas where he has no right to be and taking what he has no right to possess. To do so is to *take advantage of*, or cheat, another, with destructive consequences to the families involved. In this matter, the

Lord will act on behalf of the persons who have been cheated, and also in reprisal for the commandments violated.

This teaching was not new to the Thessalonians. They had been forewarned of these truths when the church was established. Paul had not waited until he was at a safe distance to broach these sensitive subjects.

## D. GOD CALLS ALL TO HOLINESS (vv. 7, 8)

**7, 8. For God did not call us to be impure, but to live a holy life. Therefore, he who rejects this instruction does not reject man but God, who gives you his Holy Spirit.**

The letter before us was addressed to folk who had heard and responded to being called of God through the gospel. That *call* is consistently in the upward direction, *to live a holy life.* The Christian's choices are not to be based on what he feels or thinks, what is statistically popular, or what the counsel of "professionals" and "experts" may dictate, but on the Word of God.

God has not left his hearers without help in carrying out his instructions. He has given us *his Holy Spirit.* The motivations to purity are firmly established by the command of God, the judgment of God, the upward call of God, and the empowering presence of God through his Holy Spirit.

## III. PLEA FOR THE PRACTICE OF LOVE (1 THESSALONIANS 4:9-12)

Paul now returns to a theme he introduced in chapter 3, where he prayed that the Thessalonians' love would "increase and overflow" (1 Thessalonians 3:12).

## A. YOU WERE TAUGHT LOVE BY GOD (v. 9)

**9. Now about brotherly love we do not need to write to you, for you yourselves have been taught by God to love each other.**

*Brotherly love* should be at least as natural among the children of God as among children of the same parents in a home. In Christ there is an even greater impulse toward such love, for we are *taught by God* to do so. This teaching has come from God through Jesus, who was love personified (John 3:16; 1 John 4:8-10). It is received individually through the presence of God's Spirit (Romans 5:5).

## B. YOU HAVE MADE A GOOD START (v. 10)

**10. And in fact, you do love all the brothers throughout Macedonia. Yet we urge you, brothers, to do so more and more.**

Paul had already noted the Thessalonians' expressions of love both among themselves and toward others (3:6, 12). Now he acknowledges that it has extended *throughout Macedonia* to other *brothers.* Acts records the establishment of three churches in Macedonia (Philippi, Berea, and Thessalonica); however, in 1:8 Paul stated that the impact of the Thessalonians' faith had been felt in Achaia also.

This should cause us to examine our own interest in, and love for, Christians outside our immediate circle or community. Some people seem to fear that spreading their Christian compassion and fellowship too widely might cause it to thin out at home. But this is not the way the love of Christ works. Love is like light, and the light that shines farthest is the one that is brightest near its source. So Paul had no hesitation in urging the Christians in Thessalonica to intensify and expand their love *more and more.* A few years later, he would write to the Christians in Corinth, calling their attention to the relatively poor churches in Macedonia who were demonstrating an overflowing generosity toward their still poorer brethren in Judea (2 Corinthians 8:1-7). The apostle's exhortation toward continual growth in love was not in vain.

### WHAT DO YOU THINK?

Paul says the God who wants us to live a holy life also gives us the Holy Spirit help us. How does the Spirit help us in that regard. (See John 16:13, 14; Ephesians 6:17; Romans 8:26; Galatians 5:22, 23.)

### DAILY BIBLE READINGS

**Monday, Mar. 3**—Love As God Loves (1 Corinthians 13:1-13)

**Tuesday, Mar. 4**—Live to Please God (Philippians 1:21-30)

**Wednesday, Mar. 5**—Seek the Mind of Christ (Philippians 2:1-8)

**Thursday, Mar. 6**—Be Glad for Christian Obligations (Philippians 2:12-18)

**Friday, Mar. 7**—Walk in Love and Light (Ephesians 5:1-14)

**Saturday, Mar. 8**—Serve Others As If Serving God (1 Peter 4:1-11)

**Sunday, Mar. 9**—Love One Another Sincerely (1 Peter 1:13-22)

## WHAT DO YOU THINK?

*How tragic it is when non-Christians can say, "Christians are no different from anyone else! They will lie and cheat and take advantage of you!" Unfortunately some church members have been guilty of such charges, and that reflects badly on all of us. Why are some Christians apparently unable to recognize the superiority of spiritual and heavenly treasures over material and temporal ones? What happens to the church's witness when her members "bend the rules" and "cut corners" like everyone else to increase their material wealth? How can the church uphold spiritual values and better challenge believers to hold to them even if that means taking a smaller profit or even a loss in one's business?*

## PRAYER

*We bring joyful thanks, dear God, for the revelation of your grandeur through our Lord Jesus and the written Word that tells of him. May we understand him more fully and follow him more faithfully, step by step, in purity and in patient, unassuming service. Amen.*

## THOUGHT TO REMEMBER

*"Let the beauty of Jesus be seen in me, All his wonderful passion and purity."*    —T. M. Jones

## C. YOU MUST PUT LOVE TO WORK (vv. 11, 12)

Christian love is found, not only in material generosity, but in the unassuming toil that earns what is to be given.

**11. Make it your ambition to lead a quiet life, to mind your own business and to work with your hands, just as we told you.**

Perhaps Paul has received word from Timothy and Silas of a problem that he now proceeds to address. It appears that the Thessalonians were given to wandering about and meddling in the affairs of their neighbors, and that they were quick to excuse themselves from hard work while they let someone else support them. This is something Paul would not tolerate.

That the Thessalonians should *mind* their *own business* is an admonition hard to misunderstand. He who is occupied with his own work has little time left to become meddlesome. Paul repeats this point in 2 Thessalonians 3:10-12 and 1 Timothy 5:11-14. The hard-working Christian is not unmindful of his brothers' needs, however. Ephesians 4:28 stipulates that a part of the earnings from his work should go to help others.

**12. . . . so that your daily life may win the respect of outsiders and so that you will not be dependent on anybody.**

At least two desirable results would come from the kind of daily diligence just prescribed. The *outsiders* (non-Christians), whether pagan or Jewish, would have to respect that kind of behavior. They would appreciate dependable integrity, and would likely take note of the fact that the people involved were Christians. Honest behavior in the midst of a dishonest society had the potential to open doors of opportunity for witnessing—and still does!

The industrious Christian, moreover, would enjoy the same kind of honorable independence that Paul found so satisfying for himself (1 Corinthians 9:14-19). He would not be in need of daily requirements, nor stagger under the pressure of excessive debt. Neither would he need help from people around him. But, when such a quiet, clean-living, hard-working, helpful person falls prey to illness or accident, he often finds others quick to lend him a hand (Luke 6:38). Love is a two-way street, and it is never overcrowded.

## CONCLUSION

At both the beginning and the end of our Scripture text for today is the apostle's injunction to "increase and overflow . . . more and more" in the practice of Christian virtue (3:12; 4:1, 10). The Thessalonian Christians were doing well; Paul wanted them continually to do better. But to what end? What is the goal?

The Christian's goal is clear: it is the perfection of God (Matthew 5:48) as it is revealed in his Son Jesus Christ (Ephesians 4:15). This is enough to keep one going and growing for a lifetime, until he reaches the perfection of Heaven.

The whole of Jesus' perfection cannot be grasped in a single concept. Today's lesson has dealt with two outstanding concepts, so important that they are sometimes said to be largely responsible for the wide acceptance of the gospel during the first centuries of the Christian era. These were the Christians' remarkable love for one another and their pure and holy manner of life.

Even these, however, are too broad to provide single, reachable steps in the upward path. So today we have been challenged regarding certain important parts of the whole: *purity* in using God's gift of sex and in following his provision for the marriage relationship; and *love* represented by minding one's own business while earning a living through honest toil and behaving with integrity before the pagans.

Now, what specific goals in Christ-like love and purity will you strive to attain this week?

# Discovery Learning

*This page contains an alternate lesson plan emphasizing learning activities. Classes desiring such student involvement will find these suggestions helpful. The next page is a reproducible activity page to further enhance discovery learning.*

## LEARNING GOALS

As a result of participating in today's lesson, a student will be able to:

1. Summarize Paul's explanation of the importance of personal purity and of brotherly love in the Christian life.

2. Explain how a person may rejoice in present spiritual accomplishments and yet still see the need for ongoing development in Christian maturity.

3. Set and pursue specific goals for personal purity and Christian love.

## INTO THE LESSON

Ask the students to think of as many items as they can for which the following statement would be true: "A little is good, but a lot is terrible." Have some of them share their answers, which may include: castor oil, time spent with your in-laws, food (overeating), debt, exercise, dieting, sermons (long ones!), and talking. Have some fun with this and get class members involved.

Make the transition into the lesson by pointing out that there are other items that are good and of which it could be said, "The more, the *better*."

## INTO THE WORD

Read 1 Thessalonians 3:12—4:12 aloud to the class. Ask them to separate into two teams. Give one team the assignment of developing reasons why "purity is the most important goal of the Christian life," using 3:13 and 4:3-8. The other team is to develop reasons why "love is the most important goal of the Christian life," using 3:12 and 4:9, 10. Allow several minutes for each group to prepare. Call on one or two individuals from each group to share its responses. At some point in the discussion, raise these questions: "If holiness is pursued, will love naturally follow?" "If love is pursued, will holiness automatically follow?" Have the class address these issues for a few minutes.

Ask the class, "Why do you think Paul places such an emphasis on increasing our love and holiness? Why is *increasing* them so important?" Have the students search the text from 1 Thessalonians for answers, and as each of the following responses is suggested, write it on a chalkboard or on poster board: the resulting positive relationships in the church (see the "each other" passages in 3:12 and 4:9); the expanded testimony to other believers (4:10); our witness to non-Christians (4:12); our readiness for Christ's return (3:13); our having received the *Holy* Spirit (4:8); being pleasing to God (4:1, 3, 8); distinguishing ourselves from those who do not know God (4:5); avoiding punishment (4:6); and obeying God's instructions (4:1, 2, 7-9). You may want to refer to the commentary for assistance in defining and discussing such words as *sanctification* (4:3, 4).

Have the class work in teams again, and give each team one of the following questions to answer and report on:

1. What do the actions described in 4:11 have to do with love and purity? How can we be loving if we are quiet and attending to our own business?

2. What is the effect of one's sexual conduct on his or her spiritual life? Why is this such a crucial issue in today's world? How can the church more effectively address it?

Give each group time to develop a response, then ask a spokesperson to summarize its conclusions for the benefit of the other group.

## INTO LIFE

Ask, "When have you experienced the most growth in Christian love and/or your commitment to personal purity?" Give people time to think; then ask for volunteers to tell their stories. What prompted the growth? How did fellow believers help? What Scriptures were especially helpful? Was there a church program that was instrumental? Encourage them to praise God for the growth that has been seen and to celebrate that level of achievement, no matter how small or slow that growth might have been.

Next, point out that no matter how much we have grown, we never outgrow the need to continue growing! We all need to be a little more loving from time to time. We all wrestle with the temptations of impurity in thought if not also in action. We can all grow a little more. But it will not happen unless we deliberately plan for it to happen.

Finally, distribute paper and pens or pencils as needed. Ask each person to write one specific step that he or she will take this week to move forward in the expression of Christian love and/or personal purity. Ask the students to hang on to these papers as reminders. (These need not be shared publicly unless you feel your group has such a high level of trust that members will not feel intimidated.) Close with prayer for each one to continue to grow in love and purity.

# Growing and Growing

Several times in Today's text Paul mentions the need for growth. Words like "increase," "strengthen," and "more and more" are common. Read each verse cited below. In what area or virtue does Paul say the Christian should grow? Write that on the blank line next to the reference.

| Reference | | Scale |
|---|---|---|
| 1 Thessalonians 3:12 | _____ | 1  2  3  4  5  6  7  8  9  10 |
| 1 Thessalonians 3:13 | _____ | 1  2  3  4  5  6  7  8  9  10 |
| 1 Thessalonians 4:1 | _____ | 1  2  3  4  5  6  7  8  9  10 |
| 1 Thessalonians 4:3 | _____ | 1  2  3  4  5  6  7  8  9  10 |
| 1 Thessalonians 4:6 | _____ | 1  2  3  4  5  6  7  8  9  10 |
| 1 Thessalonians 4:7 | _____ | 1  2  3  4  5  6  7  8  9  10 |
| 1 Thessalonians 4:10 | _____ | 1  2  3  4  5  6  7  8  9  10 |
| 1 Thessalonians 4:11 | _____ | 1  2  3  4  5  6  7  8  9  10 |
| 1 Thessalonians 4:12 | _____ | 1  2  3  4  5  6  7  8  9  10 |

Now look at each item on your list. On the scale to the right of each , circle the number where you think you were twelve months ago. (1 is very weak; 10 is very strong.) Put an X over the number on each scale where you think you are now.

Are you growing? Choose the area that showed the least growth. What can you do this week to stimulate growth in this area?

What can you begin within the month that will be of long-term assistance to you as you seek to grow in this area?

Who can help you? Is there a Christian leader, a peer, or someone else with whom you can meet to encourage one another and to be built up by each other?

Set a goal. What rating would you like to be able to give yourself next year in this area?

## Hope for the Future
### Unit 1. Stand Fast in the Lord
#### (Lessons 1-5)

# PRAY FOR OTHERS
### LESSON 3

**DEVOTIONAL READING:**
**1 TIMOTHY 1:1-8**
**LESSON SCRIPTURE:**
**2 THESSALONIANS 1**
**PRINTED TEXT:**
**2 THESSALONIANS 1**

Mar
16

## WHY TEACH THIS LESSON?

"Let us then approach the throne of grace with confidence, so that we may receive mercy and find grace to help us in our time of need" (Hebrews 4:16). Approaching the throne of grace is one of the most awesome privileges the Christian might enjoy. Unfortunately, far too many enjoy it far too little. And even when they do, it is often for shallow reasons. (See James 4:2, 3.)

We need a lesson in prayer. We need to learn to pray for the eternal purposes of God—evangelism, righteousness, justice, the advance of God's kingdom, the exaltation of the Lord Jesus Christ. These themes were at the heart of Paul's prayers. When he prayed for Christian friends, he prayed for their perseverance, for their role in God's plan for the ages. Today's lesson puts your students in touch with one of his prayers. Use it to challenge your students to include in their prayers Paul's kind of concern for others and for the kingdom of God.

## INTRODUCTION

### A. PRAYER LISTS

Church publications often include prayer lists, naming persons for whom prayer is suggested. These often deal with matters of sickness, sorrow, or safety. While Scripture encourages that kind of concern among the members of God's family (James 5:14, 15; 3 John 2), matters of health and safety are not ends in themselves. They are related to the more important issues of an individual's faith and his relationship with God.

Today's lesson addresses this subject, in the words of an apostle who prayed continually for many fellow Christians. In addition, his other writings were filled with expressions of prayer and exhortations to prayer on behalf of others. For what did he pray? Seldom did he mention physical health. On one occasion he prayed three times for his own relief from an unnamed "thorn in [his] flesh," and God responded, "My grace is sufficient for you" (2 Corinthians 12:9). The thorn remained as a reminder that the Lord's presence was more important than physical comfort. That may have helped to shape Paul's priorities in prayer.

Jesus' life and teaching reflected such spiritual priorities. He taught, "Do not be afraid of those who kill the body but cannot kill the soul. Rather, be afraid of the one who can destroy both soul and body in hell" (Matthew 10:28). Perhaps we should invite the Lord and his apostles to shape our prayer lists, first personally and then publicly. Today's lesson may help.

### B. LESSON BACKGROUND

The setting of 2 Thessalonians is virtually the same as that of 1 Thessalonians. Written from Corinth, and addressed by the same three messengers to the same body of believers, it recognizes the same steadfast faithfulness and spiritual growth in the face of persecution. It also acknowledges a similar need for additional instruction and maturity; thus, the need for a second letter.

Interim reports from Thessalonica had reached Corinth. The Thessalonian Christians, already anticipating Christ's coming in glory and judgment, had

## LESSON AIMS

*As a result of participating in today's lesson, a student will be able to:*

*1. Tell briefly what Paul gave thanks for and what he requested in his prayers for the Thessalonian Christians.*

*2. Compare the content of Paul's prayers with the typical prayers of Christians today.*

*3. Choose one specific item from Paul's prayer list to pray each day this week in behalf of fellow believers.*

## KEY VERSE

*We constantly pray for you, that our God may count you worthy of his calling, and that by his power he may fulfill every good purpose of yours and every act prompted by your faith.*

— *2 Thessalonians 1:11*

*LESSON 3 NOTES*

*The visual for lesson 3 in the visual packet sets the theme for this lesson. Have it on display as you begin the session.*

seized on Paul's instruction about this matter in 1 Thessalonians 4 and 5 to create a misguided excitement about the event. Some had even ceased their daily work to wait in idleness for the final day (2 Thessalonians 3:11). The church needed encouragement, assurance of God's perfect justice, and the understanding that glorifying Jesus through continued faithful service was the best way to prepare for his return.

## I. GREETING (2 THESSALONIANS 1:1, 2)

The apostle opened this prayerful epistle by invoking God's eternal blessing on his readers.

**1, 2. Paul, Silas and Timothy,**

**To the church of the Thessalonians in God our Father and the Lord Jesus Christ: Grace and peace to you from God the Father and the Lord Jesus Christ.**

In writing to the *Thessalonians*, *Paul* was joined by *Silas*, his companion throughout his second missionary journey (Acts 15:40). *Timothy* had joined the missionary party at Lystra (Acts 16:1-3). The three had worked together at Thessalonica, and Timothy had maintained the communication between Paul and *the church of the Thessalonians* (1 Thessalonians 3:2, 6).

The apostles' blessing is couched in language meaningful to both Greeks and Jews. *Grace*, or favor, is a Christian application of a common Greek greeting of good wishes. *Peace* is the traditional Jewish greeting (the Hebrew word is *shalom*), indicating wholeness in God. The source of these blessings is spiritual; they can come only *from God the Father and the Lord Jesus Christ*.

## II. THANKS FOR STEADFASTNESS (2 THESSALONIANS 1:3-5)

Paul's gratitude shows that he considered the people of God more important than anything else in creation. He was thankful for the growing faith and love of the Thessalonian believers.

### A. OCCASION FOR REJOICING (vv. 3, 4)

**3. We ought always to thank God for you, brothers, and rightly so, because your faith is growing more and more, and the love every one of you has for each other is increasing.**

The obligation to give thanks does not come from an outward compulsion; it springs from within. Paul recognized that all credit for the Thessalonians' enthusiastic response to earlier teachings had to go to God. He had prayed that he and his team would "supply what is lacking in your faith" (1 Thessalonians 3:10), and that God would "make your love increase and overflow for each other" (1 Thessalonians 3:10, 12).

Concerning the great triad of faith, hope, and love (1 Corinthians 13:13; 1 Thessalonians 1:3), these believers matched ongoing persecution with expanding *faith*, and they supported one another with abundant *love*. Their hope, especially in expectation of Christ's immediate return, needed some additional sharpening and training. But thanks be to God, they were growing up! Nothing is said about prayers for the Thessalonians' physical safety or relief from persecution. Would an easier life really have been that beneficial to them?

**4. Therefore, among God's churches we boast about your perseverance and faith in all the persecutions and trials you are enduring.**

Pursued by enemies as a hare is chased by hounds, the Christians in Thessalonica encountered all kinds of *persecutions and trials*. We have no record that Paul ever asked God to make their situation easier for them; he thanked God for their *perseverance and faith* through it all! Perhaps Christians today should not

## WHAT DO YOU THINK?

*We pray often for the physical health of loved ones, but when is the last time you heard someone pray for another's spiritual health? Why do we not more often pray about spiritual health? How can we combine concern for one's physical health with concern for his or her spiritual health of intercessory prayer?*

## OPTION

*Use the reproducible activity, "Prayer List," on page 254 to introduce this discussion.*

complain too loudly when the public media make uncomplimentary remarks about them.

## B. PREVIEW OF THE KINGDOM (v. 5)

**5. All this is evidence that God's judgment is right, and as a result you will be counted worthy of the kingdom of God, for which you are suffering.**

A faith that triumphs over difficulties becomes a clear indication that the *judgment of God is right*. Contrary to the world's opinion, it proves the power of godliness, surviving and advancing in the face of all odds and foreshadowing the ultimate defeat of God's enemies. (See Philippians 1:28.) Furthermore, it declares the necessity of final judgment, in which the scales of justice, so long apparently unbalanced in the suffering of innocent folk at the hands of the wicked, will at last be set right. What seems to be the status quo will be reversed in accord with eternal truth. Tried, purified, and proved in the fires of affliction, the saints will be *counted worthy of the kingdom of God*—a worthiness bestowed by divine grace through Christ.

The suffering of the Thessalonian Christians linked them with the apostles who had suffered earlier for the same cause. Together they were participants in an ongoing fellowship of saints who "chose to be mistreated along with the people of God rather than to enjoy the pleasures of sin for a short time" (Hebrews 11:25).

### BEING WORTHY

We all have had experiences that have caused us to evaluate the worthiness or unworthiness of some activity or product. Sometimes we have attended a lecture or gone to a party that turned out to be hardly worth our time and effort. Perhaps we purchased a new, highly advertised pen and found that it failed to write any better than some we already had. It wasn't worth what we paid for it.

At times, however, our evaluations are quite different. We may go reluctantly to some gathering and find it inspiring, uplifting, and invigorating. We all know of different items we purchased that ended up lasting far longer than we anticipated, thereby giving us our money's worth and more.

Paul prayed that the Thessalonian Christians would be "counted worthy of the kingdom of God" (2 Thessalonians 1:5). The great blessings of his kingdom are ours as well. Our past sins have been forgiven. We have a fellowship with people of honest hearts, devoted wills, transformed minds, and spiritual purposes. We have hope for an eternity full of gladness, grace, and glory. Surely we can believe that inconveniences, persecution, difficulties, and even disasters are not too much to pay so that we too may "be counted worthy."                                        —J. G. V. B.

## III. COMFORT IN DIVINE JUSTICE (2 THESSALONIANS 1:6-10

There was more to be said about the sustaining assurance of God's righteous judgment.

## A. CORRECTING THE BALANCES (vv. 6, 7)

**6. God is just: He will pay back trouble to those who trouble you.**

"For after all it is only just for God to repay with affliction those who afflict you" (*New American Standard Bible*). This theme is at least as old as the cry of Abraham: "Will not the Judge of all the earth do right?" (Genesis 18:25). There is no other way for us to be sure that sin will be punished, and righteousness rewarded, except by the *just*, or righteous, nature of God.

One of the purposes of divine justice is to provide compensation for the injustices of this life. This involves retributive justice, which will *pay back trouble to those who trouble you*. Such judgment is infinitely better than the awkward, sin-tainted

---

### WHAT DO YOU THINK?

When Christians persevere in the face of trials, it testifies to the authenticity of their faith. At the same time, followers of pagan religions and members of cults have also stood firm in the midst of persecution. What is different about the Christian's suffering? How can we be sure our faithfulness is seen as a testimony for the Lord Jesus not simply great devotion to a human ideal or, worse yet, mere stubbornness?

---

### HOW TO SAY IT

apokalupsis (Greek). uh-POCK-uh-LOOP-sis.
Corinth. KOR-inth.
Lystra. LISS-truh.
parousia (Greek) par-oo-SEE-uh.
Philippians. Fih-LIP-pee-unz.
shalom (Hebrew). shah-LOME.
Silas. SIGH-lus.
Thessalonica. THESS-uh-loe-NYE-kuh.

## WHAT DO YOU THINK?

The idea of God's giving rest or relief to his people is an appealing one. What kind of rest does God promise us?

(See Hebrews 4:6-11; Revelation 14:13; 22:3.)

efforts of men and women to work personal vengeance on private enemies. "I will repay, says the Lord" (Romans 12:19). God's justice is also remunerative, supplying to his people what they have lacked.

**7. . . . and give relief to you who are troubled, and to us as well. This will happen when the Lord Jesus is revealed from heaven in blazing fire with his powerful angels.**

Besides bringing trouble upon the troublers, God will provide *relief* to those who have been *troubled*. This relief will be enjoyed along with *us*, for Paul and his companions also suffered trouble for the Lord and anticipated the coming relief from that trouble. Relief for God's people, sometimes described by the word *rest*, is a prominent theme in Scripture, as Hebrews 3:7—4:11 explains.

The promised rest will come *when the Lord Jesus is revealed from heaven*. The Greek word used to describe this revelation is not the same one that was was used in 1 Thessalonians 3:13. That word was *parousia*, which signifies a coming or an appearing. Here the term is a form of the word *apokalupsis,* meaning a disclosure or uncovering, such as is accomplished by removing the covering from a long-concealed work of art. (It is the word that gives the book of "Revelation" its title.) Then and only then will human eyes see the Lord Jesus as he comes *from heaven*. "Look, he is coming with the clouds, and every eye will see him" (Revelation 1:7).

The accompanying *angels* are described in this verse not as "holy" (Mark 8:38), but as *powerful*. They will be active participants in the events of judgment, gathering the weeds for destruction, and gathering the good grain for the Lord's use (Matthew 13:30, 41).

*Blazing fire* may describe either the brilliant glory of the revealed Judge or the instrument of punishment meted out to those who have rejected his mercy (verse 8). In either case, we may be sure that the ultimate reality is greater and far more severe than the material figure in which it is expressed. The fire of Sinai (Exodus 19:18) signified the glory of God's presence to the children of Israel. An even greater display of fire will be most appropriate for the hour of Christ's return.

### B. PUNISHMENT OF THE WICKED (vv. 8, 9)
**8. He will punish those who do not know God and do not obey the gospel of our Lord Jesus.**

Those *who do not know God* and those who *do not obey the gospel of our Lord Jesus* may well describe the same individuals, who have taken the fatal step of rejecting the final revelation of God's grace through his Son. Others believe that the first phrase is describing pagan Gentiles who have stubbornly refused to acknowledge God while the second includes Jews who rejected Jesus as Messiah and became persecutors of his followers. Whether the two words make up the whole or whether each word describes the whole makes little difference—all who reject the Lord Jesus Christ will be punished, whether Jew or Gentile.

## WHAT DO YOU THINK?

The subject of Hell will never be a tremendously popular one. Today many pulpits are silent regarding it. Many people embrace the doctrine of universalism, which maintains that all people will ultimately be saved; or they will merely affirm that they believe that "God is too loving to condemn anyone to an eternal Hell." But 2 Thessalonians 1:6-9 speaks clearly of an eternal punishment for the wicked.

Why is this such an unpopular doctrine? What dangers do you think we risk when we fail to teach this? Do you think it is possible to overemphasize it? Why or why not? What do you think is the proper balance between teaching of Hell and teaching of more positive topics?

### OBEYING THE GOOD NEWS

I know a pair of grandparents who came up with an interesting idea. They wanted to leave some money for their grandchildren when they died. But since they were growing older and older, as were their grandchildren, they decided that the grandchildren should have the money earmarked for them before, instead of after, their death. They believed that these grandchildren, most of whom were either married and rearing children or in college, could better use this money now than at some future time.

The immediate reception of the thousands of dollars involved in this decision was, of course, great news to the grandchildren. However, while the money was a "free gift," the gifts were in the form of checks. These had to be endorsed in order to make the money available to the grandchildren. So conditions had to be met, even though the money was a gift.

Surely we have "good news," or the gospel, which tells us of Jesus' coming as our Redeemer, his life of goodness, his death on the cross, and his resurrection. This is good news of salvation that is a gift, it comes "not by works, so that no one can boast" (Ephesians 2:9).

Yet this is a gospel that must be "obeyed," as verse 8 of our printed text affirms. As Christians we proclaim "good news," but it is something that not only must be heard, but also heeded. Confession of faith, baptism, and Christian living are all responses that show one is "obeying the gospel."                          J. G. V. B.

**9. They will be punished with everlasting destruction and shut out from the presence of the Lord and from the majesty of his power.**

The faithless and disobedient ones will receive the penalty of *everlasting destruction,* being banished forever from God's *presence* and *majesty.* Fulfilled in them will be the words of Matthew 25:41: "Depart from me, you who are cursed, into the eternal fire, prepared for the devil and his angels." Having rejected God and the gospel, they will be shut out forever from the presence of the One whom they have spurned.

### C. CHRIST'S GLORIOUS RETURN (v. 10)

**10. . . . on the day he comes to be glorified in his holy people and to be marveled at among all those who have believed. This includes you, because you believed our testimony to you.**

The revelation of Christ *on the day* of judgment will occur with glory indescribable. Every eye will see him as he comes with the clouds (Revelation 1:7). Scoffer and believer alike will witness the event, but it is only *his holy people* who will glorify him. For "those who do not know God and do not obey the gospel of our Lord Jesus" (verse 8), the sight will be a terror. But *those who have believed* will marvel and worship as this will be the culmination of all their hopes. The Thessalonian Christians, Paul affirms, will be in the latter group because they *believed* the truth Paul and his companions preached.

### IV. PRAYER OF FULFILLMENT (2 THESSALONIANS 1:11, 12)

From assurance that God will set all things right by his judgment, the apostle now turned to a prayer that the Thessalonians might enjoy a full portion of the blessings prepared for the saints.

### A. FULFILLMENT OF GOD'S PLEASURE (v. 11)

**11. With this in mind, we constantly pray for you, that our God may count you worthy of his calling, and that by his power he may fulfill every good purpose of yours and every act prompted by your faith.**

Paul's continual prayers constituted a very important part of his ministry to his converts. Here his prayer was that God would *count* (some versions say "make") *you worthy of this calling.* Either translation is accurate, for if a person is to be counted worthy in God's sight, it is because he has been made worthy by God's grace. The believer remains in this God-provided worthiness as he continues to accept the power and guidance of God's Word for his spiritual nourishment.

The *calling* Paul mentions comes through the gospel. Let the hearer honor that call, making it his vocation to live in a way that shows a proper respect for it: "I urge you to live a life worthy of the calling you have received" (Ephesians 4:1). Such should be the resolute purpose of every sincere believer.

### WHAT DO YOU THINK?

*The Lord Jesus Christ will be glorified in us when Christ returns (2 Thessalonians 1:12). He should also be glorified in us now! What can we do specifically to glorify him?*

*Do you think most Christians set out each day consciously planning to glorify the Lord Jesus Christ? Why or why not? How can we be more deliberate about glorifying Jesus in our daily lives?*

## PRAYER

*We give thanks, our Father, for the courage of faithful saints, and for the apostles whose word instructed them and us. May we become increasingly mature in making our prayer requests. May we honor you as we continually accept your gracious provisions for our spiritual growth. We glorify your name and the name of your Son, Jesus Christ. Amen.*

## THOUGHT TO REMEMBER

*"Keep alert and never give up; pray always for all God's people"* (Ephesians 6:18, *Today's English Version*).

## DAILY BIBLE READINGS

*Monday, Mar. 10—Pray in Humility (2 Chronicles 7:11-18)*

*Tuesday, Mar. 11—Pray As Jesus Prayed (John 17:6-12)*

*Wednesday, Mar. 12—Pray in Private (Matthew 6:5-15)*

*Thursday, Mar. 13—Pray in the Holy Spirit (Jude 17-23)*

*Friday, Mar. 14—Pray for the Sick (James 5:13-16)*

*Saturday, Mar. 15—Pray for Friends (Acts 8:14-24)*

*Sunday, Mar. 16—Pray for the Penitent (1 Samuel 12:19-25)*

Paul then prayed that God would fulfill *every good purpose of yours and every act prompted by your faith*. Once again the emphasis is upon the need for divine aid in pleasing God. The Christian needs God's power, not only during times of suffering, but in carrying out the daily responsibilities of goodness and faith. Perhaps the *power* of the Holy Spirit to enable Christian living may be compared with power steering in an automobile. The person at the wheel (the Christian) chooses to walk in a direction pleasing to God; the machinery (the Holy Spirit) provides the energy to follow the chosen course.

### B. FULFILLMENT OF GLORY (v. 12)

The theme of verse 10 is repeated in the conclusion to which this chapter has been building.

**12. We pray this so that the name of our Lord Jesus may be glorified in you, and you in him, according to the grace of our God and the Lord Jesus Christ.**

A *name* in biblical usage represents the essence of the person who is named. To honor the name is to honor the person. When God's purpose is fulfilled through the life and testimony of the saints, *the name of our Lord Jesus* is *glorified*. In addition, when the believer develops a character reflecting the qualities of *Christ*, that believer is *glorified . . . in him*. Here the emphasis is upon the present glory of the Christian life, as experienced by one who knows and walks with Christ. Could a greater request than this be made for one's friends?

## CONCLUSION

### A. WHEN THE GOING GETS TOUGH

"When the going gets tough, the tough get going!" The high school football coach drummed this slogan into his players from the first practice session to the last game of the season. Never did he say, "Take it easy." Comfort was not the goal. The team was not content with victories over weak opponents. The players went out to win over teams that would try their mettle. Nothing less would satisfy the purpose for which they donned their gear and ran onto the field.

Should we be satisfied with a lesser commitment as we engage in God's eternal campaign for human redemption? Paul was never so easily satisfied, and his readers seemed to get the idea. How about us?

### B. WHO BENEFITS FROM PRAYER?

"Pray for Others." So exhorts our lesson title in developing the larger theme of this unit, "Stand Fast in the Lord." Our text makes it clear that Paul and his partners spent much time in prayer for the people among whom they labored. Their prayers brought many benefits to those for whom they prayed. We may be sure that their praying brought many benefits to the pray-ers as well—Paul, Silas, and Timothy. They were saved from any pride in their accomplishments among the Thessalonians. They were prevented from losing sight of their priorities. Their focus was kept on Christ and on the building of his church.

Paul also requested prayer for himself, not that he would be kept safe or be blessed physically or materially, but "that whenever I open my mouth, words may be given me so that I will fearlessly make known the mystery of the gospel . . . as I should" (Ephesians 6:19, 20). That kind of praying was clearly effective for Paul, and it surely benefited those who responded to his appeal.

Praying for preachers, teachers, missionaries, and Christian writers and editors—both at home and abroad—is surely in order. Paul's request to the Ephesians is an ideal guide for the content of such praying. A major benefit may be expected for all, including the one who prays.

# Discovery Learning

*This page contains an alternate lesson plan emphasizing learning activities. Classes desiring such student involvement will find these suggestions helpful. The next page is a reproducible activity page to further enhance discovery learning.*

## LEARNING GOALS

As a result of participating in today's lesson, a student will be able to:

1. Tell briefly what Paul gave thanks for and what he asked for in his prayers concerning the Thessalonian Christians.

2. Compare the content of Paul's prayers with the typical prayers of Christians today.

3. Choose one specific item from Paul's prayer list to pray each day this week in behalf of fellow believers.

## INTO THE LESSON

Does your church publish prayer requests in your weekly bulletin or your mid-week or monthly newsletter? If so, review that list as you begin your class. If not, ask for prayer requests. Have the class think of more than just the needs of your class, but of the needs of the whole church. Write these on the chalkboard as people mention needs. Or have the students record them on the activity sheet, copied from page 254. (You could also use this page to make an overhead transparency and lead the discussion by using it.)

When you have a sizable list, say, "We are going to pray for these in a little while, but first let's think about where our focus is in our prayers. Let's go back over this list and just note whether we are praying for a physical matter in each case or a spiritual one."

Try to get consensus on each item; then mark a "p" or an "s" next to each request. Note how many physical concerns you have and how many spiritual.

Make the transition to Bible study by saying, "Today's text gives us one of Paul's prayers for some believers. Let's see how his prayer list compares with our own."

## INTO THE WORD

Have someone read 2 Thessalonians 1:1-12; then divide the class into groups of four to six and give half the groups the first assignment below; the other half, the second. Be sure each group has a recorder/reporter assigned to write down and report on the ideas that come up in the group discussion.

1. For what did Paul specifically thank God when he prayed for the Thessalonians? (Answers they should find in this passage include their growing faith and love, v. 3, and their patience and faith in the midst of suffering, v. 4.)

2. For what did he specifically ask in prayer concerning these Christians? (Answers should include that they would be counted worthy of their calling, v. 11, that they would please God, v. 11, that they would do the works of faith with power, v. 11), and that God would be glorified, v. 12.)

Give the groups about ten minutes to work; then ask for reports. Use the lesson commentary to clarify any terms and phrases that the students are having trouble with.

Take some time to compare Paul's prayer with your requests listed earlier. How much of Paul's prayer is about spiritual matters and how much is about physical ones? How does that balance compare with the balance in your own list? Probably your list leans heavily to the physical side. If so, point out that the focus of Paul's prayer becomes a challenge to us to be more spiritual in our prayers. If your list is more spiritual, observe that your group seems to be on the right track. The way Paul prayed becomes an affirmation of your group's prayer life.

## INTO LIFE

Have the class work in the same small groups as before. Those who found Paul's thanksgivings should identify one fellow believer for whom the same kind of thanks might be offered (e. g., one who is growing in faith and love—perhaps a new believer who is growing rapidly—or one who is demonstrating patient faith in spite of opposition). The groups who identified Paul's requests should identify one fellow believer for whom the same request is appropriate. Everyone in each group should be asked to pray daily for the person identified by his or her group.

Encourage your students also to think in terms of one another's spiritual growth every time they pray. If they keep a prayer journal, for example, perhaps they could include a heading, "Spiritual Requests," as a reminder to pray often for such needs. Parents should be especially encouraged to pray for their children's faith, not just that they will grow up and find "good jobs" or even "happiness."

Close with prayer, being sure to include thanksgiving for what your class is learning and demonstrating in regard to faithfulness and a request that each member of the class continue to grow spiritually.

# Prayer List

The apostle John prayed for both the physical health and the spiritual health of his friend Gaius: "Dear friend, I pray that you may enjoy good health and that all may go well with you, even as your soul is getting along well" (3 John 2). Paul's prayer for the Thessalonian Christians (2 Thessalonians 1) was also loaded with intercessions for their spiritual health. Is spiritual health a significant topic in our intercessory prayers?

| REQUEST | PHYSICAL | SPIRITUAL |
|---|---|---|
| Read 2 Thessalonians 1. For what did Paul give thanks concerning the Thessalonians and what did he request on their behalf? List these below. Indicate whether the expressed concern is for a physical or spiritual need. | | |
| List some of the prayer requests from your church below. (Check your Sunday bulletin or your midweek or monthly newsletter.) Indicate whether the expressed concern is for a physical or spiritual need. | | |

Do your own prayers need to focus more on spiritual matters? What one issue for spiritual growth—for you or a fellow believer—do you most need to pray about this week?

Hope for the Future
*Unit 1. Stand Fast in the Lord*
(Lessons 1-5)

# DO WHAT IS RIGHT

**LESSON 4**

## WHY TEACH THIS LESSON?

*Burnout.* A generation ago the word couldn't be found in the dictionary. Now, it seems, everyone's got it! And that includes people in the church.

What causes burnout? How is it that people get tired of Christian service? What happened to those "wings of eagles" Isaiah promised?

Our lesson today addresses this issue. There is little doubt someone in your class is beginning to feel burnt out. He or she may be about ready to drop out of the life of the church. Use this lesson as a challenge to hang in there, anticipating the Lord's return, and serving with renewed zeal.

## INTRODUCTION

### A. "TAKE ME OUT TO THE BALL GAME"

This well-known baseball song contains casual lyrics about peanuts and Cracker Jack, to be munched without thought of healthful diets, and with the attitude, "I don't care if I never get back." The fan has come to the ball park for a day of fun and relaxation and a break from the daily routine.

The same fan, however, expects something different on the field. The players are to perform to perfection—hitting line drives, pitching with pinpoint accuracy, and turning the quick double play. Woe to the umpire who is less than perfect in seeing and calling the close pitch or play. Woe to the base runner who gets picked off. And everyone expects the game to be played by the rules with which he is acquainted. Three strikes means "you're out," no matter who the batter is. No one can avoid the need for order and discipline, even in a place where one goes to relax.

The need for order also holds true in religion, despite the insistence of some who may question the importance of time schedules, prepared lessons, meaningful songs, understandable speech, or correct grammar. "For God is not a God of disorder but of peace" (1 Corinthians 14:33).

### B. LESSON BACKGROUND

The Thessalonian letters deal extensively with Jesus' future coming in glory and judgment. The expectation of his return is presented in 1 Thessalonians 4:13-18 as a prime source of comfort for afflicted believers. Chapter 5 then warns that the time of the Lord's coming is totally unknown, so Christians must always be ready. Some in Thessalonica seem to have assumed that the Lord would appear almost immediately. From this they concluded that they need not make any further provisions for life on earth, and ceased any productive labor. They lived only on what they and their brethren had at hand and likely engaged in much excited discussion of the subject of Christ's return.

In 2 Thessalonians 2:1-12, the apostle writes a vigorous correction: "We ask you, brothers, not to become easily unsettled or alarmed . . . that the day of the Lord has already come" (vv. 1, 2). First, there must come a falling away and the appearance of the Lord's ultimate enemy, the "man of lawlessness" (v. 3). Then, lest his description of such a powerful enemy overly frighten his readers, Paul reminds them of God's still greater protective power and saving grace. The chapter

DEVOTIONAL READING:
EPHESIANS 4:25-32 *183*

LESSON SCRIPTURE:
2 THESSALONIANS 3 *197*

PRINTED TEXT:
2 THESSALONIANS 3:1-16

Mar
23

## LESSON AIMS

This study should prepare the student to:

1. Tell why Paul said the Thessalonians should be diligent to provide for their own needs.

2. Describe the kind of problems that come when Christians do not take responsibility for their own needs.

3. Initiate a plan of action by which she will seek to do her share of work in the church and community.

## KEY VERSE

And as for you, brothers, never tire of doing what is right.
— 2 Thessalonians 3:13

**LESSON 4 NOTES**

concludes with a prayer that God will "encourage your hearts and strengthen you in every good deed and word" (v. 17).

## I. PRAYER REQUESTED (2 THESSALONIANS 3:1-5)

Chapter 3 opens with a request for prayer that God's power would meet the apostles' continued needs.

### A. APOSTLES IN NEED (vv. 1, 2)

**1. Finally, brothers, pray for us that the message of the Lord may spread rapidly and be honored, just as it was with you.**

*Finally* provides a transition from the statements in chapter 2 to the request now being made. Brothers and sisters in Christ are asked to pray for their teachers in the faith. The appeal is not merely for personal advantage, but for success in God's work. The *message of the Lord* is viewed as something alive and powerful (cf. Hebrews 4:12; Psalm 147:15). Paul's prayer is that obstacles may not prevent the word from accomplishing its goal in the saving of many, and that, like an athlete winning a race, it may be *honored* in the accomplishment. If God's word continues to triumph, the apostles will count themselves blessed and their work a success.

**2. And pray that we may be delivered from wicked and evil men, for not everyone has faith.**

Prayers for personal safety are requested only for the sake of the gospel. Opposition from men who hated the gospel and its messengers was well known to the Thessalonian Christians. Such men had persecuted Paul and his partners before, during, and after their time of ministry in Thessalonica. Even as he wrote this letter, unbelieving Jews were making life difficult for him in Corinth (Acts 18:5, 6, 12-17).

*Not everyone has faith.* Paul did not expect pagans to act like Christians nor Jewish opponents of Christ to love his ambassadors. The best Paul could expect was that God would keep him going in spite of their opposition. In Corinth, he received that assurance (Acts 18:9, 10). Paul also met with resistance from folk who acknowledged Jesus as Messiah but continued to indulge in their old habits. In addition, he suffered "danger from false brothers" (2 Corinthians 11:26).

### B. GOD SUFFICIENT FOR ALL NEEDS (vv. 3-5)

**3, 4. But the Lord is faithful, and he will strengthen and protect you from the evil one. We have confidence in the Lord that you are doing and will continue to do the things we command.**

In contrast to the faithless men just mentioned stands *the Lord,* who is always *faithful.* Here Paul expresses his *confidence* that his prayer at the conclusion of the previous chapter (2:16, 17) would be answered. The request to *protect you from the evil one* echoes the prayer Jesus taught his disciples (Matthew 6:13) and applies both to Satan and to his works—to evil in general.

*Confidence in the Lord* becomes confidence in the Lord's people. Their steadfastness depends on their identification with him. As they dwell in him, they will be found doing—both now and in the future—what he desires. God's resources are entirely sufficient to sustain his people.

**5. May the Lord direct your hearts into God's love and Christ's perseverance.**

The Thessalonian Christians needed to be guided (as do all of us) into a continually deeper understanding of God's all-sufficient *love*—both his love for us and our love in responding to him. We also need a deeper understanding of Jesus' *perseverance*—both the perseverance he exhibited and the perseverance he creates in his followers. We are to love because God loves us; we are to endure suffering patiently because Jesus endured for us.

---

✳ **WHAT DO YOU THINK?**

*Paul asked for prayers that the word of the Lord would "spread rapidly" (2 Thessalonians 3:1). What are some of the barriers that might prevent the spread of God's Word and the gospel message? Do church members erect some of these barriers, or are they all from outside the church? If some come from inside, what are they? What work can we add to our prayers to tear down such barriers?*

### LOOKING TO THE LORD

In a certain retirement home, there are many rooms and apartments where the residents live. These are cleaned once a week: carpets are vacuumed, furniture is dusted, linens are changed, bathroom fixtures are cleaned, and wastebaskets are emptied. Each resident has certain preferences about some of those things: there are some items he wants "left alone" or rearranged in a particular way. He leaves these directions with the "executive housekeeper," who tells the various cleaning women how these rooms or apartments are to be treated. The individual workers follow the directives given them. Occasionally one will hear an employee say, "I wouldn't really do it this way on my own, but Eva says this is how it has to be done." ("Eva" is the executive housekeeper.)

In his letters to the church at Thessalonica, Paul is telling the believers there how Jesus wants them to order and arrange their lives. Again and again he refers to "the Lord" because he is the One who has given Paul the authority to tell them how they are to act. In the section covered in today's lesson text, we see evidence of Paul's constant awareness of the presence, purpose, and power of the Lord Jesus. Notice especially verses 1-6, 12, and 16.

Certainly this says something significant to us. We are to clean up and order our lives as our Lord directs us. We are not to do as we please, but as he pleases. We are not "on our own"; we are servants and workers in the house of faith we inhabit. He is a co-worker with us, aware of our tasks. He is not just an austere authoritarian, but a loving, joyous comrade in an eternal quest.     —J. G. V. B.

## II. IDLENESS REBUKED (2 THESSALONIANS 3:6-13)

Now Paul turns his attention to a specific area in which a lack of Christ's perseverance was found in Thessalonica.

### A. AVOID THE IDLE BROTHER (v. 6)

**6. In the name of the Lord Jesus Christ, we command you, brothers, to keep away from every brother who is idle and does not live according to the teaching you received from us.**

*Command* is a military term, used in the manner of a commissioned officer speaking with the authority of the highest commander (Matthew 28:18). It contrasts with the milder words "ask" and "urge" (used in 1 Thessalonians 4:1 and 5:14), but it deals with the same problem: unruly or undisciplined behavior, such as that of a soldier who has broken ranks. The earlier admonition in 1 Thessalonians 5:14 was to "warn" any such brother. This passage, addressed to a worsening situation, directs the church to *keep away from* the offender, in order to avoid any appearance of approving his behavior. First Corinthians 5:11 commands such social discipline, or peer pressure, to be used in the case of a brother who was flagrantly disregarding the Lord's directives. No one in the church is to coddle the offender with misplaced sympathy, thus creating division and destroying the corrective power of the action. The word must go out clearly: such undisciplined behavior is simply not tolerated in the body of Christ!

The pattern of acceptable behavior was established in the *teaching* delivered by the apostles of Christ. The Thessalonians had *received* it from the apostles, but Christ himself was the divine source.

### B. FOLLOW PAUL'S EXAMPLE (vv. 7-9)

**7, 8. For you yourselves know how you ought to follow our example. We were not idle when we were with you, nor did we eat anyone's food without paying for it. On the contrary, we worked night and day, laboring and toiling so that we would not be a burden to any of you.**

### HOW TO SAY IT

*Corinth.* KOR-inth.
*Dorcas.* DOR-kus.
*Galatians.* Guh-LAY-shunz.
*Philippians.* Fih-LIP-pee-unz.
*Thessalonica.* THESS-uh-loe-
   NYE-kuh.

### WHAT DO YOU THINK?

*In the New Testament, the church would withdraw fellowship from an erring church member to urge him or her to repent. (See 1 Corinthians 5.) Have you ever heard of such a practice in modern times? If so, with what result?*

*What are the dangers of attempting such a practice today? Do you think it is practical to attempt it? Why or why not? If not, then how can the church uphold the biblical standards of morality and sound doctrine?*

## DAILY BIBLE READING

*Monday, Mar. 17—Turn Away From Evil (Colossians 3: 1-11)*

*Tuesday, Mar. 18—Do Everything in Jesus' Name (Colossians 3:12-17)*

*Wednesday, Mar. 19—Be Gracious to Others (Colossians 4:1-5)*

*Thursday, Mar. 20—Live in Harmony With Others (Romans 15:1-6)*

*Friday, Mar. 21—Live Peacefully Within the Church (Ephesians 4:1-6)*

*Saturday, Mar. 22—Live Peacefully Within the Family (Ephesians 5:22—6:4)*

*Sunday, Mar. 23—Rules for Christian Living (1 Peter 3:8-12)*

## WHAT DO YOU THINK?

*Government-sponsored programs to provide temporary assistance to people without work have all but replaced the church's role in helping such people. Yet, from the beginning, these programs have been exploited by lazy people eager to collect the money and not try to find work. Fraud is commonplace as people not entitled to such payments find ways to get the money anyway.*

*What can the church do to reawaken our society to the values of working for a living?*

*Do you think such programs should be dropped from the list of government programs and returned to the church? Why or why not? Do you think your church would make a sizable increase in its benevolence budget if such programs were cut from the federal budget? Why or why not?*

In Thessalonica, the Lord's messengers had proved themselves to be holy, righteous, and blameless (1 Thessalonians 2:10) among the citizens while showing genuine affection for them. The missionaries had not been *idle* but diligent.

Paul was not claiming that he had never accepted any "free lunches" from anyone, but that he had refused to receive any kind of assistance in earning a living. No one could ever call him a freeloader. To avoid any hint of this, he worked a double shift, *night and day,* first at preaching and teaching and then at earning an income, perhaps making tents as he did at Corinth (Acts 18:3).

**9. We did this, not because we do not have the right to such help, but in order to make ourselves a model for you to follow.**

Paul was the kind of leader who stayed ahead of the competition, doing more than he expected of others. His *right* to live at the expense of those he served was established by Jesus himself, who said, "The worker deserves his wages" (Luke 10:7). God established that they who preach the gospel should live of the gospel (1 Corinthians 9:14). Yet in order to avoid any hint of appearing to be self-serving and to *model* the best possible example, Paul refused to exercise the laborer's right to his salary. He was willing to go far beyond what was required of him in order to persuade his Gentile converts to do the same in overcoming their aversion to manual labor. Such was the intensity of Paul's desire to become "all things to all men" (1 Corinthians 9:22).

### C. AN IMPORTANT PRINCIPLE (v. 10)

**10. For even when we were with you, we gave you this rule: "If a man will not work, he shall not eat."**

This teaching concerning the importance of honest labor had been emphasized in the first Thessalonian letter (2:9; 4:11). Such an attitude toward *work* is grounded in God's earliest dealings with mankind (Genesis 2:15; 3:19). It is stressed in various portions of the Old Testament, especially in the book of Proverbs with its repeated injunctions against laziness and the careless attitude of the sluggard. Jesus enforced this principle with his condemnation of the "wicked, lazy servant" (Matthew 25:26). He declared, "My Father is always at his work to this very day, and I, too, am working" (John 5:17).

Adherence to this principle does not imply the denial of help to those who are unable to help themselves. Paul promoted the most generous giving to Jewish Christians who were experiencing severe poverty (Romans 15:26, 27; 2 Corinthians 8, 9). But for those who choose to live at public expense because it is easier or more lucrative than working at an available job, there is no word of approval in Scripture.

Productive labor is something any Christian can do to the glory of God (1 Corinthians 10:31). It builds and fulfills one's physical, mental, and emotional capacities. It produces a sense of satisfaction and worth never available to those who deliberately avoid productive exertion. Besides this, honest labor makes one's bread taste better and digest more comfortably.

### D. COMMAND TO THE IDLE (vv. 11, 12)

**11. We hear that some among you are idle. They are not busy; they are busybodies.**

Once again a charge of idleness is addressed. Engaged in no productive work of their own, the idle ones were spending their time meddling in their neighbors' business—the definition of *busybodies.* (See 1 Timothy 5:13.) Such individuals had become a hindrance and a source of disturbance to the church.

**12. Such people we command and urge in the Lord Jesus Christ to settle down and earn the bread they eat.**

Corrective measures are addressed directly to the offenders, no matter what their number may have been. The orders are couched in whatever terms may be most effective, whether brotherly urging or authoritative *command* in the full name and power of Heaven's King. The careless ones are to cease their idle chatter, calm their turbulent spirits, and *settle down* to work, so as to *earn* an honest living and bring credit rather than shame to him whose name they wear (1 Thessalonians 4:11, 12).

## E. CONTINUE IN GOOD WORKS (v. 13)

**13. And as for you, brothers, never tire of doing what is right.**

Faithful believers are not to give up on *doing what is right* simply because some people live bountifully and gain notoriety by doing wrong. Paralyzing weariness comes more often from discouragement than from physical exhaustion. Nothing so clogs the channels of honest charity as the demands of human parasites who think the world owes them a living. Nothing so destroys incentives to honest labor as the advertised fact that some people live in luxury through dishonest dealing. Temptations to such discouragement demand steadfast resistance, through constant prayer (Luke 18:1; 1 Thessalonians 5:17) and constant attention to the goal in Christ (Philippians 3:13, 14). "Let us not become weary in doing good, for at the proper time we will reap a harvest if we do not give up" (Galatians 6:9).

*Doing what is right* is much more than the avoidance of doing what is wrong. It is a fulfilling, positive, and active life-style. The Scripture says Dorcas "was always doing good" (Acts 9:36), and that Jesus "went around doing good" (Acts 10:38). "Lord, please help me to be good—for something" is the prayer of a Christian who recognizes that, while *being* is the foundation for *doing, being* is not complete without the *doing*.

### TIRED OF GOODNESS

Sometimes while one is standing in line at a salad bar in a restaurant, he hears complaints from those ahead of him as they look over the available foods. "Oh, it's the same old thing—lettuce, tomatoes, green peppers, etc." No one denies the tomatoes are red and luscious, the lettuce green and crisp, the peppers fresh and spicy. The items are both nutritious and delicious. The problem is that these patrons have become tired of good things.

In the same way, it is possible to become tired of helping others, weary of trying to cheer up the disturbed, and discouraged about giving help to the needy. It may well be as harmful to be bored about doing good as it is to be inclined to do evil. So it is that Paul writes to the Thessalonians, "Never tire of doing what is right" (2 Thessalonians 3:13). The same challenge is offered in Galatians 6:9.

Have we ever felt tired of "doing what is right"? Perhaps many times we become bored simply because of repetition. We take people with us in our car—the same people, to the same place, at the same time. We give, as individuals or as a church, to someone who does not seem to be appreciative or who seems to be taking advantage of our generosity.

An anonymous poet has written in a poem entitled "How Long Shall I Give?":

"Go break to the needy sweet charity's bread;
For giving is living," the angel said.
"And must I be giving again and again?"
My peevish and pitiless answer ran.
"Oh, no," said the angel, piercing me through,
"Just give till the Master stops giving to you."

—J. G. V. B.

## WHAT DO YOU THINK?

"Never tire of doing what is right." Paul must have considered this an important exhortation since he also challenged the Galatians with essentially the same words (6:9). How can we encourage church members to follow this injunction?

How does a brother live up to this when he sees other church members shirking responsibility? How does a sister live up to this when she is unfairly criticized for the way she performs her duties? What can you do this week to encourage a fellow believer not to "tire of doing what is right"?

As for you..., never tire of doing what is right.

The visual for lesson 4 in the visuals packet suggests a variety of ministries we might undertake for the Lord. Display it as you discuss verse 13. Discuss the different activities pictured. Is there some ministry your class could take on?

## III. DISCIPLINE FOR THE LAZY (2 THESSALONIANS 3:14, 15)

The saints also have some responsibility beyond their own good behavior. They are to take specific action concerning the lazy and meddlesome brethren.

### A. WITHDRAW SOCIAL CONTACTS (v. 14)

**14. If anyone does not obey our instruction in this letter, take special note of him. Do not associate with him, in order that he may feel ashamed.**

If someone in the church ignored what Paul had just written and continued to be a meddlesome freeloader, others in the church were to note this and take appropriate action. Elders in particular are directed to "keep watch over . . . the flock of which the Holy Spirit has made you overseers" (Acts 20:28), but the action commanded in the verse before us cannot be accomplished by the elders alone. Disapproval of the offender's behavior is to be made obvious enough to make him *feel ashamed* of his conduct and thus repent and do what is right.

### B. WARN THE ERRING BROTHER (v. 15)

**15. Yet do not regard him as an enemy, but warn him as a brother.**

The offender is still a *brother*—a member of the family of God. The purpose of discipline is not to destroy him or drive him away, but to motivate him to repentance and to restore him, as directed in Galatians 6:1: "If someone is caught in a sin, you who are spiritual should restore him gently." Such discipline is not only for the sake of the disciplined one. It also affects the church and its influence on its members and on the community. In addition, it conveys a message to prospective members, so that they do not gain a distorted view of the gospel, the body of Christ, or the demands of the Christian life.

## IV. BENEDICTION (2 THESSALONIANS 3:16)

The text, which began with a request for prayer on behalf of the writers, now concludes with a prayer for the readers.

**16. Now may the Lord of peace himself give you peace at all times and in every way. The Lord be with all of you.**

*Peace* does not mean the avoidance of difficult situations, such as the one just addressed by Paul. Peace comes when such situations are handled in a manner pleasing to the *Lord of peace*. Such a blessing is not limited to the mature and well-disciplined saints; it is asked for *all of you*—the ones commanded with rebuke as well as those commended with praise.

## CONCLUSION

Disorders in the body of Christ are certainly not limited to the problem of freeloading busybodies. This problem and others may become especially acute where stirred up by obsessive speculation about the "end times"—the schedule and specific details of the Lord's appearing in glory and judgment. Other disorders, such as sexual immorality, greed, gossip, drunkenness, extortion, and strife (1 Corinthians 5:11; Galatians 5:19-21), do not seem limited to certain times and seasons.

Biblical prescriptions for these ailments include many of the same ingredients. One is a firm rejection of such evils, from oneself and from the family of Christ. Another is regular exercise in godliness (1 Timothy 4:7, 8) coupled with prayer and nourishment from God's Word. Also crucial is the encouragement that comes from Christian fellowship. Waiting for the Lord's return is not to be spent in idleness, but in diligent pursuit of the Lord's business (Matthew 25:14-46). The same may be said of waiting for a loved one coming from a distance. The time goes much better if spent in productive work rather than in clock-watching, nail-biting worry!

# Discovery Learning

*This page contains an alternate lesson plan emphasizing learning activities. Classes desiring such student involvement will find these suggestions helpful. The next page is a reproducible activity page to further enhance discovery learning.*

## LEARNING GOALS

After today's lesson, a student should be able to:

1. Tell why Paul said the Thessalonians should be diligent to provide for their own needs.

2. Describe the kinds of problems that come when Christians do not take responsibility for their own needs.

3. Initiate a plan of action by which she will seek to do her share of work in the church and community.

## INTO THE LESSON

On a chalkboard or poster write: "No matter what else is going on, it is always right to _____." Ask people to complete the sentence in as many ways as possible. Possible answers include *love, honor your parents, pay your debts, blow your nose,* etc. Make the transition into the lesson by pointing out that the challenge (and the title) of today's lesson is, "Do What Is Right!"

### OPTION

Use the "Unscrambling the Word" activity on the next page to introduce the theme.

## INTO THE WORD

Ask the class members to work individually or in small groups to study 2 Thessalonians 3:1-5 and suggest how Paul might have completed the opening sentence. After a few minutes, ask for responses and for the specific verse on which each response is based. Answers include: pray (v. 1), honor God and his Word (v. 1), have faith (v. 2), avoid the evil one (v. 3), have confidence in the Lord (v. 4), obey commands (v. 4), love (v. 5), and patiently wait for Christ's return (v. 5). Summarize by saying that God's people must always be ready to do what is right rather than what is convenient, easy, or popular.

Next, ask someone to read 2 Thessalonians 3:6-15. Again, either individually, in small groups, or as a class, determine what the Scripture says is right to do. Answers include: behave in a responsible fashion (v. 7), eat one's own food (v. 8), work hard (v. 8), be a good example (v. 9), mind one's own business (v. 11), and continually do good (v. 13). Mention that Paul worked—probably as a tentmaker—so that he could model this teaching. (See the lesson commentary on verses 7-9, and refer to Acts 18:3 and 20:34, 35.)

Raise these questions: (1) What seems to have been the problem? *People had quit working, apparently in the belief that the Lord would return immediately. They were meddling in other people's business and using up other people's resources. It's not hard to believe that those who had quit working may have been questioning the faith of those who had not.* (2) Why was this so bad? *It put a burden on those who had to support them and gave a negative witness for the church.* (3) What was Paul's solution? *Work for what you eat; mind your own business. Withdraw fellowship from any who would not accept this teaching.* (4) What was the desired result? *Peace in the church, a united witness to the world of the grace of Jesus Christ, and repentance and restoration on the part of the erring ones.*

## INTO LIFE

Have the class form groups of three to five. Ask each group to develop a role play for presentation to the rest of the class. Use the situations on the next page to get started, and have each group expand on one of the situations, add dialogue, and carry its play to a conclusion. After each group presents its play, lead the rest of the class in applause, and then ask them to respond briefly to what they saw. Was it realistic? Did they relate to one of the characters? Would they handle the situation in the same way as the characters did? The point is to develop an awareness of how we can best implement what Paul is telling us to do (shun the disorderly and the disobedient), with attitudes and approaches that will be the most productive.

Situation 5 on the next page will help you address the question: What about those who truly cannot work? Keep the emphasis on those who, for legitimate reasons, cannot support themselves or their families. Discuss the church's responsibility to help those who cannot help themselves. Refer to Acts 2:44-46; 4:34-37; and 6:1-6 for additional biblical teaching on this topic. (Also note the "What Do You Think" discussion question on page 258.)

(*Option:* You can use the situations as case studies instead of role plays if you prefer.)

In closing, ask each person to answer the following questions personally: (1) To what extent am I focused on doing what is right, rather than easy, convenient, or popular? (2) Do I work hard at home, on the job, and in the church? (3) What specifically can I do to improve my conduct and example to others? Allow several minutes for reflection. Conclude the session by reading 2 Thessalonians 3:16.

# Unscrambling the Word

The Thessalonians were confused; their thinking had become a bit "scambled." The message below is part of what Paul told them, but it has become scrambled. Unscramble the message. Check yourself by reading 2 Thessalonians 3:13.

doing for right brothers what you never as tire of is

# Role Plays

Use the following role plays to present some possible situations in which Paul's advice to the Thessalonians in 2 Thessalonians 3 would be relevant.

### SITUATION 1

Ed is working in a garden. Lyn stops by and suggests Ed is wasting his time; when the Lord returns, this effort in the garden will have been useless. When Ed suggests the Lord might not return before harvest, Lyn says he just has to have faith. They ought to be out winning the lost instead of wasting time planting seeds.

### SITUATION 2

Sue is working at a desk. Theresa stops by and remarks she is going home. Sue has to work late. Theresa suggests that is pointless. "In a hundred years, who'll know the difference?" Somewhere in the conversation it becomes apparent Theresa is not a very productive worker. She excuses it by saying her job is merely a "necessary evil." She'd rather be able just to spend time with people and share the love of Jesus with everybody.

### SITUATION 3

A small group is discussing the church's need for Sunday school teachers. Carl says the church spends too much time and effort on teaching doctrine. "We just need to love people." Diane suggests it's not very loving not to tell people—especially the young people—the truths of God's Word. Carl persists. He feels it's better to have a big crowd in the worship assembly than to have other classes going on. He really enjoys **sitting** in the service.

### SITUATION 4

A stranger shows up at the church just as people are leaving the service. He says he has no money, no food,

and no job, but he is a believer and he knows the church is supposed to look after its own. Somewhere in the discussion it becomes obvious he has no intention of working; he wants the church to provide for his needs.

### SITUATION 5

Frank is retired, but his pension is small because he had to take disability before the pension plan had accrued to full value. He is unable to work, but he is embarrassed to accept anything from the church. Ed, a deacon, wants to use the church benevolent fund to help Frank, but the latter refuses the help, quoting 2 Thessalonians 3:10.

### SITUATION 6

Tom and Andrea are a young couple with no children. Each is quick to give advice to parents, however, especially when a child is a bit unruly. Karen is a single mom (widowed) with two young children. She is faithful and involved, but very sensitive to Tom and Andrea's criticism. Her children have been the focus of their remarks more than once.

### SITUATION 7

Dave is a Sunday school teacher for a children's class, but he spends little time preparing lessons. He says he doesn't want to "quench the Spirit's leading." He reads the lesson text and then lets the kids tell what they think the passage means. They frequently finish early, so they play games to fill the hour. Bill is a parent who wants more for his daughter than Dave is offering. Dave, however, argues that his approach is more spiritual and that Bill is too tied to "programs" instead of people.

*Hope for the Future*
*Unit 1. Stand Fast in the Lord*
(Lessons 1-5)

# THE RESURRECTION HOPE

**LESSON 5**

## WHY TEACH THIS LESSON?

The future is always a source of fascination. What if we could know the future? Better yet, what if we could control it? Visions of grandeur, or at least fabulous wealth, generally accompany such dreams.

Today's lesson assures us we can! Because of the resurrection of Jesus—of which we can be absolutely certain—we can know, even control, our future. We can be sure to be included in that great reunion in the sky Paul tells us about. Encourage your students to dream of Heaven, eternity with Jesus. That's a vision of grandeur unmatched by any that is tied to this world and its puny offerings of wealth!

## INTRODUCTION

### A. A MATTER OF DEATH AND LIFE

The siren of ambulance screams in the night, demanding the right of way. It is a matter of life and death. When it reaches its destination, the paramedics scramble from it, employing every ounce of effort and every available piece of technology to prolong human life.

Man has always tried to keep death under control and to stave off its arrival for as long as possible. The reason for this is quite simple: death is a fearful and frightening prospect. Unless an individual is prepared to face death through the victory secured by Jesus' resurrection, that dismal prospect still looms before him.

The Christian gospel has turned the most important human experiences inside out. Life and death matters have been turned into matters of *death and life*; for death no longer signals the end of life, but the passageway *to* life. Jesus himself blazed the trail: "I lay down my life—only to take it up again. No one takes it from me, but I lay it down of my own accord. I have authority to lay it down and authority to take it up again" (John 10:17, 18).

The victorious way in which Christ leads is the way in which his disciples willingly follow: "Don't you know that all of us who were baptized into Christ Jesus were baptized into his death? We were therefore buried with him through baptism into death in order that, just as Christ was raised from the dead through the glory of the Father, we too may live a new life" (Romans 6:3, 4). "If we died with him, we will also live with him" (2 Timothy 2:11). Through Jesus, the dread of physical decline and death is transformed into the glad expectation of life eternal with him.

### B. LESSON BACKGROUND

Since today is Easter Sunday, our focus in today's lesson is quite naturally upon the resurrection of Jesus. Our text from the Thessalonian epistles is taken from 1 Thessalonians 4:13-18. Paul penned these words in order to allay fears among some of the Thessalonian believers that those of their number who had died would be excluded from the events surrounding the return of Christ. While Paul's teaching offers much that is important to an understanding of the doctrine of Jesus' second coming, he also meant for his words to provide practical help to the Thessalonians: "Therefore encourage each other with these words" (v. 18). Such encouragement can sustain believers today as well.

DEVOTIONAL READING:
ROMANS 5:1-11

LESSON SCRIPTURE:
MATTHEW 28:1-10; 1 THESSALONIANS 4:13-18

PRINTED TEXT:
MATTHEW 28:1-10; 1 THESSALONIANS 4:13-18

Mar
30

## LESSON AIMS

As a result of today's lesson, students will be able to:

1. Show how the resurrection account in Matthew lays the groundwork for Paul's letter of assurance to the Thessalonian Christians.

2. Show how 1 Thessalonians 4:13-18 offers courage and strength to Christians in any age.

3. Name one way in which faith in Jesus' resurrection and his coming again will make a difference in their lives during the coming week.

## KEY VERSE

We believe that Jesus died and rose again and so we believe that God will bring with Jesus those who have fallen asleep in him.

1 Thessalonians 4:14

LESSON 5 NOTES

## HOW TO SAY IT

Arimathea. Air-uh-muh-THEE-uh
   (th as in thin).
Galilean. Gal-uh-LEE-un.
Golgotha. GAHL-guh-thuh.
Greco-Roman. GRECK-oh–
   ROE-mun.
Joses. JOE-sez
Lazarus. LAZ-uh-russ.
Magdalene. MAG-duh-leen or
   Mag-duh-LEE-nee.
Salome. Suh-LOE-me.
shalom (hebrew). shah-LOME.
Thessalonica. THESS-uh-loe-
   NYE-kuh.

## WHAT DO YOU THINK?

The angel reminded the women that Jesus had predicted he would rise from the dead ("he has risen, just as he said"). Why were Jesus' followers so slow to understand all this? What possible reasons can you suggest?

Do you think this should be taken as a caution to believers today? That is, if the disciples who spent so much time in intimate contact with Jesus could fail to understand what now seems so clear, might we be missing a thing or two? If so, how should we handle our differences of understanding?

The first portion of our printed text records the account of Jesus' resurrection as found in the Gospel of Matthew. It is this event that gave to Paul and the Thessalonians, and gives to today's Christian, the assurance that the future is filled with hope, not despair. Death may close the door to earth; but in Christ, it opens another door—to Heaven!

## I. JESUS IS RISEN (MATTHEW 28:1-10)

### A. WOMEN SEE THE EMPTY TOMB (vv. 1-4)

**1. After the Sabbath, at dawn on the first day of the week, Mary Magdalene and the other Mary went to look at the tomb.**

After Jesus died, his body was entombed before *the Sabbath* began on Friday evening. The Galilean women then left Golgotha and returned home to prepare spices to embalm the body (Luke 23:56). They observed the Sabbath rest, and then came at the earliest opportunity to visit the *tomb* on the morning of *the first day of the week.* Mark 16:1 and Luke 24:10 mention other women (including Salome and Joanna) as participating in the visit, besides those named here. The name of *Mary Magdalene,* "out of whom he had driven seven demons" (Mark 16:9), figures prominently in John's account of the resurrection (John 20:1-18). *The other Mary* was probably the mother of James and Joses (Matthew 27:56, 61).

**2-4. There was a violent earthquake, for an angel of the Lord came down from heaven and, going to the tomb, rolled back the stone and sat on it. His appearance was like lightning, and his clothes were white as snow. The guards were so afraid of him that they shook and became like dead men.**

When the women arrived at the *tomb,* they discovered what had already happened. As an *earthquake* had marked the death of Jesus (Matthew 27:51), so now an earthquake marked his resurrection, terrifying the *guards* who had been posted to prevent Jesus' body from being removed.

A large, heavy *stone* was sometimes placed in a groove or trough before the entrance of a tomb to keep animals or thieves from going inside. Such a stone had been rolled into place by Joseph of Arimathea after he laid the body of Jesus in "his own new tomb" (Matthew 27:57-60). That it became a seat for the *angel of the Lord* showed dramatically who was now in charge.

The angel's brilliant appearance brings to mind the description of Jesus at his transfiguration (Matthew 17:1, 2). Luke 24:4 mentions "two men in clothes that gleamed like lightning" at the tomb. Matthew writes of the one who spoke to the women. These heavenly visitors terrified the guards to such an extent that they *shook and became like dead men* (even strong men faint when sufficiently frightened). These men seem to have recovered enough to return to Jerusalem (vv. 11-15) before the women arrived.

### B. AN ANGEL EXPLAINS AND DIRECTS (vv. 5-8)

Mark 16:5 and Luke 24:3, 4 indicate that the angels were not on the doorway stone, but had moved inside the tomb when one of them spoke to the women.

**5, 6. The angel said to the women, "Do not be afraid, for I know that you are looking for Jesus, who was crucified. He is not here; he has risen, just as he said. Come and see the place where he lay.**

*The angel* responded, not to anything the women had said, but to their unspoken fears and questions. He whose appearance had struck terror to the soldiers now spoke comfort to the friends of Jesus: *He is not here; he has risen.* Jesus could not and cannot be found among the dead. Both the cross and the tomb were and are empty. He arose as he had repeatedly predicted (Matthew 16:21; 17:9, 23; 20:19), but the predictions were not comprehended by the disciples until after they were fulfilled. *The place where* the Lord *lay,* its grave clothes now empty and its head covering neatly folded (John 20:6, 7), still bears the kind of testimony that cannot be successfully contested or denied.

**7. "Then go quickly and tell his disciples: 'He has risen from the dead and is going ahead of you into Galilee. There you will see him.' Now I have told you."**

Having seen the evidence that the *disciples* had not yet seen, these women were commissioned as the first human proclaimers of the great news. Their glad tidings, however, would be met with disbelief (Luke 24:10, 11).

Next came word that Jesus would be going to *Galilee.* This region was home to most of the apostles. Jesus and they had worked there throughout most of their time together. There the living Lord would give instructions for the ongoing ministry that they would carry out in his name.

*Now I have told you* concluded the angel's message to the women. Extending it to answer any questions they may have had would have been unwise at this point. The women simply needed to convey the important information they had been given.

**8. So the women hurried away from the tomb, afraid yet filled with joy, and ran to tell his disciples.**

The women followed the angel's instructions, driven by a mixture of emotions as well as by the heavenly command. Fear kept them from telling anyone along the way about the resurrection, but *joy* led them to seek out the *disciples* and convey their message. Would that we possessed such excitement, instead of the dull indifference that characterizes all too much of religion in our present time!

### D. THE LORD ASSURES AND COMMANDS (vv. 9, 10)

**9. Suddenly Jesus met them. "Greetings," he said. They came to him, clasped his feet and worshiped him.**

Exactly at what point in the women's journey to the city this meeting occurred is uncertain. John 20:11-18 speaks of Jesus' appearance to Mary Magdalene, who was alone. *Greetings* is not the usual Jewish greeting of peace (which is *shalom*). Rather, it is a word calls on the hearer to "rejoice" or "be glad." The mood of the women's morning visit to the tomb had been completely reversed.

The women seem to have recognized Jesus immediately, but knelt to clasp him by the *feet.* By this gesture of worship, they could assure themselves that his risen body was real and tangible. Thus they experienced the kind of proof that was similar to that which was granted to Thomas and which brought his confession, "My Lord and my God" (John 20:28).

**10. Then Jesus said to them, "Do not be afraid. Go and tell my brothers to go to Galilee; there they will see me."**

The angel's earlier message was now reinforced with the highest possible authority. With the women now fully convinced of the reality of Jesus' triumph over death, they were filled with an even greater zeal to convey the news of his resurrection to the disciples.

That Jesus referred to his disciples as *brothers* speaks of his tenderness toward them. It also foreshadowed the special relationship that all future believers would have with him (Hebrews 2:11, 12).

### II. JESUS IS RETURNING (1 THESSALONIANS 4:13-18)

#### A. PAUL'S PURPOSE IN WRITING

Forty days after the events recorded in Matthew 28:1-10, the ascension of Jesus into Heaven took place. Two angels on the nearby Mount of Olives told the amazed apostles what they needed to know about the event unfolding before

*OPTION*

*The reproducible page for this lesson (page 270) provides a harmony of the various resurrection appearances recorded in the four Gospels, Acts 1, and 1 Corinthians 15. If your students are troubled by the differences in these accounts, this resource will help them see how the differences need not be seen as contradictions.*

## WHAT DO YOU THINK?

*What are some ways in which the grief of a Christian at the death of a loved one differs from the grief of a non-Christian?*

*Even people who show little interest in the gospel will often speak of going to Heaven and being reunited there with deceased family members and friends. What is the difference between their "hope" and Christian hope?*

*Since we know him who called himself "the resurrection and the life" (John 11:25), we have a sure hope for ourselves and our loved ones who die in the Lord. We also know "the God of all comfort" (2 Corinthians 1:3). How does his comfort help us even when we lose an unsaved family member or friend to death?*

## OPTIONAL DISCUSSION IDEA

*If you have class members who have lost loved ones and feel free to talk about their experiences, perhaps they could share how their Christian hope sustained them.*

For if we believe that Jesus died and rose again, even so them also which sleep in Jesus will God bring with him.

I Thessalonians 4:14

*The visual for lesson 5 illustrates 1 Thessalonians 4:14. Display it as you discuss that verse.*

them: "This same Jesus, who has been taken from you into heaven, will come back in the same way you have seen him go into heaven" (Acts 1:11). Ten days later the church was born and the apostles went forth preaching the Christ who died for our sins, arose from the tomb, and is coming in judgment. Paul became one of these apostles, and Thessalonica was one of the cities where he planted a church. Through his writings to the Thessalonians, he was eager to complete what was lacking in their faith (1 Thessalonians 3:10). One area in which they were lacking in understanding was the doctrine of Jesus' coming in glory to receive his own to himself. It is significant that every one of the five chapters in 1 Thessalonians closes with a positive reference to the Lord's return.

One of the primary misunderstandings that Paul had to address was the fear that anyone who died before Jesus' return would have no part in that glorious occasion. The passage before us was written to correct that error.

### B. CHRIST'S RESURRECTION AND OURS (vv. 13, 14)

**13. Brothers, we do not want you to be ignorant about those who fall asleep, or to grieve like the rest of men, who have no hope.**

The apostle was not willing to leave his readers *ignorant,* or without instruction, on such an important theme. In several other passages Paul introduces new or important subjects in the same manner (Romans 1:13; 11:25; 1 Corinthians 10:1; 12:1; 2 Corinthians 1:8). The reference to those who are *asleep* refers to those who have died. Jesus used it concerning Lazarus (John 11:11). It suggests rest from one's labors and the expectation of resurrection.

It is significant that Paul's desire for the Thessalonians is not that they experience no grief at all, but that they not *grieve like the rest of men.* Grief is a natural part of the human experience. Even Jesus wept at the tomb of Lazarus (John 11:35). Paul himself experienced sorrow over the illness of a friend (Philippians 2:27). It is the misguided friend who encourages someone who has lost a loved one to death, "Don't cry."

Christians will experience grief, but there is a great difference between their grief and the bitter emptiness of those who see only the end of everything with the final heartbeat. The grief of those whose faith in Jesus provides an infinitely joyous expectation of a new beginning is different in every way from that of those *who have no hope.* Such a difference, when exhibited in circumstances of death or suffering, can provide a persuasive testimony to the power of Christian faith.

### NO HOPE

In his work, "An Essay on Man," Alexander Pope wrote, "Hope springs eternal in the human breast." This may well be true, but the "hope" about which he spoke was the hope of many blessings and favorable outcomes in this life. It is immeasurably more difficult for man, in the limits of his own intelligence, to entertain a valid hope for anything *beyond* this life. The official religion of the Romans contained a whole pantheon of gods and goddesses that were to be adored and placated with offerings. They were worshiped in lovely colonnaded temples; their officiating priests dressed in flowing robes. But there was no note of hope in the vast array of supplications and ministrations. Nothing was offered regarding death, but a crossing of the mythological river Styx (pronounced *Sticks*) and an entrance into a gray and shadowy existence. There was no note of certainty, no anticipation of glory.

G. K. Chesterton, the famous British essayist, said, "The fierce poet of the Middle Ages [Dante] wrote, 'Abandon hope, all ye who enter here,' over the gates of the lower world. The emancipated poets of today have written it over the gates of this world." Paul indicated that such was certainly true of the Greco-Roman world in which he and his readers lived.

How closely are these two realities linked together—"without hope" and "without God" (Ephesians 2:12)! Godlessness and hopelessness will always be twins. Only those who have faith in Jesus as God's Son—living, loving, crucified, risen, and returning—can have genuine hope.             —J. G. V. B.

**14. We believe that Jesus died and rose again and so we believe that God will bring with Jesus those who have fallen asleep in him.**

Here Paul begins to address the primary question troubling the Thessalonians. What had become, and what would become, of those who had already died in Christ? The answer is this: *God will bring with Jesus those who have fallen asleep in him.*

This statement can be understood one of two ways. The first possibility is that those who *have fallen asleep* in Jesus will be included among those "holy ones" who will return with Jesus when he comes (1 Thessalonians 3:13).* The second possibility involves taking the word *bring* to refer to what will happen to the dead after Jesus has returned; that is, God will *bring* them back to Heaven with Jesus. With either understanding comes the assurance that the future of those who die in Christ is secure. Believing that God will bring Christians from the grave is surely not difficult after knowing that he has brought Jesus from the tomb.

### C. WHAT WILL HAPPEN WHEN HE COMES? (vv. 15-17)
**15. According to the Lord's own word, we tell you that we who are still alive, who are left till the coming of the Lord, will certainly not precede those who have fallen asleep.**

The highest possible authority is cited for what is to follow. It comes from *the Lord,* whether by some otherwise unrecorded teaching of Jesus during his earthly ministry (compare the statement cited in Acts 20:35), or by direct revelation to Paul himself (note 1 Corinthians 11:23; Galatians 1:11, 12; 2:2; Ephesians 3:3).

The *word* is this: at *the coming of the Lord,* those who are *still alive* will not *precede* the ones who have already died (*have fallen asleep*) in Christ. Thus, those Christians who have died will share fully in the glory of Christ's return.

Some believe that this statement reveals Paul's belief that the return of Jesus would take place in his lifetime. However, it is more accurate to say that he believed that it *could* take place in his lifetime; on the other hand, were Paul to die before that day, he was perfectly content to "depart and be with Christ" (Philippians 1:23).

**16, 17. For the Lord himself will come down from heaven, with a loud command, with the voice of the archangel and with the trumpet call of God, and the dead in Christ will rise first. After that, we who are still alive and are left will be caught up together with them in the clouds to meet the Lord in the air. And so we will be with the Lord forever.**

Jesus *himself* will one day come down from Heaven, fulfilling what the angels had spoken at his ascension (Acts 1:10, 11). The *loud command* is that of an officer addressing his troops. This command probably will be uttered by Jesus, although it may be the same sound as *the voice of the archangel,* heralding the coming of Jesus. *The trumpet call of God* will call forth those who sleep (1 Corinthians 15:52).

The *dead in Christ* are *in Christ* as surely in death as they were in life. Death cannot separate anyone from the love of God (Romans 8:38, 39). The spirits of these who have died in Christ will have been alive all the time, although absent from their physical bodies. (See 2 Corinthians 5:8; Philippians 1:23.) At Christ's return, their bodies will arise immortal (1 Corinthians 15:53). These saints will thus be prepared to "inherit the kingdom of God" (v. 50). They will then be joined by the

---

***NOTE***

*See comments on the "holy ones" of 1 Thessalonians 3:13 on pages 240 and 241.*

---

**WHAT DO YOU THINK?**

*The lesson writer says Paul lived with the expectation that Jesus could come in his lifetime. Do you think most Christians live with that same expectancy? Why or why not? What can we do to heighten that expectation among believers? How can we enhance it in our worship services, study times, personal devotions, and other times?*

---

**PRAYER**

*Thanks and praise to you, dear God, for the fulfilled promises that provide a sure and certain hope. You have promised a Savior and given your Son. You promised his resurrection and raised him in power. Thank you beforehand for your presence in all of life, for your comfort in death, for Jesus' coming in glory, and for the endless, glorious joy of your dwelling place in Heaven. Amen.*

### DAILY BIBLE READINGS

**Monday, Mar. 24**—*Jesus Christ Died for Sinners (Romans 5:1-11)*

**Tuesday, Mar. 25**—*God's Gift of Grace for All (Romans 5:12-19)*

**Wednesday, Mar. 26**—*The Fact of the Resurrection (1 Corinthians 15:1-11)*

**Thursday, Mar. 27**—*The Need for the Resurrection (1 Corinthians 15:12-19)*

**Friday, Mar. 28**—*The Assurance of the Resurrection (1 Corinthians 15:20-28)*

**Saturday, Mar. 29**—*The Nature of the Resurrection (1 Corinthians 15:35-44)*

**Sunday, Mar. 30**—*The Victory of the Resurrection (1 Corinthians 15:51-58)*

### WHAT DO YOU THINK?

*It is interesting that Paul closes 1 Thessalonians 4 with the exhortation to "encourage each other with these words." How can we gain comfort and encouragement from a passage that has often caused debate among believers with differing views regarding Christ's return?*

*What one fact do you find most comforting or encouraging in this passage? How can you share that with someone else?*

### THOUGHT TO REMEMBER

*Because Jesus lives, I too shall live.*

saints who are living at Jesus' return, but who will be instantly changed into their glorified spiritual bodies (1 Corinthians 15:51, 52). Together, both the dead and the living will *meet the Lord in the air,* and *will be with the Lord forever.*

It should be noted that this is not a full discourse on Christ's return. Certain subjects (for example, what will happen to the earth itself) are not covered. It was enough for Paul to deal with the Thessalonians' most pressing question: will a believer miss out on the glory of Christ's return if he dies before it happens? Clearly he will not.

#### TOGETHER

To those whose relationship is characterized by genuine love, the most glorious word in all our human vocabulary is the word *together.* Many times those who love are separated—by illness, for example. One person is confined to a hospital; the spouse must remain at home. While they can see each other whenever the spouse visits the hospital, the yearning of both is for a degree of recovery that will allow them to be together in the manner to which they have become accustomed.

Perhaps the clouds of war gather overhead and a responsibility in terms of military service must be met. The tides of war pull a couple apart, but letters and telephone calls make some communication possible. One can be sure that a predominant wish is expressed again and again— "Someday, before long, we can be *together* again."

When our loved ones are severed from us by death, we find the separation a source of bitterness and grief. The greatest wish we have is not to know what all the conditions of a future life may be. We desire to know one thing above all: "Can we be *together* again?" If we can, love is content with that assurance alone.

Paul tells the Thessalonians, regarding those who have gone before in relation to those who are left, "We . . . will be caught up *together* with them" (1 Thessalonians 4:17). For love, this is enough!     —J. G. V. B.

### D. GAINING STRENGTH FROM THE ASSURANCE (v. 18)

**18. Therefore encourage each other with these words.**

It is not enough for the words of Scripture to instruct, establish, and encourage the people who read them. Those same Scriptures are to be shared, reviewed, and discussed in gatherings of the church (Hebrews 10:25) and in personal contacts, so that all may receive comfort. Let us use the Word to quiet anxieties over the fate of departed saints, to strengthen faith in the promises of God, and to encourage the kind of living that is prepared to receive those promises.

### CONCLUSION

Many church buildings have been designed to highlight the essential facts of the gospel message and to call the worshipers' attention to them. Centrally located on the worshipers' level in the church building where this writer worships is the Communion table, inviting us to "proclaim the Lord's death until he comes" (1 Corinthians 11:26). Behind the table is the pulpit, dedicated to the proclamation of Christ giving his life, conquering death, interceding in Heaven, and coming in glory to claim his own. Highly visible behind the pulpit is the baptistery, where believers, dying to sin in repentance, are buried with their Lord in baptism that they may rise to walk with him through time and eternity. Having understood the purpose of his first coming, they are now fully prepared for his second.

Someone has said, "If the outlook is bad, try looking up." Because of Jesus' resurrection and promised return, our future is certain. He holds "the keys of death and Hades" (Revelation 1:18). May we, like the Thessalonians, learn to "wait for his Son from heaven, whom he raised from the dead—Jesus" (1 Thessalonians 1:10).

# Discovery Learning

*This page contains an alternate lesson plan emphasizing learning activities. Classes desiring such student involvement will find these suggestions helpful. The next page is a reproducible activity page to further enhance discovery learning.*

## LEARNING GOALS

As a result of today's lesson, students will be able to:

1. Show how the resurrection account in Matthew lays the groundwork for Paul's letter of assurance to the Thessalonian Christians.

2. Show how 1 Thessalonians 4:13-18 offers courage and strength to Christians in any age.

3. Name one way in which faith in Jesus' resurrection and his coming again will make a difference in their lives during the coming week.

## INTO THE LESSON

Ask for volunteers among the class to tell briefly about a time when they were very joyful. Then ask for responses relating a time when someone was scared, very sad, or felt left out. Take as many brief responses as possible. Make the transition into today's lesson by saying that many of those same emotions were at work when Jesus rose from the dead. They have continued to be a part of our experience ever since, and will continue until the Lord returns. But since he has risen, and since he is returning, we have the power to change the sorrow to joy!

## INTO THE WORD

Divide the class in half. Ask the first half to study Matthew 28:1-10 and list the emotions they find being experienced there. (They should find fear, vv. 4, 5, 8; joy, v. 8; worship, v. 9. Implied but not stated might be grief, surprise, excitement, and possibly others.)

The other half should study 1 Thessalonians 4:13-18 and list the emotions mentioned there. (They should find ignorance, v. 13; grief, v. 13; hope, v, 13; faith or belief, v. 14; encouragement or comfort, v. 18.)

Give the groups (each half of your class could be divided into smaller groups with the same assignment if you have a large class) about five minutes to complete this activity. Then read the text aloud and ask for reports from the groups. Be sure a verse number is cited for each emotion given, and read the verse again. Comment on the context so that in the course of discussing the emotions you give a full picture of the content of each passage.

Ask, "How does the information presented in our text from Matthew lay the foundation for what we read in 1 Thessalonians 4?" Point out verse 14 during in the discussion. (If the class is slow to respond, this might be a good way to "prime the pump.") "We believe that Jesus died

and rose again." The hope we have of his return and of our own resurrection is founded on the resurrection of Jesus! This is what makes our celebration of what we call "Easter" significant. If Jesus' resurrection were significant only to him, there would be no cause for celebration. Since it signals the truth of his promise in John 14:1-4, it brings us great joy and comfort. (Have a student read John 14:1-4.)

## OPTION

Use the reproducible page that follows to provide additional information about the resurrection. It gives a harmony of the various resurrection appearances cited in the New Testament.

## INTO LIFE

Ask, "What turned the women's sorrow to joy on the resurrection morning?" (The angel's message; seeing the Lord.) Observe that we cannot witness the empty tomb or the witness of angels firsthand as they did. We cannot see with our eyes the risen Lord or clasp his feet. In that, we are more like the Thessalonian Christians to whom Paul wrote. Ask, "What was expected to turn the Thessalonians' sorrow to joy?" (Faith in the resurrection and return of Christ.)

Continue the discussion and personal application of these Scriptures with these questions: "How do the passages in today's text help us when a family member dies?" ". . . when a job is lost?" ". . . when a family is breaking apart?"

As Christians we are not insulated from sadness, grief, and fear, but we are equipped with a certainty of victory. The joy and assurance we receive from knowing that the past and the future are in God's hands will help us confront present situations from his perspective.

Discuss, "If more Christians had an unwavering faith in the fact that Jesus will soon return and take us all to be with him forever, what kind of difference would that make in our world?"

Distribute index cards to your students. Assure them what they write on the cards can remain private if they choose. Then ask each of them to write one way in which his faith in Jesus' resurrection and coming again will make a difference in his life during the coming week. Ask the students to keep the cards as reminders of what they have written.

# Resurrection Harmony

All four Gospels record the resurrection and several appearances by Jesus after the resurrection. Acts 1 and 1 Corinthians 15 also mention appearances. But these sources do not cite the same appearances. As a result, some have alleged error and discrepancy in the Bible on this issue. The following is offered as a possible harmony of all the reports, giving a fuller picture of the events than any single source records.

| Event | Matthew | Mark | Luke | John | Acts | 1 Cor. |
|---|---|---|---|---|---|---|
| Several women start for the tomb | 28:1 | 16:1, 2 | 24:1 | 20:1 | | |
| Mary Magdalene goes to get Peter & John | | | | 20:2 | | |
| Angels tell the other women Jesus is alive | 28:5-7 | 16:5-7 | 24:2-8 | | | |
| The women leave the tomb | 28:7, 8 | 16:8 | | | | |
| Peter and John inspect the tomb | | | 24:12 | 20:3-10 | | |
| Jesus appears to Mary | | 16:9 | | 20:11-17 | | |
| Jesus appears to the other women | 28:9, 10 | | | | | |
| Mary Magdalene tells the apostles | | 16:10, 11 | | 20:18 | | |
| The other women report | | | 24:9-11 | | | |
| Jesus appears on the road to Emmaus | | 16:12, 13 | 24:13-33 | | | |
| Jesus appears to Peter (Cephas) | | | 24:34 | | | 15:5 |
| Jesus appears to the apostles | | 16:14 | 24:36-43 | 20:19-24 | | |
| Jesus appears to the apostles 1 week later | | | | 20:26-31 | | 15:5 |
| Jesus appears to 7 apostles by Sea of Galilee | | | | 21:1-23 | | |
| Jesus appears in Galilee to 500 | 28:18-20 | | | | | 15:6 |
| Jesus appears to James | | | | | | 15:7 |
| Jesus appears to apostles in Jerusalem | | 16:15-18 | 24:44-49 | | 1:3-8 | 15:7 |
| The ascension | | 16:19, 20 | 24:50-53 | | 1:9-12 | |
| Jesus appears to Saul of Tarsus | | | | | | 15:8 |

# COMMANDED TO WRITE

**LESSON 6**

## WHY TEACH THIS LESSON?

The study of the book of Revelation often meets with one of two extreme reactions. Some are eager to study it—maybe too eager. Certain they will find some secret key that will give them insight into the end times, these are ever hungering for new and more exciting presentatons of its message. Others are wary. Perhaps they have heard too much wild speculation about the images in the book. Perhaps they have tried unsuccessfully to decipher the figurative language. For whatever reason, they have given up on understanding the book.

Each approach is wrong. The writer was "commanded to write," so the readers were expected to understand. The writing was addressed to suffering saints to encourage them in their present distress, not simply to give details of the by and by. Events of the future are, indeed, foreshadowed, but with the view to encouraging the reader in his or her present distress.

Assure your class members that today's study, as each of the remaining lessons in this quarter, will approach the book of Revelation from this practical starting point. They should find hope in whatever distress they are suffering in their Christian walk as well.

## INTRODUCTION

### A. IT IS WRITTEN!

What a marvelous gift is the ability to write, and thus to convey information, thoughts, and feelings to people you may never see! From earliest times God made certain that his people wrote down what he deemed essential for them to remember, since it contained a message for all people in all times (Romans 15:4). These writings, which became part of the Scriptures, were preserved and transmitted, often with great difficulty.

In the New Testament, writing was crucial to the preservation of the life and message of Jesus. Two Gospel writers, Luke and John, offer personal testimony as to the process and purpose of their efforts (Luke 1:1-4; John 20:30, 31). Luke continued the story begun in his book of the life of Christ with the book of Acts (Acts 1:1, 2). The New Testament epistles gave encouragement and instruction to both congregations and individuals, and were meant to be distributed for the benefit of others (Colossians 4:16). As we will see in today's lesson, it was vital that John write what Jesus wanted to be conveyed to the seven churches in Asia.

The commonly used phrase, "It is written," reflects the consistent concern of God throughout Scripture that his revelation be carefully copied and preserved. Let us never take for granted our precious privilege of being able to read and to know the *Word* of God.

### B. LESSON BACKGROUND

God's people are no strangers to difficulty. They have frequently endured physical persecution, exile, and the demand that they renounce their God and swear allegiance to false deities, including the human rulers of earthly kingdoms. Apocalyptic (that is, highly figurative and symbolic, dealing with the struggle between

---

**DEVOTIONAL READING:**
**REVELATION 21:1-4**
**LESSON SCRIPTURE:**
**REVELATION 1**
**PRINTED TEXT:**
**REVELATION 1:4-15**

**LESSON AIMS**

This study should equip the student to:

1. List the descriptions of Jesus in Revelation 1.

Apr 6

2. Explain how these descriptions show a special relationship between the Lord and his suffering saints.

3. Make a commitment to serve the Lord even when pressured to do otherwise.

The visual for lesson 6 shows an artist's concept of John writing the Revelation. Have the visual on display as students arrive.

What thou seest, write in a book, and send it unto the seven churches which are in Asia. *Revelation 1:11*

**KEY VERSE**

"Write on a scroll what you see and send it to the seven churches."
*Revelation 1:11*

LESSON 6 NOTES

## NOTE

*In addition to the Old Testament apocalyptic material, secular apocalyptic literature was common in the first century. The typical Greek approach made good and evil equals in a never-ending struggle that saw first one dominant and then the other. The inspired "Apocalypse" (the title of "Revelation" if we transliterate the word) shows God clearly in control of the good and ultimately victorious.*

## WHAT DO YOU THINK?

*In the verse just before our printed text begins is a blessing on "the one who reads the words of this prophecy" (Revelation 1:3). How have you been blessed by a study of Revelation—or have you? What problems have you encountered in studying this book? What is your favorite part of Revelation? Why?*

*The map for lesson 1 also includes the seven churches of Asia. Display it again as you discuss the location of these churches.*

good and evil) literature has often appeared as a kind of "code" writing during times of severe persecution. By this means, the faithful have been encouraged and instructed in terms that made no sense at all to their oppressors. The Old Testament books of Daniel and Zechariah abound in such language.

The earliest persecutions of the church came from Jewish sources that were familiar with the Old Testament apocalyptic material. Thus, for a time, plain language served best in strengthening the church. However, when the Roman Empire attempted to require all its subjects to worship the emperor, and intensified its persecution of the church, apocalyptic symbolism again became the style in which God's Word was communicated to God's people. This is the style found throughout most of the book of Revelation. In fact, the first word of the book is *apocalupsis:* "apocalypse." It is translated "revelation."

Most scholars believe that Revelation was written during the persecution mounted by Domitian, the Roman emperor from A.D. 81 to 96. The writer of Revelation identifies himself as John (most likely the apostle John, son of Zebedee). The style of writing differs considerably from that of his Gospel and his three brief epistles; however, one must keep in mind that the circumstances behind the writing of Revelation differed considerably. John was already separated from his friends by exile because of his preaching. How would he communicate to them a written message of ultimate triumph over their Roman oppressors without getting himself and them into greater difficulties? The Holy Spirit provided John with visions of the victory of Christ in words and symbols familiar from Old Testament Scripture but meaningless to the literal Roman mind.

This suggests, of course, a familiarity with the Old Testament on the part of John's readers. This would not surprise us if the readers were Jewish. The churches of Asia, however, were in large part Gentile. Paul labored in some of these cities, as we read in the bok of Acts, and his converts among the Jews were few. The Gentiles were more receptive to his message. Thus, we conclude that these Gentile believers were urged to become familiar with the Jewish Scriptures.

## I. GREETINGS TO THE CHURCHES (REVELATION 1:4, 5a)

The message to be delivered took the form of an extensive letter to groups of Christians in the Roman province of Asia.

### A. WRITER AND READERS (v. 4a)
**4. John,**
   **To the seven churches in the province of Asia:**
*John,* who had served for years among the churches around Ephesus (the principal city of *Asia*), was known well enough among them to require no further introduction. The province of Asia occupied much of the western one-fourth of Asia Minor, or modern Turkey.

Churches were found in at least ten cities of Asia in New Testament times. Since *seven* in the Bible frequently symbolizes perfection or completeness, some have suggested the *seven churches* mentioned here and addressed individually in Revelation 2 and 3 represent all churches in every place and time. Others believe each church represents the church in one of seven different time periods. The book of Revelation is, indeed, applicable to all congregations in all times, but its message speaks particularly to those suffering under conditions similar to what was experienced by these seven churches in the first century. Just as we can learn and apply lessons written by Paul specifically to churches in Rome, Corinth, Galatia, Ephesus, Philippi, Colosse, and Thessalonica, so we can learn and apply lessons written specifically to the seven churches named in Revelation 2 and 3.

Another way to look at this issue is to see the letter as written first to seven churches, but having a fulfillment beyond them as well. When we read "Out of Egypt I called my son" in Hosea 11:1, our first thought is that the reference is to the exodus. The context makes that clear. Yet Matthew, by the inspiration of the Holy Spirit, tells us Mary, Joseph, and Jesus' flight to Egypt and subsequent return fulfills this prophecy (Matthew 2:15). Does it refer to the exodus or to Jesus? Both. Was Revelation written to seven churches or to all churches in all times? Both.

## B. BLESSINGS AND THEIR SOURCE (vv. 4b, 5a)

**4b, 5a.** *Grace and peace to you from him who is, and who was, and who is to come, and from the seven spirits before his throne, and from Jesus Christ, who is the faithful witness, the firstborn from the dead, and the ruler of the kings of the earth.*

John's petition for *grace and peace* upon his readers combines the Greek wish for goodness and beauty (grace) with the Jewish prayer for God's wholeness (peace). New Testament language (as in Ephesians 2:7) adds the assurance of God's love in Jesus Christ to grace, and the wholeness that can come from none but Christ (John 14:27) to the idea of peace.

John also includes a majestic description of the Godhead within his greeting. The words *who is, and who was, and who is to come* are reminiscent of the name by which God (the Father) revealed himself in Exodus 3:14, 15 (I AM WHO I AM). The Holy Spirit is identified by the term *seven spirits*. According to one writer, this term describes the Holy Spirit as "sevenfold in his operations." Perhaps the number *seven* was used in conjunction with the seven churches to which the letter was being sent. *Jesus Christ*, who is the primary focus of this writing (see 1:1, 2), is the only one of the three persons of the Godhead named directly.

Here three aspects of Jesus' ministry are highlighted. Jesus told Pilate that he had come to "testify to the truth" (John 18:37), and his *faithful* commitment to this mission led to his death. Death, however, could not hold him. Through his resurrection he became *the firstborn from the dead*. Similar titles are "the firstfruits of those who have fallen asleep" (1 Corinthians 15:20) and "the firstborn from among the dead" (Colossians 1:18). Jesus was not the first person to be raised from the dead. The Old Testament records a few resurrections, and Jesus himself raised several. But he is the first to be brought back to life never to die again. This makes him *the ruler of the kings of the earth*. He is the supreme ruler over all earthly rulers—"Lord of lords and King of kings" (Revelation 17:14; Ephesians 1:20, 21).

The all-out conflict between this ruler and the kings of the earth is described later in vivid apocalyptic language.

### ATTENTION TO TENSES

John begins the book of Revelation with greetings from the One "who is, and who was, and who is to come." This is an interesting sequence to apply to our own lives. We are what we are, and are doing what we are doing, in terms of right now. Yet all that we are now has grown out of what we were and did in the past. Likewise, it is true that what happens in the future will be in large part determined by what we are and what we do in the present.

We also find this to be true occupationally. If one is a secretary to an important businessman, usually he or she has concentrated on the study of typing, word processing, and other business subjects in the past. If more career advances take place in the future, they will be based on the work being done now.

In our Christian lives, the same sequence of verb tenses comes into play. Our sense of forgiveness, fellowship, and fruitfulness in the present is dependent on the

## HOW TO SAY IT

*Aegean.* Ay-JEE-un.
*apokalupsis (Greek).* uh-POCK-uh-LOOP-sis.
*apocalyptic.* uh-POCK-uh-LIP-tik.
*Colosse.* Kuh-LAHSS-ee.
*Domitian.* Doe-MISH-un.
*Ephesus.* EFF-uh-suss.
*Hierapolis.* High-er-AP-uh-liss.
*Josephus.* Joe-SEE-fuss.
*Laodicea.* Lay-ODD-uh-SEE-uh.
*Miletus.* My-LEE-tuss.
*Pergamum.* PER-guh-mum.
*Smyrna.* SMUR-nuh.
*Troas.* TROE-az.

## DAILY BIBLE READINGS

**Monday, Mar. 31**—Jesus, God's Eternal Word (John 1:1-4)

**Tuesday, Apr. 1**—Jesus, the Light of the World (John 1:5-18)

**Wednesday, Apr. 2**—We Live Through Jesus Christ (Romans 6:1-11)

**Thursday, Apr. 3**—Christ, the Head of All Things (Colossians 1:15-20)

**Friday, Apr. 4**—Give Thanks to the Lord (Psalm 100)

**Saturday, Apr. 5**—God Honors Those Who Serve him (John 12:20-26)

**Sunday, Apr. 6**—A Savior for All People (Luke 2:25-32)

past. What Jesus did for us enables us to stand as we do—complete in him. All the benefits and bliss of the future come from the life and joy we find in him in our life's present. The One who is, and was, and is to come makes *us* what we are and were and are to become! —J. G. V. B.

## II. GLORY TO THE SAVIOR (REVELATION 1: 5b, 6)

Christ, the source of blessing to the saints in the seven churches, is now presented as the object of adoration among those communities of faith.

### A. HE IS BLESSED (vv. 5b, 6)

**5b, 6. To him who loves us and has freed us from our sins by his blood, and has made us to be a kingdom and priests to serve his God and Father—to him be glory and power for ever and ever! Amen.**

Some translation say "loved us" here to keep the tense consistent with the past tense of *freed*. But the Greek text changes tenses, and this is given in the ongoing present tense—*loves us*. Jesus' love is not limited to the sacrifice on Calvary that freed us from our sins, but it continues in that "he always lives to intercede" for his own (Hebrews 7:25; 1 John 2:1).

A choice between two words found in ancient manuscripts (both of which sounded much the same) has led some translators (as in the *King James Version*) to say that Christ has "washed us from our sins." Either word, *washed* or *freed*, expresses essentially the same truth: in Jesus our sins are gone!

Christ has established his people as a *kingdom*, made up of *priests* who have direct access to God in Jesus' name (see 1 Peter 2:5). All this is reason to celebrate and to give him *glory and power for ever and ever!*

### B. HE IS COMING (v. 7)

**7. Look, he is coming with the clouds, and every eye will see him, even those who pierced him; and all the peoples of the earth will mourn because of him. So shall it be! Amen.**

Just as a cloud was present when Jesus ascended (Acts 1:9), so will *clouds* be part of the background when he returns (Matthew 26:64). Paul mentions *clouds* in his description of Christ's return in 1 Thessalonians 4:17.

That *every eye will see him* means that his audience will include reluctant foes (they who *pierced him*, as predicted in Zechariah 12:10), as well as eager friends. The word *mourn* is "wail" in some translations. It pictures the bitterness of the cry of those who must confront divine judgment unprepared (Matthew 13:42, 50).

### C. HE IS ETERNAL (v. 8)

**8. "I am the Alpha and the Omega," says the Lord God, "who is, and who was, and who is to come, the Almighty."**

*Alpha*, or A, is the first letter of the Greek alphabet, and *Omega*, or long O, is the last. Thus, *the Lord* declares himself to be the eternal One (as he did in v. 4), living before all else began and after all created matter has been extinguished. Near the end of Revelation, Jesus describes himself with the words *Alpha and Omega*, and uses other titles that affirm his deity (Revelation 22:13, 16).

## III. ASSIGNMENT TO JOHN (REVELATION 1:9-11)

### A. THE MAN AND THE PLACE (v. 9)

**9. I, John, your brother and companion in the suffering and kingdom and patient endurance that are ours in Jesus, was on the island of Patmos because of the word of God and the testimony of Jesus.**

---

**WHAT DO YOU THINK?**

*Revelation 1:7 promises that at Christ's second coming "every eye will see him." Suppose an unbeliever challenged this and said, "This proves the Bible is not true. It would be a physical impossibility for everyone on a round earth to see Jesus return. The people who wrote the Bible obviously thought the world was flat—and who knows what else!" How would you answer?*

Although he was an elderly and respected apostle at this point, John did not consider himself above or superior to those he addressed. He was their *brother*, sharing their experiences. He understood what it was like to experience *suffering* for one's faith. He and Peter had suffered persecution not long after the church began (Acts 4:18-21; 5:40-42). Later he had lost his brother James during the persecution initiated by king Herod Agrippa I (Acts 12:1, 2). Now, after many years, John had insisted on preaching that God, as revealed in Jesus Christ, was the only deity to be worshiped, while the emperor Domitian demanded that any worship be directed toward himself. For that reason, John had been exiled—separated from his people and confined to a desolate island prison.

Among the islands in the Aegean Sea, *the island of Patmos* is a rough and irregular cluster of three sections linked by narrow necks of land. Its total tortuous shoreline is comparable with its distance from the Asian coast—some forty miles, though Patmos contains not more than twenty-five square miles in total area. John's stay there is believed to have lasted about eighteen months and to have been concluded by the emperor Nerva after the death of Domitian in A.D. 96.

More meaningful to us is John's introduction of the threefold Christian experience of *suffering, kingdom,* and *patient endurance.* These themes echo throughout Revelation: suffering for the faith, the triumph of Heaven's kingdom over worldly realms, and the patient endurance that enables the saints to achieve Heaven's victory. This triumphant trio makes the book of Revelation of special value in times of hardship.

### B. THE PREPARATION (v. 10)

**10. On the Lord's Day I was in the Spirit, and I heard behind me a loud voice like a trumpet.**

Following Jesus' resurrection on the first day of the week, and the establishment of the church on the first day of the week (Pentecost), Christians chose that day to meet at the Lord's table (Acts 20:7) and to bring offerings for the needy (1 Corinthians 16:2). The term *Lord's Day* does not appear in Scripture until this passage in Revelation, but soon afterward Christians in general were known to call the first day of the week the Lord's Day.

John's exile kept him from meeting with fellow believers for worship (Hebrews 10:25), but he could still engage in prayer and meditation. The *loud voice* that he heard from *behind* him reminded him in an impressive way that, though in exile, he was by no means alone.

### C. THE ASSIGNMENT (v. 11)

**11. . . . which said: "Write on a scroll what you see and send it to the seven churches: to Ephesus, Smyrna, Pergamum, Thyatira, Sardis, Philadelphia and Laodicea."**

The order in which the *seven* cities are named forms a kind of circuit, from *Ephesus* northward, then eastward and southward to *Laodicea*, east of Ephesus, which is the last city mentioned. Why other cities in the region, such as Troas, Miletus, Colosse, and Hierapolis were omitted can only be surmised. Churches anywhere, however, could profit from the seven messages John was to receive.

## IV. DESCRIPTION OF THE SAVIOR (REVELATION 1:12-15)

### A. HIS PLACE WITH THE CHURCHES (vv. 12, 13a)

**12, 13a. I turned around to see the voice that was speaking to me. And when I turned I saw seven golden lampstands, and among the lampstands was someone "like a son of man."**

---

*WHAT DO YOU THINK?*

John said that "on the Lord's Day" he was "in the Spirit" (Revelation 1:10). Of course, he was on a level of communion with the Holy Spirit that made it possible for him to receive divine revelation. Even without achieving the level of divine inspiration, we can and should be enjoying regular communion or "fellowship" with the Holy Spirit (note 2 Corinthians 13:14). How can we do that? How significant are our Lord's Day activities to our fellowship with the Spirit? How can we make those activities even richer experiences of fellowship with the Spirit?

*WHAT DO YOU THINK?*

Think of our church as a lampstand or a light. (Read John 8:12; 9:5; Matthew 5:14.) What does this suggest about our mission? Where specifically do you think we should be aiming our light? How can we do that?

What kind of things jeopardize the brightness of our light? (What kind of opposition from outside the church is a threat to us right now? What kind of behavior by church members might dim the light?) How can we guard against such things?

## WHAT DO YOU THINK?

*In John's vision of Christ, the whiteness of his hair symbolized his purity and holiness. How does thinking about God's purity and holiness affect you? Is it frightening to think about standing before a pure and holy God, knowing your own impurity? Why or why not? What can help relieve such fear? (1 John 4:18)*

*How would you counsel a non-Christian who is afraid to accept Christ because he is intimidated by the Lord's holiness?*

## THOUGHT TO REMEMBER

*God, unchanging and eternal, has revealed himself through the timeless truth of his Son and his written Word.*

John gave immediate attention to *the voice* coming from behind him. At once he noticed *seven golden lampstands.* Revelation 1:20 states that these lampstands symbolized the churches to which the writing was addressed. Coming immediately to mind is Matthew 5:14, 15: "You are the light of the world. . . . Neither do people light a lamp and put it under a bowl. Instead they put it on its stand." Each congregation brings the light of the gospel to its community. Jesus is then described as present in the midst of his beleaguered churches.

*Son of man* is a title introduced in Daniel's night vision, which included "one like a son of man coming with the clouds of heaven" (7:13). Jesus referred to himself frequently by that title (Matthew 8:20; Mark 2:10; Luke 22:69; John 1:51), emphasizing his identity with humanity while at the same time affirming his divinity.

### B. HIS ROBE OF AUTHORITY (v. 13b)
**13b. . . . dressed in a robe reaching down to his feet and with a golden sash around his chest.**

Exodus 28 gives instructions on the preparation of robes for Aaron and his sons, which served to distinguish them as priests in Israel. All were to wear a special *sash* (Exodus 39:27-29). Aaron in particular, as high priest, was to be recognized by his robe and by a specially ornamented sash (Josephus says that it had "a mixture of gold interwoven") that was wound around the *chest.* Thus, what John saw in his vision was the familiar attire of the priesthood. How fitting for our great High Priest, who "has made us . . . priests to serve his God" (v. 6) to be clothed this way!

### C. HIS COUNTENANCE OF PURITY (v. 14)
**14. His head and hair were white like wool, as white as snow, and his eyes were like blazing fire.**

Pure, glistening *white* is the symbol of utmost purity and of the holiness of God. Such a one, whose *eyes were like blazing fire,* could see and understand the inmost thoughts of the human heart.

### D. HIS POSTURE OF POWER (v. 15)
**15. His feet were like bronze glowing in a furnace, and his voice was like the sound of rushing waters.**

The appearance of the Son of man's *feet* resembled *bronze*—imperishable metal, refined and burnished to a glow. The *sound* of his *voice* was not an intimidating shout, but a naturally dominant sound, like that of waves crashing on a rocky seacoast or of a mighty waterfall. Ezekiel 43:2 also speaks of such a sound coming forth from the "God of Israel."

Thus did John's vision come to his readers through figures familiar from other portions of the Scriptures. The living Lord Jesus was revealing himself to the churches through revealing himself to his exiled apostle.

## CONCLUSION

John obeyed the Lord's command to write what he saw and to convey the writing to the churches. What were they to do with it? Read it? Accept it and use it for their encouragement, spiritual growth, and victory over present and future afflictions? All this and more. They passed it along to us for the same ongoing uses.

God's purpose for the book of Revelation was only partly accomplished when John completed his work and passed it on to the seven churches. The promise of Revelation 1:3 is addressed to us as well: "Blessed is the one who reads the words of this prophecy, and blessed are those who hear it and take to heart what is written in it, because the time is near."

# Discovery Learning

*This page contains an alternate lesson plan emphasizing learning activities. Classes desiring such student involvement will find these suggestions helpful. The next page is a reproducible activity page to further enhance discovery learning.*

## LEARNING GOALS

This study should equip the student to:

1. List the descriptions of Jesus in Revelation 1.

2. Explain how these descriptions show a special relationship between the Lord and his suffering saints.

3. Make a commitment to serve the Lord even when pressured to do otherwise.

## INTO THE LESSON

Begin the class by asking volunteers to tell what nicknames they had while growing up or might still have. Who called or calls them these names? What do the names reveal about them?

Nicknames often identify a notable characteristic about the person. These are the ones that can become unkind if they focus on an embarrassing trait. Another popular kind of nickname is one that identifies a particular relationship between the one named and the one using the name. Married people often call their spouses either "Hon" or "Honey." A mother may refer to her child as "Baby" even after the child is no longer an infant.

Observe that in our lesson text for today we'll see a variety of images used to describe Jesus. These images are like nicknames; they reveal something about the relationship between Jesus and his people. Point out that the book of Revelation was written primarily to provide encouragement to suffering believers in the first century. Thus, as we look at the variety of terms used to describe Jesus and his people in today's text, we should see the significance of these terms in the context of suffering.

## INTO THE WORD

Today's lesson is the first in a series of studies from Revelation. Thus it will be important to provide a good introduction to the book. Use the information in the Lesson Background (p. 271, 272) to explain why Revelation was written in the style (apocalyptic) that it was. Note also the period in which Revelation is believed to have been written (around A.D. 95 during the reign of Domitian). In referring to the "seven churches in Asia," use the map (visual for lesson 1 in the visuals packet). Also point out the location of the isle of Patmos on this map, and use the information in the lesson commentary under Revelation 1:9 to provide additional details about Patmos.

Ask the class, "What word would you use to describe the book of Revelation?" Possible responses may include:

confusing, frightening, complicated, encouraging. Point out that this series of lessons on Revelation (there are eight all together) will focus on the practical purpose of encouraging believers, rather than the theories of interpretation surrounding the return of Jesus. (Perhaps you will want to list the upcoming lesson titles and Scripture texts on the blackboard, on poster board, or on an overhead transparency.)

Next, divide the class into two groups for the study of today's Scripture. Have each group designate a "reporter" to record the group's answers to its questions. Distribute copies of "Pictures of the Savior, " page 278, and ask one half of the class to complete the first section; the other half to complete the second.

After about ten minutes, ask for reports. Make a list on the chalkboard of all the traits, names, and acts of God that the groups find. Then discuss the third section of the reproducible page together.

## INTO LIFE

Discuss how similar the situation of modern Christians is to that of the first-century Christians. In some areas of the world, persecution against Christians is severe. In other places it is more subtle but growing. How is the encouragement of this chapter relevant to us today?

Go back over the list as you did for part three of the activity above. This time, discuss the relevance to twentieth-century Christians. What new insights come from looking at Revelation in this practical light? Discuss questions like the following. (You can add to the list.)

• What does it mean to be a "faithful witness" for the Lord today?

• What is significant about serving the eternal God in a culture dominated by a quest for "instants" and "disposables"?

• How does this pure one (in dazzling white) with the blazing eyes look at the impurity in our world? in our own lives?

Ask the class members to think without answering aloud about the following questions: "Have you been afraid to serve the Lord in some ministry because of outside pressure? Who is pressuring you? What in todays's study encourages you to make a commitment to serve in spite of the opposition?"

Close with a time of prayer for courage to serve where the Lord is leading.

# Pictures of the Savior

| ① List the description each of the following verses gives of the nature or character of God, Jesus, or the Holy Spirit—who he is as opposed to what he does. (Include names or titles.) | ③ In this column, write next to each item at the left how it would give special encouragement to one suffering for his testimony of Jesus. (A couple of ideas are provided to stimulate your thinking.) |
|---|---|
| v. 4 | |
| v. 5 | As a "faithful witness" (v. 5), Jesus has gone the same path he asks his faithful witnesses to follow. |
| v. 8 | |
| vv. 13-15 | Jesus is present among the lampstands (i.e., the churches; vv. 13, 20). He is present among his *people* who are suffering. |
| v. 17 | |
| v. 18 | |
| ② List the description each of the following verses gives of the acts of God, Jesus, or the Holy Spirit—what he has done, what he does or is doing, and what he will do. | |
| v. 5 | |
| v. 6 | |
| v. 7 | |
| v. 17 | |
| v. 18 | |

# TO SMYRNA AND PERGAMUM

### LESSON 7

## WHY TEACH THIS LESSON?

Last week's lesson described Jesus as a "faithful witness." Today's lesson expands that description to include the Lord's people.

The Christians in the city of Smyrna, poor and persecuted, needed to hold on. Things were going to get even worse. Their faithfulness was going to be tested, even to the point of death. Similarly, the saints at Pergamum were under fire. At least one "faithful witness" among them had already been martyred. False teachers were there, but they could be resisted.

What are the pressures facing Christians in your community? Assure your students that resisting those pressures will be rewarded. The "crown of life" is still promised to the faithful.

## INTRODUCTION

### A. WORTH DYING FOR

Several candidates for an attractive position with a prominent firm appeared before the board of examiners. One friendly applicant centered his preparation on finding out all he could about the members of the board, and he gave every questioner the answers he wanted to hear. One of the examiners later remarked that the man obviously did not believe anything strongly enough to stake his life on it.

The Lord is conducting an examination to determine whether those who claim to believe in him are willing to stake their lives on it. This is the message of Revelation 2:10. Christians may not be called upon to die for their faith, but they are expected to live for it, making each of their daily choices from that perspective. Having found something worth dying for, they have established themselves in something worth living for.

### B. LESSON BACKGROUND

It had been approximately forty years since the apostle Paul had spent three years preaching and teaching in Ephesus, the chief city of the province of Asia (Acts 20:17, 31). From there the gospel had gone throughout all Asia (Acts 19:10, 26), including the cities to which the letters of Revelation were addressed. The first letter was addressed to the church at Ephesus (2:1-7) where John (according to tradition) had served in recent years. The church there was praised for its faithfulness in the gospel, but was rebuked for having left its "first love" (v. 4) or its early warmth and enthusiasm. Such a condition could be fatal if not corrected. The second letter was addressed to Smyrna, on the seacoast to the north.

## I. ENCOURAGEMENT TO SMYRNA (REVELATION 2:8-11)

Only two of the seven churches in Revelation were commended without any rebuke. Smyrna was one of the two.

DEVOTIONAL READING:
**1 CORINTHIANS 8:1-13**

LESSON SCRIPTURE:
**REVELATION 2:8-17**

PRINTED TEXT:
**REVELATION 2:8-17**

Apr
13

LESSON AIMS

This lesson should equip students to:

1. Summarize the call to faithfulness given to the churches in Smyrna and Pergamum.

2. Compare the challenges to the faithfulness of these two congregations with challenges faced by churches today.

3. Encourage another believer to greater faithfulness in serving Jesus Christ.

KEY VERSE

Be faithful, even to the point of death, and I will give you the crown of life.        Revelation 2:10

LESSON 7 NOTES

*NOTE

*The term* **evangelist** *is from the same root as* **angel**. *Its meaning is, essentially, a "good messenger"—that is, a "messenger with good news."*

WHAT DO YOU THINK?

*In each message, the Lord begins, "I know. . . ." If the Lord wrote to our church, what do you think he would say he "knows" about us—our works, our faith, where we live, our afflictions, what? Why would he point to this first? Would it be positive or negative? Why?*

## A. FROM THE LIVING LORD (v. 8)

**8. "To the angel of the church in Smyrna write: These are the words of him who is the First and the Last, who died and came to life again.**

The Greek word *angelos,* transliterated *angel* in our Bibles, meant "messenger." Though it was commonly used in Greek literature of human messengers, its use to describe heavenly messengers has dominated our understanding of the term. Still the term is used of human messengers in Luke 7:24 and 9:52. The *angel of the church,* then, would seem to refer to the "messenger" who usually addressed the congregation with God's message. Perhaps we should think of someone similar to a minister* or an elder of a church. This individual would be the person who would receive and convey to the people what the Lord said in this letter.

*Smyrna* (its modern name is Izmir) was a proud and beautiful city with an important commercial harbor on the Aegean Sea about forty miles north of Ephesus. It was noted for its devotion to Dionysus, the Roman god of fertility, and also for its willingness to meet the demands of Rome for worship of the emperor. These factors, along with a large Jewish population hostile to Christianity, made Smyrna a difficult place to live as a Christian.

The source of the letter to Smyrna is identified here as *the First and the Last.* God speaks as such an eternal One in Isaiah 44:6 and 48:12. Jesus referred to himself by this title when he first appeared to John (Revelation 1:17). The words are similar in meaning to *Alpha and Omega* (1:8). That Jesus *died and came to life again* was also impressed upon John (1:18). Such a declaration was especially meaningful in Smyrna, which preserved a myth that the god Dionysus had come back from the dead.

## B. HE UNDERSTANDS THEIR TRIALS (v. 9)

**9. I know your afflictions and your poverty—yet you are rich! I know the slander of those who say they are Jews and are not, but are a synagogue of Satan.**

The believers at Smyrna could take comfort from the fact that the Lord knew the circumstances (*afflictions* and *poverty*) that made living the Christian life so challenging in their city. Relatively few wealthy or powerful individuals were found in the first-century churches (1 Corinthians 1:26-29; James 2:5). *Poverty* is not specifically mentioned in the other six letters; perhaps it was especially severe in Smyrna, where the hard-pressed Christians obviously did not share in the prosperity of their commercially thriving city.

However, Jesus reminded the Christians in Smyrna that they were *rich.* Perhaps they did not fully appreciate what they possessed. They were heirs of "the kingdom he promised those who love him" (James 2:5). Their wealth was the kind not suspected by careless observers with mere worldly pursuits. Heaven's bank account never can be overdrawn, and when spiritual wealth is shared with others, it becomes even more treasured.

The *slander* referred to here is the Greek word typically rendered *blasphemy* in the New Testament, and it is so translated in some versions (e.g. the *King James*). The Greeks used it of any sort of abusive speech, however, against men or God. Here it likely refers to a program of slander against the Lord's people, the Christians in Smyrna, rather than God himself. The false *Jews* who conducted it resembled the "children of Abraham" who opposed Jesus and to whom he said, "If you were Abraham's children, then you would do the things Abraham did" (John 8:39). He later added, "You belong to your father, the devil, and you want to carry out your father's desire" (John 8:44). By their lack of inward commitment to the Law of Moses (Romans 2:28, 29) and by their rejection of the Messiah whom God promised to Abraham, these Jews had forfeited their claim to be God's people. By rejecting God the Son, they had become guilty of *blasphemy* in the sense we normally associate with the term. To blaspheme the Son is no less a sin than to blaspheme the Father. Their synagogue, in which these Christ-rejecting Jews assembled, had become a *synagogue of Satan.*

### DANGEROUS DECEIT

John André was of Swiss-French parentage, but became a faithful and distinguished British soldier, joining the army in 1771. He was sent to Canada in 1774 and rapidly rose through the ranks. He was articulate, artistic, and witty. Eventually he was appointed an aide to Sir Henry Clinton, an important British general. It was in 1780 that Benedict Arnold negotiated with General Clinton to betray the fort of West Point to the British. Major André was disguised as a civilian and tried to pass through the colonial forces. He carried the plans of West Point, furnished by Arnold, in his boots. André was captured near Tarrytown, New York, and taken to General George Washington. A military court appointed by Washington sentenced André to be executed as a spy and he was hanged at Tappan, New York, on October 2, 1780.

The message to Smyrna included the words, "I know the slander of those *who say they are Jews and are not, but are a synagogue of Satan*" (Revelation 2:9). To pretend in time of war to be for one side while actually being a combatant for the enemy is indeed punishable by death.

In its conflict with evil and with the evil one, the church is engaged in a life-and-death struggle; it is nothing less than a spiritual war. There are forces that seek not just to damage or demean Christianity, but to destroy it. The call is not to be faithful until difficulties arise, or until it is unpleasant to be a Christian; we must be faithful "even to the point of death." Counterfeit Christianity plays right into the hands of the enemy.

—J. G. V. B.

### C. HE PROMISES LIFE BEYOND AFFLICTION (v. 10)

**10. Do not be afraid of what you are about to suffer. I tell you, the devil will put some of you in prison to test you, and you will suffer persecution for ten days. Be faithful, even to the point of death, and I will give you the crown of life.**

Although the saints at Smyrna had already been introduced to *persecution,* they were to encounter more of it. *Prison* would be the trying experience of some, as it had been for the apostles (Acts 4:3; 5:17, 18; 12:1-4; 16:19-24). Through such surroundings the Christians would be tested by *the devil.* These same circumstances also had the potential, however, to strengthen the believers (James 1:12; 1 Peter 4:12-19), even as steel gains strength through the heat of its tempering.

The *ten days* of persecution is subject to various interpretations. Is it a literal time period, is it symbolic for a longer period (ten years perhaps), or is it a general term, indicating a significant, but not unending, period of time? (Note the use of *ten* in Numbers 14:22; Nehemiah 4:12; Daniel 1:20.) In historical context, the last option seems most reasonable. If one dates the book of Revelation at around A.D. 95, as many scholars do, then Domitian's reign and attendant persecution would end in a matter of months. At the same time, any persecution a Christian endures is minor when viewed in light of his eventual reward. A generation earlier Paul had written, "Our light and momentary troubles are achieving for us an eternal glory that far outweighs them all" (2 Corinthians 4:17).

The phrase *faithful, even to the point of death,* is more explicit than "faithful unto death," as the *King James Version* renders it. The latter suggests faithfulness all one's life, which is accurate but incomplete. The former adds the idea that one's life will be challenged and may be forfeit because of his or her faithfulness. This is plainly what it meant to Stephen (Acts 7:59, 60) and to James the brother of

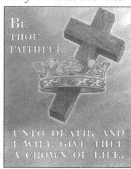

*The visual for lesson 7 illustrates verse 10 of the text. Display it as you discuss this verse.*

### HOW TO SAY IT

*Aegean.* Ay-JEE-un.
*Aesculapius.* Ess-kew-LAY-pea-us.
*angelos (Greek).* AHNG-el-loss
*Antipas.* ANN-tih-pus.
*Auca.* AWK-uh.
*Balaam.* BAY-lum.
*Balak.* BAY-lack.
*Bergama.* BUR-guh-muh.
*diadema.* dee-AH-day-muh.
*Dionysus.* Dye-oh-NISH-us.
*Domitian.* Doe-MISH-un.
*Ephesus.* EFF-uh-suss.
*Izmir.* Izz-MEER.
*Laodicea.* Lay ODD-uh-SEE-uh.
*martus (Greek).* MAR-toose.
*Moab.* MO-ab.
*Moabite.* MO-ub-ite.
*Nicolaitans.* Nick-oh-LAY-ih-tunz.
*Pergamum.* PER-guh-mum.
*Sardis.* SAR-dis.
*Smyrna.* SMUR-nuh.
*stephanos.* STEFF-uh-noss.
*Thyatira.* THIGH-uh-TIE-ruh.

John (Acts 12:1, 2). Faithfulness does not always hasten death, but it must never stop short of it.

To the faithful ones, Christ promises eternal *life* as a *crown*. The Greek word for *crown* is not the royal *diadema* worn by emperors (from which we get our word "diadem"); it is the *stephanos*—a crown that was awarded for special achievement or honor. This is the same word as used for the garland or wreath awarded to the winner in a great athletic contest. But Paul says our crown is not like that one, which soon wilts and dries up and becomes worthless. This is a "crown that will last forever" (1 Corinthians 9:24, 25). Paul anticipated it as a "crown of righteousness" to be shared by all who love and anticipate Christ's final appearing (2 Timothy 4:8).

### WHAT YOU ARE ABOUT TO SUFFER

This is one of several places in Revelation where the experience of suffering or persecution is predicted for Christians. We know from both New Testament accounts and post-Biblical historical records that many followers of Jesus were terrorized and tortured for their faith. "They met the tyrant's brandished steel, The lion's gory mane; They bowed their heads the stroke to feel: Who follows in their train?" (Reginald Heber, "The Son of God Goes Forth to War").

Yet it is not just those first-century martyrs, eulogized in Heber's great hymn, who have suffered for Jesus' sake. What about the harsh treatment many receive in Islamic countries around the world? Who can deny the grave consequences of seeking to lead people to Christian conversion in Hindu-controlled areas of India? What about the many who have given their lives for Christ in Communist China?

In Latin America, in the South Pacific islands, in Sri Lanka, in Albania, and on American Indian reservations, many have faced suffering for the Lord Jesus. It was in 1956 that five missionaries were killed by Auca Indians in western Ecuador. They were well-educated, enthusiastic servants of our Lord whose tragic deaths taught us that many of Jesus' disciples must still suffer as they seek to advance his kingdom. Speaking for all the widows of the slain men, Elisabeth Elliot (wife of martyr Jim Elliot) wrote in her powerful book *Through Gates of Splendor,* "To the world at large this was a sad waste of five young lives. But God has his plan and purpose in all things."

—J. G. V. B.

**WHAT DO YOU THINK?**

*The letters to the seven churches feature a strong emphasis on believers as overcomers (Revelation 2:7, 11, 17, 26; 3:5, 12, 21). In what ways must we be overcomers?*

*See Mark 9:24; John 16:33; Romans 12:21; 1 John 2:13, 14; 5:4, 5.*

### D. HE ASSURES THE HEARERS (v. 11)

**11. He who has an ear, let him hear what the Spirit says to the churches. He who overcomes will not be hurt at all by the second death.**

Jesus frequently concluded his parables by admonishing his hearers to use their ears for their intended purposes—receiving and considering what he had just said (Matthew 11:15; Mark 4:9, 23; Luke 14:35). Here he repeats the injunction, not only to the saints in Smyrna, but to all who would *hear* the words anywhere else at any time.

*He who overcomes* is the believer who remains steadfast through all his trials without giving in or giving up, as Jesus remained faithful all the way to the cross and was given Heaven's highest accolade (Philippians 2:5-11). His followers will be out of reach of *the second death*, which is Hell, the final and eternal separation from God and his grace (Revelation 20:6, 14; 21:8). To be twice born, first physically, then spiritually, is to die but once—physically. To be once born, only physically, is to die twice—physically and spiritually. This is the ultimate tragedy.

### II. WARNING TO PERGAMUM (REVELATION 2:12-17)

### A. FROM THE WELL-EQUIPPED LORD (v. 12)

**12. "To the angel of the church in Pergamum write: These are the words of him who has the sharp, double-edged sword.**

Whereas the opening words to Smyrna were triumphant and inspiring, here we find the makings of a full-fledged confrontation. The city of *Pergamum,* which today is known as Bergama, was made the capital of Asia by the Romans. It stood on a cone-shaped hill rising a thousand feet above the surrounding valley, some fifty miles north of Smyrna. It was, according to one writer, "a sort of union of a pagan cathedral city, a university town, and a royal residence." Here people came to worship at the temple of Zeus, to seek healing at the temple of Aesculapius (the Roman god of medicine), and to conduct emperor worship. It is not accidental therefore that the letter to Pergamum challenges the sword of the emperor with the *sword* of the Spirit: the "living and active" word of God, which is "sharper than any *double-edged sword*" (Hebrews 4:12; see also Ephesians 6:17).

## B. HE UNDERSTANDS THEIR SURROUNDINGS (v. 13)

**13. I know where you live—where Satan has his throne. Yet you remain true to my name. You did not renounce your faith in me, even in the days of Antipas, my faithful witness, who was put to death in your city—where Satan lives.**

The location of Pergamum constituted a notable handicap. The reference to *Satan's throne* may allude to the city's cluster of pagan temples, or it may reflect its position as the official center of emperor worship in Asia. Any church whose community draws heavily on gambling or the liquor business for its revenue will know something of Pergamum's predicament.

The believers in Pergamum had remained *true* and did *not renounce* their *faith* in Christ. A believer's confession made before baptism may be the easiest one he will ever make. Spoken before supportive friends, it is encouraged by the whole church. To speak up for Christ among scoffing unbelievers or zealots of an opposing religion is much more challenging, and that is what the Christians in Pergamum had done. They had not forsaken their testimony, even when *Antipas* became a *faithful* martyr because of his testimony. (The word for witness in the text is *martus,* from which we get our word *martyr.* It is so translated in Acts 22:20) Concerning this man, we know nothing except what is written here, but those in Pergamum knew all about his courage. According to one tradition, he was slowly roasted to death in a bronze kettle during the reign of Domitian. Such a violent death attested to Pergamum's reputation as a city *where Satan lives.*

## C. HE CONDEMNS FALSE TEACHINGS (vv. 14, 15)

The Lord's fervent appreciation of the Christians' steadfastness in Pergamum did not prevent his equally loving rebuke of their toleration of false teaching.

**14. Nevertheless, I have a few things against you: You have people there who hold to the teaching of Balaam, who taught Balak to entice the Israelites to sin by eating food sacrificed to idols and by committing sexual immorality.**

The account of *Balaam* and *Balak* is found in Numbers 22:1—24:25 and 31:15, 16. It is alluded to in 2 Peter 2:15 and Jude 11. Balak, king of Moab, feared the forces of Israel, advancing under Moses' leadership. So Balak hired the prophet Balaam to pronounce a curse upon Israel. Instead, God caused Balaam to bless Israel. Balaam, however, showed the Moabites another way to weaken Israel. They succeeded in enticing the Israelites to engage with them in idolatrous feasts and to engage in immoral acts. Three of the seven letters in Revelation mention false teachings that led to a toleration and even an encouragement of *sexual immorality* and the *eating* of *food sacrificed to idols.*

**15. Likewise you also have those who hold to the teaching of the Nicolaitans.**

The details of the beliefs and practices of the *Nicolaitans* have been the subject of much conjecture, but specific information is limited. Apparently they were

---

**WHAT DO YOU THINK?**

The believers at Pergamum lived "where Satan has his throne." Apparently Satan was able to exercise a significant rule over people's lives there, perhaps at the pagan temples or in the places of emperor worship. What kind of places might we associate with Satan's throne in our own community? What businesses or other establishments are extending Satan's rule over people? What can we as a church do about Satan's throne?

**WHAT DO YOU THINK?**

The church at Pergamum was praised: "You remain true to my name." At the same time, there were people there who held to false teachings ("the teaching of Balaam" and "the teaching of the Nicolaitans"). How can both truth and error exist together? What do you think that suggests about our own situation? How can we expose the false without condemning the true? How can we celebrate and honor the true without condoning the false?

**WHAT DO YOU THINK?**

The lesson writer suggests that "the teaching of the Nicolaitans" probably involved a misapplication of Christian liberty. How are Christians today tempted to abuse the freedom they have in Christ?

(See 1 Corinthians 8 and 9.)

## DAILY BIBLE READINGS

**Monday, Apr. 7**—*Repent and Return to God (Acts 3:17-26)*

**Tuesday, Apr. 8**—*Pray for Spiritual Wisdom (Colossians 1:9-14)*

**Wednesday, Apr. 9**—*Use Your Faith to Overcome (1 John 5:1-5)*

**Thursday, Apr. 10**—*Have Faith in Jesus Christ (1 John 5:6-12)*

**Friday, Apr. 11**—*Hold Firm Your Hope (Hebrews 3:1-6)*

**Saturday, Apr. 12**—*Be Wise in the Lord (Proverbs 4:1-9)*

**Sunday, Apr. 13**—*Be Faithful and Righteous (Proverbs 28:20-28)*

## WHAT DO YOU THINK?

*Manna was the wafer-like food miraculously provided by God to sustain the Israelites during the wilderness wandering (Exodus 16:14-31). Its presence proved God's ability to provide for his peoples needs. What, then, does the promise of the "hidden manna" suggest to you? What kind of assurance does it provide for you?*

## PRAYER

*Thank you, God, for this marvelous book of Revelation, with its display of the divine love that understands, appreciates, warns, and instructs. Please give us hearing ears, receptive spirits, and willing hearts, to receive and claim your promises. In Christ our Lord we pray. Amen.*

## THOUGHT TO REMEMBER

*"If we died with him, we will also live with him; if we endure, we will also reign with him" (2 Timothy 2:11, 12).*

condoning and encouraging acts similar to those mentioned in the previous verse. Perhaps they argued that Christian liberty included the freedom to participate in such hitherto-forbidden practices. The church at Ephesus was complimented for rejecting the Nicolaitan heresy (Revelation 2:6); the church at Pergamum is rebuked for tolerating it.

### D. HE COMMANDS CORRECTION (v. 16)

**16. Repent therefore! Otherwise, I will soon come to you and will fight against them with the sword of my mouth.**

The most pressing need of the believers in Pergamum was simple: *Repent!* Change your mind and change your ways! God's people must cease to tolerate and harbor among themselves teachers who disseminate teachings that God abhors. Repentance, however, is not a harsh and punitive requirement; instead, it is offered in love by the Lord of the church as the tool that will make it a stronger church.

The alternative is the sudden and unannounced arrival of Christ as the instrument of judgment. He will make war against the offending false teachers if they refuse to repent. His weapon will be the *sword* of his *mouth*, the same sword mentioned at the beginning of this letter (v. 12).

### E. HE ADMONISHES AND ASSURES (v. 17)

**17. He who has an ear, let him hear what the Spirit says to the churches. To him who overcomes, I will give some of the hidden manna. I will also give him a white stone with a new name written on it, known only to him who receives it.**

Again comes the admonition that concludes all seven letters: Let all people of all churches in all times and all places listen to what the Lord says to you. This applies both to the foregoing warnings and to the promises about to be heard.

*The hidden manna* brings to mind the miraculous supply of food provided to the Israelites as they journeyed toward the promised land (Exodus 16:14-31; Psalm 78:24). A memorial portion of this was kept in the ark of the covenant in the tabernacle (Exodus 16:32-34; Hebrews 9:3, 4). Jesus contrasted Israel's manna with himself as the bread of life (John 6:48-51), thus declaring himself to be the true nourishment from Heaven. This manna is *hidden* from the world, but will be given to those who have refused to participate in the feasts associated with idol worship.

Ancient tradition identifies a *white stone* or its equivalent as a token of acceptance or approval. It could be used as a sign of acquittal by a judge in court, as an admission to a wedding feast, or as an indication of purchasing power in the marketplace. The engraving of a secret symbol or *name* on such a stone would give it immeasurable value to the recipient. Thus the promise before us is a way of saying that each faithful saint among the multitudes of the saved will have a special and personal invitation to Heaven. No promise could be more meaningful.

## CONCLUSION

The saints in Smyrna lived in poverty, while those in Pergamum were oppressed by unfriendly forces all around them. The Lord could have provided relief supplies to Smyrna and could have worked miracles on behalf of those in Pergamum, persuading pagans there to treat Christians respectfully. But he did neither. These saints in Asia needed something else far more important. They needed to be right with God. They needed inner strength to overcome their difficulties and remain faithful, a strength that is the product of close fellowship with the Lord who bore our difficulties without seeking relief for himself. Their ultimate relief would be found with him who won glory for himself through his suffering. Sharing in that glory is the "blessed hope" (Titus 2:13) of all the faithful, both then and now.

# Discovery Learning

*This page contains an alternate lesson plan emphasizing learning activities. Classes desiring such student involvement will find these suggestions helpful. The next page is a reproducible activity page to further enhance discovery learning.*

## LEARNING GOALS

As students participate in today's class session, they should:

1. Summarize the call to faithfulness given to the churches in Smyrna and Pergamum.

2. Compare the challenges to the faithfulness of these two congregations with challenges faced by churches today.

3. Encourage another believer to greater faithfulness in serving Jesus Christ.

## INTO THE LESSON

Have seven of your class members read the following passages aloud: Revelation 2:1, 2a (stop at "perseverance"); Revelation 2:8, 9a (stop after "rich"); Revelation 2:12, 13a (stop at "throne"); Revelation 2:18, 19; Revelation 3:1; Revelation 3:7, 8a (stop at "deeds"); Revelation 3:14, 15a (stop at "hot"). Have the passages read in the order listed here. After each reading, write, "I know . . ." on your chalkboard or a large poster. When all the passages have been read, ask, "If the Lord were to write us a letter, what would he say he "knows" about us? (See the "What Do You Think? question on page 280.) Discuss some of the strengths and weaknesses of your church, which Jesus does of course "know."

Point out that today's lesson from Revelation is a call to two churches to be faithfu. Jesus knew their struggles, and he knew their faithfulness. We want to be sure he would say, "I know your faithfulness" if he wrote to us.

## INTO THE WORD

To begin this session, use the Lesson Background to provide information about the cities of Smyrna and Pergamum. Refer to the map (the visual for lesson 1) to locate them, or make copies of the map on the next page and distribute the copies to your students.

Following these comments, give each class member an index card or a piece of paper or cardboard of similar size. One side of each card should have the letter S (for Smyrna) on it; the other side should be marked with the letter P (for Pergamum). Be sure to have enough for your usual attendance (plus a few more for any guests).

Read Revelation 2:8-17, telling the class to listen carefully. Then read the following statements. Have the class members respond by showing you the S side of their card (if they think it is a statement Jesus could have made to the church at Smyrna) or the P (if they think it might have been said to the church at Pergamum).

1. "You will suffer persecution for ten days." (S) (v. 10)
2. "I have a few things against you." (P) (v. 14)
3. "Antipas was my faithful martyr." (P) (v. 13)
4. "I will give you a crown of life." (S) (v. 10)
5. "You have people there who hold to the teaching of Balaam." (P) (v. 14)
6. "Do not be afraid of what you are about to suffer." (S) (v. 10)
7. "He who has an ear, let him hear what the Spirit says to the churches." (Both)

Discuss the fact that Jesus assured the Christians at Smyrna that they would suffer. Use the commentary's discussion of v. 10 to explain the reference to "ten days." Discuss, "What truths are most important to remember when suffering for Jesus' sake? How do Christians in our community 'suffer'? How does that compare to what the Christians in Smyrna suffered? What encouragement does such a comparison give us?"

Ask, "For what was the church at Pergamum commended? For what was it rebuked?" Point out that the acceptance of false teaching had severely crippled this church's progress. Discuss, "Why is sound doctrine so important to the church? What kind of attacks are being made against sound doctrine today? How does the church most effectively guard against false doctrine?"

## INTO LIFE

Refer to Revelation 2:10. Ask, "What blessings are promised to Smyrna and to Pergamum if they remain faithful?" You may wish to comment further on the "hidden manna" and the "white stone" of v. 17, using the material in the lesson commentary. Point out that Jesus' invitation to Heaven is a personal one to every Christian.

Bring the class session to a close by asking, "What can our Sunday school class do to encourage Christians to remain faithful?" List these ideas on the chalk board or on poster board. Perhaps this would be a good time to stress the need to keep in touch with absentees.

Ask for two volunteers to lead in closing prayers. Have the first pray for the faithfulness of the class and its members to God and his Word. The second should focus on the efforts the class will make to contact others in the coming week and encourage them toward greater faithfulness.

# Seven Cities of Saints

The seven churches of Asia were located in the cities marked on the map below.

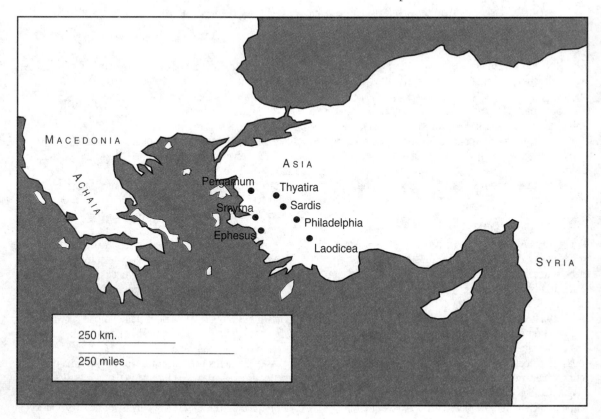

For each church, list what Jesus commended it for and what he condemned in it.

| CHURCH | + | − |
|---|---|---|
| Ephesus | | |
| Smyrna | | |
| Pergamum | | |
| Thyatira | | |
| Sardis | | |
| Philadelphia | | |
| Laodicea | | |

# TO THYATIRA

**LESSON 8**

## WHY TEACH THIS LESSON?

"Tough love." The expression has been made popular by people like Dr. James Dobson who know the importance of honesty and confronting problems in a relationship. This is what we see in the letters to the seven churches of Asia. In almost all of them there is at least some degree of censure. But it is always done in love.

This we'll see clearly in the present lesson. Thyatira is first commended, then censured, and then encouraged. There were real problems in Thyatira—serious doctrinal errors, which the Lord would not tolerate, were being tolerated in the church. This could not continue!

Probably every church member complains about his church from time to time. Perhaps there are some problems in your own congregation over which you and your class members have expressed concern. This lesson is a reminder that love does not tolerate such problems, but it deals with them with encouragement as well as censure. "Speaking the truth in love" is the motto of the church.

## INTRODUCTION

### A. POLITICALLY INCORRECT

God is not politically correct. He does not adjust his being, his behavior, his expectations, or his manner of expression to avoid irritating those who would seek to remake him into their own image. Instead, he insists on being the same I AM that he has been since before there was anything else.

God created mankind in his own image. From the first, people have not been satisfied with that but have shown a distressing tendency to make gods in their own image. Some have fashioned gods of wood or stone, which they have worshiped by acts of their own lust. Others (like the Greeks and Romans) have invented deities who became personalities larger and more lustful than themselves. Man's tendency in our time is to worship gods that reflect his technological progress and his fascination with the latest fads in entertainment. Even users of the Bible may seek to make God in their own image. "My God would never do that," they say in response to biblical warnings of judgment. But will God be manipulated and told what he may or may not do?

"That's my kind of church," one will say after shopping around for and finding a congregation that reflects his or her own special preferences in worship style or interpretation of Scripture. The Lord still makes it clear, however, that *his* kind of church—not yours or mine—offers the way to his presence.

"But that is intolerant!" cries the anything-goes multitude to whom tolerance is held as the highest virtue. Apparently the one thing they will not tolerate is intolerance. Yet these same people depend on mechanics and engineers who limit their tolerances to the thousandth part of an inch! It should not surprise us, then, that the Engineer of the universe cannot approve or welcome into his presence that which flouts and violates his plan and his very being. Neither should it surprise us that he should say to his people, "You are too tolerant of corruption among you." Let us choose acceptability with him (Romans 12:1, 2), as we are encouraged to do in today's lesson.

DEVOTIONAL READING:
ROMANS 2:1-11
LESSON SCRIPTURE:
REVELATION 2:18-29
PRINTED TEXT:
REVELATION 2:18-29

### LESSON AIMS

As students participate in today's class session, they should:

1. Tell briefly what Jesus commended and what he condemned in the church at Thyatira.

2. Explain why both sound doctrine and active ministry are important to the life of a healthy church.

Apr 20

3. Accept, or recommit to, a ministry of teaching sound doctrine or to a ministry of meeting physical needs in the name of Christ.

### KEY VERSE

Then all the churches will know that I am he who searches hearts and minds, and I will repay each of you according to your deeds.          Revelation 2:23

## How to Say It

*Akhisar. AHK-iss-ar.*

*Asherah. Uh-SHE-ruh.*

*Baal. BAY-ul.*

*Balaamites. BAY-luh-mites.*

*Ethbaal. Eth-BAY-ul.*

*Gnostics. NAHSS-ticks.*

*Laodicea. Lay ODD-uh-SEE-uh.*

*Lycus. LIKE-us.*

*Lydia. LID-ee-uh.*

*Macedonia. Mass-uh-DOE-
   nee-uh.*

*Nicolaitans. Nick-oh-LAY-
   ih-tunz.*

*Pergamum. PER-guh-mum.*

*Philippi. Fuh-LIP-pie
   or FILL-uh-pie.*

*Sardis. SAR-dis.*

*Sidonians. Sigh-DOE-nee-uns.*

*Smyrna. SMUR-nuh.*

*Thyatira. THIGH-uh-TIE-ruh.*

## What Do You Think?

*It is easy for a church to fall into a rut, putting on the same old programs in the same old way. But Christ calls us to continual improvement of our work and expansion of our efforts. Jesus said of the church at Thyatira, "I know …that you are now doing more than you did at first."*

*What are we, as a church, doing well? How can we do better what we are doing now?*

*Do you think there are things we should be doing that we are not presently doing? If so what? Why?*

## B. Lesson Background

Thyatira should not be entirely unknown to readers of the New Testament. Lydia, the "dealer in purple cloth" who was Paul's first convert in Philippi (Acts 16:11-15), came from Thyatira. This detail fits well with the fact that many highly organized trade guilds were present in Thyatira. Membership in these guilds posed special problems to those who, like Lydia, became followers of Jesus. This is because the trade guilds were closely associated with pagan worship, which included feasts in honor of idols and the accompanying immoral practices. To live as a Christian businessman or businesswoman in Thyatira demanded real commitment! We can only surmise the pressures that Lydia may have faced when she returned to her home and attempted to share her new-found faith with others.

Thyatira was located on the Lycus River in northern Asia, on the road between Pergamum (the capital of Asia) and Sardis. Its principal deity was Apollo, the mythical Roman god of light and learning. Its modern name is Akhisar, or "White Castle," so named for the rocky hill overhanging it.

## I. THE SON OF GOD SPEAKS (REVELATION 2:18)

**18. To the angel of the church in Thyatira write: These are the words of the Son of God, whose eyes are like blazing fire and whose feet are like burnished bronze.**

Once again the *angel,* or messenger (apparently one of the leaders of the congregation), was to receive, deliver, and circulate the letter. *Thyatira* was the first of four inland cities of Asia to be addressed by the Lord of the church. Earlier letters (to Ephesus, Smyrna, and Pergamum) had gone to towns located closer to the seacoast. It should be noted that this letter to Thyatira is the longest of the seven.

The title *Son of God* is not used anywhere else in Revelation. It emphasizes Christ's deity, perhaps as a direct response to the aforementioned tendency of the trade guilds to promote idol worship. The description of Jesus' *eyes* as being *like blazing fire* is reminiscent of how he first appeared to John as the Son of man (Revelation 1:14). In addition, it further challenged the belief that the god Apollo was the source of light. It emphasized that Christ is not only ever-present with his own, but also perceives their inmost thoughts. The *feet . . . like burnished bronze* again recalls Christ's initial appearance to John (Revelation 1:15).

## II. HE COMMENDS STEADFAST DEVOTION (REVELATION 2:19)

**19. I know your deeds, your love and faith, your service and perseverance, and that you are now doing more than you did at first.**

The believer's *deeds* should include such inner qualities as *love and faith,* along with the more visible attributes of *service* to others and *perseverance* when suffering affliction. At the same time, love cannot be expressed without action (1 John 3:17, 18), and neither can faith (James 2:14-18).

Thyatira's crowning achievement lay in a level of maturity that produced more and better accomplishments for Christ as the years went on. It was doing *more* than it had *at first.* This pattern of growth was the very opposite of that of Ephesus, which had lost its "first love" and had was no longer practicing "the things you did at first" (Revelation 2:4, 5). Like a good fruit tree, these believers brought forth a better crop each season. Could that be said of us?

### MORE NOW THAN AT FIRST

In many areas of life it is essential to recognize how important the final stages of any activity or project can be. In athletic competitions, quite often a team will start out like a whirlwind. The actions of the players seem almost effortless. Shots, strokes, or passes are crisp and accurate. But as the end of the game or match nears, the same team may appear droopy, dispirited, and inept, particularly if they are losing or have fallen far behind. Teams that win and are used to winning will approach the end of the game still alert, focused, and enthusiastic. They are doing more at the end of the game than at first.

This principle also holds true in nature: the oak is much greater than the acorn, the rose is more attractive than the bud, and the mature racehorse is much more graceful than the awkward, stumbling colt. It is good to begin with enthusiasm and excitement, but only persistence and disciplined growth lead to achievement and victory.

This is what John was saying about the Christians at Thyatira. Their love, service, faith, patience, and their deeds in general were "more" than they were at the beginning of their Christian walk. Sadly, this is contrary to the condition of many in our churches today. As Jesus said, testings and persecution cause some to be offended, while the "deceitfulness of wealth" causes others to become unfruitful (Matthew 13:20-22). It is one thing to accept Christ and begin the Christian life with enthusiasm. It is quite another to maintain steady growth and to do more and to be more now than at first.                                      —J. G. V. B.

## III. HE CONDEMNS ACCEPTANCE OF WRONG (REVELATION 2:20-23)

### A. JEZEBEL AND HER INFLUENCE (vv. 20, 21)

**20. Nevertheless, I have this against you: You tolerate that woman Jezebel, who calls herself a prophetess. By her teaching she misleads my servants into sexual immorality and the eating of food sacrificed to idols.**

Again, let us note the contrast with Ephesus: Ephesus had been found at fault for letting its "first love" diminish while resisting evil (Revelation 2:2-5). Thyatira is rebuked for tolerating false doctrine while increasing in good works. The saints were suffering persecution patiently, and that was to their credit. But they were also tolerating abominable teachings, and that was a serious error.

The condemnation of wrongdoing both at Ephesus and Thyatira reveals that doing good works and following sound doctrine are both important. Some today will suggest one or the other is acceptable. On the one side are those who say sound doctrine is so important that, if a church has that right, service may be sacrificed. Such people need to hear the warning to Ephesus: "Repent and do the things you did at first" (Revelation 2:5). On the other hand are those who say doctrine is unimportant as long as the church is reaching out and meeting the needs of people. These people need to read the warning to Thyatira in this verse and following.

The false teaching in Thyatira stemmed from one source: *that woman Jezebel.* The name brings to mind the daughter of Ethbaal, king of the Sidonians, who became the wife of Israel's King Ahab (1 Kings 16:30, 31). She also became the merciless enemy of God's prophets, and supporter of the prophets of Baal and Asherah (1 Kings 18:3, 4, 13, 19). Her counterpart in Thyatira has been variously identified as: (1) the wife of the "angel" or leader of the church; (2) a woman of influence in the church and community, or (3) the leader of a group of persons similar to the Nicolaitans in Ephesus and Pergamum or the Balaamites in Pergamum (Revelation 2:6, 14, 15).

This Jezebel *calls herself a prophetess*: apparently she claimed supernatural guidance in teaching and persuading the Christians in Thyatira to engage in those acts specifically forbidden to Gentile converts among the churches: *sexual immorality and the eating of food sacrificed to idols* (Acts 15:28, 29). Both of these were essential parts of the pagan worship festivals associated with the various trade guilds in Thyatira.

OPTION

Compare and contrast the messages to Ephesus and Thyatira with the reproducible activity "E.T." on page 294.

WHAT DO YOU THINK?

For a large segment of society, tolerance is the cardinal virtue of our time. Whatever practice one wants to perform, no matter how vile or repulsive, is supposed to be tolerated in our pluralistic society.

Jesus condemned the church at Thyatira for being too tolerant. At the same time, he told us to "love your enemies" (Matthew 5:44). How do we refuse to tolerate evil and still love the evildoers? Just how much tolerance is proper to meet the demands of love without becoming tolerant of evil itself?

**21. I have given her time to repent of her immorality, but she is unwilling.**

God's grace provides *time* and opportunity to acknowledge sins, to seek forgiveness, and to change direction. Some, like Thyatira's Jezebel, spurn the offer.

### TIME TO REPENT

Repentance involves change of direction. Essentially it means making an "about face," turning from one way to go in the opposite way. Many times people are confronted with the need for change. An overweight person may continue to gain pounds, as repeated trips to the scales indicate. Someone is smoking and becomes concerned about how many packs of cigarettes he is using. A college student needs to complete an assignment or prepare for an exam, but continues to neglect his responsibilities. In all such cases, there is usually a margin or space of time that is available for a change of direction.

However, there comes the point when the excess weight leads to clogged arteries, heart trouble, or breathing problems. The smoking may lead to lung or heart damage. The academic neglect can result in lower grades, possible failure of a class, and inability to achieve a degree or to graduate.

The Son of God told the Christians at Thyatira that they had been given "time to repent" (Revelation 2:21). Jesus had shown great patience with their departure from God's ways as expressed in their toleration of false teaching. This patience was not to be disregarded or misunderstood. The problems in Thyatira were known; the punishment was deferred in the hope that the church would respond accordingly.

As Jesus said to all Christians in Revelation 3:20, "Here I am! I stand at the door and knock." While he is at the door, there is a waiting period as he seeks a response. There is time for repentance, but it is an opportunity to be embraced *now*, not neglected or postponed.

                                             —J. G. V. B.

### B. JEZEBEL'S PUNISHMENT (vv. 22, 23)

**22. So I will cast her on a bed of suffering, and I will make those who commit adultery with her suffer intensely, unless they repent of her ways.**

Severe punishment is imminent for those who continue in this way. Jezebel will be *cast . . . on a bed*, apparently indicating some form of sickness. Thus, the place where Jezebel and her followers experienced their sinful pleasure will be changed into an instrument of punishment. In this instance, physical punishment is indicated (perhaps symbolically) for sins. Such are the consequences, not only for the false teacher, but also for her followers. Yet their punishment stops short of death, and opportunity to *repent* remains.

The construction of the final clause of this verse is rather curious. One normally thinks of repenting of one's own ways. Here the Lord says *they* must repent of *her* ways—Jezebel's. This does not suggest someone else is being held accountable for what this Jezebel did. Those who have followed and adopted *her ways* must repent. They must reject her counsel and return to the right kind of leadership!

**23. I will strike her children dead. Then all the churches will know that I am he who searches hearts and minds, and I will repay each of you according to your deeds.**

Here *children* probably refers to those who practice the false doctrines Jezebel has promoted (see Isaiah 57:3; John 8:44). The expression, *I will strike her children dead*, is literally, "I will kill her children with death." To kill with death seems redundant, but it depicts the severity and the assurance of the coming punishment. It means "to destroy totally," and there is no doubt about the coming of this judgment. Perhaps some kind of violent or painful death is implied. At any rate, the evident punishments will demonstrate to *all the churches* throughout Asia and elsewhere that the Lord is fully aware of all that has been going on.

I will repay each of you according to your deeds.

*The visual for lesson 8 illustrates verse 23. Display it as you discuss this verse.*

The expression *hearts and minds* is actually "kidneys and hearts." It reflects the belief that the lower portion of the body (kidneys) was the seat of one's emotions. (We still refer to someone's "gut feeling.") This function, in contemporary thought, is assigned to the *heart,* and thus the translation. The heart in Scripture is often associated with reasoning or thinking. (See Mark 2:8.) This function today is associated with the *mind.* So the idiom of first-century Greek thought, "kidneys and hearts," is here rendered by a more contemporary idiom that means the same thing: that every emotion and every thought is open to Jesus' inspection.

## IV. HE COMMANDS AND ASSURES THE FAITHFUL (REVELATION 2:24-29)

Jesus did more than just point out the problems present in Thyatira. He proceeded to tell them what to do to correct them and to make their "lampstand" burn brightly again. He also promised that perseverance on their part would be richly rewarded.

### A. HOLD TO WHAT YOU HAVE! (vv. 24, 25)

**24, 25. Now I say to the rest of you in Thyatira, to you who do not hold to her teaching and have not learned Satan's so-called deep secrets (I will not impose any other burden on you): Only hold on to what you have until I come.**

Jesus now directs his words to all those saints in Thyatira who have not followed the *teaching* of Jezebel, and thus had not been involved in *Satan's so-called deep secrets.* Perhaps the faithful recognized this teaching as coming from the pit, or the underworld (Revelation 9:1, 2). However, it may also refer to claims made by Satan and his followers to offer depths of secret wisdom, such as those offered to Eve in Eden (Genesis 3:4-6). *Deep* was a commonly used term among the Gnostics (or "knowing ones"), a heretical group just beginning to make its troublesome presence known at the time John wrote. One of their teachings was that in order to defeat Satan a person must enter his stronghold; that is, he must experience evil deeply. This was *so-called* knowledge; it was knowledge only in their own perverted thinking.

*Not . . . any other burden* seems to echo the decision of the apostles and elders in Jerusalem concerning the law and its application to Gentile Christians. These believers were directed to avoid sexual immorality and the eating of meats dedicated to idols (Acts 15:28, 29). The letter to Thyatira warns against these same sins, as we have seen from verse 20.

The Lord closes with the command to *hold on to what you have until I come.* To what must the saints at Thyatira hold with a firm grip? Certainly the virtues already commended in verse 19: their ongoing works of faith, love, service, and patient endurance. These virtues gave evidence of their loyalty to Christ and prepared them for the day when he would come. They were to live with the hope of Christ's return as their primary source of motivation.

### B. REIGN WITH CHRIST (vv. 26-28)

**26. To him who overcomes and does my will to the end, I will give authority over the nations—**

The Lord's promise, here as in the other letters, is to the one *who overcomes* the temptations to defect or simply to remain neutral. Such a person continues to do the *will* of Christ, heeding what he commands and commends. This is in direct contrast with those who are condemned for practicing the deeds of Jezebel (v. 22).

Having been fully tried and found faithful to *the end* amidst the fires of affliction and controversy, the saints at Thyatira will then be ready to accept from their Lord

### DAILY BIBLE READINGS

**Monday, April 14**—God Searches Our Hearts (Romans 8:26-30)

**Tuesday, April 15**–God Shows No Partiality (Romans 2:1-11)

**Wednesday, April 16**—God Rewards According to Works (Psalm 62:8-12)

**Thursday, April 17**—God Rescues the Godly From Trial (2 Peter 2:4-10)

**Friday, April 18**—Hold Fast to Freedom in Christ (Galatians 5:1-14)

**Saturday, April 19**—Rejoice in the Lord (Philippians 4:1-9)

**Sunday, April 20**—Test Your Faith (2 Corinthians 13:5-10)

### WHAT DO YOU THINK?

"Satan's so-called deep secrets" probably have their counterpart in the occult practices seen today. How would you respond to a fellow Christian who said it was harmless to dabble in astrology, spiritism, fortune-telling, or other such practices? How would you warn him of the dangers inherent in these practices?

See Deuteronomy 18:9-14; Isaiah 8:19, 20; Galatians 5:19, 20; Revelation 21:8. Also Romans 16:19.

### WHAT DO YOU THINK?

Jesus told the Thyatirans to "hold on to what you have until I come." Paul's advice to the Philippians was similar: "Only let us live up to what we have already attained." How? How do I objectively evaluate "what I have"? Why is that in danger, anyway, that I need to "hold on" to it? And how do I do that?

## THOUGHT TO REMEMBER

*God's people can ill afford to be tolerant of what God himself abhors.*

## WHAT DO YOU THINK?

*We live in what must be the noisiest era in history. We face what seems a continual barrage of sound from cars, trucks, trains, and airplanes. Radios and television sets constantly pour out a flood of music and spoken words. With all that, Jesus says, "He who has an ear, let him hear what the Spirit says to the churches."*

*How can we do that? What steps do we need to take, for example, to be truly ready to hear the message of Sunday school classes and sermons? How can we cut down on the barrage of worthless sound to open our ears to what God is saying to us?*

## PRAYER

*Thank you, our God and Father, for the living Word of life, Jesus our Lord. Thank you for the words he speaks to us from the book of Revelation, even though at times they are strict and demanding. Help us to recognize his absolute right to speak, to be heard, and to be obeyed. Please help us to listen with open ears and receptive hearts to all that he says, and to live by it. Amen.*

*authority over the nations.* How this authority will be exercised is explained in the next two verses.

**27. "He will rule them with an iron scepter; he will dash them to pieces like pottery"—just as I have received authority from my Father.**

As Jesus *received authority* to *rule* from his *Father,* so will he convey to his faithful ones a share in that rule. The apostles had earlier been promised "twelve thrones" at the time when Christ would sit "on his glorious throne" (Matthew 19:28). Here the promise seems to be expanded to all who follow him, even as Paul said: "If we endure, we will also reign with him" (2 Timothy 2:12; cf. Revelation 20:6).

The Greek word for *rule* in this verse literally means "to shepherd." This brings to mind the shepherd's most important piece of equipment—his rod, useful for both directing and protecting his flock. As the shepherd has his rod, so the king his *scepter,* though its use is more figurative than literal, as for the shepherd. Since this rod or scepter is made of *iron,* we are to think of an authority that is firm and unyielding. An iron rod will not bend. In the hands of God's Messiah it will accomplish his judgment, destroying the wicked and rebellious, as prophesied in Psalm 2. Our text quotes from Psalm 2:9: "You will rule them with an iron scepter; you will dash them to pieces like pottery."

**28. I will also give him the morning star.**

In the concluding chapter of Revelation are these words of the Lord Jesus: "I am the Root and the Offspring of David, and the bright Morning Star" (22:16). This continues the promise of future authority granted to believers. As the *morning star* rules the heavens, so will believers reign with Jesus. A star is linked with the scepter in Numbers 24:17 and with kingship in Matthew 2:2.

Such a promise as this possessed special meaning for the saints in Thyatira. It assured them that the Morning Star, eternal in Heaven, would forever extinguish the imaginary luster of Apollo, the city's supposed deity of light and learning.

### C. HEAR AND HEED! (v. 29)

**29. He who has an ear, let him hear what the Spirit says to the churches.**

In the first three letters to the seven churches, the promise to the faithful overcomers appeared *after* the admonition to listen to the divinely given message. Here, and in the letters to Sardis, Philadelphia, and Laodicea, these words constitute a firm and final command. It applies not only to the congregations immediately addressed, but to the Lord's people in all churches, in all places, and in all times. Listen!

## CONCLUSION

Grandpa was hard of hearing. Almost everything anyone said to him had to be repeated in response to his habitual, "Huh?" But if one was patient and did not repeat what he had said, Grandpa might reply in a way that indicated he had heard the first time. He also had a strong tendency to hear what he wanted to hear, but to be utterly oblivious of matters distasteful to him. In that respect, he was somewhat like his granddaughter, who could hear only the first half of her mother's statement: "You may watch your television program *after you get your homework done.*"

Most of us tend to hear clearly God's promises of abundant and eternal blessings, but to be oblivious to the conditions on which these blessings are based: "To him *who overcomes . . . I will give. . . .*" Because the Lord knows our "hearing problem," along with everything else about us and within us, he repeats, "If you have ears, listen!" Perhaps if we formed a habit of listening carefully to what we don't want to hear as well as to what we do, our total hearing would improve.

# Discovery Learning

*This page contains an alternate lesson plan emphasizing learning activities. Classes desiring such student involvement will find these suggestions helpful. The next page is a reproducible activity page to further enhance discovery learning.*

## LEARNING GOALS

As students participate in today's class session, they should:

1. Tell briefly what Jesus commended and what he condemned in the church at Thyatira.

2. Explain why both sound doctrine and active ministry are important to the life of a healthy church.

3. Accept, or recommit to, a ministry of teaching sound doctrine or to a ministry of meeting physical needs in the name of Christ.

## INTO THE LESSON

On a chalkboard, poster board, or flip chart, draw a line down the middle, dividing it into two sections. On the left, write, "The Sixties." On the right, put "1997." To begin the lesson, ask class members to give you examples of sin or evil from the sixties. Then ask for examples of sin or evil from the present day. After you have received several responses, take some time to compare the two lists, asking the following questions for discussion:

1. Has our society become more tolerant of evil? In what ways?

2. Have we become more idolatrous in the present day? If so, what are some evidences of this?

Observe that today's lesson deals with a church under great pressure to conform to its corrupt surroundings. As was the case with all the churches in Revelation, this one was promised a rich reward if it remained faithful to Christ.

## INTO THE WORD

Use the information in the Lesson Background to set the stage for the study of Jesus' message to the church in Thyatira. Ask the class if they know which New Testament character made her home in Thyatira. (The answer is Lydia, who was Paul's first convert in the city of Philippi; Acts 16:13-15.) Mention the pagan influences noted in the Lesson Background. The pressure on Christians to conform to pagan practices must have been great.

Divide the class into two groups. Ask the first group to list the things for which the church at Thyatira was commended. Once the group has made the list, and if the group is large enough, have the group subdivide into two smaller groups. (If your class is too small for this, the group can do both of the following activities, one after the other.)

Group A should consider the pressure or influence brought on the church by non-Christians in Thyatira that might have challenged their faithfulness in the areas listed. How would adherence to sound doctrine have been important in dealing with this pressure? What kind of difficulties might the church have faced in trying to minister to its community?

Group B should focus on the present-day church. What pressure is brought on the modern church by non-Christians that challenge our own faithfulness in the areas listed? How is adherence to sound doctrine important in dealing with this pressure? How does this pressure affect our ability to render service to our community?

Have the second large group list the things for which the church at Thyatira was condemned. Then subdivide this group. Ask group A to discuss how a greater presence of sound doctrine in the church could have helped prevent these problems. They should also discuss how these internal problems may have compromised their ability to minister to the community. Group B should discuss how the modern church may experience the same problems as those listed, and how they can correct them. What role does sound doctrine play? How can that role be established? How can the church minister to the community if it has these same problems?

After ten to fifteen minutes of discussion, bring the class together again. Point out that both groups were dealing with situations that tested a congregation's or a Christian's *faithfulness.* Two important issues revealed in this text are sound doctrine and ministry. Both are important to a church's, or an individual Christian's, faithfulness.

## INTO LIFE

Say, "If our church is going to be faithful, we need people to teach our young people, the new believers, and even the long-time Christians. We need a commitment to sound doctrine. Could you get involved in a teaching ministry? Perhaps you already are. Will you recommit yourself to sound doctrine in that ministry?

"If our church is going to be faithful, we also need active ministries meeting the physical needs of people in and out of the church. Are you involved in such a ministry? Will you commit to one?"

Lead the class into a time of silent prayer, directing them to commit, or recommit, themselves to one of these ministries.

# E. T.

Several comparisons or contrasts can be observed between the church at Ephesus (Revelation 2:1-7) and the church at Thyatira (Revelation 2:18-29). In each of the following comparisons, write "E" next to the statement that describes or applies to Ephesus and "T" next to that which describes or applies to Thyatira.

One had lost its first love and was doing less _____    The other was doing more than at first ____

One was tolerating false doctrine _____    The other was exposing false apostles _____

One had a false prophetess misleading people ____    The other hated the practices of the Nicolaitans ____

One was in danger of losing its "lampstand" _____    The other was told to "hold on . . . until I come" ____

Overcomers in one were promised fruit from the tree of life ____    Overcomers in the other were promised the "morning star" ____

One was strong in defending the faith (sound doctrine) but weak in ministry _____    The other was strong on ministry but too tolerant of false doctrine _____

E-T, T-E, T-E, E-T, E-T, E-T

# Putting Them Together

Both sound doctrine and a vital ministry to people are essential to a healthy church. Look at your own church.

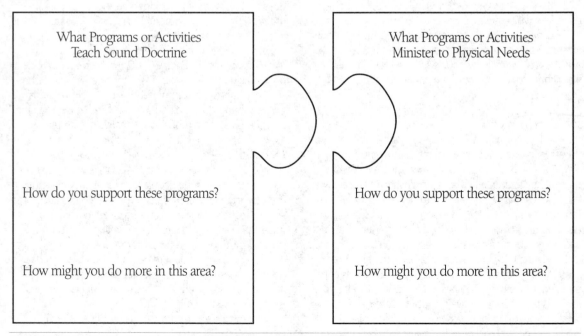

What Programs or Activities
Teach Sound Doctrine

What Programs or Activities
Minister to Physical Needs

How do you support these programs?

How do you support these programs?

How might you do more in this area?

How might you do more in this area?

# TO PHILADELPHIA AND LAODICEA

**LESSON 9**

## WHY TEACH THIS LESSON?

Things are not always what they seem. This, according to one writer, is a theme that recurs throughout the book of Revelation. We certainly see it in today's lesson. The church at Philadelphia was struggling, but the Lord said it was strong. The church at Laodicea seemed rich and strong, but the Lord said it was weak.

How about your church? Is it a strong church or a weak church? Are you sure? Use this lesson to challenge your class to look deeper than surface level to see the true status of your church—and what you can do to make it stronger!

## INTRODUCTION

### A. WHAT ARE MUSCLES FOR?

A familiar picture in many popular magazines is that of a man posed to display bulging and rippling muscles. What, we wonder, does he do with those muscles, except to develop them and display them for the admiration of viewers, beginning with himself?

Perhaps more familiar to many of us is the mental picture of a slender man, clad in overalls and toiling to coax a livelihood from his family farm. He may have walked with a limp, but this did not keep him from carrying out his daily tasks. We could not see his muscles, for they were covered by his work clothes. But they were constantly in use, laboring for those he loved. Isn't that really what muscles are for?

Today's lesson from Revelation tells of two more churches in the Roman province of Asia that were addressed by the Lord Jesus. One was limited in its size and resources, perhaps like the churches in which many of us came to Christ, but it used what it had to the glory of God. The other was wealthy, but seems to have spent its energy on posing for the admiration of its audience. And that is not what the church's resources are for.

### B. LESSON BACKGROUND

Philadelphia and Laodicea, the cities to which the last two of the seven letters in Revelation were written, lie farthest inland of the seven cities. Both occupied commanding positions on important trade routes, and both were subject to occasional earthquakes. Philadelphia was located almost directly on a line between Sardis and Laodicea. Today it is known by the name Alashehir.

In Roman times, Laodicea was known as the richest city in the district of Phrygia. Its major commodity was a glossy black textile made from the soft black wool of a now-extinct breed of sheep. Its famous medical college developed a "Phrygian powder" that was used to make a widely exported eyesalve. These and other businesses developed banking establishments that dominated the area and made the city of Laodicea wealthy and powerful. Ironically, its site is now deserted.

DEVOTIONAL READING:
2 PETER 2:4-10
LESSON SCRIPTURE:
REVELATION 3:7-22
PRINTED TEXT:
REVELATION 3:7-10, 14-21

### LESSON AIMS

*This study should prepare students to:*

*1. Compare and contrast the churches at Philadelphia and Laodicea.*

*2. Tell what constitutes a "strong" church in the eyes of Jesus.*

*3. Dedicate their resources, or lack of resources, and both their strengths and their weaknesses to the Lord's glory.*

Apr
27

### KEY VERSES

*I know your deeds.*
*Revelation 3:8, 15*

LESSON 9 NOTES

**WHAT DO YOU THINK?**

The reference to the "open door" in Revelation 3:8 sounds similar to Paul's mention in 2 Corinthians 2:12 of an open door of opportunity to preach in Troas. It is exciting when we find a similar door of opportunity for evangelism, but we must be prepared to enter it.

How does a church recognize an "open door"? What can it do to be sure it is prepared to enter such an open door? What can individual Christians do to recognize and enter an open door for ministry?

**OPTION**

Use the reproducible activity, "Two Doors," on page 302 to contrast this "door" with the one mentioned in 3:20.

**WHAT DO YOU THINK?**

Sometimes it seems an individual or a church with "little strength" is thought unimportant. Jesus' message to Philadelphia suggests otherwise. Why do some people discount a "little strength"? How can even a little strength be useful in God's kingdom? How can people with little strength be encouraged to use that for the Lord?

Laodicea, however, had a problem with its water supply. The city of Hierapolis, six miles northward, was the home of a mineral springs, which provided hot, healing waters. Colosse, ten miles to the east, was famous for its clear, cold water. But Laodicea's supply, delivered by aqueduct from both directions, was tepid and distasteful when it arrived. We will see that many of these aspects of life in Laodicea were incorporated into the language Jesus used to address the church and appeal to its spiritual needs.

Colossians 4:13-16, written some thirty years before Revelation, expressed Paul's concern for all the Christians in Hierapolis, Colosse, and Laodicea. He urged that his letter to Colosse be shared with the other two churches. Through the book of Revelation, Jesus' letters to Philadelphia and Laodicea are shared with us.

## I. PHILADELPHIA'S STEWARDSHIP (REVELATION 3:7-10)

Two of the seven letters in Revelation express approval without any rebuke. Both are addressed to "poor" churches. One is to Smyrna (Revelation 2:8-11). The other is to Philadelphia.

### A. THE VOICE OF AUTHORITY (v. 7)

**7. To the angel of the church in Philadelphia write: These are the words of him who is holy and true, who holds the key of David. What he opens no one can shut, and what he shuts no one can open.**

In most of the letters to the seven churches, Jesus introduces himself in terms found in his earlier self-revelation to John (Revelation 1:12-16). This is not the case here, although the words used carry the same tone of divine authority. *Holy* and *true* are used in Revelation as attributes of God (4:8; 6:10; 15:3; 16:7).

The phrase *key of David* calls to mind the words of Isaiah 22:22: "I will place on his shoulder the key to the house of David; what he opens no one can shut, and what he shuts no one can open." This passage was originally addressed to a man named Eliakim, whom God had designated to replace Shebna as the king's treasurer in Jerusalem. Now, Jesus applies the words to himself and draws attention to his authority to open and close doors on behalf of his church. The next verse applies this specifically to the church in Philadelphia.

### B. COMMENDING FAITHFULNESS (v. 8)

**8. I know your deeds. See, I have placed before you an open door that no one can shut. I know that you have little strength, yet you have kept my word and have not denied my name.**

Whereas Jesus had "a few things against" Pergamum (2:14) and Thyatira (2:20), he found in Philadelphia a band of saints who had remained faithful. Other churches had succumbed to the pressures of persecution from without and corruption from within, but the believers in Philadelphia had stood firm.

What was the *open door* that Christ had *placed before* this church? Was it an opportunity for fruitful service and evangelism such as Paul found at Ephesus (1 Corinthians 16:9) and Troas (2 Corinthians 2:12), and desired to find in a Roman prison (Colossians 4:3)? Or was it the door through which they were able to enter by faith, in order to find salvation and life eternal (Acts 14:27)? In either case, *no one can shut* the door that Jesus opens to those who are willing to follow him without reservation.

What made the faith of these disciples even more noteworthy was the fact that they possessed only a *little strength*. Apparently they were severely limited in numbers or resources, yet they faithfully used what they had. The small, struggling congregation has the same Lord as the large, multistaffed one!

The accolade that *you . . . have not denied my name* was another testimony to Philadelphia's tenacity. An integral part of the Roman persecution of Christians was the demand that the accused believer recant his faith and curse the name of Jesus. Those who persistently refused to do so were charged with treason and counted worthy of death.

### A LITTLE STRENGTH

Recently a story on television dealt with a young girl who had developed herself as a weight lifter. She was just five feet tall and weighed 119 pounds, yet she could lift barbell weights of about 117 pounds. Of course, she could not lift weights the way three-hundred-pound men can, but for her size she possessed considerable strength.

Jesus spoke of the church at Philadelphia as having a "little strength" (Revelation 3:8). This did not automatically make the church ineffective. In fact, Philadelphia was one of only two churches among the seven with which Jesus did not find fault. Philadelphia's strength may have been little, but it was enough to keep the word of Christ and not deny his name.

This concept of a little strength is very helpful to us as Jesus' followers today. We may not have such a dynamic faith that we can move mountains or achieve impossible victories for our Lord. Perhaps our tasks are not enormous and our challenges are rather modest. We need to realize that, whatever our level of strength, God can help us greatly if we dedicate what we have to his cause. We may have just a little strength, but it is more than enough for the many little tasks, crises, and opportunities we usually face. Even a little strength applied at the right time and place can accomplish great things for God. —J. G. V. B.

### C. REWARDING FAITHFULNESS (vv. 9, 10)

**9. I will make those who are of the synagogue of Satan, who claim to be Jews though they are not, but are liars—I will make them come and fall down at your feet and acknowledge that I have loved you.**

*The synagogue of Satan,* introduced previously in the letter to Smyrna (Revelation 2:9) was apparently a community of unbelieving, hostile Jews, who had forfeited their right to be called the people of God by their rejection of the Jews' Messiah. By thus serving their father, the devil (John 8:44), they earned the identification of their assembly with the devil. Eventually these enemies will bow humbly at the *feet* of their former victims. (See Isaiah 60:14.)

**10. Since you have kept my command to endure patiently, I will also keep you from the hour of trial that is going to come upon the whole world to test those who live on the earth.**

The Christians in Philadelphia had exhibited unshakable patience in keeping Jesus' commands and enduring affliction for his sake. This enabled them to receive his promise of preservation from an even greater *hour of trial* yet to *come upon the whole world.* The Greek word rendered *kept* means to watch or guard. Thus, the promised protection here can mean either that they will be kept from undergoing the coming trials or that they will be guarded and protected through or during the trials.

One may recall a similar promise of preservation given to the apostles: "All men will hate you because of me. But not a hair of your head will perish" (Luke 21:17, 18). Yet James, like John the Baptist and Stephen before him, met a martyr's death (Acts 12:1, 2). Others like Peter (Acts 12:6-11) experienced a miraculous deliverance from prison and death. The New Testament contains accounts of both deliverances *from* and deliverances *through* affliction.

The specific trial referred to in this verse is not known. More important is the promise of Christ's presence in the hour of trial—a promise that has sustained

*How To Say It*
*arche (Greek). ar-KAY.*
*Alashehir. AL-uh-shuh-HERE.*
*Colosse. Kuh-LAHSS-ee.*
*Eliakim. Ee-LYE-uh-kim.*
*Hierapolis. High-er-AP-uh-liss.*
*Laodicea. Lay ODD-uh-SEE-uh.*
*Pergamum. PER-guh-mum.*
*Phrygia. FRIJ-ee-uh.*
*Shebna. SHEB-nuh.*
*Smyrna. SMUR-nuh.*
*Thyatira. THIGH-uh-TIE-ruh.*
*Troas. TROE-az.*

*WHAT DO YOU THINK?*
*Have you ever prayed God would keep you from a trial but found, instead, he kept (guarded) you through it? If so, tell about the incident. At what point did you begin to appreciate that God was protecting you through the difficulty? How did you respond?*

## HOW TO SAY IT

*arche* (Greek). *ar-KAY.*
*Alashehir. AL-uh-shuh-HERE.*
*Colosse. Kuh-LAHSS-ee.*
*Eliakim. Ee-LYE-uh-kim.*
*Hierapolis. High-er-AP-uh-liss.*
*Laodicea. Lay ODD-uh-SEE-uh.*
*Pergamum. PER-guh-mum.*
*Phrygia. FRIJ-ee-uh.*
*Shebna. SHEB-nuh.*
*Smyrna. SMUR-nuh.*
*Thyatira. THIGH-uh-TIE-ruh.*
*Troas. TROE-az.*

believers throughout the history of the church. The promise may well include the great final trial of judgment, which will be an occasion of rejoicing for the faithful ones (Matthew 25:31-34).

## II. LAODICEA'S COMPLACENCY (REVELATION 3:14-21)

In contrast to Philadelphia, the last of the letters to the seven churches contains only rebuke and correction. Even so, it expresses the love of Jesus for his church.

### A. THE VOICE OF ETERNAL TRUTH (v. 14)

**14. To the angel of the church in Laodicea write: These are the words of the Amen, the faithful and true witness, the ruler of God's creation.**

The church in Laodicea is addressed, as are the other six churches, through the *angel* or messenger who was expected to carry the words to the congregation. Here Jesus emphasizes eternal truth as his credential. He calls himself *the Amen,* a title based on a Hebrew word that means "in truth" or "truly." (This is the term translated, "I tell you the truth" in John 3:3, 5, 11, and other passages.) He also calls himself *the faithful and true witness.* The importance of this title will be seen when Jesus unmasks the Laodicean church and confronts the believers there with the truth about their sad condition.

In addition, Jesus refers to himself as *the ruler of God's creation.* The word for *ruler* here is *arche,* usually translated as "beginning" or "first." (The *King James Version* has "the beginning of the creation" here.) It can mean either first in time or first in prominence. It is from this word we get our prefix *arch—,* as in *archenemy, archrival,* or *archangel.* Here it is first in prominence, as the Son was not created. He was present at the creation of the heavens and the earth and was the instrument of their creation (John 1:1-3; Colossians 1:15-17). He is Lord of the church and Lord of creation!

### B. COMPLACENCY EXPOSED (vv. 15-18)

**15, 16. I know your deeds, that you are neither cold nor hot. I wish you were either one or the other! So, because you are lukewarm—neither hot nor cold—I am about to spit you out of my mouth.**

The phrase *neither cold nor hot* brings to mind the problems with Laodicea's water supply, mentioned in the Lesson Background. The city's *lukewarm* water illustrated perfectly the spiritual condition of the church. It was not cold like the waters at Colosse, nor was it hot like the springs at Hierapolis.

Some students relate the terms *cold* and *hot* to the fervency of the Laodiceans, much like our expression of being "on fire" for the Lord. Jesus' wish for them to be hot fits well with that understanding, but his wish that they be cold is problematic. How could this be more pleasing to God than a neutral, lukewarm stance? Some have suggested the bitter atheist or the hardened sinner, like the publicans and harlots of Jesus' day, may be led to recognize his need and turn to Christ more readily than the self-satisfied nominal Christian. But this is a call to repentance—why would Jesus desire they become even worse sinners in the process of repentance? Or it may be that the nominal Christian is so unattractive that he hurts the cause of Christ more than does the outspoken enemy of the church.

Another way to view the hot-cold-lukewarm issue is to think of something other than fervency. Jesus said *I know your deeds,* not "I know your spirit." He wants them to do something useful. The cold, clear water of Colosse was refreshing on a hot day. The hot springs of Hierapolis provided medicinal value, or were appealing for a hot bath. But the lukewarm water of Laodicea was useful for neither. "I wish you were either cold and refreshing or hot and soothing, but you are neither!"

There was, however, a ray of hope for the Laodiceans. The Lord was *about to spit* them *out*. He hadn't yet! Prompt repentance, such as that urged in all the letters directed to churches with problems, would avert final judgment.

**17. You say, "I am rich; I have acquired wealth and do not need a thing." But you do not realize that you are wretched, pitiful, poor, blind and naked.**

When Laodicea suffered major damage in an earthquake some thirty years before this letter was written, the city was so financially secure that it refused assistance from the empire. They did *not need a thing*, or so they thought.

In reality, the Christians in Laodicea were sadly impoverished. They failed to recognize the need for the kind of wealth that their banks could not handle, the kind of eyesight their "Phrygian powder" could not provide, and the kind of clothing not available in their fine fabrics. Until they learned to depend on God, they would be eternally helpless and pathetic. They would have no assets beyond the grave, no ability to see beyond temporary material things, and no covering for their sins.

**18. I counsel you to buy from me gold refined in the fire, so you can become rich; and white clothes to wear, so you can cover your shameful nakedness; and salve to put on your eyes, so you can see.**

*Buy from me*, invites Jesus, for he is the only source of the riches, clothing, and vision needed by the Laodiceans. Not from deposits in their banks, but from depending upon him, would come the riches of faith "of greater worth than of gold, which perishes even though refined by fire" (1 Peter 1:7). Not from their supplies of black textiles, but from the Savior with whom they had clothed themselves at baptism (Galatians 3:27), could they receive the pure *white clothes,* signifying purity and forgiveness from the blackness of their sin and shame. Not from their famous eye *salve,* but from him who had given sight to a blind man with an ointment of spittle and clay (John 9:6, 7), could they receive the ability to see God and Heaven. Jesus is still willing to bestow spiritual sight on any willing patient (John 9:39-41).

It should be noted that this was not the first message about spiritual wealth addressed to the Laodiceans. Read of Paul's earlier concern for them in Colossians 2:1-3.

## C. LOVE SEEKS RECONCILIATION (vv. 19, 20)

**19. Those whom I love I rebuke and discipline. So be earnest, and repent.**

Purposeful chastening is one of the clearest expressions of love: (see Proverbs 3:11, 12; Hebrews 12:5-11). It is not the loving parent or teacher, but the selfish seeker of ease and comfort, who withholds correction. He does not care enough to endure the stress involved in administering discipline. He would rather avoid the pain of confrontation or the possibly negative reaction his efforts might produce.

Thus, to this church that has made Jesus sick by bragging that it does not need him or what he has to offer, Jesus declares his *love*. It is the love that prunes the fruit-bearing branch to make it still more fruitful (John 15:1, 2). As for the Laodiceans, only when their smug complacency was shattered could they effectively repent, shake off their apathy, and become *earnest* to serve the Lord with their considerable resources. The command to *repent* is not only for the unsaved; this church needed to do it!

**20. Here I am! I stand at the door and knock. If anyone hears my voice and opens the door, I will come in and eat with him, and he with me.**

There is no more touching picture than the one that shows Jesus knocking patiently at a door that must be opened from within. This is not the knock of a stranger. This is not an appeal to sinners to be saved. Jesus is addressing a church, or perhaps a church member, who has come to feel that it or he can get along without Jesus. Jesus will know. But he will not enter where he is not welcomed, even

*WHAT DO YOU THINK?*

The church at Laodicea regarded herself as being rich but was actually poor. Some churches today make the same mistake. Some churches are materially rich, with fine buildings with elaborate furnishings, but they are spiritually poor, neglecting spiritual growth, evangelism, or other vital aspects of their responsibility to Christ. Other churches are rich in programs, with a full range of activities, but at the same time they may be weak in outreach. Some churches are even doctrinally rich but spiritually poor. They may pride themselves on their biblical purity but drift into a legalism devoid of love.

How should a church measure its wealth? How can it be sure it is not substituting some other kind of wealth for spiritual wealth?


*WHAT DO YOU THINK?*

It is noteworthy that Christ emphasizes his love for the lukewarm Laodicean church. At the same time he could tell them, "You are wretched, pitiful, poor, blind and naked." Do you know anyone you could speak to so frankly and still be friends? How can we establish a depth of love that allows us to say such things to a fellow Christian—and have it accepted in love? Why is it important that we do so?


*WHAT DO YOU THINK?*

The picture of Christ knocking at the door is one that has appealed to artists, hymn writers, and Christians in general. What about this image do you find most appealing? Why?

## PRAYER

*Thank you, God our Father, for the love that seeks us and finds us where we are, and chastens and changes us according to our needs. Thank you especially for Jesus our Savior and King, who offers his love and companionship forever. Amen.*

## THOUGHT TO REMEMBER

*For lasting strength and wealth we have only one source: Jesus Christ our Lord.*

## DAILY BIBLE READINGS

*Monday, Apr. 21—Love One Another (1 John 3:11-24)*

*Tuesday, Apr. 22—Listen to God's Call (Isaiah 55:1-9)*

*Wednesday, Apr. 23—Expect Christ's Coming (2 Thessalonians 1:3-10)*

*Thursday, Apr. 24—Endure Trials to the End (Matthew 24:4-14)*

*Friday, Apr. 25—Trust God, Not Wealth (Proverbs 10:11-24)*

*Saturday, Apr. 26—Bless the Lord for His Care (Deuteronomy 8:1-10)*

*Sunday, Apr. 27—Do All for God's Glory (1 Corinthians 10:23-33)*

though he is the Lord of glory and is himself the door by which any person must enter life eternal. If the occupant responds to the voice and the knocking, and *opens the door* to welcome Jesus, he will make himself at home and will stay to *eat with him.*

### TO EAT WITH JESUS

The invasion of the island of Sicily and the mainland of Italy was one of the most significant campaigns toward the close of World War II. Among the thousands of American soldiers were many troops with an Italian background. Every once in a while a young man would enter a town where a close relative of his father or mother lived. While on a brief leave, such a soldier would visit his relatives. What a joyous meeting that would be!

Usually the hosts of these gatherings would bring out their scanty resources of bread and few scraps of food to celebrate the occasion. Not much was available, for times were hard in Italy during the Nazi occupation of their country. Very often, however, their visitor had in his knapsack supplies that he had brought with him, such as canned meat, dried vegetables, and perhaps cheese and macaroni. Many times candy bars were given to the children. All enjoyed a time of sharing and fellowship.

Jesus promises that the one who "opens the door" and lets him in will experience rich fellowship and sharing as well. It does not matter if our resources are meager, for he will share his great gifts with us. He will pour out his mercy, grace, peace, and inner spiritual power on us. He will eat with us and we with him. And as precious as this is, it is only a foretaste of the greater supper yet to come!          —J. G. V. B.

### D. VICTORY AND GLORY BECKON (v. 21)

**21. To him who overcomes, I will give the right to sit with me on my throne, just as I overcame and sat down with my Father on his throne.**

The believers in Laodicea had to overcome their pride and their self-satisfaction with their wealth. Perhaps this was harder than other churches' having to overcome poverty, persecution, false doctrine, or blatant sin. But if they failed to do so, the rewards of victory could never be theirs.

The word *throne* indicates power and authority. Jesus *overcame* all opposition to the fulfillment of his Father's plan and was then "exalted" and given a "name that is above every name" (Philippians 2:9). Likewise, his disciples must follow the same path of first overcoming on earth and subsequently reigning with Christ in Heaven.

### CONCLUSION

Often a person prepares for his departure from this life by expressing his desires concerning the distribution of his belongings. He writes a *will*—a document that says, "I will," or, "It is my serious desire." A will says a lot about what an individual wants his family to have and to be.

In the same way, we learn about the Lord Jesus from the "I wills" written within the letters to the seven churches. There is, however, a significant difference between what he wills to the church and what people will to their families. The Lord's desires are not left for someone else to carry out. He continues to be in control. When he says "I will," it means that he is going to do it, according to the conditions he has set forth. Thus, to the churches at Philadelphia and at Laodicea—and to us on the same conditions—he says, "*I will* make them . . . acknowledge that I have loved you"; "*I will also* keep you from the hour of trial"; "If anyone hears my voice and opens the door, *I will* come in and will eat with him"; and, "To him who overcomes *I will* give the right to sit with me on my throne."

What *will we* let him do for us?

# Discovery Learning

*This page contains an alternate lesson plan emphasizing learning activities. Classes desiring such student involvement will find these suggestions helpful. The next page is a reproducible activity page to further enhance discovery learning.*

## LEARNING GOALS

This study should prepare students to:

1. Compare and contrast the churches at Philadelphia and Laodicea.

2. Tell what constitutes a "strong" church in the eyes of Jesus.

3. Dedicate their resources, or lack of resources, and both their strengths and their weaknesses to the Lord's glory.

## INTO THE LESSON

Begin class by asking the students to imagine they are moving to another town and have found two churches near their new home. Doctrinally the churches are about the same. Which would they choose? Why?

Church A is small. It has a full-time minister and a part-time youth minister. It has an annual operating budget of $120,000 and gives another $35,000 per year to missions. Its facility consists of one building, with a modest auditorium and education wing. Worship services are moving but not elaborate. There is a good spirit among the members, but there is always a shortage of workers for some program or another. Visits to the church have been pleasant experiences.

Church B has a seven-acre campus and a staff of eight full-time ministers. Its budget is around 2.5 million, with $100,000 a year going to missions. Worship services are elaborate and professional; children's programs run like clockwork. Visits are exciting and memorable events.

Ask how many would choose church A and how many would choose B. Then ask for volunteers to tell why they chose the one they did. After a while, observe that nothing was said about the spirit of church B. It's possible that such a church may have exciting programs but no spiritual health. (Do **not** suggest all big churches are spiritually weak!) The smaller church, though weak by some standards, was strong in missions giving and was described as having a good spirit among its members.

## OPTION

Use the "Super-Church" activity on the next page to introduce today's topic.

## INTO THE WORD

Use the Lesson Background to provide information on the cities of Philadelphia and Laodicea. This is especially important with Laodicea, because much of what Jesus said to this church contains references to life in Laodicea that its residents would readily understand.

Divide the class into two groups. One will study Jesus' message to the church in Philadelphia; the other will examine his words to Laodicea. Move between the groups to offer assistance with any questions a group may have.

*The Philadelphia Group*

1. To what may the "open door" (Revelation 3:8) refer? How does a church know when such a door is open? How does an individual know?

2. What is the meaning of the phrase, "You have little strength"? Was this a positive or a negative quality of the church? Notice that Philadelphia is one of only two of the seven churches of which Jesus had nothing negative to say (Smyrna is the other). What does this tell you about what makes a church "strong"?

*The Laodicea Group.*

1. Explain what it meant for the church to be lukewarm instead of hot or cold (Revelation 3:15, 16).

2. How can material abundance cause a church's spiritual zeal to decline?

3. What steps can a church take to allow Christ to "come in," in response to his invitation? How can an individual do this? How can a family?

Give the groups about fifteen minutes to answer their questions. Have each group designate a "reporter," then bring the class together to hear a summary of each group's discussion.

## INTO LIFE

The extent of our resources does not determine the degree or the value of our service to Jesus. One of the hallmarks of the church at Philadelphia was its faithful use of its limited resources. Many Christians or churches minimize their effectiveness by reasoning, "If only I had more _____, or were more _____, I would be able to serve Jesus better."

Have the class offer suggestions for filling in these blanks, then allow them time to provide responses to counter their suggestions.

Have the groups that worked together earlier reconvene for closing prayer. Tell each group to form a prayer circle, offering sentence prayers that focus on the lessons learned from the two churches in today's Scripture.

# It's Super-Church! Or Is It?

How would you describe a "strong church"? List the characteristics you would expect to find in a strong church.

Review your list. Write **M** next to each item related to money, the budget, or other financial concerns. Next to each item related to the spiritual growth of the members and what the church teaches, write **T**. Next to each item related to evangelism—reaching the lost—write **E**. Next to each item that relates to opposing the works of Satan, write **S**. Finally, next to each item related to the physical plant and facilities, write **P**.

How many items did you mark **M** or **P**? How many **T**, **E**, or **S**?

The church at Philadelphia had "little strength," but it had a divinely opened door of opportunity before it. Short on **M** and **P**, perhaps, it appears to have been strong in **T**, **E**, and **S**. The church at Laodicea was rich—**M** and **P**. But the Lord had no praise for it. It was weak in **T**, **E**, and **S**.

Which is your church more like? Why do you think so? What would the Lord tell your church if he wrote you a letter today?

# Two Doors

1. What kind of door was mentioned in connection with Philadelphia? (Revelation 3:8) What is the significance of this door?

2. What kind of door was mentioned in connection with Laodicea? (Revelation 3:20) What is the significance of this door?

3. What kind of door stands open at your church today? What do you need to do to go through it?

4. What doors are closed at your church that Jesus is knocking at to have you open to him? How can you open them to the Lord?

# THE REDEEMING LAMB

**LESSON 10**

## WHY TEACH THIS LESSON?

Worthy. We don't hear this word much anymore. We would rather speak of being "qualified" or "certified." These terms don't seem to challenge our self worth as much if we don't measure up. No one wants to be unworthy!

But we are unworthy, and no amount of positive mental attitude or self imaging will compensate for what sin has done to us. It has corrupted us. It has left us unworthy of life eternal.

That's what makes this lesson so important. Here we'll meet the Lamb, who *is* worthy. And because he is worthy, he can make us worthy! Celebrate that fact with your students today.

## INTRODUCTION

### A. CAUSE FOR WEEPING

"I wept and wept," said John, while experiencing visions of Heaven's utmost glory. Why was he crying? Because no one worthy could be found to do the task at hand! The apostle's tears have been shared by God's people throughout the ages.

Consider Jeremiah, the "weeping prophet." He had to tell his beloved countrymen in Judah that their sins had brought them to defeat and captivity at the hands of the idolatrous Babylonians. Our language preserves his name in the word *jeremiad,* meaning a prolonged complaint and lamentation.

Consider the apostle Paul. This man, who coldly and brutally oversaw the killing and imprisonment of believers in Jesus, became a believer himself. He was transformed into a man of compassion, whose tears reflected his burden for a lost world and his desire that others know the Christ who had done so much for him. His tears fell for those in Ephesus (Acts 20:19, 31) and in Corinth (2 Corinthians 2:4). He writes to the Philippians of "weeping" over the "enemies of the cross of Christ" (Philippians 3:18). Paul's own tears gave him a keen awareness of the tears of others (2 Timothy 1:4).

It is not hard to find cause for weeping in the present day. Anyone can find an abundance of causes in the daily newspaper, at the grocery store magazine rack, or on the television screen.

Is the situation hopeless? No, as long as the Lamb of God is still available to take away the sin of the world (John 1:29), and to lead us back to the Father, who will one day wipe away all tears from his children's eyes (Revelation 7:17; 21:4).

### B. LESSON BACKGROUND

During his exile on the rocky island of Patmos, John was given a series of messages and visions to convey to the seven churches in Asia (Revelation 1:11). First came the letters to the churches (Revelation 2 and 3), some of which we studied during the past three Sundays. Chapter 4 begins with the opening of a door in Heaven, after which John hears a voice: "Come up here, and I will show you what must take place after this" (v. 1). The rest of the chapter then presents a description of the glory of God seated on his throne and of the response of reverent

DEVOTIONAL READING:
REVELATION 4:1-11

LESSON SCRIPTURE:
REVELATION 4, 5

PRINTED TEXT:
REVELATION 5:1-10

LESSON AIMS

*As a result of this study, the student should be able to:*

*1. List and explain the symbols used in Revelation 5 to portray the One who redeems.*

*2. Tell some reasons for worshiping the Lamb.*

*3. Implement at least one specific plan that will make the student's own personal worship more meaningful.*

May
4

KEY VERSE

*And with your blood you purchased men for God from every tribe and language and people and nation.*      Revelation 5:9

worshipers to his glory. Our lesson text for today is taken from chapter 5, which introduces God's worthy Lamb.

## I. WHO IS WORTHY? (REVELATION 5:1-4)

### A. THE SEALED SCROLL (v. 1)

**1. Then I saw in the right hand of him who sat on the throne a scroll with writing on both sides and sealed with seven seals.**

The one holding this *scroll* is referred to as *him who sat on the throne*. He is the One who has just received worship and adoration in chapter 4, and before whom the elders have laid down their crowns. This scroll was rolled together and *sealed with seven seals.*

Rolled documents of papyrus, parchment, or vellum (a more durable form of parchment) were usually inscribed on only the smoother face of the material, which became the inside of the scroll as it was unfolded and read. Only if a great amount of material had to be recorded would the back side be used as well, and this would become immediately evident to even the casual observer. Clearly, there was much to say in the book that John saw! The prophet Ezekiel was offered a similar scroll, also with writing on both sides, and was commanded to eat it (Ezekiel 2:9—3:2).

*Seals,* commonly of wax, were affixed to important documents to (1) indicate ownership, (2) assure genuineness of authorship, (3) protect against any change or abuse of the contents, or (4) conceal the contents until a properly authorized person was present for the opening. The use of *seven* seals indicates complete and perfect security against tampering. The seven seals seem to have been immediately visible, which suggests that they were aligned along the outside of the scroll. This would lead one to believe that all the seals had to be broken before any of the contents could be read.

However, the impression given in the following chapter is that as each seal was opened, a new vision was revealed to John. It appears more likely that the scroll consisted of seven separate sheets, and that when a seal was opened, a sheet was unfolded before John. At any rate, this document was secured in a manner appropriate for the wondrous mysteries of God that it contained.

### B. THE CRUCIAL QUESTION (v. 2)

**2. And I saw a mighty angel proclaiming in a loud voice, "Who is worthy to break the seals and open the scroll?"**

The business of one of God's messengers (an *angel*) is not a work for weaklings. An angel rolled the huge stone away from the entrance to Jesus' tomb (Matthew 28:2). Another angel is seen tossing a "large millstone" into the sea (Revelation 18:21). The angel introduced here may have been Michael or Gabriel, but his question is more important than his name. The candidate for breaking the seven seals and revealing its mysteries had to be *worthy* in every way: ability, character, attitude, and standing with God and man.

### C. THE FRUITLESS SEARCH (vv. 3, 4)

**3, 4. But no one in heaven or on earth or under the earth could open the scroll or even look inside it. I wept and wept because no one was found who was worthy to open the scroll or look inside.**

Strong repetition of the negatives in this verse emphasizes the hopelessness John felt in the search for one qualified to receive, open, and examine the scroll extended by the Ruler of the universe. But *no one was found:* there was *no one in heaven,* no one *on earth,* and no one *under the earth* who was *worthy.* Such was the

**HOW TO SAY IT**

*Agrippa. Uh-GRIP-puh.*

*apocalyptic. uh-POCK-uh-*
    *LIP-tik.*

*arnion (Greek). ar-NEE-ahn.*

*Corinth. KOR-inth.*

*Ephesus. EFF-uh-suss.*

*Ezekiel. Ee-ZEEK-yul*
    *or Ee-ZEEK-ee-ul.*

*Gabriel. GAY-bree-ul.*

*Herod. HAIR-ud.*

*jeremiad. jer-uh-MYE-ud.*

*Jeremiah. JAIR-uh-MYE-uh.*

*Judah. JOO-duh.*

*Patmos. PAT-muss.*

*Sardis. SAR-dis.*

*Zechariah. Zek-uh-RYE-uh.*

report after searching high and low in all the places where someone might possibly be found. (See Exodus 20:4; Philippians 2:10.)

John's frustration caused him to burst into tears and to continue weeping. Did his tears express his disappointment in not being able to see what would happen in the future (Revelation 4:1)? Did he cry out of a sense of hopelessness in realizing the present unworthiness of everything that God had originally created good and perfect? In that, we share his tears.

## II. THE ONE WHO IS WORTHY (REVELATION 5:5-7)

At this point John experienced the fulfillment of the promise recorded in one of Jesus' Beatitudes: "Blessed are those who mourn, for they will be comforted" (Matthew 5:4).

### A. THE ELDER'S ASSURANCE (v. 5)

**5. Then one of the elders said to me, "Do not weep! See, the Lion of the tribe of Judah, the Root of David, has triumphed. He is able to open the scroll and its seven seals."**

The word of assurance came to the apostle, not from one of the angels, but from an unidentified representative of the twenty-four *elders*. His admonition was, *Do not weep*; his gentle assurance was that someone totally worthy was at hand.

The phrase *the Lion of the tribe of Judah* recalls the patriarch Jacob's reference to his son Judah as a "lion's cub," and his prophecy that "the scepter will not depart from Judah . . . until he comes to whom it belongs" (Genesis 49:9, 10). Jesus, descended from the tribe of Judah (Hebrews 7:14), fulfilled this prophecy. As the Lion, he was the most noble of all the kings from that tribe.

The phrase *Root of David* recalls another Messianic prophecy, found in Isaiah 11:1: "A shoot will come up from the stump of Jesse, from his roots a Branch will bear fruit ." Jesse, as David's father, identifies the same ancestry. The word *root* can mean either a source or an outgrowth from a root (such as a shoot, stem, or branch). Near the end of the book of Revelation, Jesus refers to himself as "the Root and the Offspring of David" (Revelation 22:16). Thus, the verse before us reflects Old Testament prophecies that highlighted both the specific tribe from which the Messiah would come, and the specific individual in that tribe from whom he would be descended.

This prophesied One *has triumphed* over Satan, sin, and even death itself. He is therefore unquestionably worthy to *open the scroll* and reveal the mysteries inside it.

### B. THE LAMB IS WORTHY (vv. 6, 7)

**6. Then I saw a Lamb, looking as if it had been slain, standing in the center of the throne, encircled by the four living creatures and the elders. He had seven horns and seven eyes, which are the seven spirits of God sent out into all the earth.**

The visions in Revelation are designed primarily to convey important spiritual messages. One must keep in mind the nature of its apocalyptic contents. The language is predominantly symbolic, and the symbols can change rapidly, with little warning. So we should not be too surprised when the Lion mentioned by the elder appears as a *Lamb*.

It is with good reason that the Lamb now occupies *center* stage in John's vision. He bears the marks of having been *slain* (perhaps showing a healed scar across the throat, according to the manner of slaying the Passover sacrifice). Now,

---

**OPTION**

Use the reproducible activity, "Old Testament Imagery of the Christ," on page 310 to explore the background of the images in verses 5 and 6.

**WHAT DO YOU THINK?**

No one but Jesus was found "worthy" to open the scroll. What tasks are we worthy to perform in behalf of Christ? Jesus was worthy to open the scroll, and he stepped forward to open it. Why are people sometimes not so quick to step forward to do what they are specially gifted to do? How can we motivate them to do so?

**WHAT DO YOU THINK?**

Jesus is "the Lion of the tribe of Judah. " In 1 Peter 5:8, Satan is compared to a "roaring lion." What images come to mind when you think of both Jesus and Satan as "lions"? What insights on our spiritual warfare does this suggest to you?

**WHAT DO YOU THINK?**

The Lion is a Lamb! As impossible as this sounds, that is what John discovered. Of course, there are qualities of each animal that illustrate for us something of the nature of Christ and his redemptive work on our behalf. With which picture do you more easily relate? Why? What is it about the other image you have difficulty relating to? What, if anything, do you need to do to better appreciate or apply this image?

*The visual for lesson 10 illustrates the Lamb, who was worthy to open the scrolls. Display it as you discuss verses 6 and following, or wait until you come to verse 9, which is quoted on the poster.*

## DAILY BIBLE READINGS

*Monday, Apr. 28—The Lamb Sacrificed (Isaiah 53:4-9)*

*Tuesday, Apr. 29—The Lamb Receives a Kingdom (Daniel 7:9-14)*

*Wednesday, Apr. 30— Sinners Ransomed by Blood of Christ (1 Peter 1:18-25)*

*Thursday, May 1—The Lamb, the Light of Jerusalem (Revelation 21:22-27)*

*Friday, May 2—The Lamb, Worthy of Praise (Revelation 4:1-11)*

*Saturday, May 3—The Redeemed Worship the Lamb (Revelation 14:1-5)*

*Sunday, May 4—The Lamb, Our Final Judge (Romans 14:1-11)*

however, this Lamb is very much alive, and is not even identified by the same term as the lamb on the altar. Twenty-nine times in Revelation the Lamb is mentioned, and always with a term (Greek, *arnion*) that is found elsewhere only in John 21:15, where Jesus tells Peter, "Feed my lambs." The term seems to designate Jesus as the risen and triumphant Lamb; he appears as though slain, yet he still stands!

The *seven horns* and *seven eyes* are also strongly symbolic. As noted already, *seven* indicates completeness or perfection. Horns symbolize power, representing an animal's primary means of defending himself and his flock. The Psalms (along with other poetic passages in the Old Testament) also refer to horns in several instances as a symbol of strength. See examples in Psalms 18:2; 75:10; Jeremiah 48:25; Micah 4:13.

Having seven eyes indicates the ability to observe fully and to know completely. "These seven are the eyes of the Lord, which range throughout the earth" (Zechariah 4:10). The Lamb sees, knows, and understands everything. These eyes are identified with *the seven Spirits of God*, a phrase used in the introductory greeting to the book (1:4) and in the introduction to the letter to Sardis (3:1). It suggests the thoroughness of the work of the Holy Spirit, whose presence in Christians all over the world and in the inspired Word extends his influence *into all the earth*. The capability of this Lamb is complete!

### SLAIN, YET STANDING

A 1994 report by the National Opinion Research Center at the University of Chicago told of a study conducted in Russia. This involved three thousand persons who until recently had spent their entire lives under a Communist system where religion was banned and ridiculed. A third of these Russians under twenty-five indicated that they believed in God. Seventy percent of those surveyed expressed a confidence in church leaders, while forty percent believed in miracles. The *World Christian Encyclopedia's* editor, David Barrett, stated that these numbers reflected "one of the most enormous swings in the history of Christianity."

John tells us in verse six of our text for today that he saw "a Lamb, looking as if it had been slain, standing in the center of the throne." One would expect a slain lamb to lie fallen and lifeless. Yet here was one that to all appearances was indeed slain, but remained standing. This is a picture of the Lamb of God, Jesus of Nazareth, standing victorious after paying the ultimate price for the sins of the world.

Throughout the long history of the church, the death of Christianity often has been proclaimed. It has appeared to be slain, but has remained standing. Such was the case in ancient Rome and most recently in Communist Russia. Where Marx was exalted, our Master is proclaimed. Where the church was mocked and scorned, now Christ is preached and believers are multiplied. Behold the Lamb— slain, yet *standing!*

—J. G. V. B.

### 7. He came and took the scroll from the right hand of him who sat on the throne.

This brief verse provided the answer John was seeking to the question raised by the strong angel (v. 2). It also calmed John's anxieties concerning the book he had been shown. The Lamb, having been introduced and shown to be qualified, will do what no other being in all the world could do.

We should keep in mind as we study these symbols that the items that were part of John's vision were not as limited as the same items in the material world might be. The seven spirits were described as seven blazing lamps in chapter 4 (v. 5); in chapter 5 they are seven eyes. After taking the book, the Lamb proceeds to open one of the seals (in chapter 6), and one of the living creatures speaks to John. Such is the nature of apocalyptic literature: it is highly symbolic, but beneath the figures and symbols lies an important message. The remainder of our lesson text provides the message that gave John, and can give believers today, assurance and hope.

## III. HONORING THE LAMB (REVELATION 5:8-10)

Revelation 4 concluded with expressions of thanks and praise to the one who sat on the throne (v. 10). Now similar expressions from the same worshipers burst forth in recognition of the Lamb.

### A. BOWING IN ADORATION (v. 8)

**8. And when he had taken it, the four living creatures and the twenty-four elders fell down before the Lamb. Each one had a harp and they were holding golden bowls full of incense, which are the prayers of the saints.**

Celebration began immediately, once it had been established that *the Lamb* was worthy to open the sealed scroll. The *four living creatures* and the *elders* encircling the throne prostrated themselves in worship, expressed not only in the act but also with traditional accompaniment. The *harp,* or a lyre held in the hands, was commonly associated with songs of joyful praise, as indicated in Psalms 33:2; 43:4; 71:22; 147:7; 149:3; 150:3.

The rising of the odors of the incense, which was to be burned on an altar in the tabernacle for its fragrance (Exodus 30:7, 8), came to symbolize *the prayers of the saints* ascending toward God: "May my prayer be set before you like incense" (Psalm 141:2). Incense also could be carried and burned in small bowls. In this glorious scene, these are *golden bowls.* And *each one* present joined in the celebration; no one was a mere spectator, depending on another to express praise on his behalf. Heaven is a place of unanimous worship!

### THE FRAGRANCE OF HEAVEN

Throughout his letters, the apostle Paul refers to his prayer life (Romans 1:9, 10; 1 Corinthians 1:4; 2 Corinthians 13:7; Ephesians 1:16; 3:14-19; Philippians 1:4, 9-11; Colossians 1:3; 1 Thessalonians 1:2, 3; 2 Thessalonians 1:3; 2 Timothy 1:3; Philemon 4). He indicates that he prayed intensely and continuously for both churches and individuals. Interest in and petition for the success and stability of God's work in the world should be a constant Christian practice. We tend to emphasize the power of prayer. It does indeed "have divine power to demolish strongholds" (2 Corinthians 10:4). It can provide healing and strength in many crises of life. Yet prayer is more than power; it is a thing of beauty and blessing as well.

Our text for today tells us that the ruling Lamb had seven horns and seven eyes. The horns signify power while the eyes stand for perception and perfect understanding. The church praises the risen Lord for his ability to understand our needs, our opportunities, and our victories. This is supplemented with perfect power to effect changes in us and in our world in proportion to our trust in him and our compliance with his will.

The four living creatures and the twenty-four elders around the Lamb's throne held harps and golden bowls. The harps stand for Heaven's harmony and beautiful music. The bowls contain incense that produces a fragrance that rises toward Heaven. The fragrance represents the prayers of the saints, through which God is glorified and his church purified. Our prayers are not only an evidence of reliance on God, but are a fragrance that permeates the precincts of paradise.

—J. G. V. B.

### WHAT DO YOU THINK?

*The burning of incense was a kind of offering in the Old Testament. Perhaps it would be helpful for us to think of our prayers as offerings. The incense that was to be offered in the tabernacle was a divinely prescribed blend of spices that was to be offered continuously. Does this suggest there is a divinely established prescription or pattern for prayer? Why or why not? What do Matthew 6:5-15; Philippians 4:6, 7; James 1:5-8; 1 Thessalonians 5:17 teach us about prayer?*

## What Do You Think?

The book of Revelation shows us that Heaven will be a place of singing. On earth there is a distinct difference of taste between believers who prefer traditional hymns and those who favor simpler choruses. Sometimes that difference heats up into an argument—or something worse! What will happen to those differences as we sing in Heaven? How might we practice the heavenly art of singing here and eliminate the feud?

## Prayer

Thank you, our great God and Father in Heaven, for the spotless and death-conquering Lamb who brings us into your presence. May we praise him in joyous harmony with all who love him truly, and may we serve him with selfless abandon. Amen.

## Thought to Remember

"To him who loves us and has freed us from our sins by his blood, and has made us to be a kingdom and priests to serve his God and Father—to him be glory and power for ever and ever! Amen" (Revelation 1:5, 6).

## B. Singing in Praise (vv. 9, 10)

**9, 10. And they sang a new song: "You are worthy to take the scroll and to open its seals, because you were slain, and with your blood you purchased men for God from every tribe and language and people and nation. You have made them to be a kingdom and priests to serve our God, and they will reign on the earth."**

Next, the twenty-four elders and the four living creatures lifted their voices in a song of celebration to the victorious Lamb. A *new song* is usually composed to celebrate a great victory and honor a notable hero. We should recall the praise song of Moses and of Israel after the crossing of the Red Sea (Exodus 15:1-21). In Scripture a new song is addressed always to God (Psalms 33:3; 96:1; Isaiah 42:10).

*You are worthy*. What was the basis of the Lamb's worthiness? The primary qualification was suggested earlier when the Lamb first appeared as though it had been slain (v. 6). The Lamb had willingly sacrificed himself for others (Isaiah 53:7). By the shed blood of that sacrifice, he *purchased* and brought to *God* all those from all times and all places who would accept his sacrifice in obedient faith (John 3:16).

Not all of those invited accept the blood-bought gift of life, but some from every distinguishable group among humankind are described as having done so. They come from every *tribe* (blood-related family or clan), *language* or dialect, *people* (identifiable cultural group), and *nation* (governmental unit). These divisions, which often erect barriers and create animosities among warring factions, are erased in Christ. In him such distinctions are no longer important.

In making all believers *a kingdom and priests* of God, the Lamb has expanded on God's promise to Moses at Sinai in Exodus 19:6. Peter echoes the thought: "You also . . . are being built into a spiritual house to be a holy priesthood, offering spiritual sacrifices acceptable to God through Jesus Christ" (1 Peter 2:5).

To enjoy such a standing as *priests* and to *reign on the earth* is a marvelous privilege. It is also an awesome responsibility, with great obligations. Just as King Herod and King Agrippa in Palestine were answerable to their emperor in Rome, so anyone who would reign in the name of Christ is answerable totally to him. To reject his authority is high treason!

## CONCLUSION

Jim traveled widely in his work for a Christian organization, so he had occasion to meet on the Lord's Day with many congregations in many cities. Not surprisingly, he encountered a variety of styles in church music, some traditional and others contemporary. On one occasion he heard an excellent choral presentation of numbers from Handel's *Messiah*. Afterward he introduced himself to the choir director and said, "I like praise choruses." A shadow of disappointment clouded the director's eyes until Jim added, "Such as the ones I heard this morning!"

Christians of all musical tastes, and even of no musical training, can join wholeheartedly in the hymn to Christ that we have just examined. We can join the white-robed elders and the living creatures, along with the multitude of angels that immediately added their voices in singing, "Worthy is the Lamb, who was slain, to receive power and wealth and wisdom and strength and honor and glory and praise" (Revelation 5:12). Even that was not enough, for following this tribute, all creation blended its voices to join the chorus: "To him who sits on the throne and to the Lamb be praise and honor and glory and power for ever and ever!" (5:13).

Whether we prefer the grand repetitions of the classic hymns or the simpler repetitions of Scripture choruses and other contemporary praise choruses, we will find ways to lift our voices together in praise to the Lamb of God who loved us and bought us for the Father at the price of his own precious blood. The unity of Heaven's choir should be anticipated by voices united in praise on earth.

# Discovery Learning

*This page contains an alternate lesson plan emphasizing learning activities. Classes desiring such student involvement will find these suggestions helpful. The next page is a reproducible activity page to further enhance discovery learning.*

## LEARNING GOALS

As a result of this study, the student should be able to:

1. List and explain the symbols used in Revelation 5 to portray the One who redeems.

2. Tell some reasons for worshiping the Lamb.

3. Implement at least one specific plan that will make the student's own personal worship more meaningful.

## INTO THE LESSON

Prepare for this lesson by securing several well-known symbols to show the students. You may wish to use some of the following examples from the secular world: a dollar bill, a wedding ring, a picture of an eagle, an American flag, the insignia of a sports team that has a rich tradition, or a picture of McDonald's "golden arches." In addition to these, bring in some Christian symbols like a cross, a Bible, a picture of a dove, or the Communion emblems.

Spread the symbols out on a table so that students can see them as they enter the classroom. Lead into the lesson by saying, "We've gathered several well-known symbols that are important in our society today. What is a symbol?" Point out that a symbol is simply an item that stands for something else. Have students look at the examples that you have brought to class and offer their explanations of what these symbols represent. Save the Christian symbols that you have brought for last. As you discuss these, ask the class to comment on how these symbols better help us understand truths about God, Christ, and the church.

Observe that many people are hesitant to study the book of Revelation, for they are afraid that it contains too many strange descriptions that cannot be understood. But the symbols John uses are in some ways just like the ones we have discussed today: symbols that communicate ideas much deeper and richer than mere words can.

## OPTION

Use the reproducible activity, "Symbols," on the next page to introduce the lesson.

## INTO THE WORD

Divide the class into three or four small groups for the purpose of studying today's text and examining some of the symbols that appear there. Give each group these phrases from Revelation 5: "Lion of the tribe of Judah," "Root of David," "seven," and "the Lamb." Tell the groups to discuss what makes each of these symbols so significant (for example, as they discuss "Lion," they should consider what characteristics of a lion could be applicable to Jesus). Copies of the second activity, "Old Testament Imagery of the Christ," (page 310) will be helpful.

Next, raise the following questions with the class (answers are given in parentheses). "Where are the events mentioned taking place?" (Around the throne of God). "What images come to mind when the throne of God is mentioned?" (The place where God dwells, where he makes his judgments, and where he rules over his creation). "What is happening as the chapter begins?" (A strong angel is seeking one who would be found worthy to open a book.) "Is anyone found worthy to open the book?" (An elder mentions that One has been found worthy to open the book and break its seals.) "How is this One described?" (He is depicted as a Lion from the tribe of Judah, as the Root of David, and as a Lamb having been slain.) "What happens after this worthy One takes the book?" (The elders and the living creatures fall down before the Lamb, and they sing a song of praise to him.) "What are the reasons that the elders and living creatures give for worshiping the Lamb?" (He is worthy of worship because he has been slain; he has redeemed us to God.)

## INTO LIFE

Write the words *Personal Praise* on your chalkboard. Ask for volunteers to tell you some ways they worship the Lord in their personal quiet times. List as many ideas as you can. These may include singing, personal prayer, meditating on God's Word, memorization. Ask for details on how to do these things as well as getting general ideas.

Encourage the students to make a commitment to deepen their own personal worship time by taking advantage of at least one of the ideas they have heard this morning. Challenge them to take time out of each day during the coming week to focus on God—who he is, what he has done for them in the past, and how he continues to care for them in the present. End the study with a time of prayer, asking volunteers to offer short sentence praises to God for the great things he has done. (Make sure no one feels pressured to pray aloud, but encourage it of those who are willing.)

Perhaps a musically talented student could bring the prayer time to a close by leading the class in a stanza of "Holy, Holy, Holy!" or "Thou Art Worthy."

# Symbols

In the first box below, draw some pictures of things that symbolize your life—your family, your job, your personality. In the second box, draw pictures of the symbols that John uses to portray Christ.

# Old Testament Imagery of the Christ

Much of the symbolism of Jesus in the book of Revelation draws on imagery that was used in the Old Testament. Look up the references from Revelation and write the image that is used to describe the Christ. Then draw a line from the name of the image you have written to the appropriate Old Testament reference that is the background for that image.

1. Revelation 5:5                              Isaiah 41:4

2. Revelation 5:5                              Zechariah 1:18

3. Revelation 5:6                              Genesis 49:9

4. Revelation 5:6                              Zechariah 3:9

5. Revelation 5:6                              Isaiah 11:1, 10

6. Revelation 5:6                              Zechariah 4:2-10

7. Revelation 1:8                              Isaiah 53:7

# PROVISION FOR THE REDEEMED

**LESSON 11**

## WHY TEACH THIS LESSON?

"Redeemed—how I love to proclaim it! Redeemed by the blood of the Lamb; Redeemed thro' His infinite mercy, His child, and forever, I am." Fanny Crosby's hymn gives us all the reason we need to teach this lesson, which reminds us of the blessings of redemption. On Mother's Day, we surely want to honor our mothers. But it is an even greater privilege to recall that "*his* child, and forever, I am!"

## INTRODUCTION

### A. SECURITY FOR MOTHERS

"Well, I'm not buying any green bananas." That's the way one mother answered a friend who wanted to know how she felt about future prospects for herself and her family. And who of us would be inclined to argue with her about it? Her concern for her own advancing years and for the uncertainties facing her children and grandchildren gave her an uneasy feeling about what lay ahead. Any of us could respond with our own litany of insecurities relating to crime, national debt, moral decay, family breakdown, and other special items of concern. How about our green bananas? Will they have the opportunity to ripen and be enjoyed by others?

What lasting gift can we bestow on Mother on this, her day? In addition to the assurance of our love and prayers and our pledge of lasting support, what security can we provide or promise?

Perhaps we can begin by remembering that this particular first day of the week was the *Lord's Day* long before it became *Mother's Day*. God's revelation of eternal triumph and lasting security came to an apostle, and thus to the church, on a Lord's Day (Revelation 1:10) long ago, amid circumstances that were much less secure than ours. To all mothers and all their children of all generations, God offers the abiding security of his unchanging love and eternal presence.

### B. LESSON BACKGROUND

The vision recounted in Revelation 7 seems to interrupt a series of events recounted in chapters 4-6. Yet it is built on what is found in those chapters. Chapters 4 and 5 describe the throne room of Heaven, focusing on the glorious One who is seated on the central throne. Accompanying him is the Lamb, standing though having been slain. Surrounding the central throne appear four living creatures, suggesting the totality of created beings. Encircling all these are twenty-four thrones occupied by twenty-four white-robed elders, symbolizing either the leaders of believers from both Old and New Covenants or the believers themselves. Surrounding all of these was a throng of angels, joining in praise to God.

Chapter 6 presents a series of visions occurring with the opening of six of the seven seals. Each of the first four visions consists of a horse and rider. First comes a victorious rider on a white horse, followed by one on a red horse (representing

DEVOTIONAL READING:
HEBREWS 9:7-14

LESSON SCRIPTURE:
REVELATION 7

PRINTED TEXT:
REVELATION 7:1-3, 9, 10, 13-17

LESSON AIMS

This study should equip class members to:

1. Explain the relationship between the assurances found in Revelation 7 and the final judgment.

2. Name one assurance that is most meaningful to them.

3. Understand how the reference to "great tribulation" can apply to suffering believers throughout the history of the church.

May
11

KEY VERSE

*For the Lamb at the center of the throne will be their shepherd; he will lead them to springs of living water. And God will wipe away every tear from their eyes.*
                    *Revelation 7:17*

*LESSON 11 NOTES*

## OPTION

*Introduce the topic of security with the reproducible activity, "Security Comes From…," on page 318. Here is the solution to that activity:*

1. *Faithfulness*
2. *Righteousness*
3. *Perseverance*
4. *Humility*
5. *Trust*
6. *Steadfastness*
7. *Knowledge*
8. *Sanctification*
9. *Service*

*Key Word: Assurance*

## WHAT DO YOU THINK?

*Paul says we have been "marked in him with a seal, the promised Holy Spirit" (Ephesians 1:13). He also speaks in Romans 8:6 of our having "the mind controlled by the Spirit." How do these passages help us understand the symbol of having been sealed in our foreheads? What kind of visible demonstration of this seal should be evident in our lives?*

war), another on a black horse (representing pestilence or famine), and a fourth rider (whose name was Death) on a "pale" horse. The opening of the fifth seal results in a vision of "the souls of those who had been slain because of the word of God and the testimony they had maintained" (Revelation 6:9). The sixth introduces the terrors of final judgment, from which multitudes try to hide themselves.

The vision of the sixth seal closes with a penetrating question: "For the great day of their wrath has come, and who can stand?" Who will be able to endure the release of divine wrath against human sin? And by what means? At this point, Revelation pauses from the opening of the seals to provide the answer. The seventh and final seal will not be opened until the beginning of chapter 8.

## I. SECURITY FOR GOD'S SERVANTS (REVELATION 7:1-3)

*1. After this I saw four angels standing at the four corners of the earth, holding back the four winds of the earth to prevent any wind from blowing on the land or on the sea or on any tree.*

Matthew 13:39, 41, 42, and 24:29-31 refer to *angels* as agents of judgment. In the present vision John saw God's agents *standing at the four corners of the earth*, thus controlling all the earth. The task of these angels was to hold *back the four winds of the earth*. They were to prevent the destructive hurricanes of judgment from being released too quickly to work their devastation. For similar language used of divine judgment, see Jeremiah 49:35, 36. This act by the angels protected, at least for a time, the *land* and *sea* and the kind of growth (trees) that normally bears the brunt of destructive storms.

*2, 3. Then I saw another angel coming up from the east, having the seal of the living God. He called out in a loud voice to the four angels who had been given power to harm the land and the sea: "Do not harm the land or the sea or the trees until we put a seal on the foreheads of the servants of our God."*

This next *angel* appeared *from the east*, as does the rising sun. His mission was one of light and preservation. He carried the evidence of authority from God himself—an official *seal* such as that identifying the ambassador of a nation and serving to authenticate his message. This angel demonstrated his authority by delivering his message to the four angels *in a loud voice*.

The angel's cry kept the effects of the four winds from being felt by the *land*, *sea*, and *trees*. His words also reveal why the opening of the seventh seal had been delayed. The pause was a pause of grace, allowing the angels to *put a seal on the foreheads of the servants of our God*. Revelation 14:1 and 22:4 also refer to this marking as an important means of identifying the faithful.

Ezekiel 9:3-6 tells of a similar marking of the faithful before the punitive slaughter of those who were guilty of abominations in Jerusalem. Both markings are reminiscent of the procedure followed during the Israelite Passover. A mark was placed on the doorposts of the Israelites' homes in Egypt before the Lord carried out the plague of death on the firstborn (Exodus 11:1—12:30).

The *forehead* was an appropriate place to carry the *seal* identifying those belonging to God. Associated with the intellect, the forehead indicates a willing commitment. It is prominent and easy to see. Deuteronomy 6:4-9 directs that God's Word be bound on their foreheads.

Rather than an actual physical mark, a spiritual identification is indicated in 2 Timothy 2:19: "God's solid foundation stands firm, sealed with this inscription: 'The Lord knows those who are his.'" The seal of God's ownership may not be physically visible on our brows, but his ownership of our lives will become evident as his will guides our thoughts, directs our attention, and determines the course of our actions.

Verses 4-8, not included in our printed text, describe those who were sealed as 144,000 descendants of Jacob, with 12,000 from each of twelve tribes. The twelve tribes named are not identical with the ones who were assigned territories in the promised land. This, along with the precise pattern of exact numbers, suggests that these numbers are symbols rather than literal statistics.

What do these numbers symbolize? Some believe that the 144,000 of verses 4-8 refer to the saved who are Jews, while the "great multitude" described in verse 9 includes Gentiles who have turned to Christ. It is more likely, however, that the 144,000 and the great multitude refer to the same group of people. This understanding is in line with the tendency of the New Testament to apply Old Testament language to the church. (See Hebrews 12:22-24; 1 Peter 2:9.) Those who belong to the "Israel of God" (Galatians 6:16) are here pictured in glory with God.

## II. PRAISE FROM GOD'S SERVANTS (REVELATION 7:9, 10)

**9, 10. After this I looked and there before me was a great multitude that no one could count, from every nation, tribe, people and language, standing before the throne and in front of the Lamb. They were wearing white robes and were holding palm branches in their hands. And they cried out in a loud voice: "Salvation belongs to our God, who sits on the throne, and to the Lamb."**

What John earlier *heard* (v. 4) as the sealing of the 144,000 from the tribes of Israel, he now *saw* as a *great multitude* of saints *that no one could count*, coming from all imaginable categories of humanity—political units, families, clans, cultural groups, races, languages and dialects—and gathering *before the throne and in front of the Lamb*. In Christ there is neither Jew nor Greek, slave nor free, male nor female, but all share a common relationship to God (Galatians 3:28). While that unity remains imperfect here on earth, in Heaven it will be complete. We will be one!

The unity of the redeemed is reflected in the similarity of their clothing, equipment, and activity. *White robes* signified a God-given purity, innocence, and righteousness. The redeemed also carried *palm branches*, indicating a festive occasion like Jesus' triumphal entry into Jerusalem (John 12:12, 13; see also Leviticus 23:39, 40). Thus equipped, this throng became a mighty choir declaring praise to the Ruler of Heaven and earth, and to the Lamb who had risen in power and glory after dying as a sacrifice for the sins of the world.

The promise that such an all-inclusive throng will gather around the throne in Heaven challenges the church to take seriously Christ's command to go into all the world and make disciples of all nations (Matthew 28:18-20). If that throng will indeed be one, without divisions into separate cultural, racial, and language groups, some mingling of these within congregations and choirs here on earth would be a most appropriate preparation.

Verses 11 and 12, not included in our printed text, tell us that the multitude of redeemed persons were then joined in their praises by "all the angels." The angels' sevenfold tribute of praise is similar to that found in Revelation 5:12.

## III. BLESSINGS TO GOD'S SERVANTS (REVELATION 7:13-17)

God's devoted servants have reason enough to praise him on earth for blessings they experience in their daily walk with him. They have immeasurably greater blessings yet to come.

### A. THEY ARE KEPT AND CLEANSED (vv. 13, 14)

**13, 14. Then one of the elders asked me, "These in white robes—who are they, and where did they come from?"**

**I answered, "Sir, you know."**

*WHAT DO YOU THINK?*

*The scene in Revelation 7:9, 10 reminds us that the gospel is intended for people of all races and nations and language groups. Yet there remain several peoples with no contact with the gospel, no Bible in their own language, no missionary to tell them the good news of Jesus Christ. What demands does this put on our church? Can we honestly say we are doing everything we can to take the gospel to "all nations" (Matthew 28:19)? Why or why not? How can we increase our missions outreach?*

*WHAT DO YOU THINK?*

*The lesson writer also sees a challenge in Revelation 7:9, 10 that churches be more inclusive of various races and people groups. "If that throng will indeed be one, without divisions into separate cultural, racial, and language groups, some mingling of these within congregations . . . here on earth would be a most appropriate preparation." What is our church doing to include a variety of cultural, racial, and language groups? What more do you think we can or should do?*

## WHAT DO YOU THINK?

Our society is increasingly abandoning biblical principles of right and wrong. Whenever Christians speak against any form of immorality, they are being subjected to increasing ridicule and even hostility. Anti-Christian groups and individuals are working to limit the rights of Christians to practice their faith publicly. Does this suggest the time of "the great tribulation" for believers is near? Why or why not?

If Christians try to exercise political clout to influence society, might they be guilty of trying to prevent "the great tribulation" that God has said they must endure? Why or why not? Or do you think exercising political power might actually generate more tribulation? Why or why not? How should one's view of "the great tribulation" affect his or her participation in the political process?

## WHAT DO YOU THINK?

The lesson writer refers to "those who may feel uneasy about singing, 'Are You Washed in the Blood of the Lamb?'" How do we respond to those critics who object to our emphasis on blood atonement?

See Hebrews 9:22; Romans 3:23-26.

## HOW TO SAY IT

Ezekiel. Ee-ZEEK-yul
  or Ee-ZEEK-ee-ul.
Jeremiah. JAIR-uh-MYE-uh.
Lazarus. LAZ-uh-russ.
shekinah (Hebrew). shih-
  KYE-nuh.
Zechariah. Zek-uh-RYE-uh.

*And he said, "These are they who have come out of the great tribulation; they have washed their robes and made them white in the blood of the Lamb.*

At this point, John's role changed from that of an observer of the events in Heaven, and he became an invited participant. An otherwise unidentified member of the twenty-four *elders* may have noticed some confusion in John's expression, so he left the circle of thrones to help this observer understand what was happening. He spoke the question that was evidently on John's mind: "Who are all these white-robed singers of God's praises, and how did they get here?" John could have suggested an answer, but he preferred to learn from one who knew. So with appropriate respect he said, in effect, "I'm listening; tell me." The instructive elder responded by answering the question and going on to tell what these assembled saints could expect in the future. His response continues to the end of the chapter.

Two characteristics identified the members of the throng first mentioned in verse 9. They had endured *great tribulation* for the sake of Christ, and they had been cleansed by "him who loves us and has freed us from our sins by his blood" (Revelation 1:5). The term **the** *great tribulation* implies a definite period of affliction, perhaps calling to mind Daniel's prophecy of "a time of distress such as has not happened from the beginning of nations until then" (Daniel 12:1). One may also think of Jesus' words to his disciples: "For then there will be great distress, unequaled from the beginning of the world until now—and never to be equaled again" (Matthew 24:21; Mark 13:19).

Many have suggested a specific period of intense suffering as the fulfillment of this time of tribulation. Some believe that it refers to a period of extreme opposition shortly before Christ's second coming. It is believed that this hostility will accompany the appearance of the "man of lawlessness," whose coming will precede Christ's return (2 Thessalonians 2:3). However, it is also possible that *the great tribulation* is a general reference to any form of persecution of believers. This would make the message concerning tribulation pertinent to suffering Christians of any era and in any country, whose sufferings may well be for them the great tribulation. The important point then becomes the assurance offered to the oppressed believer, not the discovery of the clue to a particular theory of interpretation.

Thus, whatever the immediate reference may have been, this passage bears a close and timeless relationship to the assurances of Romans 8:35-37 and 2 Corinthians 4:16-18 that no difficulty on earth can separate God's people from his love, and that the worst of present afflictions for Christ's sake is insignificant when compared with future blessings.

While the idea of whitening robes with blood seems impossible from a human perspective, spiritually there is no difficulty with bleaching one's garments *white* by applying the sacrificial *blood of the Lamb*. Those who may feel uneasy about singing, "Are You Washed in the Blood of the Lamb?" need to reconsider Ephesians 1:7; 1 Peter 1:18, 19; 1 John 1:7; and Revelation 1:5.

### WHITE ROBES

You can always tell who the graduates are at any high school or college commencement. They are the ones dressed in robes. Wearing a robe indicates that a milestone in one's academic career has been reached.

John tells us that the multitude of the redeemed were distinguished by the white robes that they wore. They are said to have "washed their robes and made them white in the blood of the Lamb" (Revelation 7:14). They have responded in faith and obedience to the Son of God's sacrifice for them.

Those in the church at Sardis are told that the white garments promised to them are a token of the fact that they have overcome (3:5). Jesus tells them that "they will walk with me, dressed in white" (3:4). In Revelation 19 we are given a vision of the

Lamb's wife, who is clothed in "fine linen, bright and clean." We are also informed that the "fine linen stands for the righteous acts of the saints" (v. 8).

Just as academic achievement involves overcoming certain obstacles and challenges, spiritual achievement means conquering the daily challenges to our growth in Christ. The robe of academic accomplishment is a beggar's garment compared with the white robes awaiting those who have overcome in Jesus' name. The congratulatory words from a dean or president pale in comparison with the Master's "Well done." What a glorious "graduation ceremony" that will be!                          —J. G. V. B.

## B. THEY SERVE IN GOD'S PRESENCE (v. 15)

**15. Therefore,**

 **"they are before the throne of God**
  **and serve him day and night in his temple;**
 **and he who sits on the throne will spread his tent over them.**

Because the saints have availed themselves of Christ's cleansing sacrifice and have remained faithful through the most severe afflictions, they will experience the joy of serving God face to face without the limitations of *day and night*. It is difficult to know exactly how the saints will *serve* God in Heaven, beyond expressions of worship and praise. Since there will be no poverty or pain, acts of mercy to the needy will not be necessary. The eternal activities are a part of the divine provision that we cannot begin to fathom (1 Corinthians 2:9).

In its references to the *temple* Revelation uses a Greek word that indicates the inner shrine rather than the outer courts. It symbolizes the very presence of God. So intimate is his presence that Revelation 21:22 says of the new Jerusalem, "I did not see a temple in the city, because the Lord God Almighty and the Lamb are its temple."

Heaven's most essential ingredient (that is, what will make it Heaven) will be the very presence of the Almighty—among his people rather than on a distant throne. He will *spread his tent over* his people, sheltering them with his presence. (Compare the promises of Ezekiel 37:27 and Zechariah 2:10.) In the Old Testament, the Hebrew word *shekinah* described the glory of God that appeared over the mercy seat in the tabernacle, indicating the presence of God among his people. The eternal reality will be infinitely greater.

## C. THEY CONTINUE IN GOD'S CARE (vv. 16, 17)

**16. "Never again will they hunger;**
  **never again will they thirst.**
 **The sun will not beat upon them,**
  **nor any scorching heat.**

The elder found it easier to describe Heaven by its relief from familiar problems and difficulties than by its positive provisions. We know what hurts us here; Heaven is a place where none of that will be present. *Hunger* and *thirst* are universal and sometimes critical problems, especially among the poor. There will be no such deprivations in Heaven.

In many areas where John had ministered, the discomforts and dangers of the desert *sun* and *scorching heat* were closely related to hunger and thirst. Isaiah 49:10 promised freedom from all of these: "They will neither hunger nor thirst, nor will the desert heat or the sun beat upon them. He who has compassion on them will guide them and lead them beside springs of water." The new Jerusalem is described as having no need of the *sun*, "for the glory of God gives it light, and the Lamb is its lamp" (Revelation 21:23). Eternity in Heaven will offer benefits without limit to replace earth's difficulties.

## DAILY BIBLE READINGS

 **Monday, May 5**—Worship in Spirit and in Truth (John 4:19-26)
 **Tuesday, May 6**—The Lord, Your Keeper (Psalm 121:1-8)
 **Wednesday, May 7**—The Lord, Your Shepherd (Psalm 23)
 **Thursday, May 8**—The Lord, Your Comforter (Isaiah 25:6-9)
 **Friday, May 9**—Jesus, the Good Shepherd (John 10:11-16)
 **Saturday, May 10**—The Lord, Worthy of Worship (1 Chronicles 16:28-36)
 **Sunday, May 11**—Jesus Rewards Faithfulness (John 14:15-21)

## WHAT DO YOU THINK?

*In Heaven we will continuously serve God. Does that mean our service on earth is a preparation for our service in Heaven? Or is the nature of our service there so different that earthly service has no direct bearing? Give reasons with your answer. Consider not just the actual "tasks" associated with service, but the attitude, spirit, and faithfulness involved.*

*Do you think we say enough about preparing for serving God in Heaven when we ask people to serve in the church? Why or why not? (See Matthew 25:21.)*

## WHAT DO YOU THINK?

*Which of the description of Heaven in these verses appeals to you the most right now? Why? How might you share your feelings about Heaven in a way that will appeal to an unbeliever and help lead him or her to Christ?*

*Display the visual for lesson 11 as you conclude your Bible study. Discuss, what might this person be feeling right now? Praise God for the promise that he will wipe away those tears!*

God shall wipe away all tears.

## PRAYER

*We are frightened, O God, by circumstances around us and by our inability to overcome our own "great tribulations." Constantly we need your loving care, your guidance, and your power to gain the victories you have in store for us. May we never stray from the security of your presence. We pray in Jesus' name. Amen.*

## THOUGHT TO REMEMBER

*"Therefore, my dear brothers, stand firm. Let nothing move you. Always give yourselves fully to the work of the Lord, because you know that your labor in the Lord is not in vain" (1 Corinthians 15:58).*

**17. "For the Lamb at the center of the throne will be their shepherd;**
    **he will lead them to springs of living water.**
  **And God will wipe away every tear from their eyes."**

The *Lamb*, who had been shown worthy to open the scroll with the seven seals, now becomes the good *shepherd* of his flock (John 10:11-14). In him the promises of Psalm 23 reach their ultimate fulfillment, as do the words of Ezekiel 34:23: "I will place over them one shepherd, my servant David, and he will tend them; he will tend them and be their shepherd." The reason that hunger is absent is that the Lamb will feed them; the reason there is no thirst is that *he will lead them to springs of living water.*

Perhaps the tenderest picture presented in the Bible is that of Almighty God tenderly caressing one of his little ones and wiping away his *every tear.* This promise also applies to the sobbing of an aged saint. Again, this was foretold in Isaiah 25:8: "He will swallow up death forever. The Sovereign Lord will wipe away the tears from all faces . . . the Lord has spoken."

### TEARS WIPED AWAY

People around the world live without many possessions that we believe to be essential to our life and work. There are people who do not use knives and forks as we do, people who sleep in hammocks instead of beds, and those who wear very few or no clothes. Some do not have umbrellas, some have never seen shoes or gloves, and some have no written language. But something all peoples seem to have in common is tears. At some time or in some circumstance, everyone needs to cry.

We know that we cannot escape tears in our own lives. When loved ones die, when tragedies invade the lives of those near to us, when we know bitter defeats or disappointments, or even when some utterly unbelievable blessing comes our way, we know the presence of tears. Even the Son of God, whom we usually think of as the master of every emergency, cried unashamedly at Lazarus's grave. The shortest verse in the Bible speaks volumes: "Jesus wept."

Because tears are universal, the promise in today's text becomes one of the most comforting in the entire Bible: "God will wipe away every tear from their eyes" (Revelation 7:17). This is reinforced by a later assurance: "He will wipe every tear from their eyes. There will be no more death or mourning or crying or pain" (21:4).

Here in this present life there is no place *without* tears. In that future life in Heaven, there shall be no place *with* tears. Fear, frustration, failure all gone; pain, parting, pathos unknown; death, defeat, disappointment forever past. "God will wipe away every tear."

             —J. G. V. B.

## CONCLUSION

The process of becoming a mother is in a way comparable to the experience of the white-robed saints of Revelation—there is joy after tribulation. Jesus said, "A woman giving birth to a child has pain because her time has come; but when her baby is born she forgets the anguish because of her joy that a child is born into the world" (John 16:21).

Childbirth is not, of course, the end of difficulties or problems for a mother; it is—among other things—the beginning of altogether new ones. This is especially true for those mothers in today's society who must take on the challenge of bringing up a fatherless child. How important it becomes for such children to learn and understand that God is their heavenly Father and that where he lives, there are no fatherless children. Lonely mothers and orphaned children, washed in the blood of the Lamb and adopted into God's family, are included without discrimination or distinction in the fatherly embrace of him who will one day wipe all tears forever from their eyes. "His child, and forever, I am!"

# Discovery Learning

*This page contains an alternate lesson plan emphasizing learning activities. Classes desiring such student involvement will find these suggestions helpful. The next page is a reproducible activity page to further enhance discovery learning.*

## LEARNING GOALS

As a result of this study, a student should be able to:

1. List several assurances provided for those who are "redeemed by the blood of the Lamb."

2. Name the assurance that is most significant to the student's own experience.

3. Suggest some way to share the good news of redemption so that others might have the same assurance.

## INTO THE LESSON

Write the word *security* on your chalkboard or on a large poster before class. Begin your session by asking, "What makes people feel secure in today's world?" Write on the board as many answers as the class can suggest. (Possible answers include a good job, a nice house, health, friends, family, possessions, money in the bank, or a relationship with God.)

Discuss what's wrong with most of these answers—they are temporary, they are uncertain, and so on. Even the best security without God is of absolutely no help when it comes to eternity!

Now focus on the idea of a relationship with God. Ask, "What makes you feel secure in your relationship with God? What makes you feel insecure?" Note that God wants us to be confident and secure in our relationship with him (Hebrews 4:16; 1 John 5:13). Conclude this introduction by saying, "Today we are going to look at God's provision for the redeemed, as seen through John's vision in Revelation 7."

### OPTION

Use the first reproducible activity on page 318, "Security Comes From …" to introduce today's study.

## INTO THE WORD

Supply the context of Revelation 7 by using the material under Lesson Background in the commentary. Have three good readers in the class read today's text in the following sections: Revelation 7:1-3; Revelation 7:9, 10; and Revelation 7:13-17. Summarize these passages, using the outline provided in the commentary.

Provide paper and pencils and ask the students to write the following verse numbers in a column down the left side of the page: 2, 3, 9, 14, 14, 15, 16, 16, 17, 17, 17. Have students work individually or in small groups to review Revelation 7 for assurances that God cares for his people. Next to each verse number they should write one assurance.

(v. 2) The presence of an angel signifies that God is watching his servants in a special way.

(v. 3) The "seal": God protects his servants from harm.

(v. 9) God shows no favoritism.

(v. 14) White robes show God's power to forgive people through Jesus' blood.

(v. 14) Those who have "come out" of the tribulation prove God can preserve his people in spite of severe persecution.

(v. 15) Spreading his tent over his people means God is present, living with them.

(v. 16) No more hunger or thirst.

(v. 16) Protection from sun and heat.

(v. 17) The "shepherd" provides for the flock's needs.

(v. 17) Springs of living water, an unending supply of the most basic necessity.

(v. 17) "God will wipe away every tear!"

Allow about ten minutes for this activity; then review the results. Some of these are less obvious than others; students will likely need some help to see all of these.

Ask students to take a moment of reflection and decide which of these portraits is most meaningful to their own situations right now. You might suggest that they highlight or underline the specific passage in their Bibles.

### OPTION

The reproducible activity, "God Takes Care of Our Needs," on page 318 to explore today's text.

## INTO LIFE

Observe that perseverance through tribulation involves recognition of certain factors: *peace* (I am confident in my relationship with God and in his ability to see me through any of my circumstances); *praise* (I am willing to focus my attention on my Creator rather than on my circumstances); and a proper *perspective* on my circumstances (I look at them as opportunities for God to work rather than situations through which I must work on my own.)

Encourage students to have a time each day during which they can: (1) deepen their sense of peace in their relationship with God, (2) express their praise to God, and (3) meditate on their circumstances in order to see God's fingerprint of blessings upon their lives.

# Security Comes From . . .

Look up the following Scriptures and find in each the one key word that focuses on how we can find security. Write that word in the corresponding blanks below. The highlighted letters will spell an important concept from today's lesson. (You will find each word, or *a form of the word*, in the corresponding verse.)

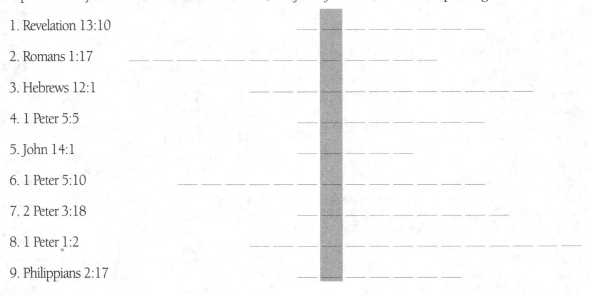

1. Revelation 13:10  ___ ___ ___ ___ ___ ___ ___

2. Romans 1:17  ___ ___ ___ ___ ___ ___ ___ ___ ___ ___

3. Hebrews 12:1  ___ ___ ___ ___ ___ ___ ___ ___ ___

4. 1 Peter 5:5  ___ ___ ___ ___ ___ ___

5. John 14:1  ___ ___ ___ ___ ___

6. 1 Peter 5:10  ___ ___ ___ ___ ___ ___ ___ ___

7. 2 Peter 3:18  ___ ___ ___ ___ ___ ___

8. 1 Peter 1:2  ___ ___ ___ ___ ___ ___ ___ ___ ___

9. Philippians 2:17  ___ ___ ___ ___ ___ ___

# God Takes Care of Our Needs

We are so fortunate to have a God who desires to take care of our needs. In today's Scripture text, look up the references and determine which of man's needs God is meeting. (You may find more than one answer in each verse.)

Revelation 7:2

Revelation 7:3

Revelation 7:9

Revelation 7:14

Revelation 7:15

Revelation 7:16

Revelation 7:17

# THE VICTORIOUS CHRIST

## LESSON 12

## WHY TEACH THIS LESSON?

Flashing lights. Ringing bells. Screaming sirens. These are all warnings, and they demand to be heeded. We need warnings. They alert us to danger before it is too late. If they are not there—or if we ignore them—the results can be tragic.

That is the reason this lesson is needed. It, too, is a warning. Along with lessons on the grace of God, we need the warnings of the judgment of God. This warning need have no terror for your students, if they are "in Christ" (Romans 8:1). But it dare not be taken lightly, either. The victorious Christ will have his victory over Satan and all who are in league with him.

## INTRODUCTION

### A. WHAT PRICE VICTORY?

You can find them all over the world, wherever a nation has gained its independence or achieved a major triumph on the field of battle. Such nations have erected statues, monuments, or other impressive structures to celebrate their victories. Included among these are memorials honoring those who made the ultimate sacrifice, giving their lives in defense of their countries. Victory comes only through conflict and sacrifice. The more meaningful victories come at the greater costs.

The theme of the book of Revelation is victory! It announces the decisive conquest of our most deadly foes: Satan, sin, and death. It tells that the victory has been won for us by Jesus our Lord at the cost of suffering and death to himself.

For every victor in conflict there must be someone or something vanquished—persons, principles, or both. Many people shudder at the thought of eternal defeat and destruction for anyone. But Satan and his minions wage their warfare relentlessly against God, seeking to destroy his influence and his people as thoroughly as possible. Victory for one side cannot be achieved without the destruction of the other. The book of Revelation faces honestly the impossibility of compromise in this arena of spiritual warfare. Victory can come no other way.

### B. LESSON BACKGROUND

Last week's lesson from Revelation 7 dealt with God's "sealing" or identifying his people to protect them from the coming judgment. They are described as having emerged from "the great tribulation," which is part of the continuing warfare between God and Satan. Chapters 8-18 depict that warfare in dramatic visions that are puzzling in detail but very clear in showing the ferocity of conflict between the forces of God and the forces of Satan. Chapters 19 and 20, from which today's lesson comes, depict the end of that warfare through Christ's coming in glory and judgment. The outcome is eternal joy for his people and the consignment of his enemies to the eternal lake of fire.

Chapter 19 opens with thunderous hymns of praise by the multitudes in Heaven (vv. 1-8), followed by the grand announcement of the marriage supper of the Lamb and his bride (v. 9). It then depicts the victorious Christ coming forth to judge the earth.

DEVOTIONAL READING:
REVELATION 19:1-10
LESSON SCRIPTURE:
REVELATION 19, 20
PRINTED TEXT:
REVELATION 19:11-16; 20:11-15

LESSON AIMS

This lesson should prepare the student to:

1. Explain how the events of the final judgment signal the final victory of Christ and the church.

2. Tell how an understanding of judgment should motivate the Christian to victorious living here and now.

3. Name a specific victory that he or she is seeking right now, and how to work this week toward achieving it.

KEY VERSE

On his robe and on his thigh he has this name written: KING OF KINGS AND LORD OF LORDS.         Revelation 19:16

May
18

**Lesson 12 Notes**

**What Do You Think?**

*Once again Jesus is called "Faithful and True." (See Revelation 3:14.) In the Gospels we witness Jesus' faithfulness to his mission in spite of the devil's temptation (Matthew 4:1-11; Luke 4:1-13) and the misguided efforts of people (John 6:14, 15).*

*Could you be called "faithful and true" to the Lord's mission? What is the biggest challenge or temptation you face that would divert you from sharing in the Lord's mission? How do you deal with that? How can the church help you—or others—to remain faithful and true?*


**What Do You Think?**

*Our lesson text depicts a warlike Christ. The world seems eager to see Jesus only as meek and mild, a symbol for peace. But as long as falsehood, immorality, injustice, violence, and other evils beset our world, we need to emphasize a Christ who brings peace by warring against those evils that destroy peace.*

*How can we do that? How can we present to the world an image of the warring Christ without tainting the picture with all the evils so often associated with human wars? How do we maintain a true picture of the grace of God at the same time we present the truth about the judgment of God?*

## I. THE VICTOR (REVELATION 19:11-16)

### A. The Mighty Warrior (vv. 11-13)

**11. I saw heaven standing open and there before me was a white horse, whose rider is called Faithful and True. With justice he judges and makes war.**

That John *saw heaven standing open* signaled that something dramatic and climactic was about to unfold before him. Ezekiel 1:1 speaks of the heavens being opened so that the prophet might see "visions of God," and Matthew 3:16 says that "heaven was opened" to Jesus at the time of his baptism.

As John watched in amazement, there appeared before him *a white horse*. The color white is a symbol of both righteousness and purity. (See Revelation 7:9-14 and 19:8.) The horse is associated with conquest and the capability of making *war*. (See 6:2.) The primary focus then turns to the identity of the rider, and the horse is quickly forgotten.

*Faithful and True* are such essential characteristics of the living Christ that they serve as his name. Jesus is described in John's initial greeting to the seven churches as the "faithful witness" (1:5). He later refers to himself as "true" (3:7) and as the "faithful and true witness" (3:14). These are the qualities of divinity, for God is eternally faithful (Deuteronomy 7:9; 1 Corinthians 10:13) and true (Revelation 6:10).

The ability to judge and make war with *justice* is one that is sadly lacking in today's world. Only Jesus possesses such an ability. In one of Isaiah's numerous Messianic prophecies, he declared, "With righteousness he will judge the needy, with justice he will give decisions for the poor of the earth. He will strike the earth with the rod of his mouth; with the breath of his lips he will slay the wicked" (Isaiah 11:4). Jesus' parables of judgment, such as those recorded in Matthew 24:30-35, 45-51 and 25:1-30 echo the same theme. The era of grace and reconciliation will end when Jesus returns to hold both Satan and the sinner accountable for their endless rebellion and to pronounce judgment (Matthew 25:41; Hebrews 9:27). God's righteous judgment is as real as his love and mercy; Hell is as real as Heaven.

**12. His eyes are like blazing fire, and on his head are many crowns. He has a name written on him that no one knows but he himself.**

The description of *eyes . . . like blazing fire* calls to mind Jesus' first appearance to John on Patmos (1:14) and his later introduction to the church at Thyatira (2:18). Such eyes as these could penetrate the dark recesses of the human mind and perceive what is normally invisible. They are fully capable of rendering final judgment.

Whereas John's vision of Jesus in Revelation 1 contained details associated with the priesthood (see the commentary on 1:13 in lesson 6), this vision magnifies his position as King. An ancient king having power over more than one country would sometimes wear a crown for each territory. Thus it is fitting that Christ, as Ruler over all kingdoms and all his enemies (Philippians 2:5-11; 1 Corinthians 15:24-28), should wear *many crowns*.

Was the unknown *name* written on a crown or garment worn by the rider or on his person? How does it relate to the name given to faithful overcomers and known only to them (Revelation 2:17)? In any case, the writing could not be read. The Lord's new and unknown name is in addition to all the familiar titles he holds— Savior, Redeemer, Master, Lord, Christ, Son of man, Son of God, and others.

We should keep in mind that new names are common to us all, in conjunction with new accomplishments or changes in our social or educational status. In parts of Africa a man becomes *Mr.* when he marries, just as his bride becomes *Mrs.* We are all familiar with titles such as *Doctor, Professor, General,* or *President.* Of course, there is that most meaningful new name (*Christian*) for the believer in Jesus (see Isaiah 62:2). Apparently Jesus' new name will be one appropriate for his triumphant return in glory.

**13. He is dressed in a robe dipped in blood, and his name is the Word of God.**

The Rider's *robe* bore evidence of the conflict through which he had gained a great victory. Some manuscripts and translations describe this robe as "sprinkled" or "spattered" with blood instead of *dipped in blood*. If the blood was Jesus' own blood freely given at the cross, the rendering here of "dipped" is preferred. However, if this was the blood of conquered enemies, a description of "sprinkled" or "spattered" would be appropriate. Either reading describes a significant aspect of the warfare waged by our Lord. Isaiah 63:3 gives this vivid account of God's wrath manifested in judgment: "I have trodden the winepress alone; from the nations no one was with me. I trampled them in my anger and trod them down in my wrath; their blood spattered my garments, and I stained all my clothing." The Lamb's victory was accomplished through a life-and-death (or, more accurately, death-and-life) struggle.

This verse adds yet another title to those already given to Jesus: *his name is the Word of God*. In John 1:1-3, 14-18 and 1 John 1:1, Jesus is referred to as the Word—the means by which God communicates his nature and his love to mankind. Only in this passage, however, does the full title, *The Word of God*, appear in Scripture. Some believe that this is the name mentioned in verse 12. But John mentions still another name for Jesus in verse 16, as well as other names and titles in the remaining chapters. The name of verse 12 is something that simply lies beyond our grasp, known only to Jesus.

### A ROBE DIPPED IN BLOOD

When Winston Churchill became Prime Minister of Great Britain, he said in his first statement to the House of Commons (May 13, 1940), "I have nothing to offer but blood, toil, tears, and sweat." Victory in World War II was achieved at just such a cost. It seems strange that the victorious Monarch of Heaven, riding in triumph and leading "the armies of heaven" (Revelation 19:14), should be wearing a bloody garment. His robe is "dipped in blood" (v. 13).

Some scholars believe that this blood is that of Christ's enemies. Others point to the emphasis throughout the book of Revelation upon the victory of the Lamb secured through the shedding of his own blood. He has "freed us from our sins by his own blood" (1:5). "You were slain, and with your blood you purchased men for God" (5:9).

The prominence of the blood of Christ in Revelation (and throughout the New Testament) teaches us that winning people to Christ is achieved only at a great cost. The victorious Lamb of God is the Lamb that was slain. Jesus instituted the New Covenant with his own blood. Great multitudes are pictured in Revelation as having made their robes "white in the blood of the Lamb" (7:14).

It is through the blood, sweat, and tears of dedicated servants of God that people of every tongue, tribe, and nation can be saved from sin and liberated to walk with God. God's victories are great and lasting, but their price is also great.

—J. G. V. B.

### B. HIS TROOPS (v. 14)

**14. The armies of heaven were following him, riding on white horses and dressed in fine linen, white and clean.**

This description does not satisfy our curiosity as to exactly who comprised *the armies of heaven*. They may have been angels; we know that Jesus will be accompanied by "all the angels" when he comes in glory to judge all nations (Matthew 25:31).

Perhaps these *armies* also included the saints—those faithful ones cited and commended in Revelation 7:14. The garments (*fine linen, white and clean*) are

### HOW TO SAY IT

*Ezekiel.*   *Ee-ZEEK-yul*
    *or Ee-ZEEK-ee-ul.*
*hades (Greek).*   *HAY-deez.*
*Patmos.*   *PAT-muss.*
*Thyatira.*   *THIGH-uh-TIE-ruh.*

## What Do You Think?

The sharp sword by which Christ is able to "strike down the nations" is obviously his Word. This description reminds us of one piece of our spiritual weaponry listed in Ephesians 6: "the sword of the Spirit, which is the word of God" (Ephesians 6:17). If the Word is so powerful, it seems we should see it striking down the growing evils in our culture. One must conclude that the sword is not being used!

What needs to be done to give the Word of God more prominence in our churches, schools, and workplaces? How can we better wield this sharp sword in our culture?

## What Do You Think?

Perhaps no title of Jesus given in Revelation is more awesome than "King of Kings, and Lord of Lords." This title occupies a prominent place in one of the most dramatic pieces of sacred music: the great "Hallelujah Chorus" in Handel's Messiah. According to tradition, even the king of England was moved to rise in tribute to the true "King of kings" when he heard this music.

But we need to do more than rise to our feet at the playing of a chorus to honor the King of kings. It needs to affect our lives. What do you think would happen if each Christian began each day with a prayer, "King of kings and Lord of lords, rule my life today"? How can we be more conscious of—and thus submissive to—the lordship of Jesus Christ in our daily lives?

exactly what the wife of the Lamb (the church) will be wearing, according to Revelation 19:8. Here they follow their blood-stained Captain, sharing his victory and riding on *white horses* similar to his. They carry no weapons; they bear no visible stains of battle. It is the Lord who bears the marks of battle—the blood and the crowns of triumph. By his power, they have come through their great tribulation and have washed their garments and made them white in his blood. Now they are prepared to ride in triumph behind their Captain.

### C. His Victorious Reign (vv. 15, 16)

**15. Out of his mouth comes a sharp sword with which to strike down the nations. "He will rule them with an iron scepter." He treads the winepress of the fury of the wrath of God Almighty.**

Jesus introduces himself, in Revelation 1:16 and 2:12, as the One with a *sharp double-edged sword* coming *out of his mouth*. Ephesians 6:17 identifies the Word of God as the sword of the Spirit, and Hebrews 4:12 says that the Word of God is living, powerful, and "sharper than any double-edged sword." Here the sword is used to *strike down the nations*. The outcome is that the kingdom of the world will "become the kingdom of our Lord, and of his Christ" (Revelation 11:15).

To *rule* these nations *with an iron scepter* calls to mind the punishment predicted for God's enemies in Psalm 2:9: "You will rule them with an iron scepter; you will dash them to pieces like pottery." A similar promise was given to the church in Thyatira to anyone who would overcome and do the will of Christ (Revelation 2:26, 27). The theme of judgment continues in the striking reference to treading *the winepress of the fury of the wrath of God Almighty.* Here, as in Isaiah 63:3, 4, divine judgment is compared with the trampling of grapes into a dry pulp as their juice is crushed out of them. So shall God's enemies be trampled and crushed in the end.

There is another side, however, to the use of the *iron scepter.* The Greek word translated "rule" literally means "to shepherd." The iron *scepter* becomes an iron *rod* in the hand of the shepherd, a rod used to destroy predators intent on harming the flock. Rather than judgment, safety and protection dominate the image. The rod is a source of constant comfort to the sheep (Psalm 23:4). Only those who are not a part of the flock have something to fear from the shepherd's rod.

**16. On his robe and on his thigh he has this name written: KING OF KINGS AND LORD OF LORDS.**

The *name* that proclaims total sovereignty for the victorious Christ appears where it would be most visible on the rider of a horse—on the *thigh*. No one could escape noticing that he has been declared superior to all other rulers.

The remainder of Revelation 19 elaborates on the utter defeat of the Lord's enemies, including the beast, those who have worshiped his image, the kings of earth and their armies, and the false prophet. Revelation 20:1-10 speaks of a much-discussed thousand-year period when Satan is to be bound, just before the consummation of all history. Then comes the vision of final judgment.

## II. JUDGMENT (REVELATION 20:11-15)

### A. The Judge (v. 11)

**11. Then I saw a great white throne and him who was seated on it. Earth and sky fled from his presence, and there was no place for them.**

The judgment *throne* that John saw was *white* (symbolic of the purity and impartiality of this judgment), and sufficiently *great* to accomplish the evaluation of all the earth. The One whom John saw sitting on the throne during his first vision of "what must take place after this" (4:1) now prepares to conduct a worldwide, history-encompassing judgment.

Terror at the prospect of such judgment will cause men of the earth to hide themselves and pray for the mountains to cover them (Revelation 6:14-17). Such an attempt will be futile, for even the *earth and sky* will not stand in the presence of the One who created them and now removes them.

An end to the material world in a cataclysm of fire is associated with Christ's coming again (2 Peter 3:10-13). John's final vision begins in this manner: "I saw a new heaven and a new earth, for the first heaven and the first earth had passed away" (Revelation 21:1). The old order is to be swept away to make way for the new one. There will be no *place* for the old; its purpose in the Creator's plan will have been fulfilled.

## B. The Books and the Book (vv. 12, 13)

**12. And I saw the dead, great and small, standing before the throne, and books were opened. Another book was opened, which is the book of life. The dead were judged according to what they had done as recorded in the books.**

The judgment scene will bring all mankind alike *before the throne* of God. Whoever is alive at the return of Christ must stand in judgment with those who have lived and died in all preceding generations. King and peasant, rich and poor, philosopher and laborer, will all be present.

We often think of *books* as the records of important transactions or financial matters. Heaven's records preserve the "official" account of what we have done, on the basis of which we will be *judged*. We should recall the words that frequently introduced the messages of Jesus to the seven churches: "I know your deeds."

*Another book,* later *opened,* is also important, for it is the *book of life,* bearing the names of those whom God recognizes as living in him. Those who have worshiped the beast will not be recorded there (Revelation 13:4, 8; 17:8), for such individuals have chosen the path of Satan and death rather than God and life. This book contains the names of those who have overcome their trials for Jesus' sake (Revelation 3:5).

**13. The sea gave up the dead that were in it, and death and Hades gave up the dead that were in them, and each person was judged according to what he had done.**

No one is excused from the judging process. Those who have been lost or buried at *sea,* whose bodies have been consumed, will be restored and will be present for the event.

The word *Hades* signifies the intermediate state for the spirits of those awaiting judgment. When Jesus returns, both the wicked and righteous dead will arise (Acts 24:15), or be given up, to face the final judgment. There the public, worldwide vindication of God's eternal purpose will occur.

The basis of judgment will be the same for each and every person: *according to what he has done.* But how, then, will any be saved? The New Testament record is clear that, on the basis of works, no one will be saved (Galatians 2:16; Ephesians 2:8-10). What is written in these books, then, will justify no one—except God, who will be justified for executing judgment (Psalm 51:4). This is the purpose of the other book, the book of life (vv. 12, 15). Those whose names are recorded there are justified, not by their works, but by the grace of God. Those who have accepted that grace are not condemned for what is written in the books; they have "crossed over from death to life" (John 5:24).

## THE BOOKS WERE OPENED

One of the interesting technological marvels of our time is the increasing development of information retrieval systems. With computers and the marvels of vari-

*The visual for lesson 12 is a dramatic illustration of Revelation 20:12. Post it as you discuss this verse—or have it on display from the beginning.*

## WHAT DO YOU THINK?

*Our lesson text ends with a stern warning: "If anyone's name was not found written in the book of life, he was thrown into the lake of fire." Such a message is today labeled "intolerant." How dare anyone suggest that people with a different set of beliefs will go to Hell! How dare we suggest our neighbor's actions are deserving of Hell!*

*Is there any way to give this warning that will not be rejected as intolerant? Is there any way to share it in such a way that people will see the love that motivates the warning so they can respond to that? If so, how?*

*Do you think we sometimes bring on ourselves the criticism of intolerance because of the way we present the warning? If so, what do we need to change?*

## PRAYER

*You are to be praised above measure, O God, for paying the price of victory for us—a victory that lasts through time and eternity. May we grow in our thanks, shaping our lives toward the eventual coming of your kingdom. We pray and trust in Jesus' name. Amen.*

## THOUGHT TO REMEMBER

*"The kingdom of the world has become the kingdom of our Lord and of his Christ, and he will reign for ever and ever"* (Revelation 11:15).

## DAILY BIBLE READINGS

**Monday, May 12**—*Praise God for His Judgments (Revelation 19:1-5)*

**Tuesday, May 13**—*Power Belongs to God (Revelation 19: 6-10)*

**Wednesday, May 14**— *Punishment of False Prophets (Revelation 19:17-21)*

**Thursday, May 15**—*Christ Will Reign One Thousand Years (Revelation 20:1-6)*

**Friday, May 16**—*A Kingdom That Cannot Be Shaken (Hebrews 12:22-29)*

**Saturday, May 17**—*Our Bodies Will Be Changed (Philippians 3:17-21.*

**Sunday, May 18**—*Jesus Shall Abolish Death (2 Timothy 1:8-12)*

ous chips, it is now possible to store millions of factual items and to call them up at will. For example, one can drop a postcard to an address in Baltimore and request a report on one's contributions to and status with the Social Security system. The report comes back with a detailed summary of contributions and of the projected amounts to be paid at certain intervals.

We are told that when the dead stand before God, the "books" will be opened (Revelation 20:12). This means that there will be an accurate accounting of our actions on file in the memory system of Heaven. Paul says in Romans 14:12, "Each of us will give an account of himself to God." He states that those who have been faithful workers in God's kingdom are those "whose names are in the book of life" (Philippians 4:3).

If men can make instruments that can record, keep, and recall millions of acts and facts, why should anyone think it impossible for God to do so?

In a sense, we stand before God every day that we live, for in him we indeed "live and move and have our being" (Acts 17:28). The time will come, however, when each one of us will actually stand before him. There the "books" will be opened, and we will be confronted with all we did, said, thought, and were. If our names are in the book of life, our sins will have been forgiven. By grace, our record will be clear, and we will be assured of a blessed future.      —J. G. V. B.

### C. THE OUTCASTS (vv. 14, 15)

**14, 15. Then death and Hades were thrown into the lake of fire. The lake of fire is the second death. If anyone's name was not found written in the book of life, he was thrown into the lake of fire.**

First Corinthians 15:26 describes *death* as the last enemy that shall be destroyed. Hades, or the dwelling place of the dead, is death's partner. Both are vanquished by Jesus (Acts 2:27, 31, where *hades* is translated "the grave"). Both are *thrown into the lake of fire* following God's judgment. Thus, our experience with Christ is a matter of death and life, with life having the final and victorious word.

Jesus' description of judgment included this preliminary reference to the lake of fire: "Depart from me, you who are cursed, into the eternal fire prepared for the devil and his angels" (Matthew 25:41). This is the place of utter and eternal terror referred to in the verses before us and in Revelation 21:8: "The cowardly, the unbelieving, the vile, the murderers, the sexually immoral, those who practice magic arts, the idolaters and all liars—their place will be in the fiery lake of burning sulfur. This is the second death."

If the lake of fire is the *second* death, the *first* death would appear to be physical death, which places a person in Hades. Since no one will suffer the first death anymore after Jesus returns, both death and Hades will be eliminated. Along with those whose names were *not found written in the book of life,* they will be thrown into the lake of fire.

### CONCLUSION

Today's text ends on a negative note, describing the tragic destiny of those who have neglected enrollment in the Lamb's book of life and have followed instead the road to destruction with the beast and the false prophet. There remains, however, "the rest of the story." That will come with next week's lesson, when we conclude the quarter by considering "A New Heaven and Earth." The grace of God provides a victorious conclusion for those who will receive his grace and the blessings that accompany it. This includes a share in the eternal reign of Christ himself. Through all the difficulties of an uncertain life in an unfriendly world, we can be "more than conquerors through him who loved us" (see Romans 8:35-39).

# Discovery Learning

*This page contains an alternate lesson plan emphasizing learning activities. Classes desiring such student involvement will find these suggestions helpful. The next page is a reproducible activity page to further enhance discovery learning.*

## LEARNING GOALS

This lesson should prepare the student to:

1. Explain how the events of the final judgment signal the final victory of Christ and the church.

2. Tell how an understanding of judgment should motivate the Christian to victorious living here and now.

3. Name a specific victory that he or she is seeking right now, and how to work this week toward achieving it.

## INTO THE LESSON

Start today's lesson with an examination of what it costs to achieve victory. Have some examples of victory for the students to see as class begins. If you have time and resources, show a video of a championship being won in a particular sport. Video rental stores should have a number of these. If such a project is not possible, bring in a newspaper clipping describing a championship sporting event, or a triumph in battle (such as World War II or the Gulf War). Whatever you use should portray personal or collective victory. After showing this, ask, "What does it take to achieve victory? To win a sports championship? To win a war? While the cost to the loser is clear, what does victory cost the winner?"

As the class responds to the question, expect to hear the following suggestions: dedication; discipline; sacrifice of time, energy, or resources; money or other physical resources; training, practice, or rehearsal; and mental preparation. Sacrifice is to be expected when one contemplates success in an undertaking.

Explain to the class that today's lesson focuses on "The Victorious Christ," as portrayed in Revelation 19 and 20. The battle between Christ and Satan, and good and evil, builds throughout the book of Revelation, with its culmination coming in these two chapters. Use the material in the Lesson Background of the commentary to prepare for discussion of today's text.

## INTO THE WORD

Divide the class into three groups. Distribute worksheets (prepared in advance) to the groups. One worksheet should be labeled, "The Victor—Revelation 19:11-13," another, "The Victor's Troops—Revelation 19:14," and the last, "The Cost of Victory—Revelation 19:15, 16." On the sheet labeled "The Victor" should be three columns with these headings: "His Name," "His Actions," and "The Cost of Victory." The following Scrip-

tures should be listed in each column: "His Name" (Matthew 1:21; Acts 4:12; Philippians 2:9-11); "His Actions" (Isaiah 11:4; 2 Timothy 4:1); and "The Cost of Victory" (Luke 9:51; Luke 22:63-65; Luke 23:44-46). On the sheet labeled "The Victor's Troops" should be two columns with these headings: "Clothing" and "Character." The following Scriptures will be listed in each column: "Clothing" (Revelation 3:5; Isaiah 61:10; Ephesians 6:13-17); and "Character" (Matthew 16:24; John 8:31; John 15:8). On the sheet labeled "The Cost of Victory" there should be two headings: "Christ" and "Followers," with the following Scriptures listed in each column: "Christ" (Isaiah 53:5; John 19:1-3; Matthew 27:30, 31; Mark 15:24-27); "Followers" (Romans 6:6; Galatians 2:20; Matthew 16:24; Philippians 3:8; Romans 6:2).

Have each group look at its portion of Revelation 19. Tell the members of the group to list phrases that fit the column headings on their paper. Then have them look up the additional Scriptures and add words or phrases drawn from these passages to their lists. Allow time for the groups to work; then ask for reports on their findings.

Next, have a good reader in the class read Revelation 20:11-15. Ask the class, "What pictures of the judgment scene are portrayed here?" The class should respond with answers of the great white throne, the judgment books of God, the book of life, and the lake of fire (the second death).

## OPTION

Use the reproducible worksheet on page 326 to explore this and other biblical references to the judgment.

## INTO LIFE

Point out that anytime there is a victory, there must also be a defeat. Ask, "If Christ is victorious, who or what is defeated?" (Satan, sin, death.) Then ask, "If the Christian is victorious, who or what is defeated?" Make a list of defeated foes as your class calls out suggestions. (Satan, old habits, fear, lust, and death are all possible answers.)

Observe that, given time, we could probably come up with a long list of such general answers. What we really need, however, is to look inside and see what foe has been stealing our victory. Ask each student to consider what victory Christ wants to achieve in his or her life and one step the student could take toward achieving it. Then close with prayer that God will give the students victory.

# Judgment Day

The Day of Judgment is described in several biblical passages as well. Look up the following references and record what each tells about the judgment.

Revelation 20:11-15

Revelation 6:14-17

Jude 14, 15

2 Peter 2:9; 3:7

John 5:22

Daniel 7:9, 10

# A Fiery End

"Fire" plays a major role in the scenes of judgment in various Scriptures. What does each of the following Scripture passages say about God's use of fire in judgment?

Revelation 20:14, 15

Revelation 19:20

2 Peter 3:5-13

1 Peter 1:7

2 Thessalonians 1:8

Matthew 25:41

2 Kings 1:10

# A NEW HEAVEN AND EARTH
### LESSON 13

## WHY TEACH THIS LESSON?

In "Rocky Mountain High" John Denver sings of someone "Goin' home to a place he'd never been before." I don't know what Denver was thinking, but it sounds like Heaven to me. Remind your class that Heaven is not just a grand city off in the sweet by and by that we want to go to someday. It is home! Challenge the students to live in such a way they will feel "at home" once they get there!

## INTRODUCTION

### A. "TALKIN' ABOUT HEAVEN"

"It was like I'd died and gone to Heaven."

How often have you heard that from someone who had just experienced something remarkably exciting or pleasant, whether it was tasting a sumptuous desert or seeing some breathtakingly beautiful scenery? Seldom is the "heavenly" experience related to God or to Jesus (as revealed in the Bible), and even more seldom is it anything like the holy city described in Revelation.

Each person is inclined to invent his or her own "Heaven," based on whatever the inventor most enjoys: a hobby, a family reunion, or even, as in Muslim tradition, a luxurious harem. In some cases, such thinking has invaded the songs we sing in church and the sermons we hear about Heaven, telling us much about the enhancement of earthly pleasures and little about the glories of God that await us.

This kind of speculation is understandable. It illustrates our human limitations as we try to grasp something beyond our ability to comprehend or describe. A more harmful side of this is the tendency of some to invent a heavenly gatekeeper who admits or rejects applicants to Heaven on the basis of the inventor's opinions. Some would make the Lamb's wedding feast an open affair, ushering in even those who have never indicated that they wanted to come!

Almost everyone talks about Heaven, but distressingly few pay much attention to what is said in the Bible. After all is said, the Bible is our only word from God about the only Heaven he has to offer. We need to respect his description and what he says about how to get there.

### B. LESSON BACKGROUND

Our lesson title, "A New Heaven and Earth," recalls Genesis 1:1, which records the creation of the original heaven and earth that have "fled" in the book of Revelation (20:11). That creation was a long time ago, and it may be a long time yet before God establishes the new Heaven and earth. That new Heaven and its inhabitants, however, will share the eternity of their Maker.

The more immediate background of our lesson this week is found in the judgment scene of last week's lesson. The verses immediately preceding our printed text tell of judgment for all mankind according to what was written in the "books" (the records of each person's "works") and in the Lamb's book of life. God's enemies are cast into the lake of fire (Revelation 20:14, 15). Today's lesson ends our quarter on a note of victory, as we consider what God has prepared for those who love and serve him.

**DEVOTIONAL READING:**
REVELATION 22:1-9

**LESSON SCRIPTURE:**
REVELATION 21:1—22:5

**PRINTED TEXT:**
REVELATION 21:1-7, 22-27

### LESSON AIMS

This study should enable the student to:

1. Describe the holy city in terms of what its inhabitants will experience for eternity.

2. List some aspects of eternal life that can be enjoyed by the Christian even now.

3. Choose one aspect of eternal life that has been neglected in his or her experience and seek to take advantage of it this week.

### KEY VERSE

Then I saw a new heaven and a new earth, for the first heaven and the first earth had passed away, and there was no longer any sea.     Revelation 21:1

May
25

LESSON 13 NOTES

*The visual for lesson 13 is an artist's rendering of John's vision of the new heaven and new earth. Display it as you begin the session.*

And I saw a new heaven and a new earth: for the first heaven and the first earth were passed away.
Revelation 21:1

## WHAT DO YOU THINK?

*Heaven is described as "a bride prepared for her husband." Consider various aspects of the bride metaphor. What does each suggest to you about Heaven?*

*The preparation.*

*The purity and faithfulness of the bride. (See Ephesians 5:25-27.)*

*The sacrificial love of the bridegroom.*

*The bride's garments (Revelation 19:8).*

*The celebration.*

## I. THE HOLY CITY (REVELATION 21:1-7)

### A. GOD'S NEW JERUSALEM (vv. 1, 2)

**1. Then I saw a new heaven and a new earth, for the first heaven and the first earth had passed away, and there was no longer any sea.**

*Then I saw* introduces a new vision, by which John is allowed to see *a new heaven and a new earth.* The word *new* stands in deliberate contrast with the old, or, as this verse reads, *the first heaven and the first earth.* But exactly what does this contrast involve? Does this speak of the cleansing and renovation of the existing heaven and earth, or of a total replacement? In the light of 2 Peter 3:10-13, which predicts the dissolution of the earth with a "roar" and "by fire," a total replacement would seem reasonable. This is also implied in one of the texts studied last week, which notes that "earth and sky fled" from the One who sits on the great white throne (Revelation 20:11). The *heaven* that will pass away is clearly not the place of God's eternal presence (Matthew 6:9), but rather the area including the atmosphere and what we consider outer space, with its sun, moon, and stars.

John notes *there was no longer any sea.* John on the island of Patmos and his readers in Asia might have considered the sea a turbulent barrier between them, as it is between many nations now. It will not divide the new earth from the new Heaven.

The *sea* in Revelation is also the symbol of unrest and turmoil. The beast with seven heads and ten horns arises from out of the sea (13:1). The absence of the sea indicates the presence of peace in the new Heaven and earth.

**2. I saw the Holy City, the new Jerusalem, coming down out of heaven from God, prepared as a bride beautifully dressed for her husband.**

*The Holy City, the new Jerusalem* stands in vivid contrast to *Babylon,* the "unholy city" representing all wickedness, which had been destroyed in God's judgment (Revelation 18:1-8). The significance of Jerusalem can be traced to the influence and efforts of David and Solomon. David had made the city his capital, and Solomon had added various improvements to it, including the building of his magnificent temple. Because of the temple's presence, Jerusalem came to hold a special place as "the city the Lord had chosen out of all the tribes of Israel in which to put his Name" (1 Kings 14:21). In the New Testament, Jerusalem becomes a symbol for the church. (See Galatians 4:26; Hebrews 12:22-24.) Its appearance in John's vision tells us that Heaven is the true holy city, the one that Abraham "was looking forward to . . . whose architect and builder is God" (Hebrews 11:10).

To this holy city, God gave a purity and a beauty like that of a radiant *bride* on her wedding day. The Bible often uses the symbol of marriage to portray the relationship between God and his people. Isaiah 54:5-8 and Hosea 2:19, 20 speak of Israel's relationship with Jehovah using the language of marriage, and Ephesians 5:23-32 uses the ties of marriage to illustrate the special relationship between Christ and his church. The Ephesians passage tells of Christ's desire to cleanse the church, that his bride might be "holy and blameless" (v. 27). Now, in Revelation, that bride appears *beautifully dressed,* prepared for the great marriage supper of the Lamb (19:9). Her radiance and purity present a sharp contrast to the rank corruption of Babylon the Great (17:5), to whom God promises, "The voice of the bridegroom and bride will never be heard in you again" (18:23).

### LIVING IN THE CITY OF GOD

All the cities of men have been *built up.* However, John saw the holy city "*coming down* out of heaven from God" (Revelation 21:2). The cities of earth are places from which many have fled because of the congestion, crime, and the confusion of moral and spiritual values that one finds in most cities. The movement of masses of people to the suburbs in countries around the world has been spurred by a belief that it is important to get away from the city. The comparative calm, coolness, and quiet surroundings of suburban living have been an irresistible attraction to millions.

Several decades before Christ, a Roman writer named Marcus Terentius Varro wrote in his work *On Agriculture,* "It was divine nature which gave the country, and man's skill that built the cities." A similar sentiment was expressed by William Cowper in his long poem, "The Task" (1785): "God made the country, and man made the town." When we think about it, the reasons we run from the city are related, not to "man's skill," but to his flaws and imperfections.

We have in the picture of the city coming down from God a perfection in beauty, glory, and holiness that can thrill and encourage us. The city is "holy" because its inhabitants are redeemed, free from sin, purified in character, and alive with the radiance of the love of God in Jesus. How wonderful it will be to move away from the "city of man" and dwell forever in the "city of God"!                    —J. G. V. B.

## B. God With His People (vv. 3, 4)

**3. And I heard a loud voice from the throne saying, "Now the dwelling of God is with men, and he will live with them. They will be his people, and God himself will be with them and be their God.**

Where our text has a *loud voice from the throne,* some manuscripts—and thus some translations—have a "great voice out of heaven" (*King James Version*). As such, the voice may have come from an angel (see verse 9) assigned to make the announcement. If it came from the *throne,* as in the reading followed by the *New International Version*, it would have come from the one seated on the throne (see verse 5) rather than the throne itself. Either way, the message comes by the authority of the Ruler of Heaven, who was seated on the throne. The message is that *God* is to *live* forever among *his people,* those who desired his presence while on earth.

The desire of God to be *with* his people is one of the most prominent themes in all of Scripture. The purpose of the tabernacle in the wilderness was to provide a place where God's presence would be recognized by the Israelites: "I will put my dwelling place among you. . . . I will walk among you and be your God, and you will be my people" (Leviticus 26:11, 12). Later God's presence was associated with Solomon's temple (1 Kings 8:12, 13). After this temple was destroyed by the Babylonians, the prophet Ezekiel reassured those who wondered whether this meant that God had forsaken his people: "Then the nations will know that I the Lord make Israel holy, when my sanctuary is among them forever" (Ezekiel 37:28).

When Jesus came to earth, he was designated as Immanuel, meaning "God with us" (Isaiah 7:14; Matthew 1:23). Christians are to recognize that the Spirit of God dwells in them, making their bodies his temple (1 Corinthians 3:16; 6:19). The perfect and eternal fulfillment of God's plan to dwell with his people will come only when his presence is directly experienced by all, without the limitations of time or space. In the Greek text, the final clause before us is emphatic in declaring this fulfillment: "God himself will be with them—their God!"

**4. He will wipe every tear from their eyes. There will be no more death or mourning or crying or pain, for the old order of things has passed away."**

Where is there a picture to match that of the heavenly Father drying the tears of his children? The primary cause of tears (and the first mentioned here) is *death*—the last enemy to be destroyed when Jesus returns (1 Corinthians 15:24-26). Those tears include the tears of a child whose pet has died as well as the uncontrolled sobbing caused by the death of an aged one's infant grandchild. From such circumstances, and from lesser causes, springs much of the *mourning* in the world and the *crying* that expresses grief and frustration. Also removed in Heaven is that nagging companion of advancing age—the *pain* that reminds us when our physical

*What Do You Think?*

*Many people have a difficult time appreciating the presence of the Lord in their lives, in spite of promises like that in Matthew 28:20. How does the promise that "the dwelling of God [will be] with men, and he will live with them" in Heaven encourage you and give you hope? How can you share that hope with another?*

*What Do You Think?*

*The promise of the cessation of death, mourning, crying, and pain is one of the Bible's most precious promises. And yet, some Christians are unable to appreciate it fully. A Christian with an unsaved spouse, or unsaved parents or children may fear that the absence of an unsaved loved one will cause bitter sorrow. How would you answer a fellow believer who was concerned about such a loved one?*

machinery is damaged or worn. All of these difficulties will be in the forgotten past, wholly replaced by the glory of God in the endless future of the holy city.

### C. GOD'S FAITHFUL PROMISE (v. 5)

**5. He who was seated on the throne said, "I am making everything new!" Then he said, "Write this down, for these words are trustworthy and true."**

God himself speaks from the *throne* of Heaven to make a brief, but inclusive statement and promise: "*I am making everything new.*" He is not only the architect and builder, but the furnisher and decorator, of every detail in the new Jerusalem.

What more could he say at this point? We know the harsh reality of death, grief, and pain, but how could we even begin to understand what totally new experiences will replace them? All our efforts to describe Heaven in terms of earthly delights simply reveal our limitations.

The final words of this verse seem to be a directive from God himself. Apparently seeing some hesitancy in John (perhaps John was expecting to hear more at this point), he commands, "Write that down! It's important! I will do exactly as I have promised." The word *trustworthy* is the same as *faithful* in Revelation 3:14 and 19:11. In English people, not words, are "faithful," but the association of these words with the one who is faithful and true is clear.

### D. GOD'S ETERNAL PROVISION (vv. 6, 7)

**6. He said to me: "It is done. I am the Alpha and the Omega, the Beginning and the End. To him who is thirsty I will give to drink without cost from the spring of the water of life.**

Again we hear the words of God: *It is done.* The making of all things new for the children of God is complete. *Alpha* and *Omega* are the first and last letters of the Greek alphabet. The phrase is God's declaration that he is eternal; he is the one "who is, and who was, and who is to come" (Revelation 1:8). Thus, the one who introduced himself at the beginning of this book as *the Alpha and the Omega* now speaks again as the book nears its conclusion. (See also 22:13, 16).

The presence of *the water of life* in the city calls to mind Jesus' discussion with the Samaritan woman at the well of Sychar (John 4:10-15). He is as essential for spiritual life as water is for physical life. Later John sees a "river of the water of life, as clear as crystal, flowing from the throne of God and of the Lamb" (Revelation 22:1). Here is one good hint of what to expect in Heaven: provisions for life and refreshment given *without cost* out of the loving Father's care for his children.

**7. He who overcomes will inherit all this, and I will be his God and he will be my son.**

The overcoming ones are identified in the letters to the seven churches as those who remain faithful to Christ in spite of persecution, evil influences, and false teaching, even to the point of dying for his sake. Every letter concludes with a promise to him *who overcomes* (Revelation 2:7, 11, 17, 26; 3:5, 12, 21). Now the patience and diligence of the saints are rewarded. At the same time, they are not said to have earned what they receive; they *will inherit all this*. They enter the holy city, not because of their virtue, but by their relationship to the Father as his children (see John 1:12). While every Christian is a *son* or child of God through faith in Christ (Galatians 3:26), both his fatherhood and our sonship will take on a new dimension when we enter the city where he resides.

## II. THE CITY OF GOD AND THE LAMB (REVELATION 21:22-27)

Verses 9-21 (not in our printed text) describe what might be called (for lack of a better term) the "material" aspects of the holy city as John saw it from a distance.

### WHAT DO YOU THINK?

How are the references to the *spring of the water of life* (Revelation 21:6) and the *river of the water of life* (Revelation 22:1) especially appealing? (See John 4:13, 14; 6:35; 7:37-39.)

### NOTE

In John's day, sons were especially favored with inheritances. A daughter received little or nothing by inheritance. She was expected to marry and thus share her husband's inheritance. That each one who overcomes is called God's "son" is not a case of gender discrimination, as some will allege, but the opposite. Male and female overcomers are all "sons"; they all get an equal inheritance from the Father!

Its walls, gates, and streets are made of the most precious items known to man. Its vast measurements show it to be a cube, just as the Holy of Holies in Solomon's temple was equal in all three dimensions (1 Kings 6:19, 20). Such a mind-boggling description of the city should convince us that we are viewing something that is actually immeasurable and indescribable. The city's true glory, however, is the very presence of God within. To this John now returns.

## A. THE CITY'S TEMPLE (v. 22)

**22. I did not see a temple in the city, because the Lord God Almighty and the Lamb are its temple.**

The word translated *temple* refers to the inner portion, or sanctuary. The Old Testament equivalent would be the Holy Place in the tabernacle, where only priests were permitted to enter. In Heaven's immeasurable city, the true Holy Place (see Hebrews 9:24), no such special area was needed or appropriate, since *God* and *the Lamb* were everywhere and totally accessible to all.

Glimpses of this degree of access to God had been seen in Jesus' teaching that worship is not a matter of special places, but of spirit and of truth (John 4:21, 23), and in Peter's statement that all Christians comprise a "holy priesthood, offering spiritual sacrifices acceptable to God through Jesus Christ" (1 Peter 2:5). Our access to God will reach its highest level when we "see his face" (Revelation 22:4).

### NO TEMPLE THERE

Most of us have become accustomed to having a building where the congregation of the faithful can meet for worship, fellowship, and witness. While it is true that God's presence is everywhere and that he cannot be confined within any walls, still a lovely church building can be an ever-present testimony in a community to the reality of Christian faith.

Our world contains many beautiful and striking edifices of worship. These include the Church of St. Peter's in Rome, the Cathedral of Notre Dame in Paris, and the Cathedral of St. Mark in Venice. Simpler, yet possessing elegance and charm, are the white spires of wooden church buildings that beautify the "commons" of New England colonial towns.

Perhaps it comes as something of a shock to learn that there is "no temple" in the city of God that descends before John and glistens with the eternal luster of Heaven. However, this city is his home, so it is not necessary to invite him to be present. He himself is with the city's inhabitants. His glory is everywhere. Where he lives, "nothing impure will ever enter . . . nor will anyone who does what is shameful or deceitful" (Revelation 21:27). His servants are always blessed by the light of his presence, and their thirst for God's beauty and bounty is forever quenched.

Our earthly "temples" and sanctuaries speak of our need to worship God and of our testimony to and for him. The absence of a temple there assures us that what these temples mean to us will be everlastingly fulfilled.                —J. G. V. B.

## B. THE CITY'S LIGHT (vv. 23, 24)

**23. The city does not need the sun or the moon to shine on it, for the glory of God gives it light, and the Lamb is its lamp.**

Heaven will offer a manifestation of *the glory of God* unlike anything ever witnessed by man. Isaiah foretold this: "The sun will no more be your light by day, nor will the brightness of the moon shine on you, for the Lord will be your everlasting light, and your God will be your glory" (Isaiah 60:19).

**24. The nations will walk by its light, and the kings of the earth will bring their splendor into it.**

## WHAT DO YOU THINK?

*Has your home ever been broken into, or have you ever had anything stolen? Do you check the locks and double check them at night? How many have security systems? What is the point of all this? How, then, do you feel about the promise that the gates of the new Jerusalem will never be shut? (See Proverbs 29:25.) How might this be an especially appealing promise that might assist in evangelizing some segments of society?*

The light of the gospel will have made it possible for those of many *nations* to be enrolled in the Lamb's book of life and to experience the *light* of God shining in the holy city.

The members of this diverse multitude, including *the kings of the earth,* acknowledge that they are in the presence of the King of kings. This, too, was foretold by the prophet of old: "In the last days the mountain of the Lord's temple will be established . . . and all nations will stream to it" (Isaiah 2:2). "Nations will come to your light, and kings to the brightness of your dawn" (Isaiah 60:3).

### C. THE CITY'S SECURITY (vv. 25-27)

Locked gates and doors, alarm systems, and security guards and patrolmen will be unnecessary and inappropriate in the holy city. The acknowledged presence of God and the Lamb provides all the security it needs.

**25, 26. On no day will its gates ever be shut, for there will be no night there. The glory and honor of the nations will be brought into it.**

The city is described as having twelve *gates*, three on each of its four sides, but there is never any reason to close any of them. The light of God's presence is constant, never to be extinguished, so there is no darkness from which to be protected. There is no danger from enemies, for the archenemy (Satan) and his minions have been cast into the lake of fire.

Once more the presence of *nations* in the holy city is emphasized. Here too, the prophet Isaiah looked ahead, by God's Spirit, to "the glories that would follow" (1 Peter 1:11): "Your gates will always stand open, they will never be shut, by day or night, so that men may bring you the wealth of the nations—their kings led in triumphal procession" (Isaiah 60:11).

**27. Nothing impure will ever enter it, nor will anyone who does what is shameful or deceitful, but only those whose names are written in the Lamb's book of life.**

Here is the reason Heaven deserves the title of the "holy" city. Everything evil—everything contrary to God's righteous character and standards—will have no opportunity to *enter* that city.

Not only is this verse *exclusive*; it is also *inclusive*, telling us how to plan and live so that we may enter there. Enrollment in *the Lamb's book of life* is a lifelong commitment to learning the love and the way of God so that we will be prepared for the indescribable pleasure of his eternal presence. Enroll, and don't be a dropout!

### CONCLUSION

You may have heard the classic story of the mother who tried for years to tell her blind daughter about the world she could not see. Then came that wonderful day when a newly developed surgical procedure brought sight to the girl and gave her the opportunity to view her world for the first time. She could not understand why her mother had not told her that the world was so beautiful. Tenderly the mother replied, "I did my best, honey, but you just didn't have any way to understand."

Through the book of Revelation, God's apostle has done his best to depict Heaven through the visions of the holy city. We gain a strong impression of the grandeur and glory that await us in the presence of God and our Savior, but we simply do not have any way to understand fully those spiritual delights that are beyond our experience or imagination. Truly a vast array of delightful surprises await the faithful followers of Christ.

We are given a clear understanding, however, about the means of access to Heaven. We must go through him who is the way, the truth, and the life (John 14:6)—believing, loving, trusting, obeying, and following Jesus. That information is beyond question!

## PRAYER

We love and praise you, our Father eternal, as the giver of life, for time and eternity. Increase our desire for life everlasting with you, so that we may have a contagious excitement for it. Preserve us from counterfeit "heavens," and give us patience as we approach what Christ has gone to prepare for us. Amen.

## THOUGHT TO REMEMBER

"God himself will be with them and be their God" (Revelation 21:3).

# Discovery Learning

*This page contains an alternate lesson plan emphasizing learning activities. Classes desiring such student involvement will find these suggestions helpful. The next page is a reproducible activity page to further enhance discovery learning.*

## LEARNING GOALS

As a result of participation in the class, the adult student should be able to:

1. Describe the holy city in terms of what its inhabitants will experience for eternity.

2. List some aspects of eternal life that can be enjoyed by the Christian even now.

3. Choose one aspect of eternal life that has been neglected in his or her experience and seek to take advantage of it this week.

## INTO THE LESSON

During the week before class, contact several students and ask them to bring in pictures and stories of the most beautiful places they have ever visited. As class begins, have these people display their pictures and tell about the places and what impressed them most concerning them.

Make the transition into today's lesson by observing that it is difficult to tell another person about what that one has not experienced. If that is difficult with natural places, it is even harder to describe Heaven! John tries to describe it in terms appropriate for his day, but there are many things about Heaven that we cannot now comprehend, for we simply have no frame of reference.

## INTO THE WORD

Before class, secure several concordances for your students to use. Recite for your students the first words of the printed text: "Then I saw a new Heaven and a new earth. . . ." Continue by saying, "Let's begin to develop our concept of Heaven." Have the students break into small groups. Give each group a concordance and the instructions to find passages that portray what Heaven is like. Some Scriptures that the students might include are: Matthew 6:20 (location of true treasures); Luke 10:20 (contains register of the saints); John 14:2 (a place prepared with dwelling places); Acts 7:55, 56 (dwelling of the glorified Christ); 2 Corinthians 5:1 (built by the hand of God; everlasting); Hebrews 12:22 (compared to Mt. Zion and Jerusalem); Ephesians 2:6 (we have been raised to sit with Christ in Heaven); Hebrews 11:10, 16 (compared to a city and a country); Matthew 3:12 (compared to a barn); Matthew 25:34 (compared to a kingdom); Luke 20:34-36 (no marriage in Heaven); Revelation 7:16, 17 (no problems in Heaven); Revelation 21:2, 3 (God's home among his people); Revelation 21:4 (no sorrow or pain); Revelation 21:6 (water of life available); Revelation 21:22 (no temple, for God's presence will surround all); Revelation 21:23 (God will provide the needed light there); Revelation 21:25-27 (gates will never be shut; nothing unclean will ever abide there); Revelation 22:15 (nothing wicked in Heaven); and Luke 23:43 (paradise).

After giving the students time to explore the Scriptures, have everyone return to a large group setting. Ask for representatives from each group to mention a couple of verses they discovered. Write the verses and a brief explanation of their meanings on the blackboard. Mention to the class that although it is difficult to describe the glory of Heaven, the Bible does give us a lot of insight into what life will be like when we get there.

Distribute copies of "Contrasting Creations" on page 334, and have the students follow the directions given there. They should find the following contrasts: 1. Genesis 1:16, sun and moon created—no need for sun or moon (Revelation 22:5). 2. Genesis 3:6, people sin—sin is defeated (Revelation 21:8); 3. Genesis 3:8, people hide from God—God is among his people (Revelation 21:3). 4. Genesis 2:17, death—no more death (Revelation 21:4). 5. Genesis 3:16, pain and sorrow—no pain or mourning (Revelation 22:3). 6. Genesis 3:22-24, fruit of the tree of life is not to be eaten—fruit of the tree of life is to be eaten freely (Revelation 22:2).

## INTO LIFE

Read Revelation 21:1-4 again. Discuss, "How does the fact that God has promised us an eternal life free of these things help us with coping with a sin filled life right now?" People may share that God's better future is the basis for our hope. Next, read John 17:3. Ask, "According to Jesus, when does eternal life begin?" Answer: At the moment we begin our walk with God through accepting Jesus. How does knowing this help us deal with everyday problems and pressures? How does it help us prepare for death? Encourage specific and practical answers.

Conclude the session by saying, "One of the best ways to make our eternal life real right now is to constantly remember that Jesus is coming again." Read Revelation 22:12-17 and offer a prayer thanking God for all that he's done to prepare Heaven for us and that we are eager for the day when his Son Jesus will come again!

# Contrasting Creations

Read Revelation 22:1-7, 22-27. Then look up the Scriptures listed under "First Creation" below. For each one, write a feature of the current creation that is in contrast to what Revelation 21 or 22 says of the new creation—the new Heaven and new earth. List the contrasting feature in the "New Creation" column, along with the verse number where it is mentioned.

| First Creation | New Creation |
|---|---|
| 1. Genesis 1:16 | |
| 2. Genesis 3:6 | |
| 3. Genesis 3:8 | |
| 4. Genesis 2:17; 3:19 | |
| 5. Genesis 3:16 | |
| 6. Genesis 3:22-24 | |

"Behold, I will create new heavens and a new earth. The former things will not be remembered, nor will they come to mind" (Isaiah 65:17).

"Then I saw a new heaven and a new earth, for the first heaven and the first earth had passed away, and there was no longer any sea" (Revelation 21:1).

# Looking Forward to That City

What is it about Heaven that you most eagerly anticipate. List your top three items.

1.

2.

3.

Read John 17:3. What can you do to begin enjoying the things on your list even *now*?

# Summer Quarter, 1997

## Special Feature

## Lessons

## *Theme: Guidance for Ministry*

## *Theme: A Call to Faithfulness*

### Unit 1. The Greatness of Christ

### Unit 2. Be Faithful Followers of Christ

## ABOUT THESE LESSONS

The lessons for this quarter are divided into two main studies. The first five lessons are taken from 1 and 2 Timothy and Titus. They focus on what it means to be a true servant of Christ, particularly when circumstances are less than ideal. The remaining nine lessons are taken from the book of Hebrews. Emphasis is placed on Jesus as the superior revelation of God to man, and upon how we can serve Jesus faithfully and responsibly.

Jun 1

Jun 8

Jun 15

Jun 22

Jun 29

July 6

July 13

July 20

July 27

Aug 3

Aug 10

Aug 17

Aug 24

Aug 31

# Christian Theology and Christian Living

*by John W. Wade*

This is a rather unusual quarter, in that it includes fourteen lessons instead of the ordinary thirteen. What is not unusual is the balance that you will find in this quarter between a strong emphasis on theology and an equally strong emphasis on practical Christian living. Christian theology and Christian living go together. Whenever one is separated from the other, problems are certain to arise.

## GUIDANCE FOR MINISTRY

JUNE

The first unit of this quarter, entitled "Guidance for Ministry," gives us five lessons from what we call the Pastoral Epistles—1 and 2 Timothy and Titus. These epistles were written by the apostle Paul to two of his younger co-workers. The title for this unit could very well have been "Christ's Servant," for each lesson deals with some aspect of the duties and responsibilities of those who would serve Christ.

Lesson 1 urges the Lord's servant to be an example to others in sound doctrine and in living a godly life. Lesson 2 focuses on Christ's servant as a teacher of godliness. In lesson 3 the emphasis is on suffering, "like a good soldier of Jesus Christ" (2 Timothy 2:3). Lesson 4 continues this theme, stressing faithfulness on the part of the Christian servant. Lesson 5 discusses how a Christian ought to respond to the society about him. While he must be "subject to rulers and authorities" (Titus 3:1) and deal gently with all, he must never compromise the faith.

## A CALL TO FAITHFULNESS

The rest of the quarter covers the topic, "A Call to Faithfulness." This study is based on selected Scriptures from the epistle to the Hebrews. The nine lessons are grouped into two units, the first of which is "The Greatness of Christ."

JULY

Lesson 6 affirms that "Jesus Is God's Son." This should provide strength for those who feel threatened by those who deny the deity of Jesus today. Lesson 7 presents Jesus as Savior. He became a human being and suffered death to free men from the power of sin and the fear of death. Jesus is seen as our great High Priest in lesson 8. Demonstrating the superiority of Christ's priesthood over the Levitical one is one of the main thrusts of Hebrews. In lesson 9 Jesus is seen as the perfect sacrifice who died in our place to take away sin "once for all."

AUGUST

"Be Faithful Followers of Christ" is the final unit. In lesson 10 the writer urges his readers to "Grow in Faithfulness," rebuking those who are content to live on milk when they ought to be maturing by eating strong meat. Lesson 11 urges Christians to "Remain Near to God." The writer warns the Hebrew believers of the consequences that await those who turn back to Judaism. Lesson 12 is based on Hebrews 11, the great faith chapter of the Bible. The readers are encouraged to exhibit the same faith as those who had preceded them. In lesson 13 the writer depicts the Christian life as a race that must be run with patience and strength. Lesson 14, "Live Responsibly," is a much-needed lesson in our age, when so many do everything they can to avoid responsibility for their actions.

Summertime will be vacation time for many of your students, so it may be difficult to maintain the kind of continuity you desire. At the same time, there is enough power in each lesson for it to stand alone. Teach each lesson faithfully, and let God's Word do its work on the hearts of your students!

# CHRIST'S SERVANT SETS AN EXAMPLE

## LESSON 1

## WHY TEACH THIS LESSON?

Timothy and the letters addressed to him have long been a model for vocational ministers who "preach the Word" (2 Timothy 4:2). Is there a word here for those who hear the Word preached?

Yes! Use this lesson to encourage your students in whatever ministries they perform. The charge to be "a good minister" is not just for preachers. We can all be good ministers if we faithfully serve the Lord with the gifts he has given us.

## INTRODUCTION

### A. A CAREFUL EXAMPLE

Several years ago we were leading a group of young people on a backpacking trip along the Appalachian Trail. At one point we came to a fork in the trail. The shorter route led up the side of the mountain, almost reaching its summit before coming down and rejoining the longer trail. This shorter trail was a challenge even for experienced hikers, for it was narrow and led over large boulders, some of which had to be scaled with the aid of a rope.

I preferred to follow this trail because it was two miles shorter and would have taken me less time, had I been alone. But I took the longer trail because some of the younger members of the party would have had great difficulty when they encountered some serious hazards on the steeper trail.

This is the way a good Christian ought to lead. He should not choose the path that best satisfies himself. Instead, he should lead along the trail that best protects and guards those who look to him for guidance. This was the kind of ministry that Paul urged Timothy to pursue.

### B. LESSON BACKGROUND

By the time Paul wrote 1 Timothy, his young friend and co-worker had been recognized for some time as having great potential for Christ and his kingdom. In addition to working with Paul in many of his missionary endeavors, he had also been dispatched by the apostle to provide counsel for troubled churches. (See 1 Corinthians 4:17; Philippians 2:19-23; 1 Thessalonians 3:1-3.)

Timothy was the child of a mixed marriage; his father was a Greek pagan, while his mother Eunice was a devout Jewish woman who (along with his grandmother Lois) taught him the Hebrew Scriptures. Timothy joined Paul during Paul's second missionary journey (Acts 16:1-3), and continued to be his faithful companion until the apostle's death. So strong was the bond between the two men that Paul often referred to Timothy as his "son" (1 Corinthians 4:17; Philippians 2:22; 1 Timothy 1:2, 18; 2 Timothy 1:2; 2:1).

Most scholars believe that 1 Timothy was written after Paul's house arrest in Rome (Acts 28:16, 30, 31) had ended (about A.D. 63). It may have been written in Macedonia after Paul left Rome (1 Timothy 1:3). Although the letter is addressed to

DEVOTIONAL READING
PSALM 37:1-11

LESSON SCRIPTURE
1 TIMOTHY 4:6-16

PRINTED TEXT
1 TIMOTHY 4:6-16

LESSON AIMS

*After studying this lesson, each student will be able to:*

*1. List the characteristics of the exemplary Christian servant as enumerated in the text and outline.*

*2. Explain the value, both to oneself and to others, of living a life consistent with the truth.*

*3. Identify and commit to applying personally at least one of the ministry characteristics that needs to be developed in his or her own life.*

*See pages 219-226 for more background information on Timothy.*

KEY VERSE

*Train yourself to be godly. For physical training is of some value, but godliness has value for all things, holding promise for both the present life and the life to come.* 1 Timothy 4:7, 8

**Lesson 1 Notes**

**What Do You Think?**

It has been said that, while our message—i.e., sound doctrine—must never change, our methods of communicating the message must always be changing. What new methods are required to reach a culture where people are accustomed to being entertained, and where there is such a low tolerance for communication that is dry or difficult?

Are there certain methods that are inconsistent with the message? If so what and why?

If money were no object, what technology would you like to see included in the educational program of our church? Why is money an object?

**What Do You Think?**

There have always been competing religious ideas that are at odds with true Christian faith and doctrine. Perhaps the most dangerous are those that have the most in common with Christianity, so that believers are ensnared without recognizing the heresy. The "health and wealth" gospel and the "name it and claim it" theology are examples. The New Age Movement, which teaches reincarnation and makes all people gods unto themselves, constitutes another threat to true doctrine. Who is most at risk of being deceived by these "myths"? Why? How can the church protect believers from being deceived by such false teaching?

Timothy, whom Paul calls "my true son in the faith" (1 Timothy 1:2), it seems that much of its content was designed to be shared with other Christians and churches. In the first chapter, Paul warns against false doctrines that were already beginning to assail the faith of new Christians. In the second chapter, he gives instructions about prayer. In the third chapter, he sets forth the qualifications of overseers (elders) and deacons. In the fourth chapter, from which today's lesson text is taken, Paul offers some practical counsel that Timothy needed to heed if he wanted to become an effective minister. These suggestions are just as important to us today as they were to Timothy in the first century.

## I. THE SERVANT'S TRADEMARK (1 TIMOTHY 4:6-8)

### A. Faithfully Instructs Others (v. 6)

**6. If you point these things out to the brothers, you will be a good minister of Christ Jesus, brought up in the truths of the faith and of the good teaching that you have followed.**

The word translated here as *minister* is the Greek word *diakonos*. This is a multi-purpose word, the basic meaning of which is "servant." Frequently it is used in a general sense, focusing on the servant's relationship to the task at hand. Sometimes, however, it is used in an official sense. It is the word used in the previous chapter (vv. 8-13) to refer to the office of "deacon." A form of the word is found when Paul tells Timothy to "do the work of an evangelist, discharge all the duties of your 'ministry'" (2 Timothy 4:5). Whether the word refers to an official "minister" or merely someone performing a "ministry" is not always easy to determine.

A key part of Timothy's ministry was teaching (1 Timothy 1:3; 2 Timothy 2:2). Thus, to be a *good minister* he had to *point these things* that Paul was writing *out to the brothers* in Ephesus. Anyone today whose ministry is teaching must also point out to the believers what Paul and other inspired writers have written, as recorded in the Bible. This is not necessarily true of one whose ministry is benevolence or keeping a building in good repair. Such a one is a good minister or servant when he faithfully discharges the duties assigned him to the glory of God.

The knowledge of the Scriptures had been an instrumental part of Timothy's upbringing (2 Timothy 3:15). The Scriptures, containing *the truths of the faith and of the good teaching that* he had *followed,* were still his most important tool in serving Christ and building his church. .

### B. Shuns Useless Myths (v. 7)

**7. Have nothing to do with godless myths and old wives' tales; rather, train yourself to be godly.**

Paul urged Timothy to reject all forms of false teaching. The teachings mentioned here were not necessarily blasphemous or sacrilegious; they did, however, turn one's attention away from the gospel. For that reason Timothy was to *have nothing to do with* them. These *myths* may have included either some of the tales that had become a part of the Jewish literature of that day, or the pagan stories that abounded in the Greco-Roman literature. Whatever they were, their presence in Ephesus seems to have been at the heart of Timothy's purpose for being there. (See 1 Timothy 1:3-7.) Timothy was to draw a clear line between these false teachings, having *nothing to do with* them, and the truth, by which Timothy and others could be trained to be *godly*.

### C. Strives for Personal Piety (v. 8)

**8. For physical training is of some value, but godliness has value for all things, holding promise for both the present life and the life to come.**

Paul often made reference to athletic activities to illustrate a spiritual point. We know that proper *training* can help us maintain good health. Such exercise is especially important to those of us who follow a more sedentary life-style. It is likely to make us feel better and to prolong our lives.

While these benefits are indeed important, Paul states, literally, that *physical training is of little value.* (Most other versions translate it that way.) How little becomes apparent when it is compared with the joys that *godliness* can bring not only in *the present life,* but in the life *to come.* At best, physical exercise can prolong our lives only a few years, but godliness can prepare us for an eternity of joy.

Physical exercise and the effort to attain godliness offer some interesting parallels. First, one who trains for an athletic contest must subject his body to hours of strenuous and exhausting exercise. In the same way, one must exert himself spiritually to grow in godliness, agonizing as we struggle against sin and temptation. Second, the successful athlete must have a goal, whether it be running faster, jumping higher, or hurling the discus farther, than his competitors. To train without a goal would be foolish. In the same way, the Christian must keep ever before him the ultimate goal—Heaven. Finally, the athlete who expects to succeed in his contest must lay aside other conflicting interests that will keep him from his goal. The Christian who expects to see his Lord face to face someday must turn aside from the distractions of the world and give himself exclusively to that one goal.

While physical exercise and spiritual exercise are similar in these respects, they are quite different in one very important respect. The rewards for physical exercise are temporal. In the Olympic games of Paul's day, the prize was a simple wreath. Today the prize for a successful athlete may amount to worldwide fame and an annual income of millions of dollars. As impressive as this may seem, it is just as temporal as the Olympic wreath; it will all too quickly pass away. Spiritual exercise promises blessings not only during *the present life,* but eternal joy in *the life to come.*

Godliness is profitable unto all things, having promise of the life that now is, and of that which is to come.
1 Timothy 4:8

*The visual for lesson 1 is based on 1 Timothy 4:8. Display it as you discuss this verse.*

### FIT OR FAT

Covert Baily has become one of the most popular fitness experts in America. His book *Fit or Fat* and his lectures carried over the public television network have exposed his insights to millions. Bailey has popularized what health experts have known for years: that small daily changes in diet and exercise determine whether a person is fit or fat.

We gain weight and become flabby over time, one cheeseburger or one donut at a time. We lose our muscle tone and fitness gradually, one missed workout at a time. We also regain or maintain fitness in the same way—by small daily acts. If you eat a low-fat diet of moderate portions today, tomorrow, and the next day, and if you exercise regularly this week, next week, and the next, then over time you will be fit.

In several New Testament passages, the apostle Paul uses sports and fitness analogies to teach us about the Christian life, as he does in 1 Timothy 4:8. Like physical fitness, spiritual fitness comes through small daily habits maintained consistently over time. A daily time of prayer and Bible study, steady involvement in a ministry that exercises our spiritual gifts, unfailing faithfulness in attending the worship and study opportunities provided by the local congregation, and a consistent application of the spiritual disciplines prescribed in God's Word make us spiritually fit. And the lack of these things makes us spiritually fat.     —C. B. Mc.

## II. THE SERVANT'S EXAMPLE (1 TIMOTHY 4:9-14)

### A. SUFFERS REPROACH (vv. 9, 10)

**9. This is a trustworthy saying that deserves full acceptance.**

This seems to be a formula used by Paul when he wanted to call a reader's attention to something important (see 1 Timothy 1:15; 2 Timothy 2:11; Titus 3:8).

**10. . . . (and for this we labor and strive), that we have put our hope in the living God, who is the Savior of all men, and especially of those who believe.**

The price that Paul paid for being a committed spokesman for the gospel included strenuous *labor* that was often met by opposition from those he hoped to win. For Paul this involved physical suffering that on more than one occasion almost led to his death. He assures Timothy that as a true minister of Christ, he may very well have to face a similar set of circumstances.

Across the centuries, such has been the experience of countless numbers of Christians who have stood against false religions and violent rulers. The valorous deeds of these faithful may be hidden in the dusty pages of history, but God has not forgotten them. Furthermore, these martyrs are not limited to the past; our own times have produced their share.

The phrase *the Savior of all men* is sometimes quoted to prove that God will save all, regardless of the lives they have lived. This kind of universalism flies in the face of many other teachings in the Bible. It is best to understand Paul's words in the sense that God is potentially the Savior of all men. That potential is realized only in the lives of those who *believe* in him.

### B. PERSISTS DESPITE HIS YOUTH (vv. 11, 12)

**11, 12. Command and teach these things. Don't let anyone look down on you because you are young, but set an example for the believers in speech, in life, in love, in faith and in purity.**

Paul urged Timothy to *teach* what he had learned from Paul. In doing this, one of the barriers Timothy might encounter was his youth. Timothy was probably in his thirties at this time, not a mere teenager as some have suggested. But in a culture that had great respect for the elderly, Timothy was considered a young man. Since Christianity was still a relatively new religion at this point, many would be especially reluctant to receive it from someone as young as he. To overcome this obstacle, Timothy had to speak and act carefully and with patience. Timothy could command respect from those he taught, because he came to them with the authority vested in him by Paul. (See 2 Timothy 1:6.) But he still had to earn their respect by his own conduct. Paul proceeded to highlight some areas that Timothy needed to attend to if he was to do this.

He was to be an example in *speech*. One can offend others, not only by the words he uses, but also by the tone of voice with which he speaks. Timothy was to avoid giving offense in this way. Timothy was to embrace a life-style that reflected his Christian calling. He was to act *in love* toward the people he was serving, always seeking to work for their welfare. Timothy was to act *in faith,* for what one believes determines in a large measure how he will behave. Timothy must not only uphold sound doctrine; he must translate sound doctrine into a godly life.

Finally, Paul concluded with an admonition to live a life of *purity.* This admonition was especially necessary for those who lived in the Greco-Roman world—a culture that was saturated with all kinds of illicit sexual activities. Such an admonition is certainly needed today, as well, because the same problems persist in our society. Unfortunately, many Christian leaders have failed to heed Paul's warning and have succumbed to impurity, thereby destroying their ministries.

### FOLLOW THE PATTERN

In 1859 an American manufacturer named Ebenezer Butterick invented the first standardized paper pattern for clothing. Ten years later Butterick's factory in Brooklyn, New York, was turning out dress patterns by the thousands. He even founded a fashion magazine, *Metropolitan,* to promote pattern sales.

---

### WHAT DO YOU THINK?

*IF YOU HAVE A CLASS OF YOUNG ADULTS, ASK THIS:*

*Paul told Timothy not to let anyone look down on him because of his youth. Isn't that a lot easier said than done? After all, how does one control how other people respond to him or her?*

*Have you ever felt older people did not take you seriously? If so, why do you think they didn't? How did—do—you respond?*

*How can a young adult gain the credibility needed to be a spiritual leader in the church?*

*IF YOU HAVE A CLASS OF MIDDLE OR OLDER ADULTS, ASK THIS:*

*Paul told Timothy not to let anyone look down on him because of his youth. Why is it sometimes hard for older people to accept leadership from younger people? What can we do to help younger people become effective leaders?*

*Do you think we should sometimes "go along with" a younger leader's idea even if we know it's not the best way to do something—as long as it is not wrong? Why or why not? What possible good might come from that? What possible harm?*

More than one hundred years later, seamstresses still use Butterick patterns to sew clothing. The pattern is pinned to a piece of fabric, which is then cut to the exact size and shape of the pattern. These pieces can then be sewn together to produce a dress or shirt or suit that looks just like the original design.

A pattern serves as a plan or model to be followed in making something. In 1 Timothy 4:12, Paul reminds Timothy that because he is in the disciple-making business, he is to be a pattern or example for the church he is leading. In speech, in life, in love, in faith, and in purity, church leaders and mature believers should be models worthy of imitation. —C. B. Mc.

## C. READS AND EXHORTS (v. 13)

**13. Until I come, devote yourself to the public reading of Scripture, to preaching and to teaching.**

Paul anticipated joining Timothy in Ephesus. Until he arrived, Timothy was to give particular attention to *the public reading of Scripture*. Since few persons owned copies of the Scriptures in that day, it was a common practice for someone to read them aloud for the benefit of others. *Preaching* and *teaching* were the primary activities to which Timothy was to devote himself.

## D. EXERCISES HIS SPIRITUAL GIFT (v. 14)

**14. Do not neglect your gift, which was given you through a prophetic message when the body of elders laid their hands on you.**

This *gift* was probably not a miraculous gift, though the word used is the one commonly employed to designate one.* In this context, it seems to refer to those activities mentioned in verse 13: reading, preaching, and teaching. Perhaps it is a reference to his ministry, even as Paul considered his own ministry something entrusted to him (1 Corinthians 4:1, 2). The term *gift* would be consistent with that.

Miraculous spiritual gifts were conferred by the laying on of hands by the apostles (Acts 8:18), but it is the *body of elders*, not the apostles, who are mentioned here. Apparently this refers to an ordination of Timothy by a group of elders, probably in Lystra during Paul's second missionary journey. It was a public service before fellow Christians, setting Timothy apart to accompany Paul as he continued on his missionary endeavors. By reminding Timothy of that special moment in his life, Paul hoped to encourage him not to *neglect* the gift he had received at that time.

## III. THE SERVANT'S GROWTH (1 TIMOTHY 4:15, 16)

### A. OBVIOUS TO OTHERS (v. 15)

**15. Be diligent in these matters; give yourself wholly to them, so that everyone may see your progress.**

Paul urged Timothy to give himself *wholly*, or totally, to his growth in the ministry. A variety of obstacles could turn him aside from this path. He could be distracted by the cares of the world, or his success in the ministry could turn his head and cause him to become a victim of his own pride. In his own ministry, Paul knew just one pace—full steam ahead—and he wanted every other servant of the Lord to serve with the same level of commitment. In this he was echoing the words of the Master: "No one who puts his hand to the plow and looks back is fit for service in the kingdom of God" (Luke 9:62). If Timothy committed himself to his personal spiritual growth with a similar zeal, his *progress* would be obvious to others. This did not imply that Timothy should call attention to his growth. Genuine maturity in Christ should speak for itself without having to be "advertised."

## WHAT DO YOU THINK?

*Paul tells Timothy to make preaching and teaching a priority. In today's church we often lay many additional expectations on our ministers, like shepherding, music, youth programming, stewardship, and other areas. Some work with little or no secretarial help. In what ways can a church protect its minister's preparation time for preaching and teaching so that these things remain a priority? What if the budget will not allow for a paid secretary or additional ministerial staff?*

## *NOTE (v. 14)

*In 2 Timothy 1:6 Paul mentions a "gift" Timothy had by the laying on of his own hands. This was likely a miraculous gift, since Paul was an apostle. If Paul participated with the elders in the laying on of hands mentioned in 1 Timothy 4:14, then these two passages likely refer to the same "gift," a miraculous gift. These may have been separate events, however. There is no way to be certain.*

## HOW TO SAY IT

diakonos (Greek). dee-AH-ko-nos.
Ephesus. EFF-uh-suss.
Eunice. YOU-nis.
Greco-Roman. GRECK-oh–ROE-mun.
Lystra. LISS-truh.
Macedonia. Mass-uh-DOE-nee-uh.

## WHAT DO YOU THINK?

We are always disappointed when people we have respected as leaders are convicted of criminal activities, abuse their power, or display some moral weakness. We consider this a compromise of their integrity and a violation of the trust we have placed in them. Thus did Paul tell Timothy, "Watch your life and doctrine closely" (1 Timothy 4:16).

Beyond our own personal disappointment, what problems are caused when a leader fails in this way? What harm does it do the local church? What does it do for the leader's own life? What can the church do to help its leaders "persevere" in these things to help prevent a failure? What should it do after a failure occurs?

## PRAYER

Help us, dear Father, that we may all become good and effective ministers for you. Help us to keep our lives pure, our message true, and our commitment untiring, that we might save ourselves and those who hear us. In our Master's name we pray. Amen.

## THOUGHT TO REMEMBER

Be a good example!

### B. TO BE REWARDED (v. 16)

**16. Watch your life and doctrine closely. Persevere in them, because if you do, you will save both yourself and your hearers.**

The final victory belongs to the person who persists to the end. Those who turn back or are distracted by the allurements of this world will never stand in the victor's circle. But there was more at stake here than Timothy's own salvation. By his faithful teaching and preaching, he could offer others the hope of salvation that he himself enjoyed. By the same token, a leader who is unfaithful not only stumbles himself, but causes others to stumble.

## CONCLUSION

### A. MODELS

We are hearing much these days about the importance of children having good models as they grow up. Most children do pattern their lives after some person they look up to or even idolize. Such an individual may be a parent, an older brother or sister, or a sports hero. Children often try to imitate their heroes in the way they walk or talk, the way they play a game, or in their values. This is a perfectly healthy, acceptable thing for children to do—unless the hero turns out to be less than heroic. Unfortunately, in recent years we have seen several of these heroes betray the trust others have placed in them by becoming involved in drugs and violent crimes. This has led to the disillusionment of many young people, or worse, their own tragic downfall as they tried to imitate their fallen heroes.

Some seem to think that "role modeling" is a new concept recently discovered by child psychologists. Of course they are wrong, for this is exactly what Paul was talking about when he encouraged Timothy to be "an example for the believers" (1 Timothy 4:12). Paul knew quite well that Christ was the perfect example; on one occasion he wrote, "Live a life of love, just as Christ loved us" (Ephesians 5:2). But Paul also recognized that people need someone close at hand—someone they can watch daily. For many in Ephesus, Timothy was that person.

Timothy was not to be a one-dimensional model as some of our contemporary heroes are. He was to be a model in his correct doctrine. He was to demonstrate moral purity in his life. He was to show other believers how to handle rejection and persecution. He was to use the spiritual gift that God had given him, thereby encouraging other Christians to use their gifts.

What Paul wrote to Timothy applies with equal force to us. After all, we really do not have much choice about being models. Whether we like it or not or are even aware of it, others are looking to us as models. The real issue is what kind of models we will be.

### B. DESPISED YOUTH

Paul was concerned that the Christians in Ephesus might reject Timothy's teaching because of his youth. Older people today sometimes have a similar problem when younger people suggest new ideas. "We've never done it that way before," they complain. They then proceed to oppose or reject the idea.

Youthfulness on the part of the messenger may be one barrier to the transmission of the gospel, but there are others. Some may reject a messenger because he speaks with a different accent. Others may have trouble accepting a message from a man who has long hair or is not dressed in a suit and tie. There is no way that a messenger can overcome all of the biases of his listeners. But when we go out as ambassadors of our Lord, we should make every accommodation we can to the sensitivities of our hearers. At the same time, we must never compromise sound doctrine in order to please others.

# Discovery Learning

*This page contains an alternate lesson plan emphasizing learning activities. Classes desiring such student involvement will find these suggestions helpful. The next page is a reproducible activity page to further enhance discovery learning.*

## LEARNING GOALS

After studying this lesson, each student will be able to:

1. List the characteristics of the exemplary Christian servant as enumerated in the text and outline.

2. Explain the value, both to oneself and to others, of living a life consistent with the truth.

3. Identify and commit to applying personally at least one of the ministry characteristics that needs to be developed in his or her own life.

## INTO THE LESSON

Recruit a young man in his thirties to come to your class, preferably in biblical garb, either to deliver a monologue on "I am Timothy" in which he answers all the following questions, or to answer these questions, which you will have prepared and given to class members for use in an "interview of Timothy." (1) "What is your religious background?" (2) "What was your first experience with Paul?" (3) "What are some of the experiences you shared with Paul as you traveled with him?" (4) "Where were you when you received this letter (1 Timothy) from Paul?" (5) "How would you characterize your relationship with Paul?" (6) "What in this letter was most surprising to you, if anything?" (7) "Why would Paul caution you about your youth? You aren't all that young!" Feel free to develop other questions that you believe to be relevant and answerable. Advise your role-player to read the lesson writer's commentary, Acts 16, and 2 Timothy 1:5, 6.

## INTO THE WORD

Though the following activity can be done on a chalkboard, it might have greater instructional effect as word strips mounted one by one on the wall or line by line on an overhead projector. Prepare a title, "THE TRUE MINISTER," for whichever format you choose, then reveal each of the following phrases, in random order, and ask your students to identify a verse that says something relevant to that phrase. (Verse numbers are given here after each phrase for your convenience.) (1) "instructs others," v. 6; (2) "avoids false doctrine," v. 7; (3) "trains for godliness," v. 8; (4) "labor and strive," vv. 9, 10; (5) "persists in spite of obstacles," vv. 11, 12; (6) "reads and preaches," v. 13; (7) "exercises gifts given," v. 14; (8) "considers the life to come," v. 8; (9) "is rewarded," v. 16. As each is introduced and matched with the text, you will have opportunity to expand on the meaning of the text.

As each verse is suggested, read the verse and comment on the relevant phrase. Ask students to suggest how each characteristic is valuable first to the person displaying it and then to others who will follow his or her example.

To help define the concept of what we call a full-time *minister*, ask your class to help you prepare an acrostic. On the chalkboard (or poster board or an overhead) put the letters of the word vertically. Ask students to look directly at the text to identify "What a minister does," beginning with each letter. Here is a sample of key words or phrases that may be suggested: M—models, meditates; I—ignores fables; N—nourished; I—instructs; S—suffers, saves; T—trusts, teaches; E—exemplifies, exercises; R—reads, reminds. Once you complete your acrostic, ask the class, "What does a minister do that our acrostic does not represent?" List these answers, and as you do, try to fit each under one of the descriptions already given.

Discuss, "To what extent do these characteristics apply to those of us who are not professional 'ministers'?" Note the explanation of the term *minister* as "servant" on page 338. Note that each of us is a minister in some sense, called to serve the Lord as he has gifted us.

Paul's admonition to Timothy is full of warning. Hand out index cards with the word WARNING printed with black marker on each. Ask the adults, individually or in pairs, to write out a WARNING sign related to the text. Give them two to three minutes and then have all the signs read. Collect them and post them somewhere outside your classroom where passersby will have the opportunity to be duly warned. Some samples: "WARNING: Bodily exercise profits less than godly exercise!" or "WARNING: Do NOT neglect your gift!"

## INTO LIFE

Distribute half-sheets of paper with 1 Timothy 4:7, 8 written at the top. Comment on the popularity of exercise programs, equipment, clubs, and the like designed to provide physical training. Ask the students to come up with their own spiritual training programs.

Each student should identify a ministry characteristic from today's lesson that needs to be developed in his or her own life. Then the student should list three or four steps that can be taken to develop this characteristic.

Allow about five minute for this activity, but do not ask for public reporting. Close with prayer that God will help the students develop the needed qualities.

# Not-So-Hidden Truths

In each of the following sentences there is a "hidden" word from today's text. The first one is identified to show you how you might look for the others. Each of the thoughts expressed is also related to today's text. When you finish the search, also decide how the thoughts are a part of today's Scripture lesson.

1. Give me an <u>exam, ple</u>ase; let me prove myself.
2. One big if threatens your ministry: "if you neglect. . . ."
3. With open minds, we visualize all that the living God will do for us.
4. I want each of your disciples to learn all these things.
5. It is okay to exercise, but I want you to have extra investments in the spiritual disciplines.
6. Will A, B, or C characterize our effort? No, we work much harder than such an easy answer would imply; D might be better . . . for drudgery!
7. We want none of our words to be lie; veracity is our watchword.

# Letter to a Minister

Consider the following as a "computer template" for a letter to a minister. Each item comes from a letter Paul wrote to his young minister friend Timothy. "Click" on each advice/command statement you want in your letter.

Dear Minister:

❏  Be true to your Christian heritage.

❏  Avoid foolish stories and tales.

❏  Persevere in all things.

❏  Read Scripture in public.

❏  Use the gifts you have been given.

❏  Be love personified.

❏  Keep yourself pure.

❏  Watch to make life & doctrine consistent.

❏  Put your hope God.

❏  Train yourself in godliness.

❏  Remember what has eternal value.

❏  Set an example in good speech.

If you do these things, you will be a good minister of Christ Jesus.

In him,

_____

Now go back and identify the verse in which each of these is found. Or, if you like, number the items from one to twelve based on how important you think each is for anyone trying to be a good minister in the end of the twentieth century.

**Not-So-Hidden Truths:** 1. example; 2. gift; 3. hope; 4. teach; 5. train; 6. labor; 7. believe

# CHRIST'S SERVANT TEACHES GODLINESS

**LESSON 2**

## WHY TEACH THIS LESSON?

One commercial dairy used to advertise its products as made from the milk of contented cows. I don't know what makes a cow content or even how one could discover such a secret. But today's text reveals something about contentment for the Christian.

Perhaps if the world saw more of what the church has to offer as coming from contented Christians, our witness to the world would be more effective. If believers seem no happier as they pursue godliness than the world is with its pursuit of material success, what reason have they given for anyone to take seriously the gospel's claims?

Helping your students to provide that reason is your goal in today's lesson.

## INTRODUCTION

### A. YOU CAN'T TAKE IT WITH YOU

Jack Benny, a popular comedian of a generation ago, was usually depicted on stage as a penny-pinching tightwad. During one performance, another character asked him what would happen to all his money when he died.

"I intend to take it with me," replied Jack.

"But, Jack," replied his questioner, "you can't take it with you."

"Well, then," responded Jack, "I just won't go!"

Of course, Jack Benny eventually did go, and he did *not* take his money with him. No one can, for in the words of a portion of today's text, "We brought nothing into the world, and we can take nothing out of it" (1 Timothy 6:7). Generosity with material possessions is not the only mark of godliness, but it is an important one, for one's attitude toward possessions will determine how conscientious and successful he is in developing other marks of godliness.

### B. LESSON BACKGROUND

The historical setting for the first epistle to Timothy was discussed in last week's lesson. The theme of that lesson was the example of a Christian leader; the theme of today's lesson is godliness. Several verses in our text give special attention to riches and the danger they pose to godliness. This emphasis was especially needed because Ephesus, where Timothy was serving, was a very wealthy city. Located in western Asia Minor (now a part of modern Turkey), Ephesus was the western terminus of an important trade route that originated in the East. Trade items passed through its port to destinations all over the Mediterranean world, creating considerable wealth for the city. In addition, the famous and impressive temple of the Roman goddess Diana (also known by her Greek name Artemis) was located there. Her presence brought a booming business to the silversmiths, who made images of the goddess to sell to her worshipers. (See Acts 19:24, 25.)

DEVOTIONAL READING
1 TIMOTHY 6:12-20
LESSON SCRIPTURE
1 TIMOTHY 6:2b-21
PRINTED TEXT
1 TIMOTHY 6:2b-21

## LESSON AIMS

After studying this lesson, each student should:

1. Contrast ungodly pursuits with the pursuit of godliness with contentment.

2. Identify what the godly person is to flee and what he is to follow.

3. Declare a commitment to pursue godliness in his or her life.

## KEY VERSE

*Pursue righteousness, godliness, faith, love, endurance and gentleness. Fight the good fight of the faith.* —1 Timothy 6:11, 12

## I. THE DANGER OF FOOLISH DISPUTES (1 TIMOTHY 6:2b-5)

### A. DISPUTERS DESCRIBED (vv. 2b-4)

**2b. These are the things you are to teach and urge on them.**

Paul is beginning to conclude his letter. *These…things* that he has written are important; they must be communicated to the believers. More than mere teaching is required, however; Timothy is to *urge* the believers to heed the instruction. The word *urge* is from a Greek word often translated as "exhort" or "encourage." It pictures one coming alongside another to give direction or assistance.

**3, 4. If anyone teaches false doctrines and does not agree to the sound instruction of our Lord Jesus Christ and to godly teaching, he is conceited and understands nothing. He has an unhealthy interest in controversies and quarrels about words that result in envy, strife, malicious talk, evil suspicions.**

Now Paul turns to discuss the importance of "these things" from the negative side. What if one refuses to heed Paul's *sound instruction*? What if one *teaches* something opposed to Paul's *godly teaching*? Such a one is described in very uncomplimentary terms!

Paul was not just suggesting a hypothetical situation. The church in the first century faced some of the same problems that the church faces today. Then, as today, foolish and misguided individuals disturbed the church with their *false* doctrines. Teaching the truth is essential to the health of the church. This was one of the reasons Timothy was left in Ephesus in the first place (1 Timothy 1:3, 4).

We do not know for certain the content of these *false doctrines* or the *controversies and quarrels*. Some of the false teachers may have come from Jewish backgrounds. Rabbis in that day loved nothing better than to engage in lengthy, intricate, hairsplitting debates. However, since the membership of the church in Ephesus was drawn largely from pagan backgrounds, this seems the more likely source of the contentions. Ultimately their source lay in human pride and ignorance (*conceited and understands nothing*), a combination that almost always spells trouble. The bitter fruit of these deliberations is seen in the list of negatives that concludes verse 4.

### B. ROBBED OF TRUTH (v. 5)

**5. . . . and constant friction between men of corrupt mind, who have been robbed of the truth and who think that godliness is a means to financial gain.**

Paul's denunciation of these false teachers is not what we would call gentle, indicating that we today must deal firmly with such teachers lest they beguile the innocent. In this verse Paul reveals their motivation: they *think that godliness is a means to financial gain*. In other words, they are in it for the money.

Some manuscripts include a command to withdraw from such false teachers. While these words quite possibly were not in the original, they do seem appropriate to this situation and are in keeping with Paul's instructions given elsewhere. (See 2 Thessalonians 3:6; 2 Timothy 3:5.) It was the way Paul himself handled brothers who rejected sound teaching (1 Timothy 1:19, 20).

## II. THE SECRET OF CONTENTMENT (1 TIMOTHY 6:6-8)

### A. THE REWARD OF GODLINESS (v. 6)

**6. But godliness with contentment is great gain.**

The godly person has learned to resist the enticements of material gain. He knows how fragile and temporary such wealth can be. He also knows that it tends to cause strife and envy. Today, more than at any time in history, many have allowed themselves to be seduced by the idolatry of things. Plunging hopelessly into debt, they try to buy happiness but settle instead for items that can never bring real *contentment*. Some people are willing to sell their bodies and even their souls to

### WHAT DO YOU THINK?

*What would you do if you suspected a Sunday school teacher was teaching false doctrine? How would you confirm whether it was, indeed, false doctrine or merely a difference of opinion? What action would you take if you confirmed the teacher was guilty of teaching false doctrine? Would this action protect the church, redeem the false teacher, or both? Explain.*

*See 1 Timothy 6:3-5.*

### WHAT DO YOU THINK?

*To what extent should the church be refuting the error of false religions and cult groups—groups that are outside the control of the church itself? Is simply upholding the true and genuine enough? Why or why not? Are direct attacks on the specific errors of specific groups appropriate? Why or why not? Can a person arguing for the truth be guilty of "an unhealthy interest in controversies and quarrels," or is Paul only talking about the false teachers? Explain or support your answer.*

*Suppose a sister congregation took a public stand against a local cult group and was sued by the cult. To what extent do you think our church should support the sister church's efforts and defense? Why?*

accumulate things, only to have these so-called treasures turn to ashes in their hands. Never has a society had so much and enjoyed so little.

## B. MATERIAL GAIN IS TEMPORARY (v. 7)
**7. For we brought nothing into the world, and we can take nothing out of it.**

A Brink's truck never follows a hearse to the cemetery. Nothing should be more obvious than the fact that "you can't take it with you." Yet Satan with his clever enticements keeps many blinded to this truth.

## C. TRUE CONTENTMENT (v. 8)
**8. But if we have food and clothing, we will be content with that.**

We live in a world where many lack enough *food and clothing* to sustain life. Television has made us painfully aware of people by the millions, especially children, who are starving to death. Ironically, one of the biggest health problems in our land is overeating. In a nation that God has blessed with such abundance, how can we learn to be *content* with just the necessities of life? It is vital that we keep the "big picture" in view and give eternal matters priority. Paul experienced both abundance and poverty, and in the process "learned to be content whatever the circumstances" (Philippians 4:11).

## III. THE DANGERS OF WEALTH (1 TIMOTHY 6:9, 10)
### A. A DEADLY SNARE (v. 9)
**9. People who want to get rich fall into temptation and a trap and into many foolish and harmful desires that plunge men into ruin and destruction.**

This *trap* is a snare, the kind used to catch birds or small animals. In its simplest form it is nothing but a loop of wire or a strong cord anchored to a stake, tree, or rock. Without even being aware of it, the animal passes through the loop, causing it to draw tightly about its neck or leg. As the animal tries to escape, its struggles only cause the loop to draw tighter, making the animal's escape almost impossible.

The desire for wealth operates in much the same way. Without realizing what is happening, we allow ourselves to be drawn into the loop. Once snared, we find it increasingly difficult to break free. The desire for money or the things it will buy leads to other sins. Because of it a company will cut corners and produce a defective product or will misrepresent its value. Because of a desire for money people will make agreements they have no intention or ability to fulfill. Some will steal or traffic in drugs or even kill for money. This covetous desire has become so pervasive in our society that many tend to consider it normal rather than a deadly sin.

Jesus directed some of his most pointed warnings toward the rich (Luke 6:24; Matthew 19:23-26). But as Paul indicates, the dangers are great not just for the rich but for those who *want to get rich*. The desire for wealth does not produce godliness, but a godlessness that will lead to ultimate *destruction*.

## B. ALL KINDS OF EVIL (v. 10)
**10. For the love of money is a root of all kinds of evil. Some people, eager for money, have wandered from the faith and pierced themselves with many griefs.**

Obviously, evil arises from other sources as well. Sexual lust and pride have their origins in something other than a love for money. At the same time, we must recognize that greed is not totally unrelated to sexual lust, pride, and a lust for power. Where greed is present, these other sins are likely to be lurking nearby. Greed frequently leads to a departure from *the faith* and numerous other *griefs*. The testimonies of the wealthy tell of loneliness, restlessness, and sadness, even leading in some cases to suicide.

### WHAT DO YOU THINK?

Paul says, "If we have food and clothing, we will be content with that." Could he still say that today? Are Christians generally content merely with food and clothing? Why or why not?

What does this kind of contentment require? Should a Christian worker never go on strike for better wages? Why or why not? Are investing, saving, and trading on the stock market okay, or do these activities indicate one is not content with food and clothing? Explain.

Believers over the centuries have used fasting as a way of gaining mastery over physical appetites. How might occasional fasting increase one's contentment with what he or she has? What things besides food might we give up periodically to improve our sense of contentment with the level of physical comfort with which God has blessed us?

### WHAT DO YOU THINK?

Paul says some people, eager for money, have wandered from the faith. Wandering suggests a slow progression, perhaps not noticeable at first. A child who wanders off from his mother doesn't know he is getting lost until he is lost. What does this suggest about the deceptiveness of wealth? How can we identify "wandering saints" and draw them back before they have wandered away? How can we identify the wandering of our own hearts?

### HOW TO SAY IT

Artemis. *AR-teh-miss.*

Caesarea Philippi. *Sess-uh-REE-uh Fuh-LIP-pie.*

gnosis *(Greek). NO-sis.*

Gnosticism. *NOSS-tih-sizm.*

Elijah. *Ee-LYE-juh.*

Elisha. *Ee-LYE-shuh.*

Ephesus. *EFF-uh-suss.*

Pontius Pilate. *PON-shus PIE-lut.*

*Use the visual for lesson 2 to summarize "all this" that Paul says to "flee" (v. 11) and to discuss the things we ought to "pursue."*

### HOW MUCH LAND DOES A MAN NEED?

The Russian author Leo Tolstoy wrote a short story that tells of a rich man who was never satisfied. He was consumed with the desire for more and more. One day he heard of a wonderful offer to acquire more land. For a thousand rubles he could have all the land that he could cover on foot in a day. But he had to return to the starting point by sundown or he would lose everything.

The man arose early and began his journey. He walked on and on, always thinking he could go just a little farther and get just a little more land. Eventually he went so far that he realized he would have to walk very fast if he was to return to the starting point in time to claim the land.

As the sun sank lower in the sky, he quickened his pace. Then he began to run. As he came within sight of the starting point, he expended his last energies, plunged over the finish line—and dropped dead.

The man's servant then took a spade and dug a grave for his master. He made it just long enough and just wide enough to bury the man. The title of Tolstoy's story is, *"How Much Land Does a Man Need?"* Tolstoy concludes by saying, "Six feet from his head to his heels was all he needed."

We do well to remember that this world is not our home. The great aim of life is not found in amassing possessions. We are here to know God and to prepare to spend an eternity with him.

—C. B. Mc.

## IV. THE PURSUIT OF GODLINESS (1 TIMOTHY 6:11-20)

### A. FLEE FROM GREED (v. 11)

**11. But you, man of God, flee from all this, and pursue righteousness, godliness, faith, love, endurance and gentleness.**

In the previous verses, Paul had warned against greed and all the troubles that come with it. Timothy was instructed not just to avoid this vice, but to flee. This is the same command he gave in regard to immorality (1 Corinthians 6:18). Many times people seem to rank immorality as a "major" sin, but covetousness or greed is tolerated as "minor." It is interesting that Paul makes no such distinction, but recommends the same attitude toward each.

As Timothy runs from the troubles associated with greed, Paul says, he is run toward a number of virtues. Virtue does not come by accident or merely by staying away from evil. One must *pursue* these qualities if he is to become an effective leader in the Lord's church.

In addressing Timothy as a *man of God,* Paul picks up an Old Testament expression. In 1 Kings 17:24 this title is applied to Elijah, and in 2 Kings 7:17 and 8:2, to Elisha. Both of these men were stalwart spokesmen for God. In using this title, Paul indicates he expects Timothy to follow their examples of godliness and faithfulness.

### B. FIGHT THE GOOD FIGHT (v. 12)

**12. Fight the good fight of the faith. Take hold of the eternal life to which you were called when you made your good confession in the presence of many witnesses.**

Depicting the pursuit of *eternal life* as an athletic contest, Paul encourages his young comrade to enter the struggle with fervor. Timothy first entered this contest when he *made a good confession in the presence of many witnesses.* At an early date in the history of the church, one who desired to become a Christian made a public confession of his faith. We do not know what form this public statement may have taken, but it was probably a simple statement, similar to that of Peter at Caesarea Philippi: "You are the Christ, the Son of the living God" (Matthew 16:16). Perhaps Paul's statement in Romans 10:9 hints at the confession made by believers in the first century: "If you confess with your mouth, 'Jesus is Lord,' and believe in your heart that God raised him from the dead, you will be saved."

This reminder of Timothy's earlier statement of faith would give him strength for the struggles that lay ahead in his ministry. That it was made before witnesses helped him to realize that he did not stand alone.

### FIGHT ONE MORE ROUND

On September 7, 1892, in New Orleans, James Corbett and John L. Sullivan fought for the world's heavyweight boxing title. Their match was the first in which the boxers used gloves rather than "bare knuckles." "Gentleman Jim" Corbett, as he was known, became the American heavyweight champion when he knocked out Sullivan in the twenty-first round. Corbett held the title for five years until 1897.

When asked later for his advice on becoming a champion, Corbett said:

"Fight one more round. When your feet are so tired that you have to shuffle back to the center of the ring, fight one more round. When your arms are so tired that you can hardly lift your hands to come on guard, fight one more round. When your nose is bleeding and your eyes are black and you are so tired that you wish your opponent would crack you in the jaw and put you to sleep, fight one more round. Remember that the man is never whipped who always fights one more round." —C. B. Mc.

## C. BE FAITHFUL (vv. 13-16)

**13. In the sight of God, who gives life to everything, and of Christ Jesus, who while testifying before Pontius Pilate made the good confession, I charge you.**

Paul presents Timothy with a solemn *charge*—solemn because it was made *in the sight of God*, the giver of all life, and *of Christ Jesus*, whose *confession* affirmed his authority. Jesus acknowledged that he was a king, and that his kingdom was not of this world (John 18:36, 37). He further informed Pilate that the Roman governor had no authority over him except what God had allowed (John 19:10, 11). The confession Jesus made before *Pontius Pilate* was essentially that "Jesus is Lord" (cf. Romans 10:9).

**14, 15a. . . . to keep this command without spot or blame until the appearing of our Lord Jesus Christ, which God will bring about in his own time—**

Paul charges Timothy to keep the commitment he had made without compromise and in a manner that was above reproach *until the appearing of our Lord Jesus Christ*. Many in that day anticipated an early return of Christ, perhaps within a generation. Nothing in Paul's statement (or in any of his other teachings) necessarily indicates belief in an early return*. He clearly states that *God will bring about* the Lord's return *in his own time*. Paul is not saying when Jesus will return, but he challenges Timothy to remain faithful, regardless of when Christ returns.

**15b, 16. . . . God, the blessed and only Ruler, the King of kings and Lord of lords, who alone is immortal and who lives in unapproachable light, whom no one has seen or can see. To him be honor and might forever. Amen.**

Paul suddenly breaks into a doxology of praise to Almighty God—even before he finishes his exhortation. Some have suggested that these words may have been part of a hymn used by the early Christians. Regardless of their source, Paul so lived in the presence of God that such words of praise flowing from his pen seemed appropriate at almost any time. (See 1 Timothy 1:17.)

## D. TEACH THE RICH (vv. 17-19)

**17-19. Command those who are rich in this present world not to be arrogant nor to put their hope in wealth, which is so uncertain, but to put their hope in God, who richly provides us with everything for our enjoyment. Command them to do good, to be rich in good deeds, and to be generous and willing to share. In this way they will lay up treasure for themselves as a firm foundation for the coming age, so that they may take hold of the life that is truly life.**

---

### WHAT DO YOU THINK?

*It is not uncommon in Paul's writings for him to insert a doxology, as he does here in verses 15 and 16. When was the last time you broke out in spontaneous praise? How can we make praising God a more common element in our daily lives? What kind of reaction do you think it would get from people around us if we occasionally uttered genuine expressions of praise to God for his grace and providence?*

### *NOTE

*It's probably safe to say Paul believed the Lord could have returned in his lifetime, but not to say he necessarily expected it. We should have the same attitude, believing the Lord could return at any moment, but not trying to set a time when he must return.*

### OPTION

*Use the reproducible activity, "Rich or Poor?" on page 352 to explore the difference between being "rich in this present world" and spiritually rich.*

## PRAYER

*Thank you, dear God, for inspiring the apostle Paul to write this letter to Timothy, setting forth your standards for godliness. As we study and meditate upon them, give us the wisdom and courage to apply them to our lives. In our Master's name we pray. Amen.*

## THOUGHT TO REMEMBER

*"Godliness with contentment is great gain" (1 Timothy 6:6).*

## DAILY BIBLE READING

*Monday, June 2—Keep Above Reproach (1 Timothy 6:13-21)*

*Tuesday, June 3—Keep Yourself Pure (1 Timothy 5:17-22)*

*Wednesday, June 4—Approve That Which Is Good (Philippians 1:3-11)*

*Thursday, June 5—Do Not Love the World (1 John 2:12-17)*

*Friday, June 6—Accept the Love of Christ (Ephesians 3:14-21)*

*Saturday, June 7—Follow Christ's Example (John 13:12-17)*

*Sunday, June 8—God's Divine Power Grants Godliness (2 Peter 1:3-11)*

In verses 9 and 10, Paul had warned against the dangers of riches. Now he discusses this issue further. It is noteworthy that while Paul warns against the dangers of wealth, he does not condemn wealth as such. He condemns putting *their hope in wealth*, which becomes a substitute for putting *their hope in God*. In addition, wealth often causes people to become arrogant toward others. Possessing wealth gives them power over people—a power that many do not hesitate to use. The Christian's perspective is that if God has blessed him with material wealth, he is to use that wealth to help others, thereby glorifying God.

Some have used verse 19 as a basis upon which to build a theology of salvation by works. Such a theology flies in the face of other Scriptures and is certainly not Paul's emphasis here. One cannot buy his way into Heaven. The point is that one who shows true generosity with his wealth is investing in spiritual riches, and will thus be better prepared to enjoy the blessings of eternal *life*.

### E. A FINAL CHARGE (vv. 20, 21)

**20, 21. Timothy, guard what has been entrusted to your care. Turn away from godless chatter and the opposing ideas of what is falsely called knowledge, which some have professed and in so doing have wandered from the faith. Grace be with you.**

Paul shows his deep affection for Timothy as he closes this letter with some words of wisdom and warning. These words were necessary, for some had already *wandered from the faith* and had fallen away. (See 1 Timothy 1:19, 20.) The word *knowledge* is *gnosis* in the Greek, and was a key concept in a heretical teaching called Gnosticism. This heresy posed a serious threat to the church toward the close of the first century, and Paul's reference to *ideas of what is falsely called knowledge* may well be an attack on an early form of this heresy.

In order to guard the faith that had been entrusted to him, Timothy had to live it, preach it, and defend it against its enemies. One can scarcely imagine more timely advice than this for our age—a time when all kinds of strange teachings are drawing men and women away from the true faith.

*Grace be with you.* In one form or another, the blessing of *grace* appears at the close of all of Paul's epistles.

## CONCLUSION

A friend of mine once had a "fisherman's ruler." It was only about six inches long, but the markings on it indicated that it was eighteen inches long. When he used this ruler, even a good-sized minnow would be long enough legally to keep. When he came back from fishing trips, he could boast that he had caught several fish more than eighteen inches long, according to his special ruler. Of course, all of this was a joke, and we always got a good laugh out of it.

Some in our society today, however, are guilty of a similar form of deception when it comes to evaluating godliness—and they aren't joking! They have decided that God's standards for morality revealed in the Bible are too limited and too narrow, so they use their own ruler. An unborn baby is now called a "product of conception," not a human being; thus there is nothing wrong in destroying him or her. Alcoholism is now a "disease," so an alcoholic has no moral responsibility for his sad plight. Homosexuality is just an "alternative life-style," so it should no longer be condemned by obvious biblical teachings.

Although this list could be easily enlarged, these examples demonstrate how all too often one can establish his or her own moral values. Today's lesson emphasizes the importance of godliness. The question we must answer is simple: do we measure godliness by our ruler, or by the ruler God has given us in the Bible?

# Discovery Learning

*This page contains an alternate lesson plan emphasizing learning activities. Classes desiring such student involvement will find these suggestions helpful. The next page is a reproducible activity page to further enhance discovery learning.*

## LEARNING GOALS

After studying this lesson, each student should:

1. Contrast ungodly pursuits with the pursuit of godliness with contentment.

2. Identify what the godly person is to flee and what he is to follow.

3. Declare a commitment to pursue godliness in his or her life.

## INTO THE LESSON

Prepare for this class by cutting out some small arrows, six or eight inches long, from either paper or cardboard. On half of these write the word *flee*; on the other half, write *follow*. Place one of these on each of the seats where your class members will sit.

Enlarge the following puzzle onto a chalkboard, poster, or overhead transparency, for use as a group activity.

```
R  I  G  H  T  E  O  U  S  N  E  S  S
D  O  F  A  I  T  H  S  R  G  E  E  C
E  E  S  U  O  R  E  N  E  G  I  T  O
E  C  S  Y  V  N  E  N  M  S  S  O  N
A  C  A  T  I  E  T  V  R  E  U  Q  T
T  I  N  L  R  L  C  E  I  N  S  U  E
A  N  D  A  E  U  V  A  O  L  P  A  N
R  O  A  N  R  O  C  I  R  T  I  R  T
G  E  E  G  R  U  T  T  R  G  C  R  M
T  S  V  T  O  C  D  U  I  L  I  E  E
S  L  N  I  I  R  T  N  E  O  O  L  N
U  O  S  R  V  H  R  E  E  V  N  S  T
C  E  F  I  R  T  S  A  T  E  S  L  C
```

Divide your class into two groups, according to the FLEE and FOLLOW arrows. The FLEE group is to find words in the puzzle related to ungodliness; the FOLLOW group is to locate words related to godliness. There are nine of the former: *controversies, quarrels, envy, strife, suspicions, friction, evil, arrogant, destruction*. There are ten in the latter: *contentment, faith, godliness, gentleness, love, endurance, righteousness, truth, generous, grace*. List the words as they are noted, in separate columns.

## INTO THE WORD

Divide your class into three to seven work groups (depending on your class size). Give each group one (or more) of the following statements, each of which is a comment by the lesson writer. Ask each group, "What evidence or examples can you cite that confirms the statement your group has."

(1) "The church in the first century faced some of the same problems that the church faces today"—vv. 3, 4.

(2) "We today must deal firmly with [false] teachers lest they beguile the innocent. . . . They are in it for the money"—v. 5.

(3) "Today, more than at any time in history, many have allowed themselves to be seduced by the idolatry of things"—v. 6.

(4) "One of the biggest health problems in our land is overeating"—v. 8.

(5) "The desire for money . . . has become so pervasive in our society that many tend to consider it normal or even virtuous rather than a deadly sin."—v. 9.

(6) "Greed is not totally unrelated to sexual lust, pride, and a lust for power. Where greed is present, these other sins are likely to be lurking nearby"—v. 10.

(7) "Wealth often causes people to become arrogant toward other people. Possessing wealth gives them power over people—a power that many do not hesitate to use"—vv. 17-19.

After groups have a few minutes to discuss, have each report in the order of the lesson text. Add explanations and insights as you choose.

## INTO LIFE

Read 1 Timothy 6:15, 16. The lesson commentary notes that these verses were possibly "part of a hymn used by the early Christians." Divide the class into the *flee* and *follow* groups used earlier. Have one group try to think of as many hymns, Christian songs, or choruses as possible that use the word *King* in the title. Have the other group do the same with the word *Lord*. Give each group five minutes to complete its list, then call time and see which team has won.

Ask each student to focus on a statement from one of the songs investigated in the previous activity. The statement should express submission to the lordship or kingship of Christ. Let this statement declare the student's commitment to godliness in his or her life.

Close the class session by singing a stanza of one song or hymn from each group. Encourage class members to hum, sing, or reflect on the words of one of these songs during the coming week.

# Rich or Poor?

Decide whether the person saying each of the following remarks is *rich* or *poor*. Use *R* or *P* to identify; consider today's text as you decide.

_____ 1 "If I follow God closely enough, I know I'll be financially successful."

_____ 2. "I know 'you can't take it with you,' but having it while I'm here is important."

_____ 3. "What more could I want? I have today's bread and today's clothes."

_____ 4. "What it all comes down to in the end is this: whoever has the most toys wins!"

_____ 5. "What little I have is yours . . . if you need it."

_____ 6. "I don't have time for Bible reading, Sunday school, or prayer; my two jobs and my family keep me too busy."

_____ 7. "If I could just win one of those magazine or state lotteries, then I'd be happy . . . and I'd be generous, too."

_____ 8. "Take the world . . . but give me Jesus."

_____ 9. "I've seen too many of my friends wander away from the church and faith to 'make more money.' That wouldn't be worth it to me."

_____ 10. "Which would I rather have: money or contentment? don't they go together?"

# Gotta' Run!

Paul reminds Timothy there are things to be fled and things to be pursued. Fill in the following table chart with some of the modern person's "Flee" and "pursue" objects.

|  | GOOD THINGS | BAD THINGS |
|---|---|---|
| MEN RUN *FROM* | | |
| MEN RUN *TO* | | |

# CHRIST'S SERVANT ENDURES SUFFERING

**LESSON 3**

## WHY TEACH THIS LESSON?

"Take two aspirin and call me in the morning." That's the kind of solution we like for pain and suffering. Quick. Easy. And, especially, painless!

Fortunately, it doesn't always work that way. If suffering could always be avoided or terminated so easily, we would never know the joy of victory over it. Paul's advice to Timothy made no mention of escape or avoidance. The apostle, facing death, told his colleague to endure.

It's a sobering thought, but it's one your students need to think about.

## INTRODUCTION

### A. NO PAIN, NO GAIN

One often sees the words, "No Pain, No Gain," posted on the walls of locker rooms in gymnasiums and health clubs. This slogan suggests that if athletes and exercisers are going to accomplish anything worthwhile, they must be willing to suffer the rigors of training and practice. Muscle tone is not developed without stretching the muscles past the point of comfort. Precision performance is not achieved without hours of bone-wearying practice.

Few athletes may recognize that this is a thoroughly Christian concept. It is a point stated clearly by the apostle Paul in our text for today's lesson. Paul knew from personal experience what he was talking about. (Read his personal litany of suffering in 2 Corinthians 11:24-29.) With such credentials, Paul was certainly qualified to explain to Timothy the suffering he was likely to experience as a servant of the Lord. The apostle's words are just as applicable to us today.

### B. LESSON BACKGROUND

Paul's first imprisonment in Rome began in about A.D. 61. It appears that, following a two-year period under house arrest (Acts 28:16, 30, 31), he was released. Paul then resumed his travels, visiting such places as Macedonia (1 Timothy 1:3). He may even have made his way to Spain, fulfilling a desire he had expressed in Romans 15:24, 28. During this period, he wrote the letters of 1 Timothy and Titus. However, the great apostle's activities came to an abrupt end around A.D. 67, when he was seized by the emperor Nero and once more imprisoned in Rome. Conditions this time were far worse than during the first imprisonment; one of Paul's friends had difficulty even locating him (2 Timothy 1:17). The second epistle to Timothy was written during this second imprisonment, as Paul awaited his execution.

## I. EXHORTATION TO FAITHFULNESS (2 TIMOTHY 2:1-7)

### A. BE STRONG (v. 1)

1. **You then, my son, be strong in the grace that is in Christ Jesus.**

DEVOTIONAL READING
1 TIMOTHY 2:14-26
LESSON SCRIPTURE
2 TIMOTHY 2:1-13
PRINTED TEXT
2 TIMOTHY 2:1-13

LESSON AIMS

*Having studied this lesson, each adult will be able to:*

*1. Enumerate Paul's basic exhortations to Timothy in this text.*

*2. Explain why suffering for one's faith is to be expected.*

*3. Serve Christ effectively in one's daily position or occupation.*

KEY VERSE

*Endure hardship with us like a good soldier of Christ Jesus.*

*2 Timothy 2:3*

WHAT DO YOU THINK?

How does grace make it easier for us to "be strong" (2 Timothy 2:1)?

See 2 Corinthians 12:9; Hebrews 4:16; 1 John 1:9.

WHAT DO YOU THINK?

What provision have we made in our church to train up those who will be able to teach God's truth to the next generation? Do you think we are doing enough? Why or why not? Who is responsible for recruiting and training potential teachers? What standards do we expect our teachers to live up to?

The writer of Hebrews complained to his readers, "Though by this time you ought to be teachers, you need someone to teach you the elementary truths of God's word all over again" (Hebrews 5:12). What can we do to be sure those who "ought to be teachers" are?

WHAT DO YOU THINK?

What kind of "civilian affairs" (verse 4) do Christian soldiers sometimes get involved in that weaken their witness for the Lord? How can we encourage one another to avoid such entanglements and serve the Lord without distraction?

At the beginning of this epistle, Paul addressed Timothy as "my dear son" (1:2). In the first chapter he mentioned that he prayed for Timothy "night and day" (1:3). He reminded Timothy of his upbringing, and the faith Timothy had received from his mother and grandmother (1: 5). Paul encouraged him to stir up the gift of God that he had received (v. 6). Paul's admonition to be strong was based on these factors in Timothy's background.

It is difficult to overestimate the importance of early training and loving guidance in helping one develop the character necessary to stand strong in the faith. One of the reasons for the growing problems among so many of the young people in our churches today is that we have neglected to provide them the right kind of training. Until we are willing to make the sacrifices necessary to bring our children up in the faith, we cannot expect to find a solution to these problems.

Timothy had the background to stand strong in the faith, but still he needed this encouragement from Paul. Such encouragement is something that those who are active in Christian work frequently need. All Christians can and should encourage those who take the lead in ministry.

### B. BE A TEACHER (v. 2)

**2. And the things you have heard me say in the presence of many witnesses entrust to reliable men who will also be qualified to teach others.**

From a human point of view, the church stands always just one generation away from extinction. If any one generation fails to pass its faith on to the next generation, the end is at hand. That is the reason every congregation must be concerned about evangelism and Christian education.

Paul's charge here to Timothy applies to all Christians. One does not have to be a Sunday school teacher in order to pass his faith along to others. Teaching is not confined to formal classroom settings. In fact, often the most effective teaching occurs in one-on-one situations. Any Christian may find himself with ample opportunities to share his faith with family members, friends, or co-workers—opportunities that no one else has.

Timothy is instructed to entrust what he has heard from Paul to reliable men. Reliable for what? To pass the message on to others. Part of the Christian leader's job is teaching people generally. But a significant part of the job is training, seeking out those who are can be trusted to teach others and making sure they become qualified to do so.

### C. BE TOUGH (vv. 3, 4)

**3, 4. Endure hardship with us like a good soldier of Christ Jesus. No one serving as a soldier gets involved in civilian affairs—he wants to please his commanding officer.**

In verses 3-6, Paul uses the illustrations of a soldier, an athlete, and a farmer to impress on Timothy his responsibilities. During his many labors for Christ, Paul had had a number of encounters with soldiers. Even as he wrote this letter from prison, he was probably guarded by one. Certain aspects of a soldier's life parallel those of a Christian. The life of a soldier is not easy, especially under combat conditions. Military training is designed to make a soldier both physically and mentally tough. A good soldier is prepared not only for the expected; he must also be prepared for the unexpected.

Being a soldier in the Lord's army is no different. As Christians most of us are not called on to endure physical hardships, but we certainly need to be mentally tough to resist all the threats and challenges to our faith that we face almost daily. Just as it takes a soldier months of preparation and continuous training to be ready to meet the enemy, so we must be prepared to spend much time in study and in the proper spiritual disciplines to be able to fend off Satan and his cohorts.

A soldier's first responsibility is to carry out the orders he is given. When he allows himself to become *involved in civilian affairs*, he loses his effectiveness. He cannot live as both a civilian and a soldier. In the same way, a Christian is likely to be ineffective if he allows himself to become engrossed in seeking pleasure, fame, money, or anything else that might turn his focus from the Lord. The Christian may live in this world, but his allegiance is to the kingdom "not of this world" (John 18:36).

## D. BE FAIR (v. 5)

**5. Similarly, if anyone competes as an athlete, he does not receive the victor's crown unless he competes according to the rules.**

An athlete must prepare himself for competition by strenuous practice, proper diet, and adequate rest. Even such conscientious preparation, however, is not enough. If the athlete expects to receive the wreath of victory, he must compete *according to the rules*. Some modern athletes have attempted to enhance their prowess by the use of illegal drugs. When they are caught, in almost every case they must give up their awards and in some cases they are barred from future competition.

In the same way, a servant of the Lord must conduct himself properly. He will not cut corners to achieve success, nor will he serve for gain or fame. And he certainly will not compromise the faith in order to please others.

## E. BE BLESSED (vv. 6, 7)

**6, 7. The hardworking farmer should be the first to receive a share of the crops. Reflect on what I am saying, for the Lord will give you insight into all this.**

The third figure that Paul offers as a model for Timothy is that of a *farmer*. Farming has always been hard work. Furthermore, it involves numerous risks. The weather must be just right in order for the farmer to work up the soil to sow the seeds. Then the rains must come at the right time and in the right amounts. If the rains come too soon, the seed may rot in the ground. If they come too late, the plants will be stunted. If there is too little rain, the crops will be dry and parched. If it rains too much, the crops will be washed out or drowned. There are also various insects and diseases about which to be concerned.

If all goes well, however, the farmer's hard work and risk-taking will be rewarded. He is then entitled to *be the first to receive a share of the crops*. Just as the farmer is nourished by the crops he raises, so the Christian worker is spiritually nourished and sustained by his labor. This may refer to the joys that come to a Christian as he sees the kingdom of the Lord grow. It may also refer to the reward of Heaven that lies in his future.

### DON'T BE CHEAP WITH THE SEED

In 2 Timothy 2:6, Paul compares Christian service with the intensive labor of a farmer.

How do successful farmers plant seed? They do not reach into a bin, pull out an ear of corn, pop out the kernels, and plant them one by one. No, they buy certified seed by the truckload, fill and refill their corn planters, and plant day and night until the allotted acreage is planted. The rule for successful farming is: "If you're ever going to be cheap, *don't be cheap with the seed*." It has always been true that "whoever sows sparingly will also reap sparingly, and whoever sows generously will also reap generously" (2 Corinthians 9:6).

Likewise, the Christian life yields great rewards. But what we get out of it will depend in large part on what we are willing to put into it.      —C. B. Mc.

*The visual for lesson three illustrates verses 3-7. Display it as you begin the session, and refer to it after you have introduced the farmer, soldier, and athlete metaphors. What other metaphors can the class think of consistent with Paul's message here?*

Endure hardship as a good soldier of Jesus Christ. . . . if anyone competes in athletics, he is not crowned unless he competes according to the rules. The hard-working farmer must be first to partake of the crops. . . . May the Lord give you understanding in all things.
2 Timothy 2:3-7, *niv*

*Use the reproducible activity, "Soldier, Athlete, Farmer," on page 360 to assist in the discussion.*

## II. ENCOURAGEMENT TO ACCEPT SUFFERING (2 TIMOTHY 2:8-13)

### A. Remember Jesus Christ (v. 8)

**8. Remember Jesus Christ, raised from the dead, descended from David. This is my gospel.**

In the previous verses, Paul had tried to prepare Timothy for the suffering that he, like Paul, would probably face. Now, to provide further encouragement, the apostle challenges Timothy to *remember Jesus Christ*. Jesus was *descended from* King *David*. Timothy, as a keen student of the Old Testament, knew some of the prophecies indicating that the Messiah would be a descendant of David. One of the most significant was this promise from God to David: "I will raise up your offspring to succeed you, who will come from your own body, and I will establish his kingdom. He is the one who will build a house for my Name, and I will establish the throne of his kingdom forever" (2 Samuel 7:12, 13).

At the heart of the *gospel* that Paul preached were the foundational truths that Jesus had died, was buried, and was *raised from the dead*. If Timothy were to face suffering or even death for the cause of Christ, he could find assurance in the fact that his Master had also suffered and died, yet the tomb could not hold him. Christ's resurrection gives a similar hope to every Christian.

### B. Paul's Example (vv. 9, 10)

**9, 10. . . . for which I am suffering even to the point of being chained like a criminal. But God's word is not chained. Therefore I endure everything for the sake of the elect, that they too may obtain the salvation that is in Christ Jesus, with eternal glory.**

Paul discusses the subject of *suffering* in other passages in this epistle (1:8, 12; 3:11, 12; 4:5). This does not suggest that Paul had some kind of psychotic fixation about suffering. He never implies that Christians ought to seek suffering for suffering's sake. He is trying to prepare Timothy and other Christians for the suffering that they are likely to face in the future. Paul was then *chained like a criminal*, awaiting execution as if he were a violent lawbreaker. Suffering had been and still was a fact of life for him.

Paul's play on words in this verse is noteworthy, and is conveyed in the English translation as well as in the original Greek. Although he had been *chained*, yet *God's word is not chained*. When Paul had been imprisoned the first time in Rome, he continued to teach and preach (Acts 28:23-31). His opportunities to do so were greatly restricted during his second imprisonment in Rome, but even there he was not completely silenced. Though in chains, he could still write to those outside, as this epistle shows. Furthermore, the word that he had proclaimed earlier was still loose in the world, touching the lives of people all across the Roman Empire. Men may bind the messenger, but the message continues to run free!

*I endure everything for the sake of the elect.* Again, Paul is not boasting of his efforts or exhibiting a "martyr complex." Rather, he is calling Timothy's attention to the higher purpose of suffering: that others might have the opportunity to receive *the salvation that is in Christ Jesus.* When viewed from the perspective of *eternal glory*, suffering for Christ is never in vain.

### No Reserves, No Retreats, No Regrets

In 1904 William Borden, heir to the Borden Dairy estate, graduated from a Chicago high school as a millionaire. As a graduation present, his parents gave him a trip around the world. Traveling through Asia, the Middle East, and Europe gave Borden a burden for the world's hurting people. Writing home, he said, "I'm going to

### What Do You Think?

The death and resurrection of Christ was central to the gospel message Paul preached (1 Corinthians 15:3, 4). The resurrection gives hope to every believer (1 Corinthians 15:19-22). The resurrection of Jesus is a unique claim among world religions. Because of the resurrection, Christians claim preeminence for Jesus as the only Son of God and the only way to God. Unbelievers react to this claim as exclusionary and intolerant—two of the greatest "sins" of this postmodern world.

What should believers do to reach out to those who are offended by the gospel's exclusive claims? Without compromising the gospel, how can we become "all things to all men" in this situation?

give my life to prepare for the mission field." When he made this decision, he wrote in the back of his Bible two words: "No Reserves." After graduating from Yale University, he continued to turn down high-paying job offers, entering two more words in his Bible: "No Retreats."

Following completion of his studies at Princeton Seminary, Borden sailed for China to work with Muslims there. While on the mission field, Borden was stricken with cerebral meningitis and died within a month. Many of his family and friends thought, "What a tragedy—such a promising young man, dying in a foreign place so far from home!" But shortly before he died, underneath the words "No Reserves" and "No Retreats," Borden had written in his Bible two more words: "No Regrets."

In 2 Timothy 2:3 Paul tells Timothy to "endure hardship with us like a good soldier of Christ Jesus." No matter what obstacles or hardships we may face, we must serve Christ with no reserves, no retreats, and no regrets. —C. B. Mc.

## C. A FAITHFUL SAYING (vv. 11, 12)

**11, 12. Here is a trustworthy saying: If we died with him, we will also live with him; if we endure, we will also reign with him. If we disown him, he will also disown us;**

These two verses, along with verse 13, have given rise to two different interpretations. Some see these verses as parallel to Paul's teaching in Romans 6:1-11, in which he spells out the significance of baptism. One who decides to become a Christian figuratively dies to sin and is symbolically buried with Christ in baptism. Then, just as Christ arose from the tomb, the Christian arises from his watery grave to walk in a new life with Christ. Such an interpretation would not be foreign to Paul's thought.

Others suggest that these verses are from an ancient Christian hymn. It is true that their structure seems poetic. The theme of this hymn is that those who suffer martyrdom for Christ's sake will be made alive in him and will reign with him. Since in the immediate context of these verses, Paul has been discussing suffering, this second view may be preferable.

## D. A FAITHFUL SAVIOR (v. 13)

**13. If we are faithless, he will remain faithful, for he cannot disown himself.**

The Scriptures affirm that God is *faithful* and that he cannot go back on his promises (1 Thessalonians 5:23, 24; 1 John 1:9). In this verse, however, the reference is to Jesus Christ. In his very character he shares in the faithfulness of his Father. Such faithfulness does not depend on our faithfulness. Even if we become faithless, he will not *disown himself*. What he has promised us he will provide. If we remain faithful, he has promised us eternal life. If we disown him, he has promised that he will disown us (Matthew 10:33).

## CONCLUSION

### A. HANG TOUGH!

When Paul wrote his second letter to Timothy, he was in prison facing execution because of his proclamation of the gospel. Paul knew that his death could present a rather serious test of Timothy's faith. Timothy, on learning of the death of his mentor and father in the faith, might be tempted to abandon his faith, or at least compromise his message so that it would be more acceptable to the Roman authorities. So Paul, instead of wallowing in self-pity, sent words of encouragement to Timothy. Simply put, his message was, "Hang tough!"

Timothy was urged to "endure hardship." These words apply equally to us today, but we often have difficulty in accepting them. We have tried to remove

---

### WHAT DO YOU THINK?

In recent years there has been a growing contempt expressed for what is referred to as "the religious right." When Christians uphold and promote absolute values such as the sanctity of life, the biblical view of marriage, and abstinence from sex outside of marriage, those who disagree paint us as judgmental and as enemies of personal rights. How similar do you think this is to Paul's suffering . . . like a criminal? Why? Do you know of cases that are more parallel, when Christians have been arrested for practicing their faith? If so, what? What do you think Paul would write to Christians who suffer this way today?

### WHAT DO YOU THINK?

Does 2 Timothy 2:11 mean that anyone who expects eternal life must be a martyr for Jesus? Why or why not?

See Galatians 2:20; Colossians 3:1-3.

## PRAYER

*We thank you, Father, that Christians who have lived before us were willing to suffer so that we today may enjoy the blessings of the faith. We pray that we may not have to face such suffering. But, Father, if suffering should be our lot, give us the strength to face it courageously as did Paul. In Jesus' name we pray. Amen.*

## THOUGHT TO REMEMBER

*"I consider that our present sufferings are not worth comparing with the glory that will be revealed in us"* (Romans 8:18).

## DAILY BIBLE READING

*Monday, June 9—Jesus' Suffering Foretold* (Luke 9:18-27)

*Tuesday, June 10—Christ Suffered for Us* (1 Peter 2:18-25)

*Wednesday, June 11—Suffer for Righteousness* (1 Peter 3: 13-22)

*Thursday, June 12—Be Proud to Suffer for Christ* (1 Peter 4:12-19)

*Friday, June 13—Rejoice in Suffering* (Colossians 1:24-29)

*Saturday, June 14—Suffering Produces Character* (Romans 5: 1-11)

*Sunday, June 15—God Is Our Comforter* (2 Corinthians 1:3-11)

the idea of hardship from our vocabulary and experience. Our culture has surrounded us with so many "creature comforts," that any suggestion that we break out of our cocoons and confront a hostile world sends shock waves through our systems.

We should also recognize that the lack of physical comforts is not the only source of suffering. Indeed, some of our most painful experiences result from "people problems." Many of us have been so conditioned to avoid anything that might be offensive to anyone that we are afraid to speak to others about the Lord and his kingdom. Or we so compromise our Christian commitment that no one will take offense.

We need to hear and heed Paul's challenge to Timothy. Most of us do not face situations where we are physically threatened for defending our faith, but we do live in a culture that is increasingly antagonistic to Christians who take the Bible seriously enough to try to live by its teachings. We often hear the challenge: "When the going gets tough, the tough get going!" Hang tough, Christians!

### B. PASSING THE BATON

In last summer's Olympic games, we watched runners, both individuals and members of relay teams, compete for honors. The relay teams that won the medals not only had to have fast runners; they also had to pass the baton from one member to another quickly and smoothly. The act of passing a baton may seem simple enough, but teams spend many hours practicing it in order to do it effectively.

Sharing our Christian faith with others is in some ways like passing the baton to the member of a relay team. Runners are often awkward at it the first time they try, but they gain experience through practice. So it is when we try to communicate our faith to non-Christians. Expert soul winners did not start out that way. They gained their ability through experience, and so must we.

Often when we try to share our faith, we fail miserably. We drop the baton. It is likely that members the Olympic medal-wining teams have all experienced at some time the frustration that comes from dropping the baton. But they refused to quit! They came back and practiced all the harder, and eventually became champions. Let us take courage and learn from them.

### C. WINNING IS THE ONLY THING

Vince Lombardi, who became a legend in football as coach of the Green Bay Packers, once remarked, "Winning isn't everything; it's the only thing!" Unfortunately, some have taken this to mean that one should do anything he can to win, ignoring whatever regulations exist. "Win at all costs" is the only standard many seem to know. Professional athletes have been fined and suspended for breaking the rules. Prominent universities have had their athletic programs restricted or even terminated because the pressure to win led them to violate rules and codes of ethics.

What has all this to do with our lesson today? Just this: Paul went all out to achieve victory for the Lord, and he expected other Christians to do the same. In his zeal to win, however, he insisted that we must compete *according to the rules* (2 Timothy 2:5). At times we may be tempted to take shortcuts in our efforts to advance the Lord's kingdom. In the past, men have mistakenly used military might, clever promises, or political pressure to accomplish this. When Satan tempted Jesus, he offered him shortcuts that would have allowed Jesus to establish his kingdom without having to confront the cross. Of course, Jesus resisted such temptations to "bargain" over his Father's will, and so should we.

# Discovery Learning

*This page contains an alternate lesson plan emphasizing learning activities. Classes desiring such student involvement will find these suggestions helpful. The next page is a reproducible activity page to further enhance discovery learning.*

## LEARNING GOALS

Having studied this lesson, each adult will be able to:

1. Enumerate Paul's basic exhortations to Timothy in this text.

2. Explain why suffering for one's faith is to be expected.

3. Serve Christ effectively in one's daily position or occupation.

## INTO THE LESSON

As class members arrive, hand each a small peel-and-stick label (name tags available at office supply stores will work well) with one of these words written on it: *soldier, athlete, farmer.* Attempt to use an equal number of each; these will be used to divide the class for a later activity.

Give class members the following list of "Reasons a Christian Should Expect and Accept Suffering." Direct the class to number the reasons from one to eight as "most significant" to "least significant". (Though the list is numbered here, if you reproduce it, do not number the entries.) (1) Suffering offers an example to others. (2) Christ suffered on our behalf. (3) Suffering builds personal faith and strength. (4) Suffering can strengthen and reinforce one's witness. (5) Paul and other first-century Christians suffered. (6) Suffering is only temporal. (7) Evil resents the presence of righteousness and always reacts to it with violence. (8) Suffering is evidence that one's witness is being noticed by the world. Do not expect complete agreement in these ratings. Briefly discuss the validity of the statements and the reasons the students give for their rankings. Ask if there are other statements that should be in the list.

## INTO THE WORD

Take some time to provide the background of 2 Timothy (use the Lesson Background on page 353). Mention how much Paul's surroundings had changed since the time he wrote 1 Timothy. Note that even though Paul was facing certain death when he wrote 2 Timothy, the letter begins with a reference to "the promise of life that is in Christ Jesus" (2 Timothy 1:1).

Divide the class into three groups, according to the stickers used earlier. (If groups exceed five or six each, consider splitting each group into two other groups.) Direct each group to make two lists: how the occupa-

tion on the sticker is an appropriate description of a Christian and how it is not. If your groups need assistance with this, use the lesson writer's insights in the commentary or suggest the following: (1) *Soldier*—must submit to the authority above him/must face the possibility of violence or death; (2) *Athlete*—must train and abide by the rules/considers a healthy body a priority; (3) *Farmer*—works hard/gets to enjoy the fruit of his work/suffers from the uncertainty of weather patterns. Add this directive: "Be sure to include the similarities that the Scripture text notes." Let the groups work for five minutes or so, then add this challenge: "Now select another occupation that might offer other comparisons with being a Christian. Make the same lists you have made for the three occupations mentioned by Paul." If your groups need help, offer these suggestions: *carpenter, fireman, electrician, stonemason, physician.* After four or five minutes, ask the groups to give their responses. As figures are identified, list them on the chalkboard or on poster board. (Suggest that your students develop this list on their own. Such consideration will keep the concepts of today's text in their minds. The "Into Life" activity is similar and can also be a part of such review and reinforcement.)

## OPTION

Use the reproducible page that follows to provide a guide to study today's text.

## INTO LIFE

Display the following incomplete statement: "Being a Christian is like being a _____." Ask each person to fill in his or her own vocation or position in life and then to consider the way(s) it is an appropriate symbol. For example, if one filled in *retiree*, he could say it is appropriate in that he is living on an investment made earlier, much as a Christian is living on an investment that *God* made earlier. If someone says *housewife*, she could make the comparison with the Christian life, since both involve caretaking, managing, and nurturing (plus a lot of hard work!).

Encourage your class members to continue developing their personal parallelism through the coming week. Lead in a closing prayer that each may use his or her position in life as a means of glorifying God and serving as an ambassador for Christ.

# Soldier, Athlete, Farmer

Paul uses three figures for the Christian walk in today's text: soldier, athlete, farmer. Decide in what way(s) each of the following *could* be a figure of the Christian life and ministry.

| ASTRONAUT | MAIL CARRIER | QUILT MAKER |
|---|---|---|
| SANITATION WORKER | HOMEMAKER | COMPUTER PROGRAMMER |

# Unbroken Chains

Verse 2 of this text pictures the basic process by which the gospel passes. How far can you go in a chain of those from whom you learned the gospel? Consider relatives, teachers, preachers, Bible college professors, and others.

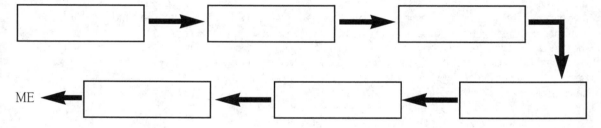

ME

The chain below can help you identify a statement about the gospel from today's text. Write the statement, one word per link.

God's Word is not chained.

## Guidance for Ministry
### (1 and 2 Timothy, Titus)
### (Lessons 1-5)

# CHRIST'S SERVANT TEACHES FAITHFULNESS

**LESSON 4**

Jun 22

## WHY TEACH THIS LESSON?

A good start is important to a runner. The determined runner will spend hours perfecting his or her start, hoping to gain a fraction of a second's advantage on the other runners. A good start is important, but they don't give any prizes for it. The prize comes at the finish.

This lesson is a reminder that, having made a start in our Christian life, we have done well. But we have not done all. We need to finish well, also. Paul's example was an encouragement to Timothy, and it is an encouragement to your students today, to finish the course.

## INTRODUCTION
### A. FAITHFUL UNTO DEATH

When Italy's Mount Vesuvius erupted in A.D. 79, the volcanic ash completely covered the nearby town of Pompeii. Centuries later the town was excavated. Among other finds, the archaeologists uncovered the remains of a Roman soldier standing erect at his post. Though his body has long since disintegrated, the impression of his body can be seen in the lava that surrounds him. His helmet, armor, and sword are still in place just as they were when he died. Many other inhabitants of the town escaped, and the soldier might have been able to escape had he been willing to leave his post. But he was willing to die rather than disobey his orders.

The apostle Paul displayed similar bravery. He was under orders to carry the gospel to the world. He was busy carrying out those orders when the persecution of Christians intensified. No doubt he could have gone into hiding and escaped the persecutors, but to do so would have meant betraying his Commander, Jesus Christ. That kind of faithfulness gave him a calm assurance as he faced death, knowing that there was a "crown of righteousness" awaiting him.

### B. LESSON BACKGROUND

In A.D. 64 Rome was swept by a terrible fire. The people blamed the emperor Nero for the inferno, and he, in order to shift the blame away from himself, accused Christians of the deed. Many of them were subsequently arrested and executed. Whether Paul was in Rome when he was captured we do not know, but he was held in prison in Rome awaiting his execution.

It is likely that Timothy was in Ephesus when Paul wrote 2 Timothy (that Timothy was there at the writing of 1 Timothy is clear from 1 Timothy 1:3). We may very well refer to the closing chapter of 2 Timothy as Paul's "farewell address." There we learn that except for Luke he was alone, everyone else having left him (2 Timothy 4:11). Some apparently had been sent away to carry out other tasks in the service of the Lord. A tragic note surrounds the absence of Demas who had forsaken Paul, "because he loved this world" (4:10). While urging Timothy to join

DEVOTIONAL READING
PHILIPPIANS 4:8-20

LESSON SCRIPTURE
2 TIMOTHY 4:1-18

PRINTED TEXT
2 TIMOTHY 4:1-8

### LESSON AIMS

After studying this lesson, each student should:

1. Summarize Paul's charge to Timothy to serve faithfully in his ministry, even as Paul had done to the very end.

2. Compare the responsibilities Timothy had with those faced by the student.

3. Respond to Paul's charge to Timothy with renewed commitment to faithfulness in ministry.

### KEY VERSES

I give you this charge: Preach the Word; be prepared in season and out of season.
—2 Timothy 4:1, 2

*LESSON 4 NOTES*

### WHAT DO YOU THINK?

*Paul made Timothy answerable to God for the "charge" he gave him (2 Timothy 4:1). Those who are ordained to the ministry certainly must consider that they are responsible to God for the fulfillment of the task to which they have committed themselves. In addition, however, every Christian has received a call to service for which he will be held accountable. What are the tasks or responsibilities for which Christians today are answerable to God?*

*See Matthew 5:14; 25:14-30; 28:19, 20; John 15:1, 2; Hebrews 13:17; 1 Peter 4:10.*

*The visual for lesson 4 asks, "How shall they hear without a preacher?" (Romans 10:14). Display it as the session begins. Call attention to it as you discuss verse 2. Discuss, "What do you think the man in the poster is thinking about? Is he a preacher thinking about the solemn charge here in verse 2? Is he considering becoming a preacher? Is he contemplating his financial commitment to world missions to send preachers where they are needed?"*

him in Rome and to come "before winter" (v. 21), Paul also encouraged his "dear son" (1:2) to remain faithful in his ministry.

## I. PAUL'S CHARGE TO TIMOTHY (2 TIMOTHY 4:1-5)

### A. AUTHORITY FOR THE CHARGE (v. 1)

**1. In the presence of God and of Christ Jesus, who will judge the living and the dead, and in view of his appearing and his kingdom, I give you this charge:**

Paul lays on Timothy the solemn *charge* of faithfully carrying out his ministry. This sacred responsibility is not based on any personal whim of Paul. It is made *in the presence of God and of Christ Jesus.* Thus it is based on the highest authority available.

When the Lord Jesus came into the world the first time, he came as Savior, "to seek and to save what was lost" (Luke 19:10), "to give his life as a ransom for many" (Matthew 20:28). When he comes the second time, he will come as judge. Numerous passages in the New Testament declare that Jesus *will judge* the world when he returns (Matthew 25:31-33; John 5:22, 25-27; Acts 10:40-42; Romans 2:16; 2 Corinthians 5:10).

Of course, the roles of Savior and Judge are intertwined. He is one because he is the other. When he was on earth as Savior, he often pronounced judgment on sinners, especially the Pharisees and legal experts. When he returns as Judge, it will mean the ultimate salvation of those who have believed in him. "Just as man is destined to die once, and after that to face judgment, so Christ was sacrificed once to take away the sins of many people; and he will appear a second time, not to bear sin, but to bring salvation to those who are waiting for him" (Hebrews 9:27, 28).

Both those who are *living* when Jesus returns and those who are already *dead* will be subjected to his judgment. The *appearing,* or return, of Jesus will signal the consummation of Christ's *kingdom.* All Christians are in that kingdom now (Colossians 1:13), but they look forward to its magnificent, heavenly fulfillment (2 Timothy 4:18; 2 Peter 1:10, 11).

### B. FIVE IMPERATIVES (v. 2)

**2. Preach the Word; be prepared in season and out of season; correct, rebuke and encourage—with great patience and careful instruction.**

Paul specifies five ways Timothy is to be faithful to his charge. The first is basic to the other four—that is, without the first, the other four are meaningless. The primary command is to *preach the Word.* This phrase may also be translated, "herald the Word" or "proclaim the Word publicly." A herald is under orders to proclaim a message just as he has received it. To argue, debate, or change it is not his prerogative.

The command *be prepared in season and out of season* speaks of Timothy's preparation to preach the Word. He should be prepared at all times to serve as God's herald. One commentator has rendered this, "Be on duty at all times." In the front lines, a soldier is not entitled to any vacations or time off. Certainly Timothy was in a combat zone, surrounded by a hostile world that seemed intent on silencing the gospel. Every Christian worker knows from experience that there are times when people appear receptive to the gospel; at other times they are completely negative and unresponsive. "Never mind the situation," Paul advises Timothy. "Proclaim the good news at all times."

The herald is to make his proclamation clear enough so that his hearers will understand the message. He is also to *correct* any misunderstandings they might have. In a world that has little or no understanding of true Christianity, we need to exercise the same care in presenting the message of salvation.

The term *rebuke* indicates stronger action than correcting. It urges one to refute error when it arises. This was no minor matter; elsewhere in this epistle Paul mentions a number of errors creeping in among the believers (2:14, 16-18, 23; 3:5-8).

Timothy is also to *encourage* his listeners to respond to the gospel and to apply it to their lives in such a way that changes are obvious. To know the truth is not enough; we must live the truth for it to be effective. Timothy's role is not just to be sure people know the Word, he is to provide that gentle encouragement characteristic of Barnabas (Acts 4:36) to motivate them to action.

Timothy is to carry out these mandates *with great patience and careful instruction*. He is to exercise patience with those under his care. Probably no advice to a preacher, elder, deacon, or teacher is more important than this. Some people may be slow to accept some of the obligations attached to the gospel message. There may be any number of misconceptions or assumptions that have formed a "wall" in the thinking of an individual. And so the teacher must be patient, teaching and encouraging, modeling and explaining, until the lessons finally sink in. Furthermore, he must not neglect sound doctrine in his teaching. Many today would try to separate Christian life and doctrine, insisting that a fruitful life is more important than doctrine. But a Christian life-style must be built on a foundation of sound doctrine, else it will collapse in times of stress.

### IT IS ALWAYS TOO EARLY TO QUIT

Paul instructed Timothy to carry out his ministry in all situations with "great patience" (2 Timothy 4:2), even to the point of enduring "hardship" (v. 5). Paul's words echo numerous biblical teachings on the necessity of perseverance.

In Luke 18 Jesus tells the story about a persistent widow who finally received justice from an unjust judge because she continually confronted him with her request. Jesus told his disciples this story "to show them that they should always pray and not give up" (Luke 18:1). In Luke 11:5-8 Jesus tells about a persistent man who woke up his neighbor in the middle of the night to borrow three loaves of bread. From behind a locked door, the neighbor refused and told the man to go away. However, said Jesus, because the man persisted in his request for bread, the neighbor got up and gave him as much as he needed.

We should remember that in ministry, as in baseball, stopping at third base adds no more to the score than striking out at the plate. When you are doing God's work, it is always too early to quit.

Never, never give up.

—C. B. Mc.

## C. BEWARE OF FALSE TEACHERS (vv. 3, 4)

**3, 4. For the time will come when men will not put up with sound doctrine. Instead, to suit their own desires, they will gather around them a great number of teachers to say what their itching ears want to hear. They will turn their ears away from the truth and turn aside to myths.**

Some think that the phrase *the time will come* refers to the "last days" mentioned in 3:1. It must be recognized, however, that a lack of *sound doctrine* has always been a problem against which the church has had to struggle. Acts 20:29, 30 records Paul's words to the elders of the church at Ephesus, warning them that "even from your own number men will arise and distort the truth in order to draw away disciples after them."

The response described in these verses is one often encountered by God's messengers. Isaiah met with a similar reaction when his hearers, stung by his preaching, responded, "Give us no more visions of what is right! Tell us pleasant things, prophesy illusions" (Isaiah 30:10). We still have our share of church members who prefer to have their ears tickled, their wrongs approved, and their egos stroked.

### WHAT DO YOU THINK?

*Timothy was to correct, rebuke, and encourage (2 Timothy 4:2). Under what circumstances are you willing to receive a word of correction or rebuke from your minister? From what other person or persons would you accept a word of rebuke? On what conditions or under what circumstances?*

*See Matthew 18:15-17; Galatians 6:1, 2.*

*Do you think you could give a word of rebuke or correction in a loving and positive way? Why or why not?*

### WHAT DO YOU THINK?

*Our culture certainly has its share of myths competing with the truth of the gospel. To what extent does each of the following myths challenge the message and mission of the church? What inroads into the church itself has each made? What does the church need most to do to address each myth?*

- *"You only go around once, so grab all the gusto you can!"*
- *New Age philosophy.*
- *Humanism*
- *"Truth is relative."*

## WHAT DO YOU THINK?

What "hardships" are common to the ministry in today's churches? How can you help your minister or ministers cope? What about those serving in volunteer ministries—what hardships do they face? What can you do for them?

## HOW TO SAY IT

Barnabas. *BAR-nuh-bus.*
Demas. *DEE-mus.*
Judaizers. *JOO-duh-IZE-ers.*
Nero. *NEE-roe or NIHR-o.*
Pompeii. *Pom-PAY.*
semper fidelis (Latin). *SEM-per fuh-DAY-lus.*
Vesuvius. *Vuh-SOO-vee-us.*

## D. ENDURE AFFLICTIONS (v. 5)

**5. But you, keep your head in all situations, endure hardship, do the work of an evangelist, discharge all the duties of your ministry.**

The behavior of Timothy's fickle audience is now contrasted with the behavior Paul expects from Timothy. Although Timothy may encounter stiff resistance to his preaching, he is to carry on his *ministry*, even as Paul's own ministry is coming to an end.

*Keep your head in all situations.* We might speak of "keeping your cool" no matter what happens. This is sound advice, especially for a church leader who finds himself surrounded by frustrating problems.

The phrase *endure hardship* repeats the instructions Paul had given earlier (2 Timothy 2:3; recall lesson 3, page 354). Paul urges Timothy to toughen himself against the trials and tribulations, both mental and physical, that he would have to endure.

*Do the work of an evangelist.* The work of an evangelist is to share the good news of salvation with sinners in order to bring them into a saving relationship with Jesus Christ. Ephesians 4:11 regards this as a specific office, including it among the tasks of apostles, prophets, pastors, and teachers. While some may indeed be specially gifted for this responsibility, evangelism should be the concern of every Christian.

### DEEP WATER

It is interesting that in his instructions to Timothy, Paul says, "endure hardship" and, "do the work of an evangelist" in the same breath (2 Timothy 4:5). Evangelism is often hard work.

Luke tells about the day Jesus called his disciples from their boats and nets by the Sea of Galilee to follow him. They had been fishing all night but had caught nothing. Jesus said, "Put out into deep water, and let down the nets for a catch" (Luke 5:4).

When these fishermen followed the Lord's instructions and cast their nets in the deep water, they caught such a large number of fish that their nets began to break. When they called for another boat to come and help them, both boats became so full of fish that they began to sink. Afterward, Jesus told Simon Peter that from then on he and his partners would catch men.

Evangelism, or "fishing for men," often requires us to launch out into deep water. Sometimes it can stretch our nets to the breaking point. Ask anyone involved in a rapidly growing church. Reaching and teaching new people is a challenge. But Jesus calls us to "do the work of an evangelist" and to join him in the great adventure of fishing for men.

—C. B. Mc.

## II. PAUL'S ACCEPTANCE OF DEATH (2 TIMOTHY 4:6-8)

### A. HIS DEPARTURE IS AT HAND (v. 6)

**6. For I am already being poured out like a drink offering, and the time has come for my departure.**

Perhaps the Roman government had set the date for Paul's execution, or God may have given Paul a special revelation that his death was imminent. This added an extra measure of urgency to Paul's advice to Timothy.

*I am already being poured out like a drink offering.* This interesting figure calls to mind certain practices under the Old Testament Law. Numbers 15:1-10 states that when an animal was offered on the altar, a vessel of wine was poured out beside the altar as the final act of the sacrificial ceremony. Timothy, who had been taught the Old Testament by his mother and grandmother, would appreciate this striking figure. By its use here, Paul is indicating that the final act of his personal sacrifice had begun. Earlier Paul had stated that Christians' whole lives ought to be considered "living sacrifices" (Romans 12:1). Now, even as Paul had offered his life to Jesus, he offers his death in one final expression of devotion.

## B. He Has Finished His Course (v. 7)

**7. I have fought the good fight, I have finished the race, I have kept the faith.**

Here, as in his other writings, Paul uses language drawn from the athletic arena and from the battlefield. The phrase *fought the good fight* probably would have called the attention of Paul's readers to a wrestling or boxing match, or perhaps a contest between gladiators. The participants in these events strained every muscle to gain victory and avoid defeat. This was especially true of the gladiators' competition, where defeat might very well mean death.

In fighting the good fight, Paul had many opponents. Satan and his cohorts were the primary foes. Satan had used a variety of people and situations to try to overwhelm and frustrate Paul. His own people, the Jews, tried several times to take his life, and the Judaizers, who wanted to make the laws of Moses binding on Gentiles, created serious problems in many churches. Paul often struggled against the presence of worldliness, divisiveness, and false teaching. Even among his friends he experienced conflict (as his dispute with Barnabas about John Mark indicates) and betrayal (as the example of Demas, mentioned in verse 10 of this chapter, demonstrates). In addition to all these conflicts, he constantly worked hard to keep himself from becoming spiritually careless and straying into the category of "disqualified" (1 Corinthians 9:27).

Yet in this lifelong struggle against numerous opponents, Paul had never quit and had never given less than his best. When he affirms that he has fought the good fight, he is not bragging. This is a fact.

*I have finished the race.* For Paul, life was not only a fight, it was also a race to be completed. We are reminded of the language used in Hebrews 12:1: "Therefore, since we are surrounded by such a great cloud of witnesses, let us throw off everything that hinders and the sin that so easily entangles, and let us run with perseverance the race marked out for us." Now the apostle prepares to cross the finish line and receive the reward that is promised to all who have completed their race.

*I have kept the faith.* Paul may be referring to his faithful proclamation of the gospel. He had not been intimidated into silence by his foes, nor had he compromised the gospel when threatened by them. Paul may also be alluding to his own personal commitment to the Lord. After his conversion in Damascus, the Lord had called him to become an apostle to the Gentiles. He was warned that accepting this call would mean much suffering (Acts 9:15, 16). Knowing this, Paul still accepted the call, and from that point on he never looked back.

## C. The Crown Awaits Him (v. 8)

**8. Now there is in store for me the crown of righteousness, which the Lord, the righteous Judge, will award to me on that day—and not only to me, but also to all who have longed for his appearing.**

The word rendered *crown* does not refer to symbol of royalty, worn by one with an inherent right to it. Paul cannot claim this crown because it is his right, but only by the grace of God. The righteousness is not Paul's but that of the Lord Jesus Christ (Philippians 3:9). Paul's crown came, not as a reward for his efforts, but as a gift from *the Lord, the righteous Judge.*

A simple laurel wreath was awarded to a victorious athlete in the ancient Olympic games. While its intrinsic worth was negligible, symbolically its value was immeasurable. The *crown of righteousness* was much more than a simple wreath of leaves. It symbolized eternal life (Revelation 2:10), and would never wither or fade, as the athlete's crown eventually would.

Whereas in most races there is only one winner, in the race of life there are many winners. Paul has no exclusive claim on the crown, but it is reserved for *all who have*

### WHAT DO YOU THINK?

Marathon runners speak of hitting a "wall" in the race where the temptation to give up is intense. If the runner can get through that wall, he or she has a good chance of being able to finish.

What are some "walls" we face in running the race of the Christian life? What causes temptation to give up? How can we run through these walls so that we, like Paul, can someday say, "I have finished the race"?

## PRAYER

*Dear Lord, help us give heed to Paul's example as we strive to live lives that will be pleasing to you. Give us knowledge and courage in this effort. Above all, help us come to life's close with a spirit of triumph. In the name of the Lord of life, even Jesus. Amen.*

## THOUGHT TO REMEMBER

*"For to me, to live is Christ and to die is gain"* (Philippians 1:21).

## DAILY BIBLE READING

**Monday, June 16**—*The Lord's Laws Are Forever (Psalm 119:89-96)*

**Tuesday, June 17**—*Praise the Lord for His Faithfulness (Psalm 31:19-24)*

**Wednesday, June 18**—*Faithful in Spite of Trials (2 Timothy 4:9-18)*

**Thursday, June 19**—*Be Faithful As God's Child (Romans 8:12-17)*

**Friday, June 20**—*Be Faithful Over Small Things (Luke 16: 1-13)*

**Saturday, June 21**—*The Lord Requires Faithfulness (Deuteronomy 10:12-22)*

**Sunday, June 22**—*Faithfulness Will Be Rewarded (1 Peter 5:1-11)*

*longed for his appearing;* that is, for those who look forward to Christ's return. What a triumphant note to sound in the face of certain death!

## CONCLUSION

### A. IT IS INEVITABLE

Occasionally we hear people say that the only things certain in this life are death and taxes. For many persons this is only a half-truth, for there are a few situations under which one may avoid paying taxes. *Every* person who has ever lived, with the rare exceptions of Enoch and Elijah, has had to face death.

In spite of death's inevitability, our culture has attempted to remove it from any serious consideration. Of course, we read or hear about death every day in our newspapers and on our televisions, but for most of us those incidents remain nothing more than dramas played out on the tube, remote from our snug little worlds. In previous generations people died at home, not in hospitals, and funerals were community affairs that almost everyone attended. It is not unusual today to find college-age persons who have never attended a funeral; if they have, it has probably been the funeral of a family member. Many parents have the notion that they need to shield their children from the harsh realities of life, especially death.

The Bible speaks often about death, and we need to help people learn the biblical view of it. Today's lesson has given us a brief glimpse of the apostle Paul, who, after a life of faithful service to the Lord, could calmly face his approaching death without fear or remorse. For Paul, death was not the end, but was, instead, a graduation to a higher realm. His was not some vain, empty hope that one grasps in desperation as death approaches. It lay at the very foundation of the apostle's unshakable faith: "Death has been swallowed up in victory. Where, O death, is your victory? Where, O death, is your sting?" (1 Corinthians 15:54, 55).

### B. "SEMPER FIDELIS"

The motto of the United States Marine Corps is "semper fidelis," which means "Always Faithful." This might also have served as the apostle Paul's motto. Many years earlier he had made a life-changing decision. He was transformed from a persecutor of Christians to a proclaimer of Christ. The honors that he had gained as a devout Jew became nothing but garbage to him after his conversion. Once that decision had been made, he held to it without wavering for the rest of his life.

Such unwavering faithfulness seems strangely out of place in our age. We live in a time that makes easy compromise a virtue and waffling an art form. What was the key to Paul's tenacity? First of all, he knew what he believed, or more precisely, *whom* he believed. Second, he had clear-cut goals for his life. He knew that Christ had called him to become an apostle to the Gentiles. He knew that Christ had commissioned his followers to carry the gospel to the "ends of the earth" (Acts 1:8). Paul could not rest until the Lord's orders, sweeping though they were, had been carried out. Third, Paul surrounded himself with comrades who shared his views, and who, with few exceptions, remained as faithful as Paul himself.

Paul's life serves as a sterling example for us today. Like him, we must know whom we believe. This involves more than just an academic belief in Jesus; it means that we must accept him as Lord of our lives. Like Paul, we must have definite goals in life. God has a plan for every one of us, "to be conformed to the likeness of his Son" (Romans 8:29). Let us pursue it with uncompromising vigor. Finally, like Paul, we need to surround ourselves with fellow Christians who will provide help and support when we are tempted to compromise or turn back. May our motto become "semper fidelis"—always faithful—to Jesus.

# Discovery Learning

*This page contains an alternate lesson plan emphasizing learning activities. Classes desiring such student involvement will find these suggestions helpful. The next page is a reproducible activity page to further enhance discovery learning.*

## LEARNING GOALS

After studying this lesson, each student should:

1. Summarize Paul's charge to Timothy to serve faithfully in his ministry, even as Paul had done to the very end.

2. Compare the responsibilities Timothy had with those faced by the student..

3. Respond to Paul's charge to Timothy with renewed commitment to faithfulness in ministry.

## INTO THE LESSON

Begin today's session by asking, "Has anyone ever been to an ordination service for a minister?" It is likely that some have. Ask what those who have witnessed such a service found most impressive or meaningful about it. Point out that most ordination services include a section known as a "charge" (if you can secure a bulletin from an ordination service, it should include a place where the charge is to be presented). Ask the class to define a charge and to tell what it should include. Explain that a charge to a new minister is a challenge often delivered by someone who has been especially close to the person being ordained or has been a strong spiritual influence.

Lead into today's Scripture observing that Paul gave to Timothy a "charge" in the concluding chapter of 2 Timothy—Paul's final letter to his "son" in Christ. This charge contains much that is timely for today's Christian leader. His words are important to those of us who follow, too.

## INTO THE WORD

Provide a brief review of the background of 2 Timothy, noting that Paul is writing from a Roman prison. His death is imminent—a fact that will become especially clear in today's Scripture.

Read (or have someone read) 2 Timothy 4:1-8, then divide the class into two groups. Provide each group with one of the following sets of questions for discussion. Have each group designate a reporter who will summarize the group's answers when you reconvene.

*Group One: The Message.* This group will focus on Paul's challenge to Timothy in verse 2 by considering the following questions:

1. What does "Preach the word" mean? How does this command apply to Christians who do not "preach" from behind the pulpit? What are some ways that the church can fulfill this command?

2. Discuss the words *correct, rebuke, encourage.* What does each mean? Why are all of these important? What happens in a church if too much attention is given to correction and rebuke without encouragement? What if too much attention is given to encouragement without correction and rebuke?

*Group Two: The Man.* This group will discuss Paul's challenge in verse 5, using the following questions:

1. What are some "hardships" that church leaders today may frequently "endure"? How are these similar to or different from those that Timothy would have faced?

2. What is "the work of an evangelist"? Is this a paid position? Why or why not? If so, what would such a person do? Isn't evangelism something for all Christians to do? How can our church better carry out this task?

Be sure to move between the groups to offer any insights or answer questions that arise. Use the material in the lesson commentary as needed. Then, after fifteen to twenty minutes, bring the groups together and have each group's reporter summarize its answers.

## INTO LIFE

Many refer to these verses as "Paul's last words," and appropriately so, as Paul realizes he is about to die. He includes both last words concerning himself and last words for his son in the faith. Give each person in the class a sheet of paper, and tell them to fold the sheet to create two columns to be headed "*I*" and "*YOU.*" Direct students to review Paul's convictions about himself (for example, "I have fought the good fight" and "There is in store for me the crown") and then write statements (under "*I*") regarding themselves and their understanding of, or preparation for, death. Also direct them to review Paul's challenge to Timothy and to write similar statements (under "*You*") that they would choose to leave for those working in Christ's service. Suggest they put these sheets in their Bibles. During the coming week, they should reflect on how their life and example demonstrate faithfulness.

Close with a time of silent prayer. Focus on thanking God for the hope we have in Christ and for the difference that it makes in our outlook on the future.

## OPTION

Use the reproducible activity "Contrasting Values" on the next page to apply this lesson to life.

# Picture This!

Each of the following small pictures is designed to represent a phrase or verse from today's text. By each, put the verse number or write the phrase.

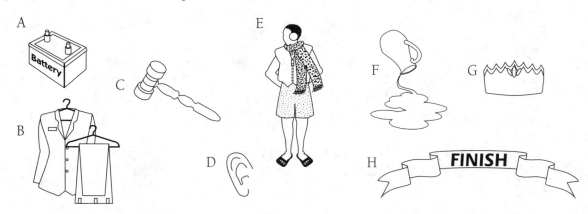

A — Battery

B

C

D

E

F

G

H — FINISH

# Contrasting Values

Finish each of the following statements. Use thoughts from today's text.

| The person of God knows that some will. . . . | But he or she will: |
|---|---|
| . . . select teachers who tell them what they want to hear. | |
| . . . turn aside to myths. | |
| . . . drop out of the race. | |
| . . . dread Christ's coming. | |
| . . . lose their heads in everyday conflict. | |
| . . . receive nothing valued at their deaths. | |

| | | | |
|---|---|---|---|
| A. v. 1. "I give you this charge" | E. v. 2. "in season and out of season" |
| B. v. 3. "to suit" | F. v. 6. "being poured out" |
| C. v. 1. "Judge the living and the dead" | G. v. 8. "the crown of righteousness" |
| D. v. 3. "what their itching ears want to hear" | H. v. 7. "finished the race" |

# CHRIST'S SERVANT ENCOURAGES COMMUNITY

## LESSON 5

## WHY TEACH THIS LESSON?

If Charles Colson is right, the world is about to see "the arrival of the mother of all crime waves." Citing statistics from the bipartisan Council on Crime in America, Colson warns in a *Wall Street Journal* editorial (February 24, 1996), "By the year 2000, the huge increase in 14- to 17-year-old males will cause violent crime to 'spiral out of control.'"

If this crime wave is to be prevented, it will not happen by the addition of more police and the building of new prisons. It will come by a renewed sense of community, people working together for the common good. Only the church can offer that vision, if it will.

This lesson could be the first step in just such a move. Challenge your students to see the need for all Christians to "devote themselves to doing what is good"—starting with them!

## INTRODUCTION

### A. AN AMBASSADOR OF THE KING

J. Hudson Taylor, founder of the China Inland Mission, was once making a trip to a town in China that he had never visited before. On his way he came to a river, and since there was no bridge, he bargained with a man in a boat to ferry him across. Taylor paid the man and was just ready to step aboard when another man rushed forward, pushed him aside, and started to step onto the boat. Taylor, who had a quick temper, started to shove the rude intruder into the river. Then he stopped and gently tapped the man on the shoulder.

"Sir," said Taylor, "I have already hired this man and his boat to take me across the river. But if you would be willing to be my guest, I would be happy to have you accompany me."

The man was so surprised by Taylor's offer that he questioned him as they crossed the river: "Why did you invite me aboard after I treated you so rudely?"

"Sir," Taylor replied, "I am on a mission for King Jesus, and so I must behave as one of his ambassadors."

"Who is this King Jesus?" asked the man. "I have never heard of him." That was all the invitation that the missionary needed to witness to the man about Christ. It has always been the case that even the smallest acts of love and kindness can open up opportunities for witnessing that we could never have imagined.

### B. LESSON BACKGROUND

The epistle to Titus was apparently written some time between Paul's release from his first imprisonment in Rome in A.D. 63 and his second imprisonment there in A.D. 67. We know little about Titus himself. Although he accompanied

DEVOTIONAL READING
ROMANS 13:1-10
LESSON SCRIPTURE
TITUS 3:1-11
PRINTED TEXT
TITUS 3:1-11

Jun 29

LESSON AIMS

*After studying this lesson, each student will be able to:*

*1. Summarize what Paul told Titus about proper Christian behavior toward those in the church and in the community.*

*2. Use the verses in today's text to confront and counter beliefs or actions that are improper for Christians.*

*3. Plan some specific plan of action to "devote themselves to doing what is good."*

KEY VERSE

*And I want you to stress these things, so that those who have trusted in God may be careful to devote themselves to doing what is good. These things are excellent and profitable for everyone.*

Titus 3:8

**LESSON 5 NOTES**

Paul on some of his missionary travels, Titus is not even mentioned in the book of Acts. He was heavily involved in the work in Corinth and must have served as a link between Paul and the church, keeping Paul informed of the church's condition (2 Corinthians 2:12, 13; 7:6, 13-15). In 2 Corinthians 8:23, Paul refers to Titus as "my partner and fellow worker among you." Titus is also mentioned in Galatians 2:1-3, in connection with Paul's stand for Christian liberty in the face of false teachers. There Paul notes that Titus was not "compelled to be circumcised" (v. 3).

At the time of the writing of Paul's letter to Titus, Titus was serving on the Mediterranean island of Crete (Titus 1:5). Paul had first visited Crete during his voyage to Rome (Acts 27:7-12), but at that point he had not had the opportunity to carry on any evangelistic work. Later, after Paul's house arrest in Rome was ended, he was able to stop at Crete and witness the work being done. When he departed, he left Titus there to continue the ministry, straightening "out what was left unfinished" and appointing elders in every city (Titus 1:5). In Paul's final letter of 2 Timothy, Paul writes that Titus has gone "to Dalmatia" (4:10), which is part of modern Croatia.

## I. A CHRISTIAN'S BEHAVIOR (TITUS 3:1, 2)

### A. TOWARD GOVERNMENT (v. 1)

**1. Remind the people to be subject to rulers and authorities, to be obedient, to be ready to do whatever is good.**

*Remind* in the Greek is literally, "Keep on reminding." Christian teaching is not something that is done once and is then completed. It is an ongoing process, not only for new students who may be hearing such teaching for the first time, but also for the most mature Christians, who still need frequent reminders of their responsibilities.

Specifically, Titus needed to remind the believers in Crete about their duty *to be subject to* the governing civil *authorities*. Paul had addressed this subject earlier (Romans 13:1-7). Thus far, the Roman government had not severely persecuted Christians. The time was approaching, however, when the emperor Nero would unleash his fury against the Christians in Rome. Other more severe and widespread persecutions would soon follow. Paul was helping Titus to prepare the Christians in Crete for this coming storm, when they would be called upon to obey officials who were determined to destroy the church. Of course, Paul is not suggesting that Christians give absolute and unquestioning support to governments—even governments that are generally favorable to Christianity. Whenever the laws of man violate the laws of God, the Christian must choose to obey God (see Acts 5:29).

In the context, the phrase *be ready to do whatever is good* probably refers specifically to a Christian's relationship to government. We might see it as a limitation on the command to obey—do whatever is good in obedience but not what is evil. It certainly has a more general application, however. Under all circumstances, Christians are to *do whatever is good* in all circumstances. Such action is right in the eyes of God and also bears witness of Christ to unbelievers.

## WHAT DO YOU THINK?

*Paul's teaching about submitting to the government is repeated in Romans 13:1, 2: "Everyone must submit himself to the governing authorities, for there is no authority except that which God has established . . . he who rebels against the authority is rebelling against what God has instituted."*

*At what point, if any, is rebellion against a godless government the right thing to do? (Remember, the Roman government was increasing its opposition when Paul write to Titus. Within four years it would execute the apostle.) Is the example of Peter and John in Acts 418-20; 5:28, 29 a model for any more than specific acts of disobedience? Why or why not?*

### SEEK THE PEACE OF THE CITY

In 597 B.C. Nebuchadnezzar and his Babylonian army invaded Jerusalem. They took King Jehoiachin of Judah prisoner, plundered the temple, and carried off some ten thousand captives to spend the rest of their lives in a foreign land. Four months later, following a nearly one-thousand-mile journey, the Jewish exiles entered Babylon.

Although the Jews may have been tempted to withdraw from such a pagan society, God gave a different set of instructions to his people through the prophet Jeremiah: "Also, seek the peace and prosperity of the city to which I have carried you into exile. Pray to the Lord for it, because if it prospers, you too will prosper" (Jeremiah 29:7).

Like the Jews in Babylon, we Christians have been called to be a positive influence on our surroundings—to be in the world but not of it. Unlike them, Christians in democratic societies have a far greater opportunity to set the moral direction of their nation and its government. As citizens we choose the national, state, and local legislators who make our laws. We select the representatives, governors, mayors, and other officials who administer those laws. We set the course of our judicial system by electing judges, or those who appoint them. We should seek to use these privileges to fulfill our Lord's command to be the salt and light of our surroundings.

—C. B. Mc.

## B. TOWARD OTHERS (v. 2)
**2. . . . to slander no one, to be peaceable and considerate, and to show true humility toward all men.**

The word translated *slander* is the root for the word *blaspheme or blasphemy*. To blaspheme, in our use of the word, is to speak evil of God, but the original was used of other people as well. This is language that intends to do a person harm. Such language does not have to be false for it to be damaging. The truth deliberately told to hurt someone can be even more devastating than lies. Of course, there are exceptions to this prohibition. A person asked to give a recommendation for another, or a witness under oath in court must tell the truth, even though it may harm the individual in question. The motive behind what we speak is all-important.

The word *peaceable* reminds us of the admonition in Hebrews 12:14: "Make every effort to live in peace with all men and to be holy." Being *considerate* and humble are all but lost in too many parts of our society, but such behavior agrees with Scripture elsewhere: "Do nothing out of selfish ambition or vain conceit, but in humility consider others better than yourselves. Each of you should look not only to your own interests, but also to the interests of others" (Philippians 2:3, 4).

Obedience to such a comprehensive commandment is possible only through God's grace and the renewing of the Holy Spirit. These are themes to which Paul now turns.

## II. A CHRISTIAN'S TESTIMONY (TITUS 3:3-7)
### A. ONCE A SLAVE (v. 3)
**3. At one time we too were foolish, disobedient, deceived and enslaved by all kinds of passions and pleasures. We lived in malice and envy, being hated and hating one another.**

The modern psychologist might diagnose Paul as having a bad self-image. He might even accuse the apostle of tearing down the self-image of his readers, with whom he identifies with the word *we*. But Paul is not concerned with image; he is stating the pure facts. If the "image" looks bad, it does so because it is compared with the image of God, who is utterly pure and holy. This stark contrast is what makes grace so necessary, and that is the matter to which Paul will turn next.

The sins listed here cover a broad range, including sins against God, against self, and against other persons. The picture of a person so enmeshed in sin contrasts starkly with that of a person who has been redeemed by grace.

NOTE

See pages 280 and 281 for more on the word slander/blasphemy.

WHAT DO YOU THINK?

The people of Crete, where Titus was serving, had a reputation for being "liars, evil brutes, lazy gluttons" (Titus 1:12). Yet Paul told the Christians there to be "considerate" and "show true humility toward all men" (Titus 3:2) What would keep the unbelievers from taking advantage of such gentle people? How can we protect ourselves from being used and taken advantage of if we are considerate and gentle with everyone?

## What Do You Think?

*Paul reminds Titus that we Christians were like the pagans once, "foolish, disobedient, deceived and enslaved by all kinds of passions and pleasures. We lived in malice and envy, being hated and hating one another." That changed, not by anything we did, not because we are better than others, but by the grace of God. How, then, would you respond to someone who says, "Christians think they are better than anyone else"? How can we live in such a way as to keep from having such an accusation made?*

## What Do You Think?

*Why is it that the myth that one is saved by being "good enough" persists? Why do some Christians even seem to think they are saved by some combination of grace and good works? How can we teach the truth in a clear and convincing way?*

### B. Saved Through God's Love (v. 4)

**4. But when the kindness and love of God our Savior appeared,**

Even though man had fallen into the depths of sin and disgrace, God did not give up on him. He showed his matchless *kindness and love* by sending his Son into the world to die for us. "While we were still sinners, Christ died for us" (Romans 5:8). Such love is beyond our understanding, but we are not required to understand all that occurred at the cross. We are challenged to believe and accept the fact that what happened there was done on our behalf.

### C. Not by Works (v. 5a)

**5a. He saved us, not because of righteous things we had done, but because of his mercy.**

Earlier in his ministry Paul had confronted and resisted the Judaizers, who taught that Gentiles must become obedient to the Law of Moses before they could be considered true Christians. Paul emphatically rejected this doctrine, as well as any teaching that advocated salvation by works rather than by grace. This is most clearly taught in Romans and Galatians. Throughout its history, however, the church has been plagued by variants of this heresy that somehow we can be saved by our good works. The good works prescribed have differed from age to age, but the idea persists that there exists a set of scales in Heaven that God will use in administering judgment. As long as our good works outweigh the bad, we are "in."

*He saved us...because of his mercy.* The idea that we are saved by grace seems too good to be true. Yet that is exactly what this verse states. "Amazing Grace," we sing, and rightly so, for this is the very heart of God's wonderful plan of salvation.

### D. Through Regeneration (vv. 5b, 6)

**5b, 6. He saved us through the washing of rebirth and renewal by the Holy Spirit, whom he poured out on us generously through Jesus Christ our Savior.**

*The washing of rebirth* refers to Christian baptism, which brings a penitent believer into the fellowship of the church. Paul uses similar language in speaking of Christ's relationship to the church: "to make her holy, cleansing her by the washing with water through the word" (Ephesians 5:26). Jesus also addressed this matter in speaking to Nicodemus: "no one can enter the kingdom of God unless he is born of water and the Spirit" (John 3:5). Baptism is much more than just a ceremony or ritual. It marks the beginning of the new life in Christ; it is a time of *rebirth*.

*The Holy Spirit* is the One who brings about our *renewal* or rebirth when we accept Christ. Baptism and receiving the gift of the Holy Spirit were shown to be connected in the first gospel sermon, preached on Pentecost (Acts 2:38). When one is "raised" to "live a new life" (Romans 6:4; Colossians 2:12), it is the Spirit that empowers that life. The Spirit then becomes actively involved in the process, by which one who has experienced rebirth continues to grow toward maturity in Christ. That the Holy Spirit was *poured out on us generously* may mean that God has given us a generous portion of the Holy Spirit. It may also mean that the Holy Spirit assists us in many different ways in the process of Christian growth.

### E. The Hope of Eternal Life (v. 7)

**7. . . . so that, having been justified by his grace, we might become heirs having the hope of eternal life.**

To be *justified* means that we are declared not guilty. In the legal system one can be justified by proving he or she is innocent or that extenuating circumstances make the act permissible. Neither of these options is available to us as we face a holy God. It is only *by his grace* that we are declared "not guilty." We thus escape the penalty of death accompanying our sins because Christ suffered that penalty for us at the cross. Because we are justified, we have *the hope of eternal life*. Though we may be tested and sorely tempted during the storms of life, this hope serves as a guiding lighthouse, providing direction through the turbulence. When everything about us seems to be falling apart, such hope can give us the calming assurance that we need.

## III. A CHRISTIAN'S FAITHFULNESS (TITUS 3:8-11)

### A. DOING GOOD WORKS (v. 8)

**8. This is a trustworthy saying. And I want you to stress these things, so that those who have trusted in God may be careful to devote themselves to doing what is good. These things are excellent and profitable for everyone.**

*This is a trustworthy saying.* Paul uses this expression several times in the Pastoral Epistles to emphasize a particular point (1 Timothy 1:15; 3:1; 4:9; 2 Timothy 2:11). In this case he is probably calling attention to the teachings he has just set forth in verses 3-7. But the expression could also apply to the words that follow, for the emphasis Paul makes on good works in the succeeding verses would certainly constitute a *trustworthy saying.*

To some, Paul might seem to be contradicting himself within the verses we are studying. In verse 5 he rejected "works of righteousness" as a basis of salvation, yet in this verse he urges believers *to devote themselves to doing what is good.* But there is really no contradiction. As Christians we do not do good works in order to be saved, but because we are saved. A person who has been saved by God's grace feels joy and gratitude toward God. It is only natural that he or she wants to share that joy and gratitude with others. What better way to do this than to help others?

*Doing what is good* includes more than works of benevolence. It includes every aspect of a noble life-style. The Christians on the island of Crete lived in a world steeped in paganism. (See Paul's description of the people in Titus 1:10-13.) It was important that the believers set good examples for those about them. Even though pagans might condemn the Christians for their religion, it was important that the life-style of believers be above reproach.

We live in an increasingly pagan world, and, like those Christians in the first century, we need to live so that those about us will observe a clear difference. One of the serious problems the church faces today is that most non-Christians cannot tell any significant difference between the way Christians live and the way pagans live. We would do well to take heed to Paul's words. In a world that has all kinds of needs, a Christian should have no trouble finding a place where he may give his service to the glory of God. Often a good work need be nothing more than a kind word to one who is discouraged, or a listening ear to one whose heart is burdened. Any congregation should be able to recognize opportunities for its members to become involved in various demonstrations of *doing what is good.*

### B. AVOIDING FALSE DOCTRINE (vv. 9-11)

**9. But avoid foolish controversies and genealogies and arguments and quarrels about the law, because these are unprofitable and useless.**

*Foolish controversies* refers to all kinds of fruitless discussions in which Christians sometimes engage. These deliberations are foolish because they have nothing to do with vital issues in living the Christian life. For example, we may think of the great energy and countless hours that were wasted by many scholars in the Middle Ages, arguing about how many angels could dance on the head of a pin.

The *quarrels about the law* apparently dealt with matters concerning the Jewish law. Probably most of the Christians on Crete came from Gentile backgrounds. But

## PRAYER

Dear Lord, we pray for your guidance as we try to live lives that are pleasing to you in a world that is becoming increasingly hostile to your kingdom. Help us to walk wisely and humbly, knowing that we are saved by grace, not by our good works. Through our Master we pray. Amen.

## THOUGHT TO REMEMBER

Although our home is in Heaven, our present responsibilities are on earth.

## DAILY BIBLE READING

Monday, June 23—Avoid Disputes (2 Timothy 2:14-19)

Tuesday, June 24—Support Faithful Workers (Philippians 4:10-20)

Wednesday, June 25—Teach Sound Doctrine (Titus 2:1-8)

Thursday, June 26—Teach With Authority (Titus 2:9-15)

Friday, June 27—Forgive One Another (2 Corinthians 2:5-11)

Saturday, June 28—All Are Guilty Under the Law (Romans 3:9-20)

Sunday, June 29—All Are Justified by God's Grace (Romans 3:21-31)

the Jewish influence was evidently widespread enough to create problems within the church.

The reference to *genealogies* likely reflects the fondness of many Jewish teachers for taking an individual from a list of names (such as one finds in the lists of descendants in Genesis) and composing a story around that person. Such efforts only served to draw attention away from the true, God-ordained purpose of Scripture.

**10, 11. Warn a divisive person once, and then warn him a second time. After that, have nothing to do with him. You may be sure that such a man is warped and sinful; he is self-condemned.**

A *divisive person* is one who creates controversies and quarrels over issues that are unprofitable, as noted in the previous verse. When such controversies disrupt the peace of the church or hinder its efforts to evangelize, then the troublemakers must be dealt with. In so doing they are to be confronted patiently and lovingly, not in an arbitrary or heavy-handed way. Such persons are to be admonished twice, according to Paul's counsel. The purpose is to save them if at all possible, to not expel them. Jesus outlined a similar approach to handling situations where one brother has sinned against another (see Matthew 18:15-17).

Church discipline of this sort is, for several reasons, rarely administered today. Certainly it should not be administered arbitrarily. It should be reserved for only the most serious cases, involving one who is *warped and sinful.*

Of course, a division demands two sides, and its not always easy to know which side is the one that is "divisive." Some in the church want to change an old tradition and some resist. Who is divisive: the changers or the resisters? Often as not, the answer is both. When warning a "divisive person," take care that the one giving the warning is not equally divisive!

## CONCLUSION

Paul presents to Titus a picture of what a servant of Christ ought to be: a gentle person who is devoted to doing good to those about him. At first glance the emphasis seems to be on personal virtues, which may appear to clash with the lesson title, "Christ's Servant Encourages *Community.*" But there is no conflict here. To suppose that we can build a solid community or a stable society except upon a foundation of upright individuals is sheer folly. Our society is in serious trouble because we have ignored this obvious truth. We have spent billions of dollars trying to eliminate poverty, supposing that if we created a better environment, we would automatically create better people.

Two thousand years ago, Paul knew that the corruption that had permeated the Roman Empire could be eliminated only one way. A law-abiding citizen who shows gentleness and meekness toward his fellow men, who avoids the lusts of the flesh, and who gives himself to good works, all because he has been given new life in the Lord, will provide a firm foundation for a stable society. The same holds true concerning changing our surroundings today. Passing laws and appropriating money may at times be helpful, but if we truly hope to change our society for the better, we must realize that this will happen only when the hearts of people are changed.

In such a setting, the message of the gospel could not be more timely. When people experience the "washing of rebirth" and the "renewal by the Holy Spirit," then they will come to know the "hope of eternal life." What is more, they will help make ours a kinder, gentler, and safer society.

Too often, however, the church's message to society is lost in the bitter words shouted at others *within* the church. The church will have no influence to rebuild community in the neighborhood if the church itself is filled with division. That is the reason Paul warns against tolerating a "divisive person."

# Discovery Learning

*This page contains an alternate lesson plan emphasizing learning activities. Classes desiring such student involvement will find these suggestions helpful. The next page is a reproducible activity page to further enhance discovery learning.*

## LEARNING GOALS

After studying this lesson, each student will be able to:

1. Summarize what Paul told Titus about proper Christian behavior toward those in the church and in the community.

2. Use the verses in today's text to confront and counter beliefs or actions that are improper for Christians.

3. Plan some specific plan of action to "devote themselves to doing what is good."

## INTO THE LESSON

Before class write the following on your chalkboard or on a large poster:

DO WHATEVER BE GOOD READY IS TO

Divide the class into small groups and ask each group to try to unscramble the sentence. After a few minutes, see what the groups came up with. The correct response is, "Be ready to do whatever is good."

Note that this is a statement from today's Scripture text. It sums up the message for Christians as they look at their relationships with other believers and with unbelievers. Just as Jesus was known for going about doing good, so should we. It is the only hope for our troubled world!

## INTO THE WORD

Have each of the following series of statements prepared on a separate card. Ask for volunteers to stand and read them. Distribute the cards and allow a couple of minutes for your readers to review their assignments. While they do that, direct the rest of the class to listen to each reading and identify a verse in today's text that addresses in some way the comments made. Then have the statements read in no particular order.

Following are the readings. Verses are noted in parentheses after each statement, but these should not be on the cards—or, at least, should not be read.

(1) "This new city leash law for dogs is stupid! No way am I going to drag my little Fifi around by the neck!" (v. 1)

(2) "Those Smiths down the street are low-life scum who live like pigs. Their yard's a mess. Their car's a disgrace." (v. 2)

(3) "You know this UFO thing? I'm convinced those aliens are up to no good. What about you?" (v. 9)

(4) "A person's got to stand up for himself. If I've got to get angry and lash out, I'll get angry and lash out!" (v. 2)

(5) "I don't need a preacher or anyone else to keep reminding me of what I'm supposed to do and not to do. I'm an adult!" (v. 1)

(6) "Well, I know Johnson's come and gone regarding his faith several times. But everybody deserves one more chance. I say we make him a deacon." (v. 10)

(7) "Why shouldn't I go to Heaven? I think I've been pretty good, and I've done a lot of things here at church over the years" (v. 5)

(8) "If I had half the money Elder Jones has, I'd give a lot more to the church. He ought to share some of that with the rest of us. If I had it, I would." (v. 3)

Call the students' attention to Titus 3:4-7. You may want to write these verses on the chalkboard or on an erasable marker board. Have your group read the verses together. Take a few moments to discuss the meaning of the words *rebirth*, *renewing*, and *justified*, using the lesson commentary as needed. These words convey some very crucial doctrines.

## OPTION

Use the reproducible activity "Searching for Change" on the next page to facilitate your study of today's Scripture text.

## INTO LIFE

Read Titus 3:8, in which Paul stresses the importance of *doing what is good* in the life of a Christian. Ask, "Why are good works so important to 'maintain,' as Paul states in this verse? How do you resolve the apparent contradiction between this verse and verse 5?" Use the material in the lesson commentary under verse 8 to help explain the critical relationship between verses 5 and 8.

Now ask, "What are some examples of 'doing good' in which we as a class could participate as a class project?" Make a list of these ideas, based on both church needs and community needs. Try to be as creative and imaginative as possible. If interest in a specific project seems to surface, meet later with interested class members to pursue this. Encourage the class to devote a few moments at the beginning of each class period to monitoring the progress of their project. Be sure to stick with it!

## OPTION

Use the reproducible activity "Building Community" on the next page to help with application of the text.

# Searching for Change

Titus 3:1-11 pictures the drastic differences the gospel has made in our lives. In the puzzle grid below find seven attributes of the former nature; list these to the left. Then find seven attributes of the Christian nature; list them to the right.

| AT ONE TIME<br>WE WERE | | BUT NOW<br>WE ARE |
|---|---|---|

```
T H E K S U O I V N E I N D
N C E S S A N D L V O V E E
O F O G O D T H I E K I N N
D N E N S S A S N D L S O O
H V E L S O S F G O L D B T
D U T H U I E K I A O N E N
D N M E M F D E V O T E D E
S S A B N D E E G L L O I I
V H U E L O D T R B F G E D
O S D T H E E K A A I N N E
D I N E S S A E N H T D T B
L L S U O I C I L A M E O O
V O E O F A G O D T H E K S
I O N D E N E S S A N D L I
O F V P E O D E V I E C E D
```

The unused letters in the puzzle repeat the phrase Paul says, in verse 4, made the difference. Write the phrase here:

_____ _____ _____ _____ ____ _____ Indeed, that makes all the difference in the world—and in the world to come!

# Building Community

What in today's text could you use to deal with a brother or sister who . . .

. . . argues that the Sabbath regulations are required of the Christian on Sunday?

. . . insists that bad laws should be intentionally ignored?

. . . likes to discuss the flaws and seeming flaws in an immature brother/sister in Christ?

. . . maintains one must continually forgive and fellowship with one who continuously creates division in the body?

Left side: foolish, disobedient, deceived, enslaved, malicious, envious, hateful. Right side: obedient, peaceable, considerate, humble, submissive, good, devoted. Unused letters: The kindness and love of God

# JESUS IS GOD'S SON

**LESSON 6**

## WHY TEACH THIS LESSON?

"Anything you can do, I can do better. I can do anything better than you!" From childish playground arguments to classic Broadway musicals, this argument goes on and on. But there is one who can make that claim without argument or contradiction. The Son of God is better—period. Today's lesson shows he is better than the prophets, better than the angels, even better than Moses, the great lawgiver of Israel. He is God's Son.

The practical implications of that truth are at the heart of what you want your students to grasp today. God himself summed up the matter on the Mount of Transfiguration" "This is my Son, whom I love; with him I am well pleased. Listen to him!" (Matthew 17:5). Let this lesson be a time when you and your students "listen to him!"

## INTRODUCTION

### A. COMMUNICATING WITH ANTS

A Christian and an atheist were once discussing the existence of God. The atheist offered this challenge: "If there is a God like the one you claim to worship, how could he possibly communicate with us? His intellect would be so vastly superior to ours that we couldn't begin to understand him." As they walked along, they came to an anthill. "Look at those ants," said the atheist. "How could we possibly speak to them in a way that they could understand us? Why, we would have to become an ant and live among them to be able to speak to them!"

"You are quite correct," responded the Christian. "And that's exactly what God did. When he wanted to speak to us in a way that we could really understand, he sent his Son as a man."

### B. LESSON BACKGROUND

The first five lessons of this quarter, drawn from 1 and 2 Timothy and Titus, dealt with the topic, "Guidance for Ministry." Today's lesson begins a two-unit section entitled, "A Call to Faithfulness," based on the book of Hebrews. The first four lessons in this unit develop the theme, "The Greatness of Christ." In August we'll consider the challenge to "Be Faithful Followers of Christ."

While most of the epistles of the New Testament begin by identifying the writer, Hebrews is quite different. In fact, it begins more like a tract than a letter. The writer is not identified. This has led to abundant speculation as to the author's identity; among the most frequent suggestions are Paul, Apollos, and Barnabas. On the other hand, the destination of the book seems certain: it was directed to Jewish, or Hebrew, Christians. Exactly where these believers lived is yet another mystery. Some scholars suggest Palestine, while others believe the book was destined for Alexandria (in Egypt) or Rome.

These questions concerning the book's authorship and destination should not be allowed to detract from its great value to us. Hebrews is both a theological treatise and a guidebook for practical Christian living. Christians today can find valuable instruction and encouragement from both of these emphases.

**DEVOTIONAL READING**
HEBREWS 1:6-14
**LESSON SCRIPTURE**
HEBREWS 1:1–3:6
**PRINTED TEXT**
HEBREWS 1:1-5; 3:1-6

## LESSON AIMS

By completing this study, students will:

July 6

1. Explain how Jesus the Son is superior to prophets, angels, and Moses.

2. Refute specific doctrinal errors, using today's text.

3. Resolve to remain firm in their commitment to follow and serve the Lord Jesus Christ

## KEY VERSE

Therefore, holy brothers, who share in the heavenly calling, fix your thoughts on Jesus, the apostle and high priest whom we confess. He was faithful to the one who appointed him.     Hebrews 3:1, 2

**LESSON 6 NOTES**

The visual for lesson 6 illustrates Hebrews 1:1, 2. Display it as you begin the session.

**WHAT DO YOU THINK?**

In the past God spoke through the prophets, but now he has spoken through his Son. How would you respond if a fellow Christian said, "That means we don't need the Old Testament anymore—all we need are the words of Jesus in Matthew, Mark, Luke, and John"? What value are "the prophets" now that we have the "final word" in Jesus?

(Be sure to consider the "prophets"—i.e., inspired men—who wrote the New Testament, too.)

**WHAT DO YOU THINK?**

Our text says Jesus is the "exact representation of [God's] being. Paul told the Philippians that Jesus is "in very nature God." How is this identification of Jesus with God important to your faith? How would you answer one who said Jesus was merely a prophet—like Moses or Elijah?

## I. JESUS IS SUPERIOR TO PROPHETS AND ANGELS (HEBREWS 1:1-5)
### A. SUPERIOR TO THE PROPHETS (vv. 1, 2)
**1. In the past God spoke to our forefathers through the prophets at many times and in various ways.**

A fundamental proposition of Christianity is that God has spoken to man. That revelation has come *at many times*. Since the writer was addressing Hebrew Christians, who were familiar with the Old Testament, they would immediately call to mind how God spoke to Adam in the Garden of Eden, how he called Abram from Ur of the Chaldeans, and how he thundered forth his commandments on Mount Sinai. They would also remember how he used various spokesmen, called *prophets*, to speak to kings and to the people at large. *Prophet* does not primarily mean one who predicts the future, but one who speaks for another—in this case, for God. The Hebrews referred to their Scriptures (the Old Testament) as "the Law and the Prophets." All inspired writings can be said to have come *through the prophets*.

The phrase *in various ways* highlights the many different ways in which God spoke to man. Sometimes he spoke in audible words. On other occasions he spoke through dreams, visions, signs, or miracles. The prophets frequently use expressions such as, "This is what the Lord says," "The word of the Lord came to me," and "Hear the word of the Lord," indicating that God communicated directly with them.

**2. But in these last days he has spoken to us by his Son, whom he appointed heir of all things, and through whom he made the universe.**

Frequently the Bible divides the history of God's redemptive work into two segments of time. The Old Testament era is considered the "former days." The New Testament era, beginning with Christ's first coming and ending with his return, is viewed as the *last days*. For other uses of this phrase and similar terminology in the New Testament, see Acts 2:16, 17; 1 Corinthians 10:11; Hebrews 9:26; 1 Peter 1:20; and 1 John 2:18. While we do not know when Jesus will return, we know that when he does come back, he will judge the nations (Matthew 25:31-33). We need to pay special attention to God's message for the *last days*, just as the Hebrew Christians did. This message is found only in *his Son*.

Jesus has been *appointed heir of all things*. We are not to think of this inheritance as one in which the father must die before the son can receive it. This expression indicates the close relationship of the divine Son to the heavenly Father. One aspect of this kinship is the Son's participation in the creation of *all things*. This doctrine is stated, not only in this verse, but in other New Testament passages as well (see John 1:1-3; 1 Corinthians 8:6; and Colossians 1:14-17). *All things* will one day come under the dominion of Jesus, and then of the Father, when Jesus returns (1 Corinthians 15:24-28).

### B. EQUAL WITH THE FATHER (v. 3)
**3. The Son is the radiance of God's glory and the exact representation of his being, sustaining all things by his powerful word. After he had provided purification for sins, he sat down at the right hand of the Majesty in heaven.**

The writer expresses the Son's relationship to the Father through a series of striking phrases. The Son is *radiance of God's glory*. Translators have struggled to find a way to express this idea in English. The *Revised Standard Version* uses "he reflects the glory of God," but this is unsatisfactory because it suggests Jesus is something less than God, as the moon "reflects" the light of the sun but has no light of its own. The *New English Bible* has "the effulgence of God's splendour," but how many people know what *effulgence* means? The Father and the Son, though distinct personalities, share the same radiant glory. John 1:14 tells us, "The Word became flesh and made his dwelling among us. We have seen his glory, the glory of the One and Only, who came from the Father, full of grace and truth."

The unity of the Father and the Son is also expressed in the next phrase: *the exact representation of his being.* We think of representation as a process where one person or thing stands for another, someone or something different from the representative. This is not quite accurate in this case. Jesus represents God to man because he is God, who took on human flesh. Philippians 2:6 tells us Jesus is "in very nature God." Hear Jesus' own words: "Anyone who has seen me has seen the Father" (John 14:9).

The Son is described as the Creator, even as God is Creator. Genesis 1:1 says, "*God* created the Heavens and the earth." John 1:3 says "Through him ["the Word," i.e., Jesus] all things were made; without him nothing was made that has been made." The Son is the Creator.

Furthermore, the Son is described as *sustaining all things by his powerful word.* To the Colossians Paul wrote that through Jesus, "all things hold together" (Colossians 1:17). He is not only our Creator; he is also our Sustainer.

The Son came to earth for the purpose of purging, or cleansing us, to provide *purification for sins.* Once this was accomplished by his death on the cross, he returned to his proper place *at the right hand of the Majesty in heaven.*

## C. SUPERIOR TO ANGELS (vv. 4, 5)
**4. So he became as much superior to the angels as the name he has inherited is superior to theirs.**

*Angels* were held in high regard by the ancient people. The Jews especially held them in esteem because of their participation in the giving of the Law at Mount Sinai (Acts 7:53; Galatians 3:19). They were obedient servants of God. Yet the Son was superior to any of the angels, not only because of his obedience in carrying out God's will in human redemption, but because of the divine inheritance that belonged exclusively to him as the Son.

**5. For to which of the angels did God ever say, "You are my Son; today I have become your Father"? Or again, "I will be his Father, and he will be my Son"?**

The writer of Hebrews quotes from the Psalms five times in this first chapter, one of those occurring in this verse. The book of Psalms was the hymnbook used in the Jewish synagogue. When Jews became Christians, they no doubt continued to use these songs in their worship. Thus, these quotations would strike a familiar chord with them. This one is taken from Psalm 2:7.

The second half of the verse contains a quotation from 2 Samuel 7:13, 14, where God promised that David's seed would be given an everlasting kingdom. The writer of Hebrews declares its fulfillment to be in Jesus Christ. When God proclaimed Jesus to be his *Son,* he declared Christ to be superior to the angels. No angel was ever entitled to be addressed in this manner.

### LORD, LIAR, OR LUNATIC?
The great confession that sets a Christian apart from adherents to other religions is that *Jesus Christ is God's Son.* Throughout history, unbelievers have attempted to portray Jesus as something other than the Son of God or to define that expression as meaning Jesus was something less than divine. Many will readily accept him as a good man or a great teacher, but not as God in the flesh. The problem with such an approach is that Jesus never left any of those options open to us.

In John 5:25 and 11:4, Jesus referred to himself as "the Son of God." Jesus said that to know him is to know God (John 8:19). He said that to believe in him is to believe in God (John 14:1). He said that to receive him is to receive God (Mark 9:37).

## WHAT DO YOU THINK?
If Jesus were just one of thousands of angels, or if he were any part of the created order, he would not be unique, and his intercession for us would not satisfy the claims of justice against sinners. The fact that Jesus was and is the unique and perfect Son of God—God incarnate—and that he laid down his life for unworthy sinners, makes his story not just good news but great news.

It's great news, but it also puts certain demands on us, doesn't it? What obligations or responsibilities do you feel because of Jesus' unique role of God incarnate and the sacrifice for our sin?

### How to Say It

Abram. AY-brum.
Apollos. Uh-POLL-lus.
Barnabas. BAR-nuh-bus.
Chaldeans. Kal-DEE-unz.
Darius. Duh-RYE-us.
effulgence. ih-FUL-junts.
Elijah. Ee-LYE-juh.
Levitical. Lih-VIT-ih-kul.
Melchizedek. Mel-KIZ-eh-dek.
Ur. Er.

### What Do You Think?

Jesus is described in our text as "the apostle and high priest" (Hebrews 3:1). These terms indicate his role of being "sent out" with a mission of redemption, offering the sacrifice of himself for sin. The Hebrews were familiar with these word pictures, so the language was clearly understood.

What original word pictures might you suggest if you were trying to explain the unique role of Christ to someone unfamiliar with biblical terminology? Explain the word pictures you suggest.

When Philip said, "Show us the Father," Jesus answered, "Anyone who has seen me has seen the Father" (John 14:9). Jesus continually equated a person's attitude toward him with that person's attitude toward God.

C. S. Lewis stated the issue this way: "A man who was merely a man and said the sort of things Jesus said would not be a great moral teacher. He would either be a lunatic—on a level with the man who says he is a poached egg—or else he would be the Devil of Hell. You must make your choice. Either this man was, and is, the Son of God: or else a madman or something worse. You can shut him up for a fool, you can spit at him and kill him as a demon; or you can fall at his feet and call him Lord and God. But let us not come up with any patronizing nonsense about his being a great human teacher. He has not left that open to us. He did not intend to."

—C. B. Mc.

## II. JESUS IS SUPERIOR TO MOSES (HEBREWS 3:1-6)

In the closing verses of chapter 1, the writer of Hebrews uses other Old Testament quotations to support his argument that Christ is superior to the angels. His readers needed such teaching, because chapter 2 indicates that they were becoming somewhat lax in their commitment. He urges them to "pay more careful attention, therefore, to what we have heard, so that we do not drift away" (v. 1). He warns about neglecting "such a great salvation" (v. 3). In the later verses of chapter 2, he deals with the incarnation of Christ, explaining that he had to be "made a little lower than the angels," so that he could suffer and die for our sins (v. 9). Thus he became our "merciful and faithful high priest" (v. 17).

### A. A Faithful High Priest (vv. 1, 2)

**1. Therefore, holy brothers, who share in the heavenly calling, fix your thoughts on Jesus, the apostle and high priest whom we confess**

Christians have been made *holy* by the sacrificial death of Christ. This special relationship to Jesus identifies them with Jesus and with each other as *brothers*. Together they *share in the heavenly calling*, a calling that originated *in* Heaven and directs people *to* Heaven.

The word *apostle* means "one who is sent out." We think immediately of the twelve whom Jesus sent out with the good news of the gospel, and of the apostle Paul, who was sent to the Gentiles with the same message. Here it is applied to *Jesus*, whom God sent into the world to bring salvation (see John 20:21).

Christ is also our *high priest*. Under the Law of Moses, the high priest was an intermediary between God and man. One of his duties was to offer sacrifices to God, as prescribed by the Law. The Jewish readers of this letter would be quite familiar with this function. According to the Law, the high priest had to come from the tribe of Levi. This meant that Jesus, since he was from the tribe of Judah, was not eligible to be a priest under the Old Covenant (Hebrews 7:14). However, Jesus' priesthood was not of the Levitical order, but of the order of Melchizedek—that mysterious priest who appears rather suddenly in the Old Testament to bless Abram after his victorious return from battle (Genesis 14:17-20).

**2. He was faithful to the one who appointed him, just as Moses was faithful in all God's house.**

The place of Moses in Jewish history is hard to overestimate. His roles in the founding of the nation, in providing the Law, and in leading the people to the promised land confirm his faithfulness. Though reluctant at first, Moses was faithful in fulfilling the task God called him to do. Moses was declared by God to be faithful (Numbers 12:7).

Jesus, too, was faithful. He said he came not to do his own will, but the will of the One who had sent him (John 6:38). Later in Hebrews we read, "When Christ came into the world, he said: . . . 'Here I am . . . I have come to do your will, O God'" (10:5-7). Jesus, too, was faithful to his task, and without hesitation.

## B. THE BUILDER IS SUPERIOR TO THE BUILDING (vv. 3, 4)

**3, 4. Jesus has been found worthy of greater honor than Moses, just as the builder of a house has greater honor than the house itself. For every house is built by someone, but God is the builder of everything.**

Although both Moses and Christ were faithful in their duties, Christ was *worthy of greater honor than Moses*. The writer uses the analogy of a *house* and its *builder* to make his point. A house that is both sturdy and attractive is worthy of honor, but the individual who built the sturdiness and attractiveness into the house is worthy of *greater honor*.

The writer then proceeds to apply his analogy to Moses and Christ. The *house* that Moses built was the Hebrew nation. At the same time, Moses himself was a part of that house and a part of the vast universe created by *God, the builder of everything*. Earlier in this lesson we learned that Jesus the Son participated with God in the creative process. Thus, as the builder, he is superior to others (such as Moses) who are but parts of that building.

## C. THE SON IS SUPERIOR TO THE SERVANT (vv. 5, 6)

**5, 6. Moses was faithful as a servant in all God's house, testifying to what would be said in the future. But Christ is faithful as a son over God's house. And we are his house, if we hold on to our courage and the hope of which we boast.**

Here the writer continues to affirm the superiority of Jesus to Moses. Moses was but a *servant in all God's house*. Note the prepositions used in the verse: Moses served *in* God's house, but Christ is *over* his house. As a faithful servant, Moses was given considerable responsibility, yet he still remained only a servant. Christ is superior because *as a son* he exercises authority over the servants in God's house. Moses' ministry prepared for the superior ministry of Jesus and the New Covenant that he would establish.

With the phrase *we are his house*, the writer now turns from his theological discussion to its practical implications. Christians are now Christ's *house*. They became his house by the process of believing in and obeying him. That relationship, however, is a conditional one. It is in force only as long as *we hold on* in our faith and obedience. This warning is in harmony with the major thrust of the book of Hebrews, which is to encourage Jewish Christians to stand firm in their new faith rather than return to the Judaism they had left. To abandon Christianity is to abandon their *hope*.

### GREATER THAN MOSES

He was raised in Pharaoh's house. He was quite possibly an adopted heir to the throne of Egypt. He was skilled in all the arts, languages, and wisdom of one of the greatest nations of the ancient world.

Yet God had an even greater calling for Moses. He led an entire nation out of bondage in Egypt. He became recognized as Israel's lawgiver, having received God's commandments on Mount Sinai. These were written down in what came to be the first five books of the Bible, or "the Law of Moses."

When the day of God's deliverance of Israel came, he sent Moses to confront Pharaoh. At that time Egypt was at the pinnacle of her power and influence in world affairs. Pharaoh himself was considered a god by his own people. No other king could match the strength of his armies or his wealth. When Moses strode into Pharaoh's court to demand, "Let my people go," he was confronting the most powerful man on earth.

## WHAT DO YOU THINK?

The concept of hope in the New Testament is much stronger than the vague sense implied by our usual use of the term. Hope is confident expectation, not just a mere wish. It is based on the reliability of the God who promises, for he cannot lie.

The text says, "We are his house, if we hold on to our courage and the hope of which we boast." Of course, this does not suggest we who have hope should boast arrogantly in the face of those without hope! It suggests a confidence that encourages us in the face of difficulty.

In what situations has your hope in Christ given you courage to go on? How do you demonstrate your hope in Jesus—God incarnate, superior to prophet, angel, and even Moses—in practical situations?

## PRAYER

*Gracious God, we praise you for Jesus Christ, your divine Son, who he is the Creator and Sustainer of the universe. Thank you that he has made atonement for our sins, and that even now he sits at your right hand. Amen.*

## THOUGHT TO REMEMBER

*If Christ is not divine, every impulse of the Christian world falls to a lower octave.*

—Henry Ward Beecher

## DAILY BIBLE READING

*Monday, June 30*—Christ Is Eternal (Hebrews 1:5-14)

*Tuesday, July 1*—Christ Is Over All (Ephesians 1:15-23)

*Wednesday, July 2*—Christ Has Come From God (John 8: 37-42)

*Thursday, July 3*—Christ, Son and Heir of God (Galatians 4:1-7)

*Friday, July 4*—To Know Christ Is to Know God (John 14:1-11)

*Saturday, July 5*—Confess Christ As God's Son (1 John 4:13-21)

*Sunday, July 6*—Christ Has Come to Do God's Will (John 6:35-40)

Without question, Moses was the greatest figure of the Old Testament. Yet Moses was only a man—an extraordinary man for certain, but still just a man. In these latter days, the writer of Hebrews says, God has spoken to us through one far greater than Moses: his own Son. With power, wisdom, and glory far beyond that of Moses, Jesus came to make of us what no one else could: a people prepared to live for eternity with God.

—C. B. Mc.

## CONCLUSION

### A. WHO'S IN CHARGE?

One of the decisive battles of the ancient world pitted Alexander the Great against Darius III, king of Persia. Darius had carefully selected the site of the battle—a level plain where he could most effectively deploy his cavalry and chariots. His forces outnumbered Alexander and the Macedonians four or five to one. To strike fear into the hearts of his enemies, Darius lined up his troops in battle array the night before the battle and reviewed them by torch light. The ploy seemed to work, for Alexander's generals came to him in a state of panic. Some urged a retreat, while others suggested a surprise attack by night. To the latter suggestion Alexander supposedly replied, "I will not steal a victory. We will attack in the morning as planned!" The generals were then sent back to their tents for a good night's rest, reassured that they had nothing to fear. The attack was carried out according to plan, and it was so successful that Darius fled from the field of battle. The Macedonians were victorious because they knew Alexander was in charge. They had enough confidence in him to follow him wherever he led them.

In today's world, the forces of evil seem to be winning against the forces of good on every hand. We seem to be hopelessly outnumbered. But before we flee in panic or resort to foolish tactics born out of desperation, we need to stop and consider who is in charge. Christ Jesus is our Commander and *he* is in charge! This lesson has reminded us that he "made the universe," and that he upholds "all things by his powerful word." Knowing this, we can enter the battle with renewed confidence, realizing that temporary losses will not alter the fact that the ultimate victory belongs to him and his kingdom.

### B. "WHAT DO YOU THINK ABOUT THE CHRIST?"

The writer of Hebrews makes a concerted effort to convey what the deity of Christ encompasses. Rather than try to offer a detailed analysis of Christ's deity, he demonstrates that Jesus is far superior to any other means by which God has communicated his message to mankind.

First of all, we are told that Christ is God's final revelation to us. In earlier ages God spoke through the prophets, whose messages prepared the way for Jesus to come as the culmination of all that they prophesied. We are told also that Jesus is the "heir of all things." Furthermore, Christ was active with God in the creation of all things, and with God he continues to sustain all things.

Second, as noble as the angels might be, Christ is superior to them. He is our great high priest. Through his death on the cross, he has purged us of our sins, and now he sits at the right hand of God in a position of absolute authority.

On one occasion Jesus asked the Pharisees, "What do you think about the Christ? Whose son is he?" (Matthew 22:42). Unwilling to acknowledge him as the Son of God, they called him David's son. We, on the other hand, are quick to affirm with our lips that Jesus is God's Son, but with our actions we often deny what our lips affirm. The Pharisees stood condemned for their unbelief. Can we expect to escape similar condemnation for our practical denial?

# Discovery Learning

*This page contains an alternate lesson plan emphasizing learning activities. Classes desiring such student involvement will find these suggestions helpful. The next page is a reproducible activity page to further enhance discovery learning.*

## LEARNING GOALS

By completing this study, students will:

1. Explain how Jesus the Son is superior to prophets, angels, and Moses.

2. Refute specific doctrinal errors, using today's text.

3. Resolve to remain firm in their commitment to follow and serve the Lord Jesus Christ

## INTO THE LESSON

Recruit seven men to act out the events of Matthew 17:1-8 for the class. (Use men from the class or bring in some "extras." Bible costumes are great, but simply pinning an index card on each actor with his character name on it is sufficient. Of course, the one who does the voice of God will not need a card—he should be "off stage.")

After the drama, point out that Moses and Elijah were outstanding Old Testament characters. Representing "the Law and the Prophets," they stand for all that God communicated to his people throughout the Old Testament era. These were great men!

But God declares that Jesus is greater. Now that he had come, God expected people to listen to him. He had brought the "final word," as it were. No one could compare with Jesus.

That is the message of today's text from the book of Hebrews.

## INTO THE WORD

Provide a little background information on the book of Hebrews. (See the Lesson Background on page 377. Read Hebrews 1:1-5; 3:1-6. Ask the class to compare the message here with what they witnessed in the Bible drama earlier. List their ideas on the chalkboard.

Have each person write the letters of the alphabet vertically on a sheet of paper. Direct them to find words, either quoted or interpreted from today's text, for as many letters as they can, that will describe or identify Jesus. (They should not expect to find something for every letter.) Give them ten to fifteen minutes and then compare/contrast lists orally. The following may be found in the text (verse numbers indicated): Apostle (3:1), Builder (3:3), Faithful (3:2), Glory (1:3), Heir (1:2), Priest (3:1), Radiance (1:3), Son (1:2), Superior (1:4), Worthy (3:3). Such designations as the following might be used (based on words or thoughts in the text): Excellent (1:4),

Householder (3:6), Inheritor (1:4), Upholder (1:3), Word (1:2), Creator (1:2). Expect and accept other reasonable ones.

The epistle to the Hebrews combats many of the false doctrines of the first century and of centuries since. Give your class members each of the following "statements of faith," and ask them to refute them from today's texts. Appropriate verses are given following each statement.

(1) "Jesus was only a man, adopted by God to be his Son" (1:2-4).

(2) "Jesus did not do exactly what God wanted him to do" (3:2).

(3) "God may have created us, but if he did, he left us on our own to resolve the issues of life" (1:1, 2).

(4) "Angels, as heavenly spiritual beings, deserve our worship" (1:4, 5).

(5) "All of creation can be scientifically explained as purely natural events" (1:2).

(6) "Moses, as a prophet of God, should be counted equal with Jesus, another of God's prophets" (3:3).

(7) "I accepted Christ years ago—that's all that really affects how I stand with God" (3:6).

As each statement is discussed and refuted, note or ask how these doctrines have been or are promoted today. For example, the sixth statement expresses a belief of the Muslim faith, but it is wholly contrary to what Hebrews 3:3 says.

### OPTION

Use the reproducible activity "He Is Great!" on page 384 to lead your class in a study of today's text.

## INTO LIFE

Give copies of the preceding seven false doctrinal statements to the students. Challenge them to consider one a day throughout the next week and, in their personal Bible study, to find other key Bible verses that refute the statement. Suggest that they look for expressions of any of these erroneous ideas in what they read or hear this week.

Close with a prayer of thanks that "God has spoken" through his Son Jesus.

### OPTION

Use the reproducible activity "Fix Your Thoughts on Jesus" on page 384 to provide class members with personal reminders of today's lesson.

# He Is Great!

Today's study begins a unit on the greatness of Christ. Using each letter of the word *great* to get you started, and ideas from Hebrews 1:1-5, list five adjectives that describe the greatness of God.

He is     G _____

                R_____

                E_____

                A _____

                T_____

If opportunity is available in class, walk around the classroom as other classmates do. Show them your acrostic as you look at theirs. See how many different words you see. Discuss the choices as a group.

Write something good here about MOSES:

Write something *better* here about CHRIST:

Do it one more time here:

MOSES—

CHRIST—

# Fix Your Thoughts on Jesus

Clip the six letters below. Put each one someplace you will notice it each day this week. (For example: bathroom mirror, a favorite mug, on a radio you often listen to.) As you notice each, think of an attribute of Jesus. See how many you can come up with during the week.

He is great, you know!

# JESUS IS SAVIOR

**LESSON 7**

## WHY TEACH THIS LESSON?

Outside the church, salvation is an unpopular concept. It flies in the face of humanism, which claims people can solve their own problems, given enough time and enough "positive thinking." To express a need for a savior is negative, and it denies that people have the power to solve their own problems.

But that is the message of the Bible. Popular or not, it must be proclaimed. The writer to the Hebrews summed up the saving role of Christ to be sure his Jewish readers did not lapse into a system that claimed they could save themselves. The system is different, but humanism makes the same claim. Perhaps something in this lesson will equip your students to share the saving message of Christ with their friends and neighbors.

## INTRODUCTION

### A. THE MURDERED HOSTAGE

According to an old story set in the Middle Ages, a powerful duke rebelled against his king. To advance his cause, the duke took scores of the king's loyal followers hostage. When he threatened to execute them one by one if the king did not give in to his demands, the king sent his son to investigate the situation. When the prince arrived at the duke's castle, he saw how desperate the situation was and offered himself as a hostage if the duke would set the other hostages free. The duke agreed and the exchange was made, but as soon as he had the prince in his custody, he murdered him.

In a way this resembles how God dealt with us through his Son. We were captives of sin, held hostage by Satan. When God's Son came to rescue us, the forces of evil seized him and put him to death. At this point, however, what happened to God's Son and what happened to the prince are noticeably different. Jesus was able to break the shackles of death and rise again. Now he sits at the right hand of God, making intercession for us.

### B. LESSON BACKGROUND

In the previous lesson we learned that angels, although they enjoy an exalted and privileged position in God's order, are still inferior to God's Son (Hebrews 1). Furthermore, we learned that Moses, honored giver of Israel's Law, was also inferior to the Son (Hebrews 3:1-6).

The first four verses of chapter 2 contain an exhortation to the Hebrew Christians to hold fast to the gospel they had received. Apparently there was some danger that they might abandon the salvation offered through the gospel and return to their former way of life in Judaism.

The writer's argument is eloquent. Having displayed Christ's superiority to the angels, he is ready to describe how he could appear "a little lower than the angels" (2:9). No doubt, these Jewish believers were troubled by the idea of a humbled Messiah. It had been a stumbling block for the Jews' acceptance of Jesus in the first place (1 Corinthians 1:23). We can imagine the how the Jewish friends and relatives of the Hebrew Christians would continually question and challenge their faith

## DEVOTIONAL READING
**HEBREWS 10:1-10**

## LESSON SCRIPTURE
**HEBREWS 2**

## PRINTED TEXT
**HEBREWS 2:5-11, 14-18**

July
13

## LESSON AIMS

*As a result of studying this lesson, students should:*

*1. List the benefits that come to us by the incarnation.*

*2. Explain why it is only in Christ that a person can become what he or she was created to be.*

*3. Use to the fullest the resources they have in Christ for living the Christian life.*

## KEY VERSE

*But we see Jesus, who was made a little lower than the angels, now crowned with glory and honor because he suffered death, so that by the grace of God he might taste death for everyone.*

Hebrews 2:9

## What Do You Think?

*In recent years there has been a renewed interest in angels. We know that they were a part of the created order (Psalm 148:2-5). We know that they are capable of carrying out assignments in this world, including fighting battles or delivering messages from God (2 Kings 19:35; Luke 1:11-13). At times they are associated with a brilliant appearance (Luke 2:9); at other times their presence is undetected (Hebrews 13:2). We also understand that angels are capable of rebelling against the rule and will of God (2 Peter 2:4; Jude 6).*

*While we can know much about angels, there are still many unanswered questions. What is the danger of speculating about the role of angels? How might too much talk of angels distract us from our purpose?*

## What Do You Think?

*Man was "crowned . . . with glory and honor" by being made the ruler of God's creation. But, because of sin, everything is not subject to him. So Jesus became man, suffered death, and is himself "now crowned with glory and honor" at the right hand of God. Through his glory, we, too, will be glorified (Colossians 3:4).*

*How do worldly people seek "glory and honor"? Why do Christians sometimes get caught up in the same pursuits? How can we help each other to seek Christ's glory instead?*

in such a Messiah. They probably quoted Scriptures of the great messianic reign and questioned, "Where is the messianic kingdom if this Jesus is really the Christ?"

This is the kind of question and challenge the writer is attempting to answer. Jesus had to identify with man, a little lower than the angels, so that man could identify with him in glory. He became our brother, sharing our weakness, so that we could share his strength and glory.

## I. RECLAIMING MAN'S PLACE (HEBREWS 2:5-10)

### A. God's Purpose for Man (vv. 5-8)

**5. It is not to angels that he has subjected the world to come, about which we are speaking.**

In these verses the writer links the ensuing discussion with the foundation laid in chapter 1 by referring again to *angels*. His interlude (2:1-4) was not meant to introduce a separate subject, but to emphasize how important the present discussion is.

In this present age, angels have certain responsibilities, many of which we are unaware. We are simply told that they are "sent to serve those who will inherit salvation" (Hebrews 1:14). They are not sent as rulers, but as servants. This may suggest that some of the problem was not only a danger of falling back into Judaism, but that some might "drift away" (2:1) toward the rising heresy of gnosticism, with its angel worship and other blasphemous practices. The warning here is that angels are not the rulers of *the world to come;* they deserve no worship. In the heavenly realm, which may be what the writer means by *the world to come*, the angels will no doubt also have responsibilities, but there they will still be subject to the Son.

It is also possible that *the world to come* means the New Covenant system instituted by Jesus, which stands in contrast to the Old Covenant, referred to in verse 2 of this chapter. That word was "spoken by angels," but the salvation of the New Covenant focuses not on angels, but on the Son. Whereas Jews who rejected Christ were (and are) still looking for that "world to come," the writer of Hebrews demonstrates that it has come to pass in Jesus.

**6, 7. But there is a place where someone has testified: "What is man that you are mindful of him, the son of man that you care for him? You made him a little lower than the angels; you crowned him with glory and honor.**

The writer introduces this quotation from Psalm 8:4-6 with the words, *there is a place where someone has testified*. We may be tempted to conclude that the writer of Hebrews was only vaguely familiar with the Old Testament. But such a conclusion is unwarranted. In that day the Scriptures were not divided into chapters and verses—a device that makes it more convenient for us to cite a particular passage. And while he seldom names the specific author of any Old Testament passage that he quotes, it is the message of the text that is his primary concern.

The point of this quotation is to call attention to the fact that man was created by God with great potential: *a little lower than the angels*. David's words in this psalm echo the "rule" given to man in the beginning, according to Genesis 1:28.

**8. . . . . and put everything under his feet." In putting everything under him, God left nothing that is not subject to him. Yet at present we do not see everything subject to him.**

*You. . .put everything under his feet.* The ideal, in creation, was for man to rule over everything in the created universe. This changed radically with the entrance of sin into the world. Man lost the dominion he had been given. Death entered, over which man has little or no control. What control man did retain became tainted by sin. The harmony God intended for man to enjoy has not been fully restored: *Yet at present we do not see everything subject to him.*

## B. GOD'S PURPOSE REALIZED IN CHRIST (vv. 9, 10)

**9. But we see Jesus, who was made a little lower than the angels, now crowned with glory and honor because he suffered death, so that by the grace of God he might taste death for everyone.**

The writer of Hebrews, even as we who read it, sees something in Psalm 8 that David did not see: *we see Jesus.* There is a crucial difference between Jesus and man: Jesus is the Creator; man is created. Jesus, who is "superior to the angels" (Hebrews 1:4), humbled himself to be *made a little lower than the angels.* Christ laid aside a measure of his glory to enter the world as a human being—a man, who is "a little lower than the angels." In thus becoming the true *son of man* mentioned in Psalm 8, Jesus effected God's plan to restore to man the dominion lost through sin.

The way in which Jesus made it possible for man to regain his position of dominion was to *taste death for everyone.* Death then lost its bitter taste when Jesus arose from the tomb. He returned to Heaven where he was *crowned with glory and honor.* Eventually Jesus' full authority will be recognized and his people will reign with him. That time will occur when Christ returns to claim his own and declare victory over his enemies. The purpose for which God created man will thus be realized when we actually *see Jesus* on that day.

**10. In bringing many sons to glory, it was fitting that God, for whom and through whom everything exists, should make the author of their salvation perfect through suffering.**

God desired to create a family of *sons* who would one day live with him in *glory.* To accomplish this, it was fitting that he *make the author of their salvation perfect through suffering.* The idea of a suffering Messiah was repugnant to the Jews; Paul calls the crucifixion of Christ a "stumbling block" to them (1 Corinthians 1:23). Thus these Jewish Christians required some explanation as to why it was necessary for the Messiah to experience this.

We also may need some explanation: how could Jesus be made *perfect*? As God, wasn't he already perfect? The word translated here as *make . . . perfect* means "to bring to completion." It does not speak of Christ's character as much as it speaks of his calling. When God laid the foundations of the world, he already had a plan for human redemption (1 Peter 1:18-20). This plan required that his Son would suffer and die. Until Christ completed his suffering, his mission to make atonement for mankind remained incomplete. This is what Jesus referred to on the cross when he prayed, "It is finished" (John 19:30).

## II. MAKING US HIS BROTHERS (HEBREWS 2:11, 14-18)

In identifying with us by becoming human and tasting death, Jesus made it possible for us to identify with him. We are his brothers. As such, we share the blessings of holiness, freedom, forgiveness, and help.

## A. MAKING US HOLY (v. 11)

**11. Both the one who makes men holy and those who are made holy are of the same family. So Jesus is not ashamed to call them brothers.**

To be *made holy* means to be set apart to a holy purpose. Through his sacrifice for us, Christ gave us the opportunity to be set apart for service to God. Being made holy does not mean that one is perfect or never falls into sin. It means that one has made a commitment to become more Christlike.

Christians *are of the same family* as Jesus, the one who makes us holy. Under ordinary circumstances we would consider it most unusual for one so holy and exalted as Jesus to accept sinners like us as members of his family. But Jesus *is not*

*The visual for lesson 7 illustrates Jesus, "crowned with glory and honor." Display it as you discuss verses 9 and following.*

CROWNED WITH GLORY AND HONOR

### WHAT DO YOU THINK?

*We know that the Son holds preeminence over the angels, but he willingly chose to take the role of a mortal, a little lower than the angels," for the purpose of redeeming lost mankind. It is always a sign of character strength to voluntarily set aside privilege and position in the interest of serving the welfare of another.*

*What demands does Jesus' act of self sacrifice put on us? Who are the people in our community that—by human standards— might be said to be "beneath us," people we often do not want to, or are afraid to, minister to? What does Jesus' act of humbling himself for us demand of us in their behalf? Try to be specific.*

*"Whoever finds his life will lose it, and whoever loses his life for my sake will find it" (Matthew 10:39).*

WHAT DO YOU THINK?

The "author" of our salvation was made "perfect through suffering" (Hebrews 2:10). The plan of salvation was incomplete until Jesus "finished" it. We might say it is still incomplete until we finish it by following the Great Commission. If Jesus was "made perfect" by his suffering, how can we be "made perfect," that is, complete the work he has given us?

WHAT DO YOU THINK?

How do you feel about being numbered among Jesus' "brothers"? What does that suggest about our relationship with all other believers? Why does it sometimes seem we are "ashamed" to call some believers "brothers," perhaps those of a different race or economic level? How can we remove the barriers between brothers and sisters in Christ?

WHAT DO YOU THINK?

How do we see the "fear of death" exhibited in our world today? How can we bring the good news of freedom to those who continue to be "held in slavery by their fear of death"?

ashamed to call us brothers. Fallen and sin-stained creatures that we are, he is still willing to forgive us and to welcome us as his brothers and sisters.

## B. SETTING US FREE (vv. 14, 15)

**14, 15. Since the children have flesh and blood, he too shared in their humanity so that by his death he might destroy him who holds the power of death—that is, the devil—and free those who all their lives were held in slavery by their fear of death.**

The previous verse affirmed that Christ is our brother. For that relationship to be completely realized, it was necessary for Jesus to become fully human, assuming all the weaknesses of the flesh. This verse elaborates on this point.

Since his fall, man has lived under the curse of sin, which has subjected him to unceasing suffering and sorrow. The most dreadful of all these threats has been the pall of *death* that has cast a shadow over every human being who has set foot on the earth. It was necessary that Christ come in *flesh and blood* and suffer death himself, in order that the shackles of *the devil* might be broken. This is one of the most striking paradoxes of the gospel: Christ limited himself so that we could be freed from our sin-imposed *slavery*. He was bound so that we could be free. He came to die so that we could live. It was Christ's death and his resurrection that led Paul to cry out triumphantly, "Death has been swallowed up in victory. Where, O death, is your victory? Where, O death, is your sting?" (1 Corinthians 15:54, 55).

### PRISONERS NO MORE

Thomas Costain's historical adventure, *The Three Edwards,* describes the life of Raynald III, a fourteenth-century duke in what is now Belgium. Raynald was grossly overweight. After a violent quarrel, Raynald's younger brother Edward captured Raynald but did not kill him. Instead, he built a room around Raynald in the Nieuwkerk castle, and promised him he could regain his title and property as soon as he was able to leave the room.

This would not have been difficult for most people, since the room had several windows and a door of near-normal size, and none was locked or barred. The problem was Raynald's size. To regain his freedom he needed to lose weight. But Edward knew his older brother, and each day he sent a variety of delicious foods to him. Instead of dieting his way out of prison, Raynald only grew fatter.

When Duke Edward was accused of cruelty, he had a ready answer: "My brother is not a prisoner. He may leave when he so wills."

Raynald stayed in that room for ten years and was not released until after Edward died in battle. By then his health was so ruined that he died within a year—a prisoner of his own appetite.

Hebrews 2:14, 15 tells us that Jesus took upon himself flesh and blood, so that through his death, "he might destroy him who holds the power of death—that is, the devil—and free those who all their lives were held in slavery by their fear of death." Jesus has provided the way of escape from the vicious cycle of sin and death. We need not be prisoners anymore. We can be freed from the cycle—if we so will.

—C. B. Mc.

## C. OFFERING US FORGIVENESS (vv. 16, 17)

**16. For surely it is not angels he helps, but Abraham's descendants.**

This verse has given translators some difficulty. The word for *helps* is, literally, "to take hold of," "to seize," "to reach" or "come within reach of," or "to receive." The *King James* translators took it to mean the incarnation—Jesus' "taking hold" of human flesh to become human. The *New International Version* and the *New American Standard Bible* agree in using the word *helps*—Jesus "came within reach" of man in order to help.

Either translation essentially means the same thing. The incarnation made it possible for Jesus to become the sacrifice for our sin. This is the "help" being discussed. Nothing is said of any plan for the redemption of fallen angels; only punishment (2 Peter 2:4). The forgiveness offered in Christ is for *Abraham's descendants*, that is, those who are by faith Abraham's children (Romans 4:16; 9:7, 8; Galatians 3:29).

**17. For this reason he had to be made like his brothers in every way, in order that he might become a merciful and faithful high priest in service to God, and that he might make atonement for the sins of the people.**

Jesus' being *made like his brothers in every way* is clearly a reference to the incarnation. This was necessary in order for him to become their *high priest*. Having been one with them in the flesh and having experienced the frailties of the flesh, he could be a *merciful* high priest, sympathetic to their weaknesses (see Hebrews 4:15). He was *faithful* in two ways: to God because he faithfully carried out the mission that God sent him to accomplish, and to his brethren because he faced death on the cross on their behalf.

The writer also notes that Jesus came to *make atonement for the sins of the people.* Every sin is an affront to God's holy nature and deserves eternal punishment. Yet God mercifully chose to send his Son into the world to atone for man's sin. Man does not and cannot atone for his own sin. Our only hope was for God to take the initiative and send his Son, which he did. Even the Old Testament atonement sacrifices were insufficient; only Jesus' sacrifice of himself could provide true atonement (Hebrews 9:9-14).

## D. HELPING US IN OUR TEMPTATIONS (v. 18)

**18. Because he himself suffered when he was tempted, he is able to help those who are being tempted.**

Because Christ *suffered* temptations similar to those that we suffer, he can not only sympathize with us; he can also *help* us. We are told of certain temptations that he faced (Matthew 4:1-11; Luke 4:1-13), but certainly there were many others. Indeed, because he was the Son of God, Jesus faced the full fury of Satan in a way that no human being can ever face. At the time the book of Hebrews was written, these Hebrew Christians were being tempted to return to Judaism, thus compromising their Christian commitment. Satan placed a similar temptation before Jesus by encouraging him to abandon his mission and thus compromise his commitment to his Father's will.

Whatever temptation we encounter, we are assured that Jesus encountered it as well. He was "tempted in every way, just as we are—yet was without sin" (Hebrews 4:15). Because he passed successfully through the fires of temptation, he can now offer sympathy and support to his brethren who face similar fires. What a glorious blessing to know that there is always "grace to help us in our time of need" (4:16)!

## CONCLUSION

### A. HE HAS BEEN THERE

During the Vietnam War, an American officer compiled an outstanding record of service. He was wounded twice and received a medal for special courage in combat. Furthermore, he received a number of commendations from his commanding officer. But the greatest tribute to his skill and courage was the fact that men asked to be transferred to his unit. This was especially surprising, because his unit was usually given the most hazardous assignments in the area. When one of the men who wanted to be transferred to the officer's unit was asked why, his answer was short and to the point: "He's been there!"

*WHAT DO YOU THINK?*

If you were held hostage by terrorists, is there anyone who would offer to take your place? If so, how would you feel toward that person? How would you show those feelings?

Is that the way you demonstrate your love for Jesus? Why or why not?

*WHAT DO YOU THINK*

Jesus wants to help us when we are tempted. God has already promised there will always be a "way of escape" whenever we are tempted (1 Corinthians 10:13). How can we take advantage of the Lord's help? Aside from what he has already done on the cross, what "help" does he offer, and how do we get it? What are some ways of dealing with temptation that you have found helpful?

## PRAYER

*We give you thanks, dear God, that in your great mercy you saw fit to send your Son into the world as a servant, that we could have the hope of eternal life. In the name of our great High Priest, we pray. Amen.*

## THOUGHT TO REMEMBER

*We are saved because Christ did for us what we could not do for ourselves.*

## DAILY BIBLE READING

*Monday, July 7—Jesus Christ Gives Eternal Life (John 10:22-30)*

*Tuesday, July 8—Jesus Christ Is from God (1 John 4:1-6)*

*Wednesday, July 9—Jesus Christ Is Love (1 John 4:7-11)*

*Thursday, July 10—Jesus Christ Resists Temptations (Matthew 4:1-11)*

*Friday, July 11—Jesus Christ Was Sent by God (John 3:16-21)*

*Saturday, July 12—Jesus Christ Is Our Advocate (1 John 2:1-6)*

*Sunday, July 13—Jesus Christ Was Faithful (Hebrews 3:1-6)DE-*

What he meant was that this officer had been in combat, had suffered the difficult conditions in the field along with his men, had been wounded, and had survived. Through his actions he had won the respect and trust of those who served under him in the only way that a combat officer can win genuine respect: he had been there.

This is similar to the reasons that men and women in every age have respected and trusted Jesus Christ. Our Lord is not some remote deity residing in a distant Heaven, isolated from the events of our lives. Christ has been there! He left his heavenly home and became a human being, subject to human problems and limitations. When we suffer, we know that he empathizes, for he has suffered also. When we are tired, he understands, for he has known fatigue. When we are tempted, he can help us because he was tempted. Christ has been there, because he has been *here!*

### B. JESUS SAVES

Under the Mosaic Law, the high priest was the religious leader of the Israelites. He had many functions, but none was more important than his entrance once a year into the Holy of Holies of the tabernacle or temple, where he sprinkled blood upon the ark of the covenant for the sins of the people. In preparation for this ceremony, the high priest had to go through a process of ritualistic cleansing that symbolically made him pure when he represented the people before God.

In the Christian era, Christ is our High Priest. In many ways the high priesthood of the Old Testament was similar to Christ's high priesthood. There are, however, striking differences. The Old Testament priest had to come from the tribe of Levi, whereas Christ came from the tribe of Judah. The Old Testament high priest had to purge himself of sin ceremonially before he could stand before God. For Christ, however, no such cleansing was necessary, for he was without sin. The Old Testament high priest entered a physical Holy of Holies, whereas Christ entered the heavenly Holy of Holies (Hebrews 9:24).

In one very important respect, the high priest of the Old Testament and Christ, our great High Priest, have one item in common. Both had to deal with man's universal problem of sin. In many circles it is no longer "politically correct" to speak of sin. Those who violate accepted moral codes are said to be "socially maladjusted" or "ethically challenged." Actions that the Bible clearly marks as sinful have now become acceptable by clever changes in terminology. Taking the life of an unborn child has now become a matter of "choice" and no longer a sin. Homosexuality, condemned in the Scriptures, has become an "alternate life-style" that is widely defended even in some religious circles.

In all of these discussions, one very important element is often overlooked: personal responsibility for our actions. All of us on occasion have tried to shift the blame for our moral failures onto other persons or onto society as a whole. Again and again the Bible thunders out the warning sounded centuries ago by the apostle Paul: "The wages of sin is death" (Romans 6:23). God has never altered or withdrawn that pronouncement. All of us, because of our sins, fall under this death sentence (Romans 3:23).

There is no way that we can save ourselves. We know very well that on the basis of our works we do not deserve salvation. A lifetime of good works cannot atone for even one sin. Our situation is hopeless except for—and what a wonderful exception it is—Jesus Christ, our matchless Lord and Savior. Because he gave himself as a sacrifice for our sins, he has made reconciliation between God and mankind. He has welcomed us as a part of his family, even calling us brethren. Is there any reason we should not love him, trust him, and give our lives in service to him?

# Discovery Learning

*This page contains an alternate lesson plan emphasizing learning activities. Classes desiring such student involvement will find these suggestions helpful. The next page is a reproducible activity page to further enhance discovery learning.*

## LEARNING GOALS

As a result of studying this lesson, students should:

1. List the benefits that come to us by the incarnation.

2. Explain why it is only in Christ that a person can become what he or she was created to be.

3. Use to the fullest the resources they have in Christ for living the Christian life.

## INTO THE LESSON

On eleven index cards, write the word INCARNATION, one letter per card, on one side. On the reverse side, write the word *SUPERIORITY*, matching the *S* with the *I*, *U* with *N*, and so forth. (Use a blue marker for one word and a red marker for the other.) Display the cards spelling the word *superiority* (the dust tray of a chalkboard might be a good place). Point out to your class that last week's lesson emphasized that Jesus the Son is superior to the angels and to Moses.

Point out that last week's emphasis makes the theme of this week's lesson all the more amazing. Ask class members, one at a time, to select a letter from the word *superiority* (randomly and none in sequence), and as each calls a letter, turn that card over to show the letter on the other side. As the cards are turned, allow guesses as to the word concealed. Once guessed, turn all the cards over to show the word *incarnation*. Note that this is the emphasis of today's study: Christ—the glorious and superior Son of God—became human on our behalf.

## INTO THE WORD

Introduce the following as "headlines" in a newspaper. Ask your class to examine today's Scripture text from Hebrews 2:5-11, 14-18, and to identify the relevant verse for each headline. Though they are given here in verse order, you will want to mix them up.

2:5—"Angels Not in Charge in Heaven"; 2:6—"Man Hardly Worth God's Time"; 2:7—"Man Created Lower Than Angels"; 2:8—"All Things Are Not Under Man's Authority"; 2:9—"Jesus Tastes Death"; 2:9—"Jesus Made Lower Than Angels"; 2:10—"Jesus Is Declared 'Author'"; 2:11—"Jesus Calls the Holy His 'Brothers'"; 2:14—"Jesus: Devil Destroyer"; 2:15—"Fear of Death Subjects Many to Slavery"; 2:16—"Jesus Saves Humans; Not Angels"; 2:17—"Jesus As High Priest Makes Atonement His Goal"; 2:18—"Jesus Just Like Us: Tempted!"

Ask the students to suggest other "headlines" that they see within the truths of these verses. They may offer such suggestions as "Jesus Crowned With Glory and Honor" from verse 9, "Deliverance—at Last!" from verse 15, or "Jesus: Helper of the Tempted" from verse 18. Encourage the class to be creative in their ideas.

*OPTION*

Give just one or two headlines as samples and expand the time of having the students suggest more of the ideas.

*OPTION*

Use the reproducible activity "Speechless" on page 392 to guide your students in a study of the text.

Next (after any of the options you choose from above) ask the students to work in groups of four to six to list the benefits that come to us because of Jesus' incarnation. The following should be noted: Makes us holy (v. 11), calls us his brothers (v. 11), destroys the one who wants to destroy us—the devil (v. 14), sets us free (v. 15), makes atonement for our sins (v. 17), helps us when we are tempted (v. 18). After allowing six or eight minutes for the groups to work, ask for volunteers to tell some of the items they found in their groups. Write each one on the chalkboard as it is suggested. Use the list that is compiled to sum up the Scripture lesson.

## INTO LIFE

Give each student a copy of the following list of seven truths to use, one per day, in their daily devotional time for the next week. Suggest a time of pondering and a time of praying related to each. (1) Jesus was crowned with glory and honor after he had tasted death for everyone. (2) The author of our salvation fulfilled his mission by suffering. (3) We are one with Jesus through the process of being made holy; he calls us his "brothers." (4) Jesus became like us in order to die for us. (5) Jesus has destroyed the one who had the power of death, so that we need fear death no longer. (6) Jesus is a merciful and faithful High Priest who made atonement for us to God. (7) Jesus has been tempted and can help us in our temptations.

*OPTION*

Use the reproducible activity "Praise the Lord" on page 392 to help your students apply today's lesson.

# Speechless!

*Amazing! Stupendous! Marvelous!* Words fail for the Christian to honor the magnificent truths of Hebrews 2:5-18. How would you rate the following truths? Score them from ten to one, with 10 being the most astounding; 9, next most and so on down to a score of 1.

\_\_\_ God is mindful of man.

\_\_\_ Jesus tasted death on behalf of all men.

\_\_\_ There is no need to fear death.

\_\_\_ Jesus became fully human.

\_\_\_ Jesus knows the suffering of temptation.

\_\_\_ All creation is subjected to Christ.

\_\_\_ God made Jesus perfect through suffering.

\_\_\_ Jesus' death ensured the destruction of the devil.

\_\_\_ Jesus can help those who are being tempted.

\_\_\_ Jesus, the Son of God, is not ashamed to call us "brothers."

# Praise the Lord!

"Thanks be to God! Jesus is my Savior!" If you can exult in this truth, make a "prayer list" here to help you consider the blessings and responsibilities of your state in Christ.

| Jesus saved me **from**: | Jesus saved me **to**: | Jesus saved me **for**: |
|---|---|---|
| | | |

Us a hymnal to identify seven hymns or choruses that emphasize the grand truth of today's study: Jesus is Savior! Write them down here. Use one each day this week in your personal time of devotion. One is given to get you started.

"A Wonderful Savior is Jesus My Lord"

# JESUS IS THE HIGH PRIEST

**LESSON 8**

## WHY TEACH THIS LESSON?

Of all the word pictures for Jesus, possibly the image of Jesus as high priest is the richest. Since the Levitical priesthood, including the office of high priest, is so clearly spelled out in the Old Testament, there is a wealth of instruction available to us in this comparison.

Of course, your students are not so well versed in the priesthood and the role of the high priest as were the original Hebrew readers of this epistle. For today's readers, a little background and explanation are needed. That is the purpose of this lesson: to provide the background needed to understand Jesus' role as high priest and to challenge your students to respond to that appropriately.

## INTRODUCTION

### A. ABOUT PRIESTS

For many people, the concept of priest and priesthood often conjures up negative images. We think of ancient pagan religions in which priests wielded almost absolute power, often serving as kings as well as priests. Some of these priests presided over religious rites that included sexual abuses and even human sacrifice.

The biblical images of priests are sometimes almost as negative. The Old Testament speaks of the priests of the false god Baal (2 Kings 10:19) and of pagan peoples such as the Philistines (1 Samuel 6:2). Even though the Mosaic Law created a priesthood among God's own people, many of these turned out to be scoundrels (see 1 Samuel 2:12-17, 22-24; Jeremiah 2:26, 27). In Jesus' day, the priests were among his most bitter enemies. In fact, the priests, including the high priest, spearheaded the plot to crucify him.

But these negative images of priests do not tell the whole story. There are many good and noble priests within the pages of Scripture. We read of Jehoiada, who counseled young Joash when he became king at age seven (2 Kings 12:2). A high priest named Hilkiah found the book of the Law in the temple of the Lord (2 Kings 22:8). Later, when King Josiah heard what the Law said, he ushered in a period of revival and reformation throughout Judah. We are told that in the early church, many priests became "obedient to the faith" (Acts 6:7).

It is important to note that Christians are called a "holy priesthood" (1 Peter 2:5) and a "royal priesthood" (1 Peter 2:9). Most important of all, Jesus Christ is set forth as our great high priest. Our Lord bears many different titles and serves in many different capacities, but among the most important of these is his function as high priest—our mediator before Almighty God.

### B. LESSON BACKGROUND

The Jewish Christians who were the recipients of the book of Hebrews would have been quite familiar with the office of priest. It is likely that many of them had watched the priests offer sacrifices on the altar. They had probably attended the services led by priests on some of the great Jewish holy days, such as the feasts of Passover and Pentecost. A few may even have watched the high priest prepare to enter the hidden and mysterious Holy of Holies on the Day of Atonement.

---

**DEVOTIONAL READING**
**HEBREWS 7:20-28**

**LESSON SCRIPTURE**
**HEBREWS 4:14–5:10; 7**

**PRINTED TEXT**
**HEBREWS 4:14–5:10**

July 20

**LESSON AIMS**

*After studying this lesson, each student should be able to:*

*1. Compare the work of Jesus with that of the high priest.*

*2. Explain what makes Jesus a superior high priest.*

*3. Accept the role of priest, serving under the high priest Jesus on behalf of others.*

**KEY VERSE**

*Let us then approach the throne of grace with confidence, so that we may receive mercy and find grace to help us in our time of need.* Hebrews 4:16

**LESSON 8 NOTES**

*The visual for lesson 8 illustrates Hebrews 4:16. Have it on display as your students arrive in the classroom.*

Let us therefore come boldly unto the throne of grace.

**WHAT DO YOU THINK?**

*Some people say that since Jesus always resisted temptation to sin, he can't really empathize with our struggles with temptation. Others have noted, however, that Satan only pressures a person until the person either gives in or wins a decisive victory over the temptation. Since we sometimes give in, the pressure we face in those temptations is less than what Jesus faced, who always forced Satan to try his hardest in his temptations.*

*How does knowing Jesus endured every temptation to the extreme and still did not give in encourage you? Aren't there some temptations we give in to easily— those associated with habits, for example. How can Jesus' resistance encourage us to fight harder to win over those temptations? What can we do to encourage and remind each other of Jesus' faithfulness?*

When Jews became Christians, their view of these religious traditions changed. In many cases, however, this did not involve a complete break from their past. Paul, for example, continued to observe the Jewish feasts (Acts 20:16). He even paid the expenses of four men who had taken a Jewish vow (Acts 21:23-26). It should not surprise us that many Jewish Christians still harbored nostalgic feelings about priests and the temple. Their memories of inspiring worship services shared with family and friends likely moved many of them to want to return to Judaism. It was just this situation that served as the occasion for the book of Hebrews. The writer attempts to show his readers that something better had been provided by God to replace the Old Covenant system. Becoming Christians was not an abandoning of their Jewish faith; it was an acknowledgment that the New Covenant that God had promised had now arrived. As Christians they could enjoy the benefits of a great high priest, who is now in Heaven: Jesus the Son of God.

## I. JESUS, OUR HIGH PRIEST (HEBREWS 4:14-16)
### A. HAS PASSED INTO THE HEAVENS (v. 14)
**14. Therefore, since we have a great high priest who has gone through the heavens, Jesus the Son of God, let us hold firmly to the faith we profess.**

In previous lessons we have learned that Jesus serves as our *high priest* (Hebrews 2:17; 3:1). Here the writer notes that he has *gone through the heavens.* This contrasts sharply with the practice of the high priest under the Old Covenant, who once a year entered the Holy of Holies, having "gone through" a heavy curtain, to make atonement for the people's sins. There he was symbolically in the presence of God, but just for a few minutes. On the other hand, Jesus has entered Heaven (the true Most Holy Place), where he sits at the right hand of God (Hebrews 1:3; 9:24) and enjoys a "permanent priesthood" (7:24).

Christ's superior priesthood had important consequences for the recipients of the book of Hebrews. These Jewish Christians, who were thinking about returning to Judaism with its inferior priesthood, needed to be reminded of this and admonished to *hold firmly to the faith* they professed. The word for *profess* is the same word used in 3:1 and translated "confess." It literally means "to say the same thing." As such, it may reflect both the private and the public aspects of one's commitment to Christ. The private aspect is the acceptance of Jesus as Lord and Savior. The public dimension is the acknowledgment of this faith before witnesses.

### B. WAS TEMPTED AS WE ARE (v. 15)
**15. For we do not have a high priest who is unable to sympathize with our weaknesses, but we have one who has been tempted in every way, just as we are—yet was without sin.**

When we seek someone to represent us before God, we want someone who understands our problems, who has stood where we have stood, and who hurts when we hurt. Were Christ only divine, he could not fully meet this requirement. But he was also human, and this makes the crucial difference. He was *tempted in every way, just as we are.* We are told of certain specific temptations that Jesus successfully faced (Matthew 4:1-11; Luke 4:1-13). But Luke's record of these temptations states that the devil "left him until an opportune time" (Luke 4:13), indicating that there were other temptations during Jesus' ministry.

This verse does not suggest that Jesus was tempted with every specific temptation we face, but *in every way.* Jesus was never tempted to drive in excess of the speed limit, but were there laws in his day that everyone assumed were "made to be broken"? John suggests temptation comes in three categories: "the lust of the flesh and the lust of the eyes and the boastful pride of life" (1 John 2:16, *New*

*American Standard Bible*). Jesus was certainly tempted in each of these ways. Several studies have been done to link each of the recorded temptations in Matthew 4 and Luke 4 with one of these areas. The important point is that although he was tempted, he *yet was without sin.*

The Greek for this last clause actually contains no verb; it is merely "without sin" or "apart from sin." This suggests another possibility for understanding its meaning. Jesus, who had no sin (2 Corinthians 5:21) was not tempted by past sins, as we are. For us, each failure becomes a new temptation to yield again. But Jesus never yielded; thus he was tempted in every way we are apart from sin—in every way but that one.

## C. PROVIDES MERCY AND GRACE (v. 16)

**16. Let us then approach the throne of grace with confidence, so that we may receive mercy and find grace to help us in our time of need.**

Because Christ is now in the presence of God in Heaven, all Christians enjoy a sacred privilege. For a sinful human being to be able to come into the presence of Almighty God seems inconceivable. But Jesus our high priest has changed all of this. Now we can *approach the throne of grace with confidence.* When we do so through our prayers, we are assured that we will receive *mercy* and *help* for whatever *need* we might have. We will discover, as did Paul, that God's grace is sufficient (2 Corinthians 12:9).

### ACCESS TO THE THRONE OF GOD

Imagine it is the end of time. From somewhere comes the sound of a trumpet so loud and clear that every mortal ear hears its call. From the eastern sky a great archangel descends to declare that time is no more. The earth quakes. The moon darkens. The stars are extinguished. The very sky rolls up like a scroll. All human activity comes to an end, as every man and woman who has ever lived stands before the Creator, either to be separated forever from him, or to live eternally with him.

Suddenly you find yourself entering a magnificent city of gold through a gate made of a single pearl. Its walls glimmer with precious stones and gems. There is no sun nor moon, but the city is brighter than a summer noon because the glory of God fills every portion of it. A magnificent river flows down the great street of the city, and the tree of life blooms on either side.

At the center of the city, behind the sparkling sea of glass, is the throne of Almighty God. At his right hand stands our high priest, Jesus Christ. With a nail-scarred hand he bids you draw near. As millions of angels and the saints of all the ages lean forward to hear, Jesus calls your name and presents you to his Father.

Such is the direct access to God awaiting those who confess Christ as their Lord and Savior. Let us come boldly to his throne now, as the writer of Hebrews instructs us to do, that we may come before his heavenly throne and stand in his presence some day.

—C. B. Mc.

## II. THE WORK OF THE HIGH PRIEST (HEBREWS 5:1-3)

### A. OFFERS GIFTS AND SACRIFICES (v. 1)

**1. Every high priest is selected from among men and is appointed to represent them in matters related to God, to offer gifts and sacrifices for sins.**

In this and the verses that follow, the Hebrew Christians were reminded of the role of the Aaronic priesthood. Although they were familiar with these requirements, this reminder served to show that Jesus also met these qualifications. One of the primary functions of a priest is to serve as a mediator between God and man. If he is to do this adequately and thereby represent his fellowmen well, he must share in their experiences; that is, he must be *selected from among men.* Christ fully

---

### WHAT DO YOU THINK?

The concept of approaching God's throne confidently to make our requests is an awesome picture. It's tells us we have an incredible privilege. Imagine trying to approach the head of state in any nation—even a small one, much less a world power—without an appointment or invitation. Yet the God of the universe allows just such access.

Then why don't we take advantage of this privilege more—why don't we pray more? How much confidence do you think the average Christian has that his or her prayers can make a difference? Why? How can we develop a more confident and consistent prayer life?

### HOW TO SAY IT

*Aaronic. Air-AHN-ik.*
*Abraham. AY-bruh-ham.*
*Abram. AY-brum.*
*Augustine. AW-gus-teen.*
*Baal. BAY-ul*
*Gethsemane. Geth-SEM-uh-nee.*
*Hilkiah. Hill-KYE-uh.*
*Joash. JOE-ash.*
*Jehoiada. Jeh-HOY-uh-duh*
*Jeremiah. Jair-uh-MYE-uh.*
*Josiah. Jo-SIGH-uh.*
*Levitical. Lih-VIT-ih-kul.*
*Melchizedek. Mel-KIZ-eh-dek.*

met this qualification. He was born of a woman, he grew to maturity in a normal way, and he suffered the limitations that beset every other human being.

A very important function of a priest was to *offer gifts and sacrifices for sins*. Some scholars draw a distinction between the gifts (consisting of grain offerings) and the sacrifices (involving animals whose blood was shed). It seems better, however, to understand *gifts and sacrifices* as simply a summary of the various ceremonial activities of the priest.

### B. HAS COMPASSION ON OTHERS (v. 2)
**2. He is able to deal gently with those who are ignorant and are going astray, since he himself is subject to weakness.**

The priest in ancient Israel served not only in formal and public functions; he also had what might be called a pastoral responsibility toward his people. He was to be a teacher and an example for them. He was to rebuke the rebellious and wayward. He had a special obligation to those *going astray* because they were *ignorant*. For them, patient guidance and loving nurture were more appropriate than stern rebuke. The priest was able to offer this kind of ministry, because he himself was *subject to weakness*.

### C. IS ALSO A SINNER (v. 3)
**3. This is why he has to offer sacrifices for his own sins, as well as for the sins of the people.**

Even as the priest offered sacrifices for the *sins of the people*, he also had to offer sacrifices *for his own sins*. Although the priest dealt with holy things every day, this did not exempt him from sin. Indeed, a priest faced certain temptations that were unique to his office. For example, he was tempted to lose his sense of reverence for the holy functions he performed. He might be tempted by spiritual pride to feel himself superior to those who were not involved with spiritual activities every day. These are temptations to which Christian leaders can still fall prey. In view of this fact, it is most appropriate and important to keep our leaders in constant prayer.

### III. JESUS' HIGH PRIESTHOOD (HEBREWS 5:4-10)
### A. CALLED OF GOD (vv. 4, 5)
**4, 5. No one takes this honor upon himself; he must be called by God, just as Aaron was. So Christ also did not take upon himself the glory of becoming a high priest. But God said to him, "You are my Son; today I have become your Father."**

The priesthood was a part of God's plan to provide spiritual direction to his people. Thus, only *God* had the right to call a person to fill the office. One could not elevate himself to the position, or be voted into office by his friends. To fill the office, one not only had to be a member of the tribe of Levi; he also had to be a member of the family of *Aaron*, the first high priest. Some scholars suggest that the writer had in mind some of the Jewish religious leaders of his own day, who had played politics and connived with the Romans in order to gain their offices.

In contrast, the writer points out that *Christ* did not use political maneuvering to gain the office. Nor did he carry on a political campaign among the people to win their respect. Furthermore, since Jesus was not a descendant of Aaron or a member of the tribe of Levi, he was not qualified according to the Law to fill the office of priest. The only way he could serve in this capacity was to be *called by God*.

### B. HAS AN ETERNAL PRIESTHOOD (v. 6)
**6. And he says in another place, "You are a priest forever, in the order of Melchizedek."**

---

**WHAT DO YOU THINK?**

*When the writer says the high priest was "subject to weakness," he means the high priest was tempted and sometimes sinned, just as everyone else does. Still, he was able to minister to the spiritual needs of his people.*

*Church leaders today, however, often struggle with the idea they must be perfect. They fear if people saw them as "sinners," they would lose their ministries.*

*How can we reassure church leaders they are allowed to be human? How can we grant them freedom to fail on occasion without fear of rejection? What do you think would be the result of such freedom?*

*(Encourage prayer for your leaders, who deal with temptation but who want to set an example, a difficult tension to live with.)*

---

**WHAT DO YOU THINK?**

*The high priest was "called" to his position by God, as were Aaron, Moses, and many others we read of in the Bible. Usually, these were dramatic calls—a direct word from God, a burning bush, etc. Christian ministers often talk about their "call" to the ministry, yet their stories are generally less dramatic than that of Moses, for example! How does one recognize a call to ministry? Is it only professional ministers God calls, or is each of us called to a ministry? Explain. How does Paul's analogy of the body in 1 Corinthians 12 help? (See especially verse 18.)*

Here the writer quotes Psalm 110:4 to show that Christ's priesthood is unique in two respects. First, it lasts *forever*. Any person called to the Aaronic priesthood held office only until his death. By contrast, Christ's priesthood actually *began* with his death, when he offered himself as the perfect sacrifice for the sins of the world.

Second, the priesthood of Jesus is *in the order of Melchizedek* rather than the order of Aaron. What little we know about Melchizedek, we learn from Genesis 14:17-20. When Abram returned home after a victory over a coalition of Near Eastern kings, he was met by Melchizedek, who is identified as "king of Salem" and the "priest of God Most High" (Genesis 14:18). In what was apparently some kind of a religious ceremony, Melchizedek "brought out bread and wine" (v. 18), and Abraham in turn "gave him a tenth of everything" (v. 20). Since Melchizedek had obviously been appointed to his office by God and because his priesthood preceded that of Aaron's, the implication is that his priesthood is superior to Aaron's.

## C. LEARNED THROUGH SUFFERING (vv. 7, 8)

**7, 8. During the days of Jesus' life on earth, he offered up prayers and petitions with loud cries and tears to the one who could save him from death, and he was heard because of his reverent submission. Although he was a son, he learned obedience from what he suffered.**

*During the days of Jesus; life on earth* refers to Christ's incarnation, a subject that we saw the writer discuss in last week's text from Hebrews 2:5-11, 14-18. That "the Word became flesh" (John 1:14) brought many limitations. One of these was the suffering Jesus experienced. The mention of *prayers and petitions with loud cries and tears* brings to mind Jesus' prayers in the Garden of Gethsemane (Matthew 26:36-46; Mark 14:32-42; Luke 22:39-46). Jesus' spiritual and emotional agony during that experience is graphically expressed in Luke's Gospel: "His sweat was like drops of blood falling to the ground" (22:44).

The mention of Jesus' prayers and suffering is designed to show how completely he identified with the human race. As our great high priest, he knew the agony that we suffer and much more, for his suffering greatly surpassed anything that we might experience. When he prayed in Gethsemane, he prayed for far more than just the avoidance of the pain of physical death. His agony involved bearing the weight of human sin, a burden beyond our ability to comprehend.

The writer then observes that Jesus *learned obedience from what he suffered*. This does not mean he was disobedient before and had to learn obedience in the sense of learning how to obey. He learned obedience by experience. Had he remained in Heaven and not taken human flesh, he would have had no occasion for obedience. By becoming a man, he voluntarily subjected himself and became obedient. He did it for our benefit, so that we who are obedient (verse 9) would benefit from his obedience. As he was made perfect through suffering (2:10) on behalf of mankind, even so he became obedient through suffering to benefit mankind.

### SURRENDERING TO THE WILL OF GOD

Hebrews 5:7 tells us that when Jesus prayed he was heard because of his "reverent submission" to his Father's will. What does it mean to pray according to the will of God? It means much more than just mindlessly tacking on the phrase, "if it be your will." It involves telling God what we honestly want but letting him choose what he will do and how he will answer.

As a young man, Augustine, the brilliant theologian of the early church, led a wild and profligate life. His family was living in North Africa when Augustine told his mother that he was going to Rome to study rhetoric and public speaking. She immediately began to pray for God to keep Augustine from going to Rome. She was sure the evils of that great city would destroy him. But despite his mother's prayers, Au-

OPTION

The writer says, "During the days of Jesus' life on earth, he offered up prayers and petitions with loud cries and tears." Use the reproducible activity "Prayers of Jesus" on page 400 to explore some of those prayers.

WHAT DO YOU THINK?

Jesus prayed "to the one who could save him from death," but suffered a violent death anyway. Yet we are told his prayers were heard. How does that reassure us when it seems our prayers are not heard? How can we remain confident that God is working for our good, as he promised, even when that requires a difficult trial to be endured? How can we encourage struggling brothers and sisters?

## PRAYER

*Almighty God, we give you thanks for sending your Son into the world, not only to die for our sins but to return to Heaven to be our great high priest before the throne of grace. Give us the wisdom and strength to share this wonderful good news with those all about us. In Jesus' name we pray. Amen.*

## THOUGHT TO REMEMBER

*Jesus is the author of salvation to all who obey him.*

## DAILY BIBLE READING

*Monday, July 14—Melchizedek Is King of Peace (Hebrews 7:1-10)*

*Tuesday, July 15—High Priests Offer Blood Sacrifices (Hebrews 9:1-10)*

*Wednesday, July 16—Christ's Prayer to Be Glorified (John 17: 1-5)*

*Thursday, July 17—Christ Is High Priest Forever (Hebrews 7:11-19)*

*Friday, July 18—Christ Sits at God's Right Hand (Hebrews 8:1-6)*

*Saturday, July 19—Christ Intercedes for Us (Hebrews 7: 20-28)*

*Sunday, July 20—Nothing Can Separate Us From God's Love (Romans 8:31-39)*

gustine went. While there, some of Augustine's friends encouraged him to go to Milan, Italy, to study the great preacher Ambrose, who was acknowledged as the greatest public speaker of his day. Augustine went and returned again and again. Eventually he was converted to Christianity and became a powerful spokesman for the Christian faith.

Scholars today doubt whether anyone else in the world but Ambrose could have reached a brilliant young mind like Augustine's. Yet all that time Augustine's mother was praying, "Don't let Augustine go to Rome."

Did God answer her prayer? Yes. Did God give her what she asked? No, but he gave her something better. We should pray with a willingness to accept the greater good that God may give us when, in his infinite wisdom, his answer comes in a form different from what we have asked. Let us cultivate an attitude of "reverent submission" to him in our prayer life.

—C. B. Mc.

### D. OFFERS ETERNAL SALVATION (vv. 9, 10)

**9, 10. And, once made perfect, he became the source of eternal salvation for all who obey him and was designated by God to be high priest in the order of Melchizedek.**

This demonstrates the tie between Jesus' obedience through suffering and his being made perfect through suffering (Hebrews 2:10) commented on above. Through his obedience Christ was *made perfect*—he completed his mission. Having completed his mission, *he became the source* of our *eternal salvation*. As the spotless Lamb of God, he provided the perfect sacrifice that was needed to forgive every sin. This offer of salvation, however, is not universal. It is available only to those who *obey him*. Thus the writer has returned to the point where we began in our printed text. His call to "hold firmly to the faith we profess" is, after all, a call to continued obedience.

The writer of Hebrews mentions *Melchizedek* once again at the end of this verse, and then observes that of him, "we have much to say about this, but it is hard to explain" (v. 11). Most of these additional details regarding Melchizedek are found in chapter 7.

### CONCLUSION

Although many church hymnals have been updated and have left out some of the more traditional hymns, most of them still include an old favorite, "What a Friend We Have in Jesus." And for good reason! Countless believers have found strength and reassurance in its words. The hymn also reflects some of the main points of today's lesson. The first stanza reminds us of our Friend, Jesus, who bears "all our sins and griefs." Whereas the Old Testament priest offered "gifts and sacrifices for sins" (Hebrews 5:1), Jesus offered but one sacrifice: his own life, given on the cross as an atonement for our sins.

As our great high priest, Jesus serves as the mediator between man and God. Because of this we may "approach the throne of grace with confidence" (Hebrews 4:16). We often fail to take advantage of this great privilege, and as a result we "often forfeit" peace and bear "needless pain. . . . All because we do not carry Ev'rything to God in prayer."

In addition, our great high priest has been "tempted in every way, just as we are" (Hebrews 4:15). The hymn reminds us that we can take our problems to Jesus in prayer because he "knows our ev'ry weakness." When we have "trials and temptations," we know that Jesus will understand, because he was "tempted in every way, just as we are—yet was without sin" (v. 15).

You may want to consider closing the class period by singing this hymn.

# Discovery Learning

*This page contains an alternate lesson plan emphasizing learning activities. Classes desiring such student involvement will find these suggestions helpful. The next page is a reproducible activity page to further enhance discovery learning.*

## LEARNING GOALS

After studying this lesson, students should be able to:

1. Compare the work of Jesus with that of the high priest.

2. Explain what makes Jesus a superior high priest.

3. Accept the role of priest, serving under the high priest Jesus on behalf of others.

## INTO THE LESSON

To begin the session, ask how many remember the old TV game show "Truth or Consequences." It was a show where the host asked a question, and, if the contestant could not answer correctly, he or she had to pay the consequences. Ask for a volunteer to play the game.

Ask your contestant, "What was the most important function of the high priest?" Tell the contestant to think about it before answering. Say, "Take all the time you need." Pause about a second and then make a buzzer sound. Say, "I'm sorry. Time's up!"

Tell them that today's lesson will explain more about the role of the high priest, and how Jesus fulfills that role perfectly. "But first, our contestant has to face the consequences!" Have the contestant perform something he or she would not normally do, like sing a solo (a children's song, perhaps), whistle a song—something in good taste but mildly embarrassing!

## INTO THE WORD

Number the people in your class: 14, 15, 16, and then 1 through 10, so that you can assign the verses of today's text. Give a student more than one verse if necessary. Have the following questions written on separate cards. Notice that there is one question for each verse.

4:14: Since Jesus has gone through the heavens, what should we do?

4:15: What is different about the effects of temptation in our lives and in the life of our high priest?

4:16: What attitude is appropriate when we approach the throne of God?

5:1: What two items does the earthly high priest offer?

5:2: Why can the priest have compassion on the weak?

5:3: For whose sin does the priest make an offering?

5:4: What Mosaic priest is named in today's text?

5:5: What words from the Psalms does the writer of Hebrews say were spoken to Jesus?

5:6: To what order of priests does Christ belong?

5:7: With what did the Son offer prayers and petitions?

5:8: How did the Son learn obedience?

5:9: How does one gain the eternal salvation Jesus offers?

5:10: Who called Jesus to be high priest?

Call on another class member, especially one who was not given a verse to read, to ask the questions. Direct those who were given verse numbers to answer from the appropriate verse. At the end of the question and answer time, ask, "How did this activity resemble the role of a priest?" Answer: "I, the teacher, had someone act on my behalf to ask the questions. This is what a priest does; he acts on behalf of others."

## INTO LIFE

Most Scriptures contain "Whats" and "So Whats," or, truths and consequences. Read each of the following "Whats" from today's text and ask the students to identify some of the corresponding "So Whats." If they need help, suggest that they think in terms of, "If Jesus . . . ," then "we ought to . . ."

(1) Jesus is our high priest. (2) Our high priest is touched by our weaknesses. (3) Jesus learned obedience by the things he suffered. (4) Jesus promises eternal salvation to all who obey him. (5) Jesus prayed with tears. (6) Jesus is a priest in the order of Melchizedek. (7) A high priest does for another what that person cannot do for himself. (8) Christ did not glorify himself.

The students should see and offer a variety of responses; the following are given as examples (the numbers match the above statements). (1) We ought to use his services to the fullest. (2) We should never imagine ourselves abandoned or ignored by God. (3) We must continue to trust God, even in difficult circumstances. (4) We must obey God. (5) Our prayers must not be casual or thoughtless. (6) We must know and understand Melchizedek's role, according to the Scriptures. (7) We must never be so self-assured that we believe we have no need for Jesus. (8) We must allow God to glorify us, never seeking to glorify ourselves.

The apostle Peter says that all Christians are part of a "royal priesthood" (1 Peter 2:9). In closing, discuss with the class what it means to fulfill that calling on a daily basis.

## OPTION

Use the reproducible activity "Be a Priest" on page 400.

# Prayers of Jesus

"During the days of Jesus' life on earth, he offered up prayers and petitions" (Hebrews 5:7). Use your Bible to verify what Jesus prayed for in each of the occasions represented by the following references. Draw a line connecting each reference to its proper object.

Matthew 11:25—                    —for forgiveness for his tormentors

Matthew 14:19—                    —for glory in his own death

Matthew 26:39—                    —unity for his church

Mark 14:22, 23—                   —that Peter's faith would not fail

Luke 11:2-4—                      —thanksgiving for loaf and cup

Luke 22:31, 32—                   —for giving the gospel to "little children"

Luke 23:34—                       —the "cup" of suffering to be removed

John 11:41, 42—                   —a "model" prayer

John 17:1-5—                      —blessing on food for a multitude

John 17:20, 21—                   —thanks for hearing his prayer

# Be a Priest!

A priest represents another person to God. He intercedes for spiritual blessings. He pleads for mercy and grace. Peter, by the Spirit, has called all of us in Christ "a royal priesthood." Read 1 Peter 2:4-9. How do you see yourself filling your duties as a "holy priest"? How can you call down spiritual blessings on those you love? How will you plead for God's forgiveness for the sinners you most care for? Make a list here of people you can minister to and specific ways of doing so.

| PERSON | WAYS OF MINISTERING TO HIM OR HER |
|---|---|
|  |  |

**Prayers of Jesus:** The Scriptures, if listed in the same order as the prayers, would be in this order: Luke 22:31, 32; Mark 14:22, 23; Matthew 11:25; Matthew 26:39; Luke 23:34; John 17:1-5; John 17:20, 21; Luke 11:2-4; Matthew 14:19; John 11:41, 42.

# JESUS IS THE SACRIFICE

**LESSON 9**

## WHY TEACH THIS LESSON?

Say the word *sacrifice* today and many people think first of baseball. When a batter deliberately puts himself in a position to be put out in such a way that it advances a runner, that is called a sacrifice. It is a noble task, rewarded by not being tallied as an official "at bat," which would lower the batter's batting average.

Of course, this is a sanitized version of the original, but it is still instructive. When we think of Jesus' sacrifice, we recall that he gave himself deliberately to advance the cause of others. It is important to recall that, for it was the only way that "cause" could be advanced. We could not earn our own way, we could not atone for our own sin. We needed Jesus to sacrifice himself.

But perhaps that baseball scene is too sanitary. At least the blood and the smell of slaughtered animals showed us just how nasty sin is. This lesson will help your students see something of the Old Testament sacrificial system and contrast that with the sacrifice of Christ. Help them to see both the ugliness of sin and the beauty of God's grace given at Calvary.

## INTRODUCTION

### A. TO SACRIFICE A SON

Many incidents recorded in the Old Testament give us a preview of what is to be revealed more fully in the New Testament. For example, God gave Abraham a son through Sarah in his old age. No doubt Abraham experienced a sense of pride as he watched Isaac grow to maturity. But then came a commandment from God that must have devastated the aged father: he was ordered to offer Isaac as a sacrifice. Although Abraham must have been overwhelmed by his sadness, he prepared to carry out God's order. Isaac, too, was a willing participant in this test of Abraham's faith, for he could easily have run from his father when he realized what was about to happen. Of course, the story had a happy ending: Isaac was not sacrificed, and a substitute was found for him.

This touching story should lead us to a greater appreciation of what Jesus came to do for us. Though we cannot fully comprehend all that occurred at the cross, we know that Jesus was dying there in our place, in obedience to his Father. But whereas God intervened to spare Isaac, he did not spare his own Son, but permitted him to suffer the agonies of the cross as a sacrifice for our sins.

### B. LESSON BACKGROUND

Jewish Christians in the first century were under various pressures to abandon their Christian faith and return to Judaism. The writer of Hebrews advances several arguments why they should resist this temptation. His major thrust is that Christianity is superior to Judaism. In the first lesson of this unit, we noted that Christianity is superior because it is based on a fuller revelation; in the former days God spoke through the prophets, but in "these last days" he has spoken through his Son (Hebrews 1:1, 2). In the second lesson, Jesus was presented as our Savior, God becoming a man that he might release mankind from bondage to Satan and to death. In last week's lesson, Jesus was presented as the great high priest after the

DEVOTIONAL READING
HEBREWS 9:23-28

LESSON SCRIPTURE
HEBREWS 9:11–10:18

PRINTED TEXT
HEBREWS 10:1-14

LESSON AIMS

From today's study, each student should:

1. Contrast the system of Aaronic sacrifices with the sacrifice of Christ.

2. Explain why the sacrifice of Jesus is sufficient "once for all."

3. Be able to share with others his or her experience of forgiven sin.

July
27

KEY VERSE

By one sacrifice he has made perfect forever those who are being made holy.　Hebrews 10:14

*Have the visual for lesson 9 on display as students arrive. It is a dramatic picture of three crosses with the triumphant statement: "It is finished!"*

## WHAT DO YOU THINK?

*Some people seem to think they need to perform acts of devotion to God or kindness to others, in addition to those one might normally do, in order to receive forgiveness for their sins. This concept of "doing penance" is like the hours of "community service" that judges sometimes require from someone convicted of a crime. But such a plan for earning "extra credit" is tied to a belief in works salvation. No one can earn saving grace from God. Christ's sacrifice has atoned for sin "once for all"!*

*How would you counsel a fellow believer who was feeling guilty for some past sin and was wanting your advice on what he or she could do to "make up for" that sin?*

order of Melchizedek, and as superior to the Hebrew priests who were descendants of Aaron.

Today's lesson focuses on still another aspect of Christ's superiority: Jesus was a better *sacrifice*. The countless sacrifices offered under the Mosaic Law were never adequate because the blood of animals could not take away sin. Only the perfect sacrifice, Jesus Christ, could do that.

## I. IMPERFECT SACRIFICES (HEBREWS 10:1-6)

### A. ONLY A SHADOW (v. 1)

**1. The law is only a shadow of the good things that are coming—not the realities themselves. For this reason it can never, by the same sacrifices repeated endlessly year after year, make perfect those who draw near to worship.**

In previous chapters, the author of Hebrews had set forth Jesus Christ as the perfect sacrifice for man's sins (2:9, 17; 7:26-28; 9:26-28). Our printed text is something of a summary of the writer's argument up to this point.

*The law* and its various details were but *a shadow of the good things that are coming.* A shadow is never a very good representation of reality, because it does not show color. A shadow provides no details, only an outline of what is real. But the presence of a shadow proves there is something of substance nearby. The New Covenant is the "something of substance," *the realities*, indicated by the Law.

In this verse the writer of Hebrews sees the shadowy nature of the Law specifically in the sacrifices that it required. He places particular emphasis on the sacrifices associated with the Day of Atonement, which were offered *endlessly year by year*. The very fact that these had to be repeated is clear evidence that they could not *make perfect those who draw near to worship.* Although these ceremonies were impressive, they could not free worshipers from the guilt and the tyranny of their sins.

### B. TEMPORARY (vv. 2, 3)

**2, 3. If it could, would they not have stopped being offered? For the worshipers would have been cleansed once for all, and would no longer have felt guilty for their sins. But those sacrifices are an annual reminder of sins,**

Had the sacrifices required by the Law been able to address man's real need, *the worshipers . . . would no longer have felt guilty for their sins.* The frequent offerings were a continual reminder of the people's sin and its accompanying guilt.

But Christians, who have been *cleansed once for all,* sometimes still feel guilty. This feeling may deny them the joy that comes from being cleansed from one's sins, and it can very well cripple their effectiveness as servants of the Lord. The proper understanding of two points can perhaps solve this problem. The first point is theological: God has promised, under certain conditions, to remove our sins completely. These conditions are spelled out in such passages as Acts 2:38; 10:43; 22:16; Ephesians 1:7; Colossians 2:11-14). As Christians we then have "one who speaks to the Father in our defense" who pleads our case (1 John 2:1). We have this assurance: "If we confess our sins, he is faithful and just and will forgive us our sins and purify us from all unrighteousness" (1 John 1:9).

The second point is more practical. If we are to know the joy of forgiven sins, we must make restitution for them. If we have stolen, we ought to return what we have stolen. If we have cheated, we need to reimburse those whom we have cheated. Of course, no adequate restitution can be made for certain sins, such as murder. It is impossible for one to restore a life he has destroyed. At best, all he can do is to try to alleviate some of the consequences of such a terrible sin.

A note of caution must be inserted here. Restitution must not be seen as a form of paying for one's sins. One should never allow good deeds to serve as a salve to deaden his or her conscience to the seriousness of sin. Yet many forms of restitution, conscientiously pursued, can help restore the joy that sin has stolen and the sense that one's life can still be used of God.

## C. INEFFECTIVE (vv. 4-6)

**4. Because it is impossible for the blood of bulls and goats to take away sins.**

It should have been quite obvious that the sacrifice of animals was inadequate. Animals lacked any consciousness of sin; they were but innocent victims of a process that they could not understand. Furthermore, *it is impossible* for such material or physical items to make any lasting impact on man's standing with God. They are simply a shadow (v. 1), pointing out the need for something more effective. Only a perfect sacrifice could atone for sin.

**5. Therefore, when Christ came into the world, he said: "Sacrifice and offering you did not desire, but a body you prepared for me; with burnt offerings and sin offerings you were not pleased.**

Here the writer turns to the Old Testament Scriptures to strengthen his argument. He quotes from Psalm 40:6-8. Apparently the writer is quoting from the Septuagint (a Greek translation of the Old Testament), rather than the Hebrew text. As a result there is a slight difference in the quotation before us. Our translation reads, *but a body you prepared for me*, whereas the Psalms passage, based on the Hebrew, reads, "my ears you have pierced."

We may question why these translations are so different or why the writer of Hebrews would quote from a reading so different from the Hebrew text. The Hebrew reading calls to mind the practice, recorded in Exodus 21:5, 6, of piercing the ear of a servant who wanted to remain with his master for life. This would reflect Jesus' singular commitment to his heavenly Father's will. Ultimately that devotion resulted in Jesus giving his *body* as the sacrifice for the sins of the world.

The Septuagint reflects the pre-incarnate Christ receiving a *body* in order to live on earth and effect the plan of salvation. He did this by giving his life on the cross.

Thus, both readings find their fulfillment in the death of Jesus, by which he carried out his Father's plan and brought salvation to mankind. That offering accomplished what none of those items offered by the Law could ever accomplish. We may wonder why the author, writing to Hebrews, would quote the Greek translation instead of the original Hebrew. That we cannot answer, except to reaffirm that he did so by inspiration of the Holy Spirit (2 Timothy 3:16).

That God was *not pleased* with *sacrifice and offering* needs to be studied carefully, in light of the fact that God did command Israel to bring these (cf. verse 8), and that they constituted "an aroma pleasing to the Lord," as the laws in Leviticus 1-4 state repeatedly. But this was a temporary system, a shadow. Since these sacrifices simply could not take away sins (as v. 4 states), God was not content to continue this system; he was *not pleased* with it. *When Christ came into the world*, he brought a better sacrifice, for he brought himself. Ephesians 5:2 says, "Christ . . . gave himself up for us as a fragrant offering and sacrifice to God." The superiority of Christ's sacrifice is what the writer turns to next.

### THE WORLD'S MOST EXPENSIVE SACRIFICE

Because we do not live in a culture that offers animal sacrifices, it is hard to comprehend just how expensive the whole Old Testament sacrificial system was. Consider the cost of just the ordinary public temple sacrifices offered for the whole community (excluding whatever private sacrifices were made).

### WHAT DO YOU THINK?

There are those today who think they can atone for personal offenses through material sacrifices or gifts. Of course, this is absolutely wrong! How should we respond to such people? Suppose our church launched a major building program, and a wealthy non-Christian offered a gift of $100,000 and said, "I know I don't get to church much, but I try to treat people right and do good, and just hope that is 'enough.' Here's a token of my good intentions. I hope you can use it."

Should we accept the gift? Why or why not?

Every day of the year the priests sacrificed two lambs: one in the morning and one in the evening. On the Sabbath Day two additional lambs were sacrificed. At each new moon (signifying the beginning of a new month), the priests added two bulls, one ram, one goat, and seven lambs. They added a bull, a ram, a goat, and seven lambs for the Day of Atonement, and seventy-one bulls, fifteen rams, eight goats, and one hundred five lambs for the Feast of Tabernacles.

The Feast of Unleavened Bread (Passover) required another fourteen bulls, seven rams, seven goats, and forty-nine lambs, excluding the thousands of Passover lambs slain for all the families of Israel. (See the requirements for these sacrifices in Numbers 28, 29.) The Jewish historian Josephus estimated that at the A.D. 70 Passover 256,500 lambs were sacrificed in Jerusalem. At current prices, that Passover sacrifice cost almost thirty million U.S. dollars!

The world's most expensive sacrifice, however, is the one described in today's text from Hebrews 10. Jesus Christ paid the ransom for our sins, not with the blood of bulls and goats, but with his own blood. His single precious sacrifice cost more and did more than all others ever offered.        —C. B. Mc.

## II. THE PERFECT SACRIFICE (HEBREWS 10:7-14)

### A. FULFILLS GOD'S WILL (vv. 7, 8)

**7, 8. "Then I said, 'Here I am—it is written about me in the scroll—I have come to do your will, O God.'" First he said, "Sacrifices and offerings, burnt offerings and sin offerings you did not desire, nor were you pleased with them" (although the law required them to be made).**

Verse 7 continues the quotation from Psalm 40:6-8. Here the contrast is stated. God *did not desire* to continue the *sacrifices and offerings, burnt offerings and sin offerings.* These are intended to represent the entire sacrificial system of the Mosaic Law. Instead he sent his Son, who said, *I have come to do your will, O God.* The shadow of the old system (verse 1) could not accomplish God's will. Only the reality of the perfect sacrifice of Christ could fulfill God's will.

### B. PERMANENT (vv. 9-12)

**9, 10. Then he said, "Here I am, I have come to do your will." He sets aside the first to establish the second. And by that will, we have been made holy through the sacrifice of the body of Jesus Christ once for all.**

Through the obedience of Jesus Christ *the first,* that is, the Old Covenant, has been superseded by *the second,* or the New Covenant. This is the reason that it was such a serious mistake for the Hebrew Christians to return to the Old Covenant. God had set it aside. The only way to be faithful to that Old Covenant was to accept the New, for the purpose of the Law was to bring us to Christ! (See Galatians 3:24, 25.)

The process of being *made holy,* or set apart, now comes *through the sacrifice of the body of Jesus Christ.* This offering was made *once for all.* Since his sacrifice was perfect, it did not have to be repeated.

**11, 12. Day after day every priest stands and performs his religious duties; again and again he offers the same sacrifices, which can never take away sins. But when this priest had offered for all time one sacrifice for sins, he sat down at the right hand of God.**

These two verses set forth three ways in which the Aaronic priests differed from Christ. First, the Aaronic priests *stands* while Christ *sat down at the right hand of God.* This means that their work was never-ending, whereas Christ's work is completed. Second, the Aaronic priests *again and again* offered *the same sacrifices,* whereas Christ *offered for all time one sacrifice.* Third, the many sacrifices of the Aaronic priests

## WHAT DO YOU THINK?

*Suppose the youth of our church are planning to go on a retreat and you've been asked to review the program. One night a "sacrifice service" is planned, in which a lamb is to be offered as a sacrifice in the same manner as the Old Testament sacrifices. The program explains this is not an attempt to atone for sins, but is a visual demonstration of our need for atonement.*

*Would you support or oppose such an idea? Why? How do verses 6-8 of our text address the issue, if at all?*

## WHAT DO YOU THINK?

*While the slaughter of animals in a religious service is foreign to us, the idea of sacrifice is common. We see it in parents who sacrifice to send their kids to college or to give their children a "good Christmas." We see it in person who donates a kidney or other organ so that a loved one can live. If you have ever been the recipient of some such act of sacrificial love, you are undoubtedly grateful.*

*How might we demonstrate our gratitude for such acts? How can we demonstrate our gratitude to God for his greater sacrifice?*

*can never take away sins,* while Christ's sacrifice is sufficient to take away sins forever. A thousand years from now, if Christ has not returned, his blood will still be sufficient to forgive anyone.

### REBEL WITHOUT A CROSS

Barabbas was guilty of insurrection and murder. He and some of his cohorts had been caught and imprisoned. There Barabbas awaited his execution. As an enemy of the state, he knew he would be crucified.

Day after day Barabbas sat in the darkness of his cell and thought about dying on a cross. But when the Romans came for him, he was led from his cell, not to the cross, but to freedom. An angry mob and a band of religious power brokers had persuaded a spineless governor to nail a Galilean carpenter to a cross that should have belonged to Barabbas.

Looking at the larger picture, Barabbas stands for each of us. He was a condemned criminal who was freed because someone else took his place. Each of us is a condemned sinner who can be freed and forgiven if we accept the Christ who died in our place.

For Jesus did not die only on Barabbas's cross. He died on yours and mine.

—C. B. Mc.

## C. MAKES US PERFECT AND HOLY (vv. 13, 14)

**13, 14. Since that time he waits for his enemies to be made his footstool, because by one sacrifice he has made perfect forever those who are being made holy.**

Verse 13 uses the language of Psalm 110:1, a psalm with obvious Messianic implications. This psalm sets forth two aspects of the Messiah's work: the royal and the priestly. On the one hand, the Messiah is viewed as a conquering king, while on the other he is "a priest for ever after the order of Melchizedek" (Psalm 110:4). We see the same two aspects of Christ's ministry in the two verses before us.

Through Christ's *one sacrifice*, he *has made perfect forever* those who have accepted his sacrifice. They have been cleansed of their past sins, and thus stand perfected, or complete, before him. This does not mean that they are sinless. They *are being made holy*: they have been set apart for the Lord's service, and they are part of the ongoing process by which one becomes more like Jesus.

## CONCLUSION

### A. WHAT SACRIFICE MEANS

Years ago it was quite common for farmers to raise animals such as cows or pigs for their meat supply. When cold weather came, the animals would be butchered and the meat preserved by smoking, sugar curing, or canning. (In those days the only way that meat could be preserved by freezing was when the weather turned cold and stayed cold.) I was about six or seven when I first witnessed the butchering process. Late in the winter a calf had been born to one of our neighbor's cows. We watched him the first few days as he awkwardly made his way about the barnyard on unsteady legs. We continued to watch during the spring and summer, and were amazed at how quickly he grew and how agile he became. When fall came, we passed the barnyard each day on our way to and from school. Occasionally we would throw him a handful of grass or an apple. He repaid our kindness by coming to greet us when we came by.

Then came that fateful day. My brother and I did not realize what Dad meant when he said that the calf would be butchered. On a cold, crisp Saturday morning we witnessed the whole terrible process. We boys were heartbroken because even though the calf did not belong to us, it had become our pet. Dad tried to explain to us that life was like that—that some things had to be sacrificed in order for others

## PRAYER

*Holy and loving Father, we come before you giving our thanks for sending your Son to die for us. We thank you that this sacrifice will never have to be repeated. May this wonderful truth be the guiding light of our lives. In Jesus' name we pray. Amen.*

## THOUGHT TO REMEMBER

*"By one sacrifice he has made perfect forever those who are being made holy" (Hebrews 10:14).*

## DAILY BIBLE READING

*Monday, July 21—The New Covenant Superior to First (Hebrews 8:7-13)*

*Tuesday, July 22—Christ Sacrificed One Time Only (Hebrews 9:23-28)*

*Wednesday, July 23—The New Covenant Verified (Hebrews 9:11-22)*

*Thursday, July 24—God Does Not Want Sacrifices (Psalm 40:4-10)*

*Friday, July 25—To Obey Is Better Than Sacrifice (1 Samuel 15:16-23)*

*Saturday, July 26—To Love Is Better Than Sacrifice (Mark 12:28-34)*

*Sunday, July 27—Walk Humbly With Your God (Micah 6:1-8)*

to live. What he said to us did not make much sense to us then, but as the years passed, we ourselves became involved in the fall butchering ritual and came to accept it as just another part of rural life.

Few young people today have this experience. In fact, few farmers do their own butchering these days. The preparation of meat has become a sanitized manufacturing process performed out of the sight of most people. When we see cuts of meat neatly displayed in the grocery store, or eat a hamburger or chicken sandwich, we hardly give a thought to the process that was involved in making these foods available to us.

To some degree, this resembles our response to the death of our Lord on the cross. The early disciples who witnessed his crucifixion were overwhelmed by his death. Their leader—the best individual they had ever known—had been brutally slain by his enemies for no other reason than to maintain their control over the people. Only later, when the disciples began to learn the real meaning of Jesus' death, did they begin to understand what seemed at the time to have been a complete tragedy. What a difference it made when they came to realize that he died to save them from their sins! This frightened little band of followers was transformed into a spiritual force that challenged the Jewish leaders, took on the Roman Empire, and eventually spread throughout the whole world.

Insulated by two thousand years of history, have we lost our ability to feel either the tragedy or the power of Jesus' sacrificial death? Many have managed to encase his sacrifice in creeds, rituals, and traditions to the point that they no longer feel the impact of it. The Hebrew Christians, some of whom may even have witnessed Christ's death, were in danger of falling into the same trap, abandoning their Christian faith and returning to their former way of life.

Perhaps our appreciation of Christ's sacrifice for us would deepen if we could climb into some magical time machine and be transported back to the first century. Standing at the foot of the cross and watching Jesus die there would certainly give a deeper meaning to the words, "We have been made holy through the sacrifice of the body of Jesus Christ once for all" (Hebrews 10:10). Of course, we cannot go back in time. But we can give renewed diligence to our study of the Scriptures that tell us who Jesus is and what he did for us. May we never forget what his sacrifice means.

### B. ONCE FOR ALL

Under the Mosaic Law, the priests regularly conducted numerous sacrifices. Across the centuries multiplied thousands of animals were offered, first in the tabernacle worship and later in the temple worship. All of these were limited in their impact, for the blood of animals could not take away sin. At best these sacrifices could only remind the people of their continual guilt before God. From a positive standpoint, the sacrifices looked ahead to the perfect sacrifice of Jesus. As the spotless Lamb of God, Jesus gave himself "once for all" on the cross. His sacrifice does not need to be repeated.

"Once for all" has another application. Jesus was sacrificed for all—for everyone. The sacrifices in the tabernacle and the temple were primarily for the benefit of the Israelite people. Some allowance was made for "strangers" to participate (see Leviticus 17:8, 9; 22:18, 19), but clearly Gentiles were considered "excluded from citizenship in Israel and foreigners to the covenants of the promise" (Ephesians 2:12).

In glorious contrast, the benefits of Christ's death on the cross reached beyond the limits prescribed by the Law. The gospel message of hope was for *everyone*. What a wonderful opportunity we have to share this good news with the whole world: Christ died once for every sin of every person.

# Discovery Learning

*This page contains an alternate lesson plan emphasizing learning activities. Classes
desiring such student involvement will find these suggestions helpful. The next page
is a reproducible activity page to further enhance discovery learning.*

## LEARNING GOALS

From today's study, each student should:

1. Contrast the system of Aaronic sacrifices with the sacrifice of Christ.

2. Explain why the sacrifice of Jesus is sufficient "once for all."

3. Be able to share with others his or her experience of forgiven sin.

## INTO THE LESSON

Write the letters of the word *sacrifice* on your chalkboard or on a large poster. Ask the class members what they think of when they hear the term. Sports fans may say "baseball," many will mention the killing of animals. Some may recall Abraham's near sacrifice of Isaac. Some may think of horrible pagan practices of the past or even alleged Satanic activity in some communities today.

Observe the common features in each idea, that of giving up something to achieve a greater good—usually for someone else. This is what Jesus did for us. Though some try to remove the "blood" from their concept of faith, to do so is to abandon true Christianity. No amount of positive thinking or humanistic self-improvement can ever replace the vital role of Jesus as sacrifice, atoning for our sin as no one and nothing else could ever do!

## INTO THE WORD

Give your class this true-false quiz on today's text aloud Answers are given here.

(1) The system of Old Testament sacrifices was designed to make the people whole before God. ........................F

(2) Animal blood fully atoned for the worshiper's sin if he offered it in sincerity. ...................................................F

(3) Animal sacrifices were a constant reminder of personal sinfulness.................................................................T

(4) Old Testament priests had a never-ending job. ...........T

(5) The sacrifice of Jesus made the first system of sacrifices obsolete.........................................................................T

(6) The onetime offering of Jesus as a sacrifice for sin perfects forever those who are made holy through it. .......T

(7) The Law was to salvation as a shadow is to the substance creating it....................................................................T

(8) The author of Psalm 40 prophesied the incarnation of Christ. ...................................................................................T

(9) After being offered as a sacrifice for sin, Jesus took his place at the right hand of God. .....................................T

Once the students have had opportunity to respond, go through the statements for discussion, especially where there is disagreement. Some statements may lend themselves to more disagreement than others. For example, some may put *false* for the fourth statement, suggesting the Old Testament priest's job *did* end when he died. Point out that during the time the priest served in that capacity, he could never consider his job of offering sacrifices "finished." And even when he died, the *job* continued; his unfinished work was carried on by another. Only Jesus had the right to say, "It is finished."

### OPTION

Use the two activities on the reproducible page that follows to lead your class in a study of Hebrews 10.

## INTO LIFE

Hand each student seven blank cards (index cards will work fine, or strips of paper cut into rectangles will do). Direct each one to take the first card and put *A* on one side, *I* on the other; second card, *D* and *P*; third, *E* and *M*; fourth, *G* and *U*; fifth, *R* and *R*; sixth, *T* and *T*; and seventh, *Y* and *H*. Use one color for the letters on one side and a different color for the letters on the other side. Read aloud or summarize the story found in the first three paragraphs under the heading, "What Sacrifice Means," on pages 405, 406. Then read aloud the final three paragraphs of that section (beginning, "To some degree, this resembles . . ."). Now have each student lay out the seven cards and attempt to form a seven-letter word from the first set of letters: *A, D, E, G, R, T, Y*. Once someone forms *tragedy*, ask all to arrange their cards in the same way. At your direction have all turn their cards over, one at a time, to form the word *triumph*. Relate this to the material under "What Sacrifice Means," pointing out that the death of Jesus, which at first seemed an utter *tragedy*, was ultimately seen as a grand *triumph*.

Discuss, "How might comparing Christ's work with baseball sacrifices and the butchering of cattle help unbelievers see the practical value of Christ's sacrifice for sin?" Many people have negative views of the word *sacrifice*. If we can get them to consider the idea through one of these—or some other comparison—it might open a door to share one's personal "triumph" through the blood of Christ. Challenge the class to think of specific people with whom they can share this good news this week.

# What's the Difference?

Prepare an acrostic describing the animal sacrifices of Aaron's priests. Then, in the far right column, write a contrasting word that describes the sacrifice of Christ. (The second word need not start with the same letter.) Use Hebrews 10 for ideas. (One is done for you to give you the idea. If you need to, you can borrow some words from the next activity.)

| Aaronic sacrifice | Christ's sacrifice |
|---|---|
| **S** Shadow (v. 1) | Reality |
| **A** | |
| **C** | |
| **R** | |
| **I** | |
| **F** | |
| **I** | |
| **C** | |
| **E** | |

# Old or New?

Decide whether each of the following words relates to Aaron's sacrifices or to Christ's sacrifice. Put an *A* for the former, a *C* for the latter. It is possible you will put both *A* and *C* for some.

| | | | |
|---|---|---|---|
| ___ animal | ___ anticipatory | ___ altar | ___ all-sufficient |
| ___ continual | ___ conscience-pricking | ___ cross | ___ ended |
| ___ eternal | ___ established | ___ endless | ___ effectual |
| ___ final | ___ forced | ___ forever | ___ ideal |
| ___ image | ___ imperfect | ___ impotent | ___ inadequate |
| ___ repeated | ___ remembrance | ___ redemptive | ___ required |
| ___ shadow | ___ submissive | ___ substitutionary | ___ satisfactory |

Aren't you glad you're not a Hebrew living under the Old Testament system of animal sacrifices? Write a personal prayer of thanksgiving to the Lord for his personal sacrifice on your behalf. See how many of the following phrases you can include: "once for all," "Lamb of God," "whiter than snow," "perfected forever," "on the right hand of God."

Unit 2. Be Faithful Followers of Christ
(Lessons 10-14)

# GROW IN FAITHFULNESS

**LESSON 10**

## WHY TEACH THIS LESSON?

Is your class too large? I don't mean because your classroom is too small or that there aren't enough seats—are there people in your class who should be out teaching some other classes? Most churches have an ongoing struggle to keep enough teachers involved to lead the classes they want to offer. One of the reasons is addressed in our lesson text today. Some, who ought to be teachers, are still immature and need someone to teach the elementary principles again.

Challenge your class members to evaluate their growth. Are they using their gifts in ministry, or are they still just taking in? Should one or two of them begin to consider teaching that junior boys class? By next quarter, your class might be smaller—but you won't mind, will you?

## INTRODUCTION

### A. BONSAI CHRISTIANS

The Japanese have developed great skill in the art of *bonsai*—the growing of miniature trees. These trees may be decades old and yet only a few inches tall. Gardeners are able to produce them by using a number of special techniques. The roots are cut and restricted. The branches are carefully trimmed. Then water and fertilizer are also restricted. The result is a tree that has many features of a full-grown tree, yet is small enough to sit on a table or shelf.

Many Christians resemble these bonsai. In certain respects they may look like mature believers, but in reality they are mere babes in Christ. Satan is a master at growing bonsai Christians. He seeks to restrict our progress by keeping us from the Bible, prayer, fellowship, and other means of spiritual nourishment. The result is stunted bonsai Christians.

### B. LESSON BACKGROUND

This lesson begins a new unit, "Be Faithful Followers of Christ," which continues our studies from Hebrews. This unit addresses the problems and obstacles to growth that the Hebrew Christians were facing. They were in danger of succumbing to the temptation to abandon their faith in Jesus and retreat back into Judaism.

Most modern Christians have never been adherents of Judaism and may not be tempted to follow this particular faith. But they are often tempted to surrender to the secularism of the society around them. In some respects the appeal of secularism poses a more dangerous threat to modern Christians than Judaism did to these early Hebrew Christians. When a Hebrew Christian returned to Judaism, he moved from a very small minority group to a group that was larger, but still a minority. He was still considered out of the mainstream of the dominant culture of his day. On the other hand, the modern Christian, when he moves from Christianity back into the secular world, has become a part of the culture that is now dominant. He becomes like his friends and neighbors, and he does not have to feel different or out of place.

Another reason that secularism is so dangerous is that its temptations are so subtle. Secularism does not require its adherents to abandon their previous faith

DEVOTIONAL READING
HEBREWS 6:13-20
LESSON SCRIPTURE
HEBREWS 5:11–6:12
PRINTED TEXT
HEBREWS 5:11–6:10

LESSON AIMS

After studying this lesson, each student should:

1. Contrast the qualities of spiritual maturity with the consequences of remaining immature in the faith.

2. State the dangers and consequences of remaining immature in their faith.

3. Choose something to eliminate from his or her life and a way to move toward greater spiritual maturity.

Aug
3

KEY VERSE

Go on to maturity.

*Hebrews 6:1*

altogether. They can still attend church and be involved in church activities; at the same time, they may live much of their lives according to secular standards. In many instances it becomes difficult to tell Christians from non-Christians.

Thus, even though our circumstances today may be quite different from those of the original readers of Hebrews, the five remaining lessons in this quarter speak to some pressing needs within our churches and the lives of Christians.

## I. EVIDENCE OF SPIRITUAL IMMATURITY (HEBREWS 5:11-14)

### A. SLOW TO LEARN (v. 11)

**11. We have much to say about this, but it is hard to explain because you are slow to learn.**

In the previous verses of chapter 5, the writer has contrasted the priestly order of Aaron with that of Melchizedek. He has shown that Christ belongs to the order of Melchizedek, which is superior to the order of Aaron. Christ is superior because he "became the source of eternal salvation for all who obey him" (v. 9). (You may want to review lesson 8, which covered Hebrews 4:14—5:10.)

The writer is aware that many of his readers will not understand the relationship between the priesthoods of Aaron and Melchizedek. This concept should not have been new to them, since it is mentioned in Psalm 110:4. But their minds were clouded; they were being distracted. The writer challenges their thinking by calling them *slow to learn*, hoping to prepare them for other truths he wants to explain.

Literally he tells them, *You **have become** slow to learn.* This suggests that at one time they were growing, eager to learn new truths in their walk with the Lord. But the attraction to return to their old way, to the Law and its rituals, had stunted their growth in Christ.

### WHAT DO YOU THINK?

*Any number of things can cause us to be "slow to learn" spiritual truth: the enticements and distractions of this world, family, possessions, health, career, material wealth, an appetite for entertainment, and others. Which of these, or some other, do you think is the greatest hindrance to learning spiritual truth? Why? How can one eliminate this problem and become "quick to learn"?*

### LAZY

When the writer of Hebrews interrupts his discussion of Jesus and Melchizedek in chapter 5, he says that he did so because his readers were "slow to learn" (v. 11).

The word "slow" translates a Greek word *nothros*, which means "lazy" or "sluggish." The Greeks used it of lazy workmen. It is also found in Hebrews 6:12: "We do not want you to become lazy, but to imitate those who through faith and patience inherit what has been promised."

Did you ever notice how negative our words for lazy people are: SLUGGARD, LOAFER, BUM, GOLDBRICK, DEADBEAT, GOOF-OFF, TRAMP? These are all hated words—words that none of us wants applied to himself. Yet this is what the Hebrew Christians had become concerning God's Word. While they had been Christians for some time, they had failed to grow in their faith and in their knowledge of essential spiritual truths.

We need the discipline of an athlete, following Paul's advice to Timothy: "Train yourself to be godly" (1 Timothy 4:7). We cannot afford to be lazy in studying the Word.                                                  —C. B. Mc.

### B. NEEDING MILK (vv. 12, 13)

**12, 13. In fact, though by this time you ought to be teachers, you need someone to teach you the elementary truths of God's word all over again. You need milk, not solid food! Anyone who lives on milk, being still an infant, is not acquainted with the teaching about righteousness.**

Growth toward maturity in the faith seldom appears to progress at a consistent rate; usually it takes place by starts and stops. Still, since some of the readers of Hebrews had been Christians for quite some time (as seems the case from Hebrews 10:32), the writer had every reason to expect to see some signs of growth. He laments the fact that some individuals should have been *teachers*, yet they still needed someone to teach them a remedial course in basics, or *elementary truths*.

This assessment sounds very much like the condition of some in our churches today. They have been in Sunday school classes and other Bible study groups all of their lives, and yet they hardly know the fundamentals of the gospel. They have not progressed from the *milk* stage to the level of being able to handle *solid food* In some cases, teachers may share some of the responsibility for these biblical illiterates, for, as someone has observed, "If the student hasn't learned, the teacher hasn't taught."

## C. NOT OF FULL AGE (v. 14)

**14. But solid food is for the mature, who by constant use have trained themselves to distinguish good from evil.**

The diet of small babies is limited to milk because they lack the ability to chew and swallow or even to digest *solid food*. However, those who are *mature* can find nourishment in meat. Through this illustration, the writer was trying to show why immature Christians were having trouble understanding the doctrine of the superiority of the priesthood of Melchizedek and, as a result, the superiority of Christ's priesthood.

This verse also gives us some insights on how Christians attain maturity. They *by constant use have trained themselves* The word translated *trained* is the source of our word *gymnasium*. It describes the rigorous exercise by which athletes prepared themselves for their contests. Such physical conditioning cannot be accomplished in one quick burst of activity or by a hit-and-miss schedule.

Spiritual maturity is gained in the same way. Occasionally important spiritual insights may seem to come like brilliant bursts of light. In reality, such sudden illumination has been preceded by long periods of study and practice. We know, too, that a high spiritual level can be maintained only by giving regular attention to spiritual disciplines. Occasional prayer, sporadic church attendance, and infrequent instances of Christian service will not accomplish this.

Learning *to distinguish good from evil* is more than developing the ability to do right. In this context, it includes understanding the theology on which right decisions are made. The writer is explaining the passing of the Old Covenant with its Aaronic priesthood and the establishing of the New, with the order of Melchizedek. This is a theological issue and required maturity to be understood. Once they understood it, they could make right decisions, including the decision not to return to their old way.

### AN OAK OR A SQUASH?

When James A. Garfield was president of Hiram College, a wealthy man brought his son to be enrolled as a student. The man was very impatient for his son to finish college and join him in his business. The man asked if his son could take a shorter course of study than usual so he could get through college quickly. "Yes," Mr. Garfield answered. "He can take a shorter course than usual, but it all depends on what you want to make of him. It takes God a hundred years to produce a mighty oak, but he can turn out a squash in two months."

To be a mature Christian requires discipline and study. Today's text from Hebrews speaks of training and using our spiritual faculties so that we might become mature disciples.

The apostle Peter describes the process this way: "For this very reason, make every effort to add to your faith goodness; and to goodness, knowledge; and to knowledge, self-control; and to self-control, perseverance; and to perseverance, godliness; and to godliness, brotherly kindness; and to brotherly kindness, love. For if you possess these qualities in increasing measure, they will keep you from being ineffective and unproductive in your knowledge of our Lord Jesus Christ." (2 Peter 1:5-8).

## WHAT DO YOU THINK?

What are some issues you would describe as part of the "milk" of the Word? What are some that you would call "solid food"? Why?

What do you think would be a proper "balance" of these two types of study for children? for teens? for adults?

## HOW TO SAY IT

*Aaronic.* Air-AHN-ik.
*bonsai.* bahn-SYE.
*Melchizedek.* Mel-KIZ-eh-dek.
*nothros* (Greek). No-THROSS.
*Pilate.* PIE-lut.

To become a spiritual oak requires great diligence and effort. Shortcuts will yield only squashes.
—C. B. Mc.

## II. A CHALLENGE TO CHRISTIANS (HEBREWS 6:1-3)
### A. LEAVING FIRST PRINCIPLES (v. 1a)
**1a. Therefore let us leave the elementary teachings about Christ and go on to maturity.**

The writer in the previous verses has rebuked his readers because they were still babies in Christ, not mature enough for anything but milk. Now he challenges them to leave behind the milk of the *elementary teachings about Christ* and *go on to maturity*. Such a challenge indicates that these believers were actually ready to grow; they simply needed someone to encourage them and instill some self-confidence in them.

When the writer tells his readers to leave these principles behind, he does not mean for these principles to be discarded altogether. Instead, they should be used as a starting point for greater knowledge. We do not, for example, forget the alphabet when we learn to read. We use it as a building block for the development of higher skills. But we don't keep reciting the alphabet, either!

### B. NOT LAYING FOUNDATIONS AGAIN (vv. 1b-3)
**1b-3. . . . not laying again the foundation of repentance from acts that lead to death, and of faith in God, instruction about baptisms, the laying on of hands, the resurrection of the dead, and eternal judgment. And God permitting, we will do so.**

Here the writer lists some specific teachings that are included within the "elementary truths" to which he has referred (5:12). *Repentance* (Luke 24:46, 47; Acts 17:30), *faith in God* (Mark 16:16; Acts 16:31), and baptism (Acts 2:38; 22:16) were all associated with conversion in the New Testament church. These were basic, fundamental to beginning one's walk with the Lord.

The presence of the plural *baptisms* has led to a variety of interpretations by scholars and commentators. Since the writer is addressing the foundational teachings of Christianity, it is probably not reference to the various ceremonial washings associated with Jewish religious practices. It may be plural because the people had witnessed many baptisms as the church reached out to the world with its evangelistic message. Still another possibility is that this term refers to the various baptisms associated with the ministry of Jesus: John's baptism (Acts 19:1-5), Christian baptism (introduced on the Day of Pentecost), and the baptism of the Holy Spirit (Acts 1:5; 2:1-4). Whatever the meaning here, the writer urges his readers to progress beyond these teachings.

The *laying on of hands* was associated with the power of the apostles to impart the Holy Spirit to a person, endowing him with special miraculous gifts (Acts 8:14-24). The teachings concerning *the resurrection of the dead, and eternal judgment* deal with the future hope possessed by all Christians. Death is not the end for any faithful follower of Jesus. Judgment, which is a dreadful prospect for the lost, holds no fear for Christians, for they will have Jesus as their advocate on that day. These may seem like advanced topics to us today, but they were part of the gospel preaching designed to lead people to Christ in the first century. (See Acts 17:29-32; 24:25.)

## III. THE DANGERS OF TURNING BACK (HEBREWS 6:4-10)
### A. IMPOSSIBILITY OF RENEWAL (vv. 4-6)
**4-6. It is impossible for those who have once been enlightened, who have tasted the heavenly gift, who have shared in the Holy Spirit, who have tasted the goodness of**

**WHAT DO YOU THINK?**

What do you find to be the greatest help to your spiritual growth? The greatest hindrance? Why? What would you like to see our church do so that the programs or other things most helpful to your spiritual growth are more available? What would you be willing to do to assist in that?

**WHAT DO YOU THINK?**

Most churches know that it is important to "make disciples," which includes "teaching them to obey" (Matthew 28:19, 20). Many churches, however, are not very intentional about getting the task done. Even though they may provide a Sunday school class and/or a midweek Bible study, many churches have not defined how individual Christians will grow, nor have they provided a systematic way for that to be accomplished.

How well do you think we are doing in that regard? Why? What specifically are we doing to provide an increasingly challenging curriculum to longtime members? What more can we do?

**WHAT DO YOU THINK?**

How can we accommodate the needs of seekers or new believers in the church, but still help others move on to maturity?

*the word of God and the powers of the coming age, if they fall away, to be brought back to repentance, because to their loss they are crucifying the Son of God all over again and subjecting him to public disgrace.*

These verses provide an additional motivation for the Hebrew Christians to leave the first principles and continue to grow toward maturity. The motivation comes in the form of a solemn warning: to fail to grow is to invite the possibility that they will *fall away*, or reach a stage of apostasy from Christ, from which there is no return. Those in such danger are not described as casual church members who once made only a shallow commitment. The warning is directed to *those who have once been enlightened*; that is, they had a sound understanding of the Christian faith. They *have tasted the heavenly gift*: they had experienced the blessings that accompany the gift of salvation. They *have shared in the Holy Spirit*: they had received the gift of the Holy Spirit that is promised to all who believe in Christ, repent, and are baptized (Acts 2:38). They *have tasted the goodness of the word of God and the powers of the coming age*: they had known the joys that the message of salvation can bring, including the hope of eternal life.

Now comes the part of this verse that is perhaps most difficult to grasp. If people who have experienced all these blessings—who, in other words, have become Christians—then *fall away*, the writer says that *it is impossible* to bring them back to *repentance*. The reason is this: *they are crucifying the Son of God all over again.* Whereas those who partake of the Lord's Supper remember the crucifixion of Jesus for them, those described in this verse actually reenact the crucifixion, subjecting Jesus *to public disgrace*. They are rejecting their Savior, just as the Jewish leaders had rejected him before and delivered him to Pilate for crucifixion. This is the kind of willful sin discussed later in Hebrews 10:26, 27. Such a deliberate rejection of Christ and his salvation brings a person to a point of no return. The problem is not God's inability to help such a person; it is that person's unwillingness to be helped.

The writer of Hebrews was not suggesting that such dreadful apostasy had actually occurred among his readers. Rather, he was pointing out the dreadful results if it should happen. He has already warned his readers of the tragic consequences of unbelief and of their need to maintain their commitment to Jesus (3:7—4:11). He returns to this issue again in 10:26-39, warning them to hold fast and to guard against apostasy.

## B. An Illustration From Nature (vv. 7, 8)

**7, 8. Land that drinks in the rain often falling on it and that produces a crop useful to those for whom it is farmed receives the blessing of God. But land that produces thorns and thistles is worthless and is in danger of being cursed. In the end it will be burned.**

To make sure that no one misses his point, the writer offers an illustration from agriculture. He depicts a plot of ground that receives *rain* and is properly *farmed*, or cultivated. This plot in turn brings forth a bountiful crop. He then describes another plot that, although it receives similar treatment, produces nothing but *thorns and thistles. In the end it will be burned.* The writer suggests that a similar end awaits apostates.

## C. The Writer's Confidence (v. 9)

**9. Even though we speak like this, dear friends, we are confident of better things in your case—things that accompany salvation.**

The previous verses carried a severe warning against apostasy. Now addressing his readers as *dear friends*, the writer offers them words of encouragement. He does not believe that they are guilty of such apostasy at this point.

Let us leave the elementary teachings about Christ and go on to maturity.

*Display the visual for lesson 10 when you are ready to discuss Hebrews 6:1. Discuss the irony pictured on the poster. Compare that with the situation in which those who "should be teachers" are still needing the elementary principles explained to them again.*

## What Do You Think?

*What is our church doing to guard against the kind of "falling away" described in verses 4-6? What more can we do to keep those who "have tasted the heavenly gift" seated at the table and in fellowship with the rest of the church?*

## PRAYER

*Dear God, help us to realize that Satan is constantly attacking, seeking to cause us to turn back from our service to you. Give us the wisdom to recognize these temptations when they arise and the strength to resist them. Through Jesus our great high priest we pray. Amen.*

## THOUGHT TO REMEMBER

*"No one who puts his hand to the plow and looks back is fit for service in the kingdom of God"* (Luke 9:62).

## DAILY BIBLE READING

*Monday, July 28—God's Covenant Promise Unchanged* (Hebrews 6:13-20)

*Tuesday, July 29—Servants Rewarded for Good Work* (Matthew 10:34-42)

*Wednesday, July 30—By Grace We Are Saved* (Ephesians 2:1-9)

*Thursday, July 31—Escape Temptations With God's Help* (1 Corinthians 10:1-13)

*Friday, Aug. 1—God Punishes the Wicked* (Job 4:1-9)

*Saturday, Aug. 2—Grow in Your Salvation* (1 Peter 2:1-5)

*Sunday, Aug. 3—Prophecy Came From the Holy Spirit* (2 Peter 1:12-21)

## D. GOD'S SURE REWARD (v. 10)

**10. God is not unjust; he will not forget your work and the love you have shown him as you have helped his people and continue to help them.**

God is not some brutal tyrant who acts whimsically. As a righteous and loving God, he will remember the *work and the love* that his people *have shown him*. The Hebrew Christians had demonstrated their love for God by ministering to *his people,* an activity that they were faithful to *continue* .

## CONCLUSION

It is an axiom of human behavior that no one becomes good or bad suddenly. On one occasion we were shocked to learn that a bank officer, who was a church member and a highly respected leader in the community where we were living, had absconded with several hundred thousand dollars of the bank's funds. How were we to account for such a sudden breakdown in a person's moral character? The only way to understand such an action is to recognize that it was *not* sudden. Had we been able to look into the man's heart, no doubt we would have discovered that he had toyed with the idea for months or even years.

The first time Satan presented the temptation to this man, it is likely that he recoiled from it in shock. Such an idea was unthinkable! But Satan returned again and again, gradually wearing away the man's resistance. Finally, on that fateful day, the man yielded and the deed was done.

It was this kind of pattern against which the writer of Hebrews was warning. Apparently his readers had not yet reached the critical stage of apostasy from Christ, but he recognized the danger signs. A little turning back here, a tiny stepping aside here, and before long the person or the group has started down the long, slippery slope ending in destruction.

Christians today face a similar threat. At some point in a person's life, he or she makes a commitment to Jesus Christ. He recognizes him as our Lord and Savior, repents of his sins, and is buried with him in Christian baptism. As time passes, he grows in his faith and becomes more involved in the work of the Lord's kingdom.

Then something happens, perhaps something seemingly minor. He misses a church service, or he fails to carry out some assignment he had promised to do for the church. His conscience bothers him about it, and he promises himself that it will never happen again. But it does. It's easier the second time, and the third. The excuses become easier, too.

At the time, these departures from what he knows is right do not seem all that serious. After all, he says to himself, next month or next year it will be different. What he fails to realize is that he has started down a long, slippery slope—the same slippery slope about which the writer of Hebrews warns.

An airplane that makes a long flight over a large body of water carries enough fuel to make the flight, plus a reserve supply just in case some unanticipated problem arises. On rare occasions a problem does arise, and the plane, if it has flown a hundred or even several hundred miles out to sea, is able to turn back to the airport where it started. But there comes a time in the flight when the plane cannot turn back. It has reached the point of no return. Regardless of the problem, it cannot go back; it must continue its flight. Today's text from Hebrews has warned us about the danger of reaching a similar point of no return in departing from the faith.

Let us move on beyond the first principles, so that we do not fall into similar danger.

# Discovery Learning

*This page contains an alternate lesson plan emphasizing learning activities. Classes desiring such student involvement will find these suggestions helpful. The next page is a reproducible activity page to further enhance discovery learning.*

## LEARNING GOALS

After studying this lesson, each student should:

1. Contrast the qualities of spiritual maturity with the consequences of remaining immature in the faith.

2. State the dangers and consequences of remaining immature in their faith.

3. Choose something to eliminate from his or her life and a way to move toward greater spiritual maturity.

## INTO THE LESSON

If you or an acquaintance grows a bonsai plant, bring one to display as class begins. Use the lesson writer's introduction, entitled "Bonsai Christians," to introduce the concept of "stunted growth."

If such a plant is unavailable, prepare the door frame in the entrance to your room as a height-measuring device. Prominently mark inches and feet and post a can't-be-missed sign asking, "How Tall Are You?" If you think your class would feel comfortable with such an activity, measure each person, write his or her height on a small piece of paper, and hand it to the person.

## INTO THE WORD

Collect and have ready for display (but keep hidden) eight or more of the following items: (1) a ruler and chalk, (2) an empty milk carton, (3) an index card on which you have written, "A.A.R.P." (4) a pair of gloves, (5) a cross in any form, (6) a toy tractor or combine, (7) a will—or reasonable facsimile, (8) a thorny branch, such as one from a rosebush, (9) a piece of exercise equipment, such as a small dumbbell, (10) a baby doll, (11) a baptismal certificate, (12) a rain gauge, and (13) "Sure®" antiperspirant.

Tell the class members that you are going to display some objects that you want them to relate in some way to today's text. Ask them to wait until all objects are displayed before responding. (Have a table on which you can lay each object once you have clearly shown it to the group.) Since the objects are small, present each slowly and carefully, even moving about with it so that all can see. Random order is best.

Here is the verse to which each of the thirteen objects listed refers (numbered in accordance with how the objects were numbered earlier): (1) teaching (5:12, "ought to be teachers"); (2) immaturity (5:12, "need milk"); (3) maturity (5:14, "the mature," or 6:1, "go on to maturity"); (4) hands (6:2, "laying on of hands"); (5) crucifix-

ion (6:6, "crucifying the Son of God all over again"); (6) farming (6:7, "produces a crop"); (7) inheritance (6:12, "inherit what has been promised"); (8) growth of something useless or unwelcome (6:8, "produces thorns and thistles"); (9) training in righteousness (5:14, "trained themselves"); (10) infancy (5:13, "being still an infant"); (11) baptism (6:2, "instruction about baptisms"); (12) being fruitful for God (6:7, "land that drinks in the rain"); (13) assurance (6:11, "make your hope sure").

Once all of your objects have been introduced and displayed, ask the class to establish the relationships. Remember, even if they suggest ideas other than those listed, they *are* considering the text and its ideas closely. As the objects and the text are thus matched, you will have opportunity to ask whatever key questions or make whatever appropriate comments you choose.

## OPTION

Use the reproducible activity "Possibilities or Impossibilities" on page 416 to explore today's text.

## INTO LIFE

Have a class member dress in exercise clothes ("sweats") and be prepared to give the following "pep talk" on the elements of good health and fitness. Ask the person to exaggerate his or her talk in the hyperactive fashion of a TV "info-mercial" host or hostess and to include the following statements: (1) "You must eat the right foods...in the right amounts!" (2) "You must avoid the wrong foods...in any amounts!" (3) "You've got to get the blood pumping!" (4) "Your program must be regular, daily, constant!" (5) "There are no gimmicks, no shortcuts, no magic pills or tonics!" (6) "So . . . I am confident of better things in your case!"

Have these statements written on poster board or on an overhead transparency (which you will now display). Ask how each principle relates to developing our *spiritual* health. Point out that spiritual growth is not automatic; it requires disciplined effort.

Encourage your class to strive for the "better things . . . that accompany salvation," considering something specific to eliminate from or to add to their lives.

## OPTION

Use the reproducible activity "Do You Measure Up?" on page 416 to apply the lesson of today's text.

# Possibilities or Impossibilities

Decide where in today's text each of these possibilities is included. Write verse numbers.

___ I can become a teacher of the gospel.

___ I can become skillful in the Word.

___ I can learn to discern good and evil.

___ I can leave foundational truths to move to greater ones.

___ I can put Christ to open shame by my own immaturity.

___ I can move so far from Christ I cannot be restored.

___ I can enjoy all the delights which accompany salvation.

___ I can "taste the powers" of the world to come.

___ I can be rejected, like a weed, and end up being destroyed.

___ I can be noticed and remembered by God for my good works.

# Do You Measure Up?

Read Hebrews 5:11—6:10. If you could hold a spiritual yardstick alongside each of these elements of growth and maturity in your Christian life, how far would it reach? Rate yourself for each.

___ confidence in doctrine      ___ speaking the truth

___ meaningful prayer      ___ concept & practice of worship

___ evangelistic zeal      ___ self-control

___ joy in all circumstances      ___ ability to discern good and evil

___ service to others

What are you willing to do to "raise your score"? Write that below.

Clip the "ruler" from the left edge of this page and use it as a Bible bookmark or a bookmark for a spiritual growth book you are reading.

*"Until we all reach unity in the faith and in the knowledge of the Son of God and become mature, attaining to the whole measure of the fullness of Christ." Ephesians 4:13*

# REMAIN NEAR TO GOD

**LESSON 11**

## WHY TEACH THIS LESSON?

"How far can I go without sinning?" Why is it that we even want to ask that question? Why is it that we want to live close enough to the world to enjoy its temporal pleasures and at the same time close enough to God to enjoy his eternal ones? Why do we not, instead, ask, "Just how close can I get to God—how can I get closer?"

This is the challenge of our text today. "Let us draw near to God," without compromise, without looking back, without regret. Anyone who tries to live in both worlds is doomed to failure. Jesus' warning about trying to serve two masters should be well known to all of your students (Matthew 6:24).

Use this lesson to challenge your students to wholehearted surrender to the Lord Jesus Christ.

## INTRODUCTION

### A. STAY CLOSE TO CHRIST

A young boy once accompanied his father on a hike up a wooded mountainside. When they returned, the boy's mother asked him if he was afraid at any time during the hike. "The trees were so thick at times that we could hardly see our way," he replied, "but I wasn't afraid. At other times the trail was so overgrown that we could have got lost, but I wasn't afraid. Then one time we came around a curve in the trail, and there was a big bear and her cub, but I wasn't afraid. Once the trail ran along the top of a cliff, and I could have fallen off, but I wasn't afraid."

"Well, son, it sounds like you had a rather scary morning," said the mother. "Why weren't you afraid?"

"Because, Mommy, I stayed real close to Dad all the way."

That is what the writer of Hebrews had in mind when he urged his readers to draw near to Christ. As long as they were close to him, they had no reason to fear.

### B. LESSON BACKGROUND

In our earlier lessons from Hebrews, we have seen the author's strong doctrinal emphasis. He was intent upon setting forth the superiority of Christianity over the Judaism that his readers had left behind to follow Jesus. He showed how the high priesthood of Christ is superior to the high priesthood under the Mosaic Law. He also showed how Christ's sacrifice of himself is superior to all the animal sacrifices offered under the Law.

The writer brings his argument to a climax in the first eighteen verses of chapter 10. (Most of that passage comprises our text for lesson 9.) He concludes his contrast between the Old Covenant priesthood and the priesthood of Jesus. He affirms that the Law was merely "a shadow of the good things that are coming" (v. 1). The sacrifices it prescribed could never fully take away sin; only the one sacrifice of Jesus was sufficient to forgive all sins (v. 12). Beginning with verse 19 (where the printed text for today begins), the writer turns his focus to exhortations of a more practical and personal nature. He urges the readers not to ignore the wonderful blessings they have in Christ.

DEVOTIONAL READING
1 CORINTHIANS 1:1-10
LESSON SCRIPTURE
HEBREWS 10:19-39
PRINTED TEXT
HEBREWS 10:19-25, 32-39

LESSON AIMS

After studying this lesson, each student should:

1. Be able to list seven imperatives given to Christians in Hebrews 10.

2. Relate these imperatives to the challenges modern Christians face.

3. Carry a reminder to obey some of the imperatives from the lesson text.

Aug
10

KEY VERSE

Let us hold unswervingly to the hope we profess, for he who promised is faithful.

*Hebrews 10:23*

# I. RESPONDING TO GRACE (HEBREWS 10:19-25)

In Romans 12, Paul begins to make practical application of the doctrinal lessons he presented in chapters 1-11. He begins with *therefore*, and relates the activity urged on Christians to the grace or "mercy" of God (Romans 12:1). This is very much like the transition here in Hebrews 10. Because of forgiveness by God's grace, *therefore* the readers are urged to persevere.

## A. DRAW NEAR TO GOD (vv. 19-22)

**19-22. Therefore, brothers, since we have confidence to enter the Most Holy Place by the blood of Jesus, by a new and living way opened for us through the curtain, that is, his body, and since we have a great priest over the house of God, let us draw near to God with a sincere heart in full assurance of faith, having our hearts sprinkled to cleanse us from a guilty conscience and having our bodies washed with pure water.**

The writer shows his warm, personal relationship with his readers by addressing them as *brothers*. He then includes himself with them in his words *let us . . .* and with other first person references. This man is not some distant theologian setting forth his doctrines while isolating himself from his readers. Instead, he is dealing with practical spiritual matters that are as relevant to him as to them.

There is a strong contrast between the worshipers who would "draw near" in the Old Covenant (Hebrews 10:1) and those who *draw near* with *confidence* under the New. The Old Covenant worshipers could only come to the outer courts; a representative (the high priest) went for them into the Most Holy Place. Christians have direct access, they *enter the Most Holy Place,* that is, the heavenly sanctuary. (See Hebrews 9:24.) In the tabernacle, and later the temple, the high priest could enter the Most Holy Place only once a year, bringing the blood of the atonement sacrifice (Hebrews 9:25). Through *the blood of Jesus*, Christians are continually granted the opportunity to "approach the throne of grace with confidence" (Hebrews 4:16). The restrictions of the Old Covenant have been replaced by joyful access to God through *a new and living way.*

*Through the curtain* refers to the curtain that separated the Holy Place from the Holy of Holies. The high priest had to pass through this curtain to present his annual offering of blood for the people's sins on the Day of Atonement. The words *his body* have created considerable discussion among scholars and commentators. Some take them to refer back to the *way*, indicating that the way by which Christians enter the true Holy of Holies is through the death of Christ's physical body. Others believe that *body* refers to the *curtain*. They see the curtain not as a barrier to the Holy of Holies but as a means of entrance into it. Both views recognize the significance of the tearing of the curtain in the temple (Matthew 27:51), and of the giving of Jesus' body so that man might "enter the Most Holy Place" (v. 19). With either interpretation, the intent of this passage is clear: Christ is the *way* to the Father, a truth that Jesus himself clearly taught (John 14:6).

The writer then uses additional Old Covenant terminology to challenge his readers toward faithfulness to Christ. *Having our hearts sprinkled to cleanse us from a guilty conscience* is a blessing not possible under the old sacrificial system. (See Hebrews 9:13, 14; 10:1, 2; and the prophecy of this sprinkling in Ezekiel 36:25.) Being *washed with pure water* calls to mind the various instances in which water was prescribed for cleansing under the Law (see, for example, Leviticus 16:4; Numbers 19). Here the reference is most likely to Christian baptism. (See Titus 3:5.)

## B. HOLD UNSWERVINGLY TO THE HOPE (v. 23)

**23. Let us hold unswervingly to the hope we profess, for he who promised is faithful.**

### WHAT DO YOU THINK?

*Because of Jesus, Christians enjoy the privilege of drawing near to Almighty God without fear. Of course, we do not want to lose the sense of awe that should accompany a visit to the throne of grace. We certainly do not want to take for granted the high price he paid to open the way for us to come to him (the death of Jesus). What measures can we take to make sure that we do not forget the glory of God and what a blessing it is to be able to approach him freely?*

The writer has already encouraged his readers to *hold* and to follow closely the truth that they have received (2:1; 3:6, 14; 4:14). The same exhortation is given to them in this verse. Their *hope* is not some vague wish for better days; it is a confident expectation based on the faithfulness of the one *who promised*. The writer has reminded them before that since "it is impossible for God to lie," they "have this hope as an anchor for the soul, firm and secure" (6:18, 19).

This hope is expressed in faithful allegiance to the Lord without compromise. This has been a recurring theme in Hebrews. The writer has urged "diligence to the very end, in order to make your hope sure" (6:11). He has reminded them their hope is anchored in the "inner sanctuary" (6:19) and that it is a "better hope" than that offered under the Old Covenant, "by which we draw near to God" (7:19).

### HOLDING FAST TO OUR PROMISES

In his book *Up From Slavery*, Booker T. Washington describes meeting an ex-slave from Virginia who, three years before the Emancipation Proclamation, had made a contract with his master to buy his freedom by making an annual payment of a certain sum. While he was paying for his freedom, the slave was permitted to work wherever and for whomever he pleased. Finding that he could secure better wages in Ohio, he went there.

When the Emancipation Proclamation was issued, the slave was still $300 in debt to his master. Even though the Proclamation freed him from any obligation to his master, this slave walked the greater part of the distance back to Virginia and placed the last dollar, with interest, in his former owner's hands.

Booker T. Washington said that this freed slave knew he had no legal obligation to pay the debt, but he did it anyway because he had given his word to his master, and he had never broken his word. He could not enjoy his freedom until he had fulfilled his promise.

When we become Christians, we make a promise to be faithful to Christ, to do his will, and to live by his Word. We have even more reason to be faithful to our Master than the slave did to his. In our Master's service lies the only true freedom.

—C. B. Mc.

### C. ASSEMBLE WITH AND ENCOURAGE OTHERS (vv. 24, 25)

**24. And let us consider how we may spur one another on toward love and good deeds.**

Spurs are used by riders to encourage their horses to move, or to move faster. The horse is motivated by pain, but that part of the analogy should not be pressed. Here the idea is that through their words and their actions, Christians are to serve as models to encourage others *toward love and good deeds.*

**25. Let us not give up meeting together, as some are in the habit of doing, but let us encourage one another—and all the more as you see the Day approaching.**

One way Christians can fulfill the exhortation of verse 24 is by setting the example of regular attendance when the church assembles for study and/or worship. While this is certainly not the only mark of a faithful Christian, ordinarily it is a pretty accurate barometer of one's spiritual state. Irregular or infrequent worship attendance is usually a sign that a person is not holding unswervingly to the hope he professes. Someone has likened Christians to coals in a fireplace. Lumped together, coals glow and give off light and warmth, but if a coal is removed from the fireplace and placed alone on the hearth, it soon grows cold.

Believers have a responsibility to exhort their fellow believers not to neglect gathering for worship. The phrase *as you see the Day approaching* may call attention to the approach of the Lord's Day each week. However, many scholars think it refers to the approaching day of judgment that would soon fall upon the Jewish

### WHAT DO YOU THINK?

*Ministers, nominating committees, ministry team leaders, Sunday school superintendents, and others charged with recruitment are always looking for the most effective methods for motivating people to love and good works. What methods or influences are most effective in encouraging people into ministries of love and good works? How could you be involved in encouraging people to get involved in such ministries?*

### WHAT DO YOU THINK?

*Why do some people get in the habit of not attending corporate worship services? What can or should we change about our meetings to encourage greater faithfulness in attendance? What can or should be changed in the infrequent attender's life? How?*

people. That day came in A.D. 70, when Jerusalem fell to the Roman legions led by the general Titus. The city was destroyed, along with its beautiful temple, which was never rebuilt. Still another view is that *the Day* refers to the day of Christ's return. We prepare for that Lord's Day by being faithful in observing the present Lord's Day.

### Why I Quit Church

A story from a small town newspaper carried the headline: "Preacher Quits Sports." In the article, a minister gave twelve reasons why he had stopped attending athletic contests. Here they are:

1. Every time I went, they asked me for money.
2. The people sitting near me didn't seem to be very friendly.
3. The games are scheduled when I want to do other things.
4. The seats are too hard and not comfortable.
5. My parents took me to too many games when I was growing up.
6. I don't want to take my children, because I want them to choose for themselves what sport they like best.
7. Some games went into overtime, and I was late getting home.
8. The band played some songs that I didn't know.
9. The coach never came to call on me.
10. The referee made a decision with which I disagreed.

These would be ridiculous excuses to quit attending sports events. They are even more ridiculous reasons for not meeting with the church. The Bible assumes that the Lord's people will be together on the Lord's Day. If you are a student, you go to school. If you are an employee, you go to work. If you belong to a sports team, you go to practices and games. Likewise, if you belong to the church, you assemble and worship with the church.       —C. B. Mc.

## II. CONTINUING IN FAITHFULNESS (HEBREWS 10:32-39)

Verses 26-31 are not included in our printed text. They carry a stern warning for those who knowingly and deliberately turn away from Jesus, similar to the warning in the text used in last week's lesson (Hebrews 6:4-8). Now we see words of encouragement to the Hebrew Christians based on their faithfulness under stressful conditions in the past.

### A. Remember and Hope (vv. 32-34)

**32, 33. Remember those earlier days after you had received the light, when you stood your ground in a great contest in the face of suffering. Sometimes you were publicly exposed to insult and persecution; at other times you stood side by side with those who were so treated.**

Receiving *the light* refers either to the act of becoming a Christian, as it identifies one with Jesus Christ, the light of the world (John 1:9; 8:12). In taking this decisive step, these believers had been involved in *a great contest in the face of suffering.* They had paid dearly for their choice to follow Jesus.

The writer then proceeds to mention some of the suffering that the Hebrew Christians had endured. Some commentators believe that, at the time of the writing of Hebrews, these persecutions had not been severe enough to involve martyrdom. This argument is based on Hebrews 12:4: "In your struggle against sin, you have not yet resisted to the point of shedding your blood." This was certainly not the case for Christians in Jerusalem. Beginning with Stephen, some had been martyred for their faith. The apostle James is another example (Acts 12:1, 2), and Paul indicates that there were others in Acts 22:4. Roman persecution of Christians was less intense before A.D. 64. Jews had been expelled from Rome by Emperor

### What Do You Think?

In our culture, Christians have not had to suffer a great deal of direct persecution for their faith. There is, however, an impatience or even intolerance on the part of some in our culture toward people of faith and conviction. More and more faith is being relegated to "personal" concerns, which means it is not supposed to come out in public. Those who take a public stand for faith are accused of "imposing a moral standard" on others.

What "insult and persecution" have you suffered as a Christian? How should Christians respond to such treatment?

Claudius in 49 (Acts 18:1, 2), affecting some Christians (such as Aquila and Priscilla if they were believers that early), but there is no evidence that any of them was martyred during this expulsion. The situation changed drastically in A.D. 64, when Emperor Nero intensified the persecution. Christians were subjected to unspeakable cruelty, and martyrdom became a common occurrence. It is likely that both Peter and Paul died in Rome during Nero's reign.

The Hebrew Christians had at one time been *publicly exposed*, meaning that they were the subjects of public ridicule. They were commended by the author, not only because they had remained faithful through such *insult and persecution*, but also because they had provided support and companionship to *those who were so treated*. Had they forgotten the thrill of serving Christ and suffering for his sake in those *earlier days*?

**34. You sympathized with those in prison and joyfully accepted the confiscation of your property, because you knew that you yourselves had better and lasting possessions.**

These Christians had reached such a level of maturity that they could actually accept *joyfully* the *confiscation* of their *property*. The word *confiscation* suggests some kind of government sponsored persecution. The believers possessed the faith of the apostles in Jerusalem, who rejoiced "because they had been counted worthy of suffering disgrace for the Name" (Acts 5:41). They were willing to suffer such loss with joy because they knew they had in Heaven *better and lasting possessions*. As long as they held this faith firmly, earthly treasures mattered little or nothing to them. How strikingly different from the attitudes of our materialistic age!

## B. PERSEVERE WITH CONFIDENCE (vv. 35, 36)

**35, 36. So do not throw away your confidence; it will be richly rewarded. You need to persevere so that when you have done the will of God, you will receive what he has promised.**

The Hebrew Christians had come to know Christ and the *confidence* that faith in him can bring. Now they were in danger of throwing all of that away. In verse 36 the writer pinpoints the believers' problem—*you need to persevere*. They had become Christians and had suffered for their faith. They had fought the good fight for a time, but they had not yet finished the course. Paul had warned the Galatians to beware of becoming "weary in doing good" (Galatians 6:9). It would seem that this lack of endurance was part of the reason that the Hebrew Christians were in danger of falling away.

Many Christians today face this same temptation. Perhaps they have spent many years in the Lord's service, but they feel frustrated because their efforts have begun to appear fruitless or unappreciated. All who are so tempted are encouraged to continue in their good work so that they *will receive what he has promised*.

## C. LIVE BY FAITH (vv. 37-39)

**37-39. For in just a very little while, "He who is coming will come and will not delay. But my righteous one will live by faith. And if he shrinks back, I will not be pleased with him." But we are not of those who shrink back and are destroyed, but of those who believe and are saved.**

To further encourage the Hebrew Christians to stand fast, the writer quotes a passage from Habakkuk 2:3, 4. Since he often quotes from the Septuagint (a Greek version of the Old Testament) in his letter, in some cases his quotations do not coincide word for word with the Old Testament versions that most of us use. We saw this in Lesson 9, where we noted the difference between Psalm 40:6-8 and the way it is quoted in Hebrews 10:5-7.

---

*HOW TO SAY IT*

*Aquila. ACK-will-uh.*
*Claudius. CLAW-dee-us.*
*Habakkuk. Huh-BAK-kuk.*
*Judaism. JOO-day-iz-um.*
*Nero. NEE-roe or NIHR-oh.*
*Priscilla. Prih-SILL-uh.*
*Septuagint. Sep-TOO-ih-jent.*

---

**WHAT DO YOU THINK?**

When are you most tempted to throw away your confidence or to "shrink back" from your faith? How do you overcome such temptations?

## PRAYER

*Dear Father, may we draw near with a true heart in full assurance of faith, knowing that you have given us a high priest who hears our every prayer. Lift up our hands when we grow weary in doing what is right. Give us strength when our faith is threatened by forces that tempt us to compromise or turn away from it. In the name of our high priest we pray. Amen.*

## THOUGHT TO REMEMBER

*"Let us hold unswervingly to the hope we profess"* (Hebrews 10:23).

## DAILY BIBLE READING

*Monday, Aug. 4—Power Belongs to God* (2 Corinthians 4:7-12)

*Tuesday, Aug. 5—Be Born of the Holy Spirit* (John 3:1-15)

*Wednesday, Aug. 6—Things of the Spirit Are Unseen* (2 Corinthians 4:13-18)

*Thursday, Aug. 7—Jesus' Prayer for the Church* (John 17:20-26)

*Friday, Aug. 8—God Speaks Through his Word* (Psalm 19: 7-14)

*Saturday, Aug. 9—A Genuine Faith Is Important* (1 Peter 1:3-9)

*Sunday, Aug. 10—God Is Faithful* (1 Corinthians 1:1-9)

Habakkuk was called to prophesy to the nation of Judah at a time when the Babylonians were poised to destroy it. This was God's punishment of his people for having turned away from him. But Habakkuk was troubled by the question of why God would use a people more wicked than Judah to punish Judah (Habakkuk 1:13). God's response was that he was in control, and would make certain that the righteous would be rewarded and the wicked punished. God's people needed to have faith that his purposes would be fulfilled.

The words *he who is coming will come* are used by the writer of Hebrews to refer to the return of Christ. Many of the early Christians looked for Jesus to return very quickly to claim his own. They did not realize that God operates within a different time frame from man's, and so some had become disappointed and discouraged. The example from Habakkuk's experience was meant to bolster their trust in God.

*But my righteous one will live by faith.* Paul quotes these same words in Romans 1:17. With these words he began his demonstration that salvation was not by works of the law, but by faith. The writer of Hebrews uses these words to show that God honors those who trust in him. At the same time, he is *not…pleased with* those who, because of lack of faith, *shrink back.*

In verse 39 the writer again identifies himself with those who stand firmly in their faith. Those who turn back *are destroyed,* and face a very unpleasant future. Thus there were two options before the Hebrew Christians: continued faithfulness to Christ, leading to salvation, or turning away from Christ, leading to destruction. Is it clear which choice we have made?

## CONCLUSION

More than fifty years ago, I visited a stretch of beach near Savannah, Georgia. Recently I returned to the same beach, and I hardly recognized it. Much of the beach had disappeared, and the waves were lapping at a road that once was a quarter of a mile from the water. This change in the beach had not occurred suddenly, but slowly over many years. Although the U.S. Army Corps of Engineers had worked to save the beach, at best they had only slowed the erosion.

This illustrates the process by which Christians sometimes turn from their allegiance to Jesus. The membership roll of almost every church will provide evidence that some Christians do fall away from the faith. Regardless of how we may explain this theologically, the obvious fact is that it does happen. Ordinarily, a Christian does not suddenly turn his back on Christ and return to the world. More often it is a slow erosion that is hardly noticeable until the process is well along. Then it is almost too late to salvage the person.

We see a similar process happening in the area of public morals. Turn back the pages of history only half a century. Murder was uncommon, as were illegitimate births. Divorce was rare, and when one did occur it shocked the entire community. Abortions were illegal, and many of us never bothered to lock our doors at night. One could even attend the movies without being embarrassed. What happened? What went wrong? Clearly, this decline did not happen all at once, but was the result of a slow erosion that became more rapid as the years passed.

What can we do about it? We could wring our hands in despair and simply give up. But this is not what Christ has commanded us to do. We are to be the salt that has the power to preserve, and the light that has the power to dispel the darkness. If we are to accomplish this task, we must be aware of the dire warnings sounded in this lesson about those who turn away from Christ. More important, we must be encouraged by the promise of rich blessings that await those who patiently and firmly remain faithful, and share their faith and hope with others.

# Discovery Learning

*This page contains an alternate lesson plan emphasizing learning activities. Classes desiring such student involvement will find these suggestions helpful. The next page is a reproducible activity page to further enhance discovery learning.*

## LEARNING GOALS

After studying this lesson, each student should:

1. Be able to list seven imperatives given to Christians in Hebrews 10.

2. Relate these imperatives to the challenges modern Christians face.

3. Carry a reminder to obey some of the imperatives from the lesson text.

## INTO THE LESSON

The word *draw*, which is important in today's study, is one of those words that has a variety of uses and meanings. Display the word prominently as the class assembles, and ask, "What does this word mean?" Expect a variety of responses (*Webster's New World Dictionary* Second College Edition, lists nearly fifty uses of *draw* as a verb and a noun, and includes its use in popular expressions). Bring a dictionary and have a student skim the uses of *draw* and give some samples.

Ask the student with the dictionary to read the first definition of draw as a "transitive verb" (one that requires a direct object). It should read something like, "to make something or someone move toward one or along with one, by or as exerting force." Then have the student read the first definition of *draw* as an "intransitive verb" (no object required). It should read something like, "to come or go gradually or steadily."

Read Hebrews 10:22. Ask, "Which use is this?" (It is intransitive: we "draw near." We do not draw anything.) Point out that even in an intransitive use of *draw*, there is still a sense that something—though not the subject of the sentence and maybe not even stated—is drawing. Have someone read John 12:32. Ask, "What is it that draws us to God?" (The drawing power of Christ crucified. We draw near to God because Jesus draws us!)

## INTO THE WORD

Prepare some index cards, half of them with the word *Do* and half with the word *Don't* (written in large letters). Have enough to give one to each class member. Shuffle and distribute the cards. Ask the class to search the text and suggest a *Do* or *Don't*, depending on the card each person holds. As they respond, make a two-column listing on the chalkboard or on poster board. Expect such *Do* entries as: Be confident, v. 19; Draw near, v. 22; Keep a sincere heart, v. 22; Hold unswervingly, v. 23; Consider

one another, v. 24; Encourage one another, v. 25; Remember the past, v. 32; Persevere, v. 36; Live by faith, v. 38. *Don't* entries should include: Don't swerve, v. 23; Don't miss when the church assembles, v. 25; Don't mourn the loss of material goods, v. 34; Don't lose confidence, v. 35; Don't shrink back, v. 38. As ideas are presented, you will have occasion to ask questions and make any appropriate comments.

Next, redirect the students' attention to the text by saying, "Now let's leave the *Dos* and *Don'ts* for a series of *twos* and *threes*. Ask them to find and identify each of the following: (1) The three verses that encourage perseverance, because Christ will return (vv. 35-37). (2) The three verses that picture the negative treatment the Hebrew Christians had received in former days, and their response to it (vv. 32-34). (3) The two verses that picture the joy of faith and the doom of disbelief (vv. 38, 39). (4) The three verses that tell how Christians have a privilege that at one time only the high priest had (vv. 19-21). (5) The two verses that state the necessity and purpose of worship assemblies (vv. 24, 25). Use the lesson commentary to elaborate on any significant words or ideas.

## OPTION

Use the activities on the next page to guide your study of today's text.

## INTO LIFE

With your class, make a list of imperatives from today's text in the form "BE ____!" (Possible responses include, "be confident, v. 19; be sincere, v. 22; be sure, v. 22; be clean, v. 22; be unswerving in hope, v. 23; be encouraging, vv. 24, 25; be regular in attending worship assemblies, v. 25; be watchful of the Day, v. 25; be firm, v. 32; be patient, v. 33; be sympathetic, v. 34; be righteous, v. 38.)

When the list is made, distribute to each student a small (three- or four-inch diameter) geometric shape with seven sides (a heptagon). Point out that the number *seven* is used in the Bible as a symbol of completeness or wholeness. Have each student write a large BE in the middle of his or her heptagon. Next, each should select seven of the imperatives that relate most to his or her Christian walk, writing one on each edge of the heptagon. Encourage students to read one of the imperatives each day of the coming week, and to seek to apply it.

# A Call to __ __ __ __ __ __ __ __ __!

Read Hebrews 10:19-25, 32-39. Refer to that passage to fill in the final word in each of these statements quoted below.

We have confidence to enter the Most Holy __ __ __ __ __.

We have a great __ __ __ __ __ __.

Let us draw near . . . with a sincere __ __ __ __ __.

Spur one another on toward love and good __ __ __ __ __.

Remember . . . when you stood your __ __ __ __ __ __.

You sympathized with those in __ __ __ __ __ __.

Your confidence . . . will be richly __ __ __ __ __ __ __ __.

You will receive what he has __ __ __ __ __ __ __ __.

We are . . . of those who __ __ __ __ __ __ __.

Use the nine letters underlined in your responses to form the word that completes the heading for this page.

# Make It Personal

To which of the following affirmations can you sincerely sign your initials? You may want to re-read the relevant verses by each.

____ 1. I feel and act like a priest on behalf of God's people. (19)

____ 2. Material things mean less to me now than they did before I knew Christ. (34)

____ 3. I am anticipating Christ's return now more than I ever have before. (37)

____ 4. My commitment to Christ is stronger now than it was from the beginning. (23)

____ 5. I miss fewer and fewer worship and study assemblies of my church as the years of my Christian life pass. (25)

____ 6. More and more, my Christian family could say I spur them on to love and good deeds. (24)

____ 7. A Christian friend can count on me to come to her side when she is insulted or persecuted. (33)

Perservere
Place, priest, heart, deeds, ground, prison, rewarded, promised, believe.

# REMEMBER THE PAST

**LESSON 12**

## WHY TEACH THIS LESSON?

"Just have faith. It will be all right." How many times have you heard that in a crisis. It's a pretty bold promise, especially when it comes from one who cannot tell you in what or whom to put your faith. The world's view of faith seems to be an entity all its own. Faith requires no object—it's just "faith." It's wishful thinking—that's what it is!

In the Bible, faith always has an object. And faith that can give confidence is faith in God. Even with that, no one can tell you your immediate crisis will be resolved to your liking or understanding. But, taking the big picture as Noah, Abraham, and others in Hebrews 11 did, things *will be* all right!

Reassure your students of that blessed hope today.

## INTRODUCTION

### A. TRUSTING THE COMPASS

Several years ago I was with a group of students on a camping trip. At one point in the trip, we had to canoe across a large lake and up a stream to our next campsite. The lake was so large that we were unable to see the other side, and there were no landmarks to guide us. As we prepared to launch our canoes, thick clouds swept over the lake, obscuring the sun. With no landmarks by which to navigate, and unable to get our directions from the sun, we had no way of knowing just where the stream was.

However, we had a map and a compass, and so we plotted our course and began our journey. Soon a strong wind arose that threatened to blow us off course, but we were able to avoid potential trouble by consulting the compass. At one point our instincts told us that we were going in the wrong direction. Again, we consulted the compass and held to the course we had plotted. After several hours of paddling, we reached our destination. Our journey was successful because we followed our compass.

Each of the Old Testament heroes we are studying today also embarked on a difficult journey—one of a spiritual nature. Each one was able to reach his destination because he followed the compass. For Noah and for Abraham, that compass was faith in God.

### B. LESSON BACKGROUND

Our lesson today includes several verses from Hebrews 11, known as the faith chapter of the Bible. In this chapter God conducts a "roll call" of faithful men and women. Those who are singled out were not necessarily wiser or more pious than others, but they had one trait that distinguished them: they trusted God! Even when God asked them to perform tasks that must have seemed foolish, they obeyed. God told Noah to build an ark to prepare for a coming flood, and as ridiculous as it certainly must have seemed, he faithfully obeyed. God told Abraham to leave his comfortable home in Mesopotamia and become a wanderer, seeking for a new home. Even without a map or a compass, Abraham acted on faith and obeyed.

DEVOTIONAL READING
ROMANS 4:1-15

LESSON SCRIPTURE
HEBREWS 11:1-40

PRINTED TEXT
HEBREWS 11:1, 2, 6-10, 13-16, 39, 40.

LESSON AIMS

Following today's study, each student will:

1. Be able to explain how each of the Old Testament persons mentioned in the text demonstrated faith in God.

2. Explain the Christian's advantage over these Old Testament faithful.

3. Suggest an answer to a specific challenge to his or her faith in "things not seen."

Aug
17

KEY VERSE

*Now faith is being sure of what we hope for and certain of what we do not see.*  Hebrews 11:1

LESSON 12 NOTES

> *Now faith is the substance of things hoped for, the evidence of things not seen.*

*The visual for lesson 12 illustrates verse 1 of the text. Have it on display as the session begins.*

**WHAT DO YOU THINK?**

*Our text calls faith "being sure of what we hope for and certain of what we do not see" (Hebrews 11:1). Have you ever had to act on faith alone, with no sight of what was ahead? Describe the experience. What gave you such faith? How did the situation turn out?*

**WHAT DO YOU THINK?**

*Chapter 11 of Hebrews recalls many of "the ancients" who were champions of faith. Each one acted on his or her faith in some dramatic way. Can you name people in your own experience who are examples of great faith? What remarkable acts did their faith move them to accomplish? What risks is faith calling you to take for God?*

God has given us even greater promises. Should we not follow the examples of these heroes and live by obedient faith?

## I. THE NATURE AND POWER OF FAITH (HEBREWS 11:1, 2)

### A. THE NATURE OF FAITH (v. 1)

**1. Now faith is being sure of what we hope for and certain of what we do not see.**

This faith chapter begins with a description of *faith*. It is a general description, not necessarily limited to religious faith. The Greek word translated *being sure* has a variety of meanings. Actually it is a noun and literally means "that which stands under" or "foundation." In Hebrews 1:3 it is translated "being," i.e., God's being, the "essence" of who God is. In 3:14 it is rendered "confidence." Faith, then, is the essence of hope; it is the foundation on which our hope is built. Faith is also what gives certainty to *what we do not see* (as Moses "persevered because he saw him who is invisible," Hebrews 11:27). For the world "seeing is believing," but the Christian lives by faith, not by sight" (2 Corinthians 5:7). Faith gives confidence to the one who is guided by it even as the stars give confidence to the trained navigator.

### B. THE POWER OF FAITH (v. 2)

**2. This is what the ancients were commended for.**

To strengthen his point about the necessity of faith, the author now turns to Old Testament history. In the verses that follow, he gives several examples of persons who, through faith, were able to triumph over difficult or seemingly impossible circumstances. These persons were not morally perfect, but God was able to use them in spite of their shortcomings because they trusted him. Their faith made them models for all future generations. Beginning with Abel, these heroes and heroines are presented in a somewhat chronological order, culminating in Jesus, "the author and perfecter of our faith" (12:2).

## II. EXAMPLES OF FAITH (HEBREWS 11:6-10)

### A. THE NECESSITY OF FAITH (v. 6)

**6. And without faith it is impossible to please God, because anyone who comes to him must believe that he exists and that he rewards those who earnestly seek him.**

*Without faith* in *God*, these heroes and heroines would not have been pleasing to him, nor could they have been able to perform their heroic deeds. The twofold aspects of faith expressed in verse 1 are reaffirmed here. Faith provides the certainty of God and the unseen spiritual world. Faith also provides the confidence that God will reward those who *earnestly seek him*. What was true for these faithful men and women of old was true for the Hebrew Christians, and is also true for us today.

Because faith is so crucial, Satan's severest attacks are often aimed at our faith. He tempts us to doubt, and when doubt seeps in, it has the potential to dilute our faith and weaken us. Like the father of the boy who was controlled by an evil spirit, we must learn to pray, "I do believe; help me overcome my unbelief!" (Mark 9:24).

### WHAT KIND OF CAR DO YOU DRIVE?

In the 1980s Lee Iacocca, then head of the Chrysler Corporation, was easily the most recognized car executive in America because he personally appeared in so many television commercials for Chrysler products. One day a man found himself riding in the same elevator with Iacocca.

"You're Lee Iacocca, aren't you?" the man asked. The auto executive acknowledged that he was.

"Mr. Iacocca," the man said, "I want to tell you how much I enjoy your television commercials."

To this compliment Iacocca replied, "Sir, I couldn't care less what you think of my commercials. What I want to know is: what kind of car do you drive?"

In the automobile business, if you don't buy the car, the commercials don't matter. The same is true of the Christian message. Perhaps, after reading Hebrews 11, we may stand in awe of the great men and women of faith mentioned therein. However, it makes little difference how much we admire these individuals if we fail to exercise faith ourselves. "By faith they" must become "By faith *we*."     —C. B. Mc.

## B. THE EXAMPLE OF NOAH (v. 7)

**7. By faith Noah, when warned about things not yet seen, in holy fear built an ark to save his family. By his faith he condemned the world and became heir of the righteousness that comes by faith.**

In verses 4 and 5, Abel and Enoch were cited as men of faith. Now Noah is held up as an outstanding example of acting *by faith*. God *warned* Noah that he was preparing a flood to destroy the world because of its unbridled wickedness (Genesis 6:13). Noah was then informed that he was to build an ark by which he and his family were to be saved. It is not hard to imagine the ridicule Noah must have heard as he began this project. At a time when a catastrophic flood was in the realm of *things not yet seen,* he was to construct a huge boat.

At least two other aspects of this endeavor give us some indication of the strength of Noah's faith. First of all, this was no short-term project; it was to last a hundred and twenty years (according to the figure given in Genesis 6:3), during which time Noah preached to onlookers (2 Peter 2:5). Second, Noah's faith was strong enough that he was able to convert *his family*—his wife, his three sons, and their wives—thus ensuring their salvation from the coming judgment.

## C. THE EXAMPLE OF ABRAHAM (vv. 8-10)

**8. By faith Abraham, when called to go to a place he would later receive as his inheritance, obeyed and went, even though he did not know where he was going.**

God first called *Abraham* when he lived in Ur of the Chaldeans (Genesis 11:31; Acts 7:2, 3). Abraham had large flocks and a number of servants, indicating that he was a wealthy man. Archaeologists who have excavated ancient Ur indicate that the wealthy in Abraham's day (approximately 2000 B.C.) lived in an abundance of ease and luxury. From such surroundings of material security, God called Abraham (named "Abram" at the time) to experience the security of living *by faith*. He left his homeland, *even though he did not know where he was going*. He exchanged the comfort of what he could see and enjoy for the challenge of "things not seen."

**9. By faith he made his home in the promised land like a stranger in a foreign country; he lived in tents, as did Isaac and Jacob, who were heirs with him of the same promise.**

Although Abraham was permitted to live in Canaan, *the promised land*, he did so as an alien. The land of promise never became for Abraham a land of possession. After a time he gained the respect of the various tribes among whom he dwelt, yet the only land he actually possessed was the field that included the cave of Machpelah, which he purchased for the burial of his wife Sarah (Genesis 23).

The word *tents* indicates that Abraham never had a permanent place of residence in Canaan. He lived *by faith* in the *promise* of a residence far grander, as the next verse states. Along the way he received assurance that his faith would be rewarded. The birth of a son in his old age, long promised and long delayed, was certainly a token that other promises would be fulfilled. That son, *Isaac*, and Isaac's son *Jacob* also lived in Canaan as *heirs . . . of the same promise*. The most important wealth Abraham bequeathed to them was spiritual.

### HOW TO SAY IT

Canaan. KAY-nun.
Chaldeans. Kal-DEE-unz.
Enoch. EE-nuk.
Hagar. HAY-gar.
Haran. HAY-run.
Iacocca. EYE-uh-COKE-uh.
Machpelah. Mack-PEA-luh.
Mesopotamia. MES-uh-puh-
   TAY-me-uh.
Rahab. RAY-hab.
Ur. Er.

**WHAT DO YOU THINK?**

Like Abraham, Christians believe that God will lead them to
"the city with foundations, whose
architect and builder is God" (Hebrews 11:10). As a result, he lived
his life as a "stranger" or "foreigner" in the land. How does that
illustrate the way we are to live in
this temporal world? Why are so
many Christians tempted to try to
fit in and not be strangers? How
can we encourage one another to
remain faithful and "foreign"?

**10. For he was looking forward to the city with foundations, whose architect and builder is God.**

The secret to Abraham's patience lay in the fact that he was able to see beyond his immediate horizons far into the future. He could tolerate living as an alien in the land of promise because *he was looking forward to* an eternal *city . . . whose architect and builder is God.* During Abraham's walk of faith, he lived in a tent—a dwelling without foundations and without permanency. This was only a slight inconvenience, however, compared with the promise of a city with *foundations* as firm as God himself. There Abraham knew, by faith, that he would dwell some day.

## FAITH'S HALL OF FAME

Hebrews 11, the faith chapter of the Bible, can be an intimidating list. Here we find the "all-stars" of faith: Noah, Abraham, Isaac, Joseph, and many others. Perhaps you may be tempted to think that the lessons taught here are for extraordinary people, or that someone like you could never have faith enough to become an "all-star."

But consider one of the "stars" of this chapter, Abraham, for a moment. Abraham was living in Ur of the Chaldeans, in southern Mesopotamia, when God first called him. Ur was an important commercial city, whose people had developed a system of writing and with it an impressive body of literature. But its people were thoroughly pagan. They were polytheistic (worshipers of many gods). This was the kind of atmosphere surrounding Abraham when God called him. With no other guarantee than God's word, Abraham left his home and friends, perhaps even a business and property, to go to a distant land that God had promised him.

But Abraham's faith at times was faulty. During a famine in Canaan he fled to Egypt in fear. Then, because he was afraid of the Pharaoh, he lied about Sarah's being his wife. When it seemed that the promised heir would never come, he followed Sarah's urging and fathered a child through her handmaid Hagar.

Yet despite Abraham's failings, God continued promising and Abraham continued believing. He passed the ultimate test of faith by his willingness to offer his son Isaac as a sacrifice. Romans 4 tells us that Abraham was not declared righteous by his good works, but by his faith. It ought to encourage us to know that if we are willing to continue believing God and seeking his forgiveness and help, he can make "all-stars" out of us as well. —C. B. Mc.

## III. LESSONS FROM THE PATRIARCHS (HEBREWS 11:13-16)
### A. STRANGERS AND PILGRIMS (vv. 13, 14)
**13, 14. All these people were still living by faith when they died. They did not receive the things promised; they only saw them and welcomed them from a distance. And they admitted that they were aliens and strangers on earth. People who say such things show that they are looking for a country of their own.**

The phrase *all these people* refers to Abraham, Sarah, Isaac, and Jacob, because the persons mentioned earlier in this chapter—Abel, Enoch, and Noah—had not received the specific *promises* that came to Abraham and his family. *They died* before they could *receive the things promised*, but they died firmly believing that they would one day receive them. They had seen them *from a distance*, not with physical eyes, but with the eyes of faith. Thus they were content to accept their status as *aliens and strangers on earth*

### B. SEEKERS OF A BETTER COUNTRY (vv. 15, 16)
**15, 16. If they had been thinking of the country they had left, they would have had opportunity to return. Instead, they were longing for a better country—a heavenly one. Therefore God is not ashamed to be called their God, for he has prepared a city for them.**

**WHAT DO YOU THINK?**

Because Noah believed God, he built an ark. Because Abraham believed God, he left his home and set out to find the land God promised him. Noah and Abraham both acted out of faith in a promise.

Perhaps the most compelling promise of God to Christians is the promise of eternal life. How do the promises God has made to people of faith today cause us to act differently from those who have no faith?

See Matthew 25:14-46; 1 Corinthians 3:12-15; 2 Peter 3:11.

Although Abraham and his family considered themselves aliens and strangers in Canaan, they never really considered Mesopotamia (the territory *they had left*) their home either. Had they considered Ur or Haran (where Abraham had resided for a while after he left Ur and before he came to Canaan) in that manner, they could have returned. In fact, on many occasions they may have been tempted to return, but their faith drove them on to seek *a better country—a heavenly one*. We are reminded of the old spiritual: "This world is not my home, I'm just a passing through."

The faithfulness of the patriarchs pleased God; thus he was *not ashamed to be called their God*. "Those who honor me I will honor" (1 Samuel 2:30). He honored them by preparing for them *a city*, the new Jerusalem (Revelation 21:2).

## IV. REWARD OF FAITH (HEBREWS 11:39, 40)

**39, 40. These were all commended for their faith, yet none of them received what had been promised. God had planned something better for us so that only together with us would they be made perfect.**

The intervening verses of Hebrews 11 mention many other champions of faith: Joseph, Moses, Rahab, Gideon, and countless others whom the writer could not take time to name, but whose lives clearly demonstrated great faith. All of these were *commended for their faith, yet none of them received what had been promised*. Through the eyes of faith they were able to see it from a distance, but they could not fully claim it.

In verse 40 the writer once again uses the word *better*, a key word throughout this epistle. The *better* thing that has been reserved for those who live in the Christian era is God's plan for man's salvation through the high priestly work of his Son, who gave himself as a sacrifice for us. The benefits of that work, however, are not limited to Christians. Through God's grace they have been extended to the faithful in every age, so that all of them will one day reside in the city "whose architect and builder is God" (v. 10).

## CONCLUSION

### A. "SHOW ME!"

Missouri is called the "Show me" state. Its residents have a reputation for needing to see evidence in order to believe. One need not hail from Missouri to be skeptical, however. The words, *show me* might well serve as the motto of our times. Our scientific age has conditioned us to believe that information about everything that we know and trust must come through the five senses. If we cannot taste it, touch it, smell it, hear it, or see it, then it cannot really exist. In such a system there is no room for a faith that goes beyond the five senses.

Of course, in our daily lives we do not, and in fact cannot, live by this scientific dogma. When we get up in the morning, we turn on the water faucet, trusting that water, not sulfuric acid, will come out. We eat a bowl of cereal, trusting that it is wholesome food, not a deadly poison. We insert the key in the ignition of the car and turn it, fully believing that the car will start (and it does most of the time). We start down the highway, trusting that the oncoming drivers will stay on their side of the road. (If we doubted that they would, we would have to pull off the road every time we met someone, making it impossible to drive anywhere.) We stop at a store, select several items, and hand the clerk a piece of paper money. That piece of paper has little or no intrinsic value, yet the clerk accepts it without hesitation.

It is perfectly obvious that we have to live by these and similar acts of faith on a daily basis. Any person who refused to engage in such acts would quickly be considered a candidate for a mental institution. If we have to act on faith in

**WHAT DO YOU THINK?**

These faithful have all gone on to be with the Lord. And yet, they apparently have not yet received all that was promised, for it is "only together with us" that they will "be made perfect" or complete. Our reward and their reward are ultimately the same.

How does knowing your reward will add to that of Abraham and Noah and all the other faithful make you feel? What action does it motivate you to take?

## PRAYER

*Gracious God, we thank you for men and women across the centuries who have faithfully committed themselves to your service. We pray that you will kindle within us that same faith that will allow us to look beyond the present to the eternal city that you have promised us. In our Lord's name we pray. Amen.*

## THOUGHT TO REMEMBER

*Without faith it is impossible to please God.*

## DAILY BIBLE READING

*Monday, Aug. 11—The Faith of Abraham and His Seed* (Hebrews 11:17-22)

*Tuesday, Aug. 12—The Faith of Moses* (Hebrews 11:23-28)

*Wednesday, Aug. 13—The Faith of the Israelites* (Hebrews 11:29-38)

*Thursday, Aug. 14—Abraham Gave God the Glory* (Romans 4:13-21)

*Friday, Aug. 15—God's Promise to Abraham* (Galatians 3:15-22)

*Saturday, Aug. 16—Righteousness Comes Through Faith* (Romans 9:27-33)

*Sunday, Aug. 17—Faith Without Works Is Dead* (James 2:14-26)

scores of different ways every day, why should it be any different with our religious lives?

The critics of Christian faith have an answer to this question. They respond that experience leads us to believe that water, not sulfuric acid, will flow out of the tap; that the cereal will be wholesome, not poisonous; that the car will start when we turn it on; that other drivers will stay on their side of the road; that the clerk will accept our money.

But Christians can offer the same kind of argument. All of us who have made a serious effort to live the Christian life can relate numerous experiences as evidence that God can be trusted. We can recount instances of answered prayer. We know the meaning that faith can give to our lives. We know the confidence that comes when we trust God's promises of a glorious life beyond this world. That confidence is strengthened when we study the lives of the great champions of faith in Hebrews 11. They lived victoriously through all kinds of difficult circumstances because they trusted God.

### B. "THIS WORLD IS NOT MY HOME"

*Home* is one of the richest words in the English language. For most of us it brings up warm feelings and happy memories. For a few, home may be a palatial mansion on a large estate. Others may find their home in an apartment in a crowded city. Many see it as a comfortable suburban dwelling surrounded by grass, flowers, and trees. For others it is a grass hut in a tropical rain forest, while still others call a frequently moved tent in an arid desert their home.

Whether it be a palace or a tent, all of these homes have one thing in common: they are all temporary. A palace may last a thousand years, while a grass hut will be gone in a few months, but sooner or later they will all succumb to the ravages of time and nature.

God promised Abraham and his descendants a land that they could call their own. Abraham was able to live in that land, but he lived there as a stranger and alien. Most of his life he lived in a tent, having little opportunity to build a more permanent dwelling. He could have returned to Ur, his original home, with its more comfortable surroundings. But he was content to live as he did, because he was able to see beyond this present world. He looked for "a better country—a heavenly one" (Hebrews 11:16). He had the faith to forgo present comforts for a far greater comfort in the future.

Today, on every hand we see restless and unhappy people. Many have acquired wealth and the trappings that wealth can bring, yet the happiness they seek has eluded them. Their problems stem from their inability to see beyond this present world. How their outlook would change if only they would realize that this world is not their home! What a difference it would make if they began to seek the city whose architect and builder is God!

### C. WOMEN OF FAITH

We often speak of the men of faith in Hebrews 11, but this chapter also calls our attention to some *women* of faith. Sarah is mentioned because she had faith that God could give her the strength to bear Isaac, even when she was past the childbearing age. Rahab, who protected the Israelite spies, survived the destruction of Jericho because of her faith. Women who "received back their dead, raised to life again" are mentioned (v. 35). This chapter also describes the suffering and martyrdom of many others, some of whom undoubtedly were women. The point is quite obvious that men have no monopoly on faith. In most cases, behind every faithful man is a faithful, God-fearing woman—usually a wife or a mother.

# Discovery Learning

*This page contains an alternate lesson plan emphasizing learning activities. Classes desiring such student involvement will find these suggestions helpful. The next page is a reproducible activity page to further enhance discovery learning.*

## LEARNING GOALS

Following today's study, each student will:

1. Be able to explain how each of the Old Testament persons mentioned in the text demonstrated faith in God.

2. Explain the Christian's advantage over these Old Testament faithful.

3. Suggest an answer to a specific challenge to his or her faith in "things not seen."

## INTO THE LESSON

Set a fan in the front of your classroom. Have it on "low" as your class assembles. Ask the class to identify two "invisible things" of which the working fan gives evidence. You are looking for the responses: *electricity* and *air*. Ask the class why they believe these two exist. They should note that though both are unseen, the results of their presence are seen daily. Point out that most of us have great faith in both, for we have experienced them repeatedly.

## INTO THE WORD

Prepare flash cards (at least five by seven inches), on each of which is written one of the following Old Testament names: ABEL, ABRAHAM, BARAK, DAVID, ELIJAH, ENOCH, ESAU, GIDEON, ISAAC, JACOB, JEPHTHAH, JOSEPH, JOSHUA, MOSES, NEHEMIAH, NOAH, RAHAB, RUTH, SAMSON, SAMUEL, AND SOLOMON.

Next, divide the class into approximately equal halves (best if done simply on the basis of seating). Tell the class that you are going to show them names of Old Testament men and women, and that you want them either to identify the verse in Hebrews 11 where each is named or to state that the name does not appear in Hebrews 11. (This will be done with Bibles open to Hebrews 11.) As soon as someone knows the answer, he or she will stand, be recognized, and tell you the verse number or say, "Not in this chapter." Promise some small treat to the "winning" side, and keep score.

Play the game and reward the winners. (Abel, v. 4; Abraham, vv. 8-19; Barak, v. 32; David, v. 32; Elijah, not named; Enoch, v. 5; Esau, v. 20; Gideon, v. 32; Isaac, vv. 19, 20; Jacob, vv. 20, 21; Jephthah, v. 32; Joseph, vv. 21, 22; Joshua, not named; Moses, vv. 23-28; Nehemiah, not named; Noah, v. 7; Rahab, v. 31; Ruth, not named; Samson, v. 32; Samuel, v. 32; and Solomon, not named.)

For the next activity designate one team the "Noah Group" and the other, the "Abraham Group." Each group will try to prove its hero deserves the title of "Champion of the Faithful." Have the first group review Genesis 6-9, and the second, Genesis 12, 15, 16, and 22. After about ten minutes, write "Noah versus Abraham" on the chalkboard or on a transparency, and call for each group's responses. Though the groups will offer a variety of statements, expect such "proofs" as the following to be offered: "Noah never 'got ahead' of God, as Abraham did concerning Hagar." "Abraham had to leave home immediately when God called him; Noah could stay where he was." "Abraham's faith did not pronounce judgment on the world; Noah's faith affected the entire world through the flood." "Abraham believed in God's power to resurrect; Noah believed in God's power to destroy." (If you believe your groups need some help to get started, use one or more of the samples given here.)

Once the "debate" is over, read aloud the following propositions based on today's text. Ask students to note how each applies to Noah and Abraham. (1) Faith involves "things hoped for." (2) Faith involves "things not seen." (3) The faithful are given a good report by God. (4) Faith involves being "moved with fear." (5) Faith involves anticipation of reward. (6) There is something "distant" about faith. (7) Faith in God involves desiring something better than what one has. (8) Faith in God pleases God.

## INTO LIFE

Read these statements aloud and ask the students to reflect briefly and prayerfully on each. (1) I was not present when God created this world, but I believe he did. (2) I am too small to understand the universe, but I believe it is sustained by *his* power and grace. (3) I am incapable of fully comprehending how God redeems me through the blood of Christ, but I believe he does. (4) The Holy Spirit is invisible, but I believe he is present. (5) The earth has not yet been destroyed by fire, but I believe it will be. (6) Jesus has not returned yet, but I believe he will. (7) I have not seen Heaven, but I believe it is real.

Have each student choose one of these statements and prepare a defense if his or her faith were challenged regarding the truth expressed. Allow two or three minutes. share some of their defenses if time allows; close with prayer.

# January Christians

The Roman god Janus, after whom the month of January is named, was the god of beginnings and endings. He was "two-faced" so he could look forward and backward. In a real sense, we should be "January Christians," looking backward to what our God has done and looking forward to what God will do.

In the right-hand column below, write some beliefs or hopes you have *because* of something God has done in the past. In the left-hand column, write those things God has done to give you that hope. One example is given to get you started.

| WHAT GOD HAS DONE | WHAT I AM EXPECTING |
|---|---|
| Created the heavens and the earth (Genesis 1:1) | A new heaven and a new earth (Revelation 21:1) |

_____     _____

_____     _____

_____     _____

# Noah-and-Abraham Christians

In Hebrews 11 Noah and Abraham (as well as several others) are used as models of godly faith. Rate yourself from 1 (low) to 5 (high) on how well you're imitating these two models.

___ The warnings of God cause me to move in holy fear (v. 7).

___ I am looking for a city "whose architect and builder is God" (v. 10).

___ I am doing what I can to save my family (v. 7).

___ Wherever God wants me to be is where I will go (v. 8).

___ The world I left behind when I claimed Christ as Lord and Savior no longer has any appeal (v. 15).

___ My life-style of faith is different enough to "condemn the world" around me (v. 7).

# Good . . . Better . . . Perfect Christians

Look at Hebrews 11:39, 40. Decide how each of these three adjectives applies to the person of faith in the Christian era.

Good _____

Better _____

Perfect _____

# Guidance for Ministry

### Unit 2. Be Faithful Followers of Christ
#### (Lessons 10-14)

# RENEW COMMITMENT

## LESSON 13

## WHY TEACH THIS LESSON?

"A journey of a thousand miles begins with a single step." Most of us have heard the ancient proverb. What it doesn't tell us is why. Why begin the journey at all? After about a hundred miles, we might well ask, "Why did I ever start this trip anyway?"

This was the case for the believers addressed in the book of Hebrews. They had begun the journey—or the race, to use the writer's metaphor—but now they weren't sure. They were thinking of dropping out. The finish line was so far away.

That attitude was not left in the first century. Some of your students have had it rough, too. They may be wondering why they ever started. They may think they cannot finish. Use this lesson to encourage and challenge them to make a fresh start—focused anew on the "joy" set before them.

## INTRODUCTION

### A. JUST KEEP RUNNING

Years ago I went out for the university track team. I made the team as a distance runner, but after a few weeks I grew tired of the monotony of the training routine. Every day we had warming up and stretching exercises. Then came time with the medicine ball and other activities to lengthen our stride and to strengthen our ankles and the arches of our feet. We ran against the clock to learn to pace ourselves. Then we ran the usual distance of a race, and on some days the dreaded "over distance." Finally, we finished by running wind sprints and occasionally running up and down the stadium steps until we almost dropped from exhaustion.

High school track had never been this demanding, and I was looking for an easier way of training. One day I approached the coach and asked about a better way to train for track. I was hoping he would prescribe a special diet or maybe a daily dose of vitamins.

"Son," he replied, "if you want to be a winner, just come out every day like you've been doing and keep going through the exercises." Then pointing to the track, he said, "Then get out there on the track and keep running!"

I can understand how the Hebrew Christians must have felt. They had been through some difficult times. Perhaps they were seeking an easier way. But the writer of Hebrews did not let them off the hook. He told them to keep on doing what they had been doing, and then get out on the track of life and keep running!

### B. LESSON BACKGROUND

Our previous lesson centered on Hebrews 11, the great faith chapter of the Bible. In that chapter the writer calls the roll of God's faithful—those who had remained true to him even under very difficult and trying conditions. Their lives served as models for those who came after them. The Hebrew Christians needed these models, for many of them were on the verge of turning back in the face of hardships and persecution. The author acknowledges that they had indeed faced difficulties, but reminds them that they had "not yet resisted to the point of shedding your blood" as had some of the great champions of the faith.

DEVOTIONAL READING
2 CORINTHIANS 4:7-17

LESSON SCRIPTURE
HEBREWS 12:1-11

PRINTED TEXT
HEBREWS 12:1-11

LESSON AIMS

After studying this lesson, each student should be able to:

1. Explain the need for perseverance in the Christian life by means of the athletic contest and disciplining father metaphors.

2. Suggest some contemporary hindrances, entanglements, and opposition that may cause Christians trouble in their faith.

3. Determine a course of action that will enable him or her to "throw off" at least one hindrance to his or her "race" of life.

KEY VERSE

Therefore, since we are surrounded by such a great cloud of witnesses, let us throw off everything that hinders and the sin that so easily entangles, and let us run with perseverance the race marked out for us.          Hebrews 12:1

Aug
24

*The visual for lesson 13 illustrates the race of life mentioned in verse 1. Display it as you begin the session.*

## WHAT DO YOU THINK?

*Most of us put pressure on ourselves to do our best when others are observing us. However, a cheering or otherwise supportive crowd can draw out the best we have to give. Thus we speak of a "home court advantage" in sports. How does it help to think of a "cloud of witnesses" (Hebrews 12:1) watching you live for Christ? How can we give one another the "home court advantage" in dealing with opposition and temptation?*

## WHAT DO YOU THINK?

*A runner wears light clothing and carries nothing that will slow him down. What kind of hindrances and entanglements are likely to slow the Christian down in his or her race of life? How can we "throw off" these things to run unhindered?*

*(Make a list of hindrances— e.g., bad habits, unwholesome TV shows, etc. Then have the class suggest specific courses of action for dealing with the temptation each one presents.)*

Using an illustration drawn from the races that were held in the great arenas of that time, the writer urges the Hebrew Christians to "run with perseverance the race marked out" for them. After nearly two thousand years, that advice is still appropriate. Most of us do not face the physical persecutions that the early Christians did (our temptations are of a different order), but often we do become discouraged. We must run our race with patience and consistency if we are to claim the victory.

## I. THE CHRISTIAN'S RACE (HEBREWS 12:1-4)

### A. OUR WITNESSES (v. 1)

**1. Therefore, since we are surrounded by such a great cloud of witnesses, let us throw off everything that hinders and the sin that so easily entangles, and let us run with perseverance the race marked out for us.**

The phrase *such a great cloud of witnesses* suggests the image of a vast stadium filled with fans cheering the athletes on as they run. The witnesses are the champions of the faith mentioned in the previous chapter, who are pictured as watching the Hebrew Christians run their race.

However, the key idea of a witness is not one who sees but one who tells, one who gives testimony. Perhaps the writer is not suggesting the faithful of the past are actually spectators, watching from Heaven the events on earth. Their lives bear witness to the power of faith. Their examples cry out to the Hebrew Christians as fans cry out at the stadium, cheering on the participants on the field. Thus they inspire the Christians of all succeeding generations to continue in faith to the Lord. Their examples cheer us on whether they are able to view the events on earth or not.

The words *throw off everything that hinders* suggest another practice common in the New Testament world. A runner sometimes strengthened his legs by running in practice with weights tied to his legs. In fact, some athletes today also train with ankle weights. In the actual contest, of course, the weights were removed. They would slow the runner down. It is obvious that *sin* is a serious handicap to a runner in the Christian race.

Even one who was not an athlete could relate to what the writer was saying about the sin that *entangles.* Men frequently wore long robes over shorter toga-like garments. Often these outer robes would be taken off for running or other strenuous activity. (Recall Peter in the boat after the resurrection, John 21:7.) These robes would hinder their efforts.

At other times, the skirt of the robe would be picked up and tucked into one's belt. This prevented the person from getting his feet entangled in the robe. An athlete or any one preparing to engage in an activity requiring easy free movement would prepare by eliminating anything that would hinder his movements or entangle him—especially his feet.

That which *entangles* may speak of a particular *sin* that threatens a Christian's ability to run victoriously. *Everything that hinders* may refer to something that in itself may or may not be sinful. The item in question may even be good, such as concern for family or involvement in one's vocation. But it becomes a hindrance when it takes precedence over one's Christian commitment.

The Christian race is not a one-hundred-meter dash; it is a marathon, requiring a tremendous amount of stamina to complete. It requires *perseverance.* Many who start the Christian race drop out because they have not trained in such a way as to build up their endurance. We do no one any favors when we try to convert people by telling them the Christian life is easy. Prospects need to be told the Christian life is challenging—but that we have adequate resources to help us.

## B. OUR EXAMPLE (vv. 2, 3)

**2, 3. Let us fix our eyes on Jesus, the author and perfecter of our faith, who for the joy set before him endured the cross, scorning its shame, and sat down at the right hand of the throne of God. Consider him who endured such opposition from sinful men, so that you will not grow weary and lose heart.**

The records set by previous champions in any sport are often held up to challenge and inspire those who come after them. The writer has just challenged his readers (in chapter 11) by highlighting the examples of men and women of great faith. Now he holds up the greatest example of all: *Jesus*, described as *the author and perfecter of our faith*. The word translated "author" is one that may mean chief, leader, pioneer (earlier editions of the *New International Version* translated it "pioneer" here), or author. It comes from a word that means first—either in time (i.e., beginning) or rank (ruler, leader). The basic idea here is that he is the originator of our faith. At the same time he is the *perfecter* of our faith. This does not mean there was something wrong with our faith and that Jesus had to perfect it as in the sense of working the bugs out of a new software program. *Perfect* here means "complete." Jesus has provided what is essential for the completion of our faith.

The twin concepts of author and perfecter may call to mind the "Alpha and the Omega, the Beginning and the End" of Revelation 21:6. Jesus is the sum and substance of our faith. Those who coined the phrase, "No creed but Christ" were in sync with the message of Hebrews 12.

Even in the suffering and *shame* of *the cross*, Jesus found *joy* because he could look forward to sitting *at the right hand of the throne of God*. The Hebrew Christians were reminded of this, lest they become *weary and lose heart* and drop out of the race. They, too, can look forward to glory at the end of suffering.

There is something especially encouraging in the idea of Jesus' looking forward to *joy*. If that simply meant being in Heaven with the Father, he could have stayed there in the first place, never becoming incarnate and living among men and women. But we could not have found a home in Heaven that way. *The joy set before him* was an eternity with the redeemed in Heaven with him and the Father!

**4. In your struggle against sin, you have not yet resisted to the point of shedding your blood.**

It seems to be a human trait to think that the hardships we suffer are more severe than the hardships suffered by others. The Hebrew Christians were guilty of this. The writer reminds them that they had *not yet resisted to the point of shedding your blood*. Jesus had died for them, and other Christians had been put to death for Jesus' sake. The Hebrew Christians had suffered various insults and persecution for Jesus' sake (Hebrews 10:32-34), but none of them who would hear this letter read had yet died for their faith. They were like the man who had no shoes and complained, until he met a man who had no feet.

This verse has been taken to mean that no one among the believers who first received this letter had been martyred. Actually, that assumption cannot be made. Even if friends and neighbors of the first readers had been killed for their faith, those still alive to read or hear this letter read had not yet resisted to that point. Confiscation of property and imprisonment (10:34; 13:3) suggest a government-sponsored persecution. Executions would certainly be possible under such a regime. At the same time, it cannot be assumed that anyone among the first readers' acquaintances had been martyred, either. But whether they had lost loved ones as martyrs or not, the same was true: until each of them had resisted to the point of bloodshed, he or she had not held out as long as was expected. "Be faithful," the Lord would later tell the church at Smyrna, "even to the point of death, and I will give you the crown of life" (Revelation 2:10).

## WHAT DO YOU THINK?

*Sitting in a safe classroom, any of us can point to Jesus' example or to the example of other faithful saints as good models of endurance. But how do we bring them to mind when we really need them, when we are tempted to drop out of the race—just for a little while—to get even with the obnoxious co-worker? How can we hear the roar of the crowd urging us on when we are in the thick of the race?*

## II. TRAINING FOR THE RACE (HEBREWS 12:5-11)

### A. THE LORD'S CHASTENING (vv. 5, 6)

**5. And you have forgotten that word of encouragement that addresses you as sons: "My son, do not make light of the Lord's discipline, and do not lose heart when he rebukes you.**

The writer now quotes from Proverbs 3:11, 12. The Hebrew Christians would be quite familiar with this Scripture. It would give them a more appropriate perspective from which to view their current hardships.

One of the most serious issues Christians have to face is the problem posed by suffering. We could sense some purpose behind it if only the wicked suffered. The problem arises when we see innocent children and good, decent people suffer.

The fact that we have become Christians does not mean we have all the answers to these issues. By faith we come to understand that suffering has a place in our spiritual growth and in the development of our testimony of our faith in Christ. An athlete becomes a champion only after he has suffered intense pain and complete exhaustion in his training program. The coach does not put his players through stressful regimens because he hates them or enjoys seeing them suffer. He does it in order to prepare them for the upcoming contest. When we come to recognize this aspect of suffering, it will help us to see suffering as a means of achieving spiritual maturity.

**6. "Because the Lord disciplines those he loves, and he punishes everyone he accepts as a son."**

**WHAT DO YOU THINK?**

*How do you know when you are suffering discipline from the Lord and when you are suffering for the Lord? What, if any, is the difference?*

In a permissive age that has come to reject almost any kind of discipline, this verse may sound harsh and excessive. The Greek word rendered *punishes* literally means "to whip." It may refer to the suffering associated with persecution, resulting from the "opposition from sinful men" (v. 3). This suggests that not all suffering comes from God. Much suffering and pain are the result of human wickedness, which is contrary to the will of God. Job did not deserve to suffer any more than anyone else. Yet when his trials were over, he was a better man because of them. Whatever the source of the suffering, God can use it for his own purpose. In "all things," the Scripture tells us, he is at work, molding us into "the likeness of his Son" (Romans 8:28, 29).

Our pain does not have to be in the form of physical suffering. Often the most painful experiences are emotional or spiritual. How we handle them, and whether we seek the heavenly perspective on them, will determine whether we are crushed by them or we grow spiritually by them.

God disciplines us because he is our Father and he loves us. The most pathetic child is one who grows up without any discipline. A parent who neglects to discipline a child is not showing love, but a selfish disregard for the child's welfare. Certainly our heavenly Father is never guilty of such neglect.

### THE DISCIPLINE OF SONS

In his book, *The Problem of Pain*, C. S. Lewis says that one of the reasons God permits his people to undergo hardships and suffering is that he desires our perfection. Lewis notes that a key element of all real love is the desire that the thing or person loved be the best it can be.

An artist may not take great care with a simple sketch made to amuse a child. But he will take infinite pains with the great masterpiece of his life. We may not care that a stray dog smells bad or rummages through other people's garbage. But a family pet is washed, house-trained, and taught not to steal or tear up objects. Because we love the dog, we will interfere with its natural state and habits to make it even more lovable.

**HOW TO SAY IT**
*Smyrna. SMUR-nuh.*

A father who loves a son will discipline him to make him the sort of man he ought to be. It would be odd, even in our permissive age, to hear a man say, "I love my son, but I don't care how rotten a man he becomes just so long as he enjoys himself."

Lewis also compares God's love for us with the love between a man and a woman. When a man falls in love with a woman, does he cease to care what she looks like or how others think of her? Isn't that the time he really begins to care? Does a woman consider it a sign of love in a man that he neither knows nor cares how she looks? Of course not.

When God says that he loves us, he really means it. We are indeed the objects of his love—a love that will not be satisfied until we are the very best we can be.

—C. B. Mc.

## B. REASON FOR DISCIPLINE (vv. 7, 8)

**7, 8. Endure hardship as discipline; God is treating you as sons. For what son is not disciplined by his father? If you are not disciplined (and everyone undergoes discipline), then you are illegitimate children and not true sons.**

When discipline comes to us because of our own willful disobedience, then we ought to accept it and learn from it. Discipline administered by parents is a normal part of growing up. While some children may rebel at being disciplined, others will receive it and benefit from it.

It is not uncommon for a father to ignore an illegitimate child, thus avoiding any responsibility for disciplining him or her. The writer seems to be suggesting that if we have not experienced suffering, then we are not really God's children. Some of us may have gone through life without experiencing any great tragedies or any severe degree of suffering. Does this mean that we are not God's children?

We should keep in mind that the words of our text were directed to the particular circumstances of Christians in a particular time and place. They were growing weary of their discipline and considering dropping out of their race. The writer urges them to remain faithful, based on the scriptural teaching that discipline indicates God's favor. Such teaching is meant to encourage those who are being disciplined. It should not be used to try to evaluate the spiritual condition of believers who are not presently undergoing discipline. Our circumstances are different, so the exact application of the Scripture will differ somewhat. We can all expect discipline from time to time, but not necessarily at any given time. We might conclude from this passage that there are two kinds of Christians: those who are being disciplined and those who will be!

## C. EXAMPLE OF FATHERS (vv. 9, 10)

**9, 10. Moreover, we have all had human fathers who disciplined us and we respected them for it. How much more should we submit to the Father of our spirits and live! Our fathers disciplined us for a little while as they thought best; but God disciplines us for our good, that we may share in his holiness.**

Jewish *fathers* usually took their parenting responsibilities very seriously. As a result, Hebrew children, until they reached maturity, were taught to accept the discipline of their fathers and to respect them. However, the fathers were not perfect, and at times their discipline may have been inappropriate. Such is true of any generation of fathers. They discipline their children *as they* think *best*. But it's not always true that "Father knows best." Sometimes he doesn't, and sometimes the discipline he exacts is not appropriate—being either too harsh or too lenient. Still, these fathers are looked on—or should be looked on—with *respect*.

If we respect earthly fathers who are far less than perfect, and whose discipline lasts but *a little while*, how much more should we reverence the perfect *Father of our*

### WHAT DO YOU THINK?

One of the biggest problems our society faces is the large number of boys who grow up without a father to discipline them. What can our church do to address that problem? What can we do to encourage fathers to exercise this role? What can we do to help families where the father is absent?

### WHAT DO YOU THINK?

Many people whose fathers abandoned or abused them have difficulty with the concept of God as Father. How can we help them see God as a loving Father who disciplines his children, and to reassure them that this is a positive image?

## WHAT DO YOU THINK?

*God is willing to sacrifice our momentary comfort for the sake of the development of our character, so we must conclude that character is more important than comfort. Do you think most Christians agree? Which do we spend more time and money on, character or comfort? What can we do to emphasize character more and comfort less?*

## PRAYER

*Dear Father, when our burdens seem to overwhelm us, remind us that few of us have "resisted to the point of shedding [our] blood" in our efforts to serve you. Help us to accept discipline and see beyond it to the glorious future you have in store for us. May we look to him who is the "author and perfecter of our faith" for strength and guidance. In his holy name we pray. Amen.*

## THOUGHT TO REMEMBER

*The Christian race is a marathon, not a sprint.*

## DAILY BIBLE READING

*Monday, Aug. 18—Be Committed to Peace (James 3:13-18)*

*Tuesday, Aug. 19—In All Things Exercise Self-control (1 Corinthians 9:19-27)*

*Wednesday, Aug. 20—Look to God for Wisdom (James 1:1-8)*

*Thursday, Aug. 21—Every Good Gift Is From God (James 1:12-18)*

*Friday, Aug. 22—Act Out Your Beliefs (James 1:19-27)*

*Saturday, Aug. 23—Trust in the Lord (Proverbs 3:1-12)*

*Sunday, Aug. 24—Pray for Renewal (Psalm 51)*

*spirits* and obey him! His discipline continues throughout our Christian walk, as he prepares us to *share in his holiness.*

## D. REWARDS OF DISCIPLINE (v. 11)

**11. No discipline seems pleasant at the time, but painful. Later on, however, it produces a harvest of righteousness and peace for those who have been trained by it.**

No child enjoys the experience of *discipline.* Even mild discipline is often resented by children. So it is not surprising that Christians, especially those who are not yet mature, often resent the discipline of the heavenly Father. This is common even today. Such trials as an illness or the loss of a job frequently bring charges that God "is not fair." Rather than see health and employment as blessings of God's grace, one begins to view them as a right, something to which he is entitled. God better have a pretty good reason if he's going to take one of them away! The immaturity of that position is obvious.

The writer urges the Hebrew Christians to think in terms of *later on*—to look beyond their immediate situation and see the long-term results of God's discipline. The athlete, if he is to become a champion, must look beyond the stress and agony of training and see the victor's prize. The Christian must likewise accept any present discipline if he is to receive its positive spiritual benefits, which include the *harvest of righteousness.*

## CONCLUSION

### A. LIFT UP YOUR HANDS

Many of the Hebrew Christians had been a part of the Lord's church for some time, during which they had suffered persecution and humiliation. (See Hebrews 10:32-34.) For many, the Christian race had become long and tiring. The excitement of their earlier commitment had slowly evaporated. Perhaps they had little to show for their efforts. They had become tired "of doing what is right" (2 Thessalonians 3:13). Most of us can identify with this feeling, for sooner or later most of us experience it. This is exactly the kind of situation that Satan knows how to exploit.

In the verses that follow, the writer offers the best solution to this problem: "Therefore, strengthen your feeble arms and weak knees. 'Make level paths for your feet'" (vv. 12, 13). In other words, get back out on the track, keep running, and take the time to encourage others who are thinking about quitting the race.

### B. TODAY'S "CLOUD OF WITNESSES"

Every Christian, unless he happens to be stranded on a deserted island, is surrounded by a cloud of witnesses. These witnesses are watching our actions to see whether we translate our faith into real life. Some of these witnesses are hostile. They would like nothing better than to see us stumble or become weary in running our race. Our failures will give them an opportunity to sneer at Christianity. For this reason we need to run our race with diligence.

Other witnesses, however, will be friendly: other Christians, family members, or those who look to us as examples. While our fundamental commitment is to Christ, we also have a commitment to these who trust us. We must so live that we never cause any of them to stumble. Such a responsibility may seem like a heavy burden, but we need to realize that these friendly witnesses will also be a wonderful blessing to us. They will cheer us on when we become weary, and they will help us up when we stumble.

# Discovery Learning

*This page contains an alternate lesson plan emphasizing learning activities. Classes desiring such student involvement will find these suggestions helpful. The next page is a reproducible activity page to further enhance discovery learning.*

## LEARNING GOALS

After studying this lesson, each student should:

1. Explain the need for perseverance.

2. Suggest some contemporary hindrances, entanglements, and opposition that may cause Christians trouble in their faith.

3. Determine a course that will enable him or her to "throw off" one hindrance to his or her "race" of life.

## INTO THE LESSON

Set up your classroom to resemble a race track with bleachers on each side of three running lanes that you have marked off on the floor with masking tape. Run a strip of crepe paper between two chairs to symbolize the finish line.

Recruit three class members to be the runners in your race. Divide the rest of the class into three groups of fans, each of which will encourage one of the runners. Inform the class you will be asking questions on the text of Hebrews 12:1-11. Only the runners can give you the answers, but the fans can call out answers to the runners.

## INTO THE WORD

Put the following questions and answers on separate cards. Keep them in the order given here.

- What word is used to describe the assembly of witnesses? (*cloud*)
- What needs to be thrown off? (*everything that hinders*)
- What "so easily entangles"? (*sin*)
- How are we to run the race? (*with perseverance*)
- Who is the "author and perfecter of our faith"? (*Jesus*)
- What motivated Jesus to endure the cross? (*the joy set before him*)
- What was Jesus' response to the shame of the cross? (*He scorned it*)
- Where has Jesus now "sat down"? (*at the right hand of the throne of God*)
- What did Jesus endure? (*the cross, v. 2, or opposition from sinful men, v. 3*)
- How are the children of God *not* to react to his discipline? (*by making light of it*)
- When God rebukes his children, what should they *not* do? (*lose heart*)
- What does the Lord do to the one he loves? (*disciplines*)
- What does the Lord do to everyone he accepts as a son? (*punishes*)

- What is a sign that God is dealing with you as a son? (*you endure hardship as discipline*)
- What attitude do we have toward earthly fathers who correct us? (*respect*)
- In contrast to our "human fathers," what is God called? (*Father of our spirits*)
- By what standard do earthly fathers punish their children? (*as they think best*)
- Of what do we share if God's discipline works in us? (*his holiness*)
- How is discipline at first perceived? (*as painful*)
- What does discipline ultimately yield? (*the harvest of righteousness and peace*).

Mix into your stack, to be selected at random, two cards with each of the following: (1) "Oops! You've fallen. Miss a turn before you resume," and (2) "Ouch! You've twisted your ankle. Miss a turn before you resume."

Ask the first question to the first runner. If you get a correct answer, ask the second question to the second runner. (If incorrect, ask the same question). Ask all the questions in order. For each correct answer, allow a runner to move a short way toward the finish line. Have your fans encourage the runners with answers.

## INTO LIFE

Have the class discuss how your race was *like* the Christian race and how it was *unlike* the Christian race? *Likes* include: there are those who encourage us to finish; occasional setbacks deter our running; one succeeds in the race by knowing Scripture. *Unlikes*: life is long and hard, not short and easy; much of life is run in secret, rather than on display; some Christians drop out and quit the race; in the Christian race, each runner is to help those about him; in the Christian race, runners join the race at various points. If your sides need help getting started, give each side one or two of these similarities or differences. When appropriate, ask for specific examples or illustrations of the things the groups suggest. For example, "occasional setbacks" that may hinder us might include trouble with a habit one finds difficult to break.

Read Hebrews 12:1. For each specific situation that relates to the hindrances, entanglements, and opposition, ask for suggestions on how to deal with the problems. For the habit one finds hard to break, perhaps an accountability partner would help.

Read Hebrews 12:1 once more as a final challenge.

# Questions for the Christian Runner

Read Hebrews 12:1-11. Then answer each of the following questions with words or by drawing a picture.

## WHO'S THAT OVER THERE CHEERING?

Whom do you picture standing along-side your racecourse cheering you on? Why are they there?

## WHAT'S THIS WEIGHT AROUND MY ANKLE?

What are the hindrances to your running the Christian race successfully? What can you do to "throw" them off?

## WHY DOES THIS HURT SO?

What are the things that "hurt the most" about your life? How does your knowledge and faith make them bearable?

## WHY SHOULD I WANT TO FINISH?

Examine Hebrews 12:1-11 to see if you can identify at least four benefits of finishing the race.

# A Call to Faithfulness
### Unit 2. Be Faithful Followers of Christ
### (Lessons 10-14)

# LIVE RESPONSIBLY
### LESSON 14

## WHY TEACH THIS LESSON?

One can almost imagine the writer of Hebrews sweating a bit as he writes chapter 13. He is running out of parchment—a precious and expensive commodity in his day. But he still has much to say. So he closes with several quick, brief exhortations, any one of which could have been expanded into an entire chapter.

The result, for us, is a handy digest of practical wisdom. These are matters for every time and place. We, too, need to be reminded to love each other, to keep ourselves sexually pure, to have a responsible attitude toward money, and to observe the many other axioms of the final chapter of Hebrews. In an age that has seen too little responsible behavior, such a digest is sorely needed.

Challenge your students to focus on at least one of the gems of practical wisdom in this chapter and to make it a part of their lives.

## INTRODUCTION

### A. READY FOR EITHER

An organization that sent missionaries to foreign countries had an interesting design on its logo. It had two pictures on it. One was of an ox hitched to a plow; the other was of an altar with a slain ox lying on it. The motto on the logo read: "The plow or the altar—ready for either."

The Hebrew Christians had gone through some extremely difficult times. Many were being tempted to abandon their faith in Jesus. We have noticed, beginning with Hebrews 10:19, a more concentrated emphasis by the writer on encouraging the Hebrew Christians to stand firm in their faith. The writer warns them that more difficult times, even death, might be in their future. Until they had resisted to that point, they could not say they had done enough. Jesus, who did lay down his life, was to be their example (12:3, 4). The opening verses of the final chapter (from which today's lesson text is taken) emphasize the importance of living a life that marks Christians as different from persons of the world.

Some in the early church deliberately sought martyrdom, believing it to be a mark of a superior faith. Yet the New Testament nowhere urges people to seek martyrdom. It does talk frequently about sacrifice. Most of us will never be called on to die for our faith, but all of us have the opportunity to offer service and praise as an acceptable sacrifice to God. Let us be prepared daily for either the plow or the altar.

### B. LESSON BACKGROUND

When we first began our studies from the letter to the Hebrews several weeks ago, we observed that it begins like a tract, not a letter. It does not have the salutation or greeting that we normally would expect in a letter. Instead, it begins with a profound theological statement: God has spoken through his Son. The chapters that follow contrast Jesus, the final revelation, with all who had come before. A specific contrast is drawn between the sacrifice of Christ and the sacrificial system of the Old Testament.

All of this profound theology has some practical, down-to-earth implications. Since "our God is a consuming fire" (Hebrews 12:29, the final verse in the chap-

DEVOTIONAL READING
JAMES 5:7-16
LESSON SCRIPTURE
HEBREWS 13
PRINTED TEXT
HEBREWS 13:1-16

LESSON AIMS

As a result of today's study, students will:

1. Summarize the practical advice for Christian living and growth in Hebrews 13:1-16.

2. Explain how relevant this advice is to today's world

3. Commit themselves to applying this message in their own lives.

KEY VERSE

Do not forget to do good and to share with others, for with such sacrifices God is pleased.
*Hebrews 13:16*

Aug
31

*LESSON 14 NOTES*

*WHAT DO YOU THINK?*

*Most churches are good at showing brotherly love sometimes. Some are especially responsive when a church member has a death in the family, others are good at meeting needs for the poor—especially around holidays.*

*What expressions of love is our church especially good at? In what areas do we really need to work to do better? How can our class initiate a ministry of love to address one of these areas?*

ter), we should expect him to make ethical demands on those who would follow him. That is what we see in chapter 13 (the final chapter of this letter). These practical applications are set forth in language that reminds us of the admonitions with which Paul often closes his letters. In addition to these challenges, there is a personal reference to "our brother Timothy" (v. 23) and a final blessing: "Grace be with you all" (v. 25). This similarity of style and the author's familiarity with Timothy suggest to many that the author is the apostle Paul. The greeting, "Those from Italy send you their greetings" (13:24) also sounds like Paul, and indicates the letter could have been written from Rome, perhaps near the end of Paul's first imprisonment. No one can say for sure, however, who wrote the book.

## I. PERSONAL EXHORTATIONS (HEBREWS 13:1-6)

### A. TO BROTHERLY LOVE (vv. 1-3)

**1, 2. Keep on loving each other as brothers. Do not forget to entertain strangers, for by so doing some people have entertained angels without knowing it.**

The writer does not supply his readers with a long list of virtues that he expects them to develop. Instead, he concentrates on a few areas of conduct and attitude that seem most appropriate to their situation.

Christians belong to the "family of believers" (Galatians 6:10); thus, it should be a common practice for them to accept and treat one another as brothers and sisters. This was much more common in the early church than it is today. It is a virtue we need to restore to our practice of Christianity.

The Hebrew Christians were also urged to *entertain*, or offer hospitality to, *strangers*. This probably referred to Christians traveling through their vicinity. Such hospitality was especially important in that day. The number of public inns was scarce, and those that existed were likely to have a questionable reputation; they could even be dangerous.

The author tells his readers that some who had offered hospitality in the past had *entertained angels without knowing it*. The examples of Abraham and Lot come to mind (Genesis 18, 19). Did any other person ever *entertain . . . angels without knowing it*? If so, did they find out later—or did they never know it? Abraham and Lot certainly discovered their guests were angels—in fact, one of his three visitors is identified as "the Lord" (Genesis 18:10, 13, 17, 20, 22, etc.). Gideon also hosted an angel (Judges 6:11, 19-22), but he seemed to know from the start that his visitor was an angel. Were there others who hosted angels? *Some people* suggests, but does not demand, more than two, so we cannot say with certainty.

This leaves us wondering, do people still entertain angels? The writer does not say so, but the implication seems to be that his original audience, at least, might do so. His point is certainly that we need to consider our homes as bases for ministry rather than merely as our "castles," safe havens from the world. Jesus' picture of judgment in Matthew 25:31-46 indicates that hospitality to strangers, whether or not we entertain "angels," is really hospitality to him.

**3. Remember those in prison as if you were their fellow prisoners, and those who are mistreated as if you yourselves were suffering.**

Another special request was that the Hebrew Christians attend to fellow believers who were suffering imprisonment because of their faith. Ancient prisons were not run by people concerned with the rights or dignity of the prisoners. There were no regulations about the number of prisoners per cell, sanitation requirements, or anything related to the prisoner's comfort. The only standards that were enforced were those that pertained to security. Prisoners, then, were often dependent on friends for the essentials of food and warm clothing. (See Paul's request in 2 Timothy 4:13.) Caring for the needs of the imprisoned was a very important ministry that Christians could fulfill. In this verse, Christians are told to identify themselves with those who suffer, *as if you yourselves were suffering*.

## B. TO SEXUAL PURITY (v. 4)

**4. Marriage should be honored by all, and the marriage bed kept pure, for God will judge the adulterer and all the sexually immoral.**

God demands purity in sexual relations. This was a difficult standard to maintain in the immoral surroundings of the first-century world. In spite of the pressures of our times, we need to realize that God's standards have not changed.

The union of one man to one woman in *marriage* has not been *honored* in our day. Promiscuity and so-called "serial monogamy" have for many replaced the one-man-one-woman for life concept that has defined marriage for centuries. Even among Christians divorce and extra-marital affairs are no longer uncommon. We need to heed what the writer tells the Hebrew believers. Sexual immorality will be judged.

The writer uses two words to describe those who engage in immoral sexual behavior. The first is a general term, usually translated "immoral" or "sexually immoral" in other places. The feminine form is always translated "prostitute(s)" in the *New International Version*. Its root word is the source of our word *pornography*.

The second is translated *adulterer*. The *adulterer* is one who violates his marriage vows by becoming intimate with someone other than his spouse. (Curiously, the translators inverted the word order from what appears in the Greek, apparently choosing to list the more specific *adulterer* first and then the general term.)

The Scriptures are unanimous in their condemnation of sexual sins. Paul states it quite bluntly in Ephesians 5:6: "Let no one deceive you with empty words, for because of such things God's wrath comes on those who are disobedient." In the presence of such firm standards, it is amazing that some religious leaders today want to compromise them.

### KILLER LUST

An old black-and-white movie showed a group of shipwrecked men drifting aimlessly on the ocean in a lifeboat. As the days passed under the scorching sun, their rations of food and fresh water gave out. The men grew deliriously thirsty. One night while the others were asleep, one man ignored all previous warnings and gulped down some salt water. He quickly died. Ocean water contains seven times more salt than the human body can safely ingest. Drinking it causes a person to dehydrate even faster, because the kidneys demand extra water to flush out the extra salt. The more salt water someone drinks, the thirstier he gets. He actually dies of thirst.

When married people indulge in lust for someone else, they become like the man in the movie. They thirst desperately for something that looks like what they want. They fail to realize, however, that what they seek is precisely the opposite of what they really need. In fact, it is deadly.

God gave us the gift of sexuality to be enjoyed within the married union of one man with one woman for life. It is to our great good to keep the marriage bed pure, and to our great peril to defile it through sexual sin.                —C. B. Mc.

## C. TO LIVE IN CONTENTMENT (vv. 5, 6)

**5, 6. Keep your lives free from the love of money and be content with what you have, because God has said, "Never will I leave you; never will I forsake you." So we say with confidence, "The Lord is my helper; I will not be afraid. What can man do to me?"**

Greed is an especially dangerous sin because it leads to other sins, such as lying, stealing, and even murder. The exhortation of this verse is appropriate for

### WHAT DO YOU THINK?

We believe that God is the author of marriage, and that when it is entered into according to his intention and design, marriage is the source of many blessings. Unfortunately, many in our culture have a very different view! How can we confront the following ideas of marriage and move our society closer to the biblical model?

- "You can't help falling in love or falling out of love, so how can you make a lifelong commitment to one person?"

- "Marriage just gives you a piece of paper. A relationship built on love doesn't need that."

- "Marriage is part of the male dominance of women that has gone on for centuries and needs to be eliminated!"

- "If two consenting adults want to have a sexual relationship, that's their business—even if one or both of them is married."

- "Divorce is so common it's obvious marriage doesn't work anymore. Why not just forget about it?"

our materialistic age, driven as it is by the desire for more and more. The problem with greed is that it is never *content*; it always wants more.

In contrast, a Christian possesses spiritual resources that allow him to resist greed. He can be content with what he has, because he has God's assurance: *Never will I leave you; never will I forsake you.* This is not a license for us to relax and do nothing, expecting God to feed and clothe us. The contentment comes from knowing that God is in control of our resources and has promised to supply our needs if we order our priorities according to his will. (See Matthew 6:31-33; 1 Timothy 6:6-8.)

Especially important in this context is the understanding that God's help is eternal; it is not limited to our earthly lives in time but is ultimately fulfilled in eternal life. *What can man do to me?* He can kill me. But he can do no more than that! Even so, I am not outside the care of the ever-present Lord. Anything less that man chooses to do can also be endured with the help and assurance of the Lord's presence.

Christians are persecuted and even killed for their faith. Others face more natural trials—storms destroy their homes, they lose their jobs, occasionally they go hungry—but they remain content (Philippians 4:12). They know the Lord is with them, and that is enough.

## II. EXAMPLES TO FOLLOW (HEBREWS 13:7, 8)
### A. TEACHERS OF THE WORD (v. 7)
**7. Remember your leaders, who spoke the word of God to you. Consider the outcome of their way of life and imitate their faith.**

The word *leaders* also appears in verses 17 and 24 of this chapter. In those places it refers to the current leaders of the congregation. However, in the verse before us it seems to call attention to former leaders, or at least to include them, since the Hebrew Christians are asked to *remember* them and to consider the *outcome of their way of life.* Perhaps these were the individuals who had led many of the Hebrew Christians to Christ through the *word of God.* If these had remained faithful, the Hebrew Christians could also.

The word here translated "outcome" is used in only one other New Testament passage, 1 Corinthians 10:13, where it is the "way out" of temptation. *The outcome of their way of life* seems to refer to the deaths of these leaders. Thayer thinks so, but says it is "not merely the end of their physical life, but the manner in which they closed a well-spent life as exhibited by their spirit in dying." On the other hand, Bauer says that, while the word may refer to the end of one's life, "it can also probably be understood as (successful) outcome, result of one's way of life." If so, then the leaders here could also include the Hebrews' current leaders, whose lives were exemplary models of proper Christian conduct.

Either way, the implications for current leaders is obvious. If those who follow are going to *imitate their faith,* then they need to be sure their way of life is worthy of imitation.

### B. THE UNCHANGING CHRIST (v. 8)
**8. Jesus Christ is the same yesterday and today and forever.**

The Hebrew Christians were urged to follow the example of their early leaders. At least some of these men were no longer with them, no longer available to speak the word of God to them. In contrast, *Jesus Christ,* the perfect leader, remains unchanged. *Yesterday*—in the past—he had died on the cross for their sins. *Today* he was guiding them through faithful leaders and through his presence in their lives. His influence is not subject to the limitations that affect human leaders; it lasts *forever*. By following him, the Hebrew Christians are assured that they will not be led astray.

## III. ADDITIONAL CHALLENGES (HEBREWS 13:9-16)

### A. THE DANGER OF INSTABILITY (v. 9)

**9. Do not be carried away by all kinds of strange teachings. It is good for our hearts to be strengthened by grace, not by ceremonial foods, which are of no value to those who eat them.**

The picture here is of a ship without a helmsman, *carried away* by changing winds. A similar Greek word with the same root is used in Ephesians 4:14, where Paul warns the Ephesian Christians not to be "blown here and there by every wind of teaching." The Hebrew Christians were in danger of being driven back to the Judaism from which they had come.

*Ceremonial foods* is literally just *foods*. Some, then, believe the reference is to the demands of an unorthodox Jewish sect that put great emphasis on the eating of certain foods. But the reference to an altar in verse 10 seems to refer to the ceremonial sacrifices under the Mosaic Law and to justify the insertion of the word *ceremonial* in our text. The point the writer is making here is that *our hearts are* nurtured by *grace*, not by the sacrifices prescribed in the Law. These sacrifices were really *of no value to those* who had offered them. Keeping in mind these believers were being lured back into Judaism, we see why the writer offers this warning about the ceremonial foods

### B. THE CHRISTIAN'S ALTAR (vv. 10, 11)

**10. We have an altar from which those who minister at the tabernacle have no right to eat.**

Since the early Christians had no visible idols, their pagan neighbors often accused them of being atheists. Jews, who had no idols, criticized Christians because they had no altar on which to offer sacrifices for sin. The author answers this charge by pointing out that Christians certainly do *have an altar*. That altar is the cross on which God's own Son was offered. The term *tabernacle* refers here to the system of sacrifices instituted by Moses along with the tabernacle itself. As long as the Jews continued to cling to this system and to reject the Christ, they had *no right to eat* from the Christian's altar; that is, they could not receive the benefits of Jesus' death.

**11. The high priest carries the blood of animals into the Most Holy Place as a sin offering, but the bodies are burned outside the camp.**

The Hebrew Christians were reminded of the ceremony that took place on the Day of Atonement. The priests were allowed to eat of ordinary sacrifices, but on the Day of Atonement the regulations were different. The blood of the animals was sprinkled in the Holy of Holies, and the carcasses were then taken *outside the camp* and *burned*.

### C. FOLLOWING JESUS (vv. 12, 13)

**12, 13. And so Jesus also suffered outside the city gate to make the people holy through his own blood. Let us, then, go to him outside the camp, bearing the disgrace he bore.**

Just as the sacrificial animals were burned outside the camp on the Day of Atonement, Jesus *suffered outside the city gate,* that is, outside the walls of Jerusalem. In so doing, he accomplished *through his own blood* what the sacrifice on the Day of Atonement could never do: made *the people holy* (Hebrews 10:10). The Hebrew Christians were urged to *go* to Jesus, leaving behind the old system under the Law of Moses.

*DAILY BIBLE READING*

*Monday, Aug. 25*—Be Responsible Husbands and Wives (Ephesians 5:22-33)

*Tuesday, Aug. 26*—Be Responsible Parents and Children (Ephesians 6:1-4)

*Wednesday, Aug. 27*—Be Responsible Citizens (Matthew 22:15-22)

*Thursday, Aug. 28*—Be Responsible To God (Hebrews 4:1-10)

*Friday, Aug. 29*—Be Responsible Leaders (Hebrews 13:17-25)

*Saturday, Aug. 30*—Be Responsible for What You Say (James 3:1-12)

*Sunday, Aug. 31*—Be Responsible With Your Wealth (Luke 12:13-21)

*WHAT DO YOU THINK?*

The Old Covenant called for the frequent offering of blood sacrifices on the altar of the tabernacle or temple. Such sacrifices could never completely forgive sin. When Jesus gave his life upon the cross of Calvary, that cross became the most important altar of all time. Christian baptism (Romans 6:3-6) and the Lord's Supper (1 Corinthians 11:26) are direct links to that "altar."

How would you explain the importance of these two ordinances if someone asked you about them?

## PRAYER

*Loving Father, we thank you for the perfect sacrifice that you have offered up for our sins. Cleanse us from our sins and send us forth to labor wherever you may need us. May we always give you the glory for the opportunities we have to serve. In Jesus' name we pray. Amen.*

*The visual for lesson 14 illustrates Hebrews 13:16. Discuss how the woman in the picture might be obeying the injunction of this verse (as opposed to just doing her job). What other opportunities do Christian health care workers have to practice their faith? What opportunities do your class members have where they work?*

## THOUGHT TO REMEMBER

*The world may not always understand a Christian's profession of faith, but it should be able to see a Christian's pure life and his unselfish service to others.*

The reference to the *disgrace* that Christ bore may give some hint at what was drawing the Hebrew believers away from Christianity and back to Judaism. The persecution they faced, coupled with the Jewish idea of a curse on anyone who is hanged on a cross (Galatians 3:13; Deuteronomy 21:23), was giving them doubts. The writer had already urged faithfulness. Now he challenges them to bear the same disgrace that Christ bore so they would share also in his exaltation.

### D. THE CITY TO COME (v. 14)

**14. For here we do not have an enduring city, but we are looking for the city that is to come.**

When Jews became Christians, they turned their backs on Jerusalem as the center of true worship. For them Jerusalem was not an *enduring city*—a truth that would become tragically evident when the Roman army destroyed the city in A.D. 70. But Christians had no need to fear, for their destination was the "city with foundations, whose architect and builder is God" (Hebrews 11:10). Their holy city was not Jerusalem, but new Jerusalem (Galatians 4:26; Revelation 21:2, 10).

### E. THE PROPER SACRIFICES (vv. 15, 16)

**15, 16. Through Jesus, therefore, let us continually offer to God a sacrifice of praise—the fruit of lips that confess his name. And do not forget to do good and to share with others, for with such sacrifices God is pleased.**

Although animal sacrifices are no longer required, God still expects his people to offer *sacrifices*. These sacrifices are the joyous words of *praise* and thanksgiving that we speak and sing to him. They are the acts of kindness done in service to God and to our fellowmen.

Christians have an altar (v. 10), an atoning sacrifice (v. 12), and sacrifices—of praise and doing good. All these are better than their counterparts in the Old Covenant, for they point us to the enduring city that is to come. Though we may bear disgrace with Christ now, we will share his glory in the new Jerusalem.

## CONCLUSION

### A. THE POWER OF PURITY

Just as the Jewish priests had to cleanse themselves before they served at the altar, so Christians must also be cleansed before they can render acceptable service to God. Through Christ's blood we are made holy, or set apart, and we are required to maintain that purity by constantly renewing our commitment to him.

Personal purity is a critical part of our witness for Christ. We serve in a lost and evil world that can ensnare even the most mature Christian. For that reason we must turn again and again to Christ's sanctifying power to protect us. We should never underestimate the impact of a consistently holy life, nor should we minimize our need for divine strength in living that life.

### B. CHANGE AND DECAY

Many of us are familiar with the hymn, "Abide with Me." One line in particular contains a sobering truth: "Change and decay in all around I see." These words express the feelings of many of us, especially those of us who have lived half a century or more. We have witnessed unbelievable changes in so many areas of life. Some of the changes are disheartening and threatening: the breakup of the traditional family, the rising crime rate, the declining moral standards, and the excessive materialism.

In the face of all these changes, we could easily give way to despair. But before we do, let us consider the next line of that hymn: "O Thou who changest not, abide with me!" Jesus Christ is the same yesterday, today, and forever.

# Discovery Learning

*This page contains an alternate lesson plan emphasizing learning activities. Classes desiring such student involvement will find these suggestions helpful. The next page is a reproducible activity page to further enhance discovery learning.*

## LEARNING GOALS

As a result of today's study, students will:

1. Summarize the practical advice for Christian living and growth in Hebrews 13:1-16.

2. Explain how relevant this advice is to today's world

3. Commit themselves to applying this message in their own lives.

## INTO THE LESSON

*Remember* is a key word in today's text. Prepare pieces of yarn or string (six to eight inches long), and hand one to each class member. Do not comment, other than to say, "Keep this for something we will do later." As class assembles, display these letters on the chalkboard or on a transparency: *B, E, E, E, M, M, R, R*. Ask the class to reassemble the letters to make a word. *Remember* should be recognized easily and quickly. Note that this is a key word in today's text. Note also how appropriate a call to *remember* key truths is, in closing a letter such as Hebrews.

## INTO THE WORD

Buy enough small stick-on notes, about two inches square, to allow you to give ten pieces to each student. Leave the pieces that you give each person stuck together as a small pad.

Assign the odd-numbered verses of today's text to half of your group; assign the even-numbered to the other half. Direct students to look at their verses, and to prepare at least five statements on their stick-on sheets (one per sheet). They should use "Don't forget" or "Remember" to preface each statement they write. Give them two examples, if needed, to get them started: "Remember that Jesus never changes" (from verse 8) and "Don't forget to praise God" (from verse 15).

After a few minutes read Hebrews 13:1 and ask the students to recall "Remembers" and "Don't forgets" that they saw for that verse. Proceed through the text, reading a verse and calling for memos. If you come to a verse for which no one can identify a related memo, stop and ask the class to suggest a possibility. (For example, if none is seen for verse 10, suggest, "Remember: we have privileges others do not!")

When you have completed verse 16, ask, "Is there any reason why some verses elicited many memos and some only a few?" Ask whether the verses that produced the most memos were chosen because of ease in prepa-

ration or because of a particular need in the lives of today's Christians for the reminders in those verses. Follow up on this point by asking why these subjects covered in today's text are especially relevant for Christians in today's society: hospitality (v. 2), helping the imprisoned and the suffering (v. 3), moral purity (v. 4), contentment (vv. 5, 6), respect for church leaders (v. 7), and false doctrine (v. 9). Ask, "What current trends or attitudes in society make it a challenge to practice each of these?" For example, the tendency of many to isolate themselves from others has made hospitality less common than it once was. Christians can make a difference in this area.

## OPTION

Use the reproducible activities, "Quick Advice!" and "What Would You Say?" on the next page to lead your Bible study today.

## INTO LIFE

Have the adults pull out the pieces of string or yarn that you distributed at the beginning of the session. Ask each to tie the piece loosely around a finger. Call for a volunteer to hold up a "tied" finger and give a "Remember" or "Don't forget" from today's study. Ask another six or eight students to volunteer their ideas. Suggest that your students also wear their reminders until at least one person asks each what it means. He or she can then select a key truth from the lesson to share with that person.

Have each student make sure he or she has at least seven stick-on notes with memos on them. Suggest that these be taken home and posted, one per day, on the bathroom mirror or some other place where the student will see a reminder daily. (Students who have more than seven can post two reminders on some days.)

If time allows, you may want to include a few moments of review of this quarter or of this study in Hebrews. Ask class members what truths have stood out most to them. How were they encouraged? Challenged? Warned? Rebuked? What specific verses from the lessons can they recall?

To close the lesson and this unit on Hebrews, call attention to the beautiful benediction that the writer uses at the conclusion of his letter: 13:20, 21. Have your class stand, form a circle, and hold hands, as you conclude by reading this blessing.

# Quick Advice!

The writer of Hebrews, as other New Testament authors, concludes his letter with some quick advice. Write the verse number from today's text for any of the following that is in chapter 13. If the idea is found somewhere else in Scripture, use a concordance to find a reference and write that reference.

Honor marriage! _____     Remember leaders! _____

Give generously! _____     Be content! _____

Don't waver! _____     Entertain strangers! _____

Do good! _____     Continually praise! _____

Remember prisoners! _____

# What Would You Say?

If you were concluding a letter to Christian friends, what would you feel compelled to say? Consider the following list—from Hebrews 13—as if it were a check box on a computer screen. "Click" an X on each one you want to include.

DEAR CHRISTIAN FRIENDS,

❑ Love each other as family.
❑ Be hospitable to strangers.
❑ Keep your sexual relationships pure.
❑ Consider the faithful lives of those who have taught you.
❑ Let grace be your crown, not good works.
❑ Bear the disgrace of Christ's death with honor.
❑ Free yourself from the love of money.
❑ Fear nothing man can do to you.
❑ Keep your lips confessing His name.
❑ Share what you have with others.

Your fellow traveler, looking for a city to come,

_____

If you could choose only four from the list above, which would they be? Why?

1. _____     2. _____

3. _____     4. _____